Fodor's 04

MONTANA, WYOMING & IDAHO

Where to Stay and Eat for All Budgets

Must-See Sights and Local Secrets

Ratings You Can Trust

Fodor's Travel Publications New York, Toronto, London, Sydney, Auckland
www.fodors.com

FODOR'S MONTANA, WYOMING & IDAHO

Editors: Deborah Kaufman, Matthew Lombardi, Mark Sullivan

Editorial Contributors: Jean Arthur, Linda Cabasin, Jo Deurbrouck, Tom Griffith, Constance Jones, Christina Knight, Candy Moulton, Amy Wang
Maps: David Lindroth, *cartographer;* Bob Blake and Rebecca Baer, *map editors*
Design: Fabrizio La Rocca, *creative director;* Guido Caroti, *art director;* Melanie Marin, *senior picture editor*
Production/Manufacturing: Robert B. Shields
Cover Photo (Jackson Lake and Grand Tetons, Wyoming): David Jensen

COPYRIGHT

Published in the United States by Fodor's Travel Publications, a unit of Fodors LLC, a subsidiary of Random House, Inc., and simultaneously in Canada by Random House of Canada Limited, Toronto. Distributed by Random House, Inc., New York.

First Edition

ISBN 1–4000–1327–5

ISSN 1549–3784

SPECIAL SALES

This book is available for special discounts for bulk purchases for sales promotions or premiums. Special editions, including personalized covers, excerpts of existing guides, and corporate imprints, can be created in large quantities for special needs. For more information, write to Special Markets/Premium Sales, 1745 Broadway, MD 6-2, New York, NY 10019 or e-mail specialmarkets@randomhouse.com.

AN IMPORTANT TIP & AN INVITATION

Although all prices, opening times, and other details in this book are based on information supplied to us at press time, changes occur all the time in the travel world, and Fodor's cannot accept responsibility for facts that become outdated or for inadvertent errors or omissions. So **always confirm information when it matters,** especially if you're making a detour to visit a specific place. Your experiences—positive and negative—matter to us. If we have missed or misstated something, **please write to us.** We follow up on all suggestions. Contact the Montana, Wyoming & Idaho editor at editors@fodors.com or c/o Fodor's at 1745 Broadway, New York, NY 10019.

PRINTED IN THE UNITED STATES OF AMERICA

10 9 8 7 6 5 4 3 2 1

DESTINATION MONTANA, WYOMING & IDAHO

From the vast northern plains to the majestic Rocky Mountains, Montana, Wyoming, and Idaho are where you come when you want to get outdoors. Here where the buffalo still roam and a cowboy sensibility endures, the main question is, how rugged do you want your trip to be? National parks—including Yellowstone, the first and still the most spectacular—give you unparalleled scenery and extensive facilities. You can rough it a little or a lot on dude ranches, mountain-biking trails, white-water rivers, and America's finest trout-fishing streams. If you really want to get away from it all, pack your tent and head into the backcountry wilderness to experience nature in its purest form. Come winter, the place to be is on a pair of skis, whether you're schussing down the slopes of Jackson Hole or following a trail through Glacier National Park. This land of big sky and big mountains really is, as the natives like to say, "the last best place." Have a great trip!

Karen Cure

Karen Cure, Editorial Director

CONTENTS

ABOUT THIS BOOK

	There's no doubt that the best source for travel advice is a like-minded friend who's just been where you're headed. But with or without that friend, you'll have a better trip with a Fodor's guide in hand. Once you've learned to find your way around its pages, you'll be in great shape to find your way around your destination.
SELECTION	Our goal is to cover the best properties, sights, and activities in their category, as well as the most interesting places to visit. We make a point of including local food lovers' hot spots as well as more modest options, and we avoid all that's touristy unless it's really worth your time. You can go on the assumption that everything you read about in this book is recommended wholeheartedly by our writers and editors. Flip to On the Road with Fodor's to learn more about who they are. It goes without saying that no property mentioned in the book has paid to be included.
RATINGS	Orange stars ★ denote sights and properties that our editors and writers consider the very best in the area covered by the entire book. These, the best of the best, are listed in the Fodor's Choice section in the front of the book. Black stars ★ highlight the sights and properties we deem Highly Recommended, the don't-miss sights within any region. Fodor's Choice and Highly Recommended options in each region are listed on the title page of the chapter covering that region. Use the index to find complete descriptions.
SPECIAL SPOTS	Pleasures & Pastimes focuses on types of experiences that reveal the spirit of the destination. Watch for Off the Beaten Path sights. Some are out of the way, some are quirky, and all are worth your while. If the munchies hit while you're exploring, look for Need a Break? suggestions.
TIME IT RIGHT	Wondering when to go? Check On the Calendar up front and chapters' Timing sections for weather and crowd overviews and best days and times to visit.
SEE IT ALL	Use Fodor's exclusive Great Itineraries as a model for your trip. (For a good overview of the entire destination, follow those that begin the book, or mix regional itineraries from several chapters.) In cities, Good Walks guide you to important sights in each neighborhood; ⚑ indicates the starting points of walks and itineraries in the text and on the map.
BUDGET WELL	Hotel and restaurant price categories from ¢ to $$$$ are defined in the opening pages of each chapter—expect to find a balanced selection for every budget. For attractions, we always give standard adult admission fees; reductions are sometimes available for children, students, and senior citizens.
BASIC INFO	Smart Travel Tips lists travel essentials for the entire area covered by the book; city- and region-specific basics end each chapter. To find the best way to get around, see the transportation section; see individual modes of travel ("By Car," "By Train") for details. We assume you'll check Web sites or call for particulars.
ON THE MAPS	Maps throughout the book show you what's where and help you find your way around. Black and orange numbered bullets ❶ ❶ in the text correlate to bullets on maps.

BACKGROUND	In general, we give background information within the chapters in the course of explaining sights as well as in CloseUp boxes.
FIND IT FAST	The book begins with a chapter on Yellowstone National Park, and subsequent chapters are arranged by state. Chapters are divided into smaller regions, within which towns are covered in logical geographical order; attractive routes and interesting places between towns are flagged as En Route. Heads at the top of each page help you find what you need within a chapter.
DON'T FORGET	Restaurants are open for lunch and dinner daily unless we state otherwise; we mention dress only when there's a specific requirement and reservations only when they're essential or not accepted—it's always best to book ahead. Hotels have private baths, phones, TVs, and air-conditioning unless otherwise indicated. We always list facilities but not whether you'll be charged extra to use them, so when pricing accommodations, find out what's included.

SYMBOLS

Many Listings

- ★ Fodor's Choice
- ★ Highly recommended
- ✉ Physical address
- ✥ Directions
- Mailing address
- ☎ Telephone
- Fax
- On the Web
- E-mail
- Admission fee
- ⏲ Open/closed times
- Start of walk/itinerary
- Credit cards

Outdoors

- Golf
- Camping

Hotels & Restaurants

- Hotel
- Number of rooms
- Facilities
- Meal plans
- ✕ Restaurant
- Reservations
- Dress code
- Smoking
- BYOB
- ✕ Hotel with restaurant that warrants a visit

Other

- Family-friendly
- Contact information
- ⇨ See also
- Branch address
- ☞ Take note

ON THE ROAD WITH FODOR'S

A trip takes you out of yourself. Concerns of life at home disappear, driven away by more immediate thoughts—about, say, what marvels will beguile the next day, or where you'll have dinner. That's where Fodor's comes in. We make sure that you know all your options, so that you don't miss something that's just around the next bend. Because the best memories of your trip might well have nothing to do with what you came to Montana, Wyoming, and Idaho to see, we guide you to sights large and small all over the three-state area. You might set out to immerse yourself in Yellowstone's geological wonders, but back at home you find yourself unable to forget an afternoon spent taking a dip in the hot springs of Thermopolis. With Fodor's at your side, serendipitous discoveries are never far away.

Our success in showing you every corner of Montana, Wyoming, and Idaho is a credit to our extraordinary writers. Although there's no substitute for travel advice from a good friend who knows your style, our contributors are the next best thing—the kind of people you would poll for travel advice if you knew them.

Jean Arthur writes for travel and adventure publications from her Montana home. Her nonfiction books include *Timberline and a Century of Skiing on Mount Hood, Hellroaring: Fifty Years on the Big Mountain,* and *Winter Trails Montana.* She is a regular contributor to *Ski Trax, Horizon Air,* and *Montana* magazines and numerous newspapers such as the *Christian Science Monitor.* When not writing, she travels Montana's frontcountry and backcountry by boot, bicycle, or backcountry ski.

Idaho Falls resident **Jo Deurbrouck** is a former high school English and journalism teacher, a 12-year Idaho white-water raft guide (retired), a kayaker, hiker, and mountain biker, and self-described beer snob. She's the coauthor of three books, including *Cat Attacks: True Stories and Hard Lessons from Cougar Country,* a cautionary look at the return of the mountain lion that, despite its alarming and politically incorrect title, was praised by naturalist writers such as David Quammen. Jo is a regular contributor to *Heartland, USA* and has written for *Paddler,* the *Calgary Sun,* the *Christian Science Monitor,* and the *Washington Post,* among others. She holds a master's degree in English from Boise State University, a school renowned for its proximity to white water.

Candy Moulton has spent years traveling through Wyoming—her native state—researching her nonfiction books: *Roadside History of Wyoming; Legacy of the Tetons: Homesteading in Jackson Hole; The Grand Encampment: Settling the High Country; Wagon Wheels: A Contemporary Journey on the Oregon Trail; Writer's Guide to Everyday Life in the Wild West From 1840 to 1900; Writer's Guide to Everyday Life: Native Americans in the 1800s;* and *Steamboat: Legendary Bucking Horse.* She has also written *Roadside History of Nebraska* and *Salt Lake City Uncovered.* She is the editor of *Roundup,* the official publication of Western Writers of America, and is a regular contributor to Fodor's. Candy makes her home near Encampment, Wyoming.

Award-winning journalist and photographer **Tom Griffith** attended the University of London and graduated from the University of Wisconsin before pursuing a career in the newspaper business that took him to Montana and Arizona. He is former director of communications for the Mount Rushmore Preservation Fund and author of three books about the memorial—*America's Shrine of Democracy, The Four Faces of Freedom,* and *A Sculptor's Son*—as well as dozens of history- and travel-related magazine articles. When he's not reading or writing, Tom enjoys mountain biking and hiking in the Black Hills and teaching his two children the intricacies of trout fishing.

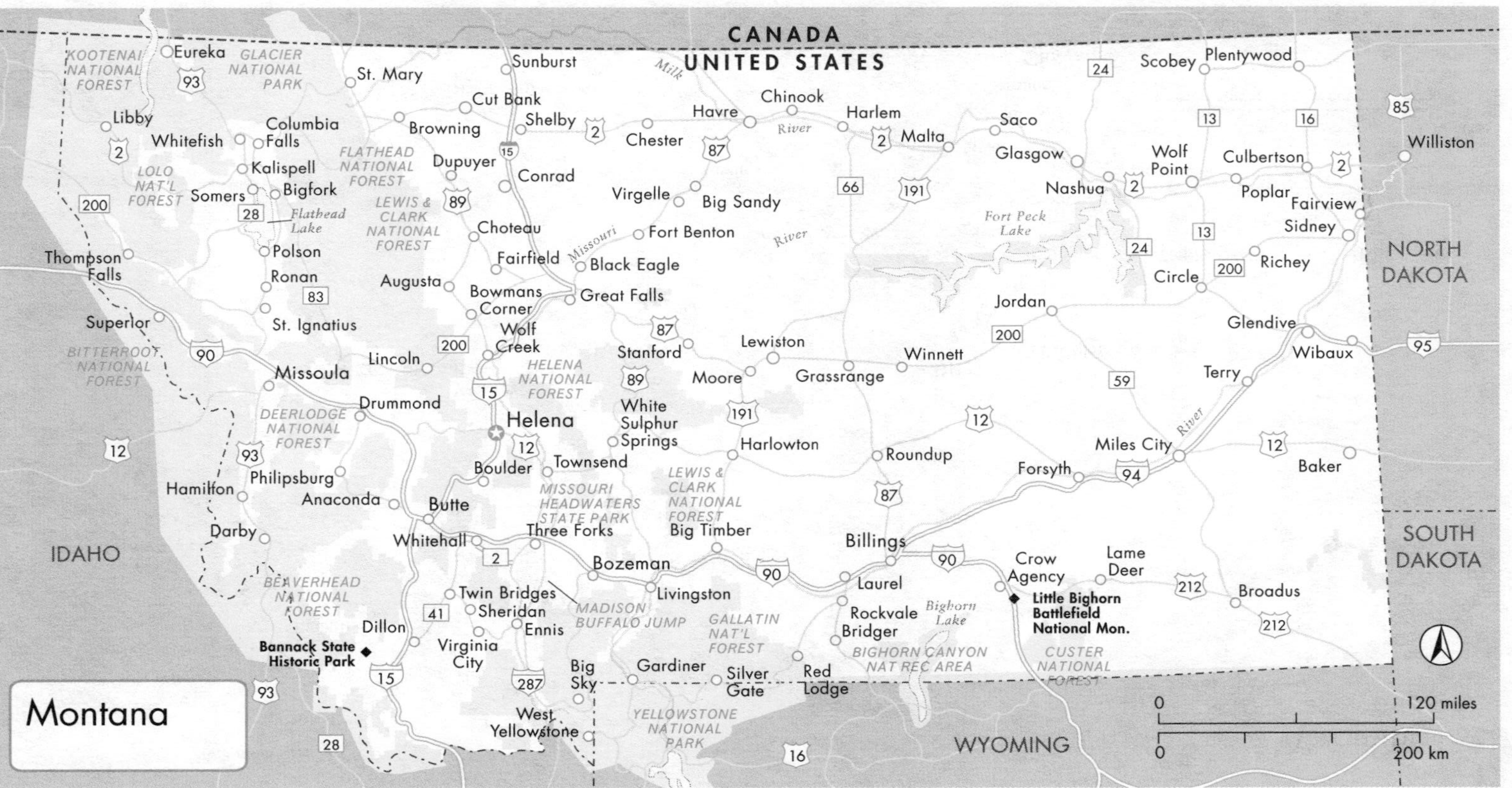
Montana
CANADA
UNITED STATES
NORTH DAKOTA
SOUTH DAKOTA
WYOMING
IDAHO
0
120 miles
0
200 km
Eureka
Libby
Whitefish
Columbia Falls
Kalispell
Somers
Bigfork
Polson
Ronan
St. Ignatius
Thompson Falls
Superior
Missoula
Hamilton
Darby
Philipsburg
Anaconda
Drummond
Lincoln
St. Mary
Browning
Cut Bank
Sunburst
Shelby
Dupuyer
Conrad
Choteau
Augusta
Fairfield
Bowmans Corner
Wolf Creek
Great Falls
Black Eagle
Chester
Havre
Chinook
Harlem
Malta
Saco
Glasgow
Nashua
Wolf Point
Scobey
Plentywood
Culbertson
Poplar
Fairview
Sidney
Richey
Williston
Circle
Glendive
Wibaux
Terry
Baker
Miles City
Forsyth
Broadus
Lame Deer
Crow Agency
Little Bighorn Battlefield National Mon.
Jordan
Winnett
Grassrange
Lewiston
Roundup
Big Sandy
Virgelle
Fort Benton
Stanford
Moore
Harlowton
White Sulphur Springs
Helena
Townsend
Boulder
Butte
Whitehall
Three Forks
Bozeman
Livingston
Big Timber
Billings
Laurel
Rockvale
Bridger
Red Lodge
Silver Gate
Gardiner
Big Sky
West Yellowstone
Ennis
Sheridan
Twin Bridges
Virginia City
Dillon
Bannack State Historic Park
Fort Peck Lake
Flathead Lake
Bighorn Lake
Milk River
Missouri River
River
KOOTENAI NATIONAL FOREST
GLACIER NATIONAL PARK
LOLO NAT'L FOREST
FLATHEAD NATIONAL FOREST
LEWIS & CLARK NATIONAL FOREST
BITTERROOT NATIONAL FOREST
DEERLODGE NATIONAL FOREST
BEAVERHEAD NATIONAL FOREST
HELENA NATIONAL FOREST
MISSOURI HEADWATERS STATE PARK
MADISON BUFFALO JUMP
GALLATIN NAT'L FOREST
YELLOWSTONE NATIONAL PARK
BIGHORN CANYON NAT REC AREA
CUSTER NATIONAL FOREST
2
93
200
28
83
90
12
15
89
287
41
191
87
24
66
13
16
85
95
59
94
212
16

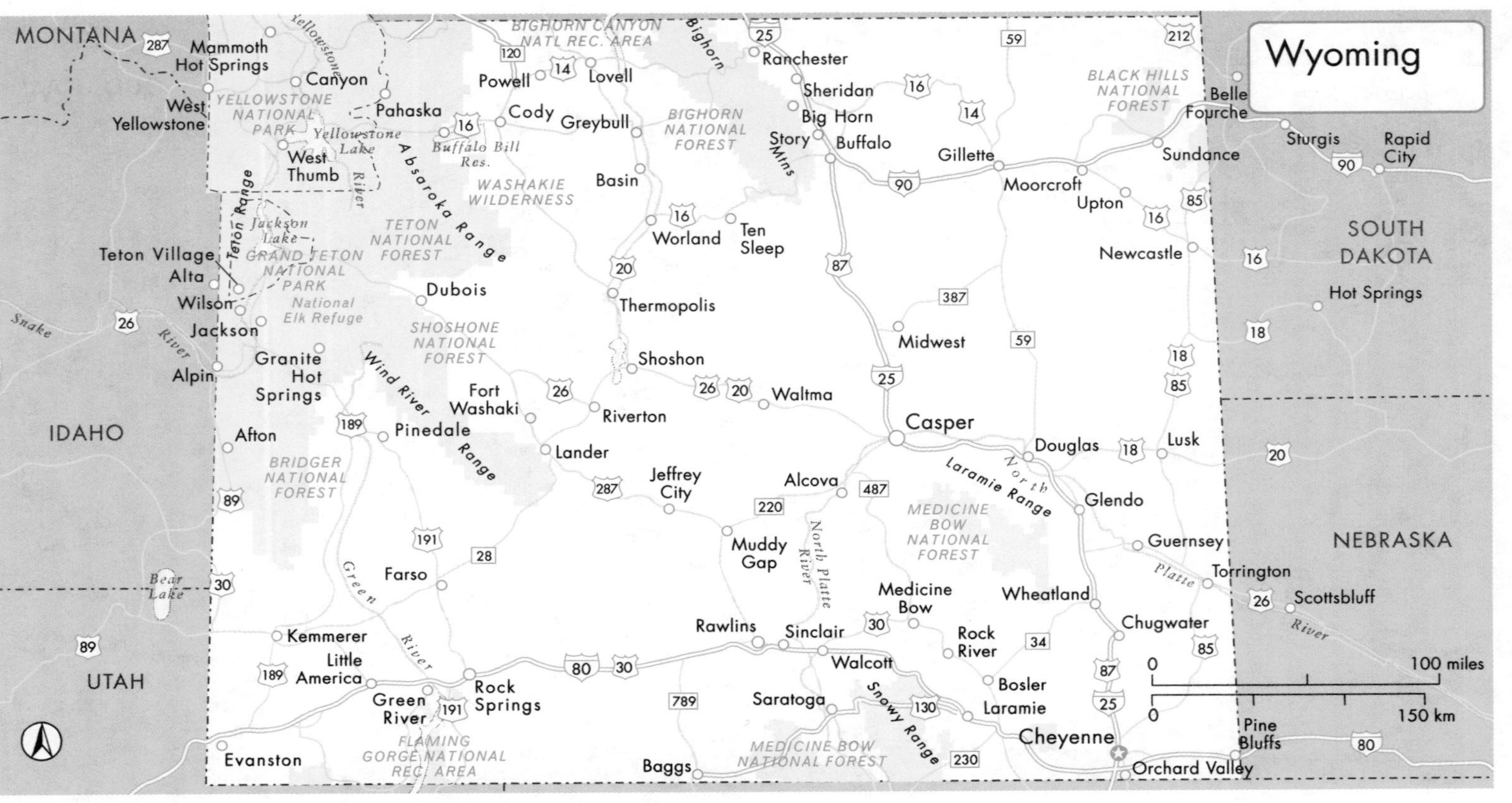
Wyoming
MONTANA
SOUTH DAKOTA
NEBRASKA
IDAHO
UTAH
Mammoth Hot Springs
Canyon
West Yellowstone
Pahaska
West Thumb
YELLOWSTONE NATIONAL PARK
Yellowstone Lake
Yellowstone River
Powell
Lovell
Cody
Greybull
BIGHORN CANYON NATL REC. AREA
Bighorn
Ranchester
Sheridan
Big Horn
Story
Buffalo
Story Mtns
BIGHORN NATIONAL FOREST
Buffalo Bill Res.
Absaroka Range
WASHAKIE WILDERNESS
Basin
Worland
Ten Sleep
Gillette
Moorcroft
Upton
Sundance
BLACK HILLS NATIONAL FOREST
Belle Fourche
Sturgis
Rapid City
Newcastle
Hot Springs
Teton Range
Jackson Lake
GRAND TETON NATIONAL PARK
TETON NATIONAL FOREST
Teton Village
Alta
Wilson
Jackson
National Elk Refuge
Dubois
Thermopolis
Snake River
Granite Hot Springs
Alpin
SHOSHONE NATIONAL FOREST
Wind River Range
Shoshon
Midwest
Fort Washaki
Riverton
Waltma
Casper
Afton
Pinedale
Lander
BRIDGER NATIONAL FOREST
Jeffrey City
Alcova
Douglas
Lusk
North Laramie Range
Glendo
MEDICINE BOW NATIONAL FOREST
Guernsey
Muddy Gap
North Platte River
Farso
Green River
Torrington
Platte River
Scottsbluff
Bear Lake
Medicine Bow
Wheatland
Chugwater
Kemmerer
Rawlins
Sinclair
Rock River
Walcott
Little America
Rock Springs
Green River
Saratoga
Snowy Range
Bosler
Laramie
Cheyenne
Pine Bluffs
Orchard Valley
Evanston
FLAMING GORGE NATIONAL REC. AREA
Baggs
MEDICINE BOW NATIONAL FOREST
0
100 miles
0
150 km
287
120
14
16
25
59
212
90
85
20
87
387
18
26
189
487
220
287
89
191
28
30
80
34
789
130
230

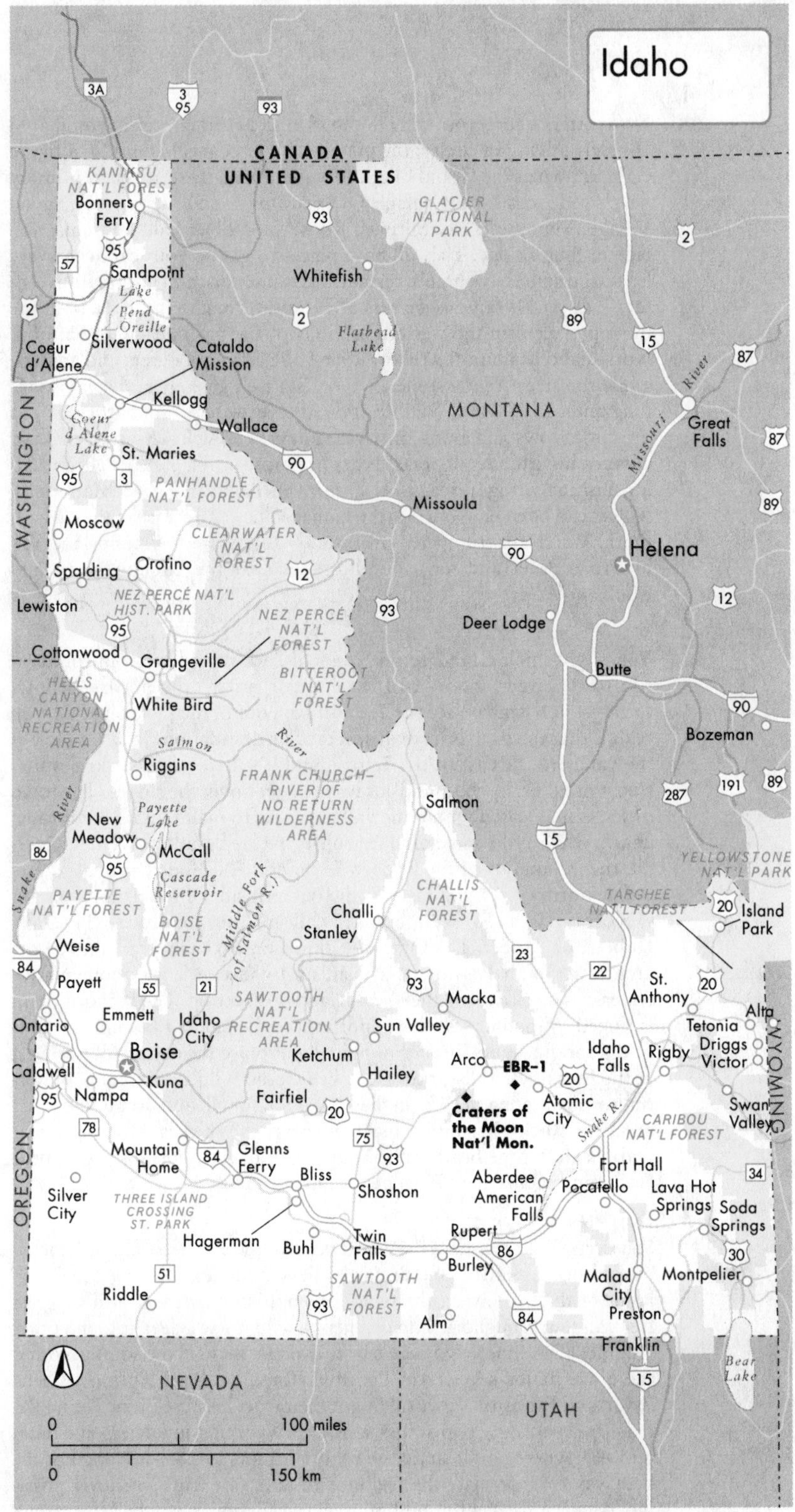
Idaho
CANADA
UNITED STATES
KANIKSU NAT'L FOREST
Bonners Ferry
Sandpoint
Lake Pend Oreille
Silverwood
Coeur d'Alene
Cataldo Mission
Kellogg
Wallace
Coeur d'Alene Lake
St. Maries
PANHANDLE NAT'L FOREST
Moscow
CLEARWATER NAT'L FOREST
Spalding
Orofino
Lewiston
NEZ PERCÉ NAT'L HIST. PARK
NEZ PERCÉ NAT'L FOREST
Cottonwood
Grangeville
BITTEROOT NAT'L FOREST
HELLS CANYON NATIONAL RECREATION AREA
White Bird
Salmon River
Riggins
FRANK CHURCH-RIVER OF NO RETURN WILDERNESS AREA
Salmon
New Meadow
Payette Lake
McCall
Cascade Reservoir
PAYETTE NAT'L FOREST
BOISE NAT'L FOREST
Middle Fork (of Salmon R.)
CHALLIS NAT'L FOREST
Challi
Stanley
Weise
Payett
Ontario
Emmett
Idaho City
SAWTOOTH NAT'L RECREATION AREA
Macka
Sun Valley
Ketchum
Hailey
Boise
Caldwell
Nampa
Kuna
Fairfiel
Arco
EBR-1
Craters of the Moon Nat'l Mon.
Atomic City
Idaho Falls
Rigby
St. Anthony
Tetonia
Driggs
Victor
Alta
Swan Valley
Island Park
YELLOWSTONE NAT'L PARK
TARGHEE NAT'L FOREST
CARIBOU NAT'L FOREST
Snake R.
Mountain Home
Glenns Ferry
Bliss
Shoshon
Silver City
THREE ISLAND CROSSING ST. PARK
Hagerman
Buhl
Twin Falls
Rupert
Burley
Aberdee
American Falls
Pocatello
Fort Hall
Lava Hot Springs
Soda Springs
Montpelier
Malad City
Preston
Franklin
Alm
SAWTOOTH NAT'L FOREST
Riddle
Bear Lake
Snake River
WASHINGTON
OREGON
NEVADA
UTAH
WYOMING
MONTANA
GLACIER NATIONAL PARK
Whitefish
Flathead Lake
Missoula
Helena
Missouri River
Great Falls
Deer Lodge
Butte
Bozeman
0 100 miles
0 150 km
3A
3
95
93
2
89
15
87
90
12
20
23
22
21
55
84
86
78
75
51
30
34
57
191
287

WHAT'S WHERE

1 Yellowstone National Park

No matter where you enter Yellowstone National Park, you'll find yourself driving in circles: the park's road system is laid out in a figure eight known as the Grand Loop. Along the road there are eight primary developed areas: Grant Village, Old Faithful, Madison, Norris, Canyon Village, Mammoth Hot Springs, Roosevelt–Tower Fall, and Lake Village/Fishing Bridge. They all have places to gas up your car at the very least, and some have hotels, restaurants, museums, and information centers. The park's famous geysers are found throughout the area but are most prevalent in the western sections of the park near Old Faithful, Norris, and Mammoth. Yellowstone Lake attracts boaters and anglers, while the steep Yellowstone Canyon is a rich geological display spanning millions of years. Wildlife abounds everywhere, but particularly in open meadows and along the river valleys. You will see bison, elk, and coyotes in virtually all areas; bears are most visible in the Pelican Valley–Fishing Bridge area, near Dunraven Pass, and near Mammoth; wolves can often be spotted in the Lamar Valley and areas south of Mammoth. Watch for trumpeter swans and other waterfowl along the Yellowstone River and for sandhill cranes near the Firehole River and Madison Valley.

2 Northwest Wyoming

You might think Grand Teton National Park would suffer in comparison to its larger, more historic neighbor just to the north—Yellowstone—but when you see the Tetons rising out of the Jackson Hole, you realize that the park is its own spectacular destination. Jackson Hole is the valley to the east of the Tetons, and it's a world-class ski destination, with literally thousands of ways to get down the slopes. The town of Jackson, located within the valley, works to maintain its small-town charm while at the same time serving as the area's cultural center. Overall, the mountains of the Bridger-Teton and Shoshone national forests define northwest Wyoming. On the western side of the region you can explore the Wind River Mountains while making your base in Pinedale, Dubois, or Lander. The Oregon-California-Mormon Trail sites in the area near South Pass merit a visit, and you can learn about Native American traditions on the Wind River Reservation. The Bighorn Basin is ringed by mountains with opportunities to soak in hot mineral pools or dig for dinosaurs in Thermopolis, or explore the culture of the West at the Buffalo Bill Historical Center in Cody. Wildlife-watching opportunities are among the best in the state: look for elk and deer in the Cody area, for Rocky Mountain bighorn sheep at Whiskey Mountain near Dubois and at the head of the South Fork of the Shoshone River near Cody, and moose near Pinedale or north of Dubois.

3 Southern Wyoming

Southern Wyoming spans the wheat fields of the southeast, the lush meadows of the Platte River and Bridger valleys, and the wide-open sagebrush lands of the southwest; the region is populated by the world's largest free-ranging pronghorn antelope herds, wild horses, deer, elk, and other wildlife. Cheyenne, Wyoming's state capital, anchors the southeast, and there are major services in Laramie, Rawlins, Rock Springs, Green River, and Evanston, towns that got their start because of the Union Pacific Railroad. Any trip across southern Wyoming involves some miles on I–80, where you'll share the road with lots of 18-wheelers, but the best way to appreciate the region is to take side trips whenever possible. Between Cheyenne and Laramie, use Wyoming Route 210 (Happy

Jack Road); follow the old Lincoln Highway—U.S. 30—between Laramie and Walcott Junction; cross the Snowy Range Scenic Byway (open from late May through early October) between Laramie/Centennial and Saratoga to see the rugged beauty of the Snowy Range mountains; and take Wyoming Route 70 (the Battle Highway) between Encampment and Baggs to explore the Medicine Bow National Forest and see the copper mines of the early 1900s. The Red Desert between Rawlins and Green River may seem stark, but in the early morning and late evening shadows lengthen, adding depth and color to the landscape.

4 Northeast Wyoming & the Black Hills

A few hundred miles east of the Rocky Mountains sit the Black Hills, an ancient mountain range that straddles the Wyoming–South Dakota border. A sacred land that was once the Great Sioux Indian Reservation, it eventually became the site of America's last great gold rush. Western legends such as Buffalo Bill Cody and the Sundance Kid roamed all over these creek-carved canyons and wind-swept prairies. A few, such as Calamity Jane and Wild Bill Hickok, never left. Today you can see their legacy in places such as Deadwood, the site of one of the country's largest ongoing historic preservation projects, and Sheridan, where Buffalo Bill ran a hotel and recruited for his Wild West Show. But most visitors come to see the heads of America's Shrine of Democracy. Mount Rushmore National Memorial, a mountain sculpture featuring the unblinking granite faces of George Washington, Thomas Jefferson, Theodore Roosevelt, and Abraham Lincoln, attracts more than 3 million visitors each year. Many also pause to examine the beauty in the weathered buttes and otherworldly canyons of Badlands National Park and the vast, untouched plains of Thunder Basin National Grasslands.

5 The Montana Plains

Nestled up against the eastern edge of the Rocky Mountains are the high plains of Montana, a vast expanse of grassy prairie where cattle often outnumber people. Though much of the land has a lonesome, empty look to it, it's rich with the history of America's last frontier in places such as the Little Bighorn Battlefield National Monument, where Lakota and Cheyenne warriors scored a major victory over government troops, and in Ekalaka, where an entire town sprang up around a log saloon in the middle of nowhere. The region is also home to two metropolitan areas that serve as bastions of education, culture, and commerce: Billings, situated along the banks of the Yellowstone River just north of Wyoming, is the state's largest community and one of the largest industrial centers between Minneapolis and Seattle; and Great Falls, nestled at the base of the Rocky Mountains in the north, prides itself on its Western art tradition and beautiful parks.

6 Southwest Montana

Montana's southwest corner was built on the promise of gold-rush riches. More than 30,000 miners and merchants arrived in the five years after the first news of gold strikes on Grasshopper Creek started circulating in 1862. The gold and silver did not last long, but the unexpected discovery of a massive vein of copper beneath Butte ushered in the greatest era of Montana's colorful mining history. Today the region's real treasures are its untamed national forests, blue-ribbon trout streams, and state parks. The Gold West Country also has an ample supply of museums and art galleries, as well as numerous historic sites—the Big Hole National Battlefield, the Grant-Kohrs Ranch, and the stately restored gold camps of Bannack, Virginia City, and Helena's Last

Chance Gulch. Wildlife, water, and wilderness are the hallmarks of the region bordering Yellowstone National Park to the south. Three of Yellowstone's five entrances are here, as are the incredible Beartooth Highway, the Absaroka-Beartooth Wilderness, and the nation's longest free-flowing river. The region's cities and towns, including Bozeman, Livingston, Red Lodge, and West Yellowstone, sponsor year-round special events and are well equipped to welcome visitors.

7 Northwest Montana

Crowned by Glacier National Park, flanked by the Bob Marshall Wilderness Area, and watered by the lakes of the Seeley Valley, northwest Montana is a wild realm encompassing nearly 3 million acres—roughly the size of Connecticut. Add to this the National Bison Range, the Jewel Basin Hiking Area, the Flathead River, and Flathead Lake—the largest body of fresh water in the West—and you can understand why Glacier Country is among the most popular tourist destinations in Montana. Tucked between the peaks and forests are numerous farms that yield such traditional crops as barley, wheat, seed potatoes, oats, and hay. But the peculiar soil and climate of the Flathead Valley also produce outstanding cherries, peppermint, Christmas trees, and champagne grapes. The largest city in the region, Missoula, is home to the University of Montana and the state's most thriving arts community.

8 Southern Idaho

The southern reaches of Idaho are defined by the Snake River plain, a stark desert crescent that swings across the bottom third of the state. Here are Idaho's most desolate stretches as well as its lushest, with more than 4,600 irrigation projects crisscrossing farm fields that grow the state's famous potatoes along with alfalfa, hay, sugar beets, legumes, and grain. Ranches in the south-central region also raise cattle and trout. (Idaho is the biggest commercial producer of trout in the world.) The Snake is the king of Idaho waterways; it carves a wide, steady course through valleys and deep canyons as the river and its aquifer, deep under the plains, pump the lifeblood to Idaho's potato fields in the southeastern and south-central regions of the state. Along the Snake's course there are waterfalls higher than Niagara Falls, springs gushing from canyon walls, and, in Hells Canyon, a gorge deeper than the Grand Canyon. Although potatoes remain the prime cash crop, chips of a different kind are driving the economy in Boise, Idaho's capital and population center. The computer giant Micron is there, along with numerous other high-tech companies.

9 Northern Idaho

Northern Idaho is wild country. The panhandle, with its northern border touching the base of Canada's British Columbia province, is a place of deep woods, mountains rich with precious ores, and huge lakes. Much of the rest of the region is dominated by the 2.3-million-acre Frank Church–River of No Return Wilderness Area, a giant expanse of mountains and raging rivers. Explorers Meriwether Lewis and William Clark supposedly nicknamed the Salmon River "River of No Return" after their boatmen witnessed the waters churning in 1805 "with great violence from one rock to another on each side foaming and roaring, so as to render the passage of any thing impossible." Today, the Salmon and its Middle Fork are ranked among the world's toughest rides by river runners.

Glacier Lakes to the Tetons Driving Tour

7 days

Day 1. Start your tour in Glacier National Park, with its 1,500 square mi of exquisite ice-carved terrain. A drive on the cliff-hugging Going-to-the-Sun Road over the Continental Divide is a must. Overnight at Lake McDonald Lodge. Opened in 1914, Lake McDonald is one of the great lodges of the West. **Day 2.** Spend a second day in Glacier to go river rafting, horseback riding, or hiking. **Day 3.** Drive southwest on U.S. 2 to Kalispell, then south on U.S. 93, where you'll hug the western shoreline of Flathead Lake for about 43 mi to the town of Polson. Flathead is the largest natural freshwater lake in the western United States—take time to breathe it all in. It's only 123 mi from Kalispell to Missoula, but the sheer beauty of the scenery amid the Flathead Indian Reservation, looking to the east at the vast Mission Range, makes the trip seem somewhat longer. Stop by the National Bison Range near Ravalli. The range is a 30-square-mi preserve of natural grasslands established in 1908 to protect one of the few surviving herds of American bison. Overnight in Missoula, at the intersection of five valleys and the junction of three great rivers. This is Montana's hippest town, with excellent galleries, gift shops, and restaurants, as well at the University of Montana and the Missoula Children's Theatre. **Day 4.** Day 4 of your trek takes you 119 mi southeast on I–90 to the century-old mining town of Butte, where the lavish Copper King Mansion reveals what you could buy with an unlimited household budget. To get to West Yellowstone from Butte, follow I–90 east 28 mi to U.S. 287; then turn south and drive 106 mi. Overnight in one of Yellowstone's old hotels, or if you don't want to drive the whole way, spend the night in Butte or Bozeman. **Day 5.** Devote the day to a tour of Yellowstone National Park. The 142-mi Grand Loop Road passes nearly every major attraction in the park, and you'll discover interpretive displays, overlooks, and short trails along the way. Most motorists easily spend a day on the Loop. You really can't go wrong with a stay at the Old Faithful Inn, where lodgepole-pine walls and ceiling beams, an immense volcanic rock fireplace, and green-tinted, etched windows provide the ideal example of what national park lodgings were originally meant to be. **Day 6.** Spend a second day in Yellowstone, this time getting off the Grand Loop to explore the park's hiking trails or to go fishing. **Day 7.** On the final day of your tour, get an early start in an easterly direction on the Grand Loop Road, turning south at Grant Village onto U.S. 89–287. Proceed 43 mi south to Grand Teton National Park, whose northern boundary is 7 mi from Yellowstone's south entrance. The sheer ruggedness of the Tetons makes them seem imposing and unapproachable, but a drive on Teton Park Road, with frequent stops at scenic turnouts, will get you up close and personal with the peaks. Overnight in one of the park lodges.

WHEN TO GO

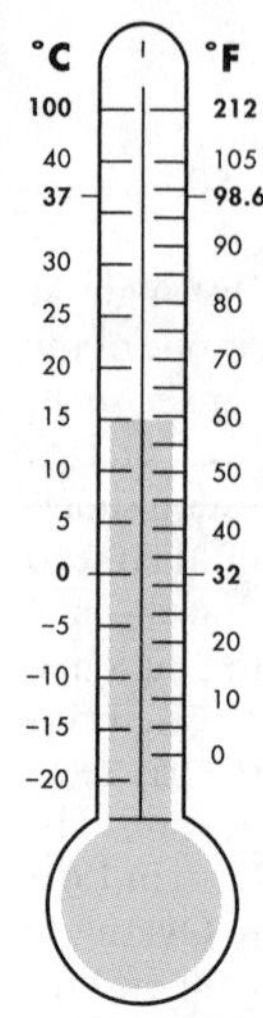

Hotels in tourist destinations book up early, especially in July and August, and hikers spread into the backcountry from June through Labor Day. Ski resorts buzz from December to early April, especially during Christmas and Presidents' holiday weeks.

If you don't mind capricious weather, spring and fall are opportune seasons to visit—rates drop and crowds are nonexistent. Spring's pleasures are somewhat limited, since snow usually blocks the high country well into June. But spring is a good time for fishing, rafting on rivers swollen with snowmelt, birding, and wildlife viewing. In fall, aspens splash the mountainsides with gold, and wildlife come down to lower elevations. The fish are spawning, and the angling is excellent.

Climate

Summer in the area begins in late June or early July. Days are warm, with highs often in the 80s, and nighttime temperatures fall to the 40s and 50s. Afternoon thunderstorms are common over the higher peaks. Fall begins in September, often with a week of unsettled weather around mid-month, followed by four to six gorgeous weeks of Indian summer—frosty nights and warm days. Winter creeps in during November, and deep snows arrive by December. Temperatures usually hover near freezing by day, thanks to the warm mountain sun, dropping considerably overnight, occasionally as low as -60°F. Winter tapers off in March, though snow lingers into April on valley bottoms and into July on mountain passes. The Rockies have a reputation for extreme weather, but no condition ever lasts for long.

Forecasts **Weather Channel Connection** ☎ 900/932–8437, 95¢ per minute from a Touch-Tone phone 🌐 www.weather.com.

Below are the average daily maximum and minimum temperatures for the region.

BOISE, ID

Jan.	37F	3C	May	71F	22C	Sept.	75F	24C
	21	– 6		44	7		46	8
Feb.	42F	6C	June	80F	27C	Oct.	64F	18C
	26	– 3		51	11		39	4
Mar.	53F	12C	July	89F	32C	Nov.	50F	10C
	33	1		57	14		30	– 1
Apr.	62F	17C	Aug.	87F	31C	Dec.	39F	4C
	37	3		55	13		24	– 4

HELENA, MT

Jan.	28F	– 2C	May	62F	17C	Sept.	66F	19C
	12	–11		41	5		44	7
Feb.	32F	0C	June	71F	22C	Oct.	55F	13C
	15	– 9		48	9		35	2
Mar.	42F	6C	July	80F	27C	Nov.	41F	5C
	23	– 5		53	12		24	– 4
Apr.	53F	12C	Aug.	78F	26C	Dec.	32F	0C
	33	1		53	12		17	– 8

SHERIDAN, WY

Jan.	33F	– 1C	May	66F	19C	Sept.	71F	22C
	6	–14		39	4		41	5
Feb.	35F	2C	June	75F	24C	Oct.	60F	16C
	10	–12		48	9		30	– 1
Mar.	46F	8C	July	86F	30C	Nov.	46F	8C
	21	– 6		53	12		19	– 7
Apr.	55F	13C	Aug.	84F	29C	Dec.	35F	2C
	30	– 1		50	10		10	–12

ON THE CALENDAR

WINTER

Dec.	*Idaho*: Sun Valley sparkles as a winter wonderland throughout the month of December with Christmas in Sun Valley (☎ 208/726–3423) festivities. The torchlight parade is a decades-old tradition followed by fireworks on Christmas Eve. Sandpoint becomes "Santapoint" for the Hometown Christmas (☎ 208/263–0887), a 10-day festival of winter activities.
	Montana: Bozeman's Christmas Stroll (☎ 406/586–4008) features sleigh rides, carolers, hot-chocolate stands, holiday lights, and late shopping hours.
	Wyoming: Take a candlelight tour of the Historic Governor's Mansion (☎ 307/777–7878) in Cheyenne to get into the holiday spirit. Members of Company I, Third U.S. Volunteer Infantry and the museum at Fort Caspar Historic Site (☎ 307/235–8462) in Casper celebrate Christmas with candlelight tours.
	Christmas celebrations blanket most Rockies towns. For the holidays, many ski areas mount torchlight parades, with large groups of torch-bearing ski instructors tracing patterns down mountainsides. Contact specific resorts for details.
Jan.	*Idaho:* The Sandpoint Winter Carnival (☎ 208/263–0887) has a snow-sculpture contest, a restaurant sampler of "best" foods, art exhibits, a torchlight parade and fireworks, and a K–9 keg pull where dogs challenge each other pulling an empty beer keg. Winter Olympics Week (☎ 800/634–3347) in Sun Valley has celebrity ski racing, a food fair, and dances. McCall (☎ 208/634–7631) stages a huge winter carnival that stretches into February. You'll find elaborate ice sculptures as well as parades, dogsled races, and fireworks.
	Montana: Settle in for cowboy music, poetry, and art at the Montana Cowboy Poetry Wintercamp (☎ 406/932–4227) in Big Timber. Introduce your children to snowboarding or skiing during Take Your Children to the Snow Week (☎ 406/862–1948) at Big Mountain Resort in Whitefish.
	Wyoming: The Wild West Winter Carnival (☎ 800/325–2732 or 800/645–6233) at Boysen State Park, near Shoshoni, has dog races, a demolition derby, softball, and golf, all on ice, as well as snowmobile races and a "snowdeo."
Feb.	*Idaho*: The Lionel Hampton Jazz Festival (☎ 208/885–6765) in Moscow attracts some of the world's top jazz musicians.
	Montana: Mid-February's Race to the Sky (☎ 406/442–4008 or 800/847–4868) begins with activities in Helena, including contests for mutt pulling and stupid pet tricks, a microbrew review, and Cool Dog Ball. The 350-mi, six-day dogsled race itself crisscrosses the Continental Divide at elevations of up to 7,000 feet, beginning and ending in Lincoln. The trail passes through Seeley Lake and Condon.
	Wyoming: On Presidents' Day weekend, horses race down the track pulling two-wheel carts at the Donald E. Erickson Memorial Chariot Races (☎ 307/326–8855), near Saratoga.

SPRING

Mar.	*Idaho*: In Pocatello, the **Dodge National Circuit Finals Rodeo** (☎ 208/233–1525) draws the top two cowboys from each of 12 national circuits for four days of bareback-riding, roping, and steer-wrestling competitions.
	Montana: Irish folk and other wearers of the green flock to Butte for the **St. Patrick's Day Parade** (☎ 406/782–0742), one of the West's largest and most rollicking, and for other Irish-accented events. Collectors from around the world attend the **C. M. Russell Auction of Original Western Art** (☎ 406/761–6453 or 800/803–3351), held in Great Falls.
	Wyoming: The **Western Spirit Art Show and Sale** (☎ 307/778–1416) at the Old West Museum in Cheyenne includes displays by top regional and national artists. The **Wyoming State Winter Fair** (☎ 307/332–5345) features livestock displays and arts and crafts for sale in Lander.
Apr.	*Idaho*: The citywide **Dogwood Festival** (☎ 208/799–2243) in Lewiston features a rodeo, concerts, and plays.
	Montana: The **International Wildlife Film Festival** (☎ 406/728–9380) in Missoula is one of two such film festivals in the world. The **Rendezvous Cross-country Ski Race** (☎ 406/646–7701) attracts 700 skiers and an entourage 1,500 strong to the 50-km (and other) races at West Yellowstone.
	Wyoming: **Cowboy Songs and Range Ballads** (☎ 307/587–4771) in Cody includes concerts, jam sessions, and a symposium all about cowboy music.
May	*Idaho*: Sandpoint marks summer's beginning with a **Waterfest** (☎ 208/263–2161), including a sand-sculpture contest, a regatta, and waterskiing events. The entire town of Wallace, in north-central Idaho's silver-mining district, is listed on the National Register of Historic Places, and the town's **Depot Day** (☎ 208/263–2161) celebrates Wallace's heritage with music and a car show in early May.
	Montana: At the annual **Big Timber Bull-A-Rama** (☎ 406/932–6228 or 406/932–6697) the West's top bull riders test their skills and spurs on 1,800-pound bucking-mad bulls. In Miles City, rodeo stock for the upcoming season is auctioned off at the **Bucking Horse Sale** (☎ 406/232–7700); the horses demonstrate their bucking prowess in rodeo competitions, and the event also features bull riding, a wild-horse race, and street dances. St. Ignatius hosts the **Buffalo Feast and Powwow** (☎ 406/745–2951) with three days of dancing and games capped by a free feast of pit-roasted buffalo. You can sample fine beers from Montana and the Northwest at the **Garden City Micro B.R.I.W. Fest** (☎ 406/721–6061) in Missoula.
	Wyoming: The huge **Flaming Gorge Fishing Derby** (☎ 307/362–3771) in Rock Springs draws 350 teams of anglers. Dubois hosts **Pack Horse Races** (☎ 307/455–2556 or 307/455–2174), where teams break camp, pack up on horses, and run an obstacle course.

SUMMER

June	*Idaho*: The Boise River Festival (☎ 208/338–8887) has a nighttime parade with animated floats, six stages of entertainment, and 300 other events over the last week of June. The International Women's Challenge (☎ 208/345–7223), statewide, is the nation's premier cycling race for women. Weiser's National Oldtime Fiddlers Contest (☎ 800/437–1280 ⊕ www.fiddlecontest.com) draws the nation's best to compete.
	Montana: The Lewis and Clark Festival (☎ 406/761–4434 or 800/735–8535) in Great Falls highlights the expedition across the West two centuries ago. Tours, kids' day camp, float trips, and courses mark the five-day event. On the third or fourth weekend in June, Great Falls puts on the Montana Traditional Dixieland Jazz Festival (☎ 406/771–1642). The Augusta Rodeo (☎ 406/562–3477) is one of the largest one-day rodeos in Montana and features the old-time Wild Cow Milking and parade. The Battle of the Little Bighorn Reenactment (☎ 406/665–3577 or 888/450–3577) in Hardin enlists more than 200 riders who portray cavalry and Native American participants in that 1876 battle. There is also a historical symposium.
	Wyoming: Bozeman Trail Days (☎ 307/684–7687 or 307/684–7629) has tours and programs about Bozeman Trail travel and Indian wars. On the third full weekend in June, competing lumberjacks make wood chips fly at the Woodchoppers Jamboree & Rodeo (☎ 307/326–8855) in Encampment.
July	*Idaho*: Thirty to forty hot-air balloons are a colorful sight over the mountains at the Teton Valley Hot-Air Balloon Races (☎ 208/354–2500) in Driggs, Idaho, around Independence Day. The Snake River Stampede (☎ 208/466–8497) in Nampa, just west of Boise, is one of the top 20 rodeos in the nation. The largest concentration of Basques in the United States has called southern Idaho home since the 1800s, and the small town of Gooding celebrates Basque heritage with music, dancing, and food during the Gooding Basque Association Picnic (☎ 208/934–4402 or 208/886–2982). The Idaho Shakespeare Festival (☎ 208/336–9221) in Boise runs all summer, presenting the Bard's work under the stars. The Festival at Sandpoint (☎ 208/263–0887), the last two weeks of July and the first two weeks of August, is a celebration of music that includes classical, pop, and jazz. The Sun Valley Ice Shows (☎ 208/622–4111) features former Olympians and professional figure skaters carving the ice from June through September.
	Montana: The Grant-Kohrs Ranch National Historic Site in Deer Lodge, Montana, celebrates cowboy lore and skills during Western Heritage Days (☎ 406/846–2070 or 406/846–3388) with roping, branding, chuck-wagon cooking, and traditional cowboy music and poetry. And don't miss the Montana State Fair (☎ 406/727–8900) in Great Falls at the end of the month.
	Wyoming: The old-fashioned Cody Stampede (☎ 307/587–5155 or 800/207–0744) in Buffalo Bill Cody's eponymous hometown is one of the Rockies' larger July 4 celebrations, complete with rodeos. The Green River Rendezvous (☎ 307/367–4101), near Pinedale,

	stages a reenactment of 1830s mountain life. For the king of outdoor rodeos, see the world's largest, **Cheyenne Frontier Days** (☎ 307/778–7222 or 800/227–6336), in late July. For something in a more arty line, check out the **Grand Teton Music Festival** (☎ 307/733–1128) in Teton Village. Celebrate cowboy and ranching heritage with music and poetry at the **Grand Encampment Cowboy Gathering** (☎ 307/327–5308 or 307/326–8855), plus living-history activities at the Grand Encampment Museum.
Aug.	*Idaho*: As common as rodeos this month are Native American events that showcase traditional songs, dances, and crafts, such as the **Shoshone-Bannock Indian Festival** (☎ 208/238–3700) in Fort Hall. The **Three Island Crossing** (☎ 208/366–2394), at Glenns Ferry on the first weekend in August, is a re-creation of the pioneers' treacherous Snake River crossing. Boise's **Western Idaho Fair** (☎ 208/376–3247) is the state's biggest and brings in a slate of nationally known entertainers. **Art on the Green** (☎ 208/664–3194), in Coeur d'Alene the first weekend in August, has arts, crafts, and dance and is one of Idaho's largest festivals.
	Montana: The **Crow Fair and Rodeo** (☎ 406/638–2601) takes place in Crow Agency—the self-styled tepee capital of the world. The Crow Indian Reservation is off I–90, 45 mi southeast of Billings. At the **Montana Cowboy Poetry Gathering** (☎ 406/538–8278) in Lewiston, U.S. and Canadian performers share verses about a man and a horse following a cow.
	Wyoming: Livestock shows, rodeos, and Western entertainers are part of the **Wyoming State Fair** (☎ 307/358–2398) in Douglas. Enjoy music and brews at the **Steinley Cup Festival** (☎ 307/326–8855), held on an island in the North Platte River in Saratoga. Top brewers from the region compete, and there is also a chili cook-off.
FALL	
Sept.	*Idaho*: You'll find lumberjack competitions at the **Clearwater County Fair and Lumberjack Days** (☎ 208/476–4335) in Orofino. **Idaho Spud Day** (☎ 208/357–3390) in Shelley sponsors the World Spud-Picking Championship. The **Nez Perce Cultural Day** (☎ 208/843–2261), in Spalding, celebrates Native American heritage. Bands from around the country come to the **Pocatello Dixieland Jamboree** (☎ 208/233–1525).
	Montana: Libby's four-day **Nordicfest** (☎ 406/293–6430) celebrates Scandinavian food, costumes, music, dance, and crafts. The **Running of the Sheep** (☎ 406/326–2288) in Reed Point is a surrealistic version of Pamplona's running of the bulls, with hundreds of sturdy Montana-bred woollies charging down Main Street. Seventeen species of raptors and magnificent golden eagles soar over the Bridger Mountains' knife-edge ridge during their southern migration. The **Bridger Raptor Festival** (☎ 406/585–1211) is arranged around the event. Celebrate with the **Labor Day Wagon Train** (☎ 406/547–2209) held at Culbertson. See arts and crafts ranging from photography to beadwork at the **Labor Day Arts Festival** (☎ 406/446–1370) in Red Lodge.

	Wyoming: The Jackson Hole Fall Arts Festival (☎ 307/733–3316) marks the season with concerts, art, poetry, dance, and crafts workshops and lectures throughout the valley. Hundreds of buckskinners gather over Labor Day Weekend for the Fort Bridger Rendezvous (☎ 307/782–3842). There is a parasol parade and dance contest as part of the Lander Jazz Festival (☎ 307/433–0662) held over Labor Day weekend.
Oct.	*Idaho*: The Swing 'N' Jazz Jamboree (☎ 208/726–3423) in Sun Valley presents both big-band and Dixieland music.
	Montana: The four-day Glacier Jazz Stampede (☎ 406/758–2800) belts out ragtime, Dixieland, swing, modern, and big-band jazz in Kalispell.
	Wyoming: Oktoberfest (☎ 307/587–2777) in Cody includes German food and drink, and polka dancing.
Nov.	*Idaho*: Steelhead are the quarry at Idaho's Great Snake Lake Steelhead Derby (☎ 208/743–3531 or 800/473–3543) in Lewiston.
	Montana: Look to the heavens in Great Falls at the Central Montana Astronomy Star Party (☎ 406/727–8733), which has plenty of large telescopes available for public viewing. See a wide array of local products at Bozeman's Holiday Festival of the Arts (☎ 406/586–3333).
	Wyoming: Horse-drawn vehicles are part of the Buffalo Christmas Parade (☎ 307/684–5544), and there is free admission to Buffalo's Jim Gatchell Museum open house and Christmas sale. Cheyenne has dozens of lighted entries, music, and other activities as part of its Christmas Parade (☎ 307/778–3133).

PLEASURES & PASTIMES

Dude Ranches

Dude ranches fall roughly into two categories: working ranches and guest ranches. Working ranches, in which guests participate in such activities as roundups and cattle movements, sometimes require horsemanship experience. Guest ranches, with a wide range of activities in addition to horseback riding, rarely do. The slate of possible activities can vary widely from ranch to ranch. At most establishments, guests are given some taste of the working-ranch experience with demonstrations of rodeo skills and the like. Fishing tends to be given second priority, and after that, almost anything goes. At a typical dude ranch, guests stay in log cabins and are served meals family style in a lodge or ranch house.

Fishing

Trout, whether they be cutthroat, brown, rainbow, Mackinaw, brook, or lake, are the prime game fish in the Rockies. This isn't exactly trophy-fish country, but what they lack in size they make up in volume, especially in stocked waters. Western Montana, the setting of Norman Maclean's fishing-permeated book *A River Runs Through It* and the subsequent film, is teeming with fishing holes along the Blackfoot, Madison, Gallatin, and Yellowstone rivers. Just over the state line in eastern Idaho, anglers in drift boats ply the water for trout at Henry's Fork. Silver Creek, a little stretch of spring water in the high country of south-central Idaho's Picabo Desert, is revered among dry-fly anglers. The Snake River in Wyoming has its own unique cutthroat trout strain. Only at Lake Pend Oreille in the far northern reaches of Idaho's panhandle do anglers catch 30-pound Kamloops trout. Across the state, in the southeastern corner, is Bear Lake, the only place that Bonneville cisco, also known as Bear Lake sardines, call home. Folks head there with dip nets (it's the only place where net fishing is allowed in the state) for the winter runs. Fishing licenses, ranging in term from daily to annual, are required in each state and are available in many convenience stores and sporting-goods shops. Local tackle shops are a good place to feel out a region's most effective lures. It's quite common to hire a knowledgeable guide or sign on with an outfitter for the best experience.

Hiking

There are literally thousands of miles of hiking trails in Montana, Wyoming, and Idaho. The national parks have particularly well marked and well maintained trails, and admittance to all trails is free. In fact, hiking is sometimes the only way to get close to certain highlights on protected land. Primarily for safety reasons, overnight hikers are usually expected to register with park or forest rangers. Also keep in mind that run-ins with bears and mountain lions have become increasingly common.

Horse-Pack Trips

Horse-pack trips are a great way to visit the Rockies' backcountry, since horses can travel distances and carry supplies that would be impossible for hikers. Northwest Montana's Bob Marshall Wilderness is the perfect example; in the state's largest stretch of roadless wilderness, a horse-packing trip is almost the only way to travel the huge expanses. Although horsemanship isn't required for most trips, it is helpful, and even an experienced rider can expect to be a little sore for the first few days. June through August is the peak period for horse-packing trips; before signing up with an outfitter, inquire about the skills they expect.

Meat & Potatoes You're in the land of the unrepentant carnivore here: fine dining means first and foremost well-prepared steaks. It's also prime hunting and fishing territory, which means antelope, elk, venison, and grouse appear regularly on menus, and you'll often have a choice of rainbow trout, salmon, and bass pulled from someone's favorite fishing spot. Microbreweries are another established phenomenon throughout the area—strong entries in the regional market are Montana's Black Dog and Idaho's Table Rock. The local fruits are exceptional: huckleberries from Montana and Idaho are used in everything from muffins to ice cream, and apples, peaches, and pears from roadside stands are full of tree-ripened goodness. And don't forget about potatoes—natives will tell you that if it's not from Idaho, it's just a spud.

Mountain Biking Mountain biking has a huge following in the Rockies—it's more popular in the region than touring on paved roads. The Montana-based Adventure Cycling Association (🌐 www.adventurecycling.org) has mapped interconnecting back roads, logging and forest-service roads, and trails stretching from Canada to Mexico. Few people ride the whole route, which covers close to 2,500 mi, but it's easy to pick a segment to suit any rider's stamina. Although the route does follow, very approximately, the Continental Divide, the riding is not all big-mountain climbing and descending. Portions of the trip are negotiable by children as young as 10. The Adventure Cycling Association leads tours or can provide detailed maps (complete with lodging and/or camping options), information, and advice for self-guided trips.

Riding the Water June through August are the principal months for rafting on the region's rivers. In general (except on dammed rivers), the flow of water lessens as the season wears on. River runners seeking the maximum white-water thrills should come early; families and those who want a gentler float should come later. To prevent overcrowding, almost all major rivers require rafters or kayakers to have permits. For individuals planning their own trips, permits on popular rivers (such as the Middle Fork of the Salmon River or the Selway River in Idaho) can be extremely hard to come by. Permits tend to be awarded first to reputable outfitters, so signing up with an appropriate company is a good way to ensure access.

Skiing Downhill skiing is the most popular winter activity by a large margin, although cross-country skiing and snowboarding have loyal followings. Resorts offer an ever-increasing range of special-interest programs, such as recreational racing and classes for women skiers and skiers with disabilities. Rockies resorts may open their lifts as early as October and close as late as July; the ski season, however, usually runs from December until early April. Christmas through New Year's Day and the month of March tend to be the busiest periods for most ski areas. The slower months of January and February often yield good package deals, as do the early and late ends of the season. Cross-country skiing generally has a shorter season owing to lack of snow, but as avalanche risks lessen in April, backcountry skiers may take advantage of the sun-baked snow. Overall, ski resorts are each area's best source of information on everything from lodging to snow conditions.

FODOR'S CHOICE

Fodor's Choice ★ The sights, restaurants, hotels, and other travel experiences on these pages are our editors' top picks—our Fodor's Choices. They're the best of their type in Montana, Wyoming, and Idaho—not to be missed and always worth your time. In the destination chapters that follow, you will find all the details.

LODGING

$$$$ **The Big EZ,** Big Sky, Montana. The most opulent lodge under the Big Sky has stone fireplaces, king-size beds, and 40-mi views.

$$$$ **Seven Lazy P Guest Ranch,** Bob Marshall Wilderness Area, Montana. From this comfortable all-inclusive ranch you can venture into the rugged Bob Marshall Wilderness, where the terrain is little changed from the days of Lewis and Clark.

$$$$ **Twin Peaks Ranch,** Salmon, Idaho. Fishing, horseback riding, and white-water rafting are the favorite activities at this 2,900-acre dude ranch, where if you want you can help herd the cattle.

$$–$$$$ **Anniversary Inn,** Boise, Idaho. The tasteful facade gives no clue to the sometimes outrageous theme rooms at this one-of-a-kind hotel.

$–$$$ **Old Faithful Inn,** Yellowstone National Park. Massive log beam construction, charmingly rustic rooms, and a reliable geyser just outside make this one of the great lodging facilities in the national park system.

$–$$$ **Paradise Valley Inn Lodge,** Bonners Ferry, Idaho. You're tucked away in the woods at this secluded retreat with a cathedral-ceilinged great room and understated contemporary furnishings.

$–$$ **Holiday Inn of the Waters,** Thermopolis, Wyoming. The rooms are standard, but the waters are something special—there's a hot mineral swimming pool and a large hot mineral soaking pool.

$–$$ **Nagel Warren Mansion,** Cheyenne, Wyoming. If you have only one night in southern Wyoming, spend it at this Victorian B & B with antique furniture, claw-foot tubs, and delectable full breakfasts.

$ **Collins Mansion B & B,** Great Falls, Montana. An 1891 mansion has been converted into one of Montana's most appealing B & Bs, with a massive porch, oak furnishings, and miles of lace.

$ **Scott Inn Bed and Breakfast,** Butte, Montana. This former miners' boardinghouse has fabulous views and modern amenities but retains its Old West charm.

¢–$ **Virginian Hotel,** Medicine Bow, Wyoming. Step back in time at this 1909 sandstone hotel, where the small guest rooms have Victorian furnishings and meals are served at antique oak tables covered with linen tablecloths.

RESTAURANTS

$$$–$$$$ **Juliano's,** Billings, Montana. Hawaiian-born chef Carl Kurokawa creates sophisticated, innovative cuisine that feels right at home in the relaxed Montana setting.

$$$–$$$$	**Rainbow Ranch,** Big Sky, Montana. Local game and fish get an upscale treatment here, complemented by Montana's largest selection of wines.
$$$–$$$$	**Svilars,** Hudson, Wyoming. This small, family-owned restaurant has become a Wyoming landmark by serving the biggest and best steaks in the state.
$$–$$$$	**Old Faithful Snow Lodge restaurant,** Yellowstone National Park. One of the few dining alternatives open year-round in Yellowstone also happens to be the park's best restaurant, with fine food and an unbeatable setting.
$$–$$$	**The Veranda,** Kellogg, Idaho. The intimate upstairs dining room here is charmingly decorated in the style of a sidewalk café, where you can indulge in some of northern Idaho's finest dining.
$–$$	**Overland Restaurant,** Laramie, Wyoming. In fair weather you can sit on the patio of this small restaurant and take in Laramie's historic district while dining on top-rate modern cuisine.
$	**Golden Phoenix,** Rapid City, South Dakota. Throughout the northern plains and Rockies there's a smattering of top-quality Chinese restaurants. Golden Phoenix is one of the best.
¢–$	**Buffalo Cafe,** Whitefish, Montana. For comfort food in a comfortable setting, you can't beat the breakfasts and lunches at this diner/café.
¢	**Purple Cow,** Hardin, Montana. Come here for burgers, shakes, and BLTs that put the fast-food chains to shame.

FESTIVALS

Cheyenne Frontier Days, Cheyenne, Wyoming. The premier event in the Cowboy State has been held the last full week of July every year since 1897; you'll see the world's top rodeo cowboys and cowgirls, parades featuring dozens of horse-drawn carriages, and nightly shows by top entertainers.

Idaho Shakespeare Festival, Boise, Idaho. At a riverside amphitheater you can bring your own picnic and take in nationally acclaimed productions of works from the Bard.

National Oldtime Fiddlers' Contest, Weiser, Idaho. The finest fiddlers from around the country congregate in Weiser every June and let their bows fly. The event has become a full-blown festival, with dances, cooking contests, a parade, and other events.

HISTORY

Deadwood, Black Hills, North Dakota. This famous Wild West town, once the epicenter of America's last great gold rush, is marked by its brick-paved streets and Victorian buildings.

Lake Yellowstone Hotel, Yellowstone National Park. Built in 1891, this white-columned hotel is now on the National Register of Historic Places. It's a great spot to soak up the atmosphere of an old-time resort, whether or not you plan on spending the night.

Sheridan Inn, Sheridan, Wyoming. Buffalo Bill Cody used to sit on the porch of this massive gabled inn—designed to resemble a Scottish hunting lodge—and recruit talent for his Wild West Show. Though you can no longer spend the night here, you can stop in for a meal or just look around.

MUSEUMS

Buffalo Bill Historical Center, Cody, Wyoming. This complex is one of the finest cultural institutions of the West, with five major museums related to Plains Indians, Western art, firearms, natural history, and, of course, Buffalo Bill.

C. M. Russell Museum Complex, Great Falls, Montana. Through an extensive collection of art and artifacts, this museum commemorates not only the life of Charlie Russell, one of the most famous Western artists, but also the passing of frontier culture and the coming of civilization.

Grand Encampment Museum, Encampment, Wyoming. Beyond doubt the best small-town museum in Wyoming, this volunteer-run pioneer town has relics from the mining, ranching, and timbering heritage of the area, including everything from a stage station to a two-story outhouse.

Museum of the Upper Missouri, Fort Benton, Montana. This small museum interprets and preserves the remains of Old Fort Benton, once the furthest inland port in the world and Montana's oldest standing structure.

National Historic Trails Interpretive Center, Casper, Wyoming. No fewer than four pioneer trails, linking civilization in the East with a wilderness full of opportunity in the West, intersected where this museum now stands.

MONUMENTS

Crazy Horse Memorial, Black Hills, North Dakota. When completed, this mountain monument to Native American leaders will be the largest sculpture in the world; until then, you can watch the carving in progress—perhaps including a few dynamite blasts.

Mount Rushmore National Memorial, Black Hills, North Dakota. America's "Shrine of Democracy," depicting George Washington, Thomas Jefferson, Theodore Roosevelt, and Abraham Lincoln on a massive scale, is one of the nation's most enduring icons.

Pictograph Cave State Monument, Billings, Montana. Hundreds of millennia-old cave paintings document the lives and culture of Montana's earliest residents.

NATURE

Grand Canyon of the Yellowstone, Yellowstone National Park. The Yellowstone River travels between the red and ocher walls of this canyon after cascading over two waterfalls; there are hiking trails along both the north and south canyon rims.

Hells Canyon, Lewiston, Idaho. Wander through depths greater than the Grand Canyon, past hills that resemble ancient Maya temples.

National Bison Range, Flathead Indian Reservation, Montana. The 19-mi loop road of the range gives you unparalleled views of elk, pronghorn, deer, mountain sheep, and a 400-head bison herd.

Norris Geyser Basin, Yellowstone National Park. In Yellowstone's hottest, most active thermal area, you'll see everything from bubbling mud pots to hissing fumaroles to geysers shooting water dozens of feet into the air.

Old Faithful Geyser, Yellowstone National Park. A visit to Yellowstone isn't complete until you've seen the world's most famous geyser spout.

Pryor Mountain Wild Horse Range, Bighorn Canyon, Montana. Set between the thousand-foot cliffs of the Bighorn River and the towering peaks of the Pryor Mountains, this isolated refuge is home to the wild descendants of horses first brought to this continent by the Spanish in the 16th century.

OUTDOOR ACTIVITIES

Boat outings from Flathead Lake Lodge, Bigfork, Montana. Take a 51-foot Q-class racing sloop built in the 1920s out onto the largest natural freshwater lake in the western United States.

Burgdorf Hot Springs, McCall, Idaho. Come here for the simple pleasure of a log-sided hot-spring pool, surrounding mountains, and not much else in the way of civilization.

The Highline Trail, Glacier National Park, Montana. The hike from Logan Pass to Granite Park Chalet is one of the highlights of spectacular Glacier National Park.

Fishing on the Gallatin River, Gallatin Canyon, Montana. You're as close as you'll get to fly-fishing heaven here, on the location where they shot the movie *A River Runs Though It.*

Jewel Basin Hiking Area, Flathead Lake, Montana. Thiry-five miles of well-maintained trails take you by 27 trout-filled alpine lakes.

Whitewater rafting on the Payette River, north of Boise, Idaho. Whether you're a beginner or an old hand, you'll find thrills on the Payette.

Route of the Hiawathas, Silver Valley, Idaho. This bike path running along an old railroad track bed is a fun, easy ride, passing through nine tunnels and across seven trestle bridges.

SKI RESORTS

Jackson Hole Mountain Resort, near Jackson, Wyoming. Skiers and snowboarders covet vertical rise and diverse terrain: they find both in abundance at Jackson Hole.

Sun Valley, Idaho. You can be pampered at the grand dame of U.S. ski resorts while you contemplate taking on the 3,400 vertical feet of Bald Mountain.

SMART TRAVEL TIPS

Finding out about your destination before you leave home means you won't squander time organizing everyday minutiae once you've arrived. You'll be more on top of things when you hit the ground as well, better prepared to explore the aspects of Montana, Wyoming, and Idaho that drew you here in the first place. The organizations in this section can provide information to supplement this guide; contact them for up-to-the-minute details, and consult the A to Z sections that end each chapter for facts on the various topics as they relate to the states' different regions. Happy landings!

AIR TRAVEL

The best connections to the region (shortest travel times) are through the Rockies hub cities, Salt Lake City and Denver. This is absolutely the case for Wyoming and most of Idaho, and often so for Montana. Idaho and Montana also receive transfer flights from Minneapolis, Seattle, and Phoenix.

BIKES IN FLIGHT

Most airlines accommodate bikes as luggage, provided they are dismantled and boxed. Airlines sell bike boxes, which are often free at bike shops, for about $15 (it's at least $100 for bike bags). International travelers can sometimes substitute a bike for a piece of checked luggage at no charge; otherwise, the cost is about $100. Domestic and Canadian airlines charge $80–$160.

BOOKING

When you book, **look for nonstop flights** and **remember that "direct" flights stop at least once.** Try to avoid connecting flights, which require a change of plane. Two airlines may operate a connecting flight jointly, so ask whether your airline operates every segment of the trip; you may find that the carrier you prefer flies you only part of the way. To find more booking tips and to check prices and make online flight reservations, log on to www.fodors.com.

CARRIERS

United and Delta have the most flights to the region. The regional carrier Big Sky serves Montana cities, and Boise, Idaho, making it possible to travel between those locations; to get in or out of the two states using Big Sky Airlines, you must connect with other airlines, primarily America West or Northwest.

Major Airlines **Air Canada** ☎ 888/247-2262 🌐 www.aircanada.com. **American Airlines** ☎ 800/433-7300 🌐 www.aa.com. **British Airways** ☎ 800/247-9297 🌐 www.ba.com. **Continental** ☎ 800/525-0280 🌐 www.continental.com. **Delta** ☎ 800/221-1212 🌐 www.delta.com. **Northwest** ☎ 800/225-2525 🌐 www.nwa.com. **United Airlines** ☎ 800/241-6522 🌐 www.united.com. **US Airways** ☎ 800/428-4322 🌐 www.usair.com.

Smaller Airlines **America Trans Air** (ATA) ☎ 800/225-2995. **America West** ☎ 800/235-9292. **Big Sky** ☎ 800/237-7788 🌐 www.bigskyair.com. **Frontier** ☎ 800/432-1359. **Horizon Air** ☎ 800/547-9308. **Mesa Airlines** ☎ 800/637-2247. **Midwest Express** ☎ 800/452-2022. **SkyWest** ☎ 800/453-9417. **Southwest** ☎ 800/435-9792.

CHECK-IN & BOARDING

Always **ask your carrier about its check-in policy.** Plan to arrive at the airport about two hours before your scheduled departure time for domestic flights and 2½ to 3 hours before international flights. You may need to arrive earlier if you're flying from one of the busier airports or during peak air-traffic times.

If you're traveling during snow season, **allow extra time for the drive** to the airport, as weather conditions can slow you down. If you'll be checking skis, arrive even earlier.

To avoid delays at airport-security checkpoints, try not to wear any metal. Jewelry, belt and other buckles, steel-toe shoes, barrettes, and underwire bras are among the items that can set off detectors.

Assuming that not everyone with a ticket will show up, airlines routinely overbook planes. When everyone does, airlines ask for volunteers to give up their seats. In return, these volunteers usually get a several-hundred-dollar flight voucher, which can be used toward the purchase of another ticket, and are rebooked on the next flight out. If there are not enough volunteers, the airline must choose who will be denied boarding. The first to get bumped are passengers who checked in late and those flying on discounted tickets, so **get to the gate and check in as early as possible,** especially during peak periods.

Always **bring a government-issued photo ID to the airport;** even when it's not required, a passport is best.

CUTTING COSTS

The least expensive airfares to the Rockies are priced for round-trip travel and must usually be purchased in advance. Airlines generally allow you to change your return date for a fee; most low-fare tickets, however, are nonrefundable. It's smart to **call a number of airlines and check the Internet;** when you are quoted a good price, **book it on the spot**—the same fare may not be available the next day, or even the next hour. Always **check different routings** and look into using alternate airports. Also, price off-peak flights, which may be significantly less expensive than others. Travel agents, especially low-fare specialists (⇨ Discounts and Deals), are helpful.

Consolidators are another good source. They buy tickets for scheduled flights at reduced rates from the airlines, then sell them at prices that beat the best fare available directly from the airlines. Sometimes you can even get your money back if you need to return the ticket. Carefully read the fine print detailing penalties for changes and cancellations, purchase the ticket with a credit card, and **confirm your consolidator reservation with the airline.**

Consolidators **AirlineConsolidator.com** ☎ 888/468-5385 🌐 www.airlineconsolidator.com for international tickets. **Best Fares** ☎ 800/576-8255 or 800/576-1600 🌐 www.bestfares.com; $59.90 annual membership. **Cheap Tickets** ☎ 800/377-1000 or 888/922-8849 🌐 www.cheaptickets.com. **Expedia** ☎ 800/397-3342 or 404/728-8787 🌐 www.expedia.com. **Hotwire** ☎ 866/468-9473 or 920/330-9418 🌐 www.hotwire.com. **Now Voyager Travel** ✉ 315 W. 49th St. Plaza Arcade, New York, NY 10019 ☎ 212/459-1616 📠 212/262-7407 🌐 www.nowvoyagertravel.com. **Onetravel.com** 🌐 www.onetravel.com. **Orbitz** ☎ 888/656-4546 🌐 www.orbitz.com. **Priceline.com** 🌐 www.priceline.com. **Travelocity** ☎ 888/709-5983, 877/282-2925 in Canada, 0870/876-3876 in U.K. 🌐 www.travelocity.com.

ENJOYING THE FLIGHT

State your seat preference when purchasing your ticket, and then repeat it when you confirm and when you check in. For more legroom, you can request one of the few emergency-aisle seats at check-in, if you are capable of lifting at least 50 pounds—a Federal Aviation Administration requirement of passengers in these seats. Seats behind a bulkhead also offer more legroom, but they don't have under-seat storage. Don't sit in the row in front of the emergency aisle or in front of a bulkhead, where seats may not recline.

Ask the airline whether a snack or meal is served on the flight. If you have dietary concerns, **request special meals when booking.** These can be vegetarian, low-cholesterol, or kosher, for example. It's a good idea to pack some healthful snacks and a small (plastic) bottle of water in your carry-on bag. On long flights, try to maintain a normal routine, to help fight jet lag. At night, **get some sleep.** By day, **eat light meals, drink water** (not alcohol), and **move around the cabin** to stretch your legs. For additional jet-lag tips consult *Fodor's FYI: Travel Fit & Healthy* (available at bookstores everywhere).

Smoking policies vary from carrier to carrier. Many airlines prohibit smoking on all of their flights; others allow smoking only on certain routes or certain departures. Ask your carrier about its policy.

FLYING TIMES

Once you have made your way to Denver or Salt Lake City, which are two of the major hubs providing air service to Idaho, Montana, and Wyoming, you will still have one or two hours of flying time to reach your final airport destination. Many of the airports in all three states are served by commuter flights that have frequent stops, though generally with very short layovers. There are no direct flights from New York to the area; most itineraries from New York take between seven and nine hours. You can reach Boise by direct flight from Chicago (four hours) and San Francisco (90 minutes).

HOW TO COMPLAIN

If your baggage goes astray or your flight goes awry, complain right away. Most carriers require that you **file a claim immediately.** The Aviation Consumer Protection Division of the Department of Transportation publishes *Fly-Rights,* which discusses airlines and consumer issues and is available online. At PassengerRights.com, a Web site, you can compose a letter of complaint and distribute it electronically.

Airline Complaints **Aviation Consumer Protection Division** ✉ U.S. Department of Transportation, C-75, Room 4107, 400 7th St. NW, Washington, DC 20590 ☎ 202/366-2220 🌐 www.dot.gov/airconsumer. **Federal Aviation Administration Consumer Hotline** ✉ for inquiries: FAA, 800 Independence Ave. SW, Room 810, Washington, DC 20591 ☎ 800/322-7873 🌐 www.faa.gov.

RECONFIRMING

Check the status of your flight before you leave for the airport. You can do this on your carrier's Web site, by linking to a flight-status checker (many Web booking services offer these), or by calling your carrier or travel agent.

AIRPORTS

The major gateways include, in Idaho, Boise Airport, and, for northern Idaho, Spokane International Airport in Washington; in Montana, Missoula International Airport and Glacier Park International Airport in Kalispell; and, in Wyoming, Jackson Hole Airport, Cheyenne Municipal Airport, Natrona County International Airport, and Yellowstone Regional Airport.

Colorado Airport Information **Denver International Airport** ☎ 303/342-2000, 800/247-2336, 800/688-1333 TTY 🌐 www.flydenver.com

Idaho Airport Information **Boise Airport** ☎ 208/383-3110.

Montana Airport Information **Glacier Park International Airport** ☎ 406/257-5994 🌐 www.glacierairport.com. **Missoula International Airport** ☎ 406/728-4381 🌐 www.msoairport.org.

Utah Airport Information **Salt Lake City International Airport** ☎ 801/575-2400.

Washington Airport Information **Spokane International Airport** ☎ 509/455-6455 🌐 spokaneairport.net

Wyoming Airport Information **Cheyenne Municipal Airport** ☎ 307/634-7071 🌐 www.cheyenneairport.com. **Jackson Hole Airport** ☎ 307/733-7682 🌐 www.jacksonholeairport.com. **Natrona County International Airport** ☎ 307/472-6688 🌐 casperwyoming.org/airport. **Yellowstone Regional Airport** ☎ 307/587-5096 🌐 www.flyyra.com.

BIKE TRAVEL

Bike travel is popular throughout the region, particularly among folks who like to ride roads that follow the Continental Divide. Generally bike travel is prohibited on interstate highways; there are few bike lanes anywhere, though you will find some in resort areas in all states in the region. As a result bike riders will be sharing the road with cars, trucks, RVs, and other traffic. In summer there is almost always construction on roads throughout the region, which can create problems for bike riders. Rentals are available in resort areas particularly, and often in other cities as well. Expect to pay $15 to $30 for a half- or full-day rental of either a mountain bike or a touring bike. Local bike shops are the best places to get bike maps and other information about cycling. For more information, see "Bicycling" under "Sports & the Outdoors" below.

Resources **Adventure Cycling Association** Box 8308, Missoula, MT 59807 406/721-1776 or 800/755-2453 www.adventurecycling.org. **National Geographic/Trails Illustrated** 800/962-1643. **Off-Road Publications** 888/477-3374.

BUS TRAVEL

Greyhound Lines has regular intercity routes throughout the region, with connections from Cheyenne, Rawlins, and Rock Springs, to Salt Lake City, which then also connects with Boise, Bozeman, and Missoula. Smaller bus companies provide service within state and local areas.

Boise-Winnemucca Stages Idaho 800/448-5692 www.northwesterntrailways.com. **Greyhound Lines** 800/231-2222 www.greyhound.com. **Coach USA/Powder River Transportation** Wyoming 800/442-3682 in Wyoming. **Rimrock/Trailways** Montana 800/255-7655.

BUSINESS HOURS

Most retail stores are open from 9 or 9:30 until 6 or 7 daily in downtown locations and until 9 or 10 in suburban shopping malls and in resort towns during high seasons. Downtown stores sometimes stay open later Thursday night. Normal banking hours are weekdays 9–5; some branches are also open on Saturday morning.

CAMERAS & PHOTOGRAPHY

Photographers love the Rockies—and with good reason. The scenery is America's best, and every season offers a multitude of breathtaking images. When you're at Native American sites, be sure to ask if taking pictures is appropriate. The *Kodak Guide to Shooting Great Travel Pictures* (available at bookstores everywhere) is loaded with tips.

Photo Help **Kodak Information Center** 800/242-2424 www.kodak.com.

EQUIPMENT PRECAUTIONS

Wind, dust, and dirt are the biggest problems you'll face with camera equipment throughout the Rockies, though if you are traveling in winter, you might experience problems because of extremely cold temperatures (it can get down to 20°F–30°F below zero and stay there for days at a time). The best way to take care of your gear is to keep it in a case or bag whenever possible, and clean it often with canned air and other lens-cleaning gear. In winter keep it out of the cold as much as possible; tuck it inside your jacket when you are not actually shooting. **Don't pack film and equipment in checked luggage,** where it is much more susceptible to damage. X-ray machines used to view checked luggage are extremely powerful and therefore are likely to ruin your film. Try to **ask for hand inspection of film,** which becomes clouded after repeated exposure to airport X-ray machines, and **keep videotapes and computer disks away from metal detectors.** Always **keep film, tape, and computer disks out of the sun.** Carry an extra supply of batteries, and **be prepared to turn on your camera, camcorder, or laptop** to prove to airport security personnel that the device is real.

CAR RENTAL

Rates in most major cities run about $50 a day and $275–$325 a week for an economy car with air-conditioning, automatic transmission, and unlimited mileage. If you plan to explore any back roads, an SUV (about $85 a day) is the best bet because it will have higher clearance. This does not include tax on car rentals, which is 5% in Boise and 6% in Jackson Hole. There is no tax in Montana, but if you rent from an airport location, there is an airport concession fee. In resort areas such as Jackson or Kalispell, you will usually find a variety of 4X4s and SUVs for rent, many of them with ski racks. Unless you plan to do a lot of mountain exploring, a four-wheel drive is usually needed only in winter.

Major Agencies **Alamo** 800/327-9633 www.alamo.com. **Avis** 800/331-1212, 800/879-2847 or 800/272-5871 in Canada, 0870/606-0100 in U.K., 02/9353-9000 in Australia, 09/526-2847 in New Zealand www.avis.com. **Budget** 800/527-0700, 0870/156-5656 in U.K. www.budget.com. **Dollar** 800/800-4000, 0124/622-

0111 in U.K., where it's affiliated with Sixt, 02/9223-1444 in Australia ⊕ www.dollar.com. Hertz ☎ 800/654-3131, 800/263-0600 in Canada, 0870/844-8844 in U.K., 02/9669-2444 in Australia, 09/256-8690 in New Zealand ⊕ www.hertz.com. National Car Rental ☎ 800/227-7368, 0870/600-6666 in U.K. ⊕ www.nationalcar.com.

CUTTING COSTS

Rental rates are similar whether at the airport or at an in-town agency. Many people fly in to Salt Lake City or Denver and rent a car there to cut travel costs. This makes sense if you're traveling to southern Idaho or southern Wyoming, but if your goal is Jackson or Cody, that's a 10- to 11-hour drive from Denver. From Salt Lake City, it's about a six-hour drive to Jackson and a nine-hour one to Cody.

For a good deal, **book through a travel agent who will shop around.** Also, **price local car-rental companies**—whose prices may be lower still, although their service and maintenance may not be as good as those of major rental agencies—and **research rates on the Internet.** Remember to ask about required deposits, cancellation penalties, and drop-off charges if you're planning to pick up the car in one city and leave it in another. If you're traveling during a holiday period, also make sure that a confirmed reservation guarantees you a car.

INSURANCE

When driving a rented car you are generally responsible for any damage to or loss of the vehicle. You also may be liable for any property damage or personal injury that you may cause while driving. Before you rent, see what coverage you already have under the terms of your personal auto-insurance policy and credit cards.

For about $10 to $25 a day, rental companies sell protection, known as a collision- or loss-damage waiver (CDW or LDW), that eliminates your liability for damage to the car; it's always optional and should never be automatically added to your bill. In most states (including Idaho, Montana, and Wyoming), you don't need a CDW if you have personal auto insurance or other liability insurance. However, **make sure you have enough coverage to pay for the car.** If you do not have auto insurance or an umbrella policy that covers damage to third parties, purchasing liability insurance and a CDW or LDW is highly recommended.

REQUIREMENTS & RESTRICTIONS

In the Rockies you must be 21 to rent a car with a valid driver's license; some companies charge an additional fee for drivers ages 21–24, and others will not rent to anyone under age 25; most companies also require a major credit card.

Child seats are compulsory for children under five (under eight in Wyoming) and cost $5 to $10 a day. Non-U.S. residents will need a reservation voucher, a passport, a driver's license, and a travel policy that covers each driver, in order to pick up a car. In most cases, cars rented in the region are not allowed to cross into Canada.

SURCHARGES

Before you pick up a car in one city and leave it in another, **ask about drop-off charges or one-way service fees,** which can be substantial. Note, too, that some rental agencies charge extra if you return the car before the time specified in your contract. To avoid a hefty refueling fee, **fill the tank just before you turn in the car,** but be aware that gas stations near the rental outlet may overcharge. It's almost never a deal to buy the tank of gas that's in the car when you rent it; the understanding is that you'll return it empty, but some fuel usually remains. You'll pay extra for child seats ($5–$10 a day) and usually for additional drivers (about $7 per day).

CAR TRAVEL

You'll seldom be bored driving through the Rockies, which offer some of the most spectacular vistas and challenging driving in the world. Idaho is home to the rockiest and most rugged stretch of the mountains, with an extraordinarily wild beauty. It is impossible to travel directly through the heart of the state—only two routes go from north to south. Montana's interstate system is more driver-friendly, connecting soaring summits, rivers, glacial valleys, forests, lakes, and vast stretches of prairie, all capped by that endless "Big Sky." Wyoming's interstate links classic, open-range cowboy country and mountain-range vistas with the geothermal wonderland of Yellowstone National Park. In Wyoming, everything is separated by vast distances, so be sure to leave each major city with a full tank of gas and be prepared to see lots of wildlife and few other people.

Before setting out on any driving trip, it's important to **make sure your vehicle is in top condition.** It is best to have a complete tune-up. At the least, you should check the following: lights, including brake lights, backup lights, and emergency lights; tires, including the spare; oil; engine coolant; windshield-washer fluid; windshield-wiper blades; and brakes. For emergencies, take along flares or reflector triangles, jumper cables, an empty gas can, a fire extinguisher, a flashlight, a plastic tarp, blankets, water, and coins or a calling card for phone calls (cell phones don't always work in high mountain areas).

BORDER CROSSING

Driving a car across the U.S.–Canadian border is simple. Personal vehicles are allowed entry into the neighboring country, provided they are not to be left behind. Drivers must have owner registration and proof of insurance coverage handy. If the car isn't registered in your name, carry a letter from the owner that authorizes your use of the vehicle. Drivers in rental cars that are permitted to cross the border should **bring along a copy of the rental contract,** which should bear an endorsement stating that the vehicle is permitted to cross the border.

GASOLINE

In major cities throughout the Rockies, gas prices are roughly similar to those in the rest of the continental United States; in rural and resort towns, prices are sometimes considerably higher. Although gas stations are relatively plentiful in many areas, you can drive more than 100 mi on back roads without finding gas.

ROAD CONDITIONS

Roads range from multilane blacktop to barely graveled backcountry trails. Many twisting switchbacks are considerately marked with guardrails, but some primitive campgrounds have a lane so narrow that you must back up to the edge of a steep cliff to make a turn. Scenic routes and lookout points are clearly marked, enabling you to slow down and pull over to take in the views.

One of the more unpleasant sights along the highway is roadkill—animals struck by vehicles. Deer, elk, and even bears may try to get to the other side of a road just as you come along, so **watch out for wildlife on the highways.** Exercise caution, not only to save an animal's life, but also to avoid possible extensive damage to your car.

Road Condition Information **Idaho** ☎ 208/336-6600 or 800/432-7623. **Montana** ☎ 406/444-6339 or 800/262-6171. **Wyoming** ☎ 307/772-0824 or 800/996-7623.

RULES OF THE ROAD

You'll find highways and the national parks crowded in summer, and almost deserted (and occasionally impassable) in winter. You may turn right at a red light after stopping if there is no sign stating otherwise and no oncoming traffic. When in doubt, wait for the green. Follow the posted speed limit, drive defensively, and **make sure your gas tank is full.** The law requires that drivers and front-seat passengers **wear seat belts**; in Montana and Wyoming **rear-seat occupants also must wear seat belts.**

SPEED LIMITS

The speed limit on U.S. interstates is 75 mph in rural areas and 65 mph in urban zones. The speed limit on most two-lane roads is 55 or 65 mph; in Montana there are lower speed limits at night.

WINTER DRIVING

Modern highways make mountain driving safe and generally trouble-free even in cold weather. Although winter driving can occasionally present some real challenges, road maintenance is good and plowing is prompt. However, in mountain areas, tire chains, studs, or snow tires are essential. If you're planning to drive into high elevations, be sure to **check the weather forecast and call for road conditions** beforehand. Even main highways can close. Be prepared for stormy weather: **carry an emergency kit** containing warm clothes, a flashlight, some food and water, and blankets. It's also good to carry a cell phone, but be aware that the mountains can disrupt service. If you do get stalled by deep snow, **do not leave your car.** Wait for help, running the engine only if needed, and remember that assistance is never far away. Winter weather isn't confined to winter months in the high country (it's been known to snow on July 4), so be prepared year-round.

CHILDREN IN MONTANA, WYOMING & IDAHO

The Rockies are tailor-made for family vacations, offering dude ranches; historic railroads; mining towns; the extreme natural features of national parks such as Yellowstone, Grand Teton, and Glacier; rafting; and many other outdoor activities. Visitor centers and lodgings are often good at recommending places to spend time with children. Attractions sometimes offer reduced family admission tickets.

The Wyoming State Tourism guide has a section geared toward children. Idaho and Montana have a small flyer for kids as well as more extensive information on children's activities in their state travel brochures. Good car reading includes the activity guidebooks *Following Lewis & Clark's Trail* ($7.95) and *Reading, Writing & Riding along the Oregon Trail*, both published by the Oregon-California Trails Association.

Guidebooks for Children **Oregon-California Trails Association** Box 1019, Independence, MO 64051-0519 816/252-2276 or 888/811-6282.

CAR TRAVEL

If you are renting a car, don't forget to **arrange for a car seat** when you reserve. For general advice about traveling with children, consult *Fodor's FYI: Travel with Your Baby* (available in bookstores everywhere).

Always **strap children under age five into approved child-safety seats.** In Wyoming, children must be in a child restraint seat if they are under age eight and less than 80 pounds. Children in Wyoming also may not ride in the front seat of any vehicle that has more than one row of seats.

FLYING

If your children are two or older, **ask about children's airfares.** As a general rule, infants under two not occupying a seat fly at greatly reduced fares or even for free. But if you want to guarantee a seat for an infant, you have to pay full fare. Consider flying during off-peak days and times; most airlines will grant an infant a seat without a ticket if there are available seats.

Experts agree that it's a good idea to use safety seats aloft for children weighing less than 40 pounds. Airlines set their own policies: If you use a safety seat, U.S. carriers usually require that the child be ticketed, even if he or she is young enough to ride free, because the seats must be strapped into regular seats. And even if you pay the full adult fare for the seat, it may be worth it, especially on longer trips. Do **check your airline's policy about using safety seats during takeoff and landing.** Safety seats are not allowed everywhere in the plane, so get your seat assignments as early as possible.

When reserving, **request children's meals or a freestanding bassinet** (not available at all airlines) if you need them. But note that bulkhead seats, where you must sit to use the bassinet, may lack an overhead bin or storage space on the floor.

LODGING

Most hotels in the Rockies allow children under a certain age to stay in their parents' room at no extra charge, but others charge for them as extra adults; be sure to **find out the cutoff age for children's discounts.** Many lodging properties that have restaurants also allow children to eat free or at reduced prices.

Although most dude ranches are ideal for children of all ages, be sure you know not only the activities a ranch offers but also which are emphasized before booking your vacation. A few ranches may have age restrictions excluding very young children.

SIGHTS & ATTRACTIONS

Places that are especially appealing to children are indicated by a rubber-duckie icon (🐤) in the margin. In all three of the region's national parks—Yellowstone, Grand Teton, and Glacier—children can participate in Junior Ranger programs that encourage learning about the natural wonders and wildlife of the area. There are interactive exhibits at the Buffalo Bill Historical Center in Cody, a chance to see elk up close at the National Elk Refuge near Jackson, and opportunities to dig for dinosaurs at various sites in Montana and Wyoming.

SPORTS & THE OUTDOORS

Altitude can be even more taxing on small lungs than on adult lungs, so **be conservative** when evaluating what level of activity your child will enjoy.

Some trip organizers arrange backpacking outings for families with small children, especially for family groups of eight or more. Short half-day or full-day bike trips with plenty of flat riding are possible at many Rocky Mountain resorts. Ask at local bike shops for recommended rides for children. Among the better resorts for biking and children's ski programs are Sun Valley Resorts in Idaho and Jackson Hole Mountain Resort in Wyoming.

It is not advisable to take children under seven on any extended rafting trip, except those specifically geared toward young children. Before taking an extended trip, you might want to test the waters with a half-day or one-day excursion. For families with younger children, trips aboard larger, motorized rafts are probably safest. Floating the gentle Snake River in Wyoming is best for young children. Outfitters designate some trips as "adults only," with the cutoff usually being 16 years old.

CONSUMER PROTECTION

Whether you're shopping for gifts or purchasing travel services, **pay with a major credit card** whenever possible, so you can cancel payment or get reimbursed if there's a problem (and you can provide documentation). If you're doing business with a particular company for the first time, **contact your local Better Business Bureau and the attorney general's offices** in your state and (for U.S. businesses) the company's home state as well. Have any complaints been filed? Finally, if you're buying a package or tour, always **consider travel insurance** that includes default coverage (⇨ Insurance).

BBBs **Council of Better Business Bureaus** ✉ 4200 Wilson Blvd., Suite 800, Arlington, VA 22203 ☎ 703/276-0100 🖷 703/525-8277 🌐 www.bbb.org.

CUSTOMS & DUTIES

When shopping abroad, **keep receipts** for all purchases. Upon reentering the country, **be ready to show customs officials what you've bought.** Pack purchases together in an easily accessible place. If you think a duty is incorrect, appeal the assessment. If you object to the way your clearance was handled, note the inspector's badge number. In either case, first ask to see a supervisor. If the problem isn't resolved, write to the appropriate authorities, beginning with the port director at your point of entry.

IN AUSTRALIA

Australian residents who are 18 or older may bring home A$400 worth of souvenirs and gifts (including jewelry), 250 cigarettes or 250 grams of cigars or other tobacco products, and 1,125 ml of alcohol (including wine, beer, and spirits). Residents under 18 may bring back A$200 worth of goods. Members of the same family traveling together may pool their allowances. Prohibited items include meat products. Seeds, plants, and fruits need to be declared upon arrival.

Australian Customs Service Regional Director, Box 8, Sydney, NSW 2001 ☎ 02/9213-2000 or 1300/363263, 02/9364-7222, or 1800/803-006 quarantine-inquiry line 🖷 02/9213-4043 🌐 www.customs.gov.au.

IN CANADA

Canadian residents who have been out of Canada for at least seven days may bring in C$750 worth of goods duty-free. If you've been away fewer than seven days but more than 48 hours, the duty-free allowance drops to C$200. If your trip lasts 24 to 48 hours, the allowance is C$50. You may not pool allowances with family members. Goods claimed under the C$750 exemption may follow you by mail; those claimed under the lesser exemptions must accompany you. Alcohol and tobacco products may be included in the seven-day and 48-hour exemptions but not in the 24-hour exemption. If you meet the age requirements of the province or territory through which you reenter Canada, you may bring in, duty-free, 1.5 liters of wine *or* 1.14 liters (40 imperial ounces) of liquor *or* 24 12-ounce cans or bottles of beer or ale. Also, if you meet the local age requirement for tobacco products, you may bring in, duty-free, 200 cigarettes and 50 cigars. Check ahead of time with the Canada Customs and Revenue Agency or the Department of Agriculture for policies regarding meat products, seeds, plants, and fruits.

You may send an unlimited number of gifts (only one gift per recipient, however) worth up to C$60 each duty-free to Canada. Label the package UNSOLICITED GIFT—VALUE UNDER $60. Alcohol and tobacco are excluded.

Canada Customs and Revenue Agency ✉ 2265 St. Laurent Blvd., Ottawa, Ontario K1G 4K3 ☎ 800/461-9999, 204/983-3500, 506/636-5064 🌐 www.ccra.gc.ca.

IN NEW ZEALAND

All homeward-bound residents may bring back NZ$700 worth of souvenirs and gifts; passengers may not pool their allowances, and children can claim only the concession on goods intended for their own use. For those 17 or older, the duty-free allowance also includes 4.5 liters of wine or beer; one 1,125-ml bottle of spirits; and either 200 cigarettes, 250 grams of tobacco, 50 cigars, *or* a combination of the three up to 250 grams. Meat products, seeds, plants, and fruits must be declared upon arrival to the Agricultural Services Department.

New Zealand Customs ✉ Head office: The Customhouse, 17-21 Whitmore St., Box 2218, Wellington ☎ 09/300-5399 or 0800/428-786 🌐 www.customs.govt.nz.

IN THE U.K.

From countries outside the European Union, including the United States, you may bring home, duty-free, 200 cigarettes or 50 cigars; 1 liter of spirits or 2 liters of fortified or sparkling wine or liqueurs; 2 liters of still table wine; 60 ml of perfume; 250 ml of toilet water; plus £145 worth of other goods, including gifts and souvenirs. Prohibited items include meat products, seeds, plants, and fruits.

HM Customs and Excise ✉ Portcullis House, 21 Cowbridge Rd. E, Cardiff CF11 9SS ☎ 0845/010-9000 or 0208/929-0152, 0208/929-6731 or 0208/910-3602 complaints 🌐 www.hmce.gov.uk.

DINING

Dining in the Rockies is generally casual. Menus are becoming more varied with such regional specialties as trout, elk, or buffalo, but you can nearly always order a hamburger or a steak. Authentic ethnic food is hard to find outside of cities. Dinner hours are from 6 PM to 9 PM. Outside the large cities and resort towns in the high seasons, many restaurants close by 10 PM.

The restaurants we list are the cream of the crop in each price category. Properties indicated by a ✕🏨 are lodging establishments whose restaurant warrants a special trip.

RESERVATIONS & DRESS

Reservations are always a good idea; we mention them only when they're essential or not accepted. Book as far ahead as you can, and reconfirm as soon as you arrive. (Large parties should always call ahead to check the reservations policy.) We mention dress only when men are required to wear a jacket or a jacket and tie—which is almost never.

SPECIALTIES

You can find all types of cuisine in the major cities and resort towns, but don't forget to try native dishes such as trout, elk, and buffalo (the latter two have less fat than beef and are just as tasty); organic fruits and vegetables are also readily available. When in doubt, go for a steak, forever a Rocky Mountain mainstay.

Rocky Mountain oysters, simply put, are bull testicles. They're generally served fried, although you can get them lots of different ways. You can find them all over the West, usually at down-home eateries, steak houses, and the like.

WINE, BEER & SPIRITS

Microbreweries throughout the region produce a diverse selection of ales such as Huckleberry Ale from Coeur d'Alene Brewing Company and Old Faithful Ale brewed by Grand Teton Brewing Company in Victor, Idaho; Moose Drool (a Montana product) and Washakie Wheat (a product of Snake River Brewing in Wyoming) are also popular.

Although the region is not known for its wines, there are some wineries to visit in Idaho.

DISABILITIES & ACCESSIBILITY

The Rockies are home to countless recreational opportunities for travelers with disabilities. Most ski areas offer adaptive ski programs. DREAM—Adaptive Recreation, Inc. serves the ski areas of Big Mountain and Blacktail in Montana. Idaho's Sun Valley Ski School area has had its own program since 1992.

The majority of United States Forest Service campgrounds have limited wheelchair-accessible sites. Access Tours leads nine-day trips for people who use wheelchairs or walk slowly and can customize trips for groups of four or more.
Local Resources **DREAM–Adaptive Recreation, Inc.** Box 4085, Whitefish, MT 59937 406/862-1817. **Grand Teton National Park** 307/739-3300 accessibility coordinator Robin Gregory, 307/733-2053 TDD. **Wyoming Tourism** 307/777-7777. **Yellowstone National Park** 307/344-7381 accessibility coordinator Doug Madsen.
Tour Operator **Access Tours** Box 499, Victor, ID 83455 800/929-4811 208/787-2332.

LODGING

Despite the Americans with Disabilities Act, the definition of accessibility seems to differ from hotel to hotel. Some properties may be accessible by ADA standards for people with mobility problems but not for people with hearing or vision impairments, for example.

If you have mobility problems, ask for the lowest floor on which accessible services are offered. If you have a hearing impairment, check whether the hotel has devices to alert you visually to the ring of the telephone, a knock at the door, and a fire/emergency alarm. Some hotels provide these devices without charge. Discuss your needs with hotel personnel if this equipment isn't available, so that a staff member can personally alert you in the event of an emergency.

If you're bringing a guide dog, get authorization ahead of time and write down the name of the person with whom you spoke.

RESERVATIONS

When discussing accessibility with an operator or reservations agent, **ask hard questions.** Are there any stairs, inside *or* out? Are there grab bars next to the toilet *and* in the shower/tub? How wide is the doorway to the room? To the bathroom? For the most extensive facilities meeting the latest legal specifications, **opt for newer accommodations.** If you reserve through a toll-free number, consider also calling the hotel's local number to confirm the information from the central reservations office. Get confirmation in writing when you can.

SIGHTS & ATTRACTIONS

People with disabilities will generally find Yellowstone National Park a great place to visit. There are many boardwalks with easy grades so you can see wildlife, geysers, and other Yellowstone attractions; lodging and dining properties are generally accessible, and there are even backcountry campsites specially designed for people with disabilities. Grand Teton and Glacier national parks aren't quite so accessible as Yellowstone, but that's due more to terrain than lack of effort on the part of the National Park Service. Larger cities usually have better services for people with disabilities. You'll often find it more difficult to get around in a wheelchair in small towns, though most places have curb cuts and designated parking areas.

Many resort towns have created opportunities for all types of visitors (on Casper Mountain in Wyoming, for example, is a short trail with sights marked in Braille for the visually impaired). However, you'll find services for people with hearing and visual impairments to be more limited in smaller communities.

TRANSPORTATION

Most major tour companies have buses that can accommodate people with disabilities; obtaining rental cars with hand controls will be more of a problem unless you get your vehicle in a major hub city such as Denver or Salt Lake City. Handicap parking is allowed with a windshield card from any state.
Complaints **Aviation Consumer Protection Division** (⇨ Air Travel) for airline-related problems. **Departmental Office of Civil Rights** for general inquiries, U.S. Department of Transportation, S-30, 400 7th St. SW, Room 10215, Washington, DC 20590 202/366-4648 202/366-9371 www.dot.gov/ost/docr/index.htm. **Disability Rights Section** NYAV, U.S. Department of Justice, Civil Rights Division, 950 Pennsylvania Ave. NW, Washington, DC 20530 ADA information line 202/514-0301, 800/514-0301, 202/514-0383 TTY, 800/514-0383 TTY www.ada.gov. **U.S. Department of Transportation Hotline** for disability-related air-travel problems, 800/778-4838 or 800/455-9880 TTY.

TRAVEL AGENCIES

In the United States, the Americans with Disabilities Act requires that travel firms serve the needs of all travelers. Some agencies specialize in working with people with disabilities.

Travelers with Mobility Problems **Access Adventures** ✉ 206 Chestnut Ridge Rd., Scottsville, NY 14624 ☎ 585/889-9096 dltravel@prodigy.net, run by a former physical-rehabilitation counselor. **Accessible Vans of America** ✉ 9 Spielman Rd., Fairfield, NJ 07004 ☎ 877/282-8267, 973/808-9709 reservations 973/808-9713 www.accessiblevans.com. **CareVacations** ✉ No. 5, 5110-50 Ave., Leduc, Alberta, Canada, T9E 6V4 ☎ 780/986-6404 or 877/478-7827 780/986-8332 www.carevacations.com, for group tours and cruise vacations. **Flying Wheels Travel** ✉ 143 W. Bridge St., Box 382, Owatonna, MN 55060 ☎ 507/451-5005 507/451-1685 www.flyingwheelstravel.com.

DISCOUNTS & DEALS

Be a smart shopper and **compare all your options** before making decisions. A plane ticket bought with a promotional coupon from travel clubs, coupon books, and direct-mail offers or purchased on the Internet may not be cheaper than the least expensive fare from a discount ticket agency. And always keep in mind that what you get is just as important as what you save.

DISCOUNT RESERVATIONS

To save money, **look into discount reservations services** with Web sites and toll-free numbers, which use their buying power to get a better price on hotels, airline tickets (⇨ Air Travel), even car rentals. When booking a room, always **call the hotel's local toll-free number** (if one is available) rather than the central reservations number—you'll often get a better price. Always ask about special packages or corporate rates.

Airline Tickets **Air 4 Less** ☎ 800/AIR4LESS; low-fare specialist.

Hotel Rooms **Accommodations Express** ☎ 800/444-7666 or 800/277-1064 www.accommodationsexpress.com. **Quikbook** ☎ 800/789-9887 www.quikbook.com. **RMC Travel** ☎ 800/245-5738 www.rmcwebtravel.com. **Turbotrip.com** ☎ 800/473-7829 www.turbotrip.com.

PACKAGE DEALS

Don't confuse packages and guided tours. When you buy a package, you travel on your own, just as though you had planned the trip yourself. Fly/drive packages, which combine airfare and car rental, are often a good deal. In cities, ask the local visitor's bureau about hotel packages that include tickets to major museum exhibits or other special events.

ECOTOURISM

Although neither the Bureau of Land Management (BLM) nor the National Park Service has designated any particular parts of the Rockies endangered ecosystems, many areas are open only to hikers; vehicles, mountain bikes, and horses are banned. It is wise to respect these closures, as well as the old adage—**leave only footprints, take only pictures.** Recycling is taken seriously throughout the Rockies, and you will find yourself very unpopular if you litter or fail to recycle your cans and bottles (locals can be strident about protecting their wilderness).

All archaeological artifacts, including rock etchings and paintings, are protected by federal law and must be left untouched and undisturbed.

U.S. Bureau of Land Management ☎ 307/775-6256. **National Park Service** ☎ 800/436-7275.

GAY & LESBIAN TRAVEL

Most resort towns are gay-friendly; smaller communities are generally tolerant if not openly friendly. For details about the gay and lesbian scene, consult *Fodor's Gay Guide to the USA* (available in bookstores everywhere).

Gay- & Lesbian-Friendly Travel Agencies **Different Roads Travel** ✉ 8383 Wilshire Blvd., Suite 520, Beverly Hills, CA 90211 ☎ 323/651-5557 or 800/429-8747 (Ext. 14 for both) 323/651-3678 lgernert@tzell.com. **Kennedy Travel** ✉ 314 Jericho Turnpike, Floral Park, NY 11001 ☎ 516/352-4888 or 800/237-7433 516/354-8849 www.kennedytravel.com. **Now, Voyager** ✉ 4406 18th St., San Francisco, CA 94114 ☎ 415/626-1169 or 800/255-6951 415/626-8626 www.nowvoyager.com. **Skylink Travel and Tour** ✉ 1455 N. Dutton Ave., Suite A, Santa Rosa, CA 95401 ☎ 707/546-9888 or 800/225-5759 707/546-9891; serving lesbian travelers.

GUIDEBOOKS

Plan well and you won't be sorry. Guidebooks are excellent tools—and you can take them with you. You may want to check out the individual *Compass American Guides* to Idaho, Montana, and

Wyoming, which are thorough on culture and history and include color photographs.

For hikers, a good guidebook for the specific region you plan to explore—no matter how well marked the trails are—can be extremely helpful. Most hikers' guidebooks provide fairly detailed trail descriptions, including length and elevation gains and recommended side trips.

Hiking Guidebooks **Adventurous Traveler Bookstore** ☎ 802/860-6667 or 800/282-3963. **The Globe Pequot Press** ☎ 800/725-8303. **The Mountaineers** ✉ 300 3rd Ave. W, Seattle, WA 98119 ☎ 206/284-6310. **Sierra Club Books** ✉ 85 2nd St., 4th floor, San Francisco, CA 94105 ☎ 415/977-5500.

HOLIDAYS

Major national holidays are New Year's Day (Jan. 1); Martin Luther King Day (3rd Mon. in Jan.); Presidents' Day (3rd Mon. in Feb.); Memorial Day (last Mon. in May); Independence Day (July 4); Labor Day (1st Mon. in Sept.); Columbus Day (2nd Mon. in Oct.); Thanksgiving Day (4th Thurs. in Nov.); Christmas Eve and Christmas Day (Dec. 24 and 25); and New Year's Eve (Dec. 31).

INSURANCE

The most useful travel-insurance plan is a comprehensive policy that includes coverage for trip cancellation and interruption, default, trip delay, and medical expenses (with a waiver for preexisting conditions).

Without insurance you'll lose all or most of your money if you cancel your trip, regardless of the reason. Default insurance covers you if your tour operator, airline, or cruise line goes out of business. Trip-delay covers expenses that arise because of bad weather or mechanical delays. Study the fine print when comparing policies.

U.K. residents can buy a travel-insurance policy valid for most vacations taken during the year in which it's purchased (but check preexisting-condition coverage).

Always **buy travel policies directly from the insurance company**; if you buy them from a cruise line, airline, or tour operator that goes out of business you probably won't be covered for the agency or operator's default, a major risk. Before making any purchase, **review your existing health and home-owner's policies** to find what they cover away from home.

Travel Insurers In the U.S.: **Access America** ✉ 6600 W. Broad St., Richmond, VA 23230 ☎ 800/284-8300 📠 804/673-1491 or 800/346-9265 🌐 www.accessamerica.com. **Travel Guard International** ✉ 1145 Clark St., Stevens Point, WI 54481 ☎ 715/345-0505 or 800/826-1300 📠 800/955-8785 🌐 www.travelguard.com.

FOR INTERNATIONAL TRAVELERS

For information on customs restrictions, *see* Customs & Duties.

CAR RENTAL

When picking up a rental car, non-U.S. residents need a reservation voucher for any prepaid reservations that were made in the traveler's home country, a passport, a driver's license, and a travel policy that covers each driver. Note that in most cases, cars rented in the region are not allowed to cross into Canada.

CAR TRAVEL

In the Rockies gasoline costs $1.59–$1.79 a gallon. Stations are plentiful. Most stay open late (24 hours along large highways and in big cities), except in rural areas, where Sunday hours are limited and where you may drive long stretches without a refueling opportunity. Highways are well paved. Interstate highways—limited-access, multilane highways whose numbers are prefixed by "I–"—are the fastest routes. Interstates with three-digit numbers encircle urban areas, which may have other limited-access expressways, freeways, and parkways as well. Tolls may be levied on limited-access highways. So-called U.S. highways and state highways are not necessarily limited-access but may have several lanes.

Along larger highways, roadside stops with rest rooms, fast-food restaurants, and sundries stores are well spaced. State police and tow trucks patrol major highways and lend assistance. If your car breaks down on an interstate, pull onto the shoulder and wait for help, or have your passengers wait while you walk to an emergency phone. If you carry a cell phone, dial *55, noting your location on the small green roadside mileage markers.

Driving in the United States is on the right. Do **obey speed limits** posted along roads and highways. Watch for lower limits in small towns and on back roads.

Bookstores, gas stations, convenience stores, and rest stops sell maps (about $3) and multiregion road atlases (about $10).

CURRENCY

The dollar is the basic unit of U.S. currency. It has 100 cents. Coins include the copper penny (1¢); the silvery nickel (5¢), dime (10¢), quarter (25¢), and half-dollar (50¢); and the golden $1 coin, replacing a now-rare silver dollar. Bills are denominated $1, $5, $10, $20, $50, and $100, all green and identical in size; designs vary. The exchange rate at press time was US$ .77 per Australian dollar, US$1.89 per British pound, US$ .75 per Canadian dollar, and US$1.24 per euro.

ELECTRICITY

The U.S. standard is AC, 110 volts/60 cycles. Plugs have two flat pins set parallel to each other.

EMERGENCIES

For police, fire, or ambulance, **dial 911** (0 in rural areas).

INSURANCE

Britons and Australians need extra medical coverage when traveling overseas.

Insurance Information In the U.K.: **Association of British Insurers** ✉ 51 Gresham St., London EC2V 7HQ ☎ 020/7600–3333 📠 020/7696–8999 🌐 www.abi.org.uk. In Australia: **Insurance Council of Australia** ✉ Insurance Enquiries and Complaints, Level 3, 56 Pitt St., Sydney, NSW 2000 ☎ 1300/363683 or 02/9251–4456 📠 02/9251–4453 🌐 www.iecltd.com.au. In Canada: **RBC Insurance** ✉ 6880 Financial Dr., Mississauga, Ontario L5N 7Y5 ☎ 800/565–3129 📠 905/813–4704 🌐 www.rbcinsurance.com. In New Zealand: **Insurance Council of New Zealand** ✉ Level 7, 111–115 Customhouse Quay, Box 474, Wellington ☎ 04/472–5230 📠 04/473–3011 🌐 www.icnz.org.nz.

MAIL & SHIPPING

You can buy stamps and aerograms and send letters and parcels in post offices. Stamp-dispensing machines can occasionally be found in airports, bus and train stations, office buildings, drugstores, and the like. You can also deposit mail in the stout, dark blue, steel bins at strategic locations everywhere and in the mail chutes of large buildings; pickup schedules are posted.

For mail sent within the United States, you need a 37¢ stamp for first-class letters weighing up to 1 ounce (23¢ for each additional ounce) and 23¢ for postcards. You pay 80¢ for 1-ounce airmail letters and 70¢ for airmail postcards to most other countries; to Canada and Mexico, you need a 60¢ stamp for a 1-ounce letter and 50¢ for a postcard. An aerogram—a single sheet of lightweight blue paper that folds into its own envelope, stamped for overseas airmail—costs 70¢.

To receive mail on the road, have it sent c/o General Delivery at your destination's main post office (use the correct five-digit ZIP code). You must pick up mail in person within 30 days and show a driver's license or passport.

PASSPORTS & VISAS

When traveling internationally, **carry your passport** even if you don't need one (it's always the best form of ID) and **make two photocopies of the data page** (one for someone at home and another for you, carried separately from your passport). If you lose your passport, promptly call the nearest embassy or consulate and the local police.

Visitor visas aren't necessary for Canadian or European Union citizens, or for citizens of Australia who are staying fewer than 90 days.

Australian Citizens **Passports Australia** ☎ 131–232 🌐 www.passports.gov.au. **United States Consulate General** ✉ MLC Centre, Level 59, 19–29 Martin Pl., Sydney, NSW 2000 ☎ 02/9373–9200, 1902/941–641 fee-based visa-inquiry line 🌐 usembassy-australia.state.gov/sydney.

Canadian Citizens **Passport Office** ✉ to mail in applications: 200 Promenade du Portage, Hull, Québec J8X 4B7 ☎ 819/994–3500 or 800/567–6868 🌐 www.ppt.gc.ca.

New Zealand Citizens **New Zealand Passports Office** ✉ For applications and information, Level 3, Boulcott House, 47 Boulcott St., Wellington ☎ 0800/22–5050 or 04/474–8100 🌐 www.passports.govt.nz. **Embassy of the United States** ✉ 29 Fitzherbert Terr., Thorndon, Wellington ☎ 04/462–6000 🌐 usembassy.org.nz. **U.S. Consulate General** ✉ Citibank Bldg., 3rd fl., 23 Customs St. E, Auckland ☎ 09/303–2724 🌐 usembassy.org.nz.

U.K. Citizens **U.K. Passport Service** ☎ 0870/521–0410 🌐 www.passport.gov.uk. **American Con-**

sulate General ✉ Queen's House, 14 Queen St., Belfast, Northern Ireland BT1 6EQ ☎ 028/9032-8239 🖷 028/9024-8482 🌐 www.usembassy.org.uk. **American Embassy** ✉ for visa and immigration information (enclose an SASE), Consular Information Unit, 24 Grosvenor Sq., London W1 1AE ✉ to submit an application via mail, Visa Branch, 5 Upper Grosvenor St., London W1A 2JB ☎ 09068/200-290 recorded visa information or 09055/444-546 operator service, both with per-minute charges, 0207/499-9000 main switchboard 🌐 www.usembassy.org.uk.

TELEPHONES

All U.S. telephone numbers consist of a three-digit area code and a seven-digit local number. Within many local calling areas, you dial only the seven-digit number. Within some area codes, you must dial "1" first for calls outside the local area. To call between area-code regions, dial "1" then all 10 digits; the same goes for calls to numbers prefixed by "800," "888," and "877"—all toll-free. For calls to numbers preceded by "900" you must pay—usually dearly.

For international calls, dial "011" followed by the country code and the local number. For help, dial "0" and ask for an overseas operator. The country code is 61 for Australia, 64 for New Zealand, 44 for the United Kingdom. Calling Canada is the same as calling within the United States. Most local phone books list country codes and U.S. area codes. The country code for the United States is 1.

For operator assistance, dial "0." To obtain someone's phone number, call directory assistance at 555–1212 or 411 (free at public phones). To have the person you're calling foot the bill, phone collect; dial "0" instead of "1" before the 10-digit number.

At pay phones, instructions often are posted. Usually you insert coins in a slot (usually 35¢ for local calls) and wait for a steady tone before dialing. When you call long-distance, the operator tells you how much to insert; prepaid phone cards, widely available in various denominations, are easier. Call the number on the back, punch in the card's personal identification number when prompted, then dial your number.

LODGING

Accommodations in the Rockies vary from the very posh resorts in ski areas such as Jackson Hole to basic chain hotels and independent motels. Dude and guest ranches often require a one-week stay, and the cost is all-inclusive. Bed-and-breakfasts can be found throughout the Rockies.

The lodgings we list are the cream of the crop in each price category. We always list the facilities that are available—but we don't specify whether they cost extra. When pricing accommodations, always ask what's included and what costs extra. Properties indicated by a ✕🏨 are lodging establishments whose restaurant warrants a special trip.

Assume that hotels operate on the **European Plan** (EP, with no meals) unless we specify that they use either the **Continental Plan** (CP, with a Continental breakfast), the **Breakfast Plan** (BP, with a full breakfast), the **Modified American Plan** (MAP, with breakfast and dinner), or the **Full American Plan** (FAP, with all meals).

i General Information **Idaho Division of Travel Promotion** ✉ Idaho Department of Commerce, 700 W. State St., Boise, ID 83720 ☎ 800/635-7820. **Travel Montana** ✉ Department of Commerce, 1424 9th Ave., Helena, MT 59620 ☎ 406/444-2654, 800/548-3390 in Montana, 800/847-4868 nationwide. **Wyoming Division of Tourism** ✉ I-25 at College Dr., Cheyenne, WY 82002 ☎ 307/777-7777 or 800/225-5996.

BED & BREAKFASTS

Charm is the long suit of these establishments, which generally occupy a restored older building with some historical or architectural significance. They're generally small, with fewer than 20 rooms. Breakfast is usually included in the rates.

i Reservation Services **Cody Lodging Co.** ✉ 927 14th St., Cody, WY 82414 ☎ 307/587-6000 or 800/587-6560 🖷 307/587-8048 🌐 www.codyguesthouses.com. **InIdaho** ✉ 307 E. Park St., McCall, ID 83638 ☎ 208/634-4787 or 800/844-3246 🖷 208/634-1268 🌐 www.inidaho.com. **Jackson Hole Central Reservations** ✉ 140 E. Broadway, Suite 24, Jackson, WY 83001 ☎ 307/733-4005 or 800/443-6931 🌐 www.jacksonholewy.com.

CAMPING

Camping is invigorating and inexpensive, and the area is full of state and national parks and forests. Sites range from rustic (pit toilets and cold running water) to campgrounds with bathhouses with hot showers, paved trailer pads that can accommodate even jumbo RVs, and full hookups. Some national forest campgrounds are free or as low as $5 for tent and RV sites, though there are fewer amenities.

Sometimes site reservations are accepted, and then only for up to seven days (early birds reserve as much as a year in advance); more often, they're not. Campers who prefer a more remote setting may camp in the backcountry; it's free but you might need a permit, available from park visitor centers and ranger stations. If you're visiting in summer, **plan well ahead.**

The facilities and amenities at privately operated campgrounds are usually more extensive (swimming pools are common), reservations are more widely accepted, and nightly fees are higher: $15 and up for tents, $28 and up for RVs.

The National Parks: Camping Guide ✉ Superintendent of Documents, U.S. Government Printing Office, Washington, DC 20402 ☎ 800/365-2267; $3.50.

CONDO & CABIN RENTALS

If you want a home base that's roomy enough for a family and comes with cooking facilities, **consider a furnished rental.** These can save you money, especially if you're traveling with a group. Home-exchange directories sometimes list rentals as well as exchanges.

There are rental opportunities throughout all three states, with the best selection in resort areas such as Sun Valley, Idaho; Big Sky and Whitefish (Big Mountain), Montana; and Jackson and Cody, Wyoming. You'll find a variety of properties ranging from one-bedroom condos to multibedroom vacation homes. The widest selection is offered by developer-owner consortiums.

International Agents **Hideaways International** ✉ 767 Islington St., Portsmouth, NH 03802 ☎ 603/430-4433 or 800/843-4433 🖷 603/430-4444 🌐 www.hideaways.com, membership $129.

Local Idaho Agents **InIdaho** ✉ 307 E. Park St., McCall, ID 83638 ☎ 800/844-3246 or 208/634-4787 🖷 208/634-1268 🌐 www.inidaho.com. **Sun Valley Company** ✉ 1 Sun Valley Rd., Sun Valley, ID 83353 ☎ 208/622-2201 or 800/786-8259 🖷 208/622-2015 🌐 www.sunvalley.com.

Local Montana Agents **Glacier Village Property** ✉ 3840 Big Mountain Rd., Whitefish, MT 59937 ☎ 406/862-3687 or 800/858-5439 🖷 406/862-0658 🌐 www.stayatbigmountain.com. **Mountain Home-Montana Vacation Rentals** 📫 Box 1204, Bozeman, MT 59771 ☎ 406/586-4589 or 800/550-4589 🌐 www.mountain-home.com. **Resortquest Big Sky** ✉ 3080 Pine Dr., Big Sky, MT 59716 ☎ 406/995-4800 or 800/548-4488 🖷 406/995-2447 🌐 www.resortquestbigsky.com.

Local Wyoming Agents **Cody Area Central Reservations** ✉ 1115 13th St., Cody, WY 82414 ☎ 307/527-6837 or 888/468-6996 🖷 307/754-3493. **Cody Lodging Co.** ✉ 927 14th St., Cody, WY 82414 ☎ 307/587-6000 or 800/587-6560 🖷 307/587-8048 🌐 www.codyguesthouses.com. **Jackson Hole Resort Lodging** ✉ 3200 McCollister Dr., Teton Village, WY 83025 ☎ 307/733-3990 or 800/443-8613 🌐 www.jhresortlodging.com.

GUEST RANCHES

If the thought of sitting around a campfire after a hard day on the range makes your heart beat faster, consider playing dude on a guest ranch. These range from wilderness-rimmed working ranches that accept guests and encourage them to pitch in with chores and other ranch activities to luxurious resorts on the fringes of small cities, with an upscale clientele, swimming pools, tennis courts, and a lively roster of horse-related activities such as breakfast rides, moonlight rides, and all-day trail rides. Rafting, fishing, tubing, and other activities are usually available; at working ranches, you may even be able to participate in a cattle roundup. In winter, cross-country skiing and snowshoeing keep you busy. Lodgings can run the gamut from charmingly rustic cabins to the kind of deluxe quarters you expect at a first-class hotel. Meals may be gourmet or plain but hearty. Many ranches offer packages and children's and off-season rates. The various state tourism offices also have information on dude ranches. *See* Dude Ranches *in* Sports & the Outdoors.

Idaho Guest and Dude Ranch Association 📫 HC 72 K, Cascade, ID 83611 ☎ 208/382-4336 or 208/382-3217. **Montana Dude Ranchers' Association** 📫 1627 West Main, Suite 434, Bozeman, MT 59715 ☎ 406/284-9933 🌐 www.montanadra.com. **Wyoming Dude Ranchers Association** ✉ Box 618, Dubois, WY 82513 ☎ 307/455-2084 🖷 307/455-2634 🌐 www.wyomingduderanchers.com.

HOME EXCHANGES

If you would like to exchange your home for someone else's, **join a home-exchange organization,** which will send you its updated listings of available exchanges for a year and will include your own listing in at least one of them. It's up to you to make specific arrangements.

Exchange Clubs **HomeLink International** Box 47747, Tampa, FL 33647 813/975-9825 or 800/638-3841 813/910-8144 www.homelink.org; $110 yearly for a listing, online access, and catalog; $40 without catalog. **Intervac U.S.** 30 Corte San Fernando, Tiburon, CA 94920 800/756-4663 415/435-7440 www.intervacus.com; $105 yearly for a listing, online access, and a catalog; $50 without catalog.

HOSTELS

Montana has hostels in Bozeman, East Glacier, Polebridge, and Whitefish that cater mainly to backpackers. Idaho has a hostel in Nampa. Wyoming has hostels in Jackson, Teton Village, Lovell, and Cheyenne.

No matter what your age, you can **save on lodging costs by staying at hostels.** In some 4,500 locations in more than 70 countries around the world, Hostelling International (HI), the umbrella group for a number of national youth-hostel associations, offers single-sex, dorm-style beds and, at many hostels, rooms for couples and family accommodations. Membership in any HI national hostel association, open to travelers of all ages, allows you to stay in HI-affiliated hostels at member rates; one-year membership is about $28 for adults (C$35 for a two-year minimum membership in Canada, £13.50 in the U.K., A$52 in Australia, and NZ$40 in New Zealand); hostels charge about $10–$30 per night. Members have priority if the hostel is full; they're also eligible for discounts around the world, even on rail and bus travel in some countries.

HI is also an especially helpful organization for road cyclists.

Organizations **Hostelling International–USA** 8401 Colesville Rd., Suite 600, Silver Spring, MD 20910 301/495-1240 301/495-6697 www.hiayh.org. **Hostelling International–Canada** 400-205 Catherine St., Ottawa, Ontario K2P 1C3 613/237-7884 or 800/663-5777 613/237-7868 www.hihostels.ca. **YHA Australia** 422 Kent St., Sydney, NSW 2001 02/9261-1111 02/9261-1969 www.yha.com.au. **YHA England and Wales** Trevelyan House, Dimple Rd., Matlock, Derbyshire DE4 3YH, U.K. 0870/870-8808 0870/770-6127 www.yha.org.uk. **YHA New Zealand** Level 3, 193 Cashel St., Box 436, Christchurch 03/379-9970 or 0800/278-299 03/365-4476 www.yha.org.nz.

HOTELS

Most city hotels cater to business travelers, with such facilities as restaurants, cocktail lounges, swimming pools, exercise equipment, and meeting rooms. Room rates usually reflect the range of amenities offered. Most cities also have less expensive hotels that are clean and comfortable but have fewer facilities. In resort towns, hotels are decidedly more deluxe, with every imaginable amenity in every imaginable price range; rural areas generally offer simple, and sometimes rustic, accommodations.

Many properties offer special weekend rates, sometimes up to 50% off regular prices. However, these deals are usually not extended during peak summer months, when hotels are normally full. The same discounts generally hold true for resort-town hotels in the off-seasons.

All hotels listed have private bath unless otherwise noted.

Toll-Free Numbers **Best Western** 800/528-1234 www.bestwestern.com. **Choice** 800/424-6423 www.choicehotels.com. **Comfort Inn** 800/424-6423 www.choicehotels.com. **Days Inn** 800/325-2525 www.daysinn.com. **Doubletree Hotels** 800/222-8733 www.doubletree.com. **Embassy Suites** 800/362-2779 www.embassysuites.com. **Fairfield Inn** 800/228-2800 www.marriott.com. **Hilton** 800/445-8667 www.hilton.com. **Holiday Inn** 800/465-4329 www.sixcontinentshotels.com. **Howard Johnson** 800/654-4656 www.hojo.com. **Hyatt Hotels & Resorts** 800/233-1234 www.hyatt.com. **La Quinta** 800/531-5900 www.laquinta.com. **Marriott** 800/228-9290 www.marriott.com. **Quality Inn** 800/424-6423 www.choicehotels.com. **Radisson** 800/333-3333 www.radisson.com. **Ramada** 800/228-2828, 800/854-7854 international reservations www.ramada.com or www.ramadahotels.com. **Ritz-Carlton** 800/241-3333 www.ritzcarlton.com. **Sheraton** 800/325-3535 www.starwood.com/sheraton. **Sleep Inn** 800/424-6423 www.choicehotels.com. **Westin Hotels & Resorts** 800/228-3000 www.starwood.com/westin. **Wyndham Hotels & Resorts** 800/822-4200 www.wyndham.com.

MOTELS

The once-familiar roadside motel is fast disappearing from the American landscape. In its place are chain-run motor inns at highway intersections and in rural areas off the beaten path. Some of these establishments offer very basic facilities; others provide restaurants, swimming pools, and other amenities.

Motel Chains **InIdaho Central Reservations** ☎ 208/634-4787. **Motel 6** ☎ 800/466-8356. **Quality Inn** ☎ 800/228-5151. **Rodeway Inns** ☎ 800/228-2000. **Shilo Inn** ☎ 800/222-2244. **Super 8 Motels** ☎ 800/800-8000. **Travelodge** ☎ 800/578-7878.

RESORTS

Ski towns throughout the Rockies—including Sun Valley, Idaho; Big Sky and Whitefish, Montana; and Jackson Hole, Wyoming—are home to dozens of resorts in all price ranges; the activities lacking in any individual property can usually be found in the town itself, in summer as well as winter. Off the slopes, there are both wonderfully rustic and luxurious resorts in the national parks: Jackson Lake Lodge and Jenny Lake Lodge in Grand Teton National Park, Lake Yellowstone Hotel and the Old Faithful Snow Lodge in Yellowstone, and Many Glacier Lodge in Glacier National Park.

MEDIA

NEWSPAPERS & MAGAZINES

The largest daily newspapers in Montana are the *Billings Gazette,* the *Bozeman Chronicle,* the *Missoulian,* and the *Great Falls Tribune.* In Wyoming the biggest newspapers are the statewide *Casper Star-Tribune* and Cheyenne's *Wyoming State Tribune-Eagle.* Idaho's biggest papers are the *Idaho Statesman* in Boise, the *Idaho State Journal* in Pocatello, the *Coeur d'Alene Press,* the *Moscow-Pullman Daily News,* and the *Lewiston Morning Tribune.*

RADIO & TELEVISION

You will find National Public Radio across the region, plus local radio stations, most targeted to country music listeners. Television stations include major affiliates, and many places also have cable or direct satellite television service. Near mountain passes or other road hazards, often a sign will offer radio station identification for road information.

MONEY MATTERS

First-class hotel rooms in Boise, Missoula, and Cheyenne cost from $75 to $175 a night, although some "value" hotel rooms go for $40–$60, and, as elsewhere in the United States, rooms in national budget chain motels go for around $40 nightly. Weekend packages, offered by most city hotels, cut prices up to 50% (but may not be available in peak winter or summer seasons). As a rule, costs outside cities are lower, except in the deluxe resorts. In cities and rural areas, a cup of coffee costs between 50¢ and $1, the price for a hamburger runs between $4 and $6, and a beer at a bar generally is between $1.50 and $3; expect to pay double in resort towns. Prices throughout this guide are given for adults. Substantially reduced fees are almost always available for children, students, and senior citizens. For information on taxes, *see* Taxes.

ATMS

You will find ATMs at banks and other locations, including grocery stores, and occasionally at lodging properties, such as those in Yellowstone National Park. You will usually be able to locate an ATM even in small communities, where they might be placed at convenience stores or lodging properties.

CREDIT CARDS

Throughout this guide, the following abbreviations are used: **AE,** American Express; **D,** Discover; **DC,** Diners Club; **MC,** MasterCard; and **V,** Visa.

Reporting Lost Cards **American Express** ☎ 800/441-0519. **Diners Club** ☎ 800/234-6377. **Discover** ☎ 800/347-2683. **MasterCard** ☎ 800/622-7747. **Visa** ☎ 800/847-2911.

NATIONAL PARKS

Look into discount passes to save money on park entrance fees. For $50, the National Parks Pass admits you (and any passengers in your private vehicle) to all national parks, monuments, and recreation areas, as well as other sites run by the National Park Service, for a year. (In parks that charge per person, the pass admits you, your spouse and children, and your parents, when you arrive together.) Camping and parking are extra. The $15 Golden Eagle Pass, a hologram you affix to your National Parks Pass, functions as an upgrade, granting entry to all sites run by the NPS, the U.S. Fish and Wildlife Service, the U.S. Forest Service, and the Bureau of Land Management. The upgrade, which expires with the parks pass, is sold by most national-park, Fish and Wildlife, and BLM fee stations. A percentage of the proceeds from pass sales funds national parks projects.

Both the Golden Age Passport ($10), for U.S. citizens or permanent residents who are 62 and older, and the Golden Access Passport (free), for those with disabilities, entitle holders (and any passengers in their private vehicles) to lifetime free entry to all national parks, plus 50% off fees for the use of many park facilities and services. (The discount doesn't always apply to companions.) To obtain them, you must show proof of age and of U.S. citizenship or permanent residency—such as a U.S. passport, driver's license, or birth certificate—and, if requesting Golden Access, proof of disability. The Golden Age and Golden Access passes are available only at NPS-run sites that charge an entrance fee. The National Parks Pass is also available by mail and via the Internet.

National Park Foundation ✉ 11 Dupont Circle NW, 6th fl., Washington, DC 20036 ☎ 202/238-4200 🌐 www.nationalparks.org. **National Park Service** ✉ National Park Service/Department of Interior, 1849 C St. NW, Washington, DC 20240 ☎ 202/208-6843 🌐 www.nps.gov. **National Parks Conservation Association** ✉ 1300 19th St. NW, Suite 300, Washington, DC 20036 ☎ 202/223-6722 🌐 www.npca.org.

Passes by Mail & Online **National Park Foundation** 🌐 www.nationalparks.org. **National Parks Pass** Box 34108, Washington, DC 20043 ☎ 888/467-2757 🌐 www.nationalparks.org; include a check or money order payable to the National Park Service, plus $3.95 for shipping and handling, or call for passes by phone.

PACKING

Informality reigns here; jeans, sport shirts, and T-shirts fit in almost everywhere, for both men and women. The few restaurants and performing-arts events where dressier outfits are required, usually in resorts and larger cities, are the exception.

If you plan to spend much time outdoors, and certainly if you go in winter, **choose clothing appropriate for cold and wet weather.** Cotton clothing, including denim—although fine on warm, dry days—can be uncomfortable when it gets wet and when the weather's cold. A better choice is clothing made of wool or any of a number of new synthetics that provide warmth without bulk and maintain their insulating properties even when wet.

In summer, you'll want shorts during the day. But because early morning and night can be cold, and high passes windy, pack a sweater and a light jacket, and perhaps also a wool cap and gloves. Try layering—a T-shirt under another shirt under a jacket—and peel off layers as you go. For walks and hikes, you'll need sturdy footwear. To take you into the wilds, boots should have thick soles and plenty of ankle support; if your shoes are new and you plan to spend much time on the trail, break them in at home. Bring a day pack for short hikes, along with a canteen or water bottle, and don't forget rain gear, a hat, sunscreen, and insect repellent.

In winter, prepare for subzero temperatures with good boots, warm socks and liners, long johns, a well-insulated jacket, and a warm hat and mittens. Dress in layers so you can add or remove clothes as the temperatures fluctuate.

If you attend dances and other events at Native American reservations, dress conservatively—skirts or long pants for women, long pants for men—or you may be asked to leave.

When traveling to mountain areas, **remember that sunglasses and a sun hat are essential at high altitudes**; the thinner atmosphere requires sunscreen with a greater SPF than you might need at lower elevations.

In your carry-on luggage, **pack an extra pair of eyeglasses or contact lenses and enough of any medication** you take to last a few days longer than the entire trip. You may also ask your doctor to write a spare prescription using the drug's generic name, as brand names may vary from country to country. In luggage to be checked, **never pack prescription drugs, valuables, or undeveloped film.** And don't forget to carry with you the addresses of offices that handle refunds of lost traveler's checks. Check *Fodor's How to Pack* (available at online retailers and bookstores everywhere) for more tips.

To avoid customs and security delays, carry medications in their original packaging. Don't pack any sharp objects in your carry-on luggage, including knives of any size or material, scissors, and corkscrews, or anything else that might arouse suspicion.

To avoid having your checked luggage chosen for hand inspection, don't cram bags full. The U.S. Transportation Security Administration suggests packing shoes on top and placing personal items you don't want touched in clear plastic bags.

CHECKING LUGGAGE

You're allowed to carry aboard one bag and one personal article, such as a purse or a laptop computer. Make sure what you carry on fits under your seat or in the overhead bin. Get to the gate early, so you can board as soon as possible, before the overhead bins fill up.

Baggage allowances vary by carrier, destination, and ticket class. On international flights, you're usually allowed to check two bags weighing up to 70 pounds (32 kilograms) each, although a few airlines allow checked bags of up to 88 pounds (40 kilograms) in first class. Some international carriers don't allow more than 66 pounds (30 kilograms) per bag in business class and 44 pounds (20 kilograms) in economy. On domestic flights, the limit may be 50 pounds (23 kilograms) per bag. Most airlines won't accept bags that weigh more than 100 pounds (45 kilograms) on domestic or international flights. Check baggage restrictions with your carrier before you pack.

Airline liability for baggage is limited to $2,500 per person on flights within the United States. On international flights it amounts to $9.07 per pound or $20 per kilogram for checked baggage (roughly $640 per 70-pound bag) and $400 per passenger for unchecked baggage. You can buy additional coverage at check-in for about $10 per $1,000 of coverage, but it often excludes a rather extensive list of items, shown on your airline ticket.

Before departure, **itemize your bags' contents** and their worth, and label the bags with your name, address, and phone number. (If you use your home address, cover it so potential thieves can't see it readily.) Include a label inside each bag and **pack a copy of your itinerary.** At check-in, **make sure each bag is correctly tagged** with the destination airport's three-letter code. Because some checked bags will be opened for hand inspection, the U.S. Transportation Security Administration recommends that you leave luggage unlocked or use the plastic locks offered at check-in. TSA screeners place an inspection notice inside searched bags, which are re-sealed with a special lock.

If your bag has been searched and contents are missing or damaged, file a claim with the TSA Consumer Response Center as soon as possible. If your bags arrive damaged or fail to arrive at all, file a written report with the airline before leaving the airport.

Complaints U.S. Transportation Security Administration Consumer Response Center ☎ 866/289–9673 🌐 www.tsa.gov.

PASSPORTS & VISAS

When traveling internationally, **carry your passport** even if you don't need one (it's always the best form of ID) and **make two photocopies of the data page** (one for someone at home and another for you, carried separately from your passport). If you lose your passport, promptly call the nearest embassy or consulate and the local police.

Idaho and Montana border Canada, and if you plan to enter Canada, have the proper papers with you (⇨ Car Travel, as well). Citizens and legal residents of the United States do not need a passport or a visa to enter Canada, but proof of citizenship (a birth certificate or valid passport) and some form of photo identification will be requested. Naturalized U.S. residents should carry their naturalization certificate. Permanent residents who are not citizens should carry their "green card." Citizens of the United Kingdom need only a valid passport to enter Canada for stays of up to six months.

U.S. passport applications for children under age 14 require consent from both parents or legal guardians; both parents must appear together to sign the application. If only one parent appears, he or she must submit a written statement from the other parent authorizing passport issuance for the child. A parent with sole authority must present evidence of it when applying; acceptable documentation includes the child's certified birth certificate listing only the applying parent, a court order specifically permitting this parent's travel with the child, or a death certificate for the nonapplying parent. Application forms and instructions are available on the Web site of the U.S. State Department's Bureau of Consular Affairs (www.travel.state.gov).

SAFETY

Regardless of the outdoor activity or your level of skill, safety must come first. Remember: **know your limits.**

Many trails are at high altitudes, where oxygen is scarce. They're also frequently desolate. Hikers and bikers should **carry emergency supplies** in their backpacks. Proper equipment includes a flashlight, a compass, waterproof matches, a first-aid kit, a knife, and a light plastic tarp for shelter. Backcountry skiers should add a repair kit, a blanket, an avalanche beacon, and a lightweight shovel to their lists. Always **bring extra food and a canteen of water,** as dehydration is a common occurrence at high altitudes. **Never drink from streams or lakes,** unless you boil the water first or purify it with tablets. Giardia, an intestinal parasite, may be present.

Always **check the condition of roads and trails, and get the latest weather reports** before setting out. In summer, **take precautions against heat stroke or exhaustion** by resting frequently in shaded areas; in winter, **take precautions against hypothermia** by layering clothing. Ultimately, proper planning, common sense, and good physical conditioning are the strongest guards against the elements.

ALTITUDE

You may feel dizzy and weak and find yourself breathing heavily—signs that the thin mountain air isn't giving you your accustomed dose of oxygen. Take it easy and **rest often for a few days until you're acclimatized.** Throughout your stay drink plenty of water and watch your alcohol consumption. If you experience severe headaches and nausea, see a doctor. It is easy to go too high too fast. The remedy for altitude-related discomfort is to go down quickly, into heavier air. Other altitude-related problems include dehydration and overexposure to the sun because of the thin air.

FLASH FLOODS

Flash floods can strike at any time and any place with little or no warning. Mountainous terrain can become dangerous when distant rains are channeled into gullies and ravines, turning a quiet streamside campsite or wash into a rampaging torrent in seconds. Similarly, desert terrain floods quickly when the land is unable to absorb heavy rain. Check weather reports before heading into the backcountry and be prepared to head for higher ground if the weather turns severe.

WILD ANIMALS

One of the most wonderful parts of the Rockies is the abundant wildlife. And although a herd of grazing elk or a bighorn sheep high on a hillside is most certainly a Kodak moment, an encounter with a bear or mountain lion is not. To avoid such an unpleasant situation while hiking, **make plenty of noise, keep dogs on a leash, and keep small children between adults.** While camping, be sure to store all food, utensils, and clothing with food odors far away from your tent, preferably high in a tree (also far from your tent). If you do come across a bear or big cat, **do not run.** For bears, back away quietly; for lions, make yourself look as big as possible. In either case, be prepared to fend off the animal with loud noises, rocks, sticks, and so on. And, like the saying goes, do not feed the bears—or any wild animals, whether they're dangerous or not.

When in any park, **give all animals their space and never attempt to feed any of them.** If you want to take a photograph, use a long lens rather than a long sneak to approach closely. This is particularly important for winter visitors. Approaching an animal can cause stress and affect its ability to survive the sometimes brutal climate. In all cases remember that the animals have the right-of-way; this is their home, and you are the visitor.

SENIOR-CITIZEN TRAVEL

Senior citizens will often find reduced rates for meals and lodging throughout the region. Many attractions also have lower fees for senior travelers.

To qualify for age-related discounts, **mention your senior-citizen status up front** when booking hotel reservations (not when checking out) and before you're seated in restaurants (not when paying the bill). Be sure to have identification on hand. When renting a car, ask about promotional car-rental discounts, which can be cheaper than senior-citizen rates.

Educational Programs **Elderhostel** ✉ 11 Ave. de Lafayette, Boston, MA 02111-1746 ☎ 877/426-8056, 978/323-4141 international callers, 877/426-2167 TTY 🖷 877/426-2166 🌐 www.elderhostel.org.

SHOPPING

Although there are plenty of modern shopping malls across the Rockies, a trip through the West is an opportunity to buy authentic memorabilia and clothing—choose from cowboy boots, cowboy hats, bolero ties, and the like. It's also a great place to find Native American crafts. Small artisan colonies often neighbor ritzy resorts. These enclaves of creative souls produce some of the finest handcrafted wares anywhere; look for local galleries and boutiques that showcase their work.

KEY DESTINATIONS

For authentic Native American products visit galleries and shops near Indian reservations in communities such as Fort Washakie, Wyoming; Browning, Montana; and Pocatello, Idaho. You'll find extensive shopping opportunities in resort areas such as Jackson, Wyoming; Coeur d'Alene, Idaho; and Kalispell, Montana. In all three states, smaller shops often feature local products ranging from huckleberry syrup and candies to jewelry and custom-designed clothing. Western items such as boots, hats, and clothing can be found throughout the region in stores such as Lou Taubert Ranch Outfitters in Billings, Montana, and Casper, Wyoming, and in Corral West stores across the area.

SMART SOUVENIRS

A quintessential Wyoming souvenir is a "jackalope" (a small mounted animal that is a cross between a jackrabbit and an antelope), which costs anywhere from $10 to $30. Other popular souvenirs include Native American products such as beaded bags or bracelets; cowboy music and artwork; or an autographed copy of a book written by a local author. Most local bookstores have a stock of signed titles by area writers, including Mary Clearman Blew, W. Michael Gear and Kathleen O'Neal Gear, Richard S. Wheeler, C. J. Box, and David Stoecklein.

SPORTS & THE OUTDOORS

The Rockies are one of America's greatest playgrounds, and many area residents make exercise a high priority. Rockies jocks can do their thing in the midst of exquisite scenery—not boxed in at a gym watching ceiling-mounted televisions.

ADVENTURE TRIP OUTFITTERS

Many trip organizers specialize in only one type of activity; however, a few companies guide a variety of active trips. (In some cases, these larger companies also act essentially as a clearinghouse or agent for smaller trip outfitters.) Be sure to sign on with a reliable outfitter; getting stuck with a shoddy operator can be disappointing, uncomfortable, and even dangerous. Some sports—white-water rafting and mountaineering, for example—have organizations that license or certify guides, and you should be sure that the guide you're with is properly accredited.

Outfitter Listings **America Outdoors** 📫 Box 10847, Knoxville, TN 37939 ☎ 865/558-3595 🌐 www.americaoutdoors.org. **Idaho Outfitters and Guides Association** 📫 Box 95, Boise, ID 83701 ☎ 208/342-1919 🌐 www.ioga.org. **Montana Outfitters and Guides Association** ✉ 2 North Last Chance Gulch, Helena, MT 59624 ☎ 406/449-3578 🖷 406/449-9769 🌐 www.moga-montana.org. **Wyoming Outfitters and Guides Association** 📫 Box 2650, Casper, WY 82602 ☎ 307/265-2376 🌐 www.wyoga.org.

BICYCLING

High, rugged country puts a premium on fitness. Even if you can ride 40 mi at home without breaking a sweat, you might find yourself struggling terribly on steep climbs and in elevations often exceeding 10,000 feet. If you have an extended tour in mind, you might want to come a couple of days early to acclimate yourself to the altitude and terrain. Pretrip conditioning is likely to make your trip more enjoyable.

On tours where the elevation may vary 4,000 feet or more, the climate can change dramatically. Although the valleys may be scorching, high-mountain passes may still be lined with snow in summer. Pack clothing accordingly. (Bicycle racers often stuff newspaper inside their jerseys when descending from high passes to shield themselves from the chill.) Although you shouldn't have much problem renting a bike (trip organizers can usually arrange rentals), it's a good idea to bring your own pair of sturdy, stiff-bottom cycling shoes to make riding easier, and your own helmet. Some experienced riders bring not only their own shoes but their own pedals if they use an interlocking shoe-and-pedal system. If you do decide to bring your own bike, be prepared to spend as much as $150 in special luggage handling. Summer and early fall are the best times to plan a trip; at other times, snow and ice may still obstruct high-terrain roads and trails.

Guided bike trips generally range in price between $80 and $150 a day, depending on lodging and meals. The Adventure Cycling Association is perhaps the best general source of information on biking in the Rockies—including detailed maps and information on trip organizers. They also guide trips stretching along the Continental Divide. Hostelling International (⇨ Lodging) is a good connection for cycling tours as well. Also, when you're in a ski resort town, check whether lifts service mountain bikes. Remember that biking is not permitted in National Wilderness areas.

Adventure Cycling Association Box 8308, Missoula, MT 59807 406/721–1776 or 800/755–2453 www.adventurecycling.org.

DUDE RANCHES

Most dude ranches don't require any previous experience with horses, although a few working ranches reserve weeks in spring and fall—when the chore of moving cattle is more intensive than in summer—for experienced riders. No special equipment is necessary, although if you plan to do much fishing, you're better off bringing your own tackle (some ranches have tackle to lend or rent). Be sure to check with the ranch for a list of items you might be expected to bring. If you plan to do much riding, a couple of pairs of sturdy pants, boots, a wide-brim hat to shield you from the sun, and outerwear as protection from the possibility of rain or chill should be packed. Expect to spend at least $150 per day. Depending on the activities you engage in, as well as accommodations, the price can exceed $300 a day. *See* Guest Ranches *in* Lodging, as well.

FISHING

Field and Stream magazine is a leading source of information on fishing destinations, technique, and equipment. For lists of guides to various rivers and lakes of the Rockies, contact the state tourism departments.

Fishing licenses, available at tackle shops and a variety of local stores, are required in all Rocky Mountain states. You can buy an Idaho license online through the Web site Great Lodge. The fishing season may vary from state to state, and from species to species. A few streams are considered "private" streams, in that they are privately stocked by a local club, and other rivers are fly-fishing or catch-and-release only, so be sure you **know the rules before making your first cast.** Tribal fishing licences are necessary on reservation land.

Rocky Mountain water can be cold, especially at higher elevations and especially in spring and fall (and winter, of course). You'd do well to **bring waterproof waders** or buy them when you arrive in the region. Outfitters and some tackle shops rent equipment, but you're better off bringing your own gear. Lures are another story, though: whether you plan to fish with flies or other lures, local tackle shops can usually give you a pretty good idea of what works best in a particular region, and you can buy accordingly.

In the mid-1990s, whirling disease—a parasitic infection that afflicts trout—began to reduce fish populations in some Rocky Mountain streams dramatically. Efforts to curb the spread of the disease have met with some success, but some waters are still suffering from a smaller fish population.

A guide will cost about $250 per day and can be shared by two anglers if they are fishing from a boat and possibly by three if they are wading. Lunch will probably be included and flies might be, although there may be an extra $15–$20 charge for these.

Orvis Fly Fishing Schools runs one of the most respected fishing instructional programs in the country and endorses other instructional programs. Summertime 2½-day programs take place in Coeur d'Alene, Idaho.

Fishing Licenses Online **www.greatlodge.com.**
Information & Licenses **Idaho Department of Fish and Game** Box 25, 600 S. Walnut St., Boise, ID 83707 208/334–3700 www2.state.id.us/fishgame. **Montana Department of Fish, Wildlife, and Parks** 1420 E. 6th St., Helena, MT 59620

☎ 406/444-2535 🌐 www.fwp.state.mt.us. **Wyoming Game and Fish Department** ✉ 5400 Bishop Blvd., Cheyenne, WY 82006 ☎ 307/777-4600 🌐 gf.state.wy.us.

Instruction **Bud Lilly's Trout Shop** ✉ 39 Madison Ave., Box 530, West Yellowstone, MT 59758 ☎ 406/646-7801 or 800/854-9559 🌐 www.budlilys.com. **Orvis Fly Fishing Schools** ☎ 800/239-2074 Ext. 784 🌐 www.orvis.com.

GROUP TRIPS

Group sizes for organized trips vary considerably, depending on the organizer and the activity. If you are planning a trip with a large group, trip organizers or outfitters will sometimes offer discounts of 10% and more, and are willing to customize trips. For example, for people specifically interested in photography or in wildlife, trip organizers have been known to get professional photographers or naturalists to join the group. Recreating as a group gives you leverage with the organizer, and you should use it.

One way to travel with a group is to join an organization before going. Conservation-minded travelers might want to contact the Sierra Club, a nonprofit organization, which offers both vacation and work trips. Hiking trails tend to be maintained by volunteers (this is more often done by local hiking clubs). Park or forest rangers are the best source of information for groups involved in this sort of work.

Individuals or groups wanting to test their mettle can learn wilderness skills through "outdoor schools."

National Outdoor Leadership School ✉ 284 Lincoln St., Lander, WY 82520 ☎ 307/332-5300 or 800/710-6657 🌐 www.nols.edu. **Sierra Club** ✉ 85 2nd St., 2nd fl., San Francisco, CA 94105 ☎ 415/977-5500 🌐 www.sierraclub.org.

HIKING

Hiking is popular throughout the Rockies, and you can get information about trails and guided trips at Forest Service offices or national park visitor centers. The national parks have guided hikes during summer and early fall. *Backpacker* magazine (Rodale Press) is the leading national magazine that focuses on hiking and backpacking, and each region in the Rockies has great local publications on places to hike. Organized-trip costs can be as little as $30 a day. *See* Guidebooks for guidebook sources.

American Hiking Society Box 20160, Washington, DC 20041 ☎ 301/565-6704 🌐 www.americanhiking.org.

KAYAKING

The streams and rivers of the Rockies tend to be better suited to kayaking than canoeing. Steep mountains and narrow canyons usually mean fast-flowing water, in which the maneuverability of kayaks is a great asset. A means of transport for less experienced paddlers is the inflatable kayak (it's easier to navigate and it bounces off the rocks). The best rivers for kayaking are in central Idaho. Cascade Kayak School features Idaho river trips and instruction, including special kids' classes, by former world-class competitors and coaches. Dvorak Expeditions (⇨ Rafting) leads trips on the rivers of Idaho and Wyoming and conducts clinics, including certification courses, for kayakers of all abilities. River Travel Center ⇨ Rafting) arranges trips in Idaho, among other destinations.

To minimize environmental impact as well as ensure a sense of wilderness privacy (riverside campgrounds are often limited to one party per night), a reservation policy is used for many rivers of the West. Often, the reserved times—many of the *prime* times—are prebooked by licensed outfitters, limiting your possibilities if you're planning a self-guided trip. For those rivers with restricted-use policies, it's best to reserve through a guide company several months or more in advance. Also, try to be flexible about when and where to go; you might find that the time you want to go is unavailable, or you may find yourself closed out altogether from your river of choice. If you insist on running a specific river at a specific time, your best bet is to sign on with a guided trip (which will cost at least $100 a day).

Outfitters provide life jackets and, if necessary, paddles and helmets; they often throw in waterproof containers for cameras, clothing, and sleeping bags. Bring bug repellent as well as a good hat, sunblock, and warm clothing for overnight trips. The sun on the river can be intense, but once it disappears behind canyon walls, the temperature can drop 30°F or

more. The best footwear is a pair of either water-resistant sandals or old sneakers.
Instruction & Trips **Cascade Kayak School** ✉ Rte. 1, Box 117-A, Horseshoe Bend, ID 83629 ☎ 800/292-7238 🌐 www.cascaderaft.com.

MAPS

If you plan to do much traveling where trails might not be well marked or maintained, you'll need maps and a compass. Topographical maps are sold in well-equipped outdoor stores (REI or Eastern Mountain Sports, for example). Maps in several different scales are available from the U.S. Geological Survey. Before ordering, you will need to request the free index and catalog, from which you can order the specific maps you need. Many local camping, fishing, and hunting stores carry U.S.G.S. and other detailed maps of the surrounding region. The U.S. Forest Service and the BLM also publish useful maps.
Maps **U.S. Geological Survey** ✉ Distribution Center, Box 25286, Federal Center, Denver, CO 80225 ☎ 303/202-4700 or 888/275-8747.

PACK TRIPS & HORSEBACK RIDING

Horsemanship is not a prerequisite for most trips, but it is helpful. If you aren't an experienced rider (and even if you are), you can expect to have some saddle discomfort for the first day or two. If you're unsure of how much of this sort of thing you can put up with, sign up for a shorter trip (one to three days) before taking on an adventure of a week or longer. Another option is to spend a few days at a dude or guest ranch to get used to life in the saddle, then try a shorter, overnight pack trip organized by the ranch.

Clothing requirements are minimal. A sturdy pair of pants, a wide-brim sun hat, and outerwear to protect against rain are about the only necessities. Ask your outfitter for a list of items you'll need. You might be limited in the gear (extra clothing) or luxuries (alcoholic beverages) an outfitter will let you bring along. Trip costs typically range between $120 and $180 per day.

Pack trips tend to be organized by local outfitters or ranches rather than national organizations. Local chambers of commerce can usually provide lists of outfitters who work in a particular area.
Outfitters **Allen's Diamond 4 Ranch** ✉ Box 243, Lander, WY 82520 ☎ 307/332-2995 🖷 307/332-7902 🌐 www.diamond4ranch.com. **Glacier Wilderness Guides** ✉ Box 535, West Glacier, MT 59936 ☎ 800/521-7238 🖷 406/387-5656 🌐 www.glacierguides.com. **Rimrock Dude Ranch** ✉ 2728 North Fork Hwy., Cody, WY 82414 ☎ 307/587-3970 or 800/208-7468 🖷 307/527-5014 🌐 www.rimrockranch.com.

RAFTING

Unless you are an expert, **pick a recognized outfitter** if you're going into white water. Even then, you should be a good swimmer and in solid general health. Different companies are licensed to run different rivers, although there may be several companies working the same river. Some organizers combine river rafting with other activities: pack trips, mountain-bike excursions, extended hikes, or fishing. In Idaho there are more than 70 licensed rafting outfitters who offer a range of trips, including kayaking, rafting, and jet boating.

"Raft" can mean any of a number of things: an inflated raft in which passengers do the paddling, an inflated raft or wooden dory in which a licensed professional does the work, or a motorized raft on which some oar work might be required. Be sure you know what kind of raft you'll be riding—or paddling—before booking a trip. Day trips typically run between $40 and $75 per person. Expect to pay between $120 and $150 per day for multiday trips.
Outfitters **Glacier Raft Company** ✉ Box 210C, West Glacier, MT 59936 ☎ 406/888-5454 or 800/235-6781 🌐 www.glacierraftco.com. **Glacier Wilderness Guides** ✉ Box 535, West Glacier, MT 59936 ☎ 406/387-5555 or 800/521-7238 🖷 406/387-5656 🌐 www.glacierguides.com. **Idaho Outfitters and Guides Association** ✉ Box 95, Boise, ID 83701 ☎ 208/342-1919 🌐 www.ioga.org. **OARS** ✉ Box 67, Angels Camp, CA 95222 ☎ 800/346-6277 🌐 www.oars.com. **Riverquest Excursions** ✉ 4203 Snake River Ave., Lewiston, ID 83501 ☎ 800/589-1129 🌐 www.riverquestexcursions.com.

ROCK CLIMBING & MOUNTAINEERING

Before you sign on with any trip, be sure to clarify to the trip organizer your climbing skills, experience, and physical condition. Climbing tends to be a team sport, and overestimating your capabilities can endanger not only yourself but other team members. A fair self-assessment of your abilities also helps a guide choose an appropriate climbing route; routes (not unlike ski trails) are rated according to their difficulty. The way to a summit may be relatively easy or brutally challenging, depending on the route selected. You may want to get some instruction at a climbing wall before a trip to the Rockies.

Guide services usually rent such technical gear as helmets, pitons, ropes, and axes; be sure to ask what equipment and supplies you'll need to bring along. (Outfitters usually rent equipment on a per-item, per-day basis.) Some mountaineering stores rent climbing equipment. As for clothing, temperatures can fluctuate dramatically at higher elevations. Bringing several thin layers of clothing, including a sturdy, waterproof/breathable outer shell, is the best strategy for dealing with weather variations.

Organized trip costs can vary considerably, depending on group size, length of climb, instruction rendered, and equipment supplied. Count on spending at least $125 a day. However, the cost of a small-group multiday instructional climb can push $300 a day. The American Alpine Institute leads trips around the world, ranging from training climbs to expeditionary first ascents. It is one of the most respected climbing organizations in the country.

Instructional Programs & Outfitters **American Alpine Institute** ✉ 1515 12th St., N-4, Bellingham, WA 98225 ☎ 360/671-1505 🌐 www.aai.cc. **Exum School of Mountaineering** 📫 Box 56, Moose, WY 83012 ☎ 307/733-2297 🌐 www.exumguides.com. **Jackson Hole Mountain Guides** 📫 Box 7477, Jackson, WY 83001 ☎ 800/239-7642 🌐 www.jhmg.com.

TOUR COMPANIES

Off the Beaten Path customizes trips within the Rockies that combine outdoor activities and learning experiences. Many trips cross the Montana–Wyoming border. The Yellowstone Association Institute offers guided tours and trips in Yellowstone National Park ranging from backcountry expeditions to "Lodging and Learning" experiences within the comfort of park lodging. Some of the trips are specifically for families. Timberline Adventures leads hiking and biking tours in the bigger national parks such as Glacier and Yellowstone.

Off the Beaten Path ✉ 27 E. Main St., Bozeman, MT 59715 ☎ 800/445-2995 📠 406/587-4147 🌐 www.offthebeatenpath.com. **Timberline Adventures** ✉ 7975 E. Harvard, Suite J, Denver, CO 80231 ☎ 303/759-3804 or 800/417-2453 🌐 www.timbertours.com. **The Yellowstone Association Institute** ✉ Yellowstone National Park ☎ 307/344-2293 🌐 www.YellowstoneAssociation.org.

STUDENTS IN MONTANA, WYOMING & IDAHO

Students can sometimes get discounts for attractions, but it is not routine.

IDs & Services **STA Travel** ✉ 10 Downing St., New York, NY 10014 ☎ 212/627-3111 or 800/777-0112 📠 212/627-3387 🌐 www.sta.com. **Travel Cuts** ✉ 187 College St., Toronto, Ontario M5T 1P7, Canada ☎ 416/979-2406, 800/592-2887, 866/246-9762 in Canada 📠 416/979-8167 🌐 www.travelcuts.com.

TAXES

Sales taxes are as follows: 5% in Idaho and 4% in Wyoming. Montana has no sales tax. Some areas have additional local sales and lodging taxes, which can be quite significant.

If you are crossing the border into Canada, be aware of Canada's goods and services tax (better known as the GST). This is a value-added tax of 7%, applicable on virtually every purchase except basic groceries and a small number of other items. Visitors to Canada, however, may **claim a full rebate of the GST** on any goods taken out of the country as well as on short-term accommodations. Rebates can be claimed either immediately on departure from Canada at participating duty-free shops or by mail within 60 days of leaving Canada. Rebate forms can be obtained from certain retailers, duty-free shops, and customs officials, or by writing to Revenue Canada (⇨ Customs & Duties).

Purchases made during multiple visits to Canada can be grouped together for rebate purposes. Instant cash rebates up to a maximum of $500 are provided by some duty-free shops when leaving Canada, and most provinces do not tax goods that are shipped directly by the vendor to the purchaser's home. Always **save your original receipts** from stores and hotels (not just credit-card receipts), and **be sure the name and address of the establishment are shown on the receipt.** Original receipts are not returned. To be eligible for a refund, receipts must total at least $200, and each individual receipt must show a minimum purchase of $50.

Canada Tax Refund **Canada Sales Tax Refunds** ✉ PMB 186, 816 Peace Portal Dr., Blaine, WA 98230-5025 🌐 www.canadasalestaxrefunds.com/.

TELEPHONES

Cell phones are generally unreliable in the backcountry, especially in canyons and in remote locations where cell towers are not within reach.

AREA & COUNTRY CODES

The telephone area codes are 208 for Idaho, 406 for Montana, and 307 for Wyoming.

LOCAL CALLS

Pay telephones cost 35¢ for local calls. Charge phones, also common, may be used to charge a call to a telephone-company calling card or a credit card, or for collect calls.

Many hotels place a surcharge on local calls made from your room and include a service charge on long-distance calls. It may be cheaper for you to make your calls from a pay phone in the hotel lobby rather than from your room.

TIME

Idaho, Montana, and Wyoming are all in the Mountain Time Zone. Mountain time is two hours earlier than Eastern time and one hour later than Pacific time. It is 1 hour earlier than Chicago, 7 hours earlier than London, and 17 hours earlier than Sydney.

TIPPING

It is customary to tip 15% at restaurants; 20% in resort towns is increasingly the norm. For coat checks and bellhops, $1 per coat or bag is the minimum. Taxi drivers expect 10% to 15%, depending on where you are. In resort towns, ski technicians, sandwich makers, coffee baristas, and the like also appreciate tips.

TOURS & PACKAGES

Because everything is prearranged on a prepackaged tour or independent vacation, you spend less time planning—and often get it all at a good price.

BOOKING WITH AN AGENT

Travel agents are excellent resources. But it's a good idea to collect brochures from several agencies, as some agents' suggestions may be influenced by relationships with tour and package firms that reward them for volume sales. If you have a special interest, **find an agent with expertise in that area**; the American Society of Travel Agents (ASTA; ⇨ Travel Agencies) has a database of specialists worldwide.

Make sure your travel agent knows the accommodations and other services of the place being recommended. Ask about the hotel's location, room size, beds, and whether it has a pool, room service, or programs for children, if you care about these. Has your agent been there in person or sent others whom you can contact?

Do some homework on your own, too: local tourism boards can provide information about lesser-known and small-niche operators, some of which may sell only direct.

BUYER BEWARE

Each year consumers are stranded or lose their money when tour operators—even large ones with excellent reputations—go out of business. So **check out the operator.** Ask several travel agents about its reputation, and try to **book with a company that has a consumer-protection program.** (Look for information in the company's brochure.) In the United States, members of the National Tour Association and the United States Tour Operators Association are required to set aside funds to cover payments and travel arrangements in the event that the company defaults. It's also a good idea to choose a company that participates in the American Society of Travel Agents' Tour Operator Program; ASTA will act as mediator in any disputes between you and your tour operator.

Remember that the more your package or tour includes, the better you can predict the ultimate cost of your vacation. Make sure you know exactly what is covered, and **beware of hidden costs.** Are taxes, tips, and transfers included? Entertainment and excursions? These can add up.

Tour-Operator Recommendations **American Society of Travel Agents** (⇨ Travel Agencies). **National Tour Association** (NTA) ✉ 546 E. Main St., Lexington, KY 40508 ☎ 859/226-4444 or 800/682-

8886 🌐 www.ntaonline.com. **United States Tour Operators Association** (USTOA) ✉ 275 Madison Ave., Suite 2014, New York, NY 10016 ☎ 212/599-6599 or 800/468-7862 📠 212/599-6744 🌐 www.ustoa.com.

TRAIN TRAVEL

Amtrak connects the Rockies to both coasts and all major American cities, with trains that run through Boise. Amtrak trains also run through northern Montana, with stops in Essex and Whitefish, near Glacier National Park. Connecting bus services to Yellowstone National Park are provided in the summer from Amtrak's stop in Pocatello, Idaho.

Canada's passenger service, VIA Rail Canada, stops at Jasper, near the Canadian entrance to Waterton/Glacier International Peace Park.

Amtrak ☎ 800/872-7245 🌐 www.amtrak.com. **VIA Rail Canada** ☎ 800/561-3949.

SCENIC TRAIN TRIPS

Both Montana and Idaho have restored unused stretches of track and refurbished turn-of-the-20th-century touring cars. These give you the chance to scout out places beyond the reach of any four-lane freeway.

Idaho Division of Travel Promotion ✉ Idaho Department of Commerce, 700 W. State St., Boise, ID 83720 ☎ 800/635-7820. **Travel Montana** ✉ Department of Commerce, 1424 9th Ave., Helena, MT 59620 ☎ 406/444-2654, 800/548-3390 in Montana, 800/847-4868 nationwide.

TRANSPORTATION IN MONTANA, WYOMING & IDAHO

Without a doubt, the best way to travel the region is by automobile because bus service is limited, there is little possibility of other public transportation, and trains provide access only to limited areas. Of course, once you are in an area, touring specific attractions by hiking, biking, or horseback riding is de rigueur and also is the way to access areas that can't be reached by vehicle.

If you have limited time, choose one area or one state to visit. To visit national parks in both Wyoming and Montana, fly into a gateway community and then rent a car. It takes only about five hours to drive between Yellowstone and Glacier, and there is plenty to see along the way.

TRAVEL AGENCIES

A good travel agent puts your needs first. Look for an agency that has been in business at least five years, emphasizes customer service, and has someone on staff who specializes in your destination. In addition, **make sure the agency belongs to a professional trade organization.** The American Society of Travel Agents (ASTA)—the largest and most influential in the field with more than 24,000 members in some 140 countries—maintains and enforces a strict code of ethics and will step in to help mediate any agent-client disputes involving ASTA members if necessary. ASTA (whose motto is "Without a travel agent, you're on your own") also maintains a Web site that includes a directory of agents. (If a travel agency is also acting as your tour operator, *see* Buyer Beware *in* Tours and Packages.)

Local Agent Referrals **American Society of Travel Agents** (ASTA) ✉ 1101 King St., Suite 200, Alexandria, VA 22314 ☎ 703/739-2782 or 800/965-2782 24-hr hotline 📠 703/739-3268 🌐 www.astanet.com. **Association of British Travel Agents** ✉ 68-71 Newman St., London W1T 3AH ☎ 020/7637-2444 📠 020/7637-0713 🌐 www.abtanet.com. **Association of Canadian Travel Agents** ✉ 130 Albert St., Suite 1705, Ottawa, Ontario K1P 5G4 ☎ 613/237-3657 📠 613/237-7052 🌐 www.acta.ca. **Australian Federation of Travel Agents** ✉ Level 3, 309 Pitt St., Sydney, NSW 2000 ☎ 02/9264-3299 📠 02/9264-1085 🌐 www.afta.com.au. **Travel Agents' Association of New Zealand** ✉ Level 5, Tourism and Travel House, 79 Boulcott St., Box 1888, Wellington 6001 ☎ 04/499-0104 📠 04/499-0786 🌐 www.taanz.org.nz.

VISITOR INFORMATION

At each visitor center and highway welcome center, you can obtain maps and information; most places have staff on hand to answer questions. You'll also find conveniences such as phones and rest rooms.

Tourist Information **Idaho Travel Council** ✉ Department of Commerce, 700 W. State St., Box 83720, Boise, ID 83720 ☎ 208/334-2470 or 800/635-7820 📠 208/334-2175 🌐 www.visitid.org. **Travel Montana** ✉ Department of Commerce, 1424 9th Ave., Helena, MT 59620 ☎ 406/444-2654 or 800/847-4868 📠 406/444-1800 🌐 www.visitmt.com or www.wintermt.com. **Wyoming Department**

of Tourism ✉ I-25 at College Dr., Cheyenne, WY 82002 ☎ 307/777-7777 or 800/225-5996 🖷 307/777-6904 🌐 www.wyomingtourism.org.

Government Advisories **Consular Affairs Bureau of Canada** ☎ 613/944-6788 or 800/267-6788 🌐 www.voyage.gc.ca. **U.K. Foreign and Commonwealth Office** ✉ Travel Advice Unit, Consular Division, Old Admiralty Building, London SW1A 2PA ☎ 020/7008-0232 or 020/7008-0233 🌐 www.fco.gov.uk/travel. **Australian Department of Foreign Affairs and Trade** ☎ 02/6261-1299 Consular Travel Advice Faxback Service 🌐 www.dfat.gov.au. **New Zealand Ministry of Foreign Affairs and Trade** ☎ 04/439-8000 🌐 www.mft.govt.nz.

WEB SITES

Do check out the World Wide Web when planning your trip. You'll find everything from weather forecasts to virtual tours of famous cities. Be sure to **visit Fodors.com** (🌐 www.fodors.com), a complete travel-planning site. You can research prices and book plane tickets, hotel rooms, rental cars, vacation packages, and more. In addition, you can post your pressing questions in the Travel Talk section. Other planning tools include a currency converter and weather reports, and there are loads of links to travel resources.

Also keep in mind that many towns, parks, and attractions have their own Web site, often jam-packed with pertinent information. Park sites are particularly helpful to read for safety precautions, as many Rocky Mountain area parks are true wilderness.

YELLOWSTONE NATIONAL PARK

FODOR'S CHOICE

Grand Canyon of the Yellowstone
Lake Yellowstone Hotel
Norris Geyser Basin
Old Faithful Geyser
Old Faithful Inn
Old Faithful Snow Lodge restaurant

HIGHLY RECOMMENDED

RESTAURANT Lake Yellowstone Hotel Dining Room

HOTELS Lake Yellowstone Hotel
Old Faithful Snow Lodge

SIGHTS Artist Point, Grand Canyon of the Yellowstone

OUTDOORS Horse Adventures
Hiking the North Rim Trail, *Grand Canyon of the Yellowstone*
Hiking Old Faithful Geyser Loop
Hiking Storm Point Trail, *Yellowstone Lake*

By Candy Moulton

WHERE ELSE BUT YELLOWSTONE can you pull off the empty highway at dawn to see two bison bulls shaking the earth as they collide in battle before the herd and an hour later be caught in an RV traffic jam? For more than 125 years the granddaddy of national parks has been full of such contradictions, stemming from its twin goals: to remain America's preeminent wildlife preserve as well as its most accessible one.

Yellowstone, in the northwest corner of Wyoming (and spilling over slightly into Idaho and Montana), was established in 1872 as America's first national park. The Continental Divide slices through it from southeast to northwest, amid a diverse terrain that includes rugged mountains, lush meadows, pine forests, free-flowing rivers, and the largest natural high-elevation lake in the United States. It's popularly believed that a Sioux description of the yellow rock varieties in the Grand Canyon of the Yellowstone gave the park its name, adopted by early-19th-century French trappers.

The Blackfeet, Crow, Bannock, Flathead, Nez Perce, and Northern Shoshone have all been aware for thousands of years of the abundance of wildlife in the park area, including elk and bison herds, black and grizzly bears, and North American wolves (which have recently been reintroduced to the environment). Only one small Shoshone band, named the Sheepeaters, lived in what is now the park. Mountain man John Colter became the first white man to explore Yellowstone, in 1807–08, and his stories about geysers and boiling rivers prompted some mapmakers to dub the uncharted region Colter's Hell. Additional stories reported from the 1820s through 1860s led eventually to government explorations and the designation of the area as a national park.

Few places in the world can match Yellowstone's collection of accessible wonders, from grazing bison and cruising trumpeter swans to rainbow-color hot springs and thundering geysers. As you visit the park's hydrothermal areas, you'll be walking on top of the Yellowstone Caldera—a 28- by 47-mi collapsed volcanic cone that last erupted about 600,000 years ago. The park's geyser basins, hot mud pots, fumaroles (steam vents), and hot springs are kept bubbling by an underground pressure cooker filled with magma. One geophysicist describes Yellowstone as "a window on the Earth's interior."

The park's attractions are as spectacular today as they were in the days of John Colter. More than 3 million people visit annually to witness the geological wonders, the beautiful scenery, and the diverse array of wildlife. Anyone traveling to Wyoming, Montana, or Idaho should make a point of fitting Yellowstone into the itinerary.

EXPLORING YELLOWSTONE

There are two major seasons in Yellowstone: summer (May–September), when by far the majority of visitors come, and winter (mid-December–February), when fewer people venture into the region, though it is no less spectacular and there are adequate services and facilities to meet most needs. The park has numerous picnic areas and campgrounds, as well as restaurants and lodgings, and there are warming huts for winter users. Except for services at park headquarters at Mammoth Hot Springs, the park closes in from October to mid-December and again from March to late April or early May.

Yellowstone has five primary entrances. The majority of visitors arrive through the South Entrance, north of Grand Teton National Park and Jackson, Wyoming. Other entrances are the East Entrance, with a main

Numbers in the text correspond to numbers in the margin and on the Western Yellowstone and Eastern Yellowstone maps.

If you have 3 days

If you have three days to visit Yellowstone, plan to spend one at **Old Faithful** 6, watching the famous geyser erupt and hiking the trails in the **Upper Geyser Basin** 5. Spend another at Canyon, taking advantage of trails on both the north and south rims of the **Grand Canyon of the Yellowstone** 26 and participating in a ranger talk or tour. On your third day, depending on your ultimate destination (south and east into Wyoming or north and west into Montana), you have two choices. Head north to Mammoth, where you can explore the **Mammoth Hot Springs Terraces** 21, learn some park history at the **Albright Visitor Center** 19, and take the self-guided tour of historic **Fort Yellowstone** 20. Or travel south to **Yellowstone Lake** 42, where you can take a sunset cruise or ride to **LeHardy Rapids** 44 in a classic 1937 touring bus.

If you have 5 days

Though in five days you can visit all the major regions of Yellowstone (Old Faithful, Mammoth, Canyon, and Lake, as outlined in the three-day itinerary), a better way to experience the park is to concentrate on just two or three of the areas and take some time to explore. There are literally dozens of trails, ranging from those that are extremely easy and suited to people with disabilities, to trails that are rigorous enough to test anyone's endurance. Good choices in the "easy" category are the boardwalks around **Old Faithful** 6, the **Upper Geyser Basin** 5, and the **Norris Geyser Basin** 17, which is the most active thermal region of the park. For moderate hikes, take the trail to Mystic Falls, with its trailhead at **Biscuit Basin** 10 between Old Faithful and Mammoth, or the **South Rim Trails** 29 at Canyon. More difficult and longer treks include hikes to Specimen Ridge, in the northeast part of the park, and the trail to the top of Elephant Back, near Lake Yellowstone. For those who prefer not to hike, consider instead a cruise on **Yellowstone Lake** 42, a cookout at Roosevelt (you can ride a horse or in a stagecoach to reach the picnic area), or participate in a photo safari that originates at **Lake Yellowstone Hotel** 43 or **Old Faithful Inn** 4.

If you have 7 days

With seven days at your disposal, a good way to see the park is to participate in a four-day "Lodging and Learning" program with the Yellowstone Association Institute (⇨ see the Cross-country Skiing & Snowshoeing and Hiking sections under "Sports & the Outdoors," below). These excursions will not only take you to the park's main sights, where you will stay in lodge or hotel rooms, but also give you a deeper appreciation for the natural cycles of Yellowstone. With your remaining three days, you can return to one or two of the areas you find most fascinating and participate in further ranger-led activities, hikes, and excursions.

Finally, seven days is plenty of time to take a real backcountry trip, either by backpacking or by horse packing (⇨ contact the backcountry office at 307/344–2160 and see Horseback Riding under "Sports & the Outdoors," below). Such journeys mean you might not see the visitor centers in the park, and you might not sleep in a bed with four walls around you, but you will gain an appreciation for the unspoiled wilderness that still exists in Yellowstone and you'll do it without running into hordes of other people. Some backcountry campsites are accessible for people with disabilities, so everyone can have a chance to see Yellowstone's wild wonders.

---

point of origin in Cody, Wyoming; the West Entrance at West Yellowstone, Montana (most used during winter); the North Entrance at Gardiner, Montana; and the Northeast Entrance at Cooke City, Montana, which can be reached from either Cody, Wyoming, via the Chief Joseph Scenic Highway, or from Red Lodge, Montana, over the Beartooth Pass. Each entrance has its own attractions: the South has the Lewis River canyon; the East, Sylvan Pass; the West, the Madison River valley; the North, the beautiful Paradise Valley; and the Northeast, the spectacular Beartooth Pass.

Within Yellowstone, the roads open to general traffic are laid out in the Grand Loop, with the Upper Loop to the north and the Lower Loop to the south forming the two halves of a figure eight. The entrance roads feed into the Grand Loop; all told, they make up 370 mi of public roads. All roads except the one linking Mammoth to Cooke City, Montana, close to automobiles in mid-October and remain closed until mid-April. Some roads may close earlier or open later due to snowfall. During winter the park roads are groomed for use by over-snow vehicles.

The park has made a significant effort to upgrade the roads, so that now they are wide and smoothly paved in most areas. Some construction is ongoing: the park road between Tower and Canyon over Dunraven Pass will have portions closed through 2005, and work will be ongoing on a segment of the East Entrance Road over Sylvan Pass through 2007, with half-hour delays most days and complete nighttime closures. On holiday weekends all road construction halts so there are no construction delays for travelers. Check with park rangers to determine where you'll encounter construction delays or closures; then give yourself plenty of time and enjoy the scenery and wildlife. Remember that snow is possible any time of year in almost all areas of the park.

Yellowstone has eight major "communities" or developed areas, all of them located on the Grand Loop Road. Grant Village, near West Thumb, is the farthest south; Old Faithful and Madison are on the western side of the Lower Loop; Norris and Canyon Village are in the central part of the park, where the two loops intersect; Mammoth Hot Springs and Roosevelt–Tower Fall lie at the northern corners of the Upper Loop; and Lake Village/Fishing Bridge is along the eastern segment of the Lower Loop.

Before you begin your visit, assess your desires and endurance level. If time is limited, don't try to cover the whole park. Instead, read through this chapter and pick an area to concentrate on, such as the Grand Canyon of the Yellowstone or Old Faithful, or plan to drive either the Lower or Upper Loop. There are summer-staffed visitor centers throughout the park, and there's a busy schedule of guided hikes, evening talks, and campfire programs, which are detailed in the park newspaper, *Discover Yellowstone*. In winter some centers and warming huts are open and distribute information about trails and activities. Pamphlets describing hot-spring basins are available for 50¢ at each site or visitor center.

In addition to enjoying frontcountry activities, you can head into Yellowstone's backcountry on your own or with a guide to hike, camp, ski,

Geological Wonders Without doubt, most people come to Yellowstone to see spouting geysers and bubbling mud pots and hear hissing steam vents—you'll find within the park the greatest concentration of thermal features in the country, nearly 10,000 of them all told. Cataclysmic volcanoes erupted here 2 million years ago, 1.3 million years ago, and again 600,000 years ago, helping to set the stage for what you see today. The heat from the magma (molten rock) under the Yellowstone Caldera continues to fuel the park's most famous geyser basins–West Thumb, Upper, Lower, Midway, and Norris–which contain most of Yellowstone's 200 to 250 active geysers. There are other geological conditions to explore as well, ranging from the basaltic columns near Tower to the hissing steam escaping from Roaring Mountain.

Wildlife Sightings If you're not here for the geysers, chances are that you've come to spot wildlife, and there's an abundance of it in Yellowstone, ranging from predators such as wolves, grizzly and black bears, coyotes, foxes, hawks, and eagles, to songbirds, rodents, bison, elk, deer, and moose. The park has 51 species of mammals, 209 species of birds, and a limited number of amphibians and reptiles. You'll spot wildlife most often in early morning and late evening, when animals move out of the forest in search of food and water. Moose like marshy areas along Yellowstone Lake and in the northeast corner of the park; wolves roam throughout but are most common in the Lamar Valley; elk and bison like river valleys and the geyser basins.

Winter Silence Stop along a trail or a road in Yellowstone during winter and simply listen to the silence. Fewer visitors—even if some of them are riding in snow coaches—mean that if you are patient, you will have an opportunity to hear the quiet nature sounds of Yellowstone. For certain the park is never totally silent; there is always the sound of a mud pot bubbling, a geyser shooting skyward, wind soughing through the pine trees, or the cry of a hawk, coyote, or, if you are lucky, a wolf to pierce the air.

---

snowshoe, or horse pack. All overnight backcountry camping requires a backcountry use permit, which must be obtained in person no more than 48 hours before the planned trip. For information, call the backcountry office (☎ 307/344–2160).

As you explore the park keep this thought in mind: Yellowstone is not an amusement park. It is a wild place. The animals may seem docile or tame, but they are wild, and every year careless visitors are injured, sometimes even killed, when they venture too close. Particularly dangerous are female animals with their young, and bison, which can turn and charge in an instant. (Watch their tails: when they are standing up or crooked like a question mark, the bison is agitated.) *Box 168, Yellowstone National Park, WY 82190* ☎ *307/344–7381, 307/344–2386 TTD* *307/344–2005* *www.nps.gov/yell* *7-day pass good for both Yellowstone and Grand Teton national parks $20 per motor vehicle, $10 on foot or bicycle, $15 on motorcycle* *Year-round to Mammoth; early May–Sept. in other areas; winter season mid-Dec.–Feb. to over-snow vehicles and transportation methods (skis/snowshoes) only.*

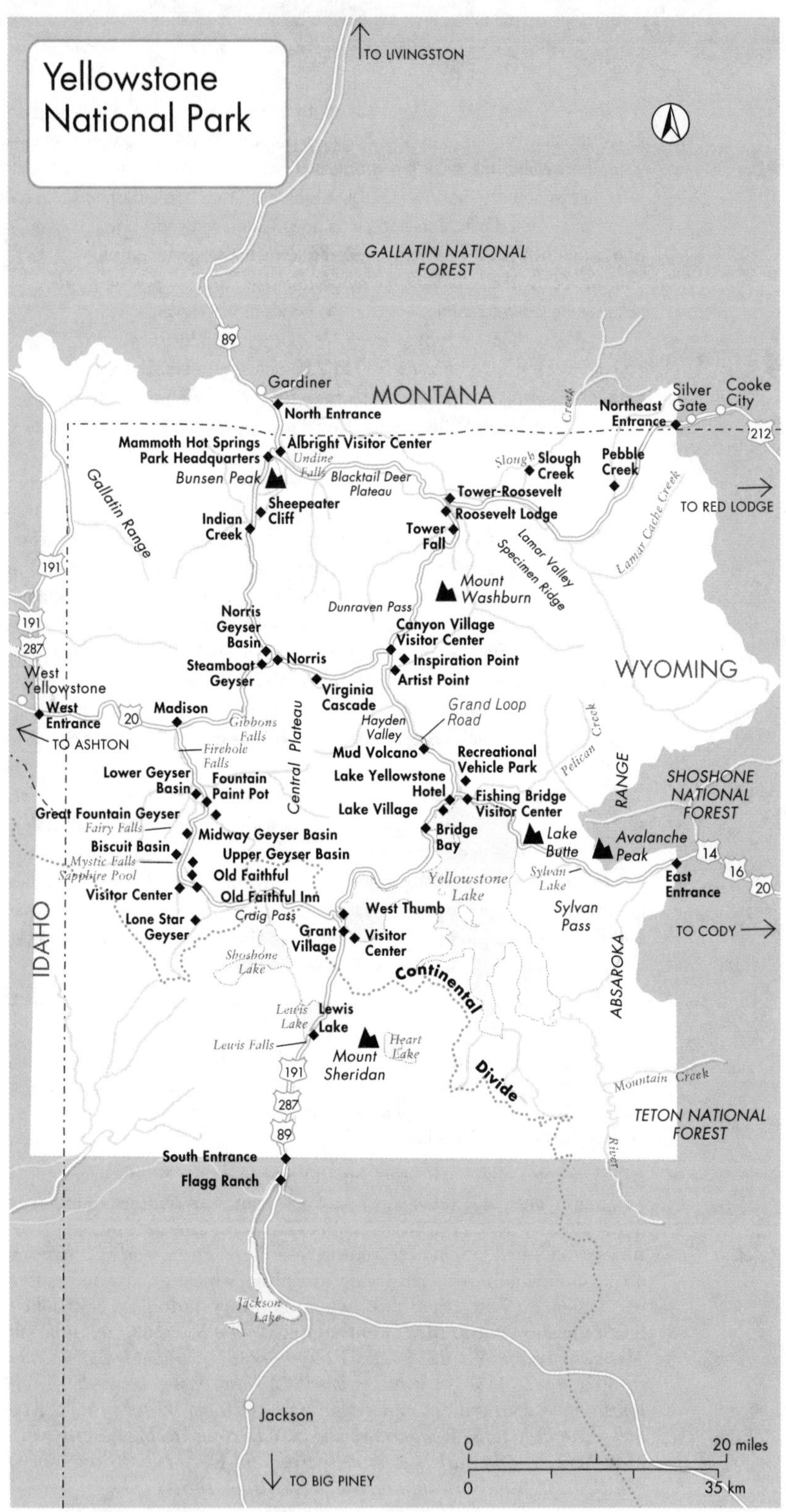
Yellowstone National Park
TO LIVINGSTON
GALLATIN NATIONAL FOREST
89
Gardiner
MONTANA
Silver Gate
Cooke City
Northeast Entrance
212
North Entrance
Mammoth Hot Springs Park Headquarters
Albright Visitor Center
Undine Falls
Bunsen Peak
Blacktail Deer Plateau
Slough Creek
Pebble Creek
Gallatin Range
Sheepeater Cliff
Tower-Roosevelt
Roosevelt Lodge
TO RED LODGE
Indian Creek
Tower Fall
Lamar Valley
Specimen Ridge
Lamar Cache Creek
191
Mount Washburn
Dunraven Pass
Norris Geyser Basin
Canyon Village Visitor Center
191
287
Norris
Inspiration Point
Steamboat Geyser
Artist Point
WYOMING
West Yellowstone
Virginia Cascade
West Entrance
20
Madison
Gibbons Falls
Grand Loop Road
TO ASHTON
Hayden Valley
Firehole Falls
Central Plateau
Mud Volcano
Recreational Vehicle Park
Pelican Creek
Lower Geyser Basin
Fountain Paint Pot
Lake Yellowstone Hotel
RANGE
SHOSHONE NATIONAL FOREST
Fishing Bridge Visitor Center
Great Fountain Geyser
Lake Village
Fairy Falls
Bridge Bay
Lake Butte
Midway Geyser Basin
Avalanche Peak
Biscuit Basin
Upper Geyser Basin
14
Mystic Falls
Sapphire Pool
Old Faithful
Yellowstone Lake
Sylvan Lake
East Entrance
16
Visitor Center
Old Faithful Inn
20
Lone Star Geyser
Craig Pass
West Thumb
Sylvan Pass
IDAHO
Grant Village
Visitor Center
TO CODY
Shoshone Lake
Continental
ABSAROKA
Lewis Lake
Lewis Lake
Lewis Falls
Mount Sheridan
Heart Lake
191
Divide
Mountain Creek
287
TETON NATIONAL FOREST
89
South Entrance
River
Flagg Ranch
Jackson Lake
Jackson
0
20 miles
0
35 km
TO BIG PINEY

Grant Village

Grant Village is the first community you'll encounter if you arrive in the park through the south entrance. This area along the western edge of Lake Yellowstone has basic lodging and dining facilities and gives you easy access to the West Thumb Geyser Basin.

Park at the **West Thumb Geyser Basin** ❶ ⚑ and have a stroll through the basin itself before taking the 1½-mi trail to **Lake Overlook** ❷. This route meanders across an area burned in previous wildfires to a point from which you can easily see the thumblike protuberance of Yellowstone Lake that gives the area its name. You're likely to spot elk as you continue the loop trail back to the trailhead.

TIMING It takes about two hours to hike to Lake Overlook and explore West Thumb Geyser Basin.

What to See

❷ **Lake Overlook.** From this hilltop northwest of West Thumb and Grant Village you get an expansive view of the southwest portion of Yellowstone. You reach the promontory by taking a 1½-mi hiking trail through forest still recovering from the massive fires of 1988; the clearing caused by the fire makes this a prime area for sighting elk. ✉ *1½ mi northwest of Grant Village.*

⚑ ❶ **West Thumb Geyser Basin.** The unusual name of this small geyser basin comes from its location along a digitlike projection of Yellowstone Lake. This area, full of geysers and hot springs, is reached by a short boardwalk loop. It is particularly popular for winter visitors who take advantage of the nearby warming hut and a stroll around the geyser basin before continuing their trip via snow coach. ✉ *Grand Loop Rd., West Thumb, 22 mi north of South Entrance.*

The **West Thumb Information Station** (⏲ June–Aug., daily 9–5; Sept., daily 9–6; Dec.–Feb., daily 8–5) is a little log cabin that houses a bookstore run by the nonprofit Yellowstone Association. There are rest rooms in the parking area, and during winter the cabin doubles as a warming hut.

Old Faithful

The world's most famous geyser, Old Faithful, is the centerpiece of this region of the park, which has extensive boardwalks through the Upper Geyser Basin and equally extensive visitor services, including several choices in lodging and dining. It is the one area of Yellowstone that almost all visitors include in their itinerary. You can get views of Old Faithful as it erupts from benches just yards away from the geyser, from a balcony or some lodging rooms at the spectacular Old Faithful Inn, and from the dining room at the lodge cafeteria, and even limited views from the Old Faithful Snow Lodge. During winter you can dine and stay in this area and cross-country ski or snowshoe through the Geyser Basin.

a good tour

Begin your tour at **Old Faithful Visitor Center** ❸ ⚑, where you can look out at Old Faithful Geyser, get maps to the region, watch a movie about geysers, and visit with park rangers about geyser activity. When you depart the visitor center walk to the century-old **Old Faithful Inn** ❹ to check out its massive log construction; late afternoon is a good time to relax with a cool drink in the lobby, on the second-floor balcony area, or on the Old Faithful observation deck.

At Old Faithful Village you're in the heart of the **Upper Geyser Basin** ❺, a mile-square area with about 140 geysers. The biggest attraction in the geyser basin is where you should begin your tour: **Old Faithful** 6, which spouts from 130 to 180 feet every 94 minutes or so. Once you've watched Old Faithful erupt, begin to explore the larger basin with a hike around **Geyser Loop Hill** 7, where you'll see a variety of wildlife as well as thermal features. Heading the list of attractions is the **Morning Glory Pool** 8, with its unique flower shape. After you have explored Geyser Hill and Morning Glory Pool, walk or drive to **Black Sand Basin** 9, which has a dozen or so hot springs and geysers.

From Black Sand Basin, return to your car and drive north 3 mi to **Biscuit Basin** 10, where you'll find the trailhead for the Mystic Falls Trail. There's a boardwalk through the Biscuit Basin geyser area, and you can get views of the basin and the Upper Geyser Basin from atop the hill on the Mystic Falls Trail. Return to your car and head farther north along **Firehole Lake Drive** 11 through an area that's sometimes populated by bison and has access to additional thermal areas. Continue north to the **Lower Geyser Basin** 12, where you'll see the Great Fountain Geyser and White Dome Geyser as well as the colorful **Fountain Paint Pots** 13.

TIMING It takes at least a day to do justice to the various sights in the Old Faithful area and geyser basins to its north.

What to See

9 **Black Sand Basin.** There are a dozen hot springs and geysers in this basin near the cloverleaf entrance from Grand Loop Road to Old Faithful. ✉ *North of Old Faithful on Grand Loop Rd.*

10 **Biscuit Basin.** Located north of Old Faithful, this basin is also the trailhead for the Mystic Falls Trail. It's an active geyser basin—sometimes there are even steam vents popping through the asphalt in the parking lot. A 2½-mi boardwalk loop takes you across the Firehole River to colorful Sapphire Pool. ✉ *3 mi north of Old Faithful on Grand Loop Rd.*

11 **Firehole Lake Drive.** About 8 mi north of Old Faithful, this one-way, 3-mi road takes you north past Great Fountain Geyser, which shoots out jets of water that occasionally reach as high as 200 feet. If you're touring the park in winter, watch for bison. ✉ *8 mi north of Old Faithful off Grand Loop Rd.*

13 **Fountain Paint Pots.** You'll see fumaroles (steam vents), blue pools, pink mud pots, and minigeysers in this geyser area. It's popular in both summer and winter because it's right next to Grand Loop Road. ✉ *Between Old Faithful and Madison on Grand Loop Rd.*

Grand Prismatic Spring. This is Yellowstone's largest hot spring, encompassing an area 370 feet in diameter. It's in the Midway Geyser Basin, and you can reach it by following the boardwalk. The spring is deep blue in color, with yellow and orange rings formed by bacteria that give it the effect of a prism. ✉ *Midway Geyser Basin off Grand Loop Rd.*

7 **Geyser Loop Hill.** Marked trails in the Upper Geyser Basin lead to Geyser Hill, and you can visit sights such as Castle Geyser and Morning Glory Pool, as well as Giantess Geyser and Giant Geyser. Be on the lookout for elk and buffalo. ✉ *Old Faithful.*

Great Fountain Geyser. This geyser erupts twice a day; rangers predict when it will shoot some 200 feet into the air, but their prediction has a window of opportunity a couple of hours long. Should you see Great Fountain spew, however, you'll be rewarded with a view of waves of water cascading down the terraces that form the edges of the geyser. ✉ *Firehole Lake Dr., north of Old Faithful.*

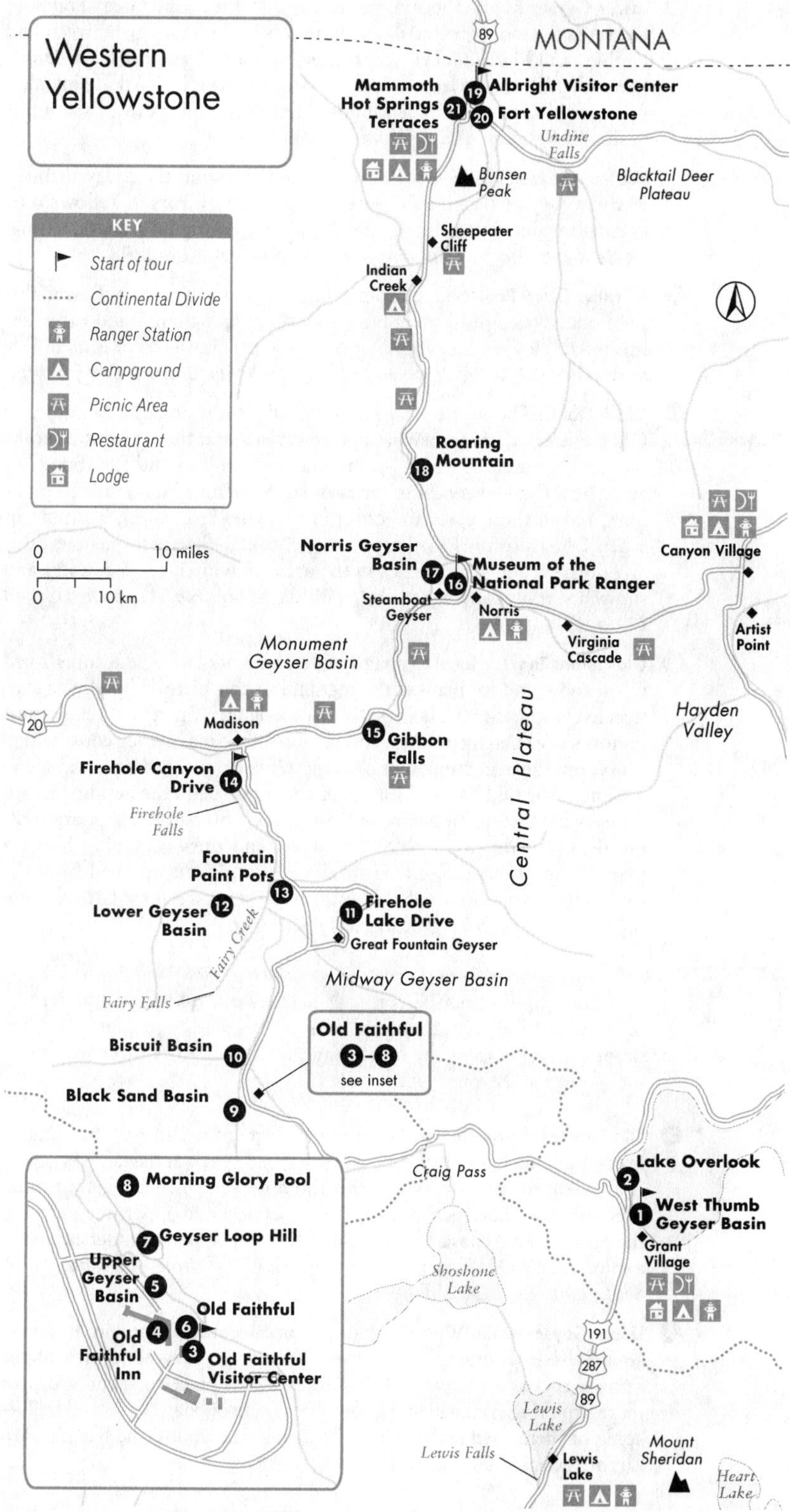
Western Yellowstone
KEY
Start of tour
Continental Divide
Ranger Station
Campground
Picnic Area
Restaurant
Lodge
0
10 miles
0
10 km
MONTANA
89
Mammoth Hot Springs Terraces
21
19 Albright Visitor Center
20 Fort Yellowstone
Undine Falls
Bunsen Peak
Blacktail Deer Plateau
Sheepeater Cliff
Indian Creek
Roaring Mountain
18
Norris Geyser Basin
17
16 Museum of the National Park Ranger
Canyon Village
Steamboat Geyser
Norris
Virginia Cascade
Artist Point
Monument Geyser Basin
Hayden Valley
20
Madison
15 Gibbon Falls
Central Plateau
Firehole Canyon Drive
14
Firehole Falls
Fountain Paint Pots
13
Lower Geyser Basin
12
11 Firehole Lake Drive
Great Fountain Geyser
Fairy Creek
Midway Geyser Basin
Fairy Falls
Old Faithful
3–8
see inset
Biscuit Basin
10
Black Sand Basin
9
8 Morning Glory Pool
7 Geyser Loop Hill
Upper Geyser Basin
5
Old Faithful
6
Old Faithful Inn
4
3 Old Faithful Visitor Center
Craig Pass
Lake Overlook
2
1 West Thumb Geyser Basin
Grant Village
Shoshone Lake
191
287
89
Lewis Lake
Lewis Falls
Lewis Lake
Mount Sheridan
Heart Lake

12 **Lower Geyser Basin.** Shooting more than 150 feet, the Great Fountain Geyser is the most spectacular sight in this basin, midway between Old Faithful and Madison. Less impressive but more regular is White Dome Geyser, which shoots from a 20-foot-tall cone. You'll also find pink mud pots and blue pools at the Fountain Paint Pots, which are a part of this basin. ✉ *Between Old Faithful and Madison.*

Midway Geyser Basin. A series of boardwalks wind their way through Midway Geyser Basin, a favorite stop of most visitors in Yellowstone, particularly in winter. Among the attractions is Grand Prismatic Spring. ✉ *Between Old Faithful and Madison on Grand Loop Rd.*

8 **Morning Glory Pool.** Shaped somewhat like a morning glory flower, this pool once was a deep blue, but tourists dropping coins and other debris into it clogged the plumbing vent. As a result, the color is no longer as striking. ✉ *At the north end of Upper Geyser Basin at Old Faithful.*

6 **Old Faithful.** The mysterious plumbing of Yellowstone has lengthened Old Faithful's cycle somewhat in recent years, but the geyser still spouts the same amount of water—sometimes reaching to 180 feet, but averaging 130 feet—every 94 minutes or so. Sometimes it doesn't shoot as high, but in those cases the eruptions usually last longer. To find out when Old Faithful is likely to erupt, check at the visitor center, or at any of the lodging properties in the area. In winter, cross-country and snowshoe trails converge at Old Faithful. ✉ *Southwest segment, Grand Loop Rd.*

Fodor'sChoice ★

4 **Old Faithful Inn.** It's hard to imagine that any work could be accomplished when snow and ice blanket the region, but this historic hotel was constructed in winter 1903. It has served as a lodging property for Yellowstone visitors since opening in 1904, and because of the massive log construction it's become an attraction in its own right. Even if you don't plan to spend a night at the Old Faithful Inn, take a walk through the building to admire its massive open-beam lobby and rock fireplace. There are writing desks on the second-floor balcony, and during evening hours a pianist plays there as well. From the outdoor deck, reached from the second floor, you can watch Old Faithful geyser as it erupts. ✉ *Old Faithful* ☎ *307/344–7901* ⊙ *Early May–late Oct.*

need a break?

Late afternoon is a good time to relax with a cool drink in the lobby or on the second-floor balcony of the **Old Faithful Inn.** You'll hear piano music floating around the massive log walls and stone fireplace, and witness the hustle and bustle of visitors from around the world swirl around you.

3 **Old Faithful Visitor Center.** Located 600 feet from Old Faithful, this A-frame building has one of the best views in the park of the famous geyser. A 100-seat theater shows a movie about geysers. You can get information from park rangers about all types of services and opportunities within the park and purchase a book that will help you better understand and explore it. ✉ *Old Faithful* ☎ *307/545–2750* ⊙ *June–Aug., daily 8–7; Sept., daily 8–6; Oct., daily 9–5.*

5 **Upper Geyser Basin.** With Old Faithful as its central attraction, this mile-square basin contains about 140 different geysers—one-fifth of the known geysers in the world. It's an excellent place to spend a day or more exploring. You will find a complex system of boardwalks and trails—some of them used as bicycle trails—that take you to the basin's various attractions. ✉ *Old Faithful.*

Madison

You'll find limited visitor services at Madison, which is notable primarily as the junction of the West Entrance Road and the Lower Loop, though there is an amphitheater for programs as well as a Yellowstone Association bookstore and a picnic area. There are no dining facilities, and the only lodging is a campground. Even so, this is a good place to take a break as you travel through the park, because you will almost always see bison grazing along the Madison River, and often elk are in the area as well.

a good tour

One mile south of Madison, take a detour onto **Firehole Canyon Drive** 14 to view the Firehole Falls. Then return to the Grand Loop Road and proceed north and east of Madison; about halfway to Norris are the **Gibbon Falls** 15, a cascade of white water in an 84-foot drop.

TIMING It will take an hour or less to see these sights.

What to See

14 **Firehole Canyon Drive.** This one-way, 2-mi detour off Grand Loop Road runs in a southerly direction just south of Madison Junction. The road twists through the 700- to 800-foot-deep canyon and passes the 40-foot Firehole Falls. ☒ *1 mi south of Madison on Grand Loop Rd.*

15 **Gibbon Falls.** Water rushes over the caldera rim in this 84-foot waterfall on the Gibbon River. ☒ *4 mi east of Madison on Grand Loop Rd.*

Norris

Norris marks the western junction of the Upper and Lower Loops, and like Madison it has limited visitor services: you'll find a museum and bookstore and a picnic area. The attraction here is the most active geyser basin in the park. The underground plumbing reached such temperatures in the summer of 2003 that a portion of the Norris Geyser Basin was closed for safety reasons. A number of new geyser areas had developed during the spring and early summer, established geysers were spewing hot water more often, and the ground itself was heated in areas to nearly 200°F.

a good tour

Begin your walk at the **Museum of the National Park Ranger** 16, where you talk to rangers about current geyser activity in the basin. From the museum head on foot into the **Norris Geyser Basin** 17, which includes the Porcelain Basin and Back Basin. (Be aware, though, that portions of the Back Basin may be closed if temperatures are at unsafe levels.) After you've explored the Norris Geyser Basin, return to your vehicle and travel 4 mi north on the Grand Loop Road to **Roaring Mountain** 18, where you might spot a bear, and you will definitely see steam vents spouting from the hillside.

TIMING Allow at least half a day to explore the basin. It's a good idea to consult with rangers at the museum about when different geysers are expected to erupt and to plan your walk accordingly.

What to See

16 **Museum of the National Park Ranger.** The former Norris Soldier Station, a historic log building that from 1886 to 1916 housed soldiers who guarded the park, is now a museum where you can see a movie telling the history of the National Park Service and exhibits related to army service in Yellowstone and early park rangers. ☒ *Grand Loop Rd. at Norris* ⏲ *June–Oct., daily 10–5.*

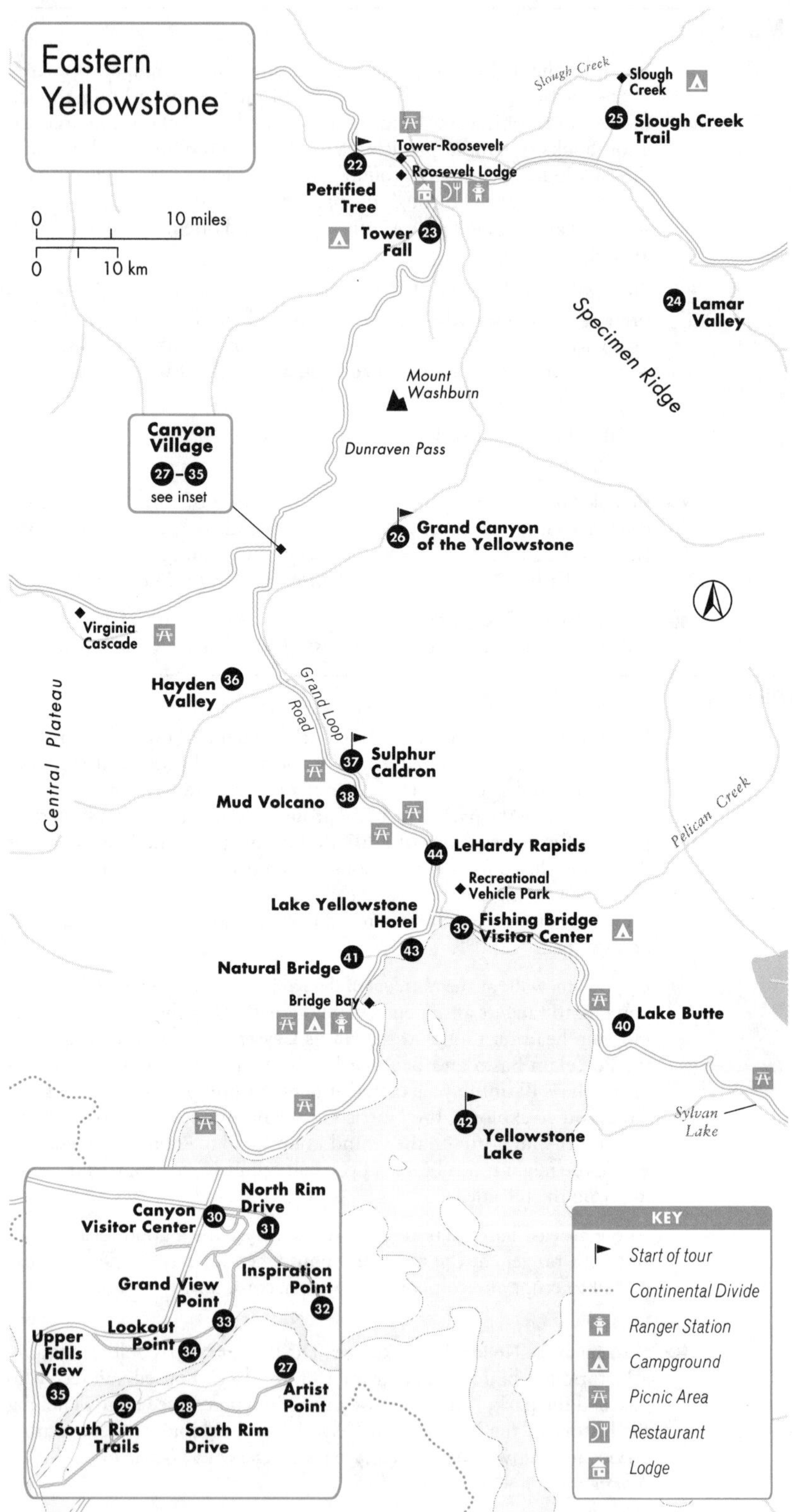
Eastern Yellowstone
0
10 miles
0
10 km
Slough Creek
Slough Creek
25 Slough Creek Trail
Tower-Roosevelt
Roosevelt Lodge
22 Petrified Tree
Tower Fall 23
24 Lamar Valley
Specimen Ridge
Mount Washburn
Dunraven Pass
Canyon Village
27–35
see inset
26 Grand Canyon of the Yellowstone
Virginia Cascade
Hayden Valley 36
Central Plateau
Grand Loop Road
37 Sulphur Caldron
Mud Volcano 38
44 LeHardy Rapids
Pelican Creek
Recreational Vehicle Park
Lake Yellowstone Hotel
39 Fishing Bridge Visitor Center
43
Natural Bridge 41
Bridge Bay
40 Lake Butte
Sylvan Lake
42 Yellowstone Lake
Canyon Visitor Center 30
North Rim Drive
31
Inspiration Point
32
Grand View Point
33
Lookout Point
34
Upper Falls View
35
27
Artist Point
29
28
South Rim Trails
South Rim Drive
KEY
Start of tour
Continental Divide
Ranger Station
Campground
Picnic Area
Restaurant
Lodge

17 **Norris Geyser Basin.** The oldest geyser basin in Yellowstone, Norris is also the most volatile of all the geyser areas of the park. It's constantly changing: some geysers might suddenly stop flowing, while new ones blow and hiss to life. Here you'll discover colorfully named features such as Whirligig Geyser, Whale's Mountain, Emerald Spring, and Arch Steam Vent. The area is accessible via an extensive system of boardwalks, some of them suitable for people with disabilities.

Fodor's Choice ★

There are several geysers of note in Norris's **Back Basin** area, the most famous being Steamboat. It performs rarely—sometimes going for years without an eruption—but when it does, it shoots a stream of water nearly 400 feet, making it the world's tallest geyser. Echinus Geyser is more dependable, erupting roughly every half hour. A portion of the Back Basin was closed temporarily in July 2003 for safety reasons because of overheating. The Steamboat Geyser was not in the area closed.

The **Porcelain Basin** in the eastern portion of the Norris area is reached by a mile-long boardwalk and trail. In this geothermal field, the earth bulges and belches from the underground pressure. You'll find bubbling pools, some milky white and others ringed in orange because of the minerals in the water.

18 **Roaring Mountain.** There is little vegetation on this bare mountain north of Norris, but the area is a good location for spotting bears, and it's known for steam vents that can be seen all across the acidic hillside. ✉ *4 mi north of Norris on Grand Loop Rd.*

Mammoth Hot Springs

Mammoth Hot Springs is headquarters for Yellowstone National Park. In the early days of the park, it was the site of Fort Yellowstone, and the brick buildings constructed during that era are still used for various park activities. Mammoth is known for its massive natural terraces, where mineral water flows continuously, building an ever-changing display. You will almost always see elk grazing in the Mammoth area. The Albright Visitor Center has information and displays about the park history, including some of the original Thomas Moran paintings, created on an 1871 government expedition to the area, that made the broader public aware of Yellowstone's beauty and helped lead to its establishment as a national park. There is a complete range of visitor services here as well.

a good tour

Begin your tour of Mammoth at the **Albright Visitor Center** 19 ⚑, where park rangers are on hand to answer your questions about the area. At the visitor center pick up a copy of the printed walking tour of historic **Fort Yellowstone** 20 and follow it. Then head to **Mammoth Hot Springs Terraces** 21, where you can spend at least an hour or two driving the one-way loop road in the upper terrace area and hiking the boardwalks of the lower terraces.

TIMING Schedule about half a day for exploring the Mammoth area. There are lots of steps on the lower terrace boardwalks, so plan to take your time there.

What to See

⚑ 19 **Albright Visitor Center.** This red-roof building, which served as bachelor quarters for cavalry officers from 1886 to 1918, now holds a museum with exhibits on the early inhabitants of the region and a theater showing films about the history of the park. There are original Thomas Moran paintings of park sites on display here as well. ✉ *Mammoth Hot Springs* ☎ *307/344–2263* ⏲ *June–Aug., daily 8–7; Sept., daily 9–6; Oct.–May, daily 9–5.*

20 **Fort Yellowstone.** The oldest buildings at Mammoth Hot Springs served as Fort Yellowstone from 1886 to 1918, the period when the U.S. Army managed the park. The redbrick buildings cluster around an open area reminiscent of a frontier-era fort parade ground. You can pick up a self-guided tour map of the area to make your way around the historic fort structures. ✉ *Mammoth Hot Springs.*

21 **Mammoth Hot Springs Terraces.** Multicolored travertine terraces formed by slowly escaping hot mineral water mark this unusual geological formation. It constantly changes as a result of shifts in water flow. You can explore the terraces via an elaborate network of boardwalks. ✉ *Northwest corner of Grand Loop Rd.*

Tower-Roosevelt

The northeast region of Yellowstone is the least-visited part of the park, giving you an opportunity to explore without running into lots of other people. The area gets its appellation from the junction of the Northeast Entrance Road and the Upper Loop, named for Theodore Roosevelt, and the Tower Fall, located to the south of the junction. You can hike or ride horseback to sights in the area, such as a petrified tree and a ridge filled with fossil specimens. This is also where wolves were first reintroduced to the park; packs are often seen in the Lamar Valley.

a good tour

Just west of Roosevelt, a spur road provides access to a **Petrified Tree** 22 ⚑, one of the many petrified life-forms found in the northeastern portion of the park. After viewing the tree return to the Grand Loop Road and travel south from Roosevelt to **Tower Fall** 23. There is ongoing road construction in this area of the park, so you may experience travel delays. Until 2005, you cannot continue south from Tower to Canyon, so backtrack to the Roosevelt and drive east into the wolf habitat of **Lamar Valley** 24.

If you want to explore this area on foot, stop 1 mi east of Roosevelt Junction and take the **Slough Creek Trail** 25.

TIMING It will take you a couple of hours to drive through this area and a full day if you decide to explore on foot.

What to See

24 **Lamar Valley.** The Northeast Entrance Road between Cooke City and Roosevelt slices through the broad Lamar Valley, where you are likely to see an abundance of wildlife, ranging from elk and moose to bison and wolves (which were transplanted in this area in 1995). The main wolf-watching activities in the park occur here during early-morning and late-evening hours year-round. ✉ *Northeast Entrance Rd. between Cooke City and Roosevelt.*

22 **Petrified Tree.** A short hike takes you to this ancient petrified redwood tree, one of the most accessible specimens of its kind in the park. ✉ *Grand Loop Rd., 1 mi west of Tower-Roosevelt.*

25 **Slough Creek Trail.** This trail climbs steeply for the first 1½ mi before reaching expansive meadows and prime fishing spots, where moose are common and grizzlies occasionally wander. From this point the trail, now mostly level, meanders another 9½ mi to the park's northern boundary. If you have all day and someone who can drive a vehicle and pick you up at the end, then it's worthwhile to walk the entire route; otherwise head out as far as you like, and then turn around and head back. Because of the variety of wildlife you might see, the return trip won't be the same even though you're following the same route. ✉ *1 mi east of Tower-Roosevelt on Northeast Entrance Rd.*

THE CHANGING WORLD OF YELLOWSTONE

YELLOWSTONE IS DEFINITELY *not a sleepy world of natural wonders. The park truly feels alive when you see mud pots, steam vents, fumaroles, and paint pots—all different aspects of the park's geyser basins, and all intriguing. Beyond the geyser activity, seasonal changes in wildlife and vegetation make Yellowstone fascinating to visit over and over again.*

Though Old Faithful continues to spew routinely, even it has changed in recent years because of various factors. The geyser now erupts about every 94 minutes (up from 78 minutes in 1990), and it may look different each time. Monitoring shows that Old Faithful almost always spews forth the same amount of water at each eruption, but how it does so varies. Sometimes it shoots higher and faster, whereas other times it lasts longer but doesn't reach so high in the sky.

Other geyser basin features aren't so reliable. The force and nature of the various geysers depend on several factors, including the complex underground plumbing at Yellowstone. Rangers say the greatest threats to the geyser basin activity are earthquakes (which occur regularly in the region, though they are usually very small tremors) and the impact caused by people. In past years, for example, people threw hundreds of coins into the bright blue Morning Glory Pool. The coins eventually clogged the pool's water vents, causing it to change color to a sickly green. Though it has been cleaned and people are warned not to throw anything into it, the Morning Glory Pool has never regained its pristine color.

Besides its unique geology related to geyser basins, Yellowstone has many other faces. There are petrified forests and fossil remains of both plants and animals. The ongoing ecological development of the region draws widespread interest. Efforts to control movement of bison—to keep them from wandering out of the park during the winter months to seek food—and the reintroduction of wolves to the ecosystem are just two examples of issues that quickly polarize people both living in and visiting the region around Yellowstone.

Bison leave the park in winter—mainly through the North and West entrances—in part because of overpopulation and the need for the animals to find adequate feed, though their movements are sometimes made easier by the fact that Yellowstone roads become groomed trails for over-snow vehicles in winter. In December 2003, a federal judge banned snowmobiles from Yellowstone, but snow coaches are still allowed, giving visitors an opportunity to enter the park in winter, where they can snowshoe and cross-country ski through geyser basins.

Wolves were returned to Yellowstone in 1995. They acclimated so well that they quickly formed several packs, some of which have ventured outside the park's boundaries. (Wolves from Yellowstone's packs have been spotted as far south as northern Utah and Colorado.) Their presence has had a lasting effect on wildlife populations. The wolves feed on both elk and buffalo, and park rangers have reported a significant decline in Yellowstone's coyote population. Since the wolves are bigger and stronger than coyotes, they kill coyotes or force them to find a new range. Researchers note that there has been a significant decline in elk calf survival as a result of wolf predation.

When massive wildfires tore through Yellowstone in 1988, some believed it would take generations for the park to recover. Already, the park has begun to renew itself. Certainly when you visit Yellowstone now you will see reminders of fires from 1988 and more recent fires in 2001 and 2002, but you will also see the new growth. Lodgepole-pine forests need fire to release their seeds, and once seeds get a start, trees grow quickly. The new growth provides excellent cover for animals, making it harder for visitors to see wildlife such as elk, deer, and bears.

The constant changes in Yellowstone, created by shifts in underground plumbing at the geyser basins, the territorial movements of animals, and the regeneration of plant life, make the park a new experience every time you visit.

23 **Tower Fall.** View volcanic pinnacles in the area of the 132-foot Tower Fall, one of the major waterfalls on the Yellowstone River. ✉ *2 mi south of Roosevelt on Grand Loop Rd.*

off the beaten path

SPECIMEN RIDGE – The world's largest concentration of standing petrified trees can be found on this ridge in the park's northeast region, to the southwest of the Lamar Valley. There are also plenty of unusual fossils, such as impressions of leaves left behind on rocks. The best way to see this area is by taking part in a ranger-led tour. ✉ *East of Tower-Roosevelt on Northeast Entrance Rd.*

Canyon

The Canyon area is located in the central part of the park, near the eastern meeting point of the Upper and Lower Loops. With its waterfalls and the steep canyon walls surrounding the Yellowstone River, this is one of the most spectacular places in Yellowstone. Here you will find all types of visitors' services and lots of hiking opportunities—as well as lots of other visitors.

a good tour

Most Canyon visitors catch their first view of the **Grand Canyon of the Yellowstone** 26 ⚑ from **Artist Point** 27, where there are two viewing levels, the lower one accessible by wheelchair. After you have peered into the canyon, take at least a short hike along the rim; then return to your vehicle and backtrack along **South Rim Drive** 28 to the Uncle Tom's parking area. If your schedule allows, park there and hike along the **South Rim Trails** 29, with impressive views of the yellow walls above the river.

After your explorations from the South Canyon rim, return to the Grand Loop Road and proceed to the Canyon Village, where you should begin explorations at the **Canyon Visitor Center** 30; there park rangers can give you specific details about hiking opportunities, and you can learn more about bison. From the village, travel south on the one-way **North Rim Drive** 31, which gives you access to **Inspiration Point** 32, **Grand View Point** 33, and **Lookout Point** 34. Farther south you'll find a spur road that takes you to the **Upper Falls View** 35.

For a great early-morning or late-evening side trip with opportunities to see a variety of wildlife, travel south of Canyon and into the open meadows of the **Hayden Valley** 36, which is home to hundreds of bison, waterbirds, and other wildlife.

TIMING Depending on how much hiking you want to do, it can take you anywhere from half a day to a couple of days to explore the Grand Canyon of the Yellowstone.

What to See

★ 27 **Artist Point.** The most spectacular view of the Lower Falls of the Yellowstone is seen from this point, which has two different viewing levels, one of which is accessible for people with disabilities. The South Rim Trail goes right past this point, and there is a nearby parking area open in both summer and winter. ✉ *East end of South Rim Rd., Canyon.*

30 **Canyon Visitor Center.** An exhibit on bison, dealing with the history of the animals and their current status in the park, is one attraction at Canyon Visitor Center, where you can also obtain park information and specific details about hiking opportunities in the Canyon area. ✉ *Canyon Village* ☎ *307/242–2552* ⊙ *June–Sept., daily 8–7.*

⚑ 26 Fodor's Choice ★ **Grand Canyon of the Yellowstone.** If you have time in Yellowstone to visit only two locations, this should be one of them (the other being Old Faithful). The cascading waterfall and rushing river carved this 24-mi-long canyon. The red-and-ochre canyon walls are topped with an emerald-green forest. The best view of the falls is from Artist Point. There are hiking trails on both the north and south rims of the canyon. ⊠ *Canyon.*

33 **Grand View Point.** You have a view of the Lower Falls of the Yellowstone from this spot on the north canyon rim. ⊠ *Off North Rim Dr., Canyon.*

36 **Hayden Valley.** You will almost always see bison grazing in this area—summer and winter—and as a result you will also often see coyotes and other predators. This broad valley was once a lake, and the rolling hills and sagebrush flats are popular grazing areas for bison, deer, and elk. A wide array of waterfowl also spends time in this area, lured by the placid waters of the Yellowstone River, which has not yet reached the canyon country, where it becomes a raging torrent. ⊠ *Between Canyon and Fishing Bridge on Grand Loop Rd.*

32 **Inspiration Point.** A spur road off North Rim Road at Canyon and a short loop walk take you to Inspiration Point, from which you can see the Grand Canyon of the Yellowstone. This is also a starting or ending point on the North Rim Trail. ⊠ *Off Spur Rd. and North Rim Dr., Canyon.*

34 **Lookout Point.** Located midway on the North Rim Trail, or accessible via the one-way North Rim Drive, Lookout Point gives you a view of the Grand Canyon of the Yellowstone from above the falls. From there you can descend a steep trail to stand above the lower falls. The best time to hike the trail is early morning, when sunlight reflects off the mist from the falls to create a rainbow. ⊠ *Off North Rim Dr., Canyon.*

31 **North Rim Drive.** This one-way, southbound road passes through Canyon Village and past Canyon Lodge to give you access to Inspiration Point, Grand View, and Lookout Point as well as to the North Rim trails. ⊠ *Canyon.*

28 **South Rim Drive.** Trailheads to Uncle Tom's Trail and the South Rim Trail can be reached from South Rim Drive, as well as Artist Point, the site most visitors head to to capture a classic view of the Yellowstone Falls on film. ⊠ *1 mi south of Canyon, off Grand Loop Rd.*

29 **South Rim Trails.** The hike along the south rim of Canyon via Clear Lake and Lily Pad Lake is a 4½-mi loop that takes you along the canyon rim, giving you impressive views of the Yellowstone falls and the canyon itself, before crossing a high plateau and then meandering through high mountain meadows, where you are likely to see bison grazing. There are many points along the canyon rim where you can take photographs of the canyon and the Yellowstone Falls, or take a break for a snack or even a picnic lunch (though you'll need to sit on the ground, as there are no picnic tables along the route). ⊠ *Off South Rim Dr., Canyon.*

35 **Upper Falls View.** A spur road off Grand Loop Road south of Canyon gives you access to the west end of the North Rim Trail and takes you down a fairly steep trail for a view of Upper Falls from almost directly above. ⊠ *¾ mi south of Canyon, off Grand Loop Rd.*

Fishing Bridge

Fishing Bridge is an important park junction, where the East Entrance Road meets the Lower Loop, and it's also an area in the park where you could see grizzly bears; they like to hunt for fish spawning or swimming near the outlet from Yellowstone Lake where it becomes the Yellowstone River. It is also a popular fishing area and a trailhead for routes headed into the Pelican Valley. There are some visitor services, including limited dining, but no lodging other than the Fishing Bridge RV Park, where only hard-sided vehicles are allowed because of the presence of grizzly bears.

a good tour

Begin your tour with a visit to **Sulphur Caldron** 37 ⚑, 4½ mi north of Fishing Bridge—the sulfurous odor will tell you that you've arrived in the area. Then either walk or return to your vehicle and drive the ½ mi south to **Mud Volcano** 38, with its burping, bubbling pots of mud. Return to your vehicle and travel south to Fishing Bridge Junction, and then turn east onto the East Entrance Road, crossing the bridge that gives the area its name before turning south into the parking lot of the **Fishing Bridge Visitor Center** 39, where you can talk to park rangers to find out what wildlife has recently been spotted in the area, which is known for its grizzly bears. From there, follow the East Entrance Road along Yellowstone Lake to **Lake Butte** 40, a particularly good spot to watch the sun go down over Yellowstone Lake. Alternatively, you can head west to the Bridge Bay area and then leave your car to visit **Natural Bridge** 41.

TIMING If you stick to the attractions near the roads, you can explore the Fishing Bridge area in a couple of hours; it will take at least a half-day or longer should you decide to hike into Pelican Valley or to Natural Bridge.

What to See

39 **Fishing Bridge Visitor Center.** With a distinctive stone-and-log design, this building, dating from 1931, has been designated a National Historic Landmark. It has exhibits on birds and other wildlife found in Yellowstone. Take note, particularly, of the overhead light made from the skulls and horns of Rocky Mountain bighorn sheep. ✉ *East Entrance Rd.*

40 **Lake Butte.** Reached by a spur road off the East Entrance Road, this wooded promontory rising 615 feet above Yellowstone Lake is a prime spot for watching the sun set over the lake. ✉ *2 mi east of Fishing Bridge on East Entrance Rd.*

38 **Mud Volcano.** The Mud Volcano Interpretive Trail loops gently around seething, sulfuric mud pots with names such as Black Dragon's Cauldron and Sizzling Basin and makes its way around Mud Volcano itself, a boiling pot of brown goo. ✉ *10 mi south of Canyon; 4 mi north of Fishing Bridge on Grand Loop Rd.*

41 **Natural Bridge.** You can take an easy 1-mi hike or bicycle ride from Bridge Bay Campground to Natural Bridge, which was formed by erosion of a rhyolite outcrop by Bridge Creek. The top of the bridge is about 50 feet above the creek, and there is a trail to its top, though travel over the bridge itself is restricted. ✉ *1 mi west of Bridge Bay Campground.*

⚑ 37 **Sulphur Caldron.** You can smell the sulphur before you even leave your vehicle to walk to the overlook of Sulphur Caldron, where hissing steam escapes from a moonscape-like surface as superheated bubbling mud. ✉ *9½ mi south of Canyon; 4½ mi north of Fishing Bridge on Grand Loop Rd.*

off the beaten path

PELICAN VALLEY – The long valley following Pelican Creek is some of the best wildlife habitat in the lower 48 states. A hike up it is likely to include sightings of bison, elk, moose, osprey, eagles, sandhill cranes, and possibly grizzly bears. There is a variety of trails in the valley, ranging from the 3.4-mi trail to Pelican Creek Bridge, to the 16-mi trail that takes you clear across the broad meadow and forest ecosystem. Because this area is so widely used by grizzly bears, there are certain restrictions, including no trail hiking during evening and night hours. For backcountry users, campsites are established outside the valley itself. The trailhead for Pelican Valley is east of Fishing Bridge; inquire at the visitor center there for trail conditions and restrictions. ✉ *3 mi east of Fishing Bridge.*

Yellowstone Lake

The tranquility of massive Yellowstone Lake, located in the southeastern segment of the park, spills over to the services at Lake Village, where you will find lodging and dining opportunities that are all geared to a slower pace, as well as opportunities to take part in water sports, including boating and fishing.

a good tour

Yellowstone Lake 42 is the primary attraction in this area, and you follow its shores for miles as you drive along the East Entrance Road to Fishing Bridge and then along Grand Loop Road between Fishing Bridge and West Thumb. Situated beside the lake just south of Fishing Bridge is the **Lake Yellowstone Hotel** 43, which is a great place to spend the night, enjoy a relaxing afternoon, have a cool drink, or eat a fine meal. From the hotel travel north on Grand Loop Road to **LeHardy Rapids** 44 to watch for wildlife, particularly grizzly bears. As an alternative to driving yourself, you can take the LeHardy Rapids-Lake Butte Bus Tour and let a driver handle the vehicle while telling you stories about Yellowstone.

TIMING The views from Lake Butte and LeHardy Rapids are best at sunset, but you can enjoy this region throughout the day. It will take a couple of hours for the sunset bus tour and an equal amount of time to explore the sites on your own.

What to See

43 **Lake Yellowstone Hotel.** Completed in 1891 and spiffed up for its centennial in 1991, this historic structure feels fresh and new as you lounge in white wicker chairs and watch the waters of Yellowstone Lake through massive windows. It got its columned entrance in 1903, when the original bland facade was reworked by the architect of the Old Faithful Inn. Now it is on the National Register of Historic Places. ✉ *Lake Village* ☎ *307/344–7901* ⏲ *Mid-May–late Sept.*

Fodor'sChoice ★

44 **LeHardy Rapids.** This is the point where Yellowstone Lake feeds into the Yellowstone River. It's a good place for an evening drive to watch for waterfowl. ✉ *2 mi north of Fishing Bridge on Grand Loop Rd.*

If you feel like letting someone else do the driving, you can opt for the **LeHardy Rapids-Lake Butte Bus Tour.** The sunset tour originates at the Lake Yellowstone Hotel, from where you travel in a 1937 touring bus to the rapids and then on to the Lake Butte Overlook in time to watch the sun go down over the western mountains. The driver delivers a narrative of historical and natural information as you travel along the shores of Yellowstone Lake. You're likely to spot a variety of wildlife, ranging from bison and elk to waterbirds or coyotes. ✉ *Lake Yellowstone Hotel* 🎫 *$19* ⏲ *Daily, sunset.*

42 **Yellowstone Lake.** Yellowstone Lake is one of the largest alpine lakes in the world, encompassing 136 square mi and located in a caldera—crater formed by a volcano—that filled with the melt from glaciers. The lake has 110 mi of shoreline, much of it followed by the East Entrance Road and Grand Loop Road, along which you will often see moose, elk, waterfowl, and other wildlife. During winter you will often see coyotes and otters along the lakeshore. Streams flowing into the lake mean it has an abundant supply of fish. ✉ *East Entrance Rd. and southeast segment, Grand Loop Rd.*

SPORTS & THE OUTDOORS

Yellowstone is filled with opportunities to enjoy the outdoors and take part in sports such as hiking, bicycling, horseback riding, and fishing in summer and cross-country skiing, snowshoeing, and snowmobiling in winter. There are more miles of trails than roads, which gives some idea of the importance of hiking and walking in the park. Only a few of the trails are accessible on bicycles, but many can be followed on skis or snowshoes.

Bicycling

More and more visitors tour Yellowstone by bicycle every year, despite the heavy traffic, large vehicles, and sometimes rough, narrow, shoulderless roads that can make the going hazardous. To be on the safe side, ride single file and wear a helmet and reflective clothing. Remember that some routes, such as those over Craig Pass, Sylvan Pass, and Dunraven Pass, are especially challenging because of their steep climbs. Bikes are prohibited on most hiking trails and in the backcountry.

Leading off Grand Loop Road at Bridge Bay along the western shore of Yellowstone Lake, **Natural Bridge Road** is an easy 1-mi bike loop leading to Natural Bridge, a 50-foot cliff cut through by Bridge Creek.

A paved 2-mi trail, **Old Faithful to Morning Glory Pool,** starts at the Hamilton Store at Old Faithful Village, loops near Old Faithful Geyser, and ends at Morning Glory Pool. The entire route is through a geyser basin, so stay on the trail. Watch for elk and buffalo.

Automobiles and bicycles share the gravel **Old Gardiner Road** running parallel to U.S. 89 between Mammoth Hot Springs and the nearby town of Gardiner; cars can travel only north, but bikes are allowed in both directions. The 5-mi route has views of the Gardiner River. Mountain bikes are recommended.

Fountain Flats Drive departs the Grand Loop Road south of the Nez Perce picnic area and follows the Firehole River to a trailhead 1½ mi away. From there, the **Fountain Freight Road** continues along the old roadbed, giving bikers access to the Sentinel Meadows Trail and the Fairy Falls Trail. The total length of the route is 5½ mi. Mountain bikes are recommended; you'll share Fountain Flats Drive with one-way automobile traffic and the Freight Road with hikers.

Running parallel to Grand Loop Road, **Blacktail Plateau Drive** is a gravel road with one-way traffic for cars traveling east, but bicycles are allowed in both directions. The road meanders through forest where you might see deer, coyotes, or elk. The west entrance is 9 mi east of Mammoth Hot Springs, and the east entrance is 2 mi west of Tower-Roosevelt. Mountain bikes are recommended.

There are no bike rentals within Yellowstone, but **Free Heel and Wheel** (✉ 40 Yellowstone Ave., West Yellowstone, MT ☎ 406/646–7744 🌐 www.freeheelandwheel.com), just outside the west entrance, rents bikes and dispenses advice, as well as sells hiking and cross-country skiing gear.

Boating

Yellowstone Lake attracts the most attention, but the park is filled with pristine waters waiting to be explored. Most of its 175 lakes, except for Sylvan Lake, Eleanor Lake, and Twin Lakes, are open for boating. You must purchase a $5 permit for boats and floatables or a $10 permit for motorized boats at Bridge Bay Marina, Grant Village visitor center, Lewis Lake Campground, or Mammoth Hot Springs visitor center.

Watercraft from rowboats to powerboats are available at **Bridge Bay Marina** by the hour or by the day for trips on Yellowstone Lake. You can even rent 22- and 34-foot cabin cruisers. ✉ *Grand Loop Rd., 2 mi south* *of Lake Village* ☎ *307/344–7311* ⏲ *Mid-June–mid-Sept., 8 AM–9:30 PM* 🎫 *$7.50–$33 per hour.*

Yellowstone Lake Scenic Cruises, run by Xanterra Parks & Resorts, operates the *Lake Queen II* from out of Bridge Bay Marina on Yellowstone Lake. Cruises make their way to Stevenson Island and then return to Bridge Bay. ✉ *Bridge Bay Marina* ☎ *307/344–7311* ⏲ *June–mid-Sept.* 🎫 *$9.75.*

Cross-Country Skiing & Snowshoeing

Even those who have visited Yellowstone many times in summer would never recognize it after the first snowfall. Rocky outcroppings are smoothed over by snow. Waterfalls that tumbled over the sides of canyons have been transformed into jagged sheets of ice. Canyon Village, West Thumb, and Madison have warming huts that are intermittently staffed; huts at Indian Creek, Fishing Bridge, and Old Faithful Village are unstaffed. All are open 24 hours.

Lone Star Geyser Trail, an easy trail leading 2.3 mi to the Lone Star Geyser, starts south of Keppler Cascades. You can ski back to the Old Faithful area. ✉ *Shuttle at Old Faithful Snow Lodge; trailhead 3½ mi west of Old Faithful Village.*

Five ski trails begin at the **Madison River Bridge** trailhead. The shortest is 4 mi and the longest is 14 mi. ✉ *West Entrance Rd., 6 mi west of Madison.*

At Mammoth Hot Springs Hotel and Old Faithful Snow Lodge, **Xanterra Parks & Resorts** rents skis and snowshoes. Skier shuttles run from Mammoth Hotel to Mammoth Terraces and to Tower and from Old Faithful Snow Lodge to Fairy Falls. ✉ *Mammoth Hot Springs Hotel or Old Faithful Snow Lodge* ☎ *307/344–7901* 🌐 *www.travelyellowstone.com* 🎫 *$11–$28.*

The **Yellowstone Association Institute** offers everything from daylong cross-country skiing excursions to multiday "Lodging and Learning" trips geared around skiing and snowshoeing treks. You bring your own personal gear; they provide group gear and instruction plus permits as needed and most meals. Ski instruction is available for those with less experience. 📫 *Box 117, Yellowstone National Park, WY 82190* ☎ *307/344–2293* 📠 *307/344–2486* 🌐 *www.yellowstoneassociation.org* 🎫 *$749–$944.*

Free Heel and Wheel, outside the West Yellowstone entrance gate, has cross-country ski gear, as well as bicycling and hiking equipment, free advice, and coffee and goodies. ✉ *40 Yellowstone Ave., West Yellowstone, MT* ☎ *406/646–7744* 🌐 *www.freeheelandwheel.com.*

Fishing

Anglers flock to Yellowstone on Memorial Day weekend, when fishing season begins. By the time the season ends in November, thousands have found a favorite spot along the park's rivers and streams. Many varieties of trout—cutthroat, brook, lake, and rainbow—along with grayling and mountain whitefish inhabit Yellowstone's waters. Popular sport-fishing opportunities include the Gardner and Yellowstone rivers as well as Soda Butte Creek, but the top fishing area in the region is Madison River, known to fly fishermen throughout the country. Catch and release is the general policy. You can get a copy of the fishing regulations at any visitor center. Fishing supplies are available at general stores found throughout the park; the biggest selection is at Bridge Bay.

Fishing permits are required for people over age 16; they cost $10 for a 10-day permit or $20 for a season permit. Anglers ages 12 to 15 must have a nonfee permit; those younger than 12 don't need a permit but must be with an adult who knows the regulations. Permits are available at all ranger stations, visitor centers, and general stores.

The park concessionaire **Xanterra Parks & Resorts** offers guided Yellowstone Lake fishing charters on boats large enough for as many as six guests. The cost of a charter includes your guide plus fishing gear. Charters are on 22- and 34-foot cabin cruisers that accommodate as many as three people fishing at one time. ✉ *Grand Loop Rd., 2 mi south of Lake Village* ☎ *307/344–7311* ⏲ *Early June–early Sept.* *$57–$74 per hour.*

Hiking

There are 1,210 mi of trails and 85 trailheads in Yellowstone. Trails are occasionally closed because of bad weather conditions or bear activity. Guided hikes are led by park rangers and concessionaires such as the Yellowstone Association Institute.

The **Yellowstone Association Institute** offers everything from daylong hiking excursions; to multiday "Lodging and Learning" trips geared around hikes, some of them designed for families; to full-blown backcountry backpacking trips. You bring your own personal gear; they provide group gear and instruction plus permits as needed and most meals. *Box 117, Yellowstone National Park, WY 82190* ☎ *307/344–2293* *307/344–2486* *www.yellowstoneassociation.org* *$490–$985.*

Starting across from a parking area, the difficult 4-mi, four-hour round-trip on **Avalanche Peak Trail** climbs 2,150 feet to the peak's 10,566-foot summit, from which you'll see the rugged Absaroka Mountains running north and south. Some of these peaks have patches of snow year-round. Look around the talus and tundra near the top of Avalanche Peak for alpine wildflowers and butterflies. Don't try this trail before late June or after early September—it may be covered in snow. At any time of year, carry a jacket: the winds at the top are strong. ✉ *19 mi east of Lake Junction on the north side of East Entrance Rd.*

The 1½-mi loop of **Back Basin Trail** passes Emerald Spring, Steamboat Geyser, Cistern Spring (which drains when Steamboat erupts), and Echinus Geyser. The last erupts 50–100 feet every 35–75 minutes, making it Norris's most dependable big geyser. ✉ *Grand Loop Rd. at Norris.*

Beaver Ponds Loop Trail is a 2½-hour, 5-mi round-trip starting at Liberty Cap. It climbs 400 feet through ½ mi of spruce and fir, passes through open meadows and past beaver ponds (look for their dams), and has spectacular views of Mammoth Terraces on the way down. Moose, antelope, and occasional bears may be sighted. ✉ *Grand Loop Rd. at Old Gardiner Rd.*

The 2½-mi round-trip **Biscuit Basin Trail** goes via a boardwalk across the Firehole River to colorful Sapphire Pool. ✉ *3 mi north of Old Faithful Village off Grand Loop Rd.*

To hear and feel the Yellowstone River's power, follow the steep side trails into the Grand Canyon of the Yellowstone. The **Brink of the Lower Falls Trail** switchbacks ½ mi one way from the parking area, 600 feet down to the brink of Lower Falls. ✉ *1¾ mi south of Inspiration Point on North Rim Trail.*

Past the entrance to Bunsen Peak Road, the moderately difficult **Bunsen Peak Trail** is a 4-mi, three-hour round-trip climbing 1,300 feet to Bunsen Peak for a panoramic view of Blacktail Plateau, Swan Lake Flats, the Gallatin Mountains, and the Yellowstone River valley. (Use a topographical map to find these landmarks.) ✉ *Grand Loop Rd., 1½ mi south of Mammoth Hot Springs.*

Fountain Paint Pot Nature Trail is an easy ½-mi loop boardwalk passing hot springs, colorful mud pots, and dry fumaroles at its highest point. ✉ *Grand Loop Rd. at Firehole Lake Dr.*

Head counterclockwise around the Old Faithful boardwalk ⅓ mi from the visitor center, crossing the Firehole River, to reach the 1⅓-mi **Geyser Hill Loop.** On your left is violent, but infrequent, Giantess Geyser. Normally active only a few times each year, Giantess spouts 100–250 feet high for five to eight minutes once or twice hourly for 12 to 43 hours. A bit farther on your left is Doublet Pool, two adjacent springs whose complex ledges and deep blue waters are highly photogenic. Near the loop's end on your right, Anemone Geyser starts as a gentle pool, overflows, bubbles, and finally erupts, 10 feet or more, repeating the cycle every three to eight minutes. ✉ *Old Faithful Village.*

The very difficult 24-mi, 13-hour round-trip on the **Heart Lake–Mt. Sheridan Trail** provides one of the park's top overnight backcountry experiences. After traversing 5½ mi of partly burned lodgepole-pine forest, the trail descends into Heart Lake Geyser Basin, reaching Heart Lake at the 8-mi mark. This is one of Yellowstone's most active thermal areas—the biggest geyser here is Rustic Geyser, which erupts 25–30 feet about every 15 minutes. Circle around the northern tip of Heart Lake and camp at one of five designated backcountry sites on the western shore (remember to get your permit beforehand). Leave all but the essentials here as you take on the 3-mi, 2,700-foot climb to the top of 10,308-foot Mt. Sheridan. To the south, if you look carefully, you can see the Tetons. ✉ *1 mi north of Lewis Lake on the east side of South Entrance Rd.*

The **Lower Terrace Interpretive Trail** leads past the most outstanding features of the multicolored, steaming Mammoth Hot Springs. Start at Liberty Cap, at the area's north end, named for its resemblance to Revolutionary War–era tricornered hats. Head uphill on the boardwalks past bright and ornately terraced Minerva Spring. Alternatively, drive up to the Lower Terrace Overlook on Upper Terrace Drive and take the boardwalks down past New Blue Springs (which, inexplicably, is no longer blue) to the Lower Terrace. This route works especially well if you can park a second vehicle at the foot of Lower Terrace. Either route should take about an hour. ✉ *Grand Loop Rd., ⅓ mi west of Mammoth Hot Springs.*

Morning Glory Pool Trail is an easy 1½-mi (one-way) boardwalk trek from Old Faithful Visitor Center, passing stately Castle Geyser, which possesses the biggest cone in Yellowstone. It erupts every 10 to 12 hours, to heights of 90 feet, for as much as an hour. Morning Glory Pool, named for its resemblance in shape and color to the flower, is a testament to human ignorance: tons of coins and trash tossed into it over the years clogged its vent, causing brown and green bacteria to spread across the surface. ✉ *Old Faithful Village.*

Mud Volcano Interpretive Trail, a ¾-mi round-trip, loops gently around seething, sulfuric mud pots with such names as Sizzling Basin and Black Dragon's Cauldron and around Mud Volcano itself. ✉ *10 mi south of Canyon Village on Grand Loop Rd.*

From the Biscuit Basin boardwalk's west end, **Mystic Falls Trail** gently climbs 1 mi (3½ mi round-trip from Biscuit Basin parking area) through heavily burned forest to the lava-rock base of 70-foot Mystic Falls. It then

CloseUp

THE GREAT SNOWMOBILE CONTROVERSY

Snowmobiles have become Yellowstone's number one controversy. There's no denying that snowmobiling is an exhilarating way to experience the park; the damage that results, in terms of air pollution, noise, and disruption to animal habitats, is the subject of heated debate. In a victory for environmentalists, the Clinton administration in 2000 implemented a plan to phase out the use of snowmobiles in the park by the winter of 2003–04. The Bush administration overturned Clinton's plan, proposing instead to maintain limits on snowmobiles and require them to have less-polluting four-stroke engines. The Bush plan, in turn, was rejected by a federal judge just days before the opening of the winter season in December 2003 and the snowmobile ban was reinstated. But that ruling was nullified by another judge, who in February 2004 declared the Clinton plan illegal. No doubt there will be further volleys in this heated battle.

switchbacks up Madison Plateau to a lookout with the park's least-crowded view of Old Faithful and Upper Geyser Basin. ✉ *3 mi north of Old Faithful Village off Grand Loop Rd.*

★ Offering great views of the Grand Canyon of the Yellowstone, the 1¾-mi **North Rim Trail** runs from Inspiration Point to Chittenden Bridge, and the 2-mi **South Rim Trail** starts at Chittenden Bridge and makes its way to Artist Point. You can wander along small sections of these trails or combine them into a three-hour trek through one of the park's most breathtaking areas. Especially scenic is the ½-mi section of the North Rim Trail from the Brink of the Upper Falls Parking Area to Chittenden Bridge that hugs the rushing Yellowstone River as it approaches the canyon. Both trails are partly paved and fairly level. ✉ *1 mi south of Canyon Village.*

Observation Point Loop, a 2-mi round-trip from the Old Faithful Visitor Center, leaves Geyser Hill Loop boardwalk and becomes a trail shortly after the boardwalk crosses the Firehole River; it circles a picturesque overview of Geyser Hill with Old Faithful Inn as a backdrop. ✉ *Old Faithful Village.*

★ Old Faithful and its environs in the Upper Geyser Basin are rich in short-walk options, starting with three connected loops that depart from Old Faithful Visitor Center. The ¾-mi **Old Faithful Geyser Loop** simply circles the benches around Old Faithful, filled nearly all day long in summer with tourists. Currently erupting approximately every 79 minutes, Yellowstone's most frequently erupting big geyser—although not its largest or most regular—reaches heights of 100 to 180 feet. ✉ *Old Faithful Village.*

The 4-mi **Osprey Falls Trail,** a two-hour round-trip, starts near the entrance of Bunsen Peak Road. A series of switchbacks drops 800 feet to the bottom of Sheepeater Canyon and the base of the Gardner River's 151-foot Osprey Falls. As at Tower Fall, the canyon walls are basalt columns formed by ancient lava flow. ✉ *Bunsen Peak Rd., 3 mi south of Mammoth Hot Springs.*

At Norris Geyser Basin, **Porcelain Basin Trail,** a ¾-mi, partially boardwalked loop, leads from the north end of Norris Museum through whitish geyserite stone and past extremely active Whirligig and other small geysers. ✉ *Grand Loop Rd. at Norris.*

Shoshone Lake–Shoshone Geyser Basin Trail is a 22-mi, 11-hour, moderately difficult overnight trip combining several shorter trails. The trail starts at DeLacy Creek Trail, gently descending 3 mi to the north shore of Shoshone Lake. On the way, look for sandhill cranes and browsing moose. At the lake turn right and follow the North Shore Trail 8 mi, first along the beach and then through lodgepole-pine forest. Make sure you've reserved one of the several good backcountry campsites—reservations can be made at any ranger station in the park. Take time to explore the Shoshone Geyser Basin, reached by turning left at the fork at the end of the trail and walking about ¼ mi. The next morning turn right at the fork, follow Shoshone Creek for 2 mi, and make the gradual climb over Grant's Pass. At the 17-mi mark the trail crosses the Firehole River and divides; take a right onto Lone Star Geyser Trail and continue past this fine coned geyser through Upper Geyser Basin backcountry to Lone Star Geyser Trailhead. ✉ *8 mi east of Old Faithful Village on north side of Grand Loop Rd.*

In the park's northwest corner, the extremely difficult 16½-mi, 10-hour **Skyline Trail** is a combination trail that climbs up and over numerous peaks whose ridgelines mark the park's northwest boundary before looping sharply back down via Black Butte Creek. ✉ *U.S. 191, 25 mi north of West Yellowstone.*

Slough Creek Trail, starting at Slough Creek Campground, climbs steeply for the first 1½ mi before reaching expansive meadows and prime fishing spots, where moose are common and grizzlies occasionally wander. From this point the trail, now mostly level, meanders another 9½ mi to the park's northern boundary. ✉ *7 mi east of Tower-Roosevelt off Northeast Entrance Rd.*

Starting at Specimen Creek Trailhead, follow the **Specimen Creek Trail** 2½ mi and turn left at the junction, passing petrified trees to your left. At the 6½-mi mark, turn left again at the fork and start climbing 1,400 feet for 2 mi up to Shelf Lake, one of the park's highest bodies of water, at 9,200 feet altitude. Stay at one of the pair of designated backcountry campsites, which you can reserve at any ranger station in the park. Just past the lake is the beginning of Skyline Trail, which follows the ridge with steep drop-offs on either side. Watch for bighorn sheep as you approach Bighorn Peak's summit. The trail's most treacherous section is just past the summit, where it drops 2,300 feet in the first 2½ mi of descent; make sure you take a left where the trail forks at the big meadow just past the summit to reach Black Butte Creek Trail. Moose and elk can be seen along this last 2½-mi stretch. ✉ *U.S. 191, 27 mi north of West Yellowstone.*

★ Well marked and mostly flat, **Storm Point Trail,** a 1½-mi loop, leaves the south side of the road for a perfect beginner's hike out to Yellowstone Lake. The trail rounds the western edge of Indian Pond, then passes moose habitat on its way to Yellowstone Lake's Storm Point, named for its frequent afternoon windstorms and crashing waves. Heading west along the shore, you're likely to hear the shrill chirping of yellow-bellied marmots, rodents that grow as long as 2 feet. Also look for ducks, pelicans, and trumpeter swans. ✉ *3 mi east of Lake Junction on East Entrance Rd.*

From the lookout point at Tower Fall, the ½-mi (round-trip) **Tower Fall Trail** switchbacks down through pine trees matted with luminous green wolf lichen to the base of the waterfall. There, you will find yourself at the northern end of the Grand Canyon of the Yellowstone. ✉ *Grand Loop Rd., 3 mi south of Tower-Roosevelt.*

Spectacular and very strenuous, the 700-step **Uncle Tom's Trail** descends 500 feet from the parking area to the roaring base of the Lower Falls of the Yellowstone. Much of this walk is on steel sheeting, which can have a film of ice in early morning or any time in spring and fall. ✉ *Artist Point Dr., about ½ mi east of Chittenden Bridge.*

Horseback Riding

About 50 area outfitters lead horse-packing trips and trail rides into Yellowstone. Expect to pay about $1,400 for a four-night backcountry trip, including meals, accommodations, and guides. A guide must accompany all horseback-riding trips.

One- and two-hour horseback trail rides run by **Xanterra Parks & Resorts** leave from three sites in the park: Mammoth Hot Springs, Roosevelt Lodge, and Canyon Village. Children must be at least 8 years old and 48 inches tall; kids 8–11 must be accompanied by someone age 16 or older. *Box 165, Mammoth Hot Springs, Yellowstone, WY 82190* ☎ *307/344–7901* *www.travelyellowstone.com* *$26–$40.*

★ Since 1968, **Gunsel Horse Adventures** has provided 4-, 7-, or 10-day pack trips into the Yellowstone backcountry. The trips are a great way to see moose, bear, deer, elk, and wolves in Yellowstone's forests. Bring only your sleeping bag and personal effects. *Box 1575, Rapid City, SD 57709* ☎ *605/343–7608* *www.sevendown.net/gunsel/yellowstone.htm* *$200 per day.*

Outfitter Gary Fales has been leading multiday pack trips into Yellowstone for decades, operating out of **Rimrock Dude Ranch** west of Cody. His favorite trip heads into the southeast corner of Yellowstone, leaving from near the East Entrance and riding up Eagle Creek into Thorofare country before following the South Fork of the Shoshone River out of the park area. Regular trips include treks between the Cody area and Jackson. Trips last a week and include backcountry camping, fishing, hiking, and horseback activities. All food and camping items are provided. ✉ *2728 Northfork Rte., Cody, WY 82414* ☎ *307/587–3970* *307/527–5014* *www.rimrockranch.com* *$200 per day; $1,600 for trips linking Cody and Jackson.*

Working with area outfitters Tory and Meredith Taylor, the **Yellowstone Association Institute** offers several backcountry horse-packing trips in Yellowstone, including "Horsepacking: Backcountry Mudpots & Hot Springs," "Wildlife Conservation," "Autumn in Yellowstone" and "Horsepacking the Nez Perce Trail," which is a trek over the route Chief Joseph and the Nez Perce took in 1877. All meals are included as well as group equipment; you will need your own sleeping bag and personal gear. *Box 117, Yellowstone National Park, WY 82190* ☎ *307/344–2293* *307/344–2486* *www.yellowstoneassociation.org* *$895–$1,495.*

With **Wilderness Pack Trips,** you can take a guided day trip, have them pack in your gear and leave it at a drop camp, or take a full multiday guided pack trip in the northeast region of the park, primarily the Lamar Valley. *Box 1146, Livingston, MT 59047* ☎ *406/222–5128* *www.wildernesspacktrips.com* *$350 per day up to $2,150 for multiday trips.*

WHERE TO EAT

When traveling in Yellowstone it's always a good idea to bring along a cooler—that way you can carry some snacks and lunch items for a picnic or break and not have to worry about making it to one of the more developed areas of the park, where there are restaurants and cafeterias.

PICNICKING IN YELLOWSTONE

THERE ARE 49 picnic areas in the park, ranging from secluded spots with a couple of tables to more popular stops with a dozen or more tables and more amenities. Only nine—Snake River, Grant Village, Spring Creek, Nez Perce, Old Faithful East, Bridge Bay, Cascade Lake Trail, Norris Meadows, and Yellowstone River—have fire grates. Only gas stoves may be used in the other areas. None have running water; all but a few have pit toilets.

You can stock up your cooler at any of the general stores in the park; there is one in each major developed area. It is also possible to purchase box lunches that include drinks, snacks, sandwiches, and fruit, or vegetarian or cheese-and-crackers selections from restaurants within Yellowstone. When you choose a picnic area, keep an eye out for wildlife; you never know when a herd of bison might decide to march through. In that case, it's best to leave your food and move a safe distance away from the big animals.

At the ***Firehole River*** *(✉ Grand Loop Rd., 3 mi south of Madison) you might see elk grazing along the banks. This picnic area has 12 tables and one pit toilet.*

There are 11 tables in the vicinity of the busy ***Fishing Bridge*** *(✉ East Entrance Rd., 1 mi from Grand Loop Rd.). The picnic area is within walking distance of the amphitheater, store, and visitor center.*

You are likely to see elk or buffalo along the ***Gibbon Meadows*** *(✉ Grand Loop Rd., 3 mi south of Norris) from one of nine tables at its area, which has a handicapped-accessible pit toilet.*

Generally you'll find burgers and sandwiches at cafeterias and full meals at restaurants. The prices in Yellowstone are comparable to what you'd pay outside the park. You will not find any chain restaurants or fast-food establishments in the park, but you will find a good selection of entrées such as free-range beef and chicken; game meats such as elk, venison, and trout; plus organic vegetables.

WHAT IT COSTS					
	$$$$	**$$$**	**$$**	**$**	**¢**
AT DINNER	over $22	$16–$22	$11–$16	$7–$11	under $7

Restaurant prices are for a main course at dinner, excluding sales tax of 5%–6%.

In Yellowstone

$$–$$$$ ✕ **Grant Village Restaurant.** The floor-to-ceiling windows of this lakeshore restaurant provide views of Yellowstone Lake through the thick stand of pines. The most contemporary of the park's restaurants, it makes you feel at home with pine-beam ceilings and cedar-shake walls. You'll find dishes ranging from fried chicken to roast beef. For a change of pace, try the fettuccine primavera. ✉ *Grant Village* ☎ *307/344–7311* ✍ *Reservations essential* ⏲ *Closed late Sept.–late May* ▭ *AE, D, DC, MC, V.*

★ **$$–$$$$** ✕ **Lake Yellowstone Hotel Dining Room.** This double-colonnaded dining room off the hotel lobby will have you gazing through the big square windows overlooking the lake. Because this is one of the park's most elegant restaurants, it tends to attract an older clientele. Try the prime rib prepared in a dry marinade of thyme, rosemary, and garlic or the chicken with wild mushroom sauce. Elk is also a special entrée here. Reservations are required for dinner. ✉ *Lake Village Rd.* ☎ *307/344–7311* ⏲ *Closed early Oct.–mid-May* 💳 *AE, D, DC, MC, V.*

$$–$$$$ Fodor'sChoice ★ ✕ **Old Faithful Snow Lodge.** From the wood and leather chairs etched with figures of park animals to the intricate lighting fixtures that resemble snowcapped trees, there's lots of atmosphere at Old Faithful Snow Lodge. The huge windows give you a view of the Old Faithful area, and you can sometimes see the famous geyser as it erupts. Aside from Mammoth Hot Springs Dining Room, this is the only place in the park where you can enjoy a full lunch or dinner in winter. The French onion soup will warm you up on a chilly afternoon; among the main courses, look for the venison special. ✉ *Old Faithful Village* ☎ *307/344–7311* ⏲ *Closed mid-Oct.–mid-Dec. and mid-Mar.–mid-May* 💳 *AE, D, DC, MC, V.*

$$–$$$$ ✕ **Roosevelt Lodge Dining Room.** At this rustic log cabin set in a pine forest, the menu ranges from barbecued ribs and Roosevelt beans to hamburgers and french fries. For a real Western adventure, call ahead to join a chuck-wagon cookout that includes an hour-long trail ride or a stagecoach ride. ✉ *Tower-Roosevelt* ☎ *307/344–7311* ⏲ *Closed early Sept.–early June* 💳 *AE, D, DC, MC, V.*

$$–$$$ ✕ **Mammoth Hot Springs Dining Room.** A wall of windows overlooks an expanse of green that was once a military parade and drill field at Mammoth Hot Springs. The art deco–style restaurant, decorated in shades of gray, green, and burgundy, has an airy feel with its bentwood chairs. Strong entrées include panfried trout topped with pecans and lemon butter, and huckleberry-Brie free-range chicken. ✉ *Mammoth Hot Springs* ☎ *307/344–7311* ✍ *Reservations essential* ⏲ *Closed mid-Oct.–mid-Dec. and mid-Mar.–mid-May* 💳 *AE, D, DC, MC, V.*

$$–$$$ ✕ **Old Faithful Inn Dining Room.** Lodgepole-pine walls and ceiling beams, a giant volcanic rock fireplace graced with a painting of Old Faithful, and green-tinted windows etched with scenes from the 1920s set the mood here. Soaked in history, the restaurant has always been a friendly place where servers find time amid the bustle to chat with diners. Don't pass up the pine nut–crusted chicken, though the menu also has old-style favorites such as chicken-fried steak, pork chops, Southern-style fried chicken, and halibut steak. ✉ *Old Faithful Village* ☎ *307/344–7311* ✍ *Reservations essential* ⏲ *Closed late Oct.–early May* 💳 *AE, D, DC, MC, V.*

$–$$ ✕ **Lake Lodge Cafeteria.** This casual eatery, popular with families, serves hearty lunches and dinners such as spaghetti, beef stew, and fried chicken. It also has a full breakfast menu. ✉ *Lake Village Rd.* ☎ *307/344–7311* ⏲ *Closed mid-Sept.–early June* 💳 *AE, D, DC, MC, V.*

¢–$ ✕ **Canyon Lodge Cafeteria.** The park's busiest lunch spot serves such traditional American fare as meat loaf and hot turkey sandwiches. For early risers, it also has a full breakfast menu. ✉ *Canyon Village* ☎ *307/344–7311* ⏲ *Closed mid-Sept.–early June* 💳 *AE, D, DC, MC, V.*

¢–$ ✕ **Old Faithful Lodge Cafeteria.** Serving family-friendly fare such as lasagna and pizza, this outdoor eatery has some of the best views of Old Faithful. ✉ *South end of Old Faithful Bypass Rd.* ☎ *307/344–7311* ⏲ *Closed mid-Sept.–mid-May* 💳 *AE, D, DC, MC, V.*

¢–$ ✕ **Pony Express Snack Shop.** When the kids are hungry, stop by this spot off the lobby of Old Faithful Inn for burgers, sandwiches, and french fries any time of day. ✉ *Old Faithful Village* ☎ *307/344–7311* ⏲ *Closed early Oct.–late May* 💳 *AE, D, DC, MC, V.*

¢–$ ✕ **Terrace Grill.** Although the exterior looks rather elegant, this restaurant in Mammoth Hot Springs serves only fast food, ranging from biscuits and gravy for breakfast to hamburgers and veggie burgers for lunch and dinner. ✉ *Mammoth Hot Springs* ☎ *307/344–7311* ⏲ *Closed late Sept.–mid-May* 💳 *AE, D, DC, MC, V.*

Near the Park

In addition to these listings, consult Chapter 2 for dining options in Jackson, Grand Teton National Park, and Cody.

$$–$$$ ✕ **Trapper's Inn.** This popular restaurant recalls the days of the mountain men with massive breakfasts featuring sourdough pancakes, biscuits, and rolls. Trout with eggs will fortify you for a day exploring Yellowstone. Lunch standouts include buffalo burgers on sourdough bread, and hearty steaks are a favorite for dinner. ✉ *315 Madison Ave., West Yellowstone, MT* ☎ *406/646–9375* ▭ *AE, D, MC, V.*

$–$$$ ✕ **Yellowstone Mine.** Decorated with mining equipment such as picks and shovels, this is a place for casual family-style dining. Town residents come in for the steaks and seafood. ✉ *U.S. 89, Gardiner, MT* ☎ *406/848–7336* ⊙ *No lunch* ▭ *AE, D, MC, V.*

WHERE TO STAY

Park lodgings range from two of the national park system's magnificent old hotels to simple cabins to bland modern motels. They are operated by **Xanterra Parks & Resorts** (📫 Yellowstone National Park, Box 165, Mammoth Hot Springs 82190 ☎ 307/344–7311, 307/344–7901 to contact a guest 🖷 307/344–7456 🌐 www.travelyellowstone.com), and all accept major credit cards. Make reservations at least two months in advance for July and August for all park lodgings. Old Faithful Snow Lodge and Mammoth Hot Springs Hotel are the only accommodations open in winter; rates are the same as in summer.

Ask about the size of beds, bathrooms, thickness of walls, and room location when you book, especially in the older hotels, where accommodations vary and upgrades are ongoing. Telephones have been put in some rooms, but there are no TVs. All park lodging is no-smoking. There are no roll-away beds available.

Prices

Prices in Yellowstone are generally comparable to costs outside the park, though some of the budget options, such as simple cabins, are often less expensive in the park. In general, accommodations in the park will have fewer amenities. For example, park lodgings have no televisions, some have no telephones, and there is no air-conditioning (though it's not needed at these elevations).

WHAT IT COSTS

	$$$$	$$$	$$	$	¢
FOR 2 PEOPLE	over $220	$160–$220	$110–$160	$70–$110	under $70

Hotel prices are for two people in a standard double room in high season, excluding service charges and 6%–9% tax.

In Yellowstone

★ **$$–$$$** 🏨 **Lake Yellowstone Hotel.** This distinguished hotel, dating from 1891, is popular with older visitors, who gather in the sunroom each afternoon to gaze at the lake while a string quartet plays. Others browse behind the etched green windows of the expensive Crystal Palace gift shop or warm themselves on chilly days before the tile-mantel fireplace in the colonnaded lobby. Rooms have white wicker furnishings giving them a light, airy feeling; some have lake views. There is one two-room suite with lake views that has been used as accommodations for more than one U.S. president. 👍 *Restaurant, snack bar, boating, fishing, hiking, bar, lobby lounge, piano bar, shops; no a/c, no room TVs, no smok-*

ing ✉ *Far end of Lake Village Rd.* ☎ *307/344–7901* 📠 *307/344–7456* 🌐 *www.travelyellowstone.com* 🛏 *158 rooms* ⏲ *Closed late Sept.–mid-May* 💳 *AE, D, DC, MC, V.*

$–$$$ **Mammoth Hot Springs Hotel and Cabins.** Built in 1937, this hotel has a spacious art-deco lobby, where you'll find an espresso cart after 4 PM. The rooms are smaller and less elegant than those at the park's other two historic hotels, but the Mammoth Hot Springs Hotel is less expensive and usually less crowded. In summer the rooms can get hot, but you can open the window and there are fans. Some rooms do not have bathrooms, so you must use a bathroom down the hall. The cabins, set amid lush lawns, are the nicest inside the park. This is one of only two lodging facilities open in winter. Some cabins have hot tubs, a nice amenity after a day of cross-country skiing or snowshoeing. *Restaurant, snack bar, hiking, horseback riding, cross-country skiing, ice-skating, ski shop, snowmobiling, bar, shops; no a/c, no room TVs, no smoking* ✉ *Mammoth Hot Springs* ☎ *307/344–7901* 📠 *307/344–7456* 🌐 *www.travelyellowstone.com* 🛏 *97 rooms, 67 with bath; 2 suites; 115 cabins, 76 with bath* ⏲ *Closed mid-Sept.–mid-Dec. and mid-Mar.–late May* 💳 *AE, D, DC, MC, V.*

$–$$$ Fodor'sChoice ★ **Old Faithful Inn.** When you breeze through the iron-latched front door, you enter a log-pillared lobby of one of the most distinctive national park lodgings. From the main building, where many gables dot the wood-shingled roof, you can watch Old Faithful erupt. Rooms in the 1904 "Old House" have brass beds, and some have deep claw-foot tubs. Rooms in the 1927 west wing contain antique cherrywood furniture, and those in the 1913 east wing have Stickley furniture and tremendous four-poster beds. First-floor rooms in the Old House are the hotel's noisiest, so ask for a rear-facing room if you are seeking some quiet. *Restaurant, snack bar, hiking, bar, lobby lounge, piano bar, shops; no a/c, no room TVs, no phones in some rooms, no smoking* ✉ *Old Faithful Village* ☎ *307/344–7901* 📠 *307/344–7456* 🌐 *www.travelyellowstone.com* 🛏 *327 rooms, 6 suites* ⏲ *Closed late Oct.–early May* 💳 *AE, D, DC, MC, V.*

$$ **Cascade Lodge.** Pine wainscoting and brown carpets set the tone in this newer motel-style facility in the trees above the Grand Canyon of the Yellowstone. The lodge is at the farthest edge of the Canyon Village, which means it's quite a hike to the nearest dining facilities, but it's quiet because it's away from the major traffic at Canyon. *Picnic area, hiking, horseback riding, bar, shops; no a/c, no room TVs, no smoking* ✉ *North Rim Dr. at Grand Loop Rd.* ☎ *307/344–7901* 📠 *307/344–7456* 🌐 *www.travelyellowstone.com* 🛏 *40 rooms* ⏲ *Closed early Sept.–early June* 💳 *AE, D, DC, MC, V.*

$$ **Dunraven Lodge.** This motel-style lodge with pine wainscoting and brown carpets is in the pine trees at the edge of the Grand Canyon of the Yellowstone, adjacent to the essentially identical Cascade Lodge. It's at the farthest edge of the Canyon Village, so it's a distance to the nearest dining facilities. *Picnic area, hiking, horseback riding, bar, shops; no a/c, no room TVs, no smoking* ✉ *North Rim Dr. at Grand Loop Rd.* ☎ *307/344–7901* 📠 *307/344–7456* 🌐 *www.travelyellowstone.com* 🛏 *41 rooms* ⏲ *Closed early Sept.–early June* 💳 *AE, D, DC, MC, V.*

★ $–$$ **Old Faithful Snow Lodge.** Built in 1998, this massive structure brings back the grand tradition of park lodges by making good use of heavy timber beams and wrought-iron accents in a distinctive facade. Inside you'll find soaring ceilings, natural lighting, and a spacious lobby with a stone fireplace. Nearby is a long sitting room where writing desks and overstuffed chairs invite you to linger. Rooms combine traditional style with modern amenities. This is one of only two lodging facilities open in winter, when the only way to get here is on over-snow vehicles. Snow Lodge also has older cabins with basic amenities. *Restaurant, snack bar, hiking, cross-country skiing, ski shop, snowmobiling, bar, shops; no a/c, no room TVs, no smoking* ✉ *Far end of Old Faithful Bypass Rd.* ☎ *307/344–7901* 📠 *307/344–7456* 🌐 *www.travelyellowstone.com* *95 rooms, 33 cabins* *Closed mid-Oct.–mid-Dec. and mid-Mar.–May* *AE, D, DC, MC, V.*

¢–$$ **Lake Lodge.** Among the pines not far from Lake Yellowstone Hotel, this lodge was built in 1920 but has been modernized so that the accommodations resemble those of a fairly standard motel. There are views of the lake from the lodge but not from the rooms. *Restaurant, snack bar, hiking, bar, shops; no a/c, no room TVs, no smoking* ✉ *Far end of Lake Village Rd.* ☎ *307/344–7901* 📠 *307/344–7456* 🌐 *www.travelyellowstone.com* *186 rooms* *Closed mid-Sept.–mid-June* *AE, D, DC, MC, V.*

¢–$$ **Lake Lodge Cabins.** Located near Yellowstone Lake, these older cabins, brightened up with yellow paint, provide basic, no-frills accommodations. *Cafeteria, boating, fishing, hiking, shops; no a/c, no room TVs, no smoking* ✉ *Lake Village Rd.* ☎ *307/344–7901* 📠 *307/344–7456* 🌐 *www.travelyellowstone.com* *186 cabins* *Closed mid-Sept.–mid-June* *AE, D, DC, MC, V.*

$ **Grant Village Lodge.** Not nearly so nice as the newer facilities at Cascade and Dunraven Lodges, the six lodge buildings that make up this facility have rough pine exteriors painted gray and rust. They remind you of a big-city motel. The rooms are basic, with few features beyond a bed and nightstand. *2 restaurants, hiking, bar, shops; no a/c, no room TVs, no smoking* ✉ *Grant Village* ☎ *307/344–7901* 📠 *307/344–7456* 🌐 *www.travelyellowstone.com* *300 rooms* *Closed mid-Sept.–late May* *AE, D, DC, MC, V.*

$ **Lake Yellowstone Hotel Cabins.** Set unobtrusively in the trees behind the Lake Yellowstone Hotel, these pine-paneled cabins with yellow exteriors provide basic accommodations. *Restaurant, snack bar, boating, fishing, hiking, bar, shops; no a/c, no room TVs, no smoking* ✉ *Lake Village Rd.* ☎ *307/344–7901* 📠 *307/344–7456* 🌐 *www.travelyellowstone.com* *102 cabins* *Closed mid-Sept.–mid-June* *AE, D, DC, MC, V.*

¢–$ **Canyon Cabins.** With clusters of plain pine-frame cabins that are all duplex or fourplex units surrounding a main lodge building, this is one of Yellowstone's most bare-bones places to stay. Cabins have beds but no other amenities to speak of. Most have no running water; instead you use a bathhouse at the main lodge. *2 restaurants, cafeteria, picnic area, hiking, horseback riding, bar, shops; no a/c, no room TVs, no smoking* ✉ *North Rim Dr. at Grand Loop Rd.* ☎ *307/344–7901* 📠 *307/344–7456* 🌐 *www.travelyellowstone.com* *532 cabins* *Closed Sept.–May* *AE, D, DC, MC, V.*

¢–$ **Old Faithful Lodge Cabins.** These older cabins located behind the Old Faithful Lodge are a good budget option. They're small and plainly decorated and have no views of Old Faithful Geyser. *Restaurant, snack bar, hiking, shops; no a/c, no room TVs, no smoking* ✉ *Far end of Old Faithful Bypass Rd.* ☎ *307/344–7901* 📠 *307/344–7456* 🌐 *www.travelyellowstone.com* *97 cabins* *Closed mid-Sept.–mid-May* *AE, D, DC, MC, V.*

¢–$ **Roosevelt Lodge.** Near the beautiful Lamar Valley in the park's northeast corner, this simple lodge dating from the 1920s surpasses some of the more expensive options. The rustic accommodations, in nearby cabins set around a pine forest, require that you bring your own bedding. Some cabins have bathrooms, but most do not. There is a bathhouse nearby. Some rooms also have woodstoves. You can make arrangements here for horseback and stagecoach rides. *Restaurant, hiking, horseback riding, shops; no a/c, no room TVs, no smoking* ✉ *Tower-Roosevelt Junc-*

tion on Grand Loop Rd. ☎ *307/344–7901* 📠 *307/344–7456* 🌐 *www.travelyellowstone.com* ⇨ *80 cabins, 12 with bath* ⏲ *Closed early Sept.–early June* 💳 *AE, D, DC, MC, V.*

Near the Park

In addition to this listing, consult Chapter 2 for dining options in Jackson, Grand Teton National Park, and Cody.

$–$$ **Pahaska Teepee Resort.** Just 2 mi from Yellowstone's east entrance, these cabins in a pine forest are a good base for summer and winter recreation, both inside and outside the park. This was Buffalo Bill's original getaway in the high country—one lodge building remains from his time. The cabins, some of which stand alone and some of which are grouped together, have two, four, or six bedrooms. With seven bedrooms and a kitchen, the Reunion Lodge is ideal for big groups. A trailhead for an extensive cross-country-ski-trail network is at Pahaska. Also here are a gas station and convenience store. ✉ *183 Yellowstone Hwy., 82414* ☎ *307/527–7701 or 800/628–7791* 📠 *307/527–4019* 🌐 *www.pahaska.com* ⇨ *48 cabins, 1 lodge* ♨ *Restaurant, hiking, horseback riding, cross-country skiing, ski shop, snowmobiling, bar, travel services* 💳 *D, MC, V.*

Camping & RV Facilities

Yellowstone has a dozen campgrounds scattered around the park. Most campgrounds have flush toilets, and some have coin-operated showers and laundry facilities. Most are operated by the National Parks Service and are available on a first-come, first-served basis. Those campgrounds run by Xanterra Parks & Resorts—Bridge Bay, Canyon, Fishing Bridge, Grant Village, and Madison—accept bookings in advance. To reserve, call 307/344–7311. Larger groups can reserve space in Bridge Bay, Grant, and Madison from late May through September.

Camping outside designated areas is prohibited, with exceptions during the winter season (October 15–May 15). There are about 300 backcountry sites available all over the park. Permits are free, and sites can be reserved for $20, regardless of the length of time spent in the park or the number of people in the group. You can make reservations by visiting any ranger station or by mail at Backcountry Office, Box 168, Yellowstone National Park, WY 82190.

All overnight backcountry camping requires a backcountry use permit, which must be obtained in person no more than 48 hours before the planned trip. For information, call the backcountry office (307/344–2160). In summer you can usually get these free permits seven days a week, from 8 to 4:30, at Mammoth Ranger Station/Visitor Center, Canyon Ranger Station/Visitor Center, Grant Village Visitor Center, South Entrance Ranger Station, Bechler Rangers Station, and Old Faithful Ranger Station. Hours vary off-season. All backcountry campsites have restrictions on group size and length of stay. Boating is prohibited throughout the backcountry, and pit fires are prohibited at certain campsites.

In Yellowstone

Bridge Bay. The park's largest campground, Bridge Bay rests in a wooded grove. You can rent boats at the nearby marina, take guided walks, or listen to rangers lecture about the history of the park. Don't expect solitude, as there are more than 400 campsites. Generators are allowed from 8 AM to 8 PM. Hot showers and laundry are 4 mi north at Fishing Bridge. ♨ *Flush toilets. Dump station. Drinking water, showers. Bear boxes, fire pits, picnic tables. Public telephone. Ranger station* ⇨ *431 sites* ✉ *3 mi southwest of Lake Village on Grand Loop*

Rd. ☎ 307/344–7311 🖷 307/344–7456 🌐 www.travelyellowstone.com 🎫 $17 ▭ AE, D, DC, MC, V ⏲ Late May–mid-Sept.

⛺ **Canyon.** The campground is accessible to Canyon's many short trails, which makes it a hit with families. The location is near laundry facilities and the visitor center. Generators are allowed from 8 AM to 8 PM. ♿ *Flush toilets. Drinking water, guest laundry, showers. Bear boxes, fire pits, picnic tables. Public telephone. Ranger station ⛟ 272 sites ✉ North Rim Dr., ¼ mi east of Grand Loop Rd. ☎ 307/344–7311 🖷 307/344–7456 🌐 www.travelyellowstone.com 🎫 $17 ▭ AE, D, DC, MC, V ⏲ Early June–early Sept.*

⛺ **Fishing Bridge RV Park.** Although Fishing Bridge is on Yellowstone Lake, there's no boat access here. Near Bridge Bay Marina, this is the only facility in the park that caters exclusively to recreational vehicles. Because of bear activity in the area, only hard-sided campers are allowed. Liquid propane is available. Generators are allowed from 8 AM to 8 PM. ♿ *Flush toilets. Full hookups, dump station. Drinking water, guest laundry, showers. Bear boxes, picnic tables. Public telephone. Ranger station ⛟ 346 sites ✉ East Entrance Rd. at Grand Loop Rd. ☎ 307/344–7311 🖷 307/344–7456 🌐 www.travelyellowstone.com 🎫 $31 ▭ AE, D, DC, MC, V ⏲ Mid-May–late Sept.*

⛺ **Grant Village.** The park's second-largest campground, Grant Village has some sites with great views of Yellowstone Lake. Some of the sites are handicapped accessible. The campground has a boat launch but no dock. Generators are allowed from 8 AM to 8 PM. ♿ *Flush toilets. Dump station. Drinking water, guest laundry, showers. Bear boxes, picnic tables. Public telephone. Ranger station ⛟ 425 sites ✉ South Entrance Rd., 2 mi south of West Thumb ☎ 307/344–7311 🖷 307/344–7456 🌐 www.travelyellowstone.com 🎫 $17 ▭ AE, D, DC, MC, V ⏲ Late June–late Sept.*

⛺ **Indian Creek.** In a picturesque setting next to a creek, this campground is in the middle of a prime wildlife-viewing area. There are some combination sites that can accommodate trailers of up to 45 feet. ♿ *Pit toilets. Bear boxes, fire pits, picnic tables ⛟ 75 sites ✉ 8 mi south of Mammoth Hot Springs on Grand Loop Rd. ☎ 307/344–2017 🎫 $10 ▭ No credit cards ⏲ Early June–mid-Sept.*

⛺ **Lewis Lake.** It's a bit off the beaten track, which means this campground south of Grant Village is quieter than most. Also, it's a good choice for boaters who don't want to fight the crowds, because it's the only campground besides Bridge Bay and Grant Village that has a boat launch. ♿ *Pit toilets. Drinking water. Bear boxes, fire pits, picnic tables ⛟ 85 sites ✉ 6 mi south of Grant Village on South Entrance Rd. ☎ 307/344–2017 🎫 $10 ▭ No credit cards ⏲ Late June–early Nov.*

⛺ **Madison.** This campground is beside the Madison River, with plenty of hiking trails nearby. It can accommodate trailers up to 45 feet. ♿ *Flush toilets. Dump station. Drinking water. Bear boxes, fire pits, picnic tables. Public telephone. Ranger station ⛟ 277 sites ✉ Grand Loop Rd. at Madison ☎ 307/344–7311 🖷 307/344–7456 🌐 www.travelyellowstone.com 🎫 $17 ▭ AE, D, DC, MC, V ⏲ Early May–mid-Oct.*

⛺ **Mammoth Hot Springs.** The sagebrush-covered hillside where Mammoth Hot Springs is located often attracts elk and mule deer. There are plenty of things to do at the nearby visitor center, including evening talks by park rangers. The campground is more exposed than most, so it gets hot on summer days. ♿ *Flush toilets. Drinking water. Bear boxes, fire pits, picnic tables. Public telephone. Ranger station ⛟ 85 sites ✉ North Entrance Rd. at Mammoth Hot Springs ☎ 307/344–2017 🎫 $12 ▭ AE, D, DC, MC, V.*

⛺ **Norris.** Because it adjoins the Gibbon River, this campground is a favorite among anglers. Brook trout and grayling are the prizes caught here. The campground can accommodate trailers up to 45 feet. Generators are allowed from 8 AM to 8 PM. *Flush toilets. Drinking water. Bear boxes, fire pits, picnic tables. Ranger station* *116 sites* *Grand Loop Rd. at Norris* *307/344–2177* *$12* *No credit cards* *Mid-May–late Sept.*

Pebble Creek. Near a 10,554-foot peak called the Thunderer, this campground offers some unforgettable views. It's also smaller than most, which means it tends to be a little quieter. It allows trailers up to 45 feet. *Pit toilets. Bear boxes, fire pits, picnic tables* *32 sites* *Northeast Entrance Rd., 22 mi east of Tower-Roosevelt Junction* *307/344–2017* *$10* *No credit cards* *June–late Sept.*

Slough Creek. Reached by a little-used spur road, this creekside campground is about as far from the beaten path as you can get without actually camping in the backcountry. It's popular among fishing aficionados, who come here for the trout. *Pit toilets. Bear boxes, fire pits, picnic tables* *29 sites* *Northeast Entrance Rd., 10 mi east of Tower-Roosevelt Junction* *307/344–2017* *$10* *No credit cards* *Late May–late Oct.*

Tower Fall. It's within hiking distance of the roaring waterfall, so this campground gets a lot of foot traffic. It can accommodate shorter trailers. Hot water and flush toilets are at Tower Store rest rooms nearby. *Pit toilets. Bear boxes, fire pits, picnic tables* *32 sites* *3 mi southeast of Tower-Roosevelt on Grand Loop Rd.* *307/344–2017* *$10* *No credit cards* *Mid-May–late Sept.*

Near the Park

In addition to these listings, consult Chapter 2 for camping options in Jackson, Grand Teton National Park, and Cody.

Flagg Ranch Village. In a wooded area near the Snake River, this sprawling complex is 2 mi from the south entrance of Yellowstone. Near the campground is a main lodge with restaurant, bar, convenience store, and gas station. *Flush toilets. Full hookups. Drinking water, guest laundry, showers. Fire pits, picnic tables. Public telephone. General store, service station* *97 full hookups, 74 tent sites* *Moran, WY 83013* *307/733–8761 or 800/443–2311* *www.flaggranch.com* *$22–$40* *D, MC, V* *Mid-May–Sept.*

Wagon Wheel Campground and Cabins. Located within West Yellowstone a few blocks west of the park, this campground has tent and RV sites along with cozy one-, two-, and three-bedroom cabins that have porches, barbecue grills, and cable TV. No pets are allowed, and there's no smoking in the cabins. *Flush toilets. Full hookups. Drinking water, guest laundry, showers. Public telephone* *408 Gibbon Ave., West Yellowstone, MT 59758* *406/646–7872* *www.wagonwheelrv.com* *40 RV sites, 8 tent sites; 9 cabins* *$26–$36 tent and RV sites; $50–$85 camping cabins, 3-day minimum rental* *No credit cards* *Memorial Day–Sept. 15.*

NIGHTLIFE & THE ARTS

Nightlife

You can listen to piano music during most summer evenings or hear a ranger talk in the large sitting room at **Mammoth Hot Springs Hotel.** Piano music resounds from the second-floor balcony of the **Old Faithful Inn** on summer evenings, and the inn has a cocktail bar. The terrace room of **Lake Yellowstone Hotel** has nightly piano music; the hotel also has a bar.

Family campfire programs are held some evenings at **Bridge Bay Campground** (Bridge Bay Campground Amphitheater), with information geared particularly to families with young children. These programs begin in early evening; later on most evenings there is another campfire talk geared more to adults and families with older children. Campfire programs occur at **Canyon** (⊠ Canyon Campground Amphitheater), including talks on Yellowstone's natural and cultural history. Rangers present some evening slide show programs at the **Grizzly and Wolf Discovery Center** (⊠ 201 South Canyon St., West Yellowstone, MT). The slide program is free, though there is a charge if you want to tour the center itself.

Take in the stars over Yellowstone at **Madison Campground Amphitheater** (⊠ Madison Junction). There are Friday and Saturday evening programs at 9, plus general night-sky observing some Friday and Saturday evenings beginning at 10:30. These talks help you find constellations and give you an opportunity to view celestial objects through telescopes. Meet west of the amphitheater; dress warmly and take a flashlight. Park rangers also present slide shows most summer evenings at the amphitheater. Details about programs are available in the park newspaper and from visitor centers.

Talks about natural or cultural history in Yellowstone take place nightly during summer at **Mammoth** (⊠ Mammoth Campground Amphitheater). Information about specific programs is available in the park newspaper and from visitor centers. Family campfire programs take place nightly during the summer at **Norris Campground** (⊠ Norris Campground Campfire Circle). Times and topics for programs are included in the park newspaper. Park rangers present slide shows most summer evenings at **Old Faithful Visitor Center** (⊠ Old Faithful Visitor Center Auditorium), with details about park history and culture. For specific times and topics, check the park newspaper and or inquire at visitor centers.

The Arts

You can learn more about photography techniques and participate in early-morning photography walks at **Canyon Village** (⊠ Canyon Visitor Center Auditorium).

Kids and adults can participate in separate photography walks and demonstrations at **Fishing Bridge** (⊠ Fishing Bridge Visitor Center). To find out about the specific times and locations for programs, check the park newspaper or a visitor center.

A one-hour or longer stroll through Geyser Hill at **Old Faithful** (⊠ Old Faithful Visitor Center) is held at least once a week with the focus on photography and how to capture images of the geysers with your camera.

A Kodak ambassador presents a program titled **Portrait of Yellowstone** (⊠ Mammoth Hotel Map Room) one evening each week with details on how to take better photos of Yellowstone attractions.

Rangers conduct morning and evening photo walks at **West Thumb Geyser Basin** (⊠ West Thumb Parking Lot), giving you ample opportunity to walk through the geyser basin and learn about taking photos of the various Yellowstone features in either morning or evening light.

SHOPPING

Some of Yellowstone's stores are interesting destinations themselves. The Old Faithful Basin Lower Store, for example, has a knotty-pine porch with benches that beckon tired hikers, as well as an inexpensive and very busy lunch counter. All stores sell souvenirs ranging from the tacky (cowboy kitsch and rubber tom-toms) to the authentic ($60 buffalo-hide moccasins and $200 cowboy coats). From May to September, most stores are open 7:45 AM to 9:45 PM; Mammoth Hot Springs is open year-round. All the stores accept credit cards.

Light meals, snacks, photography supplies, and gifts are all available at the **Canyon Nature Store** (✉ Canyon Village ☎ 307/242–7377).

Souvenirs, T-shirts and other clothing, and fishing gear are among the items you can purchase at **Fishing Bridge General Store** (✉ Fishing Bridge ☎ 307/242–7200). There's also one-hour film processing here.

Fast food, snacks, light meals, and general supplies are available at the **Grant Village General Store** (✉ Grant Village ☎ 307/242–7390).

For general supplies, including light meals, snacks, and beverages, head to the **Lake General Store** (✉ Yellowstone Lake Village ☎ 307/242–7563).

You will find a good selection of stoneware with fishing motifs and other fishy kinds of goods at the **Lake Yellowstone Gift Shop** (✉ Lake Yellowstone Hotel ☎ 307/344–7901)

Outdoor gear and clothing are sold at the **Mammoth Hot Springs Hotel Gift Shop** (✉ Mammoth Hot Springs Hotel ☎ 307/344–7901).

Top-quality Native American artwork and goods, ranging from cradle boards to jewelry, are sold at the **Old Faithful Inn Gift Shop** (✉ Old Faithful Inn ☎ 307/344–7901).

Stock up on outdoor clothing for kids and adults plus guidebooks at the **Old Faithful Lodge Gift Shop** (✉ Old Faithful Lodge ☎ No phone).

You can purchase outdoor clothing for winter and summer plus goods with a bear-related theme (stuffed animals, clothing with bear designs, carved bears) at the **Old Faithful Snow Lodge Gift Shop** (✉ Old Faithful ☎ 307/344–7901).

For goods ranging from groceries to hiking gear to camera accessories, check out the **Yellowstone General Store** (✉ Mammoth ☎ 307/344–7702).

You can get fuel, tires, and automobile accessories, as well as towing and repair services, at **Yellowstone Park Service Stations,** located at Canyon Village, Old Faithful, Grant Village, Fishing Bridge, Mammoth Hot Springs, and Tower-Roosevelt Junction.

YELLOWSTONE NATIONAL PARK A TO Z

To research prices, get advice from other travelers, and book travel arrangements, visit www.fodors.com.

AIR TRAVEL

CARRIERS There is no commercial air service to Yellowstone itself. The airlines listed here have service to neighboring regional airports.

Airlines & Contacts **Delta/Sky West** ☎ 800/221–1212. 🌐 www.delta.com. **Frontier Airlines** ☎ 800/432–1359 🌐 www.frontierairlines.com. **Great Lakes Aviation** ☎ 800/544–5111 🌐 www.greatlakesav.com. **Northwest Airlines** ☎ 800/225–2525 🌐 www.nwa.com. **United Express** ☎ 800/241–6522 🌐 www.united.com.

AIRPORTS

Yellowstone National Park is served by airports in nearby communities, including Cody, Wyoming, one hour east; Jackson, Wyoming, one hour south; Bozeman, Montana, 90 minutes north; and West Yellowstone, Montana, just outside the park's west gate, which has only summer service.

Airport Information **Gallatin Field** ✉ 850 Gallatin Field Rd., Belgrade ☎ 406/388-6632 🌐 www.gallatinfield.com.

Jackson Hole Airport ✉ 1250 E. Airport Rd., 5 mi north of Jackson off U.S. 189/191, Jackson ☎ 307/733-7682 or 307/733-4005.

Yellowstone Airport ✉ West Yellowstone, MT ☎ 406/646-7631.

Yellowstone Regional Airport ✉ 3001 Duggleby Dr., Cody ☎ 307/587-5096 🌐 www.flyyra.com.

1

BUS TRAVEL

There is no commercial bus service to Yellowstone, though several companies offer tours of the park.

Bus Information **Gray Line of Jackson Hole** ☎ 307/733-4325.

CAR RENTAL

The best places to rent cars in the region are at airports in Cody, Jackson, Bozeman, and West Yellowstone. The following companies all rent cars in the region.

All Trans Company ☎ 307/733-3135. **Aspen Rent-A-Car** ✉ 345 W. Broadway, Jackson Hole ☎ 307/733-9224 or 877/222-7736. **Avis** ☎ 800/331-1212. **Budget** ☎ 800/527-0700. **Eagle Rent-A-Car** ✉ 375 N. Cache Dr., Jackson Hole ☎ 307/739-9999 or 800/582-2128. **Hertz** ☎ 800/654-3131. **National** ☎ 800/328-4567.

CAR TRAVEL

Yellowstone National Park is well away from the interstates, so drivers make their way here on two-lane highways that are long on miles and scenery. From I–80, take U.S. 191 north from Rock Springs; it's about 177 mi to Jackson, then another 60 mi north to Yellowstone National Park. From I–90, head south at Livingston, Montana, 80 mi to Gardiner and the north entrance to the park. From Bozeman travel south 90 mi to West Yellowstone.

ROAD INFORMATION & EMERGENCY SERVICES

Contact the Wyoming Department of Transportation for road and travel reports October–April. For emergency situations dial 911 or contact the Wyoming Highway Patrol.

Montana Highway Patrol ☎ 406/388-3190 or 800/525-5555 🌐 www.mdt.state.mt.us. **Wyoming Department of Transportation** ☎ 307/777-4484, 307/772-0824 from outside Wyoming for road conditions, 888/996-7623 from within Wyoming for road conditions 🌐 www.wyoroad.info. **Wyoming Highway Patrol** ☎ 307/777-4301, 800/442-9090 for emergencies, #4357 (#HELP) from a cell phone for emergencies.

EMERGENCIES

There are hospitals with 24-hour emergency rooms in Jackson, Cody, and Bozeman. Within Yellowstone there are clinics at Lake, Mammoth, and Old Faithful. In all cases you can call 911 if you have any type of emergency.

Ambulance or Police **Emergencies** ☎ 911.

Bozeman Deaconess Hospital ✉ 915 Highland Blvd., Bozeman ☎ 406/585-5000. **Grand Teton Medical Clinic** ✉ Next to Jackson Lake Lodge ☎ 307/543-2514. **Lake Clinic** ✉ Lake Yellowstone ☎ 307/242-7241 ⏲ Mid-May–Sept., daily 8:30–8:30. **Mammoth Clinic** ✉ Mammoth Hot Springs ☎ 307/344-7965 ⏲ June–Sept., daily 8–1 and 3–5; Oct.–May, Mon., Tues., Thurs., Fri. 8:30–noon and 1–5, Wed. 8:30–noon. **Old Faithful Clinic** ✉ Old Faithful ☎ 307/545-7325 ⏲ Mid-May–mid-Sept., daily 7–7; mid-Sept.–mid-Oct., daily 8:30–5. **St. John's Hospital** ✉ 625 E. Broadway Ave., Jackson ☎ 307/733-3636. **West Park Hospital** ✉ 707 Sheridan Ave., Cody ☎ 307/527-7501.

LODGING

The best way to find accommodations in Yellowstone is to contact Xanterra Parks & Resorts, which manages all of the in-park lodging.

Xanterra Parks & Resorts ⊠ Box 165, Yellowstone National Park, 82190 ☎ 307/344-7901 general information, 307/344-7311 reservations ⊕ www.travelyellowstone.com.

CAMPING There is a variety of campgrounds both inside Yellowstone National Park and in the surrounding national forests and gateway communities.

Xanterra Parks & Resorts ☎ 307/344-7311 ⊕ www.travelyellowstone.com.

MEDIA

NEWSPAPERS & MAGAZINES There are no newspapers published in Yellowstone except the official park publication. In the park you can generally purchase regional papers such as the *Casper Star-Tribune* and *Billings Gazette* that cover major park stories.

TELEVISION & RADIO There are no radio or television stations within the park.

TOURS

A quieter way than snowmobiling to sight buffalo herds, trophy-size bull elk, moose, and other winter wildlife is within a comfortable van of the **Yellowstone Alpen Guides Co.** (⊠ 555 Yellowstone Ave. ☎ 406/646–9591 or 800/858–3502 ⊕ www.yellowstoneguides.com). The naturalist guides also lead cross-country ski trips and summer trips in and around the park.

Tour Operators **Xanterra Parks & Resorts** ⊠ Box 165, Yellowstone National Park, 82190 ☎ 307/344-7901 general information, 307/344-7311 reservations ⊕ www.travelyellowstone.com. **The Yellowstone Association Institute** ⊠ Box 117, Yellowstone National Park, 82190 ☎ 307/344-2293 ⊕ www.yellowstoneassociation.org.

VISITOR INFORMATION

Tourist Information **Bozeman Chamber of Commerce** ⊠ 2000 Commerce Way, Bozeman, MT 59715 ☎ 406/586-5421 or 800/228-4224 ⊕ www.bozemanchamber.com. **Cody Chamber of Commerce** ⊠ 836 Sheridan Ave., Box 2777, Cody, WY 82414 ☎ 307/587-2297 🖷 307/527-6228 ⊕ www.codychamber.org. **Gardiner Chamber of Commerce** ⊠ 221 Park St., Gardiner, MT 59030 ☎ 406/848-7971 ⊕ www.gardinerchamber.com. **Jackson Hole Chamber of Commerce** ⊠ 990 W. Broadway, Box E, Jackson, WY 83001 ☎ 307/733-3316 🖷 307/733-5585 ⊕ www.jacksonholeinfo.com. **Travel Montana** ⊠ 301 South Park, Helena, MT 59620-0133 ☎ 406/841-2870 or 800/847-4868 ⊕ www.visitmt.com. **West Yellowstone Chamber of Commerce** ⊠ 30 Yellowstone Ave., West Yellowstone, MT 59758 ☎ 406/646-7701 ⊕ www.westyellowstonechamber.com. **Wyoming Division of Tourism** ⊠ I-25 at College Dr., Cheyenne, WY 82001 ☎ 307/777-7777 ⊕ www.wyomingtourism.org.

WINTER TRANSPORTATION

You can't enter Yellowstone by car in the winter months, and fluctuating regulations make the use of snowmobiles uncertain. That leaves snow coaches as the only certain means of motorized transportation into the park. They range from old-style, bright yellow Bombardier coaches to modern vans with their wheels converted to tracks so they can travel over the snow. Snow coaches carry from six to a dozen passengers, make frequent stops, have guides to interpret the park's attractions, and serve as both tour vehicles and shuttles within the park.

Xanterra Parks & Resorts ⊠ Box 165, Yellowstone National Park, 82190 ☎ 307/344-7901 ⊕ www.travelyellowstone.com.

NORTHWEST WYOMING

GRAND TETON NATIONAL PARK, JACKSON HOLE, THE WIND RIVER RANGE, CODY

2

FODOR'S CHOICE

Buffalo Bill Historical Center, *Cody*

Holiday Inn of the Waters, *hotel, Thermopolis*

Jackson Hole Mountain Resort, *ski resort near Jackson*

Svilars, *restaurant in Hudson*

HIGHLY RECOMMENDED

RESTAURANTS

Bar J Chuckwagon, *Wilson*

The Blue Lion, *Jackson*

The Bunnery, *Jackson*

Club El Toro, *Hudson*

Jenny Lake Lodge, *Moran*

HOTELS

Amangani, *Jackson*

Brooks Lake Lodge, *near Dubois*

Cody Guest Houses, *Cody*

Jenny Lake Lodge, *Moran*

Parkway Inn, *Jackson*

Wort Hotel, *Jackson*

SIGHTS

Chapel of the Transfiguration, *Grand Teton National Park*

Indian Arts Museum, *Grand Teton National Park*

Jackson Lake, *Grand Teton National Park*

Menor's Ferry Historic Area, *Grand Teton National Park*

Museum of the Mountain Man, *Rock Springs*

National Bighorn Sheep Interpretive Center, *Dubois*

National Wildlife Art Museum, *Jackson*

Oxbow Bend, *Grand Teton National Park*

South Pass City State Historic Site, *South Pass*

By Candy Moulton

NORTHWEST WYOMING IS MOUNTAIN COUNTRY, with high peaks—some of which remain snowcapped year-round—and deep, glacier-carved valleys. The state's two national parks are here, both along the Continental Divide. Yellowstone National Park, with its geothermal wonders, is the state's most popular destination. Just to the south lies Grand Teton National Park, sheltering the spectacular Teton Range, which juts along the skyline above the Snake River. You might think this smaller park with a shorter history is dwarfed by its northern neighbor, but nothing overshadows peaks like these.

Name an outdoor activity and you can probably perform it here, whether it be hiking, mountain biking, climbing, fishing, picnicking, or camping in summer, or downhill skiing, cross-country skiing, dogsledding, or snowmobiling in winter. There's a rich cultural life here as well, ranging from art and music festivals in Jackson Hole to the world-class Buffalo Bill Historical Center in Cody.

Northwest Wyoming holds much for history buffs. It was a representative from South Pass City, south of Lander, who introduced legislation that made Wyoming the first territory in the nation to grant women the right to vote. The region was key to overland emigration as well: between 1843 and 1870, hundreds of thousands of pioneers made their way through the South Pass section of the Wind River range, seeking their fortunes and a better life out west. Before their passage, John Colter was the first white man known to visit this region of Wyoming; he spent the winter of 1807 here and "discovered" the area that became Yellowstone National Park. But Native Americans had already been here for centuries, and evidence of their presence can be found throughout the region, from numerous powwows to the Medicine Wheel outside of Lovell. Members of the Northern Arapaho and Shoshone tribes still reside here, on the Wind River Indian Reservation at Fort Washakie.

Exploring Northwest Wyoming

A car is necessary to see northwest Wyoming, and to really get into the spectacular backcountry a four-wheel-drive vehicle is best. Major routes through the area include U.S. 191, which runs north–south through Jackson, on the western edge of the state; U.S. 26/287, which runs east of Grand Teton National Park (also on the western edge of the state, within the Jackson Hole valley) toward Dubois; and U.S. 14/16/20, which runs east–west through Cody, in the northwest corner of the state. Much of the driving you do here will take you through the mountains—including the Absaroka, Wind River, Owl, and Bighorn ranges—that dominate the region.

The best bases for an exploration of Grand Teton National Park are the adjacent gateway towns of Jackson, Pinedale, and Dubois to the south. You can also stay at one of the lodges within the park itself.

About the Restaurants

There's a high concentration of restaurants in this region. Anyplace you go you'll find basic Western fare such as steaks, chicken, and burgers; in Jackson and Cody there's a wider selection, with menus listing everything from Chinese and Thai dishes to trout, buffalo, and elk. There are also a few fine-dining establishments in the region, such as Jenny Lake Lodge. Arguably the best steaks in all of Wyoming are prepared at Club El Toro and Svilars, two steak houses across the street from each other in the tiny community of Hudson, east of Lander.

About the Hotels

No other area of the state has such a variety of lodging properties that appeal to all budgets. Lodging options in the area include elegant and

Numbers in the text correspond to numbers in the margin and on the Northwest Wyoming, Grand Teton National Park, and Jackson maps.

If you have 3 days

If you have only three days to spend in the region, focus on the Jackson Hole area. Start your visit in **Jackson** 13–17; if you like shopping, you may want to linger here all day. If not, spend part of the day pursuing an outdoor activity in the region, such as hiking in Bridger-Teton National Forest or floating down the Snake River. Devote the next two days to exploring **Grand Teton National Park** 1–12. You can overnight in Jackson or lodge within the park itself. If you're here in winter and you're a skier, you may want to spend all three days hitting the slopes at **Teton Village & Jackson Hole Mountain Resort** 18.

If you have 5 days

Follow the three-day itinerary above. On your fourth day, head west of Grand Teton National Park on U.S. 26/287 to **Dubois** 25, site of the Wind River Historical Center and the National Bighorn Sheep Interpretive Center. Drive southwest to **Lander** 23, on Wind River Indian Reservation; spend the afternoon at Sinks Canyon State Park and overnight in Lander. On your fifth day drive south on Highway 28 to South Pass City State Historic Site, near **Atlantic City** 22. Continue southwest on Highway 28 and then northwest on U.S. 191 to **Pinedale** 21 and its excellent Museum of the Mountain Man.

If you have 7 days

Follow the three-day itinerary above. Start your fourth day with a visit to **Dubois** 25, west of Grand Teton National Park on U.S. 26/287. Continue west on U.S. 26/287 and then north on U.S. 26 and U.S. 20 to **Thermopolis** 26, where you can soak in hot mineral springs. Spend the night in Thermopolis, and before you leave the next day, visit the Wyoming Dinosaur Center. Drive north to **Cody** 27 on Highway 120. Spend the rest of the day and the next day exploring the sights and shops of this town, being sure to linger at the several museums of the Buffalo Bill Historical Center. Spend your final day visiting sights near Cody, such as the Chief Joseph Scenic Byway or Medicine Wheel National Historic Landmark, outside of **Lovell** 28.

---

expensive properties such as the Amangani resort in Jackson Hole, guest ranches in the Dubois and Cody areas, historic inns such as Cody's Irma Hotel, simple cabins, and dozens of chain motels.

It's a good idea to reserve well ahead for lodging in the Grand Teton National Park area, including the town of Jackson, in July and August. You should also reserve lodgings at Teton Village well in advance for skiing at Jackson Hole Mountain Resort.

WHAT IT COSTS

	$$$$	$$$	$$	$	¢
RESTAURANTS	over $22	$16–$22	$11–$16	$7–$11	under $7
HOTELS	over $220	$160–$220	$110–$160	$70–$110	under $70

Restaurant prices are for a main course at dinner, excluding sales tax of 4%–7%. Hotel prices are for two people in a standard double room in high season, excluding service charges and 5%–10% tax.

Timing

Most people visit northwest Wyoming in summer, although winter draws skiing enthusiasts, particularly to the Jackson Hole Mountain Resort (the ski season generally lasts December through March). The months between Memorial Day and Labor Day are the busiest, with all attractions operating at peak capacity. Temperatures can soar into the 90s in July and August, especially in the Bighorn Basin. If you don't mind a few limitations on what you can do and where you can stay and eat, the best times to visit the region are in late spring (late April and May) and early fall (September and October). Not only will you find fewer people on the roads and at the sights, but you also will have some of the best weather (although springtime can be wet, and it can and does snow in this region every month of the year). In general, spring is the best time to see wildlife, particularly young animals. Fall brings a rich blaze of colors, painting the aspen and cottonwood trees with a palette of red, gold, and orange. The days are warm, reaching into the 60s and 70s, and the nights are cool in fall. There are also fewer thunderstorms than in midsummer, plus fewer biting insects (such as mosquitoes) to bother you.

GRAND TETON NATIONAL PARK

Your jaw may well drop the first time you see the Teton Range jutting up from the Jackson Hole valley floor. With no foothills to get in the way, you'll have a close-up view of magnificent, jagged peaks capped with snow—even before you step out of your car. This massif is long on natural beauty. Before your eyes, mountain glaciers creep imperceptibly down 12,605-foot Mount Moran. Large and small lakes are strung along the range's base, multicolored wildflowers cover the valley floor, and Wyoming's great abundance of wildlife scampers about the meadows and mountains.

In Grand Teton National Park, short trails lead through willow flats near Jackson Lake, connecting with longer trails that lead into the canyons of the Teton Range. Boats skim the waters of Jackson and Jenny lakes, depositing people on the wild western shore of Jenny, and guided float trips meander down a calm stretch of the tortuous Snake River. A trip to the backcountry—which has more than 200 mi of trails, from the novice-accessible Cascade Canyon to the expert-level Teton Crest—reveals the majesty of what the Shoshone tribes called *Teewinot* (Many Pinnacles).

Exploring Grand Teton National Park

Exploration of the park generally occurs either from the south—usually out of Jackson—or from the north at Yellowstone National Park. By starting from the south, as is suggested by the tour below, you can make your first stop at Moose, which is park headquarters. The visitor center here can give you a good, quick overview of the park.

There are two main routes through the park. U.S. 26/89/191/287 runs north–south along the eastern edge of the park; it remains open year-round. Teton Park Road diverges from this highway at Moose, running north through the center of the park and hooking up with the highway again near Jackson Lake. This second route—which is open seasonally, generally from May until October—more closely hugs the Teton Range.

A seven-day pass that can also be used at Yellowstone National Park costs $20 per car, $15 per motorcycle, and $10 per hiker or biker.

Hot Springs A great way to soothe tired muscles after a hike or pack trip is with a soak in the hot mineral waters of Hot Springs State Park in Thermopolis or Granite Hot Springs, south of Jackson in Bridger-Teton National Forest. The most exhilarating time to do this is in winter, when the steam rises around you as the snow falls. You can even take a snowmobile or dogsled tour from Jackson to Granite Hot Springs, knowing that at the end of your journey, your reward will be hot-water immersion.

Museums To truly gain an appreciation for the American West, plan on spending a few hours visiting a handful of museums in the region. The Buffalo Bill Historical Center in Cody comprises five museums devoted to Buffalo Bill Cody, firearms, the Yellowstone ecosystem, Plains Indians, and the West's finest artists. Although much smaller than the Buffalo Bill Historical Center, the Museum of the Mountain Man in Pinedale nevertheless takes an informative look at trapper heritage. The Indian Arts Museum, within the Colter Bay Visitor Center at Grand Teton National Park, houses Plains Indians artifacts, including toys, clothing, and instruments, and occasionally hosts crafts demonstrations by tribal members and ranger programs on Native American culture. The Gallery of the Wind and Museum at Fort Washakie is also a good place to visit if you're interested in Native American culture.

Sports & the Outdoors One of the best ways to admire the landscape of northwest Wyoming—with mountain flowers, alpine lakes, and wildlife ranging from fat little pikas to grizzly bears—is to pick an outdoor activity and pursue it here. You can hike or ride a horse along one of the backcountry trails near Grand Teton National Park, Dubois, or Cody; scale mountain peaks in the Wind River, Absaroka, or Grand Teton ranges; or fish or float the Snake River near Jackson or the Shoshone near Cody. Come winter you can take a sleigh ride through the National Elk Refuge, snowmobile on hundreds of miles of trails, cross-country ski throughout the region, or hit the slopes at Snow King Mountain, Grand Targhee, or Jackson Hole Mountain Resort, one of the great skiing destinations in the country.

---

a good tour

Start your tour at **Moose Visitor Center** 1 ⚑, which has exhibits on the geology and wildlife of the area, plus information on the park. Follow Teton Park Road north for about 2 mi and then head east on the path to **Menor's Ferry Historic Area** 2, which illustrates how people crossed the Snake River before bridges were built. Also here is the tiny **Chapel of the Transfiguration** 3. Drive north for 10 mi on Teton Park Road to scenic **Jenny Lake** 4. The Jenny Lake Visitor Center, on the south edge of Jenny Lake, houses geology exhibits. **Jackson Lake** 5, popular with boaters and anglers, starts several miles north of Jenny Lake, off Teton Park Road. As you drive north alongside Jackson Lake, you'll come to Signal Mountain; take a detour up the mountain on **Signal Mountain Drive** 6 for a panoramic view of Jackson Hole. Return to Teton Park Road and continue north to the lakeside **Chapel of the Sacred Heart** 7. Teton Park Road intersects with U.S. 89/191/287 west of Moran Junction; follow U.S. 89/191/287 north for about 5 mi as it skirts the lake to **Colter Bay Visitor Center** 8, which hosts daily programs on wildlife

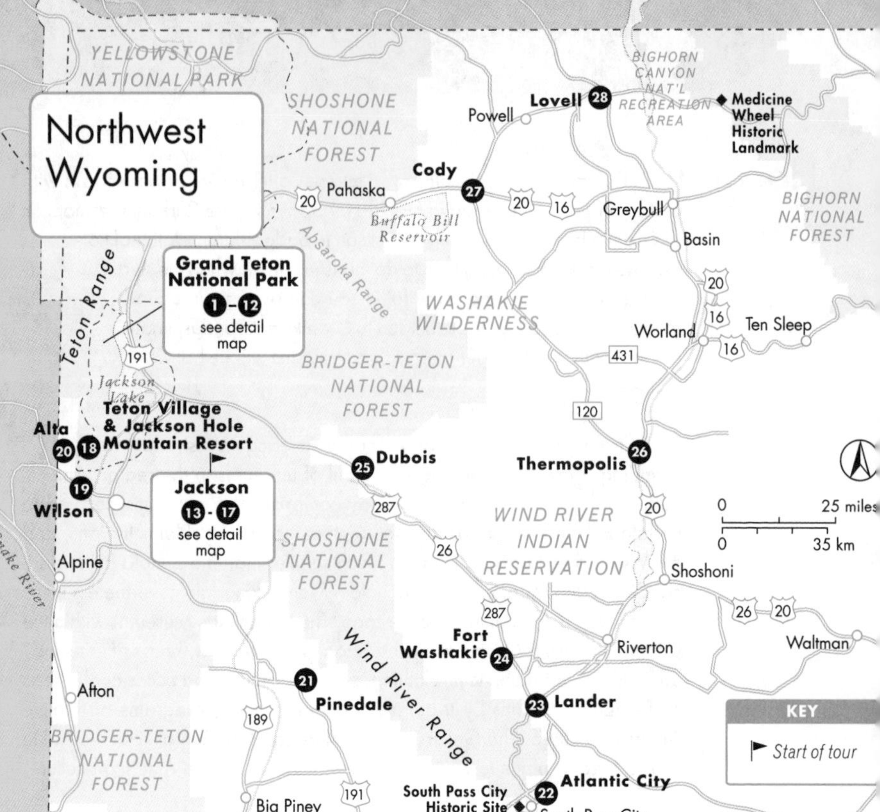

and Native American culture. Within the visitor center, the **Indian Arts Museum** 9 houses numerous Plains Indians artifacts.

From the Colter Bay Visitor Center, retrace your route south on U.S. 89/191/287 to the **Willow Flats** 10, where you have a good chance of seeing moose grazing. Continue east on U.S. 89/191/287 to the scenic **Oxbow Bend** 11, home to several species of bird. Drive southeast to Moran Junction and then head south for 6 mi on U.S. 191 to the late-19th-century cabin at **Cunningham Cabin Historic Site** 12.

TIMING Plan to spend at least a full day on this tour, and budget even more time if you want to hike or pursue other outdoor activities in the park. This tour is meant to be done between late spring and early fall, as much of the park shuts down in winter to all but skiing and snowmobiling (Teton Park Road and many of the restaurants and lodgings in the area are closed between October and April).

What to See

7 **Chapel of the Sacred Heart.** This small log chapel sits in the pine forest and affords a nice view of Jackson Lake. The chapel is open only for services, but you can appreciate the view from here at any time. ✉ *Off Teton Park Rd., ¼ mi east of Signal Mountain Lodge, 4 mi south of Jackson Lake Junction* ☎ *No phone* ⏲ *Services June–Aug., Sat. at 5:30 PM and Sun. at 8 AM.*

★ 3 **Chapel of the Transfiguration.** Still a functioning Episcopal church, this tiny chapel was built in 1925. Couples come here to exchange vows with the Tetons as a backdrop, and tourists come to take photos of the small church with its awesome view. The church is generally open, but unattended, year-round. ✉ *½ mi off Teton Park Rd., 2 mi north of Moose*

Junction ☎ *No phone* ⏲ *Late May–late Sept., Sunday services at 8* AM *and 10* AM.

8 **Colter Bay Visitor Center.** The auditorium here hosts several free daily programs about Native American culture and natural history. Ranger programs are presented hourly on topics ranging from grizzly bears and bison to nature activities in the park. The center is named for explorer John Colter, who may or may not have passed through the Grand Teton region in 1807 when he became the first white person to explore the Yellowstone area (no one is sure of his exact route). ✉ *2 mi off U.S. 89/191/287, 5 mi north of Jackson Lake Junction* ☎ *307/739–3594* ⏲ *Mid-May–mid-June and mid-Sept.–late Sept., daily 8–5; mid-June–early Sept., daily 8–8.*

12 **Cunningham Cabin Historic Site.** At the end of a gravel spur road, an easy ¾-mi trail runs through sagebrush around Pierce Cunningham's 1890 log-cabin homestead. Cunningham, an early Jackson Hole homesteader and civic leader, built his cabin in Appalachian dogtrot style, joining two halves with a roofed veranda. The cabin is closed to the public, but you can peek in through the windows. Watch for badgers, coyotes, and Uinta ground squirrels in the area. The site is open year-round, and a pamphlet is available at the trailhead. ✉ *½ mi off Jackson Hole Hwy., 6 mi south of Moran Junction.*

★ 9 **Indian Arts Museum.** You could easily spend an hour or two looking at examples of Plains Indian clothing, weapons, and other artifacts at this museum within the Colter Bay Visitor Center. Among the displays are Crow blanket strips with elegant beadwork, sashes from both the Shawnee and Hopi tribes, and various weapons, games and toys, flutes and drums, and a large collection of moccasins from many tribes. June through September, you can watch crafts demonstrations by tribal members, take ranger-led tours of the museum, and listen to a daily 45-minute ranger program on Native American culture (call for times). ✉ *2 mi off U.S. 89/191/287, 5 mi north of Jackson Lake Junction* ☎ *307/739–3594* 🎟 *Free* ⏲ *Mid-May–mid-June and mid-Sept.–late Sept., daily 8–5; mid-June–early Sept., daily 8–8.*

★ 5 **Jackson Lake.** The biggest of Grand Teton's glacier-scooped lakes at 39 square mi, this body of water in the northern reaches of the park was enlarged by construction of the Jackson Lake Dam in 1906. You can fish, sail, and windsurf on the lake, or hike trails near the shoreline. Three marinas (Colter Bay, Leeks, and Signal Mountain) provide access for boaters, and several picnic areas, campgrounds, and lodges overlook the lake. ✉ *Along U.S. 89/191/287 between Lizard Creek and Jackson Lake Junction, along Teton Park Rd. between Signal Mountain Lodge and Jackson Lake Junction.*

4 **Jenny Lake.** This alpine lake south of Jackson Lake draws boaters to its pristine waters and hikers to its tree-shaded trails. The lake is named for the Native American wife of mountain man Beaver Dick Leigh, who guided surveyors through this region in 1872. ✉ *Jenny Lake Rd., 2 mi off Teton Park Rd., 12 mi north of Moose Junction.*

Geology exhibits, including a relief model of the Teton Range, are on display at the **Jenny Lake Visitor Center.** ✉ *S. Jenny Lake Junction, ½ mi off Teton Park Rd., 7 mi north of Moose Junction* ☎ *No phone* ⏲ *Early June–early Sept., daily 8–7; early Sept.–late Sept., daily 8–5.*

★ 2 **Menor's Ferry Historic Area.** The ferry on display is not the original, but it's an accurate re-creation of the craft built by Bill Menor in the 1890s, and it demonstrates how people crossed the Snake River before bridges

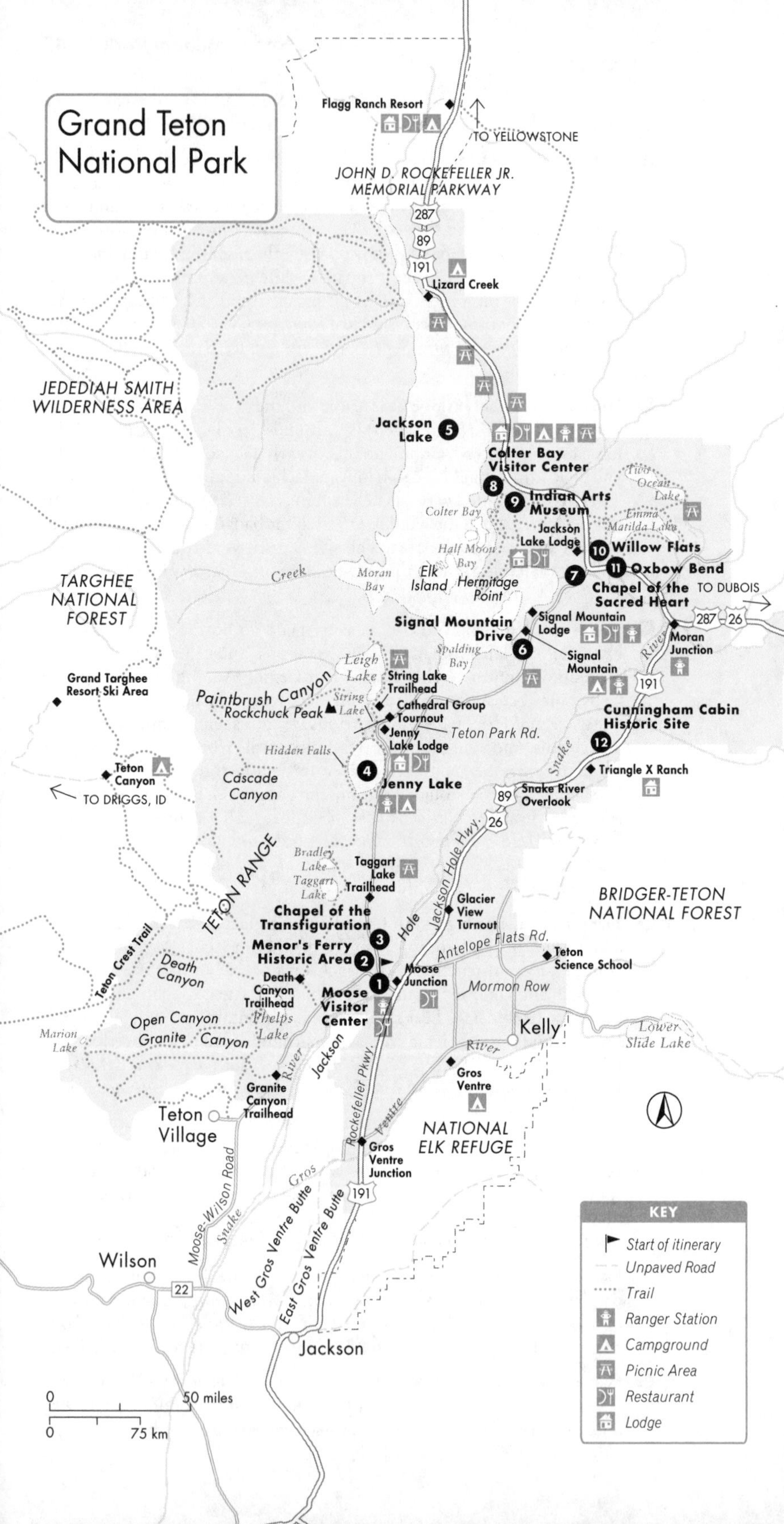

Grand Teton National Park
Flagg Ranch Resort
TO YELLOWSTONE
JOHN D. ROCKEFELLER JR. MEMORIAL PARKWAY
287
89
191
Lizard Creek
JEDEDIAH SMITH WILDERNESS AREA
Jackson Lake 5
Colter Bay Visitor Center
8
9 Indian Arts Museum
Two Ocean Lake
Emma Matilda Lake
Colter Bay
Jackson Lake Lodge
Half Moon Bay
10 Willow Flats
11 Oxbow Bend
7
Chapel of the Sacred Heart
TO DUBOIS
Creek
Moran Bay
Elk Island
Hermitage Point
TARGHEE NATIONAL FOREST
Signal Mountain Drive
6
Signal Mountain Lodge
Signal Mountain
Spalding Bay
Moran Junction
River
Leigh Lake
String Lake Trailhead
Grand Targhee Resort Ski Area
Paintbrush Canyon
Rockchuck Peak
String Lake
Cathedral Group Tournout
Jenny Lake Lodge
Teton Park Rd.
Cunningham Cabin Historic Site
12
Hidden Falls
Snake
Triangle X Ranch
Teton Canyon
4
Jenny Lake
Cascade Canyon
TO DRIGGS, ID
Snake River Overlook
26
Jackson Hole Hwy.
TETON RANGE
Bradley Lake
Taggart Lake
Taggart Lake Trailhead
BRIDGER-TETON NATIONAL FOREST
Glacier View Turnout
Chapel of the Transfiguration
3
Hole
Antelope Flats Rd.
Menor's Ferry Historic Area
2
Teton Science School
Teton Crest Trail
Death Canyon
Death Canyon Trailhead
1
Moose Junction
Moose Visitor Center
Mormon Row
Phelps Lake
Kelly
Lower Slide Lake
Open Canyon
Marion Lake
Granite Canyon
River
Jackson
Rockefeller Pkwy.
Gros Ventre
Granite Canyon Trailhead
Teton Village
Ventre
NATIONAL ELK REFUGE
Gros Ventre Junction
Moose-Wilson Road
Gros
West Gros Ventre Butte
East Gros Ventre Butte
Snake
KEY
Start of itinerary
Unpaved Road
Trail
Ranger Station
Campground
Picnic Area
Restaurant
Lodge
Wilson
22
Jackson
0
50 miles
0
75 km

were built. The original buildings used by Menor house historical displays, including a photo collection; one building has been turned into a small general store. You can pick up a pamphlet for a self-guided tour, and guided tours are available here in summer. ☒ *½ mi off Teton Park Rd., 2 mi north of Moose Junction* ☎ *No phone* *Free* *Year-round, daily 24 hrs; tours late May–early Sept., daily 8–5.*

1 **Moose Visitor Center.** With information on activities and a knowledgeable staff, this center at the south entrance is a good place to begin a visit to Grand Teton National Park. Also here are exhibits of rare and endangered species and the geology and natural history of the Greater Yellowstone area. In the auditorium you can watch a video called *The Nature of Grand Teton* and other videos on topics that range from geology to wolves. The center sells maps and books related to the history and natural history of the area. ☒ *Teton Park Rd., ½ mi north of Moose Junction* ☎ *307/739–3399* *Sept.–June, daily 8–5; June–Aug., daily 8–7.*

★ 11 **Oxbow Bend.** This spot overlooks a quiet backwater left by the Snake River when it cut a new southern channel. White pelicans stop here on their spring migration (many stay on through summer), trumpeter swans visit frequently, and great blue herons nest amid the cottonwoods along the river. Binoculars can help you locate bald eagles, ospreys, moose, beaver, and otter. In early morning in particular, look for the reflection of Mount Moran in the Oxbow's calm waters. ☒ *U.S. 26/89/191/287, 2 mi east of Jackson Lake Junction.*

6 **Signal Mountain Drive.** Climbing 800 feet up Signal Mountain, this drive leads to an overlook with spectacular panoramic views of the surrounding mountains and Jackson Hole. Note that this narrow road is unsuitable for RVs. *Off Teton Park Rd.*

10 **Willow Flats.** You will almost always see moose grazing in the marshy area of Willow Flats, in part because it has a good growth of willow trees, which moose both eat and hide in. You can also often spot birds here, including bald eagles, osprey, white pelicans, and sandhill cranes. ☒ *U.S. 89/191/287, 1 mi north of Jackson Lake Junction.*

Sports & the Outdoors

Bicycling

Jackson Hole's long, flat profile and mountain scenery attract 10-speed and mountain bikers of all skill levels. Teton Park Road and Jackson Hole Highway are generally flat with long, gradual inclines, and have well-marked shoulders. Grand Teton has few designated bike paths, so cyclists should be very careful when sharing the road with vehicles, especially RVs and trailers. A bike lane allows for northbound bike traffic along the one-way Jenny Lake Loop Road, a one-hour ride. The River Road, 4 mi north of Moose, is an easy four-hour mountain-bike ride along a ridge above the Snake River. Bicycles are not allowed on trails or in the backcountry.

May through October, **Adventure Sports** (☒ U.S. 191, Moose ☎ 307/733–3307), at Dornan's Chuckwagon in Moose, rents Diamondback, Cannondale, Giant, and Marin mountain bikes and can provide information on good places to bike in the area. May through September, **Teton Mountain Bike Tours** (☒ Jackson ☎ 800/733–0788 www.tetonmtbike.com) runs guided half-, full-, and multiday mountain-bike tours into both Grand Teton and Yellowstone national parks, as well as to the Bridger-Teton and Targhee national forests. Tours are available for all skill levels and include some specially designed for families. The Grand Teton tours are all half- or full-day outings. Prices start at $45 for half-day trips, $75 for full-day trips.

Bird-Watching

More than 300 species of birds inhabit Grand Teton National Park, and you can pick up a free bird guide at the park's visitor centers. Teton-country birds include bald eagles and osprey, which nest near Oxbow Bend throughout summer. White pelicans also stop at the Oxbow on their northerly migration in spring. Nearby Willow Flats attracts similar bird life plus sandhill cranes. You can see trumpeter swans at Oxbow Bend and Two Ocean Lake (in the northeast section of the park). Look for songbirds, such as pine and evening grosbeaks and Cassin's finches, in surrounding open pine and aspen forests. Similar songbirds inhabit Grandview Point, in the northeast section of the park, as do blue and ruffed grouse. It's a good idea to keep binoculars handy while traveling along Antelope Flats Road: you may spot red-tailed hawks and prairie falcons. Woodpeckers, bluebirds, and hummingbirds gather around Taggart Lake, which is several miles south of Jenny Lake.

Phelps Lake (✉ Moose-Wilson Rd., about 3 mi off Teton Park Rd., 1 mi north of Moose Junction) is a great spot for bird-watching. The moderate 1⅘-mi round-trip Phelps Lake Overlook Trail takes you up conifer- and aspen-lined glacial moraine to a view that's accessible only by trail. Expect abundant bird life: Western tanagers, northern flickers, and ruby-crowned kinglets thrive in the bordering woods, and hummingbirds feed on scarlet gilia beneath the overlook.

Boating

Motorboats are allowed on Jenny, Jackson, and Phelps lakes. On Jenny Lake, there's an engine limit of 7½ horsepower. On Jackson Lake you can launch your boat at Colter Bay, Leek's Marina, Signal Mountain, or Spalding Bay.

At **Colter Bay Marina** (✉ 2 mi off U.S. 89/191/287, 5 mi north of Jackson Lake Junction ☎ 307/543–2811), all types of services are available to boaters mid-May through mid-October, including free parking for boat trailers and vehicles, free mooring, boat rentals, guided fishing trips, and fuel. The marina, on Jackson Lake, is operated by the Grand Teton Lodge Company. You can rent motorboats, rowboats, and canoes from **Grand Teton Lodge Company** (☎ 307/543–3100, 307/543–2811, or 800/628–9988 🌐 www.gtlc.com) at Colter Bay Marina. Motorboats start at $22 per hour, nonmotorized boats at $10 per hour. Boats are available for rent mid-May through mid-October, and reservations are not accepted.

Both day and short-term parking for boat trailers and vehicles is available for up to three nights maximum mid-May through mid-September at **Leek's Marina** (✉ U.S. 89/191/287, 6 mi north of Jackson Lake Junction ☎ 307/543–2831). There are no boat rentals, but you can get fuel, and there's free short-term docking plus a pizza restaurant. Park concessionaire Signal Mountain Lodge operates this marina. Mid-May through mid-October, **Signal Mountain Lodge Marina** (✉ Teton Park Rd., 3 mi south of Jackson Lake Junction ☎ 307/543–2831 🌐 www.signalmtnlodge.com) rents pontoon boats ($56 per hour), deck cruisers ($38 per hour), motorboats ($21 per hour), and canoes ($10 per hour) by the hour or for full- or half-day cruising. Also available are fuel, oil, and overnight mooring ($20 per night). You can launch your boat at **Spalding Bay** (✉ 2 mi off Teton Park Rd., 7 mi south of Jackson Lake Junction) and park your trailer and vehicle for the day. There's no docking or mooring available.

Cross-Country Skiing

Grand Teton National Park has some of North America's finest and most varied cross-country skiing. Ski the gentle 3-mi Swan Lake–Heron Pond Loop near Colter Bay Visitor Center, the mostly level 9-mi Jenny Lake Trail, or the moderate 4-mi Taggart Lake–Beaver Creek Loop and 5-mi Phelps Lake Overlook trail, which have some steep descents. Advanced skiers should head for the Teton Crest Trail. In winter all overnight backcountry travelers must register at park headquarters in Moose to obtain a free permit.

Fishing

Rainbow, brook, lake, and native cutthroat trout inhabit the park's waters. The Snake's 75 mi of river and tributary are world renowned for their fishing. To fish in Grand Teton National Park you need a Wyoming fishing license. A day permit for nonresidents costs $10, and an annual permit costs $65 plus a $10 conservation stamp; for state residents a license costs $15 per season plus $10 for a conservation stamp. You can buy a fishing license at Colter Bay Marina, Dornan's General Store in Moose, Signal Mountain Lodge, and at area sporting-goods stores. Or you can get one directly from the **Wyoming Game and Fish Department** (✉ 360 N. Cache St., Box 67, Jackson 83001 ☎ 307/733–2321 ⊕ gf.state.wy.us/).

June through September, **Grand Teton Lodge Company** (✉ Colter Bay Marina or Jackson Lake Lodge ☎ 307/543–3100 or 800/628–9988 ⊕ www.gtlc.com), the park's major concessionaire, operates guided Jackson Lake fishing trips that include boat, guide, and tackle. The company also offers guided fly-fishing trips on the Snake River. Fishing trips start at $59 per hour and cost $350 per day for two people. Make reservations at the activities desks at Colter Bay Village or Jackson Lake Lodge, where trips originate. Guided half- and full-day fishing trips on Jackson Lake depart from the marina at **Signal Mountain Lodge** (✉ Teton Park Rd., 3 mi south of Jackson Lake Junction ☎ 307/543–2831 ⊕ www.signalmtnlodge.com). Trips run mid-May through September and cost $200 per half day, $386 per full day.

Golf

Jackson Hole Golf and Tennis Club (✉ 5000 Spring Gulch Rd. ☎ 307/733–3111 ⊕ www.gtlc.com) is a championship 18-hole course near the Jackson Hole Airport, with tennis, fly-fishing, horseback riding, and swimming facilities.

Hiking

Much of the spectacular mountain scenery of Grand Teton is best seen by hiking. You can get trail maps and information about hiking conditions from rangers at the park visitor centers at Moose, Jenny Lake, or Colter Bay. Popular trails are those around Jenny Lake, the Leigh and String lakes area, and Taggart Lake Trail, with views of Avalanche Canyon. Other trails let you experience the Grand Teton backcountry on longer hikes lasting from a few hours to several days. You can also do some off-trail hiking in the park. You can register for backcountry hiking and pick up backcountry trail information from any ranger station or visitor center. Wherever you go hiking in the park you may see moose and bears; keep your distance. Pets are not permitted on trails or in the backcountry, but you can take them on paved front-country trails so long as they are on a leash no more than 6 feet in length.

A 10-minute boat ride from the Jenny Lake dock ($7) takes you to the start of **Cascade Canyon Trail** (✉ Jenny Lake Rd., 2 mi off Teton Park Rd., 12 mi south of Jackson Lake Junction), a moderate, ½-mi climb to 200-foot Hidden Falls, the park's most popular and crowded trail destination. Listen here for the distinctive bleating of the rabbitlike pikas among the glacial boulders and pines. The trail continues ½ mi to Inspiration Point over a rocky path that is moderately steep. There are two points on the climb that afford good views of Jenny Lake and the surrounding area, but keep climbing; after passing a rock wall you'll finally reach the true Inspiration Point, with the best views. To avoid crowds, try to make your way to Inspiration Point in early morning or late afternoon.

Colter Bay Nature Trail Loop (✉ 2 mi off U.S. 89/191/287, 5 mi north of Jackson Lake Junction), a very easy, 1¾-mi round-trip excursion, treats you to views of Jackson Lake and the Tetons. As you follow the level trail from Colter Bay Visitor Center and along the forest's edge, you may see moose and bald eagles. Allow yourself two hours to complete the walk.

Death Canyon Trail (✉ Off Moose-Wilson Rd., 4 mi south of Moose Junction), a strenuous 7⅗-mi hike, with lots of hills to traverse, ends with a climb up into Death Canyon. The view from the top includes huge boulders and rock formations and scattered pine trees and aspens.

You can walk to Hidden Falls from the Jenny Lake ranger station by ★ following the mostly level **Jenny Lake Trail** (✉ S. Jenny Lake Junction, ½ mi off Teton Park Rd., 8 mi north of Moose Junction) around the south shore of the lake to Cascade Canyon Trail. Jenny Lake Trail continues around the lake for 6½ mi. It's an easy trail that will take you two to three hours, depending on how fast you walk.

The flat **Leigh Lake Trail** (✉ String Lake Trailhead, ½ mi west of Jenny Lake Rd., 14 mi north of Moose Junction) follows String Lake's northeastern shore to Leigh Lake's south shore, covering 2 mi in a round-trip of about an hour. You can extend your hike into an easy 7½-mi, four-hour round-trip by following the forested east shore of Leigh Lake to Bearpaw Lake. Along the way you'll have views of Mount Moran across the lake, and you may be lucky enough to spot a moose.

Lunchtree Hill Trail (✉ U.S. 89/191/287, ½ mi north of Jackson Lake Junction), one of the park's easiest trails, begins at Jackson Lake Lodge and leads ½ mi to the top of a hill above Willow Flats. The area's willow thickets, beaver ponds, and wet, grassy meadows make it prime bird-watching territory. Look for sandhill cranes, hummingbirds, and many types of songbirds. You might also see moose. The round-trip walk takes no more than a half hour.

In the shadows of 11,144-foot Rockchuck Peak and 11,430-foot Mount Saint John, the easy 3½-mi, three-hour **String Lake Trail** (✉ ½ mi west of Jenny Lake Rd., 14 mi north of Moose) loops around String Lake.

An easy to moderate path, **Taggart Lake Trail** (✉ ½ mi south of Jenny Lake on Teton Park Rd.) runs for more than 1½ mi from the trailhead to the lake. You can continue around the lake to complete the 4-mi loop, but note that the terrain becomes steeper near Beaver Creek. The loop affords views of Avalanche Canyon, and you may see moose.

Horseback Riding

June through August, Grand Teton Lodge Company arranges one-, two-, and three-hour rides from **Colter Bay Village Corral** (✉ 2 mi off U.S. 89/191/287, 5 mi north of Jackson Lake Junction ☎ 307/543–3100 or 800/628–9988 🌐 www.gtlc.com) to several destinations. Half-day trips, for advanced riders only, go to Hermitage Point. Some rides include breakfast or dinner eaten along the trail. Prices vary, from $25 for short rides to $47 for dinner rides.

Several trail rides depart daily from the **Jackson Lake Lodge Corral** (✉ U.S. 89/191/287, ½ mi north of Jackson Lake Junction ☎ 307/543–3100 or

800/628–9988 ⊕ www.gtlc.com), operated by Grand Teton Lodge Company June through August. One-hour rides give an overview of the Jackson Lake Lodge area; two- and three-hour rides go to Emma Matilda Lake, Oxbow Bend, and Christian Pond. Experienced riders can take a half-day ride to Two Ocean Lake. Some rides include breakfast or dinner eaten along the trail. Prices vary, from $25 for short rides to $47 for dinner rides.

Mountain Climbing

The Teton Range offers the nation's most diverse general mountaineering. Excellent rock, snow, and ice routes abound for climbers of all experience levels.

Started by climbing pioneers Paul Petzoldt and Glen Exum, **Exum Mountain Guides** (✉ Lupine Meadows, near Jenny Lake ☎ 307/733–2297) offers a variety of climbing experiences and instruction, ranging from one-day mountain climbs to ice climbing and backcountry adventures on skis and snowboards. Though most of their climbing is on the Teton Range, they also lead trips to other sites in Wyoming and the region, and they have an international climbing program as well. One-day climbs range from $200 to $325; climbing classes cost from $95 to $170.

Mountain climbers get a leg up in the Tetons from **Jackson Hole Mountain Guides** (✉ 165 N. Glenwood St., Jackson ☎ 307/733–4979). There are classes on rock and ice climbing for beginners and more-experienced climbers. Guided trips concentrate on the Tetons and other Wyoming locations. One-day guided climbs cost between $180 and $225; climbing classes range from $90 to $125.

River Expeditions

If you want to float the Snake River on your own, you are required to purchase a permit that costs $10 per raft and is valid for the entire season. Permits are available year-round at Moose Visitor Center and at Colter Bay, Signal Mountain, and Buffalo (near Moran entrance) ranger stations in summer. Before you set out, check with park rangers for current conditions.

You may prefer to take one of the many guided float trips through calm-water sections of the Snake; outfitters pick you up at the float-trip parking area near Moose Visitor Center for a 10- to 20-minute drive to upriver launch sites. All concessionaires provide ponchos and life preservers. Early morning and evening floats are your best bets for wildlife viewing, but be sure to carry a jacket or sweater. Float season runs mid-May to mid-September.

Barker-Ewing River Trips (✉ 45 W. Broadway, Jackson ☎ 800/448–4204 ⊕ www.barker-ewing.com) runs white-water trips down the Snake River late May through late September. A four-hour trip costs $41. If you'd like to sit back and be a passenger, travel the peaceful parts of the Snake looking for wildlife with **Barker-Ewing Scenic Float Trips** (✉ Moose ☎ 307/733–1800 or 800/365–1800 ⊕ www.barkerewingscenic.com), which operates exclusively on the scenic Snake in Grand Teton National Park. Trips run June through August and cost $40.

Grand Teton Lodge Company Snake River Float Trips (☎ 307/543–3100 or 800/628–9988 ⊕ www.gtlc.com) operates exclusively within Grand Teton National Park. Choose from a simple scenic float trip ($40.50), one that also includes lunch ($45.50), or an evening trip that includes a steak-fry dinner ($52). Make reservations at the activities desk at Colter Bay Village or Jackson Lake Lodge. To experience some wet and wild stretches of river, get in touch with the folks at **Lewis and Clark River Expeditions** (✉ 145 W. Gill St., Jackson ☎ 307/733–4022 or 800/824–5375

🌐 www.lewisandclarkexpeds.com), who put you in big rubber rafts for an exhilarating ride. You can also take a more leisurely scenic float or have a steak fry along with your river trip. Some trips are in Grand Teton National Park waters and others are outside the park. Trips run mid-May through mid-September and cost between $30 and $64.

Mad River Boat Trips (✉ 1255 S. U.S. 89, Jackson ☎ 307/733–6203 or 800/458–7238 🌐 www.mad-river.com), which worked on the movie *A River Runs Through It,* leads several white-water and scenic float trips, some combined with breakfast, lunch, or dinner. Start or end your trip with a visit to the company's river museum, which has photos and information. There are even old boats from expeditions on Wyoming waters, dating back to explorer John Wesley Powell's expedition on the Green River in the 1870s. Some trips are in park waters and others are outside Grand Teton. Trips run mid-May through August and cost between $31 and $51. **Triangle X Float Trips** (✉ 2 Triangle X Ranch Rd., Moose ☎ 307/733–2183, 307/733–6445, or 888/860–0005 🌐 www.trianglex.com) are subdued river trips in Grand Teton National Park, including short 10-mi floats and a sunset dinner float. Trips are available June through August and cost $38 to $48.

Snowmobiling

Designated unplowed sections of Teton Park Road are open to snowmobiles, and you can also snowmobile on Jackson Lake. You must first purchase an annual $15 permit at a park entrance station. The speed limit within the park is 45 mph.

North of Grand Teton, **Flagg Ranch Resort** (✉ John D. Rockefeller Jr. Memorial Pkwy., 4 mi north of Grand Teton National Park boundary 🌐 www.flaggranch.com ☎ 307/543–2861) rents snowmobiles that you can ride directly into Grand Teton National Park. The resort will also provide transportation to the Jackson-area snowmobile trails. Rentals cost $149. Snow-coach tours (in heated vans with rubber treads instead of wheels for traction on the snow) are also available, for $109.

You can rent a snowmobile at **Togwotee Mountain Resort** (✉ U.S. 26/287, Moran ☎ 307/543–2847 or 800/543–2847 🌐 www.togwoteelodge.com), on the eastern edge of Grand Teton National Park, and then ride it on an extensive trail network along the Continental Divide. Rentals cost $149; also available are snow-coach tours, which cost $109.

Where to Stay & Eat

$$–$$$ ✕ **Dornan's Chuckwagon.** An Old West theme, mountain views, and good food make this a popular local hangout. Choose from mountain red trout or salmon, barbecue chicken or baby-back ribs, and steak. There are also Mexican platters, and in summer Dornan's cooks up an outdoor Dutch-oven buffet (roast beef, ribs, and cowboy beans). Prime rib is served on weekends. Meals are eaten outside at picnic tables or inside tepees. No alcohol is served, but you can pick up something at the good wine shop next door. Another food shop on the premises prepares pizza, pasta, homemade soups, salads, and sandwiches. ✉ *U.S. 191, 12 mi north of Jackson, Moose* ☎ *307/733–2415* ▭ *MC, V* *BYOB* ⊗ *Closed Oct.–Apr.*

★ **$$$$** ✕🏨 **Jenny Lake Lodge.** In the most exclusive of the park's resorts, elegant yet rustic cabins are bedecked with handmade quilts, down comforters, and even walking sticks. You can request a phone in your room, but you may prefer to sit undisturbed in a rocker on the cabin porch and watch for moose and fox. Activities, such as riding a horse or 1950s-style bicycle along park trails, are included in the price along with breakfast and dinner. The dining room serves a set dinner menu with a choice of entrées emphasizing Rocky Mountain cuisine, including roast prime rib of buffalo and breast of pheasant. Jackets are requested for evening dining, and you should reserve ahead. ✉ *Jenny Lake Rd. (Grand Teton Lodge Co., Box 250, Moran 83013)* ☎ *307/733–3100 or 800/628–9988* 🖷 *307/543–3143* 🌐 *www.gtlc.com* ⇨ *30 cabins, 6 suites* ♁ *Restaurant, boating, bicycles, horseback riding, bar; no room phones, no room TVs* ▭ *AE, DC, MC, V* ⊗ *Closed mid-Oct.–May* 🍴 *MAP.*

$$$–$$$$ ✕🏨 **Jackson Lake Lodge.** Two large fireplaces adorn the lounge, Native American designs decorate the walls, and huge picture windows look out on Willow Flats. There are 30 rooms in the main lodge; the others, in one-story motor-lodge-style buildings, are larger and preferable. Some rooms have Teton views and a higher price tag as a result. The park's only pool is here, and you can arrange for horseback riding, float trips, and boating excursions that depart from the lodge. The Mural Room serves buffalo, cedar-plank king salmon, and rack of lamb. ✉ *U.S. 89 north of Jackson Lake Junction (Grand Teton Lodge Co., Box 250, Moran 83013)* ☎ *307/733–3100 or 800/628–9988* 🖷 *307/543–3143* 🌐 *www.gtlc.com* ⇨ *385 rooms* ♁ *2 restaurants, pool, boating, hiking, horseback riding, bar, recreation room, business services, meeting rooms, airport shuttle* ▭ *AE, DC, MC, V* ⊗ *Closed late Oct.–mid-May.*

$–$$$ ✕🏨 **Signal Mountain Lodge.** Volcanic stone and pine shingles were used in the construction of this lodge on the eastern shore of Jackson Lake. Guest rooms are clustered in cabinlike units, and many of them have lake views; some have kitchenettes. The lobby has a fireplace, a piano, and Adirondack furniture. You can rent boats, take scenic float trips, or fish. The Peaks restaurant offers buffalo steak, trout, and free-range chicken along with views of the lake and the Tetons. The Trapper Grill, which has a children's menu, serves sandwiches and burgers that can be eaten indoors or out on the deck. ✉ *Teton Park Rd. (Box 50, Moran 83013)* ☎ *307/543–2831* 🌐 *www.signalmtnlodge.com* ⇨ *79 rooms* ♁ *2 restaurants, some kitchenettes, boating, fishing, bar, shops* ▭ *AE, DC, MC, V* ⊗ *Closed mid-Oct.–early May.*

¢–$$ ✕🏨 **Colter Bay Village.** Less expensive than its posher cousins, the Colter Bay Village, near Jackson Lake, may not be fancy, but it has splendid views and an excellent marina and beach for the windsurfing crowd. (You'll need a wet suit.) A Western theme decorates the cabins. With their concrete floors, hanging bunks, canvas exteriors, and shared bathrooms, the tent cabins are by no means luxurious, but they do keep the wind and rain off. There's also an RV park with showers, a service station, and a marina. The family-oriented Chuckwagon restaurant ($–$$$$) serves lasagna, trout, and barbecue spareribs. ✉ *Off U.S. 89 (Grand Teton Lodge Co., Box 250, Moran 83013)* ☎ *307/733–3100 or 800/628–9988* 🖷 *307/543–3143* 🌐 *www.gtlc.com* ⇨ *166 cabins, 66 tent cabins with shared bath* ♁ *2 restaurants, boating, hiking, bar, shops, laundry facilities* ▭ *AE, DC, MC, V* ⊗ *Closed late Sept.–late May (tent cabins have slightly shorter season).*

$$–$$$$ 🏨 **Spur Ranch Log Cabins.** These log cabins, at the popular and busy Dornan's in Moose and adjacent to the Snake River, have views of the Teton Range. They range from small one-bedroom cabins to large two-bedroom units. Lodgepole-pine furniture fills cabins' bedrooms and living areas. ✉ *U.S. 191, 12 mi north of Jackson, Box 39, Moose 83012* ☎ *307/733–2522* 🖷 *307/739–9098* 🌐 *www.dornans.com* ⇨ *12 cabins* ♁ *2 restaurants, grocery, kitchens, boating, fishing, mountain bikes, hiking, cross-country skiing, bar, wine shop, shops; no a/c, no room phones, no room TVs* ▭ *D, MC, V.*

Camping

⛺ **Colter Bay Campground.** Busy, noisy, and filled by noon, this campground has sites for tents, trailers, or RVs and one great advantage: its central location, about ¼ mi from Jackson Lake. Try to get a site as far from the nearby cabin road as possible. This is the only national-parks-operated campground in the park that has hot showers. The maximum stay is 14 days. *Flush toilets, dump station, drinking water, guest laundry, showers, bear boxes, fire grates, picnic tables 350 sites 2 mi off U.S. 89/191/287, 5 mi north of Jackson Lake Junction 307/543–3100 www.gtlc.com $26–$39 Reservations not accepted AE, D, MC, V Mid-May–late Sept.*

Colter Bay RV Park. This campground, part of Colter Bay Village and next to Colter Bay Campground, is the only RV park in Grand Teton where you can get full hookups. There's also a marina here. *Flush toilets, full hookups, dump station, drinking water, guest laundry, showers, bear boxes, fire grates, picnic tables 112 full hookups 2 mi off U.S. 89/191/287, 5 mi north of Jackson Lake Junction 307/543–2811 AE, D, MC, V Late May–late Sept.*

Gros Ventre. The park's biggest campground is set on an open, grassy area on the bank of the Gros Ventre River, away from the mountains and in the southeast corner of the park. Try to get a site close to the river. The campground usually doesn't fill until nightfall, if at all. There's a maximum stay of 14 days. *Flush toilets, dump station, drinking water, bear boxes, fire grates, picnic tables 372 tent or RV sites 4 mi off U.S. 26/89/191, 1½ mi southwest of Kelly on Gros Ventre River Rd., 6 mi south of Moose Junction No phone $12 Reservations not accepted AE, D, MC, V May–mid-Oct.*

Jenny Lake. Wooded sites and Teton views make this the most desirable campground in the park, and it fills early. The small, quiet facility allows tents only and limits stays to a maximum of seven days. *Flush toilets, drinking water, bear boxes, fire grates, picnic tables 51 sites Jenny Lake Rd., ½ mi off Teton Park Rd., 8 mi north of Moose Junction No phone $12 Reservations not accepted No credit cards Mid-May–late Sept.*

Lizard Creek. Views of Jackson Lake, wooded sites, and the relative isolation of this campground make it a relaxing choice. There's a maximum stay of 14 days, and no vehicles more than 30 feet long are allowed. *Flush toilets, drinking water, bear boxes, fire grates 60 tent or trailer sites U.S. 89/191/287, 12 mi north of Jackson Lake Junction No phone $12 Reservations not accepted AE, D, MC, V Early June–early Sept.*

Signal Mountain. In a hilly setting on Jackson Lake, this campground has boat access. No vehicles or trailers more than 30 feet long are allowed. There's a maximum stay of 14 days. *Flush toilets, dump station, drinking water, fire grates, picnic tables 86 tent or trailer sites Teton Park Rd., 3 mi south of Jackson Lake Junction No phone $12 Reservations not accepted AE, D, MC, V Early May–mid-Oct.*

Nightlife & the Arts

Ranger programs on topics ranging from wildlife to the geology of the park are presented during summer evenings at **Colter Bay Visitor Center** (2 mi off U.S. 89/191/287, 5 mi north of Jackson Lake Junction 307/739–3594).

Shopping

Colter Bay General Store (Colter Bay Village, off U.S. 89 No phone) sells groceries, gifts, sporting goods, fishing tackle, and books, including hiking guides. Many of the items bear pictures of moose. You can buy gifts, wine, marshmallows, and other food items at **Dornan's General Store** (Teton Park Rd. near Moose Visitor Center 307/733–

2415 Ext. 301). This is also a good place to stock up on mountaineering and camping equipment.

Original watercolors by Joanne Hennes, custom jewelry, leather coats, antler knives, and hand-pressed-flower photo albums are among the unique items sold at **Jenny Lake Lodge Gift Shop** (✉ Jenny Lake Lodge, Jenny Lake Rd. ☎ 307/733–4647). **Jenny Lake Store** (✉ South end of Jenny Lake ☎ No phone) sells backpacks, waist packs, water bottles, and camping and hiking gear (socks, compasses, and even sandwiches). For a good selection of bird feeders and jewelry, head to **Needles Gift Shop** (✉ Signal Mountain Lodge, Teton Park Rd. ☎ 307/543–2831). You can purchase hiking guides, hats, and T-shirts at **Timbers Gift Shop** (✉ Signal Mountain Lodge, Teton Park Rd. ☎ 307/543–2831).

JACKSON

The largest number of visitors to northwest Wyoming come to Jackson, which remains a small Western town, "howdy" in the daytime and hopping in the evening. For active types, it's a good place to stock up on supplies before heading for outdoor adventures in Grand Teton National Park and the surrounding Jackson Hole area. For those looking to rest their feet awhile, it's a good stop for its wealth of galleries, Western-wear shops, varied cuisines, and active nightlife centering on bars and music.

Jackson's charm and popularity put it at risk. On busy summer days, traffic can slow to a crawl where the highway doglegs through downtown. Proposals for new motels and condominiums sprout like the purple asters in the spring, as developers vie for a share of the vacation market. Old-timers suggest that the town—in fact, the entire Jackson Hole—has already lost the dusty charm it had when horses stood at hitching rails around Town Square. However, with national parks and forests and state lands occupying some of the most beautiful real estate in the country, there's only so much ground on which to build. These limitations, along with the cautious approach of locals, may keep Jackson on a human scale.

Exploring Jackson

The best way to explore Jackson's downtown, which is centered on vibrant Town Square, is on foot, since parking can be a challenge during the busy summer months. To explore beyond downtown—the National Wildlife Art Museum or National Elk Refuge, for example—you'll need to hop into your car.

a good tour

Start your visit at the corner of Cache and Broadway at **Town Square** 13, easily identifiable by its elk-antler arches and bustle of activity. Stroll around the square and visit the various shops here. Walk one block west to Glenwood Street and the **Jackson Hole Museum** 14 for a lesson on local history. For even more history, head to the **Jackson Hole Historical Society** 15; to get there walk two blocks north on Glenwood to Mercill Avenue and one block west. At this point you should hop into your car and drive 3 mi north on Cache Drive to the **National Wildlife Art Museum** 16, with its wonderful collection devoted to depictions of animals. From a deck at the museum you can watch the real thing—thousands of elk in winter, plus waterfowl, coyotes, and more at various times of the year—at the **National Elk Refuge** 17. If you want to see the animals up close, you can arrange a sleigh ride to the refuge in winter through the museum. You can also drive along U.S. 191 and observe the wildlife at various pullouts along the route.

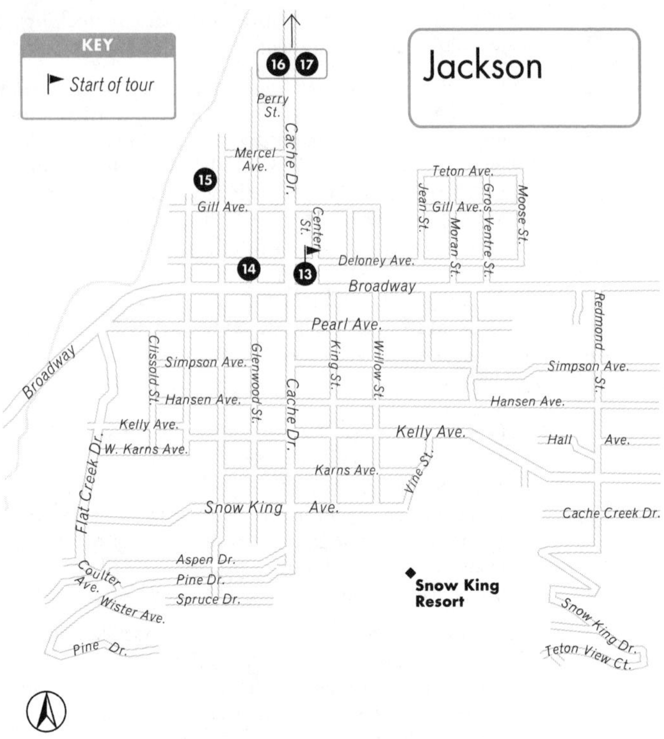

TIMING If you don't plan to shop on Town Square, you can easily do this tour in a few hours. If you want to hit the stores, budget a full day for this tour. Note that the Jackson Hole Museum is open only in summer and that the Jackson Hole Historical Society is closed weekends.

What to See

15 **Jackson Hole Historical Society.** Displays at this log cabin illuminate local history. In addition to historic artifacts and photographs, the society houses manuscripts, maps, and an oral-history collection. ✉ *105 Mercill Ave.* ☎ *307/733–9605* 🌐 *www.jacksonholehistory.org* *Free* *Weekdays 8–5.*

14 **Jackson Hole Museum.** For some local history, visit this museum, where you can get acquainted with the early settlers and find out how Dead Man's Bar got its name. You'll also learn how Jackson had the first all-female town government. Among the exhibits are Native American, ranching, and cowboy artifacts. ✉ *Corner of Glenwood and Deloney Ave.* ☎ *307/733–2414* 🌐 *www.jacksonholehistory.org* *$3* *Memorial Day–Sept., Mon.–Sat. 9:30–6, Sun. 10–5.*

17 **National Elk Refuge.** Wildlife abounds on this 25,000-acre refuge year-round, but from approximately late November through March, the real highlight is the more than 7,000 elk, many with enormous antler racks, that winter here. You can see them from various pullouts along U.S. 191, or up close by taking a horse-drawn sleigh ride through the herd, which you can arrange through the National Wildlife Art Museum. The elk stand or eat calmly as sleighs loaded with families and alfalfa pellets move in their midst. Among the other animals that make their home here are coyotes, trumpeter swans, and other waterfowl. ✉ *2820 Rungius Rd., 3 mi north of Jackson* ☎ *307/733–5771* 🌐 *nationalelkrefuge.fws.gov* *Free,*

sleigh ride $15 ⏲ Year-round; sleigh rides, generally mid-Dec.–Mar., daily 10–4.

★ 16 **National Wildlife Art Museum.** Among the paintings and sculptures of bighorn sheep, elk, and other animals of the West at this museum devoted to representations of wildlife are works by such artists as George Catlin and Charles M. Russell. The collection includes works in various media and styles, and the earliest pieces date to 2000 BC. A deck here affords views across the National Elk Refuge, where, particularly in winter, you can see wildlife in a natural habitat. ✉ *2820 Rungius Rd., 3 mi north of Jackson* ☎ *307/733–5771* 🌐 *www.wildlifeart.org* 🎫 *$6* ⏲ *Nov.–Sept., daily 8–5; Oct., Mon.–Sat. 9–5, Sun. 1–5.*

13 **Town Square.** You can spend an entire day wandering around Jackson's always-bustling Town Square, a parklike area crisscrossed with walking paths and bedecked with arches woven from hundreds of elk antlers. Various shops and restaurants surround the square, and there's often entertainment going on in the square itself, including a melodramatic "shoot-out" summer evenings at approximately 6:30. At the southwest corner of the square you can board a stagecoach for a ride around the area; it should cost about $6 per adult.

off the beaten path

GRANITE HOT SPRINGS – South of Jackson Hole, concerted local and national efforts have preserved both the wildlands and the ranches that dot the Teton Valley floor. The Snake River turns west and the contours steepen; by Hoback Junction there's white-water excitement. The drive south along U.S. 191 provides good views of the river's twists and turns and the life-jacketed rafters and kayakers who float the canyon. About 13 mi south of Jackson at Hoback Junction, head east on U.S. 189/191 and follow the Hoback River south up its beautiful canyon. A tributary canyon 10 mi south of the junction is followed by a well-maintained and -marked gravel road to Granite Hot Springs, in the Bridger-Teton National Forest, 10 mi east of U.S. 189/191 on Granite Creek Road. People come for the shady, creekside campground, the pool fed by hot springs, and moderate hikes up Granite Canyon to passes with panoramic views. In the winter, there's a popular snowmobile and dogsled trail from the highway.

Sports & the Outdoors

Bicycling

The trip up to **Lower Slide Lake,** north of town, is a favorite of cyclists. Turn east off U.S. 26/89/191 to Kelly, and then follow Slide Lake Road. Cyclists ride the **Spring Gulch Road,** part pavement, part dirt, off Route 22, along the base of Gros Ventre Butte, rejoining U.S. 26/89/191 near the Gros Ventre River.

Bike rentals for all skill levels and age groups are available at **Edge Sports** (✉ 409 W. Broadway ☎ 307/734–3916); the company also leads guided bike tours. You can rent a mountain bike to explore on your own or take a tour at **Hoback Sports** (✉ 40 S. Millward St. ☎ 307/733–5335). General tours are geared to intermediate and advanced riders, but Hoback can also custom-design a tour to suit your abilities and interests. **Teton Cyclers** (✉ 175 N. Glenwood St. ☎ 307/733–4386) rents bikes and leads tours, including family-style outings to the National Elk Refuge and intermediate or advanced tours from the top of Snow King Mountain.

Canoeing, Kayaking & Rafting

South of Jackson, where the Hoback joins the Snake River and the canyon walls become steep, there are lively white-water sections. But the Snake, whose rating is Class I and Class II, is a river for those who value scenery over white-water thrills. For the most part, floating rather than taking on rapids is the theme of running the Snake (with trips usually incorporating Jackson Lake, at the foot of the Tetons); as such, it's a good choice for families with children. What makes the trip special is the Teton Range, looming as high as 8,000 feet above the river. This float trip can also be combined with two or more days of kayaking on Jackson Lake. Raft trips take place between June and September. Experienced paddlers run the Hoback, too.

The Snake River has earned a strange footnote in history as the river that Evel Knievel tried (and failed miserably) to jump over on a rocket-powered motorcycle in the mid-1970s.

At **Snake River Kayak and Canoe** (✉ 365 N. Cache St. ☎ 307/733–9999 or 800/529–2501 🌐 www.snakeriverkayak.com) you'll receive instruction in the fine art of paddling, after which you can test yourself on the river. Canoe and kayak rentals are also available. **Teton Aquatics** (✉ 155 W. Gill Ave. ☎ 307/733–3127) offers boating lessons plus canoe and kayak rentals.

Hiking

Bridger-Teton National Forest (✉ 340 N. Cache St., Box 1888, 83001 ☎ 307/739–5500 🌐 www.fs.fed.us/btnf) covers hundreds of thousands of acres of western Wyoming and shelters abundant wildlife. Permits for backcountry use of the forest are necessary only for groups and commercial operators such as outfitters. Contact the forest office for more information.

You can take part in wilderness camping, climbing, and exploration of alpine areas with experienced guides on day trips, overnight excursions, or as part of regular classes offered by **Jackson Hole Mountain Guides** (✉ 165 N. Glenwood St. ☎ 307/733–4979 🌐 www.jhmg.com).

Dogsledding

Dogsledding excursions are available through **Iditarod Sled Dog Tours** (✉ 11 Granite Creek Rd. ☎ 307/733–7388 or 800/554–7388 🌐 www.jhsleddog.com). Frank Teasley, a veteran Iditarod racer, leads half-day introductory trips and full-day trips to Granite Hot Springs.

Skiing

Jack Dennis Sports (✉ 50 E. Broadway ☎ 307/733–3270 🌐 www.jackdennis.com) sells and rents skis and snowboards, plus outdoor gear for any season. Ski rental costs $18 to $30; snowboard and boot rental costs $25.

Snow King Resort (✉ 400 E. Snow King Ave. ☎ 307/733–5200 or 800/522–5464 🌐 www.snowking.com), at the western edge of Jackson, has 400 acres of ski runs for daytime use and 110 acres suitable for night skiing, plus an extensive snowmaking system on Snow King Mountain. Also here are a half pipe, snowboard park, and snow-tubing park. In summer there's a waterslide. Lessons and groomed cross-country trails are available for a fee at **Spring Creek Ranch** (✉ 1800 Spirit Dance Rd. ☎ 307/733–8833 or 800/443–6139).

Sleigh Rides

Sleigh rides into the National Elk Refuge last about 45 minutes and depart from in front of the **National Wildlife Art Museum** (✉ 2820 Rungius Rd. ☎ 307/733–5771) daily in winter, 10 to 4, about every 20 minutes. Dinner sleigh rides are available through **Spring Creek Ranch** (✉ 1800 Spirit Dance Rd. ☎ 307/733–8833 or 800/443–6139), with dinner at its Granary restaurant.

Snowmobiling

Numerous companies in the Jackson area rent snowmobiles. Contact the **Jackson Hole Chamber of Commerce** (✉ 990 W. Broadway, Box E, 83001 ☎ 307/733–3316 🌐 www.jacksonholeinfo.com) for information on snowmobile rentals and guides.

Rocky Mountain Snowmobile Tours (✉ 1050 S. Hwy. 89 ☎ 307/733–2237 or 800/647–2561 🌐 www.snowmobiletours.net) guides one- to five-day trips.

Where to Stay & Eat

You can make reservations for most lodgings in Jackson through two reservation services: **Central Reservations** (☎ 800/443–6931) and **Jackson Hole Vacations** (☎ 800/223–4059).

$$$–$$$$ ✕ **The Snake River Grill.** Choose from fresh fish, free-range meats, and organic produce at this restaurant overlooking Town Square. Buffalo short ribs, vegetarian pasta with mushrooms and artichokes, and grilled elk chops round out the menu, and there's an extensive wine list. ✉ *84 E. Broadway* ☎ *307/733–0557* ▭ *AE, D, MC, V* ⊗ *No lunch.*

★ **$$–$$$$** ✕ **The Blue Lion.** Consistently excellent, distinctive fare is the rule at this white-and-blue clapboard house two blocks from Town Square. Dishes range from Dijon-mustard-rubbed rack of lamb to grilled elk with a brandy-peppercorn sauce to fresh seafood, perhaps herb-crusted rainbow trout. There's patio dining in summer. ✉ *160 N. Millward St.* ☎ *307/733–3912* ▭ *AE, D, MC, V* ⊘ *No smoking* ⊗ *No lunch.*

$$–$$$$ ✕ **Off Broadway Grill.** In addition to serving seafood and pasta dishes such as Cajun shrimp with black linguine, Off Broadway Grill throws in a little Thai, wild game, and snazzy neon to spice things up. There's indoor and outdoor seating. ✉ *30 King St.* ☎ *307/733–9777* ▭ *AE, MC, V* ⊗ *No lunch.*

$$–$$$$ ✕ **Sweetwater Restaurant.** Mediterranean meals are served in a log building with antique oak furnishings, and nothing is lost in the translation. Start with smoked buffalo carpaccio or roasted red pepper hummus; then move on to roast duckling, venison tenderloin, or yellowfin tuna. ✉ *85 S. King St.* ☎ *307/733–3553* ▭ *AE, D, MC, V.*

$$–$$$ ✕ **Nani's Genuine Pasta House.** The ever-changing menu (each month the menu represents a different region) at this cozy, almost cramped restaurant may contain braised veal shanks with saffron risotto or other regional Italian cooking. Almost hidden behind a motel, Nani's is designed to attract gourmets, not tourists. Vegan dishes are also served, and you can dine in or take out. ✉ *242 N. Glenwood St.* ☎ *307/733–3888* ▭ *MC, V.*

$–$$$ ✕ **Billy's Giant Hamburgers.** True to its name, Billy's serves big—really big—burgers that are really, really good, along with several sandwiches. The portions in general are huge. The dining room is casual and noisy at this restaurant sharing an entrance with the Cadillac Grille. Seating options consist of a few booths, tall tables with stools, or the bar. ✉ *55 N. Cache Dr.* ☎ *307/733–3279* ▭ *AE, MC, V.*

★ **$–$$$** ✕ **The Bunnery.** Lunch is served year-round and dinner is served in summer at the Bunnery, but it's the breakfasts of omelets and home-baked pastries that are irresistible. All of the breads are made on the premises, mostly of a combined grain known as OSM (oats, sunflower, millet). It's elbow to elbow inside and you may have to wait to be seated on busy mornings, but any inconvenience is well worth it. There's also a decent vegetarian selection here. ✉ *130 N. Cache St., Hole-in-the-Wall Mall* ☎ *307/733–5474* ✍ *Reservations not accepted* ▭ *MC, V* ⊗ *No dinner Oct.–Apr.*

$–$$$ ✕ **Jedediah's House of Sourdough.** Friendly, noisy, and elbow knocking, this restaurant a block east of Town Square makes breakfast and lunch for those with big appetites. There are plenty of "sourjacks" (sourdough flapjacks) and biscuits and gravy. Burgers are mountain-man size, and dinners include trout, barbecue chicken, and steak. ✉ *135 E. Broadway* ☎ *307/733–5671* ✍ *Reservations not accepted* 💳 *AE, D, MC, V* ⏱ *No dinner Labor Day–Memorial Day.*

$–$$ ✕ **Bubba's Barbecue Restaurant.** Succulent baby-back ribs and mouthwatering spareribs are the specialties at this busy barbecue joint, which evokes the Old West with its large wooden porch, wooden booths, Western paintings, and antique signs. Sandwiches and a huge salad bar with plenty of nonmeat choices are also available. The desserts include homemade pies of the chocolate-buttermilk and fudge-pecan variety. The locals who started this restaurant have since gone on to open other branches throughout Wyoming. ✉ *515 W. Broadway* ☎ *307/733–2288* 💳 *AE, D, MC, V.*

★ $$$$ ✕🏨 **Wort Hotel.** This brick Victorian hotel near Town Square seems to have been around as long as the Tetons, but it feels fresh inside. A fireplace warms the lobby, and a sitting area is just up the stairs. Locally made Western-style furnishings, including lodgepole-pine beds and pine dressers, decorate the rooms, along with carpets, drapes, and bedcoverings in warm, muted tones such as blues and mauves. You can sip a drink in the Silver Dollar Bar ($–$$$)—aptly named for the 2,032 silver dollars imbedded on top of the bar—or sit down for a fine meal. Try the mixed grill of buffalo and elk medallions or the nightly veal special. ✉ *50 N. Glenwood St., 83001* ☎ *307/733–6964, 307/733–2190, or 800/322–2727* 📠 *307/733–2067* 🌐 *www.worthotel.com* 🛏 *60 rooms* 👍 *Restaurant, cable TV, gym, hot tub, bar, Internet, business services, meeting rooms, no-smoking rooms* 💳 *AE, D, MC, V.*

$$–$$$$ ✕🏨 **Spring Creek Ranch.** Outside Jackson on Gros Ventre Butte, this luxury resort has beautiful views of the Tetons. Among the numerous amenities are horseback riding, tennis, and cross-country skiing and sleigh rides in winter. Aside from hotel rooms, there's a mix of studios and condos; many of the accommodations have wood-burning fireplaces and lodgepole-pine furniture. Among the fine food served at the Granary ($$$–$$$$) are an appetizer of Dungeness crab and Havarti cheese wrapped in phyllo dough, and an entrée of poached salmon with a cucumber-dill sauce. ✉ *1800 Spirit Dance Rd., Box 4780, 83001* ☎ *307/733–8833 or 800/443–6139* 📠 *307/733–1524* 🌐 *www.springcreekranch.com* 🛏 *36 rooms, 76 studios and condos* 👍 *Restaurant, room service, kitchenettes, 2 tennis courts, pool, spa, horseback riding, cross-country skiing, sleigh rides, bar* 💳 *AE, D, DC, MC, V.*

★ $$$$ 🏨 **Amangani.** This exclusive resort built of sandstone and redwood melds into the landscape of Gros Ventre Butte, affording beautiful views of Spring Creek valley from its cliff. The warm hospitality is Western, but the setting is that of Eastern simplicity, with tall ceilings, clean lines, and rooms with platform beds, large soaking tubs, and plenty of space. The amenities here are the best in Jackson Hole and include horseback riding, tennis, and nearby cross-country skiing and sleigh rides in winter. ✉ *1535 N.E. Butte Rd., Box 15030, 83002* ☎ *307/734–7333 or 877/734–7333* 📠 *307/734–7332* 🌐 *www.amangani.com* 🛏 *40 suites* 👍 *Restaurant, room service, in-room data ports, in-room safes, minibars, refrigerators, in-room VCRs, 2 tennis courts, pool, health club, hot tub, massage, sauna, spa, steam room, horseback riding, cross-country skiing, sleigh rides, lobby lounge, library, dry cleaning, concierge, meeting room, airport shuttle, no-smoking rooms* 💳 *AE, D, DC, MC, V.*

$$$$ 🏨 **Rusty Parrot.** An imposing river-rock fireplace in the cathedral lounge lends warmth to this timber inn near the center of Jackson. You can walk

the four blocks to shops, galleries, and restaurants on Town Square. Handcrafted wooden furnishings fill the rooms, some of which have fireplaces and oversize whirlpool tubs. With body wraps, massages, and facials, the spa is a nice extra. ✉ *175 N. Jackson St., 83001* ☎ *307/733–2000 or 800/458–2004* 🖷 *307/733–5566* 🌐 *www.rustyparrot.com* *31 rooms* *Room service, some in-room hot tubs, cable TV, hot tub, spa, library, business services; no smoking* *AE, D, DC, MC, V* *CP.*

$$$–$$$$ **Antler Motel.** As real estate agents say, location, location, location, and perhaps no motel in Jackson has a better location than the Antler, one block south of Town Square. Some rooms have fireplaces, but they are otherwise standard motel rooms. In winter there's a complimentary ski shuttle. ✉ *43 W. Pearl St., 83001* ☎ *307/733–2535 or 800/483–8667* 🖷 *307/733–2002* 🌐 *www.townsquareinns.com* *110 rooms* *Restaurant, cable TV, exercise equipment, hot tub, sauna, laundry facilities, meeting room, some pets allowed, no-smoking rooms* *AE, D, MC, V.*

★ $$$ **Parkway Inn.** Each room has a distinctive look, with oak or wicker furniture, and all are filled with antiques, from 19th-century pieces onward. The overall effect is homey and delightful, especially appealing if you plan to stay several days or longer. Breakfast is served in an antiques-filled lounge. ✉ *125 N. Jackson St., 83001* ☎ *307/733–3143 or 800/247–8390* 🖷 *307/733–0955* 🌐 *www.parkwayinn.com* *37 rooms, 12 suites* *Indoor pool, gym, hot tub, sauna, no-smoking rooms* *AE, D, DC, MC, V* *CP.*

$$ **Days Inn.** Like other chains, this motel is something familiar, but the lodgepole-pine swing out front, the lobby's elk-antler chandelier, and the rooms' Teton-, Wind River–, or Snake River–range views remind you where you are. There are ski-boot and glove dryers in the lobby, plus in-room ski racks and safes. ✉ *350 S. Hwy. 89, 83001* ☎ *307/739–9010* 🖷 *307/733–0044* *91 rooms* *In-room safes, some microwaves, some refrigerators, hot tub, sauna, ski storage, no-smoking rooms* *AE, D, DC, MC, V* *CP.*

$–$$ **Cowboy Village Resort.** Stay in your own small log cabin with covered decks and barbecue grills. There is a ski-waxing room, and both the START Bus and Targhee Express buses that service the ski areas stop here. Continental breakfast is served in winter. ✉ *120 S. Flat Creek, 83001* ☎ *307/733–3121 or 800/962–4988* 🖷 *307/739–1955* *82 cabins* 🌐 *www.townsquareinns.com* *Some kitchenettes, cable TV, hot tub, laundry facilities, no-smoking rooms* *AE, D, MC, V.*

$–$$ **Trapper Inn.** This motel is within walking distance of Town Square and has some of the best-appointed rooms for people with disabilities in Jackson. ✉ *235 N. Cache St., 83001* ☎ *307/733–2648* 🖷 *307/739–9351* 🌐 *www.trapperinn.com* *54 rooms* *Cable TV, outdoor hot tub, laundry facilities, no-smoking rooms* *AE, D, DC, MC, V.*

Camping

Curtis Canyon. Numerous trees surround this simple campground northeast of Jackson Hole. Part of Bridger-Teton National Forest, the campground is near a popular mountain-biking area. *Pit toilets, drinking water, fire pits, picnic tables* *11 sites* ✉ *Off Broadway, 7 mi northeast of Jackson* ☎ *307/739–5400 or 307/543–2386* 🌐 *www.fs.fed.us/btnf/* *$12* *Reservations not accepted* *No credit cards* *May–Sept.*

Granite Creek. Part of Bridger-Teton National Forest, this wooded campground is a big, noisy place convenient to hiking and mountain-biking trails. An added bonus are the small pools of Granite Hot Springs. *Flush toilets, pit toilets, drinking water, fire pits, picnic tables* *52 sites* ✉ *Granite Creek Rd. off U.S. 189/191, 35 mi southeast of Jack-*

son ☎ *307/739–5400 or 307/543–2386* 🌐 *www.fs.fed.us/btnf* *$15* *Reservations not accepted* *No credit cards* *Late May–Sept.*

Nightlife & the Arts

Nightlife

There's never a shortage of live music in Jackson, where local performers play country, rock, and folk. Some of the most popular bars are on Town Square. At the **Million Dollar Cowboy Bar** (✉ 25 N. Cache St. ☎ 307/733–2207), everyone dresses up in cowboy garb and tries to two-step into the Old West. There's live country music most nights at the **Rancher Bar** (✉ 20 E. Broadway ☎ 307/733–3886). Various musical performers and dancing are nightly events at the **Shady Lady Saloon** (✉ 400 E. Snow King Ave. ☎ 307/733–5200) at the Snow King Resort. Folks head to the **Virginian Saloon** (✉ 750 W. Broadway ☎ 307/733–2792) to shoot a game of pool, listen to live music, and sip a drink by the fireplace.

The Arts

Artists who work in a variety of mediums show and sell their work at the **Jackson Hole Fall Arts Festival** (☎ 307/733–3316), with special events highlighting art, poetry, and dance. Festival events take place throughout town in September, and many art galleries in Jackson have special programs and exhibits.

Shopping

Jackson's peaceful Town Square is surrounded by storefronts with a mixture of specialty and outlet shops—most of them small scale—with moderate to expensive prices. North of Jackson's center, on Cache Street, is a small cluster of fine shops on Gaslight Alley.

Books

One of Gaslight Alley's best shops is **Valley Bookstore** (✉ 125 N. Cache St. ☎ 307/733–4533). It ranks among the top bookstores in the region, with a big selection and salespeople who can talk Tolstoy while guiding you to the best publications on local subjects.

Clothing

At the south edge of town, **Cattle Kate** (✉ 3530 S. Park Dr. ☎ 800/332–5382) produces some of the best designs in contemporary Western wear for women on the market today. The store also carries a few men's accessories. **Hide Out Leather** (✉ 40 N. Center St. ☎ 307/733–2422) carries many local designs and has a diverse selection of coats, vests, and accessories such as pillows and throws. Try **Jackson Hole Clothiers** (✉ 45 E. Deloney Ave. ☎ 307/733–7211) for women's Western wear and hand-knit sweaters.

Craft & Art Galleries

Jackson's art galleries serve a range of tastes. The fine nature photography of Tom Mangelson is displayed at his **Images of Nature Gallery** (✉ 170 N. Cache St. ☎ 307/733–9752). **Trailside Galleries** (✉ 105 N. Center St. ☎ 307/733–3186) sells traditional Western art and jewelry. **Wilcox Gallery** (✉ 1975 N. Hwy. 89 ☎ 307/733–6450) showcases wildlife and landscape paintings, sculpture, pottery, and other works by contemporary artists.

Sporting Goods

Jackson's premier sports shop, **Jack Dennis Sports** (✉ 50 E. Broadway ☎ 307/733–3270) is well stocked with the best in outdoor equipment for winter and summer activities. It also has a store at Teton Village.

Skinny Skis (⊠ 65 W. Deloney Ave. ☎ 307/733–6094) offers everything a cross-country skier might need. **Teton Mountaineering** (⊠ 170 N. Cache St. ☎ 307/733–3595) specializes in Nordic-skiing, climbing, and hiking equipment and clothing. **Westbank Anglers** (⊠ 3670 N. Moose-Wilson Rd. ☎ 307/733–6483) can provide all the equipment necessary for fly-fishing.

AROUND JACKSON HOLE

In this part of Wyoming, you need to keep one thing straight: there is Jackson, and then there is Jackson Hole, both named for fur trapper David Jackson, who spent a great deal of time in the area in the late 1820s and early 1830s. The first is the small town; the second is the larger geographic area surrounding the town (and called a hole because it is encircled by mountains). In addition to Jackson, Jackson Hole includes Grand Teton National Park and the small towns of Kelly, Moose, Moran, and Wilson. Also here is Teton Village, the center for the Jackson Hole Mountain Resort, best known for skiing in winter but popular for summer activities as well.

Although you might headquarter in Jackson, most of the outdoor activities in the region occur in Jackson Hole. The valley has a world-class ski mountain and hiking and biking trails, and the Snake River, ideal for fishing or floating, runs right through the middle of it.

Teton Village & Jackson Hole Mountain Resort

18 *11 mi northwest of Jackson via Hwy. 22 and Teton Village Rd.*

Although it's not an incorporated town, Teton Village is nevertheless a community that resounds with the sound of clumping ski boots in winter and the violins, horns, and other instruments of the Grand Teton Music Festival in summer. Teton Village mostly consists of the restaurants, lodging properties, and shops built to serve the skiers who flock to Jackson Hole Mountain Resort. This is potentially the best ski resort area in the United States, and the expanse and variety of terrain are incredible. In summer, folks come here to hike, ride the tram, and attend high-caliber concerts.

As it travels to the summit of Rendezvous Peak, the **Aerial Tramway** affords spectacular panoramas of Jackson Hole. There are several hiking trails at the top of the mountain. Trams depart every 15 to 30 minutes. *⊠ Teton Village ☎ 307/733–2292 or 800/333–7766 $17 ⏲ Memorial Day–late Sept., daily 9–5 or 6.*

Sports & the Outdoors

GOLF The 18-hole **Teton Pines Golf Club** (⊠ 3450 N. Clubhouse St. ☎ 307/733–1733 🌐 www.tetonpines.com) lies south of the Jackson Hole Mountain Resort.

HIKING The plus here is that much of the uphill legwork can be dispensed with by the **Aerial Tramway** (⊠ Teton Village ☎ 307/733–2292 or 800/333–7766), the same one that carries Jackson Hole skiers upward in winter. From the top of Rendezvous Peak, you can walk through high-mountain basins filled with wildflowers in summer or along cliff-line ridges, all against the stunning backdrop of the Tetons. The weather and wildflowers are best between July and August.

A loop of about 30 mi can be made by picking up the Teton Crest Trail, then branching off on the Death Canyon Trail. Don't necessarily expect solitude; most of the time, you're in Grand Teton National Park, an exceedingly popular tourist destination. However, this route keeps you well away from the visitor crush at the park's main gate, so you aren't likely to encounter hiker traffic jams, either.

Downhill Skiing & Snowboarding

Fodor'sChoice ★ A place to appreciate both as a skier and as a voyeur, **Jackson Hole Mountain Resort** is truly one of the great skiing experiences in America. There are literally thousands of ways of getting from top to bottom, and not all of them are hellishly steep, despite Jackson's reputation. First-rate racers such as Olympic champion skier Tommy Moe and snowboarder Rob Kingwill regularly train here. As Kingwill has put it, "nothing really compares to Jackson Hole . . . This place has the most consistently steep terrain. You can spend years and years here and never cross your trail."

On the resort map, about 60 squiggly lines designate named trails, but this doesn't even begin to suggest the thousands of different skiable routes. The resort claims 2,500 skiable acres, a figure that seems unduly conservative. And although Jackson is best known for its advanced to extreme skiing, it is also a place where imaginative intermediates can go exploring and have the time of their lives. It is not, however, a good place for novice skiers.

A word of caution. High snowfall some winters can lead to extreme avalanche danger in spite of efforts by the Ski Patrol to make the area as safe as possible. Before venturing from known trails and routes, check with the Ski Patrol for conditions. Ski with a friend, and always carry an emergency locator device. ✉ *Box 290, Teton Village 83025* ☎ *307/733–2292 or 800/333–7766* 🌐 *www.jacksonhole.com.*

FACILITIES 4,139-foot vertical drop; 2,500 skiable acres; 10% beginner, 40% intermediate, 50% expert; 1 aerial tram, 1 gondola, 6 quad chairs, 1 triple chair, 1 double chair, 1 surface lift.

LESSONS & PROGRAMS Half-day group lessons at the **Jackson Hole Ski School** (☎ 307/733–2292 or 800/450–0477) start at $80 for skiing or snowboarding. There are extensive children's programs, including lessons for kids 6 to 13 years old and day care. Nordic-skiing lessons start at $45. For expert skiers, the **Wild West Adrenaline Camps** (☎ 307/739–2791 or 800/450–0477), headed by such expert skiers as Tommy Moe, the 1994 Olympic gold medalist, run for five days, teaching everything from big-mountain free-skiing to racing techniques. The cost is $600 per person. Snowboarders can get expert advice from champion snowboarder Rob Kingwill and other extreme champions during weeklong courses that cost $675 per person.

LIFT TICKETS Lift tickets cost $64. You can save about 10% on five- to seven-day tickets.

RENTALS Equipment can be rented at ski shops in Jackson and Teton Village. **Jackson Hole Sports** (☎ 307/733–4005 or 800/443–6931), at the Bridger Center at the ski area, offers ski and snowboard rental packages starting at $20 a day. You can buy or rent skis or snowboards at **Pepi Stegler Sports Shop** (☎ 307/733–3270 🌐 www.jackdennis.com), a branch of the Jackson-based Jack Dennis Sports. Ski rentals cost between $18 and $30; snowboard rentals are $25. The store is at the base of Rendezvous Peak.

HELI-SKIING In general, heli-skiing is best done when there has been relatively little recent snowfall. For two or three days after a storm, good powder skiing can usually be found within the ski area. Daily trips can be arranged through **High Mountain Helicopter Skiing** (✉ Near aerial tram ☎ 307/733–3274 🌐 www.heliskijackson.com).

Nordic Skiing

BACKCOUNTRY SKIING Few areas in North America can compete with Jackson Hole when it comes to the breadth, beauty, and variety of backcountry opportunities. For touring skiers, one of the easier areas (because of flatter routes) is along the base of the Tetons toward Jenny and Jackson lakes. Telemark skiers (or even skiers on alpine gear) can find numerous downhill routes by skiing in from Teton Pass, snow stability permitting. A guide isn't required for tours to the national-park lakes but might be helpful for those unfamiliar with the lay of the land; trails and trail markers set in summer can become obscured by winter snows. When you are touring elsewhere, a guide familiar with the area and avalanche danger is a virtual necessity. The Tetons are big country, and the risks are commensurately large as well.

Alpine Guides (☎ 307/739–2663) leads half-day and full-day backcountry tours into the national parks and other areas near the resort, for more downhill-minded skiers. Arrangements can also be made through the Jackson Hole Ski School. **Jackson Hole Mountain Guides** (✉ 165 N. Glenwood St., Jackson ☎ 307/733–4979 🌐 www.jhmg.com) leads strenuous backcountry tours. The **Jackson Hole Nordic Center** (☎ 307/733–2292 or 800/450–0477) at Teton Village has cross-country, telemark, and snowshoe rentals and track and telemark lessons. The center also leads naturalist tours into the backcountry. Rental packages begin at $20.

TRACK SKIING The **Jackson Hole Nordic Center** (☎ 307/739–2292 or 800/450–0477 🌐 www.jacksonhole.com) is at the ski-resort base. The scenic 17 km (10½ mi) of groomed track is relatively flat. Because the Nordic Center and the downhill ski area are under the same management, downhill skiers with multiday passes can switch over to Nordic skiing in the afternoon for no extra charge. Otherwise, the cost is $10 for a day pass. Rentals and lessons are available; alpine lift tickets are also good at the Nordic Center.

Where to Stay & Eat

In the winter ski season, it can be cheaper to stay in Jackson, about 20 minutes away; in summer it's generally cheaper to stay at Teton Village.

$$–$$$$ ✕ **Mangy Moose.** Folks pour in off the ski slopes for a lot of food and talk at this two-level restaurant with a bar and an outdoor deck. There's a high noise level but decent food of the steaks-and-burgers variety at fair prices. The place is adorned with antiques, including a full-size stuffed caribou and sleigh suspended from the ceiling. ✉ *3295 W. McCollister St.* ☎ *307/733–4913* 💳 *AE, MC, V.*

$$$–$$$$ 🏨 **Alpenhof Lodge.** This small Austrian-style hotel is in the heart of Jackson Hole Mountain Resort, next to the tram. Hand-carved Bavarian furniture fills the rooms. All of the deluxe rooms have balconies, and some have fireplaces and Jacuzzis. Standard rooms are smaller and don't have balconies. Entrées such as wild game loaf are served in the dining room, and Dietrich's Bar and Bistro is a relatively quiet nightclub that also offers casual dining. ✉ *3255 W. McCollister Dr., 83025* ☎ *307/733–3242 or 800/732–3244* 📠 *307/739–1516* 🌐 *www.alpenhoflodge.com* 🛏 *42 rooms* 🛎 *Dining room, pool, massage, spa, ski storage, bar, nightclub* 💳 *AE, D, DC, MC, V* ⊗ *Closed Oct., Nov., and mid-Apr.–May.*

$$$–$$$$ 🏨 **R Lazy S Ranch.** Jackson Hole, with the spectacle of the Tetons in the background, is true dude-ranch country, and the R Lazy S is one of the largest dude ranches in the area. Horseback riding and instruction are the primary activities, with a secondary emphasis on fishing, either in private waters on the ranch or at other rivers and streams. You stay in log-cabin guest cottages and gather for meals in the large main lodge. There's a one-week minimum stay. ✉ *1 mi north of Teton Village, Box 308, 83025* ☎ *307/733–2655* 🖷 *307/734–1120* 🌐 *www.rlazys.com* *14 cabins* *Dining room, fishing, horseback riding; no kids under 7* *No credit cards* *Closed Oct.–mid-June* *FAP.*

¢ **The Hostel.** Although the classic hostel accommodations at this lodge-style inn are basic, you can't get any closer to Jackson Hole Mountain Resort for a better price. It's popular with young, budget-conscious people. Rooms, some of which have bunk beds, sleep two to four people. Downstairs common areas include a lounge with a fireplace, a movie room, and a ski-waxing room. ✉ *3315 McCollister Dr., Box 546, 83025* ☎ *307/733–3415* 🖷 *307/739–1142* 🌐 *www.hostelx.com* *55 rooms* *Lounge, library, recreation room, laundry facilities, Internet; no room phones, no room TVs* *MC, V* *BP.*

The Arts

In summer the symphony orchestra performances of the **Grand Teton Music Festival** (Box 490, Teton Village, 83025 ☎ 307/733–1128 or 800/959–4863 🌐 www.gtmf.org) are held outside at Teton Village. A winter series takes place in Walk Festival Hall. Tickets cost between $16 and $75.

Shopping

At the **Mountainside Mall** (✉ Teton Village ☎ No phone), not to be mistaken for a big suburban mall (to its credit), you can find goggles, snowboards, skis, and clothing ranging from parkas to swimsuits.

Wilson

19 *6 mi south of Teton Village on Teton Village Rd., 4 mi west of Jackson on Hwy. 22.*

This small town takes its name from Nick Wilson, one of the first homesteaders in the area, a man who spent part of his childhood living with the Shoshone Indians. If you want to avoid the hustle and bustle of Jackson, Wilson makes a good alternative base for exploring Grand Teton National Park or skiing at Jackson Hole Mountain Resort.

Where to Stay & Eat

$$–$$$$ ✕ **Nora's Fish Creek Inn.** Among the items served at this casual log inn are honey-hickory baby-back ribs, prime rib, and nut-crusted trout. There's also a kids' menu. You can dine in one of two large rooms, or sit at the counter for quick service. Breakfast, but not lunch, is served weekends. ✉ *Hwy. 22* ☎ *307/733–8288* *AE, D, MC, V* *No lunch weekends.*

★ **$$** ✕ **Bar J Chuckwagon.** At the best bargain in the Jackson Hole area, you'll get a true ranch-style meal along with some of the best Western entertainment in the region. The food, served on a tin plate, includes barbecued roast beef, chicken, or rib-eye steak, plus potatoes, beans, biscuits, applesauce, spice cake, and ranch coffee or lemonade. The multitalented Bar J Wranglers sing, play instruments, share cowboy stories and poetry, and even yodel. "Lap-size" children eat free. ✉ *4200 Bar J Chuckwagon Rd.* ☎ *307/733–3370* *D, MC, V.*

$–$$ ✕ **Vista Grande.** You'll get a generous portion of Mexican fare here, but if you like a lot of heat and spice, you may find this food a bit bland. Favorites include blackened-chicken tostada salad, fresh-veggie burritos, and crab chimichangas. Service can be on the slow side, but gazing at the Tetons from the window or from the deck is a great way to pass the time. This is a popular place, so it can get crowded and noisy. ✉ *2550 Teton Village Rd., near Wilson turnoff* ☎ *307/733–6964* *Reservations not accepted* *MC, V.*

$$$$ **The Painted Porch Bed and Breakfast.** Cozy, clean, and comfortable, this traditional red-and-white farmhouse built in 1901 is nestled on 3½ acres of pine and aspen about midway between Jackson and Teton Village. The rooms, both with private entrances, blend Western-style furnishings, antiques, and designer linens. ✉ *3755 N. Moose-Wilson Rd., 83002* ☎ *307/733–1981* 📠 *307/733–1564* 🌐 *www.jacksonholebedandbreakfast.com* *2 rooms* *In-room hot tubs, library* *AE, D, MC, V* *BP.*

$$–$$$ **Teton Tree House.** On a steep hillside and surrounded by trees, this is a real retreat. Ninety-five steps lead to this cozy lodgepole-pine bed-and-breakfast tucked away in the forest. Decks abound, rooms are full of wood furniture and warm Southwestern colors, and an inviting common area has a two-story old-fashioned adobe fireplace. ✉ *6175 Heck of a Hill Rd., Box 550, 83014* ☎ *307/733–3233* 📠 *307/733–3233* *6 rooms* *Dining room, hot tub; no smoking* *D, MC, V* *BP.*

Nightlife

The **Stagecoach Bar** (✉ Hwy. 22, Wilson ☎ 307/733–4407) fills to bursting Sunday when the house band—a motley bunch that includes a novelist, the first man to ski down the Grand Teton, and a changing cast of guitar aces—is playing.

Shopping

Clothing, groceries, and camping supplies are available at **Hungry Jack's General Store** (✉ 5855 W. Hwy. 22 ☎ 307/733–3561), next to the post office in Wilson.

en route

The drive between Wilson and Alta over the **Teton Pass** on Highway 22 affords outstanding views of Idaho's Teton Valley, known as Pierre's Hole to the mountain men of the 1800s on the west and Jackson Hole on the east.

Alta

20 *27 mi northwest of Wilson via Hwy. 22 to Hwy. 33 (in Idaho) to Alta cutoff (back to Wyoming).*

Alta is the site of the Grand Targhee Ski and Summer Resort, famed for its deep powder and family atmosphere. The slopes never feel crowded, but to experience complete solitude, try a day of Sno-Cat skiing in untracked powder.

Sports & the Outdoors

An average of 500 inches of powder attracts skiers to **Grand Targhee Ski & Summer Resort** (✉ Ski Hill Rd. ☎ 307/353–2300 or 800/827–4433 🌐 www.grandtarghee.com), with 2,000 acres, 1,000 of which are dedicated to powder Sno-Cat skiing. There are four lifts and one rope tow, and the vertical drop is 2,200 feet. Classes are available.

Where to Stay & Eat

$$–$$$$ ✕ **Skadi's.** Southwestern-style decor, high ceilings, and good lighting create a relaxing and roomy dining room. On the menu are tenderloin beef with poblano-chili sauce and regional game dishes such as venison and pheasant. ✉ *Grand Targhee Ski and Summer Resort, Ski Hill Rd.* ☎ *307/353–2300 or 800/827–4433* *AE, D, MC, V.*

$$–$$$$ ✕ **Grand Targhee Ski and Summer Resort.** This small but modern facility perched on the west side of the Tetons has a handsome, natural-wood look and the atmosphere of an alpine village. The motel-style rooms are simply furnished and clustered around common areas with fireplaces; the condominium rooms are brighter and more spacious. Skadi's is the resort's foremost restaurant; the Cactus Kitchen serves quicker, less ex-

pensive food. ✉ *Ski Hill Rd., Box SKI, 83422* ☎ *307/353–2300 or 800/827–4433* 🌐 *www.grandtarghee.com* *65 rooms, 32 condos* *5 restaurants, pool, hot tub, outdoor hot tub, cross-country skiing, downhill skiing, airport shuttle* *AE, D, MC, V.*

THE WIND RIVER RANGE

Rising to the east and southeast of Jackson Hole is the Wind River range, an area that remains snowcapped year-round because there are still small glaciers here. Much of this range is rugged wilderness, ideal for backcountry hiking and horseback riding. Several towns here make good bases for exploring the area, including Pinedale on the west side of the range; Atlantic City, within the range itself; and Lander, Fort Washakie, and Dubois on the east side of the range.

Pinedale

21 *77 mi southeast of Jackson on Hwy. 191.*

Fur trappers found the icy streams of the Green River watershed to be among the best places to capture beaver. They gathered on the river near what is now Pinedale for seven rendezvous during the mid-1800s, and modern-day buckskinners continue to meet in the area each summer. Pinedale is a southern gateway to Jackson Hole, but has much to offer on its own. To the east are millions of acres of Bridger-Teton National Forest, much of it off-limits to all but foot and horse traffic. The peaks reach higher than 13,000 feet, and the area is liberally sprinkled with more than a thousand high-mountain lakes where fishing is generally excellent. Contact the **Bridger-Teton National Forest, Pinedale Ranger District** (✉ 29 E. Fremont Lake Rd., Box 220, 82941 ☎ 307/367–4326 🌐 www.fs.fed.us/btnf) for more information.

Buckskinners and reenactors gather in Pinedale annually during the second weekend of July for the **Green River Rendezvous** (☎ 307/367–4101 🌐 www.pinedaleonline.com), which commemorates the get-togethers the fur trappers and traders staged between 1825 and 1843 (seven of which were in what is now Pinedale). Highlights include a parade, crafts, booths, and a historical pageant.

★ The **Museum of the Mountain Man** depicts the trapper heritage of the area with displays of 19th-century guns, traps, clothing, and beaver pelts. There's also an exhibit devoted to the pioneer and ranch history of Sublette County. In summer the museum hosts living-history demonstrations, children's events, and lectures. ✉ *700 E. Hennick Rd.* ☎ *307/367–4101* 🌐 *www.museumofthemountainman.com* *$4* *May–Sept., daily 10–5; call for winter hrs.*

Sports & the Outdoors

Encompassing parts of the Wind River range, the **Bridger-Teton National Forest, Pinedale Ranger District** (✉ Forest office, 29 E. Femont Lake Rd. ☎ 307/367–4326 🌐 www.fs.fed.us/btnf) holds hundreds of thousands of acres to explore. The fishing is generally excellent in the numerous mountain lakes, and you can also hike, snowmobile, camp, and picnic here.

Where to Stay & Eat

$$–$$$$ ✕ **Stockmen's Restaurant.** The salad bar is shaped like a tepee, and there's a 1903 map of the area at this restaurant, a local hangout since 1933. On the menu are burgers, salads, prime rib, steaks, and seafood. Smoking is allowed, so it can get hazy at times. ✉ *117 W. Pine St.* ☎ *307/367–4562 or 307/367–4563* *MC, V.*

LET'S RENDEZVOUS

I **N 1825, ANDREW HENRY MET** *and traded with beaver trappers on the Black Fork of the Green River in what came to be known as the first mountain-man rendezvous. For the next 18 years, trappers and traders, along with Native Americans and even a few missionaries, gathered annually to trade goods. The trappers sold or exchanged the furs they'd harvested during the previous winter for goods the traders provided, such as weapons, ammunition, food, clothing, and other supplies they would need for another year of trapping beaver.*

Although the first rendezvous was a quiet affair and simply an opportunity to exchange beaver pelts (called "plews") for supplies, subsequent gatherings were often raucous events, with a lot of whiskey. The rendezvous could last anywhere from a few days to several weeks. At least seven rendezvous took place on the Upper Green River near present-day Pinedale. Two others took place on the Wind River near present-day Riverton, and one small rendezvous convened near present-day Encampment, on "Potter's Fork," a stream that came to be known as the Grand Encampment River.

The fur trade petered out by 1843 because many streams had been nearly emptied of beaver, and beaver hats had gone out of style, but the era of the mountain man has not been forgotten. Each summer, present-day buckskinners load up their tepees, put on their skins, and take their black-powder guns to a rendezvous held at or near some of the historic sites: Pinedale, Riverton, Encampment, and Fort Bridger. There they have shooting contests, take part in throwing competitions with axes and frying pans, and barter with traders for skins, beads, pots, and kettles.

$–$$$ ✕ **McGregors Pub.** Built in 1905, this converted hotel has a classic Western interior with a restaurant on the ground floor. Local folks like the steaks and seafood; the menu also has Italian dishes, and there's a kids' menu. You can eat inside or outside on the patio. ✉ *21 N. Franklin St.* ☎ *307/367–4443* ▭ *AE, D, DC, MC, V.*

$–$$$ ✕ **Moose Creek Trading Company.** As the name suggests, this downtown restaurant employs a moose motif, reflected, for example, in the wrought-iron bar tables with carvings of the animal. The menu includes various sandwiches, plus homemade pies and desserts. Try the chunky chicken salad for a light summer meal. ✉ *44 W. Pine St.* ☎ *307/367–4616* ▭ *AE, D, DC, MC, V* ⊙ *No dinner.*

$–$$ **The Lodge at Pinedale.** This three-story motel is across a parking lot from the town's movie theater and bowling alley. Green carpeting and bed coverings decorate the rooms. ✉ *1054 W. Pine St., 82941* ☎ *307/367–8800 or 866/995–6343* 🖷 *307/367–8812* 🌐 *www.pinedalelodge.com* *41 rooms, 2 suites* *In-room data ports, microwaves, refrigerators, cable TV, indoor pool, hot tub, no-smoking rooms, some pets allowed (fee)* ▭ *AE, D, DC, MC, V* *CP.*

$ **Best Western Pinedale Inn.** On the north side of town, this hotel is within three blocks of downtown shopping and restaurants. The rooms aren't large, but they have contemporary furniture. ✉ *850 W. Pine St., 82941* ☎ *307/367–6869* 🖷 *307/367–6897* 🌐 *www.bestwestern.com* *58 rooms* *Some refrigerators, cable TV, indoor pool, exercise equipment, hot tub, some pets allowed, no-smoking rooms* ▭ *AE, D, DC, MC, V* *CP.*

$ **Chambers House B&B.** Huge pine trees surround this 1933 log home filled with the owner's family antiques. Downstairs there's a sitting room where you can relax with a book or chat with other guests. The master bedroom, with a fireplace, private bathroom, and private entrance, is also on the ground floor. Three of the upstairs bedrooms share bathroom facilities; a fourth has a private bathroom and a fireplace. ✉ *111 W. Magnolia St., 82941* ☎ *307/367–2168 or 800/367–2168* 🌐 *www.chambershouse.com* *5 rooms, 2 with bath* *Dining room, some pets allowed (fee); no phones in some rooms, no TVs in some rooms, no smoking* *AE, D, DC, MC, V* *BP.*

The Arts

The annual **Blues Festival** (✉ Rendezvous Rodeo Grounds ☎ 307/367–2448 🌐 www.pinedaleblues.com), highlighting blues and bluegrass, takes place the third weekend in June.

Photographs by Dan Abernathy, plus watercolors and sculpture, are on display and for sale at **Rock Rabbit Gallery** (✉ 36 W. Pine St. ☎ 307/367–2448).

Shopping

The Cowboy Shop (✉ 129 W. Pine St. ☎ 877/567–6336) stocks Western and cowpoke clothing for all ages, including hats and boots, and also sells leather goods and regional books.

en route

As you drive south of Pinedale along U.S. 191, the mountains of the Wind River range will seem to fade down to a low point. This is **South Pass,** the area through which some 500,000 emigrants traveled over the Oregon, Mormon, and California trails between 1843 and 1870.

Atlantic City

22 *36 mi south of Pinedale via U.S. 191 to Farson, then 25 mi east on Hwy. 28.*

This town was formed in 1868 when gold rushers flocked to the area seeking their fortune. Known for its red-light district, Atlantic City was the site of Wyoming Territory's first brewery. Once the gold boom had petered out less than a decade later, however, residents deserted the town. Atlantic City had a few more smaller booms over the years, but it's now a near–ghost town, with only a few residents, a couple of tourist-oriented businesses, dirt streets, late-19th-century buildings, and a whole lot of atmosphere.

South Pass City, 2 mi west of Atlantic City, was established with the discovery of gold in the region in 1867, and in its heyday it had around 1,000 residents. The town went bust in the 1870s, and the ghost town ★ that remained is now the **South Pass City State Historic Site.** You can tour many of the original buildings that survive and have been restored, and you can even try your hand at gold panning. With artifacts and photographs of the town at its peak, the small museum here gives an overview of the South Pass gold district.

South Pass City has another claim to fame. Julia Bright and Esther Hobart Morris are two of the women from the community who firmly believed that women should have the right to vote. It is suspected that they encouraged Bright's husband, Representative William Bright, to introduce a bill for women's suffrage in the Wyoming Territorial Legislature. He did so, the bill was ratified, and South Pass went down in history as the birthplace of women's suffrage in Wyoming. In 1870 Morris became the first female justice of the peace in the nation, serving South Pass City. ✉ *South Pass City Rd., off Hwy. 28, South Pass* ☎ *307/332–3684* 🌐 *wyoparks.state.wy.us/south1.htm* *$2* *Mid-May–early Sept., daily 9–5:30.*

WYOMING & WOMEN'S RIGHTS

Women's rights might not be the first subject that comes to mind when considering the Old West, but Wyoming was a pioneer on this political frontier. In 1869, Wyoming Territory enacted a law granting women the right to vote, to serve on juries, and to hold office, making it the first territory to grant women such broad political rights. The following year, 70-year-old Louisa "Grandma" Swain cast the first women's ballot in Laramie. Wyoming was not the first place in the United States to allow women to vote—Utah Territory holds that honor—but in many respects it was a leader in women's rights: It was where the first all-female jury heard a case (in Laramie) and the first female justice of the peace was appointed (Esther Hobart Morris, at South Pass City in February 1870). In 1920 an all-female town council, believed to be the first of its kind in the country, served in Jackson.

Where to Stay & Eat

$$–$$$ ✕ **Atlantic City Mercantile.** One of the town's oldest saloons, known as the Merc, serves refreshment in a room that has seen its share of gold miners, perhaps an outlaw or two, and certainly some ruffians. When you step through the doors of this 1893 building with tin ceilings, a massive back bar, and an assortment of mismatched oak tables and chairs, you may feel as though you've walked directly into an episode of *Gunsmoke*. At times a honky-tonk piano player is on hand. The menu includes steak, chicken, and seafood, plus sandwiches. If you're here on the fourth Wednesday of the month, from November through May, try the seven-course Basque dinner. ✉ *100 E. Main St.* ☎ *307/332–5143* ▭ *D, MC, V.*

¢–$ **Miner's Delight B & B.** Rooms in the lodge, which was built in 1895 as the town's hotel, are larger and have private bathrooms, but if you want to do things the way gold miners did in the boom of the late 1860s, stay in the simple, authentic, rustic cabins. Each one has a small washstand with a bowl and a pitcher of water, and there are patchwork curtains and bedcoverings. It's a short walk to the bathroom in the main lodge. ✉ *290 Atlantic City Rd., 82520* ☎ *307/332–0248 or 888/292–0248* 🌐 *www.holidayjunction.com/usa/wy/cwy0051.html* *3 lodge rooms; 5 cabins without bath* *Dining room, picnic area, no-smoking rooms; no a/c, no room phones, no room TVs* ▭ *MC, V* *BP.*

Shopping

South Pass Trading Company (✉ 50 South Pass Main ☎ 307/332–6810) sells Wyoming-made products ranging from vintage clothing to books by local and regional authors.

Lander

23 *28 mi northeast of Atlantic City via Hwy. 28.*

At the southwestern edge of the Wind River Indian Reservation and in the heart of country held dear by Chief Washakie (circa 1804–1900), one of the greatest chiefs of the Shoshone tribe, and his people, Lander has always had a strong tie to the Native American community. East of the Wind River range, Lander makes a good base for pursuing mountain sports and activities ranging from backcountry hiking to horse-packing trips.

At **Sinks Canyon State Park,** a rushing river—the Popo Agie (pronounced pa-*po*-sha)—flows into a limestone cavern, known as the Sinks, only to resurface ¼ mi downstream. In the Rise, where the water reemerges, huge fish swim in the still pool. Rocky Mountain bighorn sheep and other wildlife wander the grounds of this park 8 mi south of Lander. The park is ideal for hiking, camping, and picnicking. ✉ *8 mi south of Lander on Hwy. 131* ☎ *307/332–6333* 🌐 *wyoparks.state.wy.us/sinks1/htm* *Park free, camping $4* ⏲ *Park daily 24 hrs; visitor center Memorial Day–Labor Day, daily 9–7.*

Sports & the Outdoors

You can learn all aspects of mountaineering, from low-impact camping and hiking to horseback riding on pack trips, by taking a course from the **National Outdoor Leadership School** (✉ 284 Lincoln St. ☎ 307/332–6973 🌐 www.nols.edu).

FISHING There's great fishing on the Wind River Indian Reservation, but you must first obtain a tribal license; contact **Shoshone and Arapaho Tribes** (✉ Fish and Game Dept., 1 Washakie, Fort Washakie 82520 ☎ 307/332–7207) for more information.

Kayak, Fishing & Scenic Tours (✉ 466 Cascade St. ☎ 307/332–0305) leads guided fishing trips to area waters.

HORSEBACK RIDING **Allen's Diamond Four Ranch** (✉ Off U.S. 287, 35 mi northwest of Lander ☎ 307/332–2995) arranges mountain horse-packing trips and other horseback excursions. Some trips originate at the ranch, where you stay in cabins and take day rides; others are overnight backcountry adventures. Children must be seven or eight years old to go on extended pack trips. Also available are drop-camp services. Ride the Oregon Trail, take pack trips into the high country, or participate in an "outlaw ride" with **Rocky Mountain Horseback Adventures** (☎ 307/332–8535 or 800/408–9149).

Where to Stay & Eat

$$$–$$$$ Fodor'sChoice ★ ✕ **Svilars.** Inside this small, dark, family-owned restaurant, you'll find what many locals say is the best food in all of Wyoming. It's rivaled only by the Club El Toro steak house across the street. A meal here usually begins with *sarma* (cabbage rolls) and other appetizers. Your server will then place before you one of the biggest, if not *the* biggest, and best steaks you've likely ever seen. ✉ *175 S. Main St., Hudson, 10 mi east of Lander* ☎ *307/332–4516* ▭ *No credit cards* ⏲ *Closed Sun. and alternate Mon. No lunch.*

★ $$–$$$$ ✕ **Club El Toro.** This is one of Wyoming's best steak houses, right across the street from its rival in prestige, Svilars. People drive many miles to partake of Club El Toro's huge portions of steak and prime rib. The meat is always fresh, juicy, and tender, and with each meal you get a salad and appetizers. The family-owned restaurant also serves seafood, but most people come for the steaks. ✉ *132 S. Main St., Hudson, 10 mi east of Lander* ☎ *307/332–4627* ▭ *MC, V.*

¢–$$ ✕ **Gannett Grill.** This crowded, noisy place serves large sandwiches and hand-tossed New York–style pizzas. ✉ *148 Main St.* ☎ *307/332–8228* ▭ *D, MC, V.*

¢–$$ ✕ **Judd's Grubb.** The best Judd's has to offer is a Wimpy burger, but don't let the name fool you: the patty weighs in at a half pound, so come here with a big appetite. Also on the menu are beer-batter fries, buffalo burgers, and Mexican dishes such as enchiladas and tacos. ✉ *634 W. Main St.* ☎ *307/332–9680* ▭ *D, MC, V.*

$ **Best Western Inn at Lander.** This cabin-style motel sits on the hill overlooking Lander. The small outdoor area has picnic tables. ✉ *260 Grand-*

view Dr., 82520 ☎ 307/332–2847 📠 307/332–2760 🌐 www.bestwestern.com ⇨ 46 rooms ♨ Some refrigerators, cable TV, pool, hot tub, meeting room ▭ AE, D, MC, V 🍴 CP.

$ **Blue Spruce Inn.** Highlights of this 1920 home named for five enormous spruce trees on the property include a front porch with a swing, interior design from the Arts and Crafts period, hardwood floors, and beautiful gardens. The sunporch is a nice spot to curl up with a book and a cup of tea. The guest rooms are on the second floor, accessible only by a staircase. *✉ 677 S. 3rd St., 82520 ☎ 307/332–8253 or 888/503–3311 📠 307/332–1386 🌐 www.bluespruceinn.com ⇨ 4 rooms ♨ Dining room, library; no TV in some rooms, no smoking ▭ AE, D, MC, V 🍴 BP.*

CAMPING **Sleeping Bear Ranch.** There's a re-created Old West town at this RV park and campground that sits beside the Little Popo Agie River. There are lots of amenities here, including a restaurant, shops, and horseshoes, and you can take a hayride or swim in the river. *♨ Flush toilets, full hookups, drinking water, guest laundry, showers, grills, picnic tables, general store, play area, swimming (river) ⇨ 65 full hookups, 20 tent sites ✉ U.S. 287, 9 mi southeast of Lander, 1 mi south of junction with Hwy. 28 ☎ 307/332–3836 or 800/914–9226 Full hookups $22, tent sites $18 ▭ D, MC, V.*

Sleeping Bear RV Park. Next to a golf course, this campground and RV park has lots of grass and shade trees. You can join in various activities here, including basketball, horseshoes, and volleyball, and there's often evening entertainment in the form of campfires and storytelling. *♨ Flush toilets, full hookups, partial hookups (electric and water), drinking water, showers, fire grates, grills, picnic tables, public telephone, general store, play area ⇨ 21 full hookups, 20 partial hookups, 6 tent sites ✉ 715 E. Main St. ☎ 307/332–5159 or 888/757–2327 🌐 www.sleeping-rv-park.com Full hookups $26, partial hookups $22.50, tent sites $15.95 ▭ D, MC, V.*

Nightlife & the Arts

NIGHTLIFE On weekends the **Lander Bar** (✉ 146 Main St. ☎ 307/332–8228) gets crowded with people who come to dance and listen to live country bands.

THE ARTS Dixieland bands converge on Lander for the **Lander Jazz Festival** (✉ Lander Community Center ☎ 800/433–0662 🌐 www.landerjazz.com), with performances taking place over Labor Day weekend. June through August the **Native American Cultural Program** (☎ 307/856–7566 or 800/433–0662) has storytelling and Native American dancing at Jaycee Park each Monday evening. Native American traditional dancing is part of the **Yellow Calf Memorial Powwow** (☎ 307/856–7566 or 800/433–0662), held in late May (often over Memorial Day weekend) in Ethete, about 15 mi north of Lander.

Shopping

The shelves at **The Booke Shoppe** (✉ 160 N. 2nd St. ☎ 307/332–6221 or 800/706–4476) are lined with regional-history books and works by Wyoming authors. You can also buy cards and journals here. Antiques and one-of-a-kind treasures are sold at **Charlotte's Web** (✉ 228 Main St. ☎ 307/332–5989).

Distinctive, flamboyant women's clothing and unique jewelry are available at **Whippy Bird** (✉ 306 Main St. ☎ 307/332–3444), in an old mercantile store. Everything is for the birds at **Wild Bird Marketplace** (✉ 645 Main St. ☎ 307/332–7600), including bird feeders, birdbaths, gift items (with birds on them), and field guides.

Fort Washakie

24 *15 mi north of Lander via U.S. 287.*

This town named for Chief Washakie is the headquarters for the Eastern Shoshone tribe on the Wind River Indian Reservation. Fort Washakie was established in 1871, and some of the buildings here date to the town's early days.

A parade, rodeo, and buffalo barbecue are part of **Shoshone Indian Days** (☎ 307/856–7566 or 800/433–0662), held in mid-June.

The **Shoshone Tribal Cultural Center** examines Shoshone history, important treaties, and the development of the Wind River Indian Reservation. Tours of Fort Washakie are available; they last from one to four hours (the longer tours include visits to the Washakie and Sacajawea cemeteries). Some tours include a traditional Native American meal with such highlights as stew and fry bread, Indian tacos, and traditional berry pudding. ✉ *90 Ethete Rd.* ☎ *307/332–9106 or 307/332–3177* *Center free, tours $30–$150* ⏲ *Weekdays 8–4:45; call ahead for tour times and reservations.*

The small, private **Gallery of the Wind and Museum** displays 19th-century Native American tools, weapons, drums and musical instruments, and clothing, including headdresses and moccasins. Most of the items were gathered from the Wind River Indian Reservation. You can also purchase Native American crafts here. ✉ *U.S. 287, ½ mi south of Fort Washakie* ☎ *307/332–3267 or 307/332–4231* *Free* ⏲ *May–Sept., daily 8–7; Oct–Apr., daily 9–6.*

Beadwork, crafts, and clothing made by Arapaho tribal members from the mid-19th century through contemporary times make up the bulk of the **Arapaho Cultural Museum and Heritage Center** collection. ✉ *Off Hwy. 137, St. Stephens, 5 mi east of Fort Washakie* ☎ *307/332–3040* *Donations accepted* ⏲ *Weekdays 1–5, Sat. 1–4.*

Shopping

★ Don't let the metal exterior of **Ancient Ways Indian Arts and Tanning** (✉ U.S. 287, 1 mi south of Fort Washakie ☎ 307/332–6001) fool you. This store sells the highest-quality products made by Native Americans, including flutes, moccasins, cradle boards (used by mothers to carry babies on their backs while they worked), jewelry, and tanned hides. From squash-blossom necklaces made by Southwestern tribes to Pendleton blankets and beaded moccasins made by the Shoshone and Arapaho, you can choose any variety of Native American–crafted items at **Gallery of the Wind and Museum** (✉ U.S. 287, ½ mi south of Fort Washakie ☎ 307/332–3267 or 307/332–4231).

Dubois

25 *56 mi northwest of Fort Washakie via U.S. 287 and U.S. 26; 86 mi east of Jackson via U.S. 26 and U.S. 287.*

The mountains around Dubois attracted explorers as early as 1811, when members of the Wilson Price Hunt party crossed through the region en route to Fort Astoria in Oregon. These high peaks still attract folks who like to hike, climb, ride horses, camp, and experience wilderness. The largest herd of free-ranging bighorn sheep in the country lives here, roaming the high country in summer and wintering just above town on Whiskey Mountain.

South and east of Grand Teton and Yellowstone, Dubois is the least well known of the gateway communities to the parks, but this town of 1,000 provides all the services a visitor in Jackson or Cody might need. You can still get a room during the peak summer season without making a reservation months in advance, although it is a good idea to call a week or so before you arrive.

Displays at the **Wind River Historical Center** focus on Wind River tie hacks (individuals who cut ties for railroads), local geology, and the archaeology of the Mountain Shoshone. Outbuildings include the town's first schoolhouse, a saddle shop, a homestead house, and a bunkhouse. The center also offers Elderhostel programs for senior citizens. With advance notice you can examine the historical-photograph collection, oral-history tapes, and library. ✉ *909 W. Ramshorn Ave.* ☎ *307/455–2284* 🌐 *www.windriverhistory.org* 🎫 *$1* 🕒 *June–Sept., daily 9–5.*

★ You can learn about bighorn sheep, including Rocky Mountain bighorn, at the **National Bighorn Sheep Interpretive Center** on the north side of Dubois. Among the mounted specimens here are the "super slam," with one of each type of wild sheep in the world, and two bighorn rams fighting during the rut. Hands-on exhibits illustrate a bighorn's body language, characteristics, and habitat. Winter tours (reserve ahead) to Whiskey Mountain provide an opportunity to see the wild sheep in its natural habitat; reservations are required. ✉ *907 Ramshorn Ave.* ☎ *307/455–3429 or 888/209–2795* 🌐 *www.bighorn.org* 🎫 *$2, Whiskey Mountain tours $20* 🕒 *Memorial Day–Labor Day, daily 9–8; Labor Day–Memorial Day, daily (hrs subject to change); wildlife-viewing tours mid-Nov.–Mar., daily at 9.*

off the beaten path

BROOKS LAKE – About 20 mi west of Dubois, Brooks Lake has served tourists headed to Yellowstone since 1922 with a lodge and forest campground to support the access to hiking trails in the area of Brooks Lake Mountain and the Pinnacles. The trails lead around the lake, across alpine meadows, and through pine forest to high mountain points with expansive views. You can picnic here, and boat, fish, or swim on the lake. ✉ *20 mi west of Dubois on U.S. 26/287, then 7 mi northeast on gravel road to Brooks Lake Recreation Area.*

Sports & the Outdoors

CROSS-COUNTRY SKIING

Among the best places for cross-country skiing is **Togwotee Pass,** east of Jackson and north of Dubois on U.S. 26/287, in Bridger-Teton and Shoshone national forests.

MOUNTAIN CLIMBING

Much of the appeal of the Wind River range, which you can access from the west near Pinedale, or the east near Lander and Dubois, is the (relatively difficult) access to major peaks, the most significant of which is Gannett Peak, at 13,804 feet the highest mountain in Wyoming. The trip to the base of Gannett Peak can take two days, with considerable ups and downs and stream crossings that can be dangerous in late spring and early summer. The reward for such effort, however, is seclusion: climbing Gannett Peak might not be as dramatic as climbing the Grand Teton to the west, but you won't have to face the national-park crowds at the beginning or end of the climb. Wind River is a world of granite and glaciers, the latter (though small) being among the last active glaciers in the U.S. Rockies. Other worthy climbs in the Wind River range are Gannett's neighbors Mount Sacajawea and Fremont Peak. **Jackson Hole Mountain Guides** (✉ 165 N. Glenwood St., Jackson ☎ 307/733–4979 🌐 www.jhmg.com) leads trips in the area.

Where to Stay & Eat

$$–$$$ ✕ **Rustic Pine Steakhouse.** The bar here is one of Wyoming's more memorable spots, where locals and visitors congregate to share news about hunting or hiking. The adjoining steak house serves mouthwatering steak and seafood in quiet surroundings. Get your greens in at the salad bar. ☒ *123 Ramshorn Ave.* ☎ *307/455–2772* ▭ *MC, V* ⊗ *No lunch.*

$–$$ ✕ **Cowboy Cafe.** Among the homemade dishes served at this small restaurant in downtown Dubois are sandwiches, steaks, buffalo burgers, chicken, pork, and fish. ☒ *115 Ramshorn Ave.* ☎ *307/455–2595* ▭ *MC, V.*

¢–$ ✕ **Ramshorn Bagel and Deli.** This deli serves breakfast and lunch, including bagels, soup, and sandwiches. ☒ *202 E. Ramshorn Ave.* ☎ *307/455–2400* ▭ *No credit cards* ⊗ *No dinner.*

★ $$$$ **Brooks Lake Lodge.** This mountain lodge on Brooks Lake gives you scenery with service and amenities. The lodge, originally built in 1922, has massive open beam ceilings with lots of space, subtle lighting, and log, leather, and wicker furnishings. Each of the lodge bedrooms and cabins has handcrafted lodgepole-pine furniture. Take a guided hike, go horseback riding, or fly-fish or canoe on the lake in summer. In the winter you can take dogsled or snowmobile rides with outfitters. ☒ *458 Brooks Lake Rd., 20 mi west of Dubois, 82513* ☎ *307/455–2121* 🖷 *307/455–2121* ⊕ *www.brookslake.com* *6 rooms, 6 cabins* *Restaurant, lake, outdoor hot tub, spa, fishing, hiking, horseback riding, cross-country skiing, snowmobiling, tobogganing, bar* ▭ *AE, MC, V* *FAP.*

$$$ **Absaroka Ranch.** Traditional guest-ranch activities at this mountain-surrounded property include horseback riding, hiking, fishing, and relaxing. Five Mile Creek runs right through the property, which is 16 mi west of Dubois. There are special programs for children, and you can take an overnight pack trip deep into mountain country. The ranch takes weeklong bookings only. ☒ *Off U.S. 26/287, Box 929, 82513* ☎ *307/455–2275* 🖷 *307/455–2275* ⊕ *www.dteworld.com/absaroka* *4 cabins* *Dining room, fishing, hiking, horseback riding, recreation room, children's programs (ages 8–12); no smoking* ▭ *No credit cards* ⊗ *Closed mid-Sept.–mid-June* *FAP.*

$$$ **T Cross Ranch.** At this traditional guest ranch in an isolated valley 15 mi north of Dubois, the cozy cabins have porches with rocking chairs, fireplaces or woodstoves, and handmade log furniture. You can snuggle under a down quilt or spend your days riding horses. Hosts Ken and Garey Neal have been in the guest-ranch business for decades, and they know how to match people to horses. Only weeklong stays are available. ☒ *15 mi north of Dubois off Horse Creek Rd., Box 638 KRW, 82513* ☎ *307/455–2206* 🖷 *307/455–2720* ⊕ *www.ranchweb.com/tcross* *8 cabins* *Dining room, hot tub, fishing, hiking, horseback riding, library, recreation room, children's programs (ages 6 and up), playground, no-smoking rooms* ▭ *No credit cards* ⊗ *Closed mid-Sept.–mid-June.*

$ **Black Bear Country Inn.** The Wind River runs behind this redwood cabin-style motel, which has basic rooms with outdoor patios with tables. There's also a large seven-person apartment with a full kitchen. ☒ *505 W. Ramshorn Ave., 82513* ☎ *307/455–2344 or 800/873–2327* 🖷 *307/455–2626* ⊕ *www.blackbearcountryinn.com* *16 rooms, 1 apartment* *Cable TV, kitchenettes.*

¢–$ **Stagecoach Motor Inn.** This locally owned downtown motel has a large backyard with a picnic area and playground equipment, and there's even a reproduction stagecoach for kids to climb on. But the play area is bordered by Pretty Horse Creek, so young children need some supervision. Some rooms have full kitchens; others have refrigerators. ☒ *103 E.*

Ramshorn Ave., 82513 ☎ 307/455–2303 or 800/455–5090 🖷 307/455–3903 🌐 www.stagecoachmotel-dubois.com 42 rooms, 6 suites Picnic area, cable TV, some kitchens, some refrigerators, pool, hot tub, fishing, basketball, horseshoes, playground, laundry facilities, airport shuttle, some pets allowed, no-smoking rooms ▭ AE, D, MC, V.

Shopping

From leather couches to handmade lamps and wall hangings, you can furnish your home with the Western-style items sold at **Absaroka Western Designs** (✉ 1416 Warm Springs Dr. ☎ 307/455–2440).

2

en route

The drive from Dubois or Lander to Thermopolis takes you through **Wind River canyon** (✉ U.S. 20 between Shoshoni and Thermopolis), where you'll see geologic features that have been millions of years in the making and where canyon walls reach 2,500 feet toward the sky. At the southeast edge of the canyon is **Boysen State Park** (✉ 15 Ash Boysen Rd. ☎ 307/876–2796 🌐 wyoparks.state.wy.us/boysen1.htm) and the Boysen Reservoir, where you can boat or fish. Just before you reach Thermopolis the Wind River becomes the Bighorn River at a site known as the Wedding of the Waters.

THE BIGHORN BASIN

Flanked by the Absaroka and Owl mountains to the west and the Bighorns to the east, this broad basin is also defined by its rivers. The Bighorn River flows north along the eastern edge of the basin and up into Montana. Here, straddling the two states, is Bighorn Canyon National Recreation Area; most of the recreation area lies in Montana, but the southern portion is easily accessible via Highway 37 in Wyoming. The Shoshone and Clarks Fork rivers cut through the northwestern portion of the basin. The town of Cody, a base for exploring Yellowstone National Park but also a destination in its own right, also lies in the northwest corner of the Bighorn Basin.

Thermopolis

26 *133 mi east of Dubois via U.S. 26/287 to Shoshoni, then north on U.S. 20.*

The hot mineral springs and surrounding land in this area were considered neutral territory by Native Americans—particularly the Shoshone, who ceded the ground to the U.S. government in 1896 as a "gift of the waters." They gave the land with the stipulation that the springs should remain available for the free use of all people, which is still the case at the state bathhouse but not at the now-private pools.

The land that is now **Hot Springs State Park** was considered sacred ground by Native Americans because of its healing waters. You can partake of these waters by soaking indoors or outside at the free hot mineral pools at the Wyoming State Bath House. **Star Plunge** is a commercial facility within the park with indoor and outdoor hot mineral pools, soak tubs, and a water slide. You can hike or bike on the trails within the park, and you may even spot a bison herd. *✉ U.S. 20 ☎ 307/364–2176 or 307/864–3765 🌐 wyoparks.state.wy.us/hot.htm Park and state bathhouse free, Star Plunge $8 Park daily 24 hrs; state bathhouse Mon.–Sat. 8–5:30, Sun. noon–5:30; Star Plunge daily 9–9.*

Among the dinosaur remains displayed at the **Wyoming Dinosaur Center** is "Stan," the second-largest and most complete Tyrannosaurus rex in the world. Kids can try their hand at paleontology by digging in the dinosaur quarry; regular digs are scheduled for children ages 8–13 and 13–17. ✉ *110 Carter Ranch Rd.* ☎ *307/864–2997* 🌐 *www.wyodino.org* 🎟 *$6, dig tours $18* ⏲ *Mid-May–mid-Sept., daily 8–8; mid-Sept.–mid-May, daily 10–4. Dig tours daily 10–4, weather permitting.*

Sports & the Outdoors

GOLF **Legion Town & Country Club** (✉ 145 Airport Rd. ☎ 307/864–5294) has a 9-hole course with views of Hot Springs State Park and the Wind River canyon.

RAFTING **Wind River Canyon Whitewater** (✉ 210 Hwy. 20 S ☎ 307/864–9343 or 888/246–9343) leads white-water floats down the Wind River. Trips range from a couple of hours to full-day trips that include lunch. Scenic floats and fishing trips are also available.

Where to Stay & Eat

$–$$ Fodor'sChoice ★ **Holiday Inn of the Waters.** The rooms are standard at this hotel within Hot Springs State Park, but the extra amenities—including a hot mineral swimming pool, a large hot mineral soaking pool, and a health club—and the hotel's proximity to the commercial mineral swimming pools set it apart. There's also a nearby jogging trail, and winter lodging-meal-activity packages are available. A collection of game animals from around the world decorates the Safari Dining Room ($$–$$$$), which serves bison raised on the nearby Red Canyon Ranch, prime rib, and steaks. ✉ *Hot Springs State Park, 115 E. Park St., 82443* ☎ *307/864–3131* 🖷 *307/864–3131* 🌐 *www.holidayinnthermopolis.com/* *80 rooms* *Restaurant, room service, in-room data ports, pool, health club, outdoor hot tub, massage, sauna, spa, steam room, hiking, bar, laundry service, some pets allowed, no-smoking rooms* 💳 *AE, D, DC, MC, V.*

Cody

27 *84 mi northwest of Thermopolis via Hwy. 120; 52 mi east of Yellowstone via U.S. 14/16/20.*

Cody, founded in 1896 and named for Pony Express rider, army scout, and entertainer William F. "Buffalo Bill" Cody, is the eastern gateway community to Yellowstone National Park. The North Fork Highway, as the route leading east to Yellowstone is locally known, traverses a spectacular region, following the North Fork of the Shoshone River and offering views of amazing rock formations. Cody is also within easy reach of Shoshone National Forest, the Absaroka Range, the Washakie Wilderness, and the Buffalo Bill Reservoir.

But Cody is much more than a base for exploring the surrounding area. It's the site of several excellent museums that are part of the outstanding Buffalo Bill Historical Center. With its dude ranches, outdoor activities, and both trendy and classic Western shopping, Cody is also a prime place for people who want to experience a Western lifestyle with amenities.

A brochure with a self-guided walking tour of the town's historic sites, such as the Irma Hotel, is available from the Chamber of Commerce on Sheridan Avenue for a $1 donation.

The **Wyoming Vietnam Veterans Memorial** is a small-scale version of the Vietnam Veterans Memorial wall in Washington, D.C. The Cody memorial recognizes the Wyoming residents who died during the conflict. ✉ *U.S. 14/16/20, east of Cody.*

The **Cody Mural**, at the Church of Jesus Christ of Latter-day Saints, is an artistic interpretation of Mormon settlement in the West. Edward Grigware painted the scene on the domed ceiling in the 1950s. ✉ *17th and Wyoming Sts.* ☎ *307/587–3290 or 307/587–9258* 🎟 *Free* ⏲ *June–mid-Sept., Mon.–Sat. 8–8, Sun. 3–8.*

Fodor's Choice ★ On the west side of Cody is one of the finest museum complexes in the West: the **Buffalo Bill Historical Center,** which houses five museums in one. The **Buffalo Bill Cody Museum** is dedicated to the incredible life of William F. "Buffalo Bill" Cody. Shortly after Cody's death, some of his friends took mementos of the famous scout and Wild West showman and opened the Buffalo Bill Museum in a small log building. The museum has since been moved to the historical center and includes huge posters from the original Wild West shows, as well as personal effects such as clothing, guns, saddles, and furniture. The **Cody Firearms Museum** traces the history of firearms through thousands of models on display, from European blunderbusses to Gatling guns and modern firearms. Included are examples of Winchester and Browning arms, as well as a model of an arms-manufacturing plant. Through exhibits, outdoor activities, tours, and seminars, the **Draper Museum of Natural History** explores the Yellowstone ecosystem. There are children's discovery areas in addition to life-size animal mounts. Recordings play the sounds of wolves, grizzly bears, birds, and other animals that make their home in the Yellowstone area. At the **Plains Indian Museum,** interactive exhibits and life-size dioramas explore the history and culture of the Lakota, Blackfeet, Cheyenne, Shoshone, and Nez Perce tribes. Among the exhibits are rare medicine pipes, clothing, and an earth-house interpretive area. The **Whitney Gallery of Western Art** is devoted to the West's greatest artists. On display are works by such masters as Frederic Remington, Charles M. Russell, Albert Bierstadt, George Catlin, and Thomas Moran, plus contemporary artists such as Harry Jackson, James Bama, and Peter Fillerup. ✉ *720 Sheridan Ave.* ☎ *307/587–4771* 🌐 *www.bbhc.org* 🎟 *$15 (2 days)* ⏲ *Apr., daily 10–5; May, daily 8–8; June–mid-Sept., daily 7 AM–8 PM; mid-Sept.–Oct., daily 8–5; Nov.–Mar., daily 10–3.*

Cody Nite Rodeo, more dusty and intimate than big rodeos such as Cheyenne Frontier Days, offers children's events, such as goat roping, in addition to the regular adult events. Contact the Cody Chamber of Commerce for more information. ✉ *West Cody Strip* ☎ *800/207–0744* 🌐 *www.comp-unltd.com/~rodeo/rodeo.html* 🎟 *$10–$12; seat prices vary with location* ⏲ *June–Aug., daily at 8:30 PM.*

Summer evenings, the **Cody Gunslingers Shootout** takes place on the porch at the Irma Hotel. ✉ *1192 Sheridan Ave.* ☎ *307/587–4221* 🎟 *Free* ⏲ *June–late Sept., daily at 6 PM.*

If you give the folks at **Cody Trolley Tours** an hour of your time, they'll take you on a journey through 100 years of Cody history. The tour takes in historic sites, scenery, geology, and wildlife attractions. A combination ticket also grants you admission to the Buffalo Bill Historical Center. ✉ *Ticket booth in front of Irma Hotel, 1192 Sheridan Ave.* ☎ *307/527–7243* 🌐 *www.codytrolleytours.com* 🎟 *Tour ticket $13, combination ticket with Buffalo Bill Historical Center $22* ⏲ *Early June–Sept., Mon.–Sat. at 9, 11, 1, 3, and 6:30; Sun. at 9, 11, 1, and 3.*

Dioramas at **Tecumseh's Wyoming Territory Old West Miniature Village and Museum** depict early-Wyoming and Native American history and Western events. The gift shop sells deerskin clothing handmade on the premises. ✉ *142 W. Yellowstone Hwy.* ☎ *307/587–5362* 🎟 *$3* ⏲ *June–Aug., daily 8–8; May and Sept., daily 10–6; rest of yr by appointment.*

On Cody's western outskirts, off the West Yellowstone Highway, is **Old Trail Town,** a collection of historic buildings from Wyoming's frontier days. Also here are a cemetery for famous local mountain men and Native American and pioneer artifacts. The buildings aren't fancy and the displays are rustic, so you really get a feel for an Old West town. Sometimes in summer Bobby Bridger, great-grandnephew of mountain man Jim Bridger, performs his "Ballad of the West" ($12) in the barn here. The three-night program describes the settlement of the West and includes stories of mountain men, Buffalo Bill Cody, and the Lakota. ✉ *1831 Demaris Dr.* ☎ *307/587–5302* 🎫 *$6* ⏲ *May–Sept., daily 8–8.*

Fishing and boating on the Buffalo Bill Reservoir are popular activities at **Buffalo Bill State Park,** west of Cody. A visitor center here focuses on the history of the reservoir, which was completed in 1910. ✉ *47 Lakeside Rd., west of Cody on U.S. 14/16/20* ☎ *307/587–6076* 🌐 *wyoparks.state.wy.us/buffalo1.htm* 🎫 *Park $4, camping $4* ⏲ *Park daily 24 hrs, visitor center May–Sept., daily 8–8.*

The **Shoshone National Forest** was the country's first national forest, established in 1891. You can hike, fish, mountain bike, and ride horses in warmer weather, and snowmobile and cross-country ski in winter. There are picnic areas and campgrounds. ✉ *U.S. 14/16/20, west of Cody* ☎ *307/527–6241* 🌐 *www.fs.fed.us/r2/shoshone/* 🎫 *Free* ⏲ *Daily 24 hrs.*

off the beaten path

CHIEF JOSEPH SCENIC BYWAY – In 1877, a few members of the Nez Perce tribe killed some white settlers in Idaho as retribution for earlier killings by whites. Fearing that the U.S. Army would punish the guilty and innocent alike, hundreds of Nez Perce fled on a five-month journey toward Canada that came to be known as the Nez Perce Trail. Along the way they passed through what is now Yellowstone National Park, across the Sunlight Basin area north of Cody, and along the Clarks Fork of the Shoshone River before turning north into Montana. To see the rugged mountain area they traveled through, follow Highway 120 north 17 mi to Highway 296, the Chief Joseph Scenic Byway. The byway eventually leads to Cooke City and Red Lodge, Montana. Along the way you'll see open meadows, pine forests, and a sweeping vista of the region from the top of Dead Indian Pass.

Sports & the Outdoors

CANOEING, KAYAKING & RAFTING

Family river trips on the Shoshone River are offered by **River Runners** (✉ 1491 Sheridan Ave. ☎ 307/527–7238). **Wyoming River Trips** (✉ Buffalo Bill Village, 1701 Sheridan Ave. ☎ 307/587–6661 or 800/586–6661) arranges Shoshone River trips.

FISHING

The fish are big at the private **Monster Lake** (☎ 800/840–5137), filled with rainbow, brook, and brown trout weighing up to 10 pounds. For a fee you can fish all or part of the day at this lake on the east side of town; accommodations are available as well.

You can buy fishing tackle, get information on fishing in the area, or take a guided half- or full-day trip with **Tim Wade's North Fork Anglers** (✉ 1107 Sheridan Ave. ☎ 307/527–7274). Walk-ins are welcome.

GOLF

Olive Glenn Golf and Country Club (✉ 802 Meadow La. ☎ 307/587–5551 or 307/587–5308) is a highly rated 18-hole course open to the public; a Jacuzzi, pool, and two tennis courts are also here.

HORSEBACK RIDING

Ride for one to four hours or all day with **Cedar Mountain Trail Rides** (✉U.S. 14/16/20, 1 mi west of rodeo grounds ☎ 307/527–4966). You can ride horses into Shoshone National Forest with **Goff Creek Lodge** (✉ 995 E. Yellowstone Hwy. ☎ 307/587–3753); lunch rides are also available.

SKIING Downhill and cross-country skiing and snowboarding are available at **Sleeping Giant Ski Area** (✉ 349 Yellowstone Hwy., 50 mi west of Cody near the east entrance to Yellowstone National Park ☎ 307/587–4044 🌐 www.skisleepinggiant.com). You can rent skis and snowboards here. In the Wood River valley near Meeteetse, 32 mi south of Cody, **Wood River Ski Touring Park** (✉ 349 Yellowstone Hwy. ☎ 307/868–2603) has 32 km (20 mi) of cross-country trails.

Where to Stay & Eat

$$–$$$$ ✕ **Stephan's.** This intimate restaurant adorned with potted palms and earth-tone Western art is a Cody favorite. Specialties include Southwestern shrimp kebab grilled with jalapeños and pepper-jack cheese, penne with artichoke hearts and prosciutto in a lemon-caper sauce, and filet mignon stuffed with Gorgonzola, sun-dried tomatoes, and portobello mushrooms. Save room for the homemade chocolate cake or strawberries napoleon. *✉ 1367 Sheridan Ave. ☎ 307/587–8511 ▭ AE, MC, V.*

$–$$$ ✕ **Maxwell's.** A turn-of-the-20th-century Victorian structure with huge windows and a porch houses this upscale contemporary restaurant that serves free-range beef entrées, homemade soups, pastas, and sandwiches. The baby-back pork ribs are always a good bet, and the Mediterranean pizza with Greek olives, feta cheese, and fresh tomatoes is also a good, very filling choice. In summer there's outdoor dining on the deck. *✉ 937 Sheridan Ave. ☎ 307/527–7749 ▭ AE, D, MC, V.*

$–$$$ ✕ **Proud Cut Saloon.** At this popular downtown eatery and watering hole, owner Del Nose serves what locals call "kick-ass cowboy cuisine": steaks, prime rib, shrimp, fish, and chicken. Western paintings, vintage photographs of Cody country, and large game mounts decorate the place. *✉ 1227 Sheridan Ave. ☎ 307/527–6905 ▭ D, MC, V.*

¢–$ ✕ **La Comida.** Making no claim to authentic Mexican cooking, this restaurant nevertheless receives praise for its "Cody-Mex" cuisine. You can order enchiladas, burritos, tacos, and chiles rellenos, but they won't be as spicy as similar foods would be in the Southwest. Mexican wall hangings contribute to the festive atmosphere. *✉ 1385 Sheridan Ave. ☎ 307/587–9556 ▭ AE, D, DC, MC, V.*

$$$$ 🏨 **Rimrock Dude Ranch.** Dating to 1956, this is one of the oldest guest ranches on the North Fork of the Shoshone River. Rimrock offers both summer and winter accommodations and activities, from horseback riding in the surrounding mountain country to snowmobile trips in Yellowstone National Park. Lodging is in one- and two-bedroom cabins. There's a one-week minimum stay. *✉ 2728 North Fork Hwy., 82414 ☎ 307/587–3970 or 800/208–7468 🖷 307/527–5014 🌐 www.rimrockranch.com ⇨ 9 cabins ♁ Dining room, refrigerators, pool, fishing, horseback riding, snowmobiling, airport shuttle; no smoking ▭ MC, V 🍽 FAP.*

★ **$$–$$$$** 🏨 **Cody Guest Houses.** You have several house-rental options here, from a Victorian guest house with lace curtains and antique furnishings to a four-bedroom lodge with a fireplace. The 10 different guest houses have one to four bedrooms, and all of them have been lovingly restored and elegantly decorated. These houses are meant to make you feel truly at home, so you'll find refrigerators, full kitchens, outdoor barbecue grills, and children's play areas at most of them. *✉ 1525 Beck Ave., 82414 ☎ 307/587–6000 or 800/587–6560 🖷 307/587–8048 🌐 www.codyguesthouses.com ⇨ 10 houses ♁ Kitchens, laundry facilities ▭ AE, D, MC, V.*

$$–$$$$ 🏨 **UXU Ranch.** One of the cabins at the UXU guest ranch is a historic late-19th-century stage stop moved to the site and decorated with

Molesworth-style furnishings made by New West of Cody; other cabins here date to the 1960s or 1920s. The ranch, along the North Fork of the Shoshone River, offers outstanding horseback riding, pack trips into the nearby mountains, and the opportunity to really get away from it all. There's a minimum one-week stay. ✉ *1710 North Fork Hwy., Wapiti 82450* ☎ *307/587–2143 or 800/373–9027* 📠 *307/587–8307* 🌐 *www.uxuranch.com* *11 cabins* *Dining room, hot tub, fishing, hiking, horseback riding, bar, children's programs (ages 6 and up), playground; no a/c, no room phones* 💳 *MC, V* 🍽 *FAP.*

$$ **Best Western Sunset Motor Inn.** This inn sits on a large grassy property with shade trees and has an enclosed play area for children. Numerous amenities, clean rooms, and a quiet and relaxed atmosphere make this a favorite with families. It's a block from the Buffalo Bill Historical Center. ✉ *1601 8th St., 82414* ☎ *307/587–4265 or 800/624–2727* 🌐 *www.bestwestern.com* *116 rooms, 4 suites* *Restaurant, cable TV, indoor-outdoor pool, gym, hot tub, playground, laundry facilities, some pets allowed* 💳 *AE, D, DC, MC, V.*

$–$$ **Buffalo Bill Village.** This downtown development comprises three lodgings, which share many facilities. The Buffalo Bill Village Resort consists of log cabins with modern interiors, and the Holiday Inn Convention Center and the Comfort Inn are typical chain hotels. The downtown shopping district begins one block to the west, and there's also a grocery store a block away. ✉ *1701 Sheridan Ave., 82414* ☎ *307/587–5544* 🌐 *www.blairhotels.com* *Buffalo Bill Village Resort 83 cabins; Comfort Inn 75 rooms; Holiday Inn 184 rooms* *Restaurant, pool, gym, bar, meeting room, airport shuttle* 💳 *AE, D, DC, MC, V.*

$–$$ **Lockhart Inn.** The former home of Cody author Caroline Lockhart, this inn has rooms named after her characters and books. Western antiques decorate the rooms, many of which have claw-foot tubs. It's on the main western strip of Cody, which is convenient to area attractions. ✉ *109 W. Yellowstone Ave., 82414* ☎ *307/587–6074 or 800/377–7255* *7 rooms* *Dining room; no smoking* 💳 *D, MC, V* 🍽 *BP.*

$ **Irma Hotel.** This hotel named for Buffalo Bill's daughter retains some frontier charm, with brass beds and period furniture in many rooms, a large restaurant, and an elaborate cherrywood bar. If you want true history, be sure to stay in one of the 15 rooms of the original 1902 hotel and not in the annex, which has standard hotel-style contemporary rooms. In summer, locals stage a gunfight on the porch Tuesday–Saturday at 6 PM. ✉ *1192 Sheridan Ave., 82414* ☎ *307/587–4221 or 800/745–4762* 📠 *307/587–1775* 🌐 *www.irmahotel.com* *40 rooms* *Restaurant, bar* 💳 *AE, D, DC, MC, V.*

$ **Yellowstone Valley Inn.** Located 16 mi west of Cody and 32 mi east of Yellowstone National Park's east entrance, this sprawling and peaceful property offers basic accommodations in a mountain setting. Rooms are in the motel or duplex cabins, and campsites are available. ✉ *3324 Yellowstone Park Hwy., 82414* ☎ *307/587–3961 or 877/587–3961* 📠 *307/587–4656* 🌐 *www.yellowstonevalleyinn.com* *18 motel rooms, 18 cabin rooms* *Restaurant, picnic area, cable TV, bar, laundry facilities, meeting rooms, some pets allowed; no room phones* 💳 *AE, D, MC, V.*

CAMPING There are 32 campgrounds within **Shoshone National Forest** (☎ 307/527–6241 🌐 www.fs.fed.us/r2/shoshone); some have only limited services, and others have hookups and campground hosts.

⛺ **Cody KOA.** This campground on the southeast side of town serves free pancake breakfasts. There's also a free shuttle to the Cody Nite Rodeo, and you can arrange to take a horseback ride. *Flush toilets, full hookups, partial hookups (electric and water), drinking water, guest laun-*

dry, showers, grills, picnic tables, general store, swimming (pool) 🛏 *200 sites* ✉ *5561 U.S. 20 (Greybull Hwy.)* ☎ *800/562–8507* 🖷 *307/587–2369* 🌐 *www.codykoa.com* 💵 *Full hookups $41.95–$46.95, partial hookups $39.95, tent sites $29.95; cabins $50.95–$59.95* 💳 *AE, D, DC, MC, V* 🕒 *May–Oct.*

⛺ **Dead Indian Campground.** You can fish in the stream at this tent campground adjacent to the Chief Joseph Scenic Byway (Highway 296). There are hiking and horseback-riding trails, plus nearby corrals for horses. 👍 *Pit toilets, drinking water, bear boxes, fire grates, picnic tables, swimming (creek)* 🛏 *12 sites* ✉ *17 mi north of Cody on Hwy. 120, then 25 mi northwest on Hwy. 296* ☎ *307/527–6241* 🌐 *www.fs.fed.us/r2/shoshone* 💵 *$5* 💳 *No credit cards* 🕒 *May–Oct.*

⛺ **Deer Creek Campground.** At the head of the South Fork of the Shoshone River, this small, tree-shaded campground for tents provides hiking access to the Absaroka Range and the Washakie Wilderness. 👍 *Pit toilets, drinking water, fire pits, picnic tables* 🛏 *7 sites* ✉ *47 mi west of Cody on South Fork Hwy. (Hwy. 291)* ☎ *307/527–6241* 🌐 *www.fs.fed.us/r2/shoshone* 💵 *Free* 🕒 *May–Oct.*

⛺ **Ponderosa Campground.** Within walking distance (three blocks) of the Buffalo Bill Historical Center, this is a large facility with separate areas for tents and RVs. You can even stay in a tepee or pitch your own tent or tepee in a primitive camping area (without any nearby facilities) known as the OK Corral in the canyon above the Shoshone River. 👍 *Flush toilets, full hookups, dump station, drinking water, guest laundry, showers, grills, picnic tables, public telephone, general store, play area* 🛏 *137 full hookups, 50 tent sites; 8 tepees* ✉ *1815 8th St.* ☎ *307/587–9203* 💵 *Full hookups $38, tent sites and tepees $21* 💳 *No credit cards* 🕒 *May–Oct.*

Nightlife & the Arts

NIGHTLIFE A trip to Cody isn't complete without a chance to scoot your boots to live music, usually provided by the local band West, at **Cassie's Supper Club and Dance Hall** (✉ 214 Yellowstone Ave. ☎ 307/587–5500). The tunes are a mix of classic country, the band's Western originals, and today's hits.

THE ARTS Impromptu jam sessions, nightly concerts, and a symposium of educational and entertaining events related to cowboy music are all part of the **Cowboy Songs and Range Ballads** (☎ 307/587–4771 🌐 www.bbhc.org). In addition to classic range ballads there's original music by performers from across the West. Events are held over the course of a few days in late March or early April at the Buffalo Bill Historical Center and other venues.

The two-day **Plains Indian Powwow** (✉ 720 Sheridan Ave. ☎ 307/587–4771 🌐 www.bbhc.org), in late June, brings together hoop dancers, traditional dancers, and jingle dancers from various tribes. The performances take place at the Buffalo Bill Historical Center.

Sculptures and paintings by such artists as James Bama, Chris Navarro, and Frank McCarthy are displayed at **Big Horn Galleries** (✉ 1167 Sheridan Ave. ☎ 307/527–7587). **Simpson Gallagher Gallery** (✉ 1161 Sheridan Ave. ☎ 307/587–4022) showcases and sells contemporary representational art by Harry Jackson, Margery Torrey, and Geoff Parker.

Shopping

The **Cody Rodeo Company** (✉ 1291 Sheridan Ave. ☎ 307/587–5913) sells cowboy hats, plus housewares with a cowboy or rodeo motif. Head to ★ the **Custom Cowboy Shop** (✉ 1286 Sheridan Ave. ☎ 307/527–7300) to stock up on top-quality cowboy gear and clothing, ranging from hats and vests for men to women's shirts and jackets; there's even gear for your horse here. Also available are CDs by top Western recording artists such as Ian Tyson, Don Edwards, and Michael Martin Murphey.

What kid doesn't want a stick buffalo (think stick horse, but with a buffalo head) that actually grunts when you press on the ear? You'll find that and buffalo-hide purses, vests, and coats, as well as blankets woven of buffalo hair, at the **Diamond Eight-Eight Buffalo Ranch Store** (✉ 1210 Sheridan Ave. ☎ 307/587–3222 or 866/754–7277).

Flight West (✉ 1155 Sheridan Ave. ☎ 307/527–7800) sells designer Western women's wear, leather goods for men and women, books, gifts, and jewelry. Women shop at the **Plush Pony** (✉ 1350 Sheridan Ave. ☎ 307/587–4677) for "uptown Western clothes" ranging from leather belts to stylish skirts, jackets, and dresses. The **Wyoming Buffalo Company** (✉ 1280 Sheridan Ave. ☎ 307/587–8708 or 800/453–0636) sells buffalo-meat products, such as sausage and jerky, in addition to specialty foods such as huckleberry honey. Chock-full of souvenirs and trinkets, the **Yellowstone Gift Shop** (✉ 1237 Sheridan Ave. ☎ 307/587–4611 or 800/788–9429) also has a huge selection of turquoise jewelry.

Lovell

28 *46 mi east of Cody via Alternate U.S. 14.*

This small community makes a good base for exploring the Bighorn Mountains and Bighorn Canyon National Recreation Area, which straddles the Wyoming–Montana border. Among the attractions in and around the recreation area are the dammed lake popular with boaters and anglers and the Pryor Mountain Wild Horse Range. (For further information, *see* Chapter 5.)

The main visitor center for Bighorn Canyon National Recreation Area, the **Bighorn Canyon Visitor Center** has geological and historical exhibits on the area, as well as a film about the canyon. ✉ *U.S. 310 at Alternate U.S. 14* ☎ *307/548–2251* 🌐 *www.nps.gov/bica/* 🎫 *Free* ⏲ *Memorial Day–Labor Day, daily 8–6; Labor Day–Memorial Day, daily 8–5.*

More than 155 species of birds, including white pelicans, bald eagles, and great blue herons, inhabit the 19,424-acre **Yellowtail Wildlife Habitat Management Area,** as do numerous other animal species, including red fox, mule deer, and cottontail rabbits. ✉ *Hwy. 37 southwest of Bighorn Canyon National Recreation Area, 33 mi east of Lovell* ☎ *307/527–7125* 🎫 *Free* ⏲ *Daily.*

off the beaten path

MEDICINE WHEEL NATIONAL HISTORIC LANDMARK – A ring of rocks 80 feet in diameter, this ancient site is the best preserved of nearly 150 Native American stone wheels found in Wyoming, South Dakota, Montana, Alberta, and Saskatchewan. Evidence such as the 28 spokes (one for each day of the lunar cycle) leading from the edge of the wheel to a central cairn has persuaded some that the wheel was an ancient spiritual observatory much like England's Stonehenge may have been. To protect the area, access to the wheel is restricted to foot travel; it's a 1½-mi hike to the site from the parking lot (people with disabilities may drive to the site). Up in the Bighorn Mountains, at an elevation of 9,642 feet, the site affords views of the entire Bighorn Basin. ✉ *30 mi east of Lovell on Alternate U.S. 14* ☎ *No phone* 🌐 *wyoshpo.state.wy.us/medwheel.htm* 🎫 *Free* ⏲ *Daily 24 hrs.*

Where to Stay & Eat

¢–$$ ✕ **Bighorn.** This family-owned and -operated diner in downtown Lovell serves burgers, fried chicken, and steak. Breakfast is available all day, and there's a kids' menu. The interior is Southwestern in style. ✉ *605 E. Main St.* ☎ *307/548–6811* ▭ *AE, D, DC, MC, V.*

¢ **Cattleman Motel.** Lodgepole-pine furniture fills the clean, simple Western-style rooms at this basic one-story motel. It's near the center of town. ✉ *470 Montana Ave., 82431* ☎ *307/548–2296 or 888/548–2269* *307/548–2483* *13 rooms* *Cable TV, hot tub, some pets allowed* ▭ *AE, D, MC, V* *CP.*

NORTHWEST WYOMING A TO Z

To research prices, get advice from other travelers, and book travel arrangements, visit www.fodors.com.

AIR TRAVEL

CARRIERS American, SkyWest, and United Airlines/United Express provide multiple flights to Jackson daily, with connections in Chicago, Denver, and Salt Lake City. Scheduled jet service increases during the ski season. Great Lakes Aviation flies between Cody and Salt Lake City, and United Express connects Cody and Denver. United flies between Denver and Riverton.

Airlines & Contacts **American Airlines** ☎ 800/433-7300 🌐 www.aa.com. **Great Lakes Aviation** ☎ 307/587-7683 or 800/554-5111 🌐 www.greatlakesav.com. **Sky West Airlines** ☎ 307/587-9740 or 800/453-9417 🌐 www.skywest.com. **United Airlines/United Express** ☎ 800/241-6522 🌐 www.ual.com.

AIRPORTS

The major airports in the region are Jackson Hole Airport, north of Jackson in Grand Teton National Park and about 40 mi south of Yellowstone National Park; Riverton Airport in Riverton, 25 mi northeast of Lander and 78 mi east of Dubois; and Yellowstone Regional Airport in Cody.

Many lodgings have free shuttle-bus service to and from Jackson Hole Airport. All Star Transportation, Alltrans, and Jackson Hole Transportation are shuttle services that serve the Jackson Hole Airport. If you're coming into the area from the Salt Lake City or Idaho Falls airport, you can travel to Jackson and back on a Jackson Hole Express shuttle.

Airport Information **Jackson Hole Airport** ✉ 1250 E. Airport Rd., Jackson Hole ☎ 307/733-7682 or 307/733-4005. **Riverton Regional Airport** ✉ 4800 Airport Rd., Riverton ☎ 307/856-1307 🌐 www.flyriverton.com. **Yellowstone Regional Airport** ✉ 3001 Duggleby Dr., Cody ☎ 307/587-5096 🌐 www.flyyra.com.

Transfer Information **All Star Transportation** ☎ 307/733-2888. **Alltrans** ☎ 307/733-3135 or 800/443-6133. **Jackson Hole Express** ☎ 307/733-1719 or 800/652-9510. **Jackson Hole Transportation** ☎ 307/733-3135.

BUS TRAVEL

Greyhound Lines has very limited service to Cody.

During the ski season, START buses shuttle people between Jackson and the Jackson Hole Mountain Resort. The fare is $3 one-way, and the buses operate from 6 AM to 11 PM. In summer START buses are free, operating from 6 AM to 10:30 PM. They stop at more than 40 locations in Jackson. People with disabilities must make reservations 48 hours in advance for START buses.

The Targhee Express runs between Jackson and the Grand Targhee Ski and Summer Resort, with pickups at various lodging properties in Jackson and Teton Village. The cost is $20 per day, or you can buy a combination shuttle/Grand Targhee lift ticket for $56. Advance reservations are required. All Star Transportation runs a nightly shuttle bus between Jackson and Teton Village; the cost is $22 for up to three people.

June through September, COLT buses provide transportation to downtown Cody and surrounding attractions. The $1 fee lets you ride the buses all day.

Bus Information **All Star Transportation** ☎ 307/733-2888. **COLT** ☎ 307/587-2777. **Greyhound** ☎ 800/231-2222 🌐 www.greyhound.com. **START** ☎ 307/733-4521. **Targhee Express** ☎ 307/734-9754 or 307/733-3101.

CAR RENTAL

If you didn't drive to Wyoming, rent a car once you arrive. The airports have major car-rental agencies, which offer four-wheel-drive vehicles and ski racks. Aspen Rent-A-Car, a local agency in Jackson, rents cars, full-size vans, and sport utility vehicles; another local agency in Jackson, Eagle Rent-A-Car, provides cars and package deals with sport utility vehicles and snowmobiles. Rent-A-Wreck, in Lander, rents used cars.

Aspen Rent-A-Car ✉ 345 W. Broadway, Jackson ☎ 307/733-9224 or 877/222-7736. **Avis** ✉ Jackson Hole Airport ☎ 307/733-3422. **Budget** ✉ Yellowstone Regional Airport ☎ 307/587-6066. **Eagle Rent-A-Car** ✉ 375 N. Cache Dr., Jackson ☎ 307/739-9999 or 800/582-2128. **Hertz** ✉ Jackson Hole Airport ☎ 800/654-3131 ✉ Riverton Regional Airport ☎ 307/856-2344 ✉ Yellowstone Regional Airport ☎ 307/587-2914. **Rent-A-Wreck** ✉ 715 E. Main St., Lander ☎ 307/332-5159. **Thrifty** ✉ Jackson Hole Airport ☎ 307/734-9306 ✉ Yellowstone Regional Airport ☎ 307/587-8855.

CAR TRAVEL

Northwest Wyoming is well away from the interstates, so drivers make their way here on two-lane highways that are long on miles and scenery. To get to Jackson from I–80, take U.S. 191 north from Rock Springs for about 177 mi. From I–90, drive west from Sheridan on U.S. 14 or Alternate U.S. 14 to Cody. U.S. 14 continues west to Yellowstone National Park, and you can also hook up with U.S. 191, which leads south to Jackson.

Be extremely cautious when driving in winter; whiteouts and ice on the roads are not uncommon. Contact the Wyoming Department of Transportation for road and travel reports. For emergency situations dial 911 or contact the Wyoming Highway Patrol.

Grand Teton Park Road Conditions ☎ 307/739-3300. **Wyoming Department of Transportation Wyoming Department of Transportation** ☎ 307/777-4484, 307/772-0824 from outside Wyoming for road conditions, 888/996-7623 from within Wyoming for road conditions 🌐 www.wyoroad.info. **Wyoming Highway Patrol** ☎ 307/777-4301, 800/442-9090 for emergencies, #4357 (#HELP) from a cell phone for emergencies.

EMERGENCIES

There are hospitals in Jackson and Cody and clinics in most other towns throughout the region.

Ambulance or Police **Emergencies** ☎ 911.

Hospitals & Clinics **Grand Teton Medical Clinic** ✉ next to Jackson Lake Lodge ☎ 307/543-2514. **St. John's Medical Center** ✉ 625 E. Broadway, Jackson ☎ 307/733-3636 🌐 www.tetonhospital.org. **West Park Hospital** ✉ 707 Sheridan Ave., Cody ☎ 307/527-7501 🌐 www.westparkhospital.org.

LODGING

APARTMENT & CABIN RENTALS

Rendezvous Mountain Rentals handles condominiums and homes for vacation rentals in the Jackson Hole area, including properties at Jackson Hole Racquet Club, Teton Pines, and Teton Village. Vacation Condo Rental has town-house-style condominiums near Jackson.

Rendezvous Mountain Rentals Box 11338, Jackson 83002 307/739-9050 or 888/739-2565 307/734-2677 www.rmrentals.com. **Vacation Condo Rental** 175 S. King, Box 2228, Jackson 83001 800/992-9948 307/739-1686.

CAMPING

There are numerous campgrounds within Grand Teton National Park and Bridger-Teton, Shoshone, and Targhee national forests (Targhee National Forest borders Grand Teton National Park on the west; most of the forest lies within Idaho). Few of these campgrounds accept reservations. Campgrounds in the national forests tend to fill up more slowly than those in Grand Teton.

Reservations can be made for a small number of national-forest campgrounds near Jackson through U.S. Forest Reservations.

Bridger-Teton National Forest 307/739-5500. **Grand Teton** 307/739-3300. **Shoshone National Forest** 307/527-6241. **Targhee National Forest** 208/624-3151. **U.S. Forest Reservations** 800/280-2267.

MEDIA

NEWSPAPERS & MAGAZINES

The twice-weekly *Cody Enterprise* and weekly *Jackson Hole News & Guide* print local news as well as information on ski conditions and events in the region. Other major publications in the region, all published weekly, are the *Lovell Chronicle, Pinedale Roundup,* and *Thermopolis Independent Record.*

TELEVISION & RADIO

NBC/KCWY Channel 13, broadcast out of Casper, serves much of the area. KGWL Channel 5 is a local station based in Lander. You can pick up ABC, CBS, and NBC from Salt Lake City or Idaho Falls, depending where you are in the region.

KODI 1400 AM talk radio is broadcast out of Cody; also broadcast out of Cody is KTAG 97.9 FM, which plays pop hits as well as favorites from the '70s, '80s, and '90s. In Jackson, KSGT 1340 AM plays talk radio, KMTN 100.3 FM plays current and classic rock, and KZJH 95.7 FM plays classic rock. In Lander, KOVE 1330 AM plays country, KDLY 97.5 FM plays classic rock, and KTRZ 95.3 FM plays Top 40 music. KTHE 1240 AM in Thermopolis is a country-music station.

SPORTS & THE OUTDOORS

Northwest Wyoming has the best the state has to offer in the way of outdoor activities, including camping, climbing, fishing, mountain biking, horseback riding, hiking, cross-country and downhill skiing, snowmobiling, and even dogsledding. Grand Teton National Park and Jackson Hole Mountain Resort in particular are popular playgrounds. Throughout the region there are countless outfitters and tour guides who can help you pursue any of these activities.

FISHING

To fish in Wyoming you must obtain a fishing license, usually available at sporting-goods stores; you can also request a license through the Wyoming Game and Fish Department.

The Wind River Indian Reservation has some of the best fishing in the Rockies. A separate license is required here. Contact Shoshone and Arapaho Tribes.

Shoshone and Arapaho Tribes Fish and Game Dept., 1 Washakie, Fort Washakie 82520 307/332-7207. **Wyoming Game and Fish Department** 360 N. Cache St., Box 67, Jackson 83001 307/733-2321 gf.state.wy.us/.

SKIING For up-to-date information on ski conditions and snowfall at the Jackson Hole Mountain Resort, contact the number below or visit the Web site.

Snow report ☎ 307/733-4005 🌐 www.jacksonhole.com/today/snowreport.php.

SAFETY

You can encounter a grizzly bear, mountain lion, wolf, or other wild animal anywhere in the Yellowstone ecosystem, which encompasses the mountains and valleys around Pinedale, Dubois, Jackson, Cody, and both Grand Teton and Yellowstone national parks. If you plan on hiking on backcountry trails, be sure to carry bear repellent, make noise, and travel with a companion. Check with forest or park rangers for other tips to protect yourself. (There are different tactics, depending on the animal species.) Always let someone know where you are going and when you plan to return. There have been few fatal encounters with grizzlies and black bears in the region, but almost every summer there are incidents involving bears.

Of greater concern to most people are female animals, particularly moose, with young by their side. These animal mothers are fiercely protective of their offspring. Buffalo can and do charge visitors every year. The best safety rule with all animals is to give them plenty of space.

TOURS

Red Canyon Wild Mustang Tours, which depart daily at 8:30 AM from Cody, take you to view wild horses. For leisurely appreciation of the area, try a multiday covered wagon and horseback trip with Teton Wagon Train and Horse Adventure. Wild West Jeep Tours has naturalist guides who will show you the backcountry.

Red Canyon Wild Mustang Tours ✉ 1374 Sheridan Ave., Cody 82414 ☎ 307/587-6988 or 800/293-0148. **Teton Wagon Train and Horse Adventure** Box 10307, Jackson 83002 ☎ 888/734-6101 🌐 www.tetonwagontrain.com. **Wild West Jeep Tours** Box 7506, Jackson 83002 ☎ 307/733-9036 🌐 www.wildwestjeeptours.com.

VISITOR INFORMATION

Tourist Information **Cody Chamber of Commerce** ✉ 836 Sheridan Ave., Box 2777, Cody 82414 ☎ 307/587-2297 🖷 307/527-6228 🌐 www.codychamber.org. **Dubois Chamber of Commerce** Box 632, Dubois 82513 ☎ 307/455-2556 🖷 307/455-3168 🌐 www.dteworld.com/duboiscc. **Grand Teton National Park** Drawer 170, Moose 83012 ☎ 307/739-3300 🌐 www.nps.gov/grte. **Jackson Hole Chamber of Commerce** ✉ 990 W. Broadway, Box E, Jackson 83001 ☎ 307/733-3316 🖷 307/733-5585 🌐 www.jacksonholechamber.com. **Jackson Hole Mountain Resort** Box 290, Teton Village 83025 ☎ 307/733-2292 or 800/443-6931 🖷 307/733-2660 🌐 www.jacksonhole.com. **Lander Chamber of Commerce** ✉ 160 N. 1st St., Lander 82520 ☎ 307/332-3892 or 800/443-0662 🖷 307/332-3893 🌐 www.landerchamber.org. **Lovell Chamber of Commerce** ✉ 287 E. Main St., Lovell 82431 ☎ 307/548-7552 🖷 307/548-7614 🌐 www.lovellchamber.com. **Pinedale Chamber of Commerce** ✉ 32 E. Pine St., Pinedale 82941 ☎ 307/367-2242 🖷 307/367-6830 🌐 www.pinedalechamber.com.

SOUTHERN WYOMING

CHEYENNE, LARAMIE, THE SNOWY RANGE

FODOR'S CHOICE

Cheyenne Frontier Days, *Cheyenne*
Grand Encampment Museum, *Encampment*
Nagel Warren Mansion, *B&B in Cheyenne*
Overland Restaurant, *Laramie*
Virginian Hotel, *Medicine Bow*

HIGHLY RECOMMENDED

RESTAURANTS
Little Bear Steakhouse, *Cheyenne*
Rose's Lariat, *Rawlins*
Wolf Hotel, *Saratoga*

HOTELS
Annie Moore's Guest House, *Laramie*
Saratoga Inn Resort, *Saratoga*
Spirit West River Lodge, *Encampment*

SIGHTS
Fort Bridger State Historic Site, *Fort Bridger*
Hobo Pool Hot Springs, *Saratoga*

By Candy Moulton

A JOURNEY ACROSS SOUTHERN WYOMING takes you through a wonderfully diverse landscape, from the wheat fields of the southeast to the mountains of the Snowy Range to the stark and sometimes hauntingly beautiful Red Desert, where wild horses still roam freely. Cheyenne, the largest city in Wyoming and the state capital, is the cornerstone community at the eastern edge of the state. Evanston, a town settled by railroad workers in 1869, anchors the western edge of the state. In between are the cities of Laramie, Rock Springs, and Green River, all of which owe their origin to the construction of the Union Pacific Railroad.

Several smaller communities with unique museums, access to diverse recreational opportunities, and one-of-a-kind personality lure travelers away from I–80, the main highway access route. Medicine Bow has a rich cowboy heritage tied to Owen Wister's 1902 Western novel, *The Virginian.* Saratoga has a resort flavor and some of the best dining and lodging of any small town in the state. Encampment and Baggs are small, slow-paced, historically rich towns.

Once covered by an ocean and now rich in fossils, southwest Wyoming's Red Desert, or Little Colorado Desert, draws people in search of solitude (there's plenty of it), pioneer trails (more miles of 19th-century overland emigrant trails than anywhere else in the country), and recreation ranging from wildlife watching to fishing and boating on Flaming Gorge Reservoir, south of the town of Green River. The region is rich in history as well: here, John Wesley Powell began his 1869 and 1871 expeditions down the Green River, and Jim Bridger and Louis Vasquez constructed the trading post of Fort Bridger, now a state historic site. And all across the region, evidence remains of the Union Pacific Railroad, which spawned growth here in the 1860s as workers laid the iron rails spanning the continent.

Exploring Southern Wyoming

Once you explore this region, it becomes apparent why Wyoming has earned the nickname the "Cowboy State." The plains remain a prime grazing spot for wild horses, cattle, and sheep. As you drive west, the plains give way to the snowcapped mountains of the appropriately named Snowy Range. After a few more hours driving west you'll reach desert, with unique rock formations and herds of wild horses and pronghorn.

I–80 is the major artery through this region, running from Cheyenne at the southeast corner of the state west to Evanston in the southwest corner of the state.

About the Restaurants

Almost anywhere you dine in southern Wyoming, beef plays a prominent role on the menu; prime rib and steak are often specialties. Standard fare at many small-town restaurants includes burgers and sandwiches, and several eateries serve outstanding Mexican dishes. The pickings can be a bit slim for vegetarians, although most menus have at least one vegetable pasta dish or meatless entrée. Jeans and a T-shirt are acceptable attire for most places (even if the folks at the next table happen to be dressed up). Cowboy hats are always welcome.

About the Hotels

Because I–80 traverses this region, there are countless chain motels, but many other interesting accommodations are available. Southern Wyoming has a large number of independent lodging properties ranging from bed-and-breakfasts to lodges to historic hotels. Dude ranches are a unique lodging experience that let you sample a taste of wrangling life.

Numbers in the text correspond to numbers in the margin and on the Southern Wyoming, Cheyenne, and Laramie maps.

If you have **3 days**

Get to know Wyoming's cowboy and Old West heritage by starting your trip with a tour of **Fort Laramie National Historic Site** 7, where you can learn about the early settlers, Native Americans, and emigrant trails. Overnight in **Cheyenne** 1–6. On your second day visit Cheyenne's Old West Museum and the Wyoming State Museum before heading west on Highway 210 for an afternoon picnic and some hiking or fishing at **Curt Gowdy State Park** 6. Continue on to **Laramie** 8–13 for dinner. On your third day take a self-guided walking tour of Laramie's historic downtown area. Finish your trip with a visit to the Wyoming Territorial Prison or any of the museums at the University of Wyoming, ranging from anthropology to geology.

If you have **5 days**

Follow the three-day itinerary above. On the fourth day, head west on Highway 130 to **Centennial** 15 and across the Snowy Range Pass to **Saratoga** 16, taking time to hike, fish, or picnic (or ski, in winter) in the Medicine Bow–Routt National Forest. (In winter, when the pass closes, you'll have to backtrack to Laramie and drive west on Highway 230 to Encampment, where you can hook up with Highway 130 and drive north to Saratoga.) Spend the night in Saratoga; then head south to **Encampment** 17, where you should plan to spend at least a couple of hours at the Grand Encampment Museum with its pioneer buildings. Follow Highway 70 over Battle Pass and the Continental Divide to **Baggs** 18. In Baggs, stop at the Little Snake River Valley Museum to see Jim Baker's original mountain-man cabin. From Baggs head north on Highway 789 and then east on I–80 to **Rawlins** 19, where you can visit the Carbon County Museum and Wyoming Frontier Prison.

If you have **7 days**

A week will give you time to explore most of this region. Follow the five-day itinerary above. On the sixth day head west from Rawlins on I–80 to the melting-pot community of **Rock Springs** 20. If you'd like to view wild horses and other native wildlife, follow the Pilot Butte Wild Horse Scenic Loop Tour as far as **Green River** 21. From Rock Springs you could also drive south on Highway 191 or 530 to the spectacular canyon country of **Flaming Gorge National Recreation Area** 22. Spend the night in Rock Springs or Green River. Plan to spend your final morning at **Fort Bridger State Historic Site** 23, west of Green River on I–80. Then continue west to **Evanston** 26 for a relaxing walk at Bear River State Park.

WHAT IT COSTS

	$$$$	**$$$**	**$$**	**$**	**¢**
RESTAURANTS	over $22	$16–$22	$11–$16	$7–$11	under $7
HOTELS	over $220	$160–$220	$110–$160	$70–$110	under $70

Restaurant prices are for a main course at dinner, excluding sales tax of 4%–7%. Hotel prices are for two people in a standard double room in high season, excluding service charges and 5%–10% tax.

Timing

The best time to visit southern Wyoming is in summer or fall, when most lodging properties and attractions are open (some smaller museums, sights, and inns close between Labor Day and Memorial Day). Summer is the season for most local community celebrations, including the region's longest-running and biggest event, Cheyenne Frontier Days, held the last full week in July.

Some areas, particularly around Laramie, Centennial, Saratoga, and Encampment, are great for winter sports, including cross-country skiing, snowmobiling, and ice fishing. Bear in mind that in parts of southern Wyoming it can—and often does—snow every month of the year, so even if you're visiting in July, bring some warm clothes, such as a heavy jacket and sweater.

CHEYENNE

Born in 1867 as the Union Pacific Railroad inched its way across the plains, Cheyenne began as a rowdy camp for railroad gangs, cowboys, prospectors heading for the Black Hills, and soldiers. It more than lived up to its nickname: "Hell on Wheels." But unlike some renegade railroad tent cities, which disappeared as the railroad tracks pushed farther west, Cheyenne established itself as a permanent city, becoming the territorial capital in 1868. Its wild beginnings gave way in the late 19th century to respectability with the coming of the enormously wealthy cattle barons, many of them English. They sipped brandy at the Cheyenne Club and hired hard cases such as Tom Horn (1860–1903) to take care of their competitors—which in many cases meant killing rustlers—on the open range.

Cheyenne became the state capital in 1890, at a time when the rule of the cattle barons was beginning to weaken after harsh winter storms in the late 1880s and financial downturns in the national economy. But Cheyenne's link to ranching didn't fade, and the community launched its first Cheyenne Frontier Days in 1897, an event that continues to this day. During the weeklong celebration, which takes place in late July, Cheyenne is up to its neck in bucking broncs and bulls and joyful bluster. There are pancake breakfasts put on by locals, parades and pageantry, and parties that require the endurance of a cattle hand on a weeklong drive. Now the world's largest outdoor rodeo extravaganza, the event has been dubbed the "Daddy of 'Em All."

Exploring Cheyenne

I–25 runs north–south through the city; I–80 runs east–west. Central Avenue and Warren Avenue are quick north–south routes; the former goes north one-way and the latter runs south one-way. Several major roads can get you across town fairly easily, including 16th Street (U.S. 30), which gives you easy access to downtown. Most places of interest are in the downtown area, near the Wyoming State Capitol on Capitol Avenue. Most shopping is also downtown or along Dell Range Boulevard on the north side of town. Note that there are a few one-way streets in the downtown area.

a good tour

Park your car at the **Old West Museum** 1 ⚑, within Frontier Park; this museum houses displays on the history of the region, plus the largest collection of horse-drawn vehicles anywhere in Wyoming. After you tour the museum, cross the street for a stroll through the **Cheyenne Botanic Gardens** 2.

Cheyenne Frontier Days There is no rodeo quite like Cheyenne Frontier Days, appropriately known by the trademarked nickname the "Daddy of 'Em All." Begun in 1897 to test the ability of ranch-riding cowboys, the Cheyenne event now spans nine days at the end of July and includes three free pancake breakfasts that feed up to 12,000 people in a couple of hours, four parades with the largest collection of horse-drawn vehicles in the region, rodeos, chuck-wagon races, concerts, an art show, and a Native American village. The best cowboys and cowgirls gather here, along with top country performers, ranging from Willie Nelson to Wyoming's own Chris LeDoux, who has not only sung on Frontier Days stages but also, in his younger days, rode broncs out of its chutes.

Living History Southern Wyoming has a rich history that still lives on in its museums, forts, and buildings—establishments that occasionally not only let you observe but also relive some of that history. Medicine Bow's Virginian Hotel was built in honor of Owen Wister's classic Western novel *The Virginian,* which did much to popularize cowboy culture throughout the country. With no televisions, radios, or phones in most rooms, this 1909 lodging transports you back to a time long past when hotels shook with the rumble of Union Pacific trains. It's the perfect place to settle into an armchair with a copy of Wister's novel.

Mountain men and women, riders for the Pony Express, and pioneers headed to Oregon, California, and Utah have all trodden the grounds that are now Fort Laramie National Historic Site and Fort Bridger State Historic Site. Today costumed interpreters show and tell you about life in these areas of Wyoming in the 19th century.

You can also combine your history with a little relaxation: follow the custom of Native Americans and then pioneers who all enjoyed soaking in the hot mineral springs at Saratoga, now known as the Hobo Pools Hot Springs.

Get back into your car and head south on Carey Avenue; make a left on 24th Street to reach the **Wyoming State Capitol** ③. Find a parking place along the street or turn right onto Central Avenue to look for parking. Take a self-guided tour of the capitol building, and note the statue out front of Esther Hobart Morris, who helped make Wyoming the first state to grant women the right to vote. Cross to the east side of Central Avenue and walk a couple of blocks south to the **Wyoming State Museum** ④, housing artifacts from across the state. Return to your car and travel south on Central Avenue to 21st Street; make a left and drive a couple of blocks east to House Avenue and the **Historic Governor's Mansion** ⑤, with period furnishings from the state's first leaders. To extend your tour, take Highway 210—Happy Jack Road—west off I–25 to **Curt Gowdy State Park** ⑥, where you can fish, hike, and picnic.

TIMING You could easily visit all of the sights within the city in a day. Plan to add another half day if you want to visit Curt Gowdy State Park. Note that several sights close on Sunday.

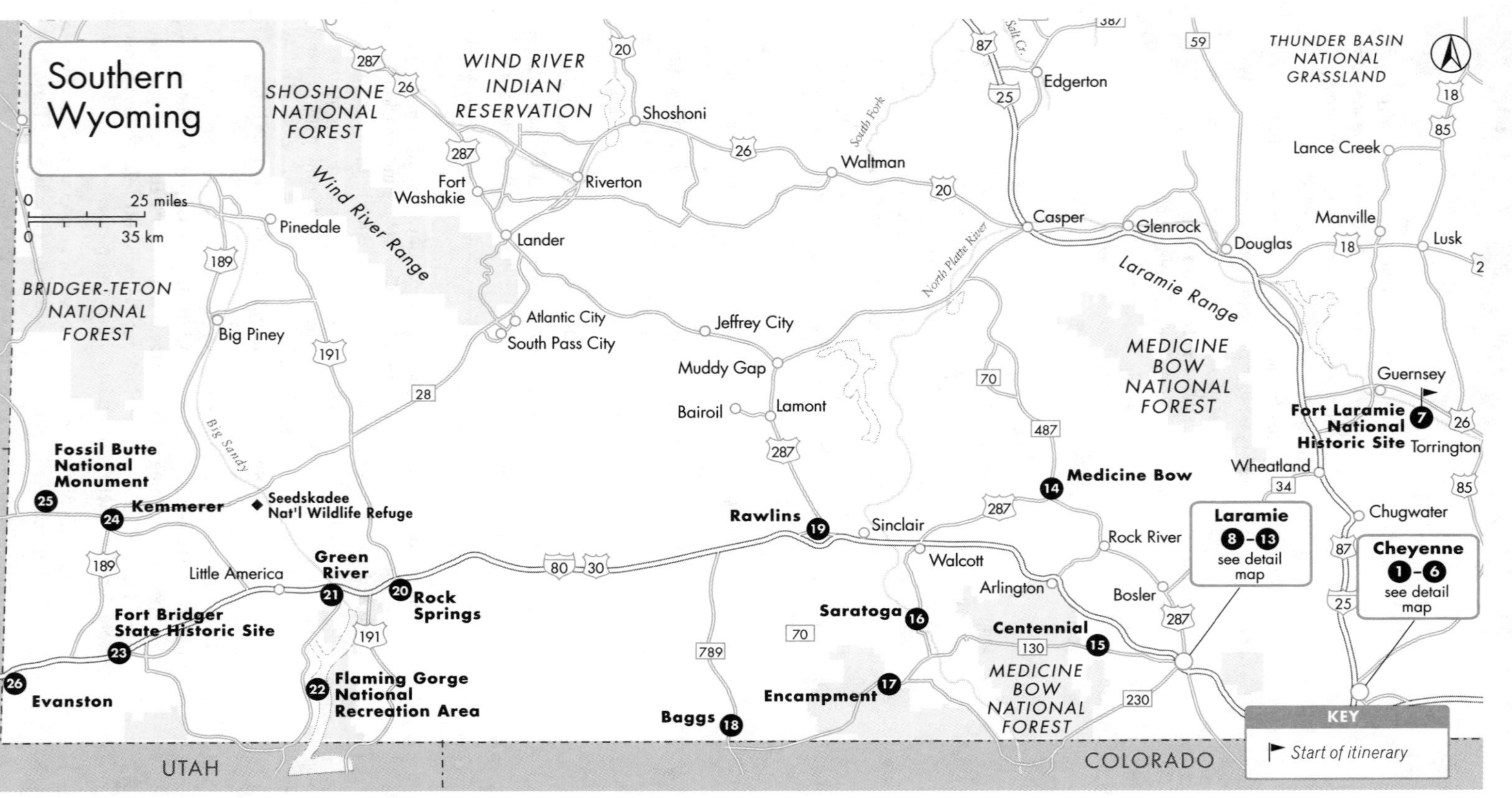

Southern Wyoming
0 25 miles
0 35 km
SHOSHONE NATIONAL FOREST
WIND RIVER INDIAN RESERVATION
THUNDER BASIN NATIONAL GRASSLAND
BRIDGER-TETON NATIONAL FOREST
Wind River Range
Laramie Range
MEDICINE BOW NATIONAL FOREST
Shoshoni
Riverton
Fort Washakie
Lander
Pinedale
Big Piney
Atlantic City
South Pass City
Jeffrey City
Muddy Gap
Bairoil
Lamont
Waltman
South Fork
North Platte River
Casper
Edgerton
Salt Cr.
Glenrock
Douglas
Lance Creek
Manville
Lusk
Guernsey
Fort Laramie National Historic Site 7
Torrington
Wheatland
Chugwater
Big Sandy
Fossil Butte National Monument 25
Kemmerer 24
Seedskadee Nat'l Wildlife Refuge
Little America
Green River 21
Rock Springs 20
Fort Bridger State Historic Site 23
Evanston 26
Flaming Gorge National Recreation Area 22
Baggs 18
Rawlins 19
Sinclair
Walcott
Saratoga 16
Encampment 17
Medicine Bow 14
Rock River
Arlington
Bosler
Centennial 15
Laramie 8–13 see detail map
Cheyenne 1–6 see detail map
KEY
Start of itinerary
UTAH
COLORADO

What to See

2 **Cheyenne Botanic Gardens.** A vegetable garden, roses and other flowers, cacti, and both perennial and annual plants bloom within the greenhouse conservatory and on the grounds here. *710 S. Lions Park Dr. 307/637–6458 www.botanic.org/ Donations accepted Conservatory weekdays 8–4:30, weekends 11–3:30; grounds stay open into the evening.*

Fodor'sChoice ★ **Cheyenne Frontier Days.** One of the premier events in the Cowboy State is Cheyenne Frontier Days, which has been held the last full week of July every year since 1897. Leading contenders in the Professional Rodeo Cowboys Association compete here. Other activities at the nine-day event include chuck-wagon races, a Native American village, dancing, free pancake breakfasts that feed as many as 12,000 people in two hours, and nightly concerts showcasing top country entertainers. Reservations for concerts and hotels are a must. *Box 2477, Cheyenne 82003 307/778–7222, 800/227–6336, 800/543–2339 in WY www.cfdrodeo.com Rodeo $10–$22, concerts $18–$40, package plans $32–$43.*

6 **Curt Gowdy State Park.** You can fish, boat, hike, and picnic at this park named for Wyoming's most famous sportscaster, who got his start at local radio stations in the 1940s. The park, which is 20 mi west of the city, is particularly pleasant in summer and spring, when the wildflowers are in bloom. *1351 Hyndslodge Rd., off Hwy. 210 (Happy Jack Rd.) 307/632–7946 wyoparks.state.wy.us/curt1.htm $2 resident vehicles, $4 nonresident vehicles Daily 24 hrs.*

5 **Historic Governor's Mansion.** Between 1905 and 1976 (when the state built a new residence for the governor), 19 Wyoming first families made their home in this Colonial Revival building. Period furnishings and ornate chandeliers remain in nearly every room. *300 E. 21st St. 307/777–7878 wyoparks.state.wy.us/govern1.htm Free Tues.–Sat. 9–5.*

1 **Old West Museum.** This museum within Frontier Park houses some 30,000 artifacts—including 125 carriages, the largest collection of horse-drawn vehicles in the state—relating to rodeos, ranching, and Cheyenne Frontier Days. Guided tours are geared toward children. During Frontier Days, the museum hosts the Governor's Invitational Western Art Show and Sale, which exhibits works by top Western wildlife and landscape artists from across the country. *4610 N. Carey Ave. 307/778–7290 or 800/266–2696 www.oldwestmuseum.org $5 Sept.–May, weekdays 9–5, Sat. 11–4; June–Aug., weekdays 8:30–5, weekends 9–5; extended hrs during Frontier Days, in late July.*

3 **Wyoming State Capitol.** Construction on this Corinthian-style building, now on the National Register of Historic Places, was authorized by the Ninth Territorial Legislative Assembly in 1886. The dome, covered in 24-karat gold leaf and visible from all roads leading into the city, is 50 feet in diameter at the base and 146 feet high. Standing in front is a statue of Esther Hobart Morris, a proponent of women's suffrage. One of Wyoming's nicknames is the "Equality State" because of its early advocacy of women's rights. Thanks to Wyoming's informal ways, it's not unusual to find the governor wandering the halls of the capitol. You can take a self-guided tour of state offices and the Senate and House chambers. *Capitol Ave. 307/777–7220 www.state.wy.us Free Sept.–Apr., weekdays 8–5; May–Aug., weekdays 8–5, Sat. 9–5.*

4 **Wyoming State Museum.** Several permanent exhibits are dedicated to exploring the heritage, culture, and landscape of Wyoming, covering everything from natural resources to wildlife to historical events. There's a

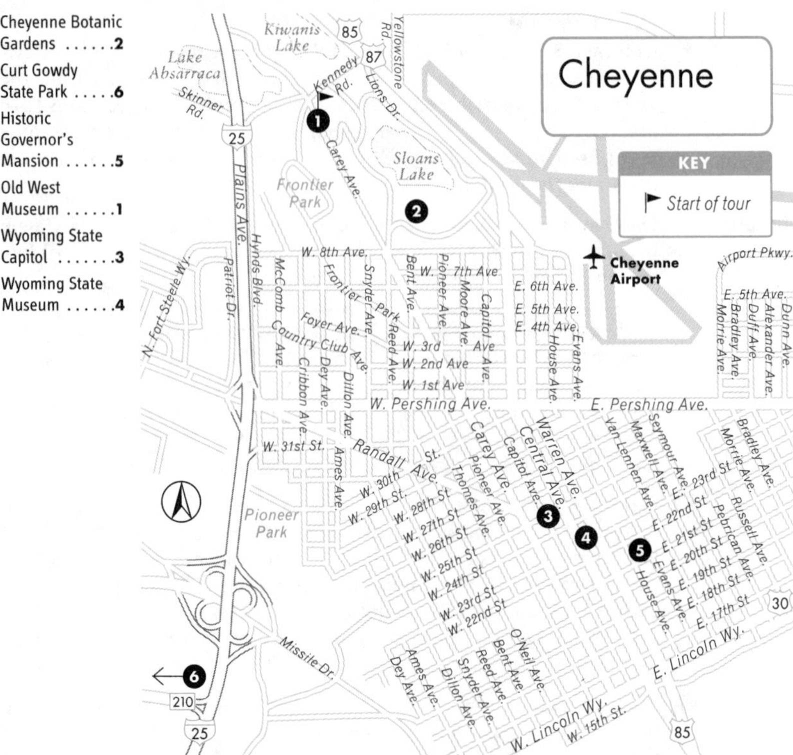

hands-on exhibit geared to children, and the museum hosts several additional temporary exhibits each year. ✉ *Barrett Building, 2301 Central Ave.* ☎ *307/777–7022* 🌐 *wyomuseum.state.wy.us* 🎟 *Free* ⏲ *May–Oct., Tues.–Sat. 9–4:30; Nov.–Apr., Tues.–Fri. 9–4:30, Sat. 10–2.*

Sports & the Outdoors

Golf

The **Airport Course** (✉ 4801 Central Ave. ☎ 307/637–6418) has 18 holes. There's a 9-hole course at **Little America Hotel and Resort** (✉ 2800 W. Lincolnway ☎ 307/775–8400). Play 18 holes of golf at **Prairie View** (✉ 3601 Windmill Rd. ☎ 307/637–6420).

Where to Stay & Eat

★ $$–$$$$ ✕ **Little Bear Steakhouse.** Locals rave about this classic American steak house decorated with a Western theme. Try the New York strip steak or the rib eye. If you're looking for something a little lighter, consider one of the seafood options on the menu. ✉ *700 Little Bear Rd.* ☎ *307/634–3684* 💳 *AE, D, DC, MC, V.*

$–$$$ ✕ **The Albany.** Historic photographs of early-day Cheyenne set the tone for this downtown icon, a place that seems as old as the city itself (the structure was built circa 1900). It's a bit dark, and the booths are a bit shabby, but the American food is solid. Now if only you could get the walls to tell their stories. No doubt they've heard it all, as many of the movers and shakers in Cheyenne's past (and a few in its present) have eaten here. The menu lists hot and cold sandwiches, salads, and burgers. ✉ *1506 Capitol Ave.* ☎ *307/638–3507* 💳 *AE, D, DC, MC, V.*

$–$$ ✕ **Lexie's Mesa Grill.** You can dine on the small outdoor patio or inside this quiet restaurant in one of the oldest extant homes in Cheyenne, dating to the turn of the 20th century. The food ranges from burgers and salads to Mexican dishes, including fajitas and enchiladas. Try the flat bread piled high with smoked turkey, black olives, portobello mushrooms, fried onions, green chilis, and cheese. ✉ *216 E. 17th St.* ☎ *307/632–9119* ▭ *D, MC, V.*

$–$$ ✕ **Los Amigos.** Mexican sombreros, serapes, and artwork on the walls complement the south-of-the-border food at this local favorite south of downtown. Deep-fried tacos and green chili are popular items, and the portions are big. ✉ *620 Central Ave.* ☎ *307/638–8591* ▭ *MC, V* ⏲ *Closed Sun.*

¢–$$$ ✕▣ **Best Western Hitching Post Inn.** State legislators frequent this hotel, known to locals as "The Hitch." With its dark-wood walls, the hotel has an elegance not found elsewhere in Cheyenne. It books country-and-western performers in the lounge. The Cheyenne Cattle Company restaurant ($$–$$$$) serves steak and other dishes in a quiet, relaxed dining room. Next door are venues for miniature golf and ice-skating. ✉ *1700 W. Lincolnway, 82001* ☎ *307/638–3301* 🌐 *www.bestwestern.com* 📠 *307/778–7194* *166 rooms* *Restaurant, coffee shop, room service, in-room data ports, refrigerators, indoor-outdoor pool, gym, lobby lounge, dance club, shop, laundry service, business services, convention center, meeting room, airport shuttle* ▭ *AE, D, DC, MC, V.*

¢–$$$ ▣ **A. Drummond's Ranch Bed and Breakfast.** At this B&B on 120 acres halfway between Cheyenne and Laramie and near Curt Gowdy State Park, outdoor hot tubs and sitting areas afford views of the mountain countryside. The large upstairs loft room has a window seat and a fireplace. Typical guests include cross-country skiers and mountain bikers (two- to six-hour tours are available for both activities), runners who want to train at the 7,500-foot elevation, and horseback riders (stalls are available to board a horse or other pets during your stay). Lunch and dinner can be provided for an extra charge, and special diets can be accommodated. ✉ *399 Happy Jack Rd., 82007* ☎📠 *307/634–6042* 🌐 *www.cruising-america.com/drummond.html* *4 rooms, 2 with bath* *Dining room, outdoor hot tub, horseback riding, library* ▭ *MC, V* *BP.*

$–$$ ▣ **Little America Hotel and Resort.** An executive golf course is the highlight of this resort at the intersection of I–80 and I–25. Most guest rooms are spread among several buildings clustered around the swimming pool, and some are attached to the common public areas via a glassed-in breezeway. ✉ *2800 W. Lincolnway, 82001* ☎ *307/775–8400 or 800/235–6396* 📠 *307/775–8425* 🌐 *www.littleamerica.com* *188 rooms* *Restaurant, coffee shop, room service, in-room data ports, some minibars, refrigerators, 9-hole golf course, pool, gym, bar, lounge, nightclub, shops, laundry service, business services, convention center, meeting rooms, airport shuttle* ▭ *AE, D, DC, MC, V.*

$–$$ ▣ **Nagel Warren Mansion.** This delightful Victorian mansion B&B, built in 1888, has gorgeous woodwork, ornate staircases, and period furniture and wallpaper. Antiques furnish the lavish rooms, which are named for figures associated with the mansion's history; some rooms have gas fireplaces. Close to downtown, the B&B is near restaurants and within walking distance of shops. ✉ *222 E. 17th St., 82001* ☎ *307/637–3333 or 800/811–2610* 📠 *307/638–6879* 🌐 *www.naglewarrenmansion.com* *12 rooms* *Dining room, in-room data ports, gym, hot tub, library, piano, meeting rooms, no-smoking rooms* ▭ *AE, MC, V* *BP.*

Fodor'sChoice ★

¢–$ ▣ **Rainsford Inn.** Elegant surroundings and a B&B atmosphere welcome you on historic "Cattleman's Row" in the heart of downtown Cheyenne. The Cattle Baron Corner suite has dark-wood furniture and ornaments ranging from ropes to boots. It overlooks 17th Street, where Cheyenne's cattle barons lived in the late 1800s. One room is suitable for people with disabilities and includes a roll-in shower. The third-floor Grandma's Attic is a very private retreat. All rooms have whirlpool tubs, one has a gas fireplace, and a full breakfast is included. ✉ *219 E. 18th St., 82001* ☎ *307/638–2337* 🖷 *307/634–4506* 🌐 *www.rainsfordinnbedandbreakfast.com* *6 rooms* *Dining room, library, no-smoking rooms* 💳 *AE, MC, V* 🍽 *BP.*

Camping

⛺ **Curt Gowdy State Park.** In rolling country with pine forest and a profusion of wildflowers during spring and summer, Curt Gowdy is a good camping spot about 20 mi west of the city. The park has picnic sites and areas for swimming, boating, and fishing. The campsites can be used for tents or trailers. *Flush toilets, pit toilets, dump station, drinking water, fire pits, picnic tables, public telephone, play area, swimming (lake)* *150 sites* ✉ *1351 Hyndslodge Rd., off Hwy. 210* ☎🖷 *307/632–7946 or 877/996–7275* 🌐 *wyoparks.state.wy.us/curt1.htm* *$6 for Wyoming residents, $12 for nonresidents* 💳 *No credit cards.*

⛺ **Terry Bison Ranch.** In addition to being a full-service campground and RV park with a restaurant and occasional entertainment, this is a working bison ranch, with nearly 2,000 head on the property. *Flush toilets, full hookups, drinking water, guest laundry* *88 full hookups, 100 tent sites; 7 cabins, 17 bunkhouse rooms* ✉ *I–25 Service Rd. near the Colorado state line* ☎ *307/634–4171* 🖷 *307/634–9746* 🌐 *www.terrybisonranch.com* *Full hookups $25, tent sites $15; cabins $79, bunkhouse rooms $38* 💳 *D, DC, MC, V.*

⛺ **Wyoming Campground and Mobile Home Park.** Two of the attractions at this campground are a swimming pool and Internet service. It's on the south side of Cheyenne. *Flush toilets, full hookups, partial hookups (electric), dump station, drinking water, guest laundry, showers, picnic tables, electricity, public telephone, play area, swimming (pool)* *50 full hookups, 20 partial hookups, 50 tent sites* ✉ *I–80, Exit 377* ☎🖷 *307/547–2244* *Full hookups $18.50–$33.50, partial hookups $16.50–$30.50, tent sites $14–$27* 💳 *AE, D, DC, MC, V* ⏲ *May–Oct.*

Nightlife

For an evening of live country music and shuffling your feet along a large dance floor, try the **Cheyenne Club** (✉ 1617 Capitol Ave. ☎ 307/635–7777). You'll find live music, dancing, and drinks at **Cowboy South** (✉ 312 S. Greeley Hwy. ☎ 307/637–3800).

Shopping

Cheyenne's **Frontier Mall** (✉ 1400 Dell Range Blvd. ☎ 307/638–2290) houses 75 specialty shops and four major department stores. It's as typical an American mall as you'll find. **Wrangler** (✉ 16th and Capitol Sts. ☎ 307/634–3048) stocks a full line of traditional Western clothing, ranging from Wrangler and Rocky Mountain jeans to Panhandle Slim shirts, Resistol hats, and Laredo boots. There are sizes and styles for the entire family.

Side Trip to Fort Laramie National Historic Site

⚑ ❼ *105 mi north of Cheyenne via Hwys. 25 and 26.*

Fort Laramie is one of the most important historic sites in Wyoming, in part because its original buildings are extremely well preserved, but also because it played a role in several significant periods in Western history. Near the confluence of the Laramie and North Platte rivers, the fort began as a trading post in 1834, and it was an important provisioning point for travelers on the Oregon Trail in 1843, the Mormon Trail in 1847, and the California Trail in 1849, when it also became a military site. In 1851 the first treaty between the U.S. government and the Northern Plains Indians was negotiated near the fort, and in 1868 a second Fort Laramie Treaty led to the end of the First Sioux War, also known as Red Cloud's War. Costumed interpreters reenact scenes of military life and talk about the fur trade, overland migration, and relations between settlers and Native Americans. ✉ *Goshen County Rd. 270, 3 mi west of town of Fort Laramie* ☎ *307/837–2221* 🌐 *www.nps.gov/fola* 🎫 *$2* 🕒 *Site daily 8–dusk; visitor center daily 8–5.*

3

en route

Although I–80 connects Cheyenne and Laramie more quickly, the drive between the two cities on **Happy Jack Road** (Highway 210) is very scenic, particularly in spring and early summer, when wildflowers are in full bloom. The road winds over the high plains, past Curt Gowdy State Park, and provides access to the Vedauwoo Recreation Area before linking back to I–80, 7 mi east of Laramie at the **Lincoln Monument.** At this state rest area you can obtain information about the region and view a larger-than-life sculpture of the 16th president.

The **Vedauwoo Recreation Area,** in the Medicine Bow–Routt National Forest, is a particularly unusual area and a great place for a picnic. Springing out of high plains and open meadows are glacial remnants in the form of huge granite boulders piled skyward with reckless abandon. These one-of-a-kind rock formations, dreamscapes of gray stone, are great for hiking, climbing, and photography. There's also camping here. ✉ *31 mi west of Cheyenne off I–80 or Hwy. 210* ☎ *307/745–2300* 🌐 *www.fs.fed.us* 🎫 *Free, camping $10* 🕒 *Daily 24 hrs.*

LARAMIE

Laramie, nestled in a valley between the Medicine Bow Mountains and the Laramie Range, was first settled when the railroad reached here in 1867. For a time it was a tough "end-of-the-rail" town. Vigilantes took care of lawbreakers, hanging them from convenient telegraph poles. Then, in 1872, the city constructed the Wyoming Territorial Prison on the bank of the Little Laramie River. One of its most famous inmates was Butch Cassidy. The prison has since closed, and things have calmed down in this city of approximately 30,000. It's now the center of open-plains ranching country and the site of the University of Wyoming, the only university in the state.

The historic downtown area has several quaint buildings, some of which date back to 1868. You can get brochures from the Laramie Chamber of Commerce, on South 3rd Street, for a self-guided tour of the late-19th-century Victorian architecture. Also available are the "Architectural Walking Tour" brochure, which focuses on the historic residences in the downtown area, and the "Laramie Antique Trail" guide, with locations of antiques shops in and around downtown.

Exploring Laramie

I–80 skirts the south and then west sides of town; U.S. 287 (3rd Street within the city) bisects Laramie from north to south. Grand Avenue, which borders the University of Wyoming, is the primary east–west route through Laramie.

American Heritage Center **13**
Laramie Plains Museum **9**
University of Wyoming **11**
University of Wyoming Geological Museum **12**
Wyoming Children's Museum and Nature Center **10**
Wyoming Territorial Park **8**

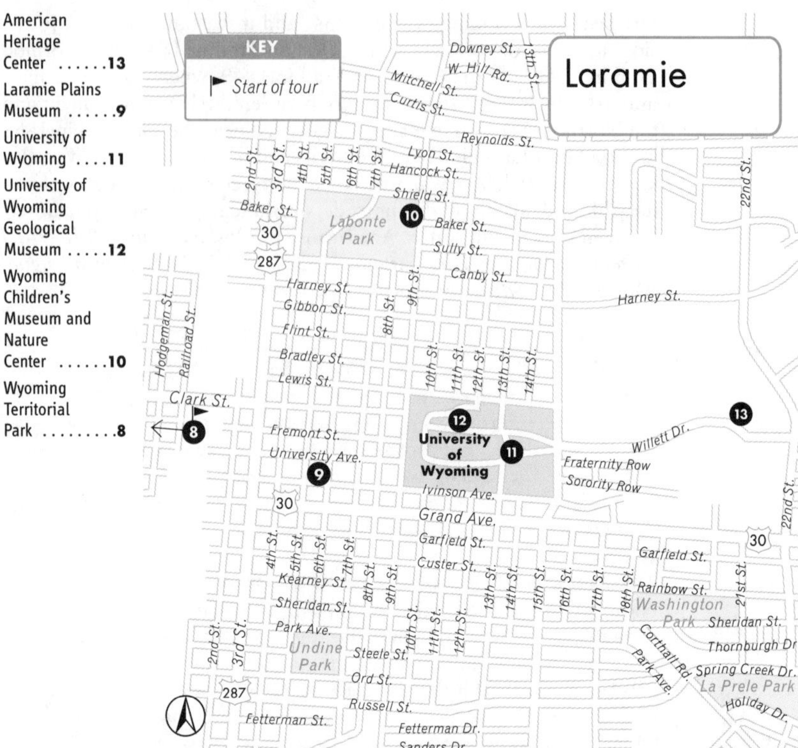

a good tour

Begin your tour of Laramie at **Wyoming Territorial Park** 8 ⚑, site of the restored Wyoming Territorial Prison and several other historic displays. When you're ready to leave the park, turn left out of the parking lot and follow Clark Street east to 6th Street; turn right and drive a few blocks south to Ivinson Avenue. The **Laramie Plains Museum** 9 stands on the corner of 6th and Ivinson. After visiting the museum, drive east three blocks on Ivinson Avenue. Turn left and head north on 9th Street; drive past the University of Wyoming to Sully Street and turn left into the parking lot of the **Wyoming Children's Museum and Nature Center** 10, on the edge of Labonte Park. Follow Sully Street east, make a right on 15th Street, and drive south to the **University of Wyoming** 11. There are parking lots off 15th Street and a visitor lot off 14th Street between Ivinson and Grand avenues. The university has several museums of note, including the **University of Wyoming Geological Museum** 12. Get back in your car and follow Willett Drive east to a large building that looks like an upside-down funnel. This is the **American Heritage Center** 13, with collections on American and Western history. Another option is to drive from the Wyoming Children's Museum and Nature Center straight to the American Heritage Center, southeast of which there's a parking lot where you can leave your car. After exploring the center, you can hop on a free shuttle bus to the campus student union, from which you can walk to the university museums.

TIMING Plan on spending a full day on this tour. Note that several museums close on Sunday and/or Monday and that the Wyoming Territorial Park is open only in summer.

What to See

13 **American Heritage Center.** The center houses more than 10,000 photographs, rare books, collections of papers, and memorabilia related to

such subjects as American and Western history, the petroleum industry, conservation movements, transportation, and the performing arts. Permanent and temporary art displays also fill the museum space. ✉ *2111 Willet Dr.* ☎ *307/766–4114* 🌐 *www.uwyo.edu/ahc* 🎫 *Free* ⏲ *Sept.–May, weekdays 8–5, Sat. 11–5; June–Aug., weekdays 7:30–4:30.*

9 **Laramie Plains Museum.** Edward Ivinson, a businessman and philanthropist and one of Laramie's first settlers, built the mansion that houses this museum in 1892; it's now on the National Register of Historic Places. Inside is a growing collection of historical artifacts from the Laramie plains area. ✉ *603 Ivinson Ave.* ☎ *307/742–4448* 🌐 *www.laramiemuseum.org* 🎫 *$4.25* ⏲ *June–Aug., Tues.–Sat. 9–5, Sun. 1–4; Sept.–May, Mon.–Sat. 1–4.*

11 **University of Wyoming.** In addition to having several museums and attractions, the university hosts year-round events—from concerts to football games. You can join a tour or just pick up information on the university at the **UW Visitor Center** (✉ 14th St. and Grand Ave. ☎ 307/766–4075). The **Anthropology Museum** (☎ 307/766–5136) houses numerous Native American exhibits. Among the artwork displayed in the **Art Museum** (☎ 307/766–6622) are paintings, sculpture, photography, and folk art from America, Europe, Africa, and Asia. Kids especially enjoy looking at the butterflies, mosquitoes, and other crawling and flying critters at the **Insect Museum** (☎ 307/766–2298). You can learn about the stars and watch laser shows at the university's **planetarium** (☎ 307/766–6514). The **Rocky Mountain Herbarium** (☎ 307/766–2236) focuses on Rocky Mountain plants but also includes other examples of flora from the Northern Hemisphere. Call individual museums for opening times and fees (most of them are free). ✉ *13th St. and Ivinson Ave.* 🌐 *www.uwyo.edu.*

12 **University of Wyoming Geological Museum.** This is one of the university's most notable museums, in a building with a dinosaur statue out front. Inside, a skeleton of an apatosaurus is 15 feet high and 75 feet long; it's believed the animal would have weighed 30 tons in its lifetime. Other exhibits explore the dinosaur family tree, meteorites, fossils, and earthquakes. ✉ *Northwest corner of University of Wyoming campus* ☎ *307/766–2646 or 307/766–4218* 🌐 *www.uwyo.edu/geomuseum* 🎫 *Free* ⏲ *Weekdays 8–5, weekends 10–3.*

10 **Wyoming Children's Museum and Nature Center.** Here, children are encouraged to explore, make noise, experiment, play, imagine, discover, and invent. The hands-on exhibits emphasize wildlife, nature, and some local history. The museum is on the edge of Labonte Park, which has playground equipment and plenty of grassy space in which children can burn off some energy. ✉ *968 N. 9th St.,* ☎ *307/745–6332* 🌐 *www.wyshs.org/mus-wychildrens.htm* 🎫 *$3* ⏲ *Memorial Day–Labor Day, Tues.–Thurs. 9–4, Fri. 1–5, Sat. 10–4; Labor Day–Memorial Day, Tues.–Thurs. 9–4, Sat. 10–4.*

8 **Wyoming Territorial Park.** Perhaps because of the bedlam of the early days, Laramie became the site of the **Wyoming Territorial Prison** in 1872. Until 1903, it was the region's federal and state penal facility, locking down Butch Cassidy and other infamous frontier outlaws. Today the restored prison is the gem of Wyoming Territorial Park, which brings to life the legends of frontier law and justice. In addition to the prison, the park contains a 19th-century railroad display, a replica of a frontier town, a living-history program, and the Horse Barn Dinner Theater. ✉ *975 Snowy Range Rd.* ☎ *307/745–6161 or 800/845–2287* 🌐 *www.wyoprisonpark.*

org *Park $10.50, dinner theater $33.95.* *Park Memorial Day–Labor Day, daily 10–5; dinner theater June–Aug., Thurs.–Sat. at 6* PM.

Sports & the Outdoors

Bicycling

Mountain-biking trails are scattered throughout the Medicine Bow–Routt National Forest and the Happy Jack recreation area, east of Laramie. For information, trail maps, and rentals, see Mike or Doug Lowham at the **Pedal House** (207 S. 1st St. 307/742–5533).

Cross-Country Skiing

The Medicine Bow–Routt National Forest and the Happy Jack recreation area have numerous cross-country trails. For information and rentals, contact **Cross Country Connection** (117 Grand Ave. 307/721–2851).

Golf

Enjoy the links at the 18-hole **Jacoby Park Golf Course** (off N. 30th St. 307/745–3111).

Where to Stay & Eat

$$–$$$$ **Cavalryman Supper Club.** It's the food, not the look of the place, that attracts people to this restaurant on the plains, 1 mi south of Laramie on U.S. 287. Menu highlights include prime rib, steak, and lobster. There is a lounge area with dining on the upper and lower floors. *4425 S. 3rd St. 307/745–4578 AE, DC, MC, V No lunch.*

$–$$ FodorsChoice ★ **Overland Restaurant.** Patio dining and a superb wine list enhance the food—pasta, chicken, quiche, beef, and seafood—at this restaurant in the historic district, right on the railroad tracks. Sunday brunch might include such unique entrées as yellowfin tuna and eggs, a buffalo-chili omelet, or avocados Benedict. *100 Ivinson Ave. 307/721–2800 AE, D, MC, V.*

¢–$ **Café Jacques 3rd Street Bar and Grill.** A casual bar and grill, Café Jacques serves sandwiches and 70 beers, including microbrews and domestic and imported brands. *216 E. Grand Ave. 307/742–5522 AE, DC, MC, V.*

$ **Laramie Comfort Inn.** On busy Grand Avenue, this Comfort Inn is close to restaurants and fast-food chains, as well as War Memorial Stadium at the University of Wyoming. The motel has a wheelchair-accessible room with the only roll-in shower in the city. One of the three suites has a whirlpool. *3420 Grand Ave., 82070 307/721–8856 or 800/228–5150 www.comfortinn.com 55 rooms, 3 suites, 1 efficiency apartment Indoor pool, gym, hot tub AE, D, DC, MC, V CP.*

★ ¢–$ **Annie Moore's Guest House.** Now a B&B, this historic home across from the University of Wyoming campus has been in its time a fraternity, a sorority, and an apartment building. Terra-cotta tiles, hardwood floors, the sounds of nesting owls, and a guest-greeting cat named Archina contribute to the coziness of the place. Continental breakfast with homemade goodies comes with good conversation. *819 University Ave., 82070 307/721–4177 6 rooms with 3 shared baths Dining room, library, recreation room AE, D, MC, V CP.*

¢–$ **Foster's Country Corner.** At this white-brick motel, the lobby and halls are rustic Western knotty pine, and the rooms are basic, with contemporary furnishings. The property includes a convenience store, a 24-hour restaurant, and a liquor store. It's on the western edge of town, at the Snowy Range Road exit off I–80. *1561 Jackson St., Exit 311 off I–80, Box 580, 82070 307/742–8371 307/742–0884 112 rooms Restaurant, indoor pool, hot tub, bar AE, D, DC, MC, V.*

WYOMING'S COWBOY SYMBOL

A **SK ANY OLD-TIMER** *in Cheyenne, Laramie, Lander, or Pinedale who the cowboy is on the Wyoming license plate's bucking-horse symbol, and you'll probably get four different answers. Artist Allen True, who designed the symbol, once said he had no particular rider in mind, but that hasn't stopped Wyoming residents from attributing the rider to regional favorites. Several well-known cowboys are often mentioned, including Stub Farlow of Lander and Guy Holt of Cheyenne (who later ranched near Pinedale).*

True was not the first person to create this bucking-horse design, however. The symbol evolved over a number of years, beginning with a 1903 photograph by Professor B. C. Buffum of cowboy Guy Holt riding Steamboat, one of five horses recognized as the most difficult bucking horses of all time. In 1921, the University of Wyoming used that photograph as a model for the bucking-horse-and-cowboy logo on its sports uniforms.

But by that time there was already another Wyoming bucking-horse symbol. During World War I, George Ostrom, a member of the Wyoming National Guard serving in Germany, had a bucking-horse-and-rider design painted on a brass drum. His 148th Field Artillery unit soon adopted the logo for its vehicles as well, and it became known as the Bucking Bronco Regiment from Wyoming. And which horse was the symbol modeled after? In the case of the Wyoming National Guard logo, the horse was Ostrom's own mount, Red Wing.

Using Allen True's design, the state of Wyoming first put the bucking bronco on its license plate in 1936, and the well-known, trademarked symbol has been there ever since.

Camping

Laramie KOA. This campground on the west side of town has lots of grassy space and some trees. Bicycles are provided for free, and for an extra fee you can have satellite TV and telephone service for your RV. Modem service is also available at no extra charge. *Flush toilets, full hookups, drinking water, picnic tables, general store, play area* *116 full hookups, 30 tent sites; 8 cabins* ☒ *1271 W. Baker St., I–80 at Curtis St. exit* ☎ *307/742–6553* *307/742–5039* *www.koa.com* *Full hookups $22–$26, tent sites $10–$16; cabins $25–$45* *D, DC, MC, V.*

Nightlife & the Arts

Nightlife

There's live country-and-western music at the **Buckhorn** (☒ 114 Ivinson Ave. ☎ 307/742–3554). You can kick up your heels on the dance floor at the **Cowboy Saloon** (☒ 108 S. 2nd St. ☎ 307/721–3165). A young set often congregates at the **Drawbridge Tavern** (☒ 1622 Grand Ave. ☎ 307/745–3490), which hosts rock bands. College students gather and shoot pool at **Mingles** (☒ 3206 Grand Ave. ☎ 307/721–2005). For rock music, head to **Shooters Saloon** (☒ 303 S. 3rd St. ☎ 307/745–7676).

The Arts

Dinner theater is performed at the **Horse Barn Dinner Theater** (☒ 975 Snowy Range Rd. ☎ 307/745–6161 or 800/845–2287).

The **University of Wyoming's Fine Arts Program** (☒ East end of Fraternity and Sorority Row ☎ 307/766–5249) regularly holds concerts by classical and popular performers. The **University of Wyoming Fine Arts Center** (☒ East end of Fraternity and Sorority Row ☎ 307/766–3327) periodically hosts productions by the University of Wyoming Department of Theater and Dance.

Shopping

Laramie's most interesting shopping is found in a shopping district called **Landmark Square** along Ivinson Avenue and Grand Avenue. Stores here sell artwork, clothing, and handcrafted items.

Books

Chickering Bookstore (✉ 203 S. 2nd St. ☎ 307/742–8609) showcases regional authors, self-help books, and a good selection of children's titles. **The Grand Newsstand** (✉ 214 Grand Ave. ☎ 307/742–5127) has the best selection of Western and regional titles in the city. **The Second Story** (✉ 105 Ivinson Ave. ☎ 307/745–4423), in an old, antiques-laden upstairs suite of offices, stocks only "personally recommended books," some of them signed by visiting authors.

Crafts & Gifts

Curiosity Shoppe (✉ 206 S. 2nd St. ☎ 307/745–4760) sells antiques, pottery, and hand-embroidered and -crocheted items. **A Touch of Country** (✉ 312 S. 2nd St. ☎ 307/721–2171) has folk art, pottery, baskets, country pine furniture, and a year-round Christmas Shoppe.

Specialty Foods

Laramie's **Whole Earth Granary** (✉ 111 Ivinson Ave. ☎ 307/745–4268) sells organic whole grains and flours, 50 varieties of coffee, herbal extracts, essential oils, and fresh seafood flown in weekly, including live Maine lobster.

IN AND AROUND THE SNOWY RANGE

The Snowy Range encompasses portions of both the Laramie and Brush Creek districts of Medicine Bow–Routt National Forest. Mountain lakes and streams, aspens and pines, camping areas, and trails for hiking, cross-country skiing, and snowmobiling draw outdoor enthusiasts here. The Snowy Range Pass, a stretch of Highway 130 running west from Centennial toward Saratoga, climbs as high as 10,847 feet; driving through the pass, which is open only in summer, takes you past stunning views of the surrounding peaks, including 12,013-foot Medicine Bow Peak. The high elevation means snow caps the mountain peaks in the range year-round.

Medicine Bow

⓮ *60 mi northwest of Laramie via U.S. 30.*

When novelist Owen Wister (1860–1938) first visited Medicine Bow—the town he would immortalize in his 1902 classic Western tale *The Virginian*—he noted that the community looked "as if strewn there by the wind." Today the town still looks somewhat windblown, although the small business district is anchored by the Virginian Hotel, built in the early 1900s and named in honor of the book. This is a community of 320 struggling for survival, with an economy based on the vagaries of agriculture and mining. Although the town sits at the intersection of U.S. 30 (Lincoln Highway) and Wyoming Route 487, you'll seldom encounter much traffic here, except during the fall hunting season (the area is particularly noted for its antelope hunting) and when there are football or basketball games at the University of Wyoming. On those days, expect a crowd on the road and fans talking of sports at the Virginian Hotel.

You can learn about the history of this small town at the **Medicine Bow Museum,** housed in an old railroad depot built in 1913. Owen Wister's summer cabin was relocated to the premises and stands next door. ✉ *405 Lincoln Pl.* ☎ *307/379–2225, 307/379–2581 tour appointments* 🌐 *www.medicinebow.org/museum.htm* 🎫 *Free* ⏲ *Memorial Day–Sept., weekdays 10–5 and by appointment.*

Where to Stay & Eat

¢–$ Fodor'sChoice ★ ✕🏨 **Virginian Hotel.** Inspired by the Owen Wister novel *The Virginian*, this sandstone hotel was built in 1909 and has been operating nearly continuously ever since. Claw-foot tubs, tulip-shape lights, and high beds with comforters fill the Victorian-style rooms. The rooms in the main hotel don't have TVs, phones, or radios (most don't even have electrical outlets), but the atmosphere more than makes up for the lack of amenities. In the main hotel, only the suites have private bathrooms; rooms in the annex have TVs and bathrooms. The dining room, with antique oak furniture and 19th-century photographs, serves American fare such as steak and chicken. ✉ *404 Lincoln Hwy., Box 127, 82329* ☎ *307/379–2377* *38 rooms, 12 with bath; 4 suites* *Restaurant, bar, no-smoking rooms; no phones in some rooms, no TVs in some rooms* 💳 *MC, V.*

Centennial

⑮ *30 mi west of Laramie via Hwy. 130; 90 mi south of Medicine Bow via U.S. 30 and Hwy. 130.*

Snuggled up against the mountains of the Snowy Range, Centennial lies at the head of the glacial Centennial Valley. As the community closest to the Snowy Range, the town makes a good base from which to take part in numerous recreational activities, including hiking, cross-country skiing, snowmobiling, and downhill skiing. This small town has a few hardy year-round residents, and many more people who summer in the area.

The former Centennial Railroad Depot now houses the **Nici Self Museum,** at the eastern edge of town. The museum displays ranching, farming, and mining equipment, plus artifacts typical of what you'd find in a pioneer home; there's also an outdoor-equipment exhibit. ✉ *2740 Hwy. 130* ☎ *307/742–7158 or 307/634–4955* 🌐 *wyshs.org/mus-nici.htm* 🎫 *Donations accepted* ⏲ *Mid-June–Labor Day, Fri.–Mon. 1–4.*

You can hike, picnic, fish, ski, snowmobile, or take photographs in the 400,000 acres of **Medicine Bow–Routt National Forest, Laramie District** (✉ Laramie office: 2468 Jackson St., Laramie 82070 ☎ 307/745–2300, 877/444–6777 for camping 🌐 www.fs.fed.us/r2/mbr/), and that is the short list. The Laramie District has 19 developed campgrounds; dispersed camping is also allowed.

Sports & the Outdoors

CROSS-COUNTRY SKIING The same trails that serve hikers in summer cater to cross-country skiers in winter in the Lower Snowy Range trail system. You can access several trails on Highway 130 west of Centennial in the Medicine Bow–Routt National Forest, including the Corner Mountain Trail (3 mi west of Centennial), Little Laramie Trail (5 mi west of Centennial), and the Green Rock Trail (9 mi west of Centennial). There is also a cross-country-skiing trail system at Snowy Range Ski and Recreation Area. Many of the trails are interconnected, so you can combine short trails for a longer ski trip.

DOWNHILL SKIING & SNOWBOARDING Downhill skiing and snowboarding are available 7 mi west of Centennial at the **Snowy Range Ski and Recreation Area** (✉ 5414 Mountain Mist Court ☎ 307/745–5750 or 800/462–7669 🌐 www.snowyrange.com).

There are slopes for beginners and experienced skiers, plus some cross-country-skiing trails.

HIKING Dozens of miles of hiking trails slice through the Medicine Bow–Routt National Forest west of town. Major trailheads are on Highway 130, including trailheads for the Corner Mountain Trail (3 mi west of Centennial), Little Laramie Trail (5 mi west of Centennial), and Green Rock Trail (9 mi west of Centennial). The 1-mi Centennial Trail takes off from the Centennial Visitor Center at the forest boundary. For a longer, more difficult hike, try the 4½-mi Barber Lake Trail, which starts at Barber Lake and incorporates ski trails and old forest roads. Most hikers follow this trail downhill one-way and instead of doubling back use two vehicles to shuttle between Barber Lake and the Corner Mountain trailhead (the Barber Lake Trail hooks up with part of the Corner Mountain trail).

Trail maps and information are available at the **Centennial Visitor's Center** (✉ Hwy. 130, 1 mi west of Centennial ☎ 307/742–6023).

Where to Stay & Eat

$ **Old Corral Hotel & Steak House.** A crowd of Western carved-wood characters greets you on the front lawn of this log restaurant and hotel. Walking into the steak house ($$–$$$$), with its woodstove and ranch decorations, is like stepping back in time into the Old West. Hand-hewn pine beds and dressers decorate the hotel rooms, and you have access to an outdoor deck with picnic tables and a hot tub, a pool room, and a TV room with videos. The lower level of the on-site gift shop sells T-shirts and Christmas decorations; upstairs there are antique replicas, including Native American pipes and outlaw paraphernalia. ✉ *2750 Hwy. 130, 82055* ☎ *307/745–5918* 📠 *307/742–6846* 🌐 *www.oldcorral.com* *35 rooms* *Restaurant, picnic area, in-room data ports, cable TV with movies, some in-room VCRs, outdoor hot tub, shop, laundry service, no-smoking rooms* *D, MC, V* *Closed mid-Oct.–mid-Dec. and mid-Apr.–mid-May.*

$–$$$ **Rainbow Valley Resort.** Just outside of town in a forest area with pine and aspen trees, these cabins afford good views of the Centennial Valley. The cabins, which have rustic pine furniture, sleep 3 to 11 people and come with full kitchens and outdoor gas grills; there's a two-night minimum stay. A common area has a basketball court and a horseshoe-pitching area. ✉ *68 Rainbow Valley Rd., Box 303, 82055* ☎ *307/745–0368* 🌐 *www.rainbowvalleyresort.com* *5 cabins* *Kitchens, basketball, hiking, horseshoes; no room phones, no smoking* *MC, V.*

CAMPING In addition to the campgrounds listed here, there are several others in both the Laramie and Brush Creek districts of the **Medicine Bow–Routt National Forest** (☎ 877/444–6777, 307/745–2300 Laramie District, 307/326–5258 Brush Creek District 🌐 www.fs.fed.us/r2/mbr/).

Nash Fork. Pine trees surround this simple campground at an elevation of 10,200 feet. Each site can accommodate an RV or a tent, but there are no hookups. *Pit toilets, drinking water, fire grates, fire pits, picnic tables* *27 sites* ✉ *Hwy. 130, 8 mi west of Centennial* ☎ *307/745–2300* 🌐 *www.fs.fed.us/r2/mbr/* *$10* *Reservations not accepted* *No credit cards* *July–Oct.*

Silver Lake. On the west side of the Snowy Range Pass at an elevation of 10,400 feet, this small campground sits beside Silver Lake and is surrounded by pine forest. You can fish in the lake. Several sites are accessible for people with disabilities. *Pit toilets, drinking water, fire grates, fire pits, picnic tables* *17 sites* ✉ *Hwy. 130, 12 mi west of Centennial* ☎ *307/326–5258* 🌐 *www.fs.fed.us/r2/mbr/* *$10* *Reservations not accepted* *No credit cards* *June–Oct.*

Shopping

Leather purses, children's and regional-history books, clothing, ice cream, and baked goods are sold at the **Country Junction** (✉ 2742 Hwy. 130 ☎ 307/745–3318), on the eastern edge of Centennial and within walking distance of the Nici Self Museum. Antiques, wood furniture, and a 5¢ cup of coffee are available at **J&N Mercantile** (✉ 2772 Hwy. 130 ☎ 307/745–0001), along with Wyoming products such as goat's-milk lotion, "cowboy bubble bath" (a bag of beans), and jewelry.

en route

Highway 130 between Centennial and Saratoga is known as the **Snowy Range Scenic Byway.** This paved road, which is in excellent condition, crosses through the Medicine Bow–Routt National Forest, providing views of 12,013-foot Medicine Bow Peak and access to hiking trails, 10 campgrounds (6 right near the road), picnic areas, and 100 alpine lakes and streams. Gravel roads lead off the route into the national forest. Maps are available from the **Centennial Visitor's Center** (✉ Hwy. 130, 1 mi west of Centennial ☎ 307/742–6023).

At the top of the 10,847-foot Snowy Range Pass, about 10 mi west of Centennial, take a short walk to the Libby Flats Observation Site for views of the Snowy Range and, on clear days, Rocky Mountain National Park to the southwest in Colorado. Lake Marie, a jewel of a mountain lake at an elevation of approximately 10,000 feet, is also here. On the Saratoga side of the mountain, the road passes through pine forest and descends to the North Platte River valley, with cattle ranches on both sides of the highway. Note that there is ongoing construction near the junction of Highways 130 and 230, 8 mi south of Saratoga. Also, the byway is impassable in winter and therefore is closed between approximately mid-October and Memorial Day.

Saratoga

16 *49 mi west of Centennial via Hwy. 130, Memorial Day–early Oct.; 140 mi west of Centennial via Hwy. 130 east to Laramie, Hwy. 230 west to Encampment, and Hwy. 130 north, rest of yr.*

Tucked away in a valley formed by the Snowy Range and Sierra Madre mountains, Saratoga is a rarely visited treasure. Fine shopping and dining happily combine with elegant lodging facilities and a landscape that's ideal for outdoor activities. This is a good spot for river floating and blue-ribbon fishing: the North Platte River bisects the region, and there are several lakes and streams nearby in the Medicine Bow–Routt National Forest. You can also cross-country ski and snowmobile in the area. The town first went by the name Warm Springs, but in an attempt to add an air of sophistication to the place, townsfolk changed the name to Saratoga in 1884 (for Saratoga Springs, New York).

★ Hot mineral waters flow freely through the **Hobo Pool Hot Springs,** and the adjacent swimming pool is heated by the springs. People have been coming here to soak for generations, including Native Americans, who considered the area neutral territory. Hardy folk can do as the Native Americans did and first soak in the hot water, then jump into the adjacent icy waters of the North Platte River. ✉ *201 S. River St.* ☎ *307/326–5417* *Free* *Hot springs year-round, daily 24 hrs; pool Memorial Day–Labor Day, daily 9–8 (sometimes closed for lessons).*

The former Union Pacific Railroad depot houses the **Saratoga Historical and Cultural Association Museum,** with displays of local artifacts related to the history and geology of the area. Outdoor exhibits include a sheep wagon and a smithy. A nearby gazebo is used for occasional musical and historical programs in summer. ✉ *104 Constitution Ave.* ☎ *307/326–5511* 🌐 *www.saratoga-museum.org* *Donations accepted* ⏲ *Memorial Day–Labor Day, Tues.–Sat. 1–4.*

Sports & the Outdoors

CANOEING & RAFTING **Great Rocky Mountain Outfitters** (✉ 216 E. Walnut St. ☎ 307/326–8750 🌐 www.grmo.com) offers guided canoe and raft expeditions on the North Platte River, plus canoe and drift-boat rentals.

CROSS-COUNTRY SKIING & SNOWMOBILING Extensive trail networks in the Medicine Bow–Routt National Forest are good for novice and experienced cross-country skiers and snowmobilers. For trail conditions, contact the **Hayden/Brush Creek Ranger District** (☎ 307/326–5258 or 307/327–5481 🌐 www.fs.fed.us/r2/mbr) of the Medicine Bow–Routt National Forest.

Snowmobile rentals, including full- and half-day guided treks into the Snowy Range or Sierra Madres, are available from **Platte Valley Outfitters** (✉ 1st St. and Bridge Ave. ☎ 307/326–5750).

FISHING Brook trout are prevalent in the lakes and streams of Medicine Bow–Routt National Forest, and you can also find rainbow, golden, cutthroat, and brown trout, as well as splake. You can also drop a fly in the North Platte River. **Great Rocky Mountain Outfitters** (✉ 216 E. Walnut St. ☎ 307/326–8750 🌐 www.grmo.com) rents tackle and runs fishing trips on the Upper North Platte.

Where to Stay & Eat

$–$$ ✕ **Lazy River Cantina.** Mexican music and sombreros greet you at this downtown restaurant, which also includes a bar and lounge where locals and visitors take their shot at darts. The entrées include tacos, enchiladas, burritos, and chimichangas, served in one of two small rooms. You can sit in a booth and watch folks and traffic on busy Bridge Avenue. ✉ *110 E. Bridge Ave.* ☎ *307/326–8472* ▭ *MC, V.*

★ ¢–$ ✕ **Wolf Hotel.** This downtown 1893 hotel on the National Register of Historic Places is well maintained by its proud owners. Although some of the guest rooms are small, all of them have simple Victorian charm (note that the rooms are on the second and third floors, and there is no elevator). The fine restaurant ($–$$$$), bar, and lounge also have Victorian furnishings, including dark-green wallpaper, antique oak tables, crystal chandeliers, and lacy drapes. Prime rib and steaks are the specialties, and seafood and lamb are also on the menu. ✉ *101 E. Bridge Ave., 82331* ☎ *307/326–5525* 🌐 *www.wolfhotel.com* *5 rooms, 4 suites* *Restaurant, bar, lounge, meeting rooms, no-smoking rooms; no TV in some rooms* ▭ *AE, DC, MC, V.*

★ $–$$$ **Saratoga Inn Resort.** With leather couches in the common areas, pole-frame beds, and Western art, this inn is as nice as any place in Wyoming. Some rooms are in the main lodge, which has a double fireplace lounge that opens both to the central sitting room and the back porch; other rooms are in separate buildings surrounding a large expanse of lawn and a hot-mineral-water swimming pool. There are five outdoor hot tubs (also hot mineral water), a 9-hole public golf course, and tennis courts. The inn coordinates year-round activities—including fishing and horseback riding—with a local guest ranch. ✉ *601 E. Pic-Pike Rd., Box 869, 82331* ☎ *307/326–5261* 📠 *307/326–5109* 🌐 *www.saratogainn.com* *50 rooms* *Restaurant, room service, cable TV, driving range, 9-hole golf course, putting green, 2 tennis courts, pro shop, pool, outdoor hot tub, fishing, horseback riding, bar, lobby lounge, shop, business services, meeting rooms, no-smoking rooms* ▭ *AE, DC, MC, V.*

Nightlife & the Arts

NIGHTLIFE Local bands often play country-and-western music on weekend nights at the **Rustic Bar** (✉ 124 E. Bridge Ave. ☎ 307/326–5965).

THE ARTS A juried art show, music, and other activities are part of the **Platte Valley Festival of the Arts,** held each year during the weekend closest to the Fourth of July. Obtain information from the **Saratoga-Platte Valley Chamber of Commerce** (✉ 115 W. Bridge Ave., Box 1095, 82331 ☎ 307/326–8855).

Shopping

Oil paintings, sculpture, and photographs are among the fine-art pieces showcased at **Blackhawk Gallery** (✉ 100 N. 1st St. ☎ 307/326–5063). The **Hat Creek Saddlery** (✉ 107 W. Bridge Ave. ☎ 307/326–5755) sells handcrafted leather goods, boots, and hats.

Encampment

17 *18 mi south of Saratoga via Hwys. 130 and 230.*

Trappers in 1838 held a rendezvous on a stream flowing from the Sierra Madre range, calling the site Camp le Grande. The name stuck, and when copper miners struck it rich in 1897, the community that sprang up became Grand Encampment. But the copper boom went bust by 1910, and Grand Encampment dropped the "Grand," even though the town survived as an agricultural and logging center. Most logging operations have since gone the way of mining here, leaving agriculture as the mainstay of the area. Recreation in the nearby Medicine Bow–Routt National Forest is a quickly emerging industry, but there's still a lot of quiet mountain country to explore, and it's not yet crowded in this town of 400 residents.

This is the gateway community to the Continental Divide National Scenic Trail, accessed at Battle Pass, 15 mi west on Highway 70. When completed, this trail will run from Canada all the way south to Mexico along the Continental Divide. Encampment is also a good place to launch trips into four nearby wilderness areas in the Hayden District of Medicine Bow–Routt National Forest—Platte River, Savage Run, Encampment River, and Huston Park—where you can go hiking, fishing, mountain biking, snowmobiling, and cross-country skiing.

Fodor'sChoice ★ The modern interpretive center at the **Grand Encampment Museum** holds exhibits on the history of the Grand Encampment copper district and logging and mining. A pioneer town of original buildings includes the Lake Creek stage station, the Big Creek tie hack cabin, the Peryam homestead, the Slash Ridge fire tower, a blacksmith shop, a transportation barn, and a two-story outhouse. Among the other relics are three original towers from a 16-mi-long aerial tramway built in 1903 to transport copper ore from mines in the Sierra Madres. You can take guided tours, and there's also a research area. A living-history day, with music, costumes, and events, takes place the third weekend in July. ✉ *817 Barnett Ave.* ☎ *307/327–5308* 🌐 *encampment.1wyo.net/GEMuseum.html* *Donations accepted* ⏲ *Memorial Day weekend 10–5; June–Labor Day, Mon.–Sat. 10–5, Sun. 1–5.*

The ranching and cowboy lifestyle is the focus of the three-day **Grand Encampment Cowboy Gathering** (✉ 817 Barnett Ave. ☎ 307/326–8855), held in mid-July. Cowboy musicians and poets perform during afternoon and evening concerts, and there's a stick-horse rodeo for children. Events take place at the Grand Encampment Museum and other venues around town.

The **Medicine Bow–Routt National Forest, Hayden District** covers 586,000 acres, including the Continental Divide National Scenic Trail and the Encampment River, Huston Park, Savage Run, and Platte River wilderness areas. The local **Forest Service office** (✉ 204 W. 9th St. ☎ 307/327–5481 🌐 www.fs.fed.us/r2/mbr) can provide information on hiking, fishing, camping, and cross-country-skiing and snowmobiling trails.

Sports & the Outdoors

CROSS-COUNTRY SKIING & SNOWMOBILING A network of cross-country trails in Medicine Bow–Routt National Forest, the **Bottle Creek Ski Trails** (✉ Hwy. 70, 6 mi southwest of Encampment ☎ 307/327–5720) include several backcountry trails suitable only for expert skiers. There are also easier routes for skiers of all levels. Some trails double as snowmobile trails. All of them are free. For more information in town, go to the Trading Post.

For ski rentals and sales as well as trail information contact Mark Rauterkus at the **Trading Post** (✉ Junction of Hwys. 70 and 230, ☎ 307/327–5720 🌐 www.wyomingcarboncounty.com/trading.htm).

HIKING There are extensive trails in the Sierra Madre range west of Encampment, ranging from developed paths around Bottle Creek to wilderness trails through Huston Park and along the Encampment River. For hiking information contact the Forest Service office of the **Medicine Bow–Routt National Forest, Hayden District** (✉ 204 W. 9th St. ☎ 307/327–5481).

HORSEBACK RIDING Rick Stevens of **Horseback Adventures** (☎ 307/326–5569 or 307/326–5751) can lead a trail ride geared to your riding level. You can choose among rides in the Snowy Range, Sierra Madres, or desert country throughout Carbon County. Horseback trips by the hour or day with **Renegade Wranglers** (✉ Riverside Ave., Riverside ☎ 307/327–5373 or 307/329–8279) include rides to Green Mountain Falls, the Encampment River Trail, Huston Park and the Continental Divide National Scenic Trail, mines, and ghost towns.

Where to Stay & Eat

$–$$$ ✕ **Bear Trap Cafe.** People come for the large portions of hearty but basic food at this log building with the look and feel of a Western hunting lodge. The menu is strong on burgers, steaks, fish, and chicken, and on selected nights there are lobster and crab specials. ✉ *120 E. Riverside Ave., Riverside, 2 mi northeast of Encampment* ☎ *307/327–5277* ▭ *MC, V* ⊗ *Closed Mon.*

¢–$ ✕ **Sugar Bowl.** Old oak-and-copper cashier booths from the original 1904 bank still adorn this delightful, old-fashioned soda fountain and eatery. The burgers are homemade, and the malts, shakes, and sundaes will satisfy any sweet tooth. ✉ *706 Freeman St.* ☎ *307/327–5720* ▭ *MC, V.*

★ $ **Spirit West River Lodge.** Beside the Encampment River, this massive log structure has walls of lichen-covered rocks and large windows overlooking the water and surrounding scenery. Stained glass and Western artwork—most of it by owner R. G. Finney, who is known for his wildlife bronzes and paintings—fill the lodge. His wife, Lynn, who serves the full breakfast, is a Senior Olympic gold medalist in cycling and a native of the area. She can direct you to the best cycling routes and cross-country-skiing trails. The lodge has a mile of private-access fishing on the Encampment River, and each room has a private entrance off a deck overlooking the river. ✉ *¼ mi east of Riverside on Hwy. 230, Box 605, 82325* ☎ *307/326–5753* *307/327–5753* *4 rooms, 1 cabin* *Pond, exercise equipment, fishing, bicycles, bar, piano* ▭ *MC, V* *BP.*

CAMPING **Lazy Acres Campground.** The Encampment River runs past this small campground with plenty of big cottonwood trees for shade. There are pull-through RV sites, tent sites, one small cabin (you provide bedding, stove, and cooking utensils), and four no-frills motel rooms. There's also an on-site fly-fishing shop. *Flush toilets, full hookups, guest laundry, showers* *34 full hookups, 5 tent sites; 1 cabin, 4 motel rooms* *Hwy. 230, Riverside* *307/327–5968* *www.wyomingcarboncounty.com/lazy.htm* *Full hookups $20.50, tent sites $15.50; cabin $26; motel rooms $34–$37* *MC, V* *Mid-May–Nov.*

Shopping

Aunt Martha's This 'n That (705 Freeman St. 307/327–5090) carries antiques and baskets, pottery, and other gift items. Roxana Johnson sells hand-knitted and hand-sewn clothing for all ages at **Ewe to You** (705 Freeman St. 307/327–5558).

3

en route

As you make your way west to Baggs over the **Battle Highway** (Highway 70), you'll cross the Continental Divide and the Rocky Mountains. This route takes you through the mining country that was developed during the 1897–1908 copper-mining boom in the Sierra Madres; interpretive signs along the way point out historic sites. In 1879, Thomas Edison was fishing near Battle Pass with a bamboo rod when he began to ponder the idea of a filament, which led to his invention of the incandescent lightbulb. Note that this section of the highway closes to car travel in winter, though it stays open for snowmobiles.

Baggs

18 *60 mi west of Encampment via Hwy. 70.*

Settled by cattle and sheep ranchers, the Little Snake River valley—and its largest community, Baggs—is still ranch country. Two emigrant trails passed nearby: the south branch of the Cherokee Trail (circa 1849–1850) crosses near the community, and the Overland Trail (1862–1865) lies farther to the north. Notorious outlaw Butch Cassidy frequented the area, often hiding out here after pulling off a train or bank robbery. To the west of Baggs, large herds of wild horses range freely on public lands.

Ranch paraphernalia and the original 1870s-era cabin of mountain man James Baker are exhibited at the **Little Snake River Valley Museum.** *No. 2 N. Savery Rd.* *307/383–7262* *lsrvmuseum.homestead.com/homepage.html* *Donations accepted* *Memorial Day–late Oct., daily 11–5.*

Where to Stay & Eat

¢–$ **Wagon Wheel Cafe.** Generous portions of steak, chicken, and seafood are dished up at low prices at this small café. Hamburgers are served on homemade buns. The café can also provide a sack lunch that is bound to assuage any appetite. *20 N. Penland St.* *307/383–7515* *MC, V.*

¢ **Drifter's Inn.** Drifter's has no-frills motel rooms adjacent to a restaurant ($$) and lounge. Menu items range from burgers and steaks to chicken and fish. Friday nights there's prime rib, and Saturday nights are reserved for steak and shrimp. *210 Penland St., 82321* *307/383–2015* *307/383–6282* *51 rooms* *Restaurant, cable TV, bar, some pets allowed, no-smoking rooms* *AE, D, MC, V.*

Rawlins

19 *70 mi northeast of Baggs via Hwy. 789 and I–80.*

Started as one of the Union Pacific's hell-on-wheels towns, Rawlins was an important transportation center as early as 1868, when miners heading for the goldfields at South Pass to the north rode the rails to Rawlins or points nearby, then went overland to the gold diggings. The town became a large sheep-raising center at the turn of the 20th century. Kingpins in the sheep industry, such as George Ferris and Robert Deal, also backed the development of the Grand Encampment Copper Mining District in the Sierra Madres after miner Ed Haggarty discovered copper there in 1897.

Declines in sheep raising, long Rawlins's mainstay industry, have hurt the community economically, as have downturns in regional mineral production. But the city of 10,000 still has many railroad workers based here and can rely on the operation of the Wyoming State Penitentiary outside of town.

About 70 mi north of Rawlins via U.S. 287 and Highway 220 are several sights of interest that are grouped together: Independence Rock State Historic Site, Devil's Gate, and Handcart Ranch (⇨ *see* Casper *in* Chapter 4).

At the **Carbon County Museum** you can see a gruesome pair of shoes made from the skin of Big Nose George Parrott. Parrott was an outlaw who was lynched in 1881 after he attempted to escape from the county jail, where he was being held awaiting execution for his role in the murder of two law-enforcement officers, the first officers to die in the line of duty in Wyoming. After his death, Parrott's body was used for "medical study," and he was ultimately skinned (which is how they made the shoes). Other more traditional articles illuminate the area's settlement. ✉ *9th and Walnut Sts.* ☎ *307/328–2740* *Free* ⏲ *May–Sept., weekdays 10–noon and 1–5; Oct.–Apr., Mon., Wed., and Sat. 1–5; tours by appointment.*

You can fish, boat, and water-ski on the Seminoe Reservoir, the primary attraction within **Seminoe State Park.** This is also a popular spot for camping and picnicking. It's on a Bureau of Land Management backcountry byway, Carbon County Road 351, which links Sinclair with Alcova. ☎ *307/320–3013* 🌐 *wyoparks.state.wy.us* *$2 resident vehicle, $4 nonresident vehicle; $6 camping* ⏲ *Daily 24 hrs.*

Cold steel and concrete, the Death House, and the Yard are all part of the tour of the **Wyoming Frontier Prison,** which served as the state's penitentiary from 1901 until 1981. There are occasional midnight tours and a Halloween tour. ✉ *500 W. Walnut St.* ☎ *307/324–4422* 🌐 *www.wyomingfrontierprison.com* *$4.25* ⏲ *Memorial Day–Labor Day, daily 8:30–5:30; Apr.–Memorial Day and Labor Day–Oct., call for limited hrs; rest of yr by appointment.*

Where to Stay & Eat

$$–$$$ ✕ **The Pantry.** The original rooms of a historic rancher's house provide a quiet setting for your meal, which may include homemade soup and bread, steak, chicken, or lasagna. ✉ *221 W. Cedar St.* ☎ *307/324–7860* ▭ *D, MC, V.*

★ **$–$$** ✕ **Rose's Lariat.** Some of the best authentic Mexican food in Wyoming is served in this tiny eatery. Try the enchiladas or tamales. If you can't handle it hot and spicy, order a sandwich, a hamburger, or one of the Italian dishes on the menu. ✉ *410 E. Cedar St.* ☎ *307/324–5261* ▭ *No credit cards* ⏲ *Closed Sun. and Mon.*

$–$$ ✕ **Su Casa.** The only place in Wyoming to rival the Mexican menu at Rose's Lariat is 6 mi east of Rawlins in Sinclair. The menu includes shrimp, beef, and chicken fajitas, green chili, enchiladas, and Navajo tacos. Try the chiles rellenos (fried cheese-stuffed peppers) or enchiladas. Takeout is available. ✉ *705 E. Lincoln Ave., Sinclair* ☎ *307/328–1745* ▭ *No credit cards* ⊙ *Closed Mon.*

$ **Best Western Cottontree Inn.** This is Rawlins's finest hotel, with spacious guest rooms decorated in greens and mauves. The inviting public areas with easy chairs are great for relaxing. The restaurant serves melt-in-your-mouth corn bread and homemade soups. ✉ *23rd and W. Spruce Sts., Box 387, 82301* ☎ *307/324–2737* *307/324–5011* 🌐 *www.cottontree.net* *122 rooms* *Restaurant, in-room data ports, cable TV, indoor pool, hot tub, sauna, bar, laundry service, business services, meeting rooms, free parking, some pets allowed, no-smoking rooms* ▭ *AE, D, DC, MC, V.*

$ **Lodge at Rawlins.** The lodge has just about everything you could ask for under one roof—from a game room to business services—and it's convenient to shops and a grocery store. ✉ *1801 E. Cedar St., 82301* ☎ *307/324–2783 or 877/729–5467* *307/328–1011* 🌐 *www.thelodgeatrawlins.com* *130 rooms* *Restaurant, in-room data ports, cable TV, pool, bar, recreation room, laundry service, business services, meeting rooms, free parking, some pets allowed (fee), no-smoking rooms* ▭ *AE, D, DC, MC, V.*

CAMPING **RV World Campground.** There are pull-through RV sites and tent sites at this campground on the west side of Rawlins. *Flush toilets, full hookups, dump station, drinking water, guest laundry, showers, grills, picnic tables, swimming (pool)* *90 full hookups, 11 tent sites* ✉ *3101 Wagon Circle Rd.* ☎ *307/328–1091* *Full hookups $22, tent sites $8* ▭ *MC, V* ⊙ *Mid-Apr.–Sept.*

Shopping

Western and wildlife art, antiques, and clothing are among the items available at **Cedar Chest Galleries** (✉ 416 W. Cedar St. ☎ 307/324–7737).

en route

If you're heading west from Rawlins to Rock Springs on I–80, you'll be following the path of the Cherokee Trail, the Overland Trail, and the Union Pacific Railroad into the **Great Divide Basin and Red Desert,** a landscape of flat sands and sandstone outcrops and bluffs. The best time to appreciate the beauty of this desert country, which spreads for thousands of acres west of Rawlins, is early morning (traveling west) and late afternoon (traveling east), when the sun creates wonderful shadows and makes the land glow. If you're headed east in the morning or west in the afternoon, you'll be driving with the sun in your eyes, so this may be a good time to take a break from driving.

SOUTHWEST WYOMING

Known as the Red Desert or the Little Colorado Desert, this is a unique area of Wyoming, with a combination of badlands, desert, and mountains. The region is known for its mineral resources and for the dinosaur fossils that have been found here. Although it may appear to be desolate, there's a wealth of wildlife in this region, including the largest free-ranging herd of pronghorn in the world (numbering around 50,000) and one of the largest herds of wild horses (numbering in the hundreds) in the United States. The far corner of southwestern Wyoming has close ties to Utah. Not only are many communities predominantly Mormon, but with Salt Lake City about an hour away, Evanston residents also shop and attend cultural events there.

Rock Springs

20 *106 mi west of Rawlins via I–80.*

Coal mining has always defined the community of Rock Springs, established when the Union Pacific Railroad pushed through the area in the late 1860s. The mines drew laborers from a variety of nationalities, making this a real melting pot of cultures. Sprawled at the base of White Mountain, Rock Springs, population 24,000, is the site of Western Wyoming Community College, a facility known for its paleontological resources.

The Red Desert to the north and east is home to hundreds of wild horses; you can often catch a glimpse of them from area highways.

Dinosaurs, placed throughout the building, are among the prehistoric animal and plant specimens on display at the **Western Wyoming Community College Natural History Museum.** Species range in age from 67 million to 180 million years old. Don't miss the fossilized fish and the baby alligator. The museum also has rotating exhibits. ✉ *2500 College Dr.* ☎ *307/382–1600* *Free* *Daily 8–7.*

Where to Stay & Eat

$–$$$ ✕ **Bitter Creek Brewery.** Choose one of 18 different burgers and wash it down with a Bob (a local brew that has won awards at brew fests in Denver and Laramie) or a Coal Porter (a beer named in honor of the coal-mining heritage of this community). Wraps, soups, steaks, and chicken are also on the menu. The brewery is in a long, narrow room with a concrete floor and blond-oak furniture. ✉ *604 Broadway* ☎ *307/362–4782* ▭ *AE, D, MC, V.*

¢–$ ✕ **Boschetto's European Market.** Rock Springs's population has been a melting pot of nationalities since its earliest settlement as a coal-mining town. With its wide selection of cheeses, sausages, spaghetti, and other foods, Boschetto's, a European-style market and deli, caters to the variety of folks living here. The dining room sparkles with a tile floor, black-and-white chairs, and small white-linen-covered tables. Takeout is available. ✉ *6717 Broadway* ☎ *307/382–2350* ▭ *AE, D, DC, MC, V.*

¢–$ ✕ **Grubs Drive-In.** Burgers and fries are the specialty at this tiny diner, and the same family has been dishing them up since the 1950s. There's not a lot of room in here: you sit at a horseshoe-shape counter elbow-to-elbow with the other diners. ✉ *415 Paulson St.* ☎ *307/362–6634* ▭ *MC, V.*

$ **Holiday Inn.** A fireplace in the lobby sets the mood at this Holiday Inn on the west side of town. An indoor pool has its own space in a separate room to the left side of the lobby. Light-color furniture fills the guest rooms; chairs and ottomans within the rooms are nice for relaxing. Note that the ground-floor rooms have exterior entrances. ✉ *1675 Sunset Dr., 82902* ☎ *307/382–9200* *307/632–1064* *www.holiday-inn.com* *113 rooms, 1 suite* *Restaurant, some refrigerators, indoor pool, gym, hot tub, bar, meeting rooms, airport shuttle, some pets allowed (fee)* ▭ *AE, D, DC, MC, V.*

$ **Ramada Limited.** Cherrywood furniture—including a desk, end tables, and an easy chair—decorates the rooms here. A free Continental breakfast is served by the fireplace in the breakfast room. Near the White Mountain Mall, the hotel is on the west side of town; take Exit 102 off I–80. ✉ *2717 Dewar Dr., 82902* ☎ *307/362–1770, 888/307–7890 reservations only* *307/362–2830* *www.ramada.com* *129 rooms, 2 suites* *In-room data ports, pool, gym, laundry service, some pets allowed* ▭ *AE, D, DC, MC, V* *CP.*

CAMPING **Rock Springs KOA.** Tent sites and plenty of RV space make up this campground on the west side of the city. *Flush toilets, full hookups, dump station, drinking water, guest laundry, showers, grills, picnic tables, swimming (pool) 100 full hookups, 20 tent sites 86 Foothill Blvd. 307/362–3063 or 800/562–8699 www.koa.com Full hookups $19–$27, tent sites $19 D, MC, V Apr.–mid-Oct.*

The Arts

Programs ranging from art shows to concerts are presented throughout the year by the **Community Fine Arts Center** (400 C St. 307/362–6212). Every June the center hosts International Day in recognition of the 56 nationalities of people who settled and live in Rock Springs. The center's Halseth Gallery houses a permanent collection of more than 400 mostly American paintings, prints, drawings, and photographs, including artwork by Norman Rockwell, Grandma Moses, and Rufino Tamayo.

en route

Wild horses, antelope, desert elk, coyotes, hawks, and sage grouse are among the wild animals you might see on the **Pilot Butte Wild Horse Scenic Loop Tour** (307/362–3771), which also takes you past such prominent features as Pilot Butte, the Killpecker Sand Dunes, and segments of the Overland Trail. Along the route there are pullouts with interpretive panels.

This loop links Rock Springs and Green River; it takes two to three hours to drive the 50-mi route, half of which is on gravel roads, between the two towns. From Rock Springs, travel north for 14 mi on Highway 191. Turn left onto Sweetwater County Road 4-14 and follow the route for 2½ mi before turning left onto Sweetwater County Road 4-53, which will take you to Green River, 33½ mi away.

Green River

21 *12 mi west of Rock Springs via I–80.*

Of all the towns along the Union Pacific Railroad, Green River is the only one that predated the arrival of the rails in the late 1860s. It began as a Pony Express and stage station on the Overland Trail. In 1869 and again in 1871, explorer John Wesley Powell (1834–1902) launched expeditions down the Green and Colorado rivers from sites near Green River. Today the town of more than 13,000 attracts those who want to explore the waterways of the Green River drainage in the nearby Flaming Gorge National Recreation Area.

A golf tournament, bull-riding competition, parade, arts festival in the park, and concerts are all part of **Flaming Gorge Days** (307/875–5711 www.flaminggorgedays.com), a four-day celebration held each June in Green River. Tickets can be purchased for individual events; it costs $6 to $8 to attend the bull-riding competition, and concert tickets start at $25.

off the beaten path

SEEDSKADEE NATIONAL WILDLIFE REFUGE – Prairie and peregrine falcons, Canada geese, and various species of hawks and owls inhabit this 25,000-acre refuge. Trumpeter swans also occasionally use the area. Within or near the refuge there are homestead and ranch sites, Oregon Trail crossings, and ferries that cross the Green River, as well as the spot where Jim Bridger and Henry Fraeb built a trading post in 1839. Visitor information and rest rooms are available 24 hours. *37 mi north of Green River on Hwy. 372 307/875–2187 www.r6.fws.gov/refuges/seedskad Free.*

Sports & the Outdoors

A stroll on the paved path by the Green River takes you along the route that John Wesley Powell followed on his expedition down the waterway in 1869. Along the way you can visit Expedition Island, the Green Belt Nature Area, and the Scotts Bottom Nature Area. Access **Expedition Island** off 2nd Street, southwest of the railroad yard in Green River; wild birds, squirrels, and rabbits inhabit the grassy, tree-shaded island. Downstream from Expedition Island on the south bank of the river is the **Green Belt Nature Area,** with interpretive signs, nature paths, and numerous birds, including waterfowl. Farther south is **Scotts Bottom Nature Area,** where you'll find more interpretive signs related to the wildlife that lives in this riparian habitat.

Where to Stay & Eat

$–$$$ ✕ **Denali Grill and Bakery.** A Mount Denali theme pervades this down-home restaurant with artificial pine trees galore, twig curtain rods, pictures of moose and bears, and iron caribou silhouettes on the walls. The owners pride themselves on their homemade breads, soups, and sandwiches. Local favorites are the baby-back barbecue ribs and salmon fillet. Bread pudding, pecan torte, and lemon crunch pie are some of the homemade desserts. ✉ *375 Uinta Dr.* ☎ *307/875–4654* ▭ *AE, D, MC, V.*

$–$$ ✕ **Penny's Diner.** The name pretty much says it all—a 1950s-style 24-hour diner with a bright shiny look, reminiscent of a railcar, and flashing neon lights. Try a burger, fries, and a milk shake. The diner is part of the Oak Tree Inn. ✉ *1172 W. Flaming Gorge Way* ☎ *307/875–3500* ▭ *AE, D, DC, MC, V.*

$–$$$ **Little America.** This one-stop facility stands alone in the Red Desert, and it can be a real haven if the weather becomes inclement. The hotel, founded in 1934, is the original of the small chain. The rooms are large and comfortable; a small number of them have only showers, and no bathtubs, in the bathrooms. A full-service fuel station and a convenience store are also on the premises. ✉ *I–80, 20 mi west of Green River, Box 1, Little America 82929* ☎ *307/875–2400 or 800/634–2401* 🖷 *307/872–2666* 🌐 *www.littleamerica.com* *140 rooms* *Restaurant, some in-room data ports, some refrigerators, pool, gym, bar, playground, laundry facilities, business services* ▭ *AE, D, DC, MC, V.*

¢–$ **Oak Tree Inn.** This two-story inn in four buildings on the west side of town is 20 mi from Flaming Gorge and has views of unique rock outcroppings above the city. Contemporary furnishings fill the rooms, which are decorated in shades of mauve and green. ✉ *1170 W. Flaming Gorge Way, 82935* ☎ *307/875–3500* 🖷 *307/875–4889* *192 rooms* *Restaurant, some refrigerators, exercise equipment, hot tub, laundry facilities, some pets allowed (fee); no smoking* ▭ *AE, D, DC, MC, V.*

Flaming Gorge National Recreation Area

❷❷ *20 mi south of Green River via Hwy. 530 or Hwy. 191.*

The Flaming Gorge Reservoir of the Flaming Gorge National Recreation Area straddles the border between Wyoming and Utah; most of the park's visitor services are in Utah. The water flow comes from the Green River and is held back by Flaming Gorge Dam. You can boat and fish, as well as watch for wildlife. The area is as rich in history as it is spectacularly beautiful. Mountain men such as Jim Bridger and outlaws such as Butch Cassidy found haven here, and in 1869, on his first exploration down the Green River, John Wesley Powell named many local landmarks: Flaming Gorge, Horseshoe Canyon, Red Canyon, and the Gates of Lodore. The recreation area has marinas, lodging, food, campgrounds, places to rent horses and snowmobiles, and trails for mountain bikes. The Ashley National Forest administers the area. ☎ *801/784–3445, 800/277–7571 for information on reservoir elevations and river flows, 877/444–6677 TDD, 877/833–6777 for campground reservations* 🌐 *www.fs.fed.us* 🎫 *Free* ⏲ *Daily 24 hrs.*

Sports & the Outdoors

BOATING **Buckboard Marina** (✉ Hwy. 530, 25 mi south of Green River ☎ 307/875–6927) provides full marina services, including boat rentals, a marina store, and an RV park.

FISHING Bob and Marsha Tynsky of **Sweetwater Fishing Adventures** (✉ 1125 Florida, Green River ☎ 307/875–9609) lead guided fishing trips within Flaming Gorge.

Camping

⛺ **Buckboard Crossing.** The campsites at this campground on the west side of Flaming Gorge can be used for tents or RVs, but there are no hookups for RVs. There's a boat dock here. ♿ *Flush toilets, dump station, drinking water, showers, fire pits, picnic tables, general store* ⛟ *68 sites* ✉ *23 mi southwest of Green River on Hwy. 530, then 2 mi east on Forest Rd. 009* ☎ *435/784–3445 for information, 307/875–6927 or 877/444–6777 for reservations* 🌐 *www.reserveusa.com* 🎫 *$13* 💳 *AE, D, MC, V* ⏲ *Early May–late Sept.*

⛺ **Firehole Canyon.** Located in the Flaming Gorge National Recreation Area, this campground has great canyon views. You can pitch a tent or park an RV on the campsites here, but there are no hookups for RVs. There's a beach area nearby, plus a boat ramp. ♿ *Flush toilets, drinking water, showers, fire pits, picnic tables* ⛟ *38 sites* ✉ *13 mi south of Green River on Hwy. 191, then 10 mi west on Forest Rd. 106* ☎ *435/784–3445 for information, 877/444–6777 for reservations* 🌐 *www.reserveusa.com* 🎫 *$13–$26* 💳 *AE, D, MC, V* ⏲ *Late Apr.–late Sept.*

Fort Bridger State Historic Site

★ 🐤 ㉓ *51 mi west of Green River via I–80.*

Started in 1843 as a trading post by mountain man Jim Bridger and his partner Louis Vasquez, Fort Bridger was under the control of Mormons by 1853 after they either purchased the fort or forced the original owners to leave—historians aren't sure which scenario occurred. As the U.S. Army approached during a conflict known as the Mormon War of 1857, the Mormons deserted the area and burned the original Bridger post. Fort Bridger then served as a frontier military post until it was abandoned in 1890. Many of the military-era buildings remain, and the Bridger post has been rebuilt and is staffed by a mountain man and woman. You can attend interpretive programs and living-history demonstrations during the summer. The largest mountain-man rendezvous in the intermountain West occurs annually at Fort Bridger over Labor Day weekend, attracting hundreds of buckskinners and Native Americans plus thousands of visitors. ✉ *Exit 34 off I–80* ☎ *307/782–3842* 🌐 *wyoparks.state.wy.us/bridger1.htm* 🎫 *$2 residents, $4 nonresidents* ⏲ *Grounds year-round, daily 8–sunset. Museum Apr. and Oct., weekends 9–4:30; May–Sept., daily 9–5:30.*

Camping

⛺ **Fort Bridger RV Camp.** There's plenty of grass for tents, and room for RVs as well at this campground near Fort Bridger. ♿ *Flush toilets, full hookups, drinking water, guest laundry, showers, grills, picnic tables* ⛟ *39 full hookups, 20 tent sites* ✉ *64 Groshon Rd.* ☎ *307/782–3150* 🎫 *Full hookups $19, tent sites $15* 💳 *No credit cards* ⏲ *Apr.–mid-Oct.*

Shopping

The fort's re-created **Bridger/Vazquez Trading Post** sells goods typical of the 1840s, when the post was first established, including trade beads, clothing, and leather items. It's open May–September, daily 9–5.

Kemmerer

24 *34 mi north of Fort Bridger via Hwy. 412, 35 mi north of Evanston via Hwy. 189.*

Probably the most important person in Kemmerer's history was James Cash Penney, who in 1902 started the Golden Rule chain of stores here. He later used the name J. C. Penney Company, which by 1929 had 1,395 outlets. Penney revolutionized merchandising in western Wyoming. Before the opening of Penney's stores, the coal-mining industry dominated the region, and miners were used to working for the company and purchasing their supplies at the company store—which often charged whatever it wanted, managing to keep employees in debt. But when Penney opened his Golden Rule, he set one price for each item and stuck to it. Later he developed a catalog, selling to people unable to get to town easily.

The **Fossil Country Frontier Museum,** housed in a former church, has fossils and displays related to early settlement in the area. ✉ *400 Pine Ave.* ☎ *307/877–6551* *Free* ⏲ *June–Aug., Mon.–Sat. 9–5; Sept.–May, Mon.–Sat. 10–4.*

At **Ulrich's Fossil Gallery** you can view fossils from around the world and even buy some specimens, particularly fish fossils. Ulrich's also runs fossil-digging excursions at private quarries; call for more information. ✉ *U.S. 30* ☎ *307/877–6466* *Gallery free, fossil-digging excursions $65* ⏲ *Daily 8–6; fossil digs June–Sept., daily at 9.*

Where to Stay & Eat

$ ✕ **Busy Bee.** This local favorite on the main street of town serves hearty homemade fare such as chicken-fried steak, chicken dinners, hamburgers, and omelets. The theme is cows: cow pictures and ceramic heifers dot the walls and counters. ✉ *919 Pine St.* ☎ *307/877–6820* *No credit cards.*

¢ **Energy Inn.** Southwestern colors decorate these basic rooms, some of which have kitchenettes. A fax and microwave are available in the lobby, and you won't have trouble finding a parking spot in the 2-acre lot. The motel is a few miles south of Kemmerer in Diamondville. ✉ *3 Hwy. 30, Diamondville 83101* ☎ *307/877–6901* *42 rooms* *In-room data ports, some kitchenettes, refrigerators, cable TV* *AE, D, DC, MC, V.*

Shopping

To understand Kemmerer's roots, stop at the **JC Penney store** (✉ 722 JC Penney Dr. ☎ 307/877–3164), which is where James Cash Penney began his merchandising career. This small retail establishment, known as the "mother store," sells clothing.

Fossil Butte National Monument

25 *15 mi west of Kemmerer via U.S. 30.*

A unique concentration of creatures is embedded in this natural limestone outcrop, indicating clearly that this area was an inland sea more than 50 million years ago. Many of the fossils—which include fish, insects, and plants—are remarkably clear and detailed. Pronghorn, coyotes, prairie dogs, and other mammals find shelter within the 8,198-acre park, along with numerous birds, such as eagles and falcons. You can hike the fossil trails and unwind at the picnic area. A visitor center here houses an information desk and exhibits of fossils found in the area, including a 13-foot crocodile. *307/877–4457 www.nps.gov/fobu Free Park daily 24 hrs. Visitor center June–Aug., daily 8–7; Sept.–May, daily 8–4:30.*

Evanston

26 *50 mi south of Fossil Butte National Monument via U.S. 189; 86 mi west of Green River on I–80; 80 mi east of Salt Lake City, Utah, on I–80.*

Like other raucous towns established as the Union Pacific laid its tracks across Wyoming, Evanston started as a tent city. Many of the rail workers were Chinese. Today Evanston celebrates that railroad and Chinese history at Depot Square, with the UP Railroad Depot and a model of a Chinese joss house. The town makes a decent base for visiting Fort Bridger State Historic Site and Fossil Butte National Monument.

Wildlife, from ducks and Canada geese to herds of bison and elk, is abundant in **Bear River State Park,** and you can hike and ski on the park's trails, which have picnic shelters. The park connects to Evanston's Bear Pathway, a paved trail that for much of its length is fully accessible to people with disabilities. *601 Bear River Dr. 307/789–6547 wyoparks.state.wy.us/bear1.htm Free Daily 24 hrs.*

The **Uinta County Historical Museum** houses displays on Chinese culture and local history, including historic photographs of the area, ranching and railroad paraphernalia, and Native American artifacts. *36 10th St. 307/783–0370 Free Memorial Day–Labor Day, weekdays 9–5, weekends 10–4; Labor Day–Memorial Day, weekdays 9–5.*

Sports & the Outdoors

The **Bear River Outdoor Recreation Alliance** (Box 2600, Evanston 82930 307/789–1770) has a series of trails used for mountain biking and hiking in summer and as Nordic ski trails in winter. These trails can be found in and around Evanston and Uinta County. There's also a system of yurts for overnight stays. The trails are a cooperative project of the Alliance, the U.S. Forest Service, Evanston Parks and Recreation Department, and the Wyoming and Utah state parks divisions. You can obtain information from Evanston's **Visitors Information Center/ Depot Square** (920 Front St., Evanston 82930 307/789–1472) or by writing Bear River Outdoor Recreation Alliance.

Where to Stay & Eat

$–$$$ **Legal Tender.** Within the Best Western Dunmar Inn, this restaurant has the most "upscale" atmosphere in the community, but it's not pretentious. It's quiet with lots of faux greenery and a floral carpet. The varied menu includes steak, seafood, chicken, and pasta, and there's a full salad bar. *1601 Harrison Dr. 307/789–3770 AE, D, DC, MC, V.*

$–$$ **Don Pedro's Family Mexican Restaurant.** This small, family-owned restaurant serves authentic Mexican food. Sombreros, serapes, and Mexican music create the appropriate mood in which to dine on sizzling fajitas or the special *molcajete,* a stew of beef and chicken. *909 Front St. 307/789–2944 AE, D, DC, MC, V.*

$ **Hunan Garden.** Evanston's Chinese culture comes through in this restaurant with green walls and Chinese lamps that serves Hunan, Szechuan, and Mandarin dishes. Among the house specialties on the extensive menu are walnut prawns, double-face noodles (chicken, prawns, and beef sautéed with vegetables), and black-pepper beef or lamb. You can also order set dinners for two or more that include hot-and-sour soup, cheese puffs, barbecue-pork egg rolls, sweet-and-sour prawns, Hunan chicken, and Mongolian beef. ✉ *933 Front St.* ☎ *307/789–3908* ▭ *MC, V.*

$ **Best Western Dunmar Inn.** The rooms are spread over a large area that's a bit mazelike (you have to drive or walk a ways to your room from the main lobby and restaurant), but they are large and well appointed, with a desk and easy chairs. The public spaces are casual and inviting. ✉ *1601 Harrison Dr., Box 0768, 82931* ☎ *307/789–3770 or 800/654–6509* 🖷 *307/789–3758* 🌐 *www.bestwestern.com* *165 rooms* *Restaurant, in-room data ports, cable TV, pool, gym, hot tub, bar, business services, meeting rooms, no-smoking rooms* ▭ *AE, D, MC, V.*

$ **Pine Gables Inn B&B.** Built in 1883 in Victorian style, this house, the only B&B in town, is on the National Register of Historic Places. The rooms have murals, hand-painted by the house owner; antique furnishings; and nooks and crannies that are a fun part of the house's architecture. There is a large Jacuzzi in one suite, and a kitchenette in another. Some of the rooms have fireplaces and claw-foot tubs. ✉ *1049 Center St., 82930* ☎ *307/789–2069 or 800/789–2069* 🌐 *www.cruising-america.com/pinegables* *3 rooms, 2 suites* *Library* ▭ *AE, MC, V* *BP.*

¢ **High Country Inn.** Dark-green carpeting, neutral-tone walls, and mauve-and-green accents decorate the rooms at this inn overlooking a golf course. The lobby has lots of oak trim and an aquarium. You can even participate in off-track betting here. ✉ *1936 Harrison Dr., 82930* ☎ *307/789–2810* 🖷 *307/789–5506* 🌐 *www.highcountryinn.net* *110 rooms, 2 suites* *Restaurant, pool, bar* ▭ *AE, D, DC, MC, V.*

SOUTHERN WYOMING A TO Z

To research prices, get advice from other travelers, and book travel arrangements, visit www.fodors.com.

AIR TRAVEL

CARRIERS Great Lakes Airlines/United Express connects Cheyenne, Laramie, and Rock Springs to Denver, Colorado.

Airlines & Contacts **Great Lakes Aviation/United Express** ☎ 307/432-7000 in Cheyenne, 307/742-5296 in Laramie, 800/554-5111 🌐 www.greatlakesav.com/.

AIRPORTS

Cheyenne, Laramie, and Rock Springs' Sweetwater County Airport are the major airports in the area, with service to and from Denver only; there is no commercial service to other communities in the region. Many visitors to southeastern Wyoming prefer to fly into Denver International Airport and drive the 90 mi north to Cheyenne.

If you only need to get to and from the airport or bus station and the capitol area from Cheyenne Airport, you can make do with cabs. Try Checker Cab or Yellow Cab.

Airport Information **Cheyenne Airport** ✉ 200 E. 8th Ave., Cheyenne ☎ 307/634-7071 🌐 www.cheyenneairport.com. **Laramie Airport** ✉ 3 mi west of Laramie off Hwy. 130 ☎ 307/742-4164 🌐 www.laramieairport.com. **Sweetwater County Airport** ✉ 382 Hwy. 370, Rock Springs ☎ 307/352-6880 🌐 www.rockspringsairport.com.

Taxis **Checker Cab** ☎ 307/635-5555. **Yellow Cab** ☎ 307/638-3333.

BUS TRAVEL

Greyhound Lines connects Cheyenne, Evanston, Laramie, Rawlins, and Rock Springs to such hubs as Denver and Salt Lake City.

Bus Information **Greyhound Lines** ☎ 800/231-2222 🌐 www.greyhound.com ✉ 1503 Capitol Ave., Cheyenne ☎ 307/634-7744 ✉ 1936 W. Lincoln Hwy., Evanston

☎ 307/789-2810 ✉ 4700 Bluebird La., Laramie ☎ 307/742-9663 ✉ 2217 E. Cedar St., Rawlins ☎ 307/324-4196 ✉ 1695 Sunset Dr., Suite 114, Rock Springs ☎ 307/362-2931.

CAR RENTAL

Rental agencies can be found at airports and at other locations in the larger cities.

Local Agencies **Avis** ✉ Cheyenne Airport ☎ 307/632-9371 ✉ Laramie Airport ☎ 307/745-7156 ✉ Sweetwater County Airport, Rock Springs ☎ 307/362-5599. **Dollar** ✉ 300 E. 8th Ave., Cheyenne ☎ 307/632-2422 ✉ 555 General Breeze Rd., Laramie ☎ 307/742-8805. **Enterprise** ✉ 800 W. Lincolnway, Cheyenne ☎ 307/632-1907 ✉ 2208 Grand Ave., Laramie ☎ 307/721-9876. **Hertz** ✉ Cheyenne Airport ☎ 307/634-2131 ✉ Laramie Airport ☎ 307/745-0500 ✉ Sweetwater County Airport, Rock Springs ☎ 307/382-3262.

CAR TRAVEL

A car is essential to explore southern Wyoming. I–80 is the major route through the region, bisecting it from east to west. In places it runs parallel to U.S. 30. Other major access roads include U.S. 287, connecting Laramie and Medicine Bow; Highway 130, serving Centennial and Saratoga; Highway 230, running through Encampment; and Highway 70, connecting Encampment and Baggs.

Although distances between towns can be extensive, gasoline and other automobile services are available in each community and at various points roughly 20 to 40 mi apart along I–80. When traveling here in winter, be prepared for whiteouts and road closings (sometimes for hours, occasionally for more than a day). Always carry a blanket and warm clothing when driving in winter, along with a safety kit that includes snack food and water. Cell-phone service is getting better but is still sporadic in areas where mountains might interfere with cell towers.

Note that the Snowy Range Pass section of Highway 130, between Centennial and Saratoga, and the Battle Highway section of Highway 70, west of Encampment, close during cold weather, generally from mid-October until Memorial Day.

Contact the Wyoming Department of Transportation for information on road conditions.

Wyoming Department of Transportation ☎ 307/777-4484, 307/772-0824 from outside Wyoming for road conditions, 888/996-7623 from within Wyoming for road conditions 🌐 www.wyoroad.info/highway/text_road.html. **Wyoming Highway Patrol** ☎ 307/777-4301, 800/442-9090 for emergencies, #4357 (#HELP) from a cell phone for emergencies 🌐 whp.state.wy.us/index.htm.

EMERGENCIES

Ambulance or Police **Emergencies** ☎ 911.

24-Hour Medical Care **Evanston Regional Hospital** ✉ 190 Arrowhead Dr., Evanston ☎ 307/789-3636 or 800/244-3537 🌐 www.evanstonregionalhospital.com. **Ivinson Memorial Hospital** ✉ 255 N. 30th St., Laramie ☎ 307/742-2141 🌐 www.invinsonhospital.org. **Memorial Hospital of Carbon County** ✉ 2221 Elm St., Rawlins ☎ 307/324-2221 🌐 www.minershospital.com. **Memorial Hospital of Sweetwater County** ✉ 1200 College Dr., Rock Springs ☎ 307/362-3711. **United Medical Center** ✉ 300 E. 23rd St., Cheyenne ☎ 307/634-2273 🌐 www.umcwy.org.

LODGING

CAMPING Just about every community in the region has private campgrounds and RV parks.The Wyoming Campground Association can provide information on these campgrounds.

You can also camp on public lands managed by the U.S. Forest Service and local Bureaus of Land Management; these camping opportunities range from dispersed camping with no facilities to campgrounds with water, fire pits, and picnic tables. Some of the best camping spots are in the Medicine Bow–Routt National Forest near the communities of Centennial, Saratoga, Encampment, and Baggs. Camping near lakes and reservoirs is possible west of Cheyenne at Curt Gowdy State Park and south of Green River at Flaming Gorge National Recreation Area.

Curt Gowdy State Park ☎ 307/632-7946 🌐 wyoparks.state.wy.us/curt1.htm. **Flaming Gorge National Recreation Area** ☎ 801/784-3445, 877/833-6777 for campground reservations 🌐 www.fs.fed.us/r4/ashley/fg_html_aw.html. **Kemmerer District Bureau of Land Management** ☎ 307/828-4500 🌐 www.wy.blm.gov/kfo/info.htm. **Medicine Bow–Routt National Forest** ☎ 307/745-8971 🌐 www.fs.fed.us/r2/mbr. **Rawlins District Bureau of Land Management** ☎ 307/328-4200 🌐 www.wy.blm.gov/rfo/. **Rock Springs District Bureau of Land Management** ☎ 307/352-0256 🌐 www.wy.blm.gov/rsfo/. **U.S. Forest Service** ☎ 303/275-5350 🌐 www.fs.fed.us/r2. **Wyoming Campground Association** ☎ 307/684-5722 🌐 www.campwyoming.org/.

DUDE RANCHES

If you want to experience a bit of the wrangling life, consider a stay at a dude ranch. Professional cattle drivers and ranchers will teach you to rope, ride, and rodeo. The Wyoming Dude Ranchers Association can help you find a ranch to suit your interests and needs.

Wyoming Dude Ranchers Association ☎ 307/455-2084 🌐 www.wyomingdra.com.

MEDIA

NEWSPAPERS & MAGAZINES

Major newspapers in the region include the *Wyoming State Tribune-Eagle,* published in Cheyenne; the *Laramie Daily Boomerang;* the *Rawlins Daily Times;* the *Rock Springs Rocket Miner;* the *Green River Star;* and Evanston's *Uinta County Herald.* The *Casper Star-Tribune* covers the entire state and includes a weekly events section each Thursday.

TELEVISION & RADIO

Cheyenne has ABC/ KKTU Channel 8 and CBS/KGWN Channel 5. NBC/KUSA Channel 9, broadcast out of Denver, reaches much of southern Wyoming. Rock Springs and Evanston pick up Salt Lake City TV stations, including ABC/KTVX Channel 4, CBS/KTUV Channel 2, and NBC/KSL Channel 5.

You can listen to country music in and around Cheyenne on the following radio stations: KFBC 1240 AM, KHAT 96.7 FM, KGYN 95.1 FM, and KOLZ 100.7 FM. Cheyenne's KLEN 106.3 FM and KIGN 101.9 FM play rock and roll; KGAB 650 AM has talk radio. Evanston's KEVA 1240 AM and KOTB 106.1 FM play country. In Green River listen to KFRZ 92.1 FM for country music. Among the stations broadcast out of Laramie are KOWB 1290 AM and KCGY 95.1 FM, both of which play country music. Kemmerer is served by KMER 950 AM, which plays oldies. Rock Springs has oldies on KRKK 1360 AM, country on KQSW 96.5 FM, and rock and roll on KSIT 104.5 FM.

SPORTS & THE OUTDOORS

SKIING & SNOWMOBILING

Numerous trail systems in the Medicine Bow–Routt National Forest, Snowy Range, and Sierra Madres are popular with cross-country skiers and snowmobilers. Centennial, Encampment, Laramie, and Saratoga make particularly good bases for cross-country skiing, and you can access some downhill-skiing terrain from Centennial as well.

TOURS

The Cheyenne Trolley takes a $6, two-hour tour of the historic downtown area and Frances E. Warren Air Force Base, including 20–25 minutes at the Old West Museum. The trolley runs from mid-May to mid-September, Monday–Saturday at 10 and 1:30, Sunday at 11:30. Tickets are sold at the Cheyenne Area Convention and Visitors Bureau on weekdays and at the Wrangler shop on weekends. For a self-guided walking tour of the downtown and capitol area in Cheyenne, contact the Cheyenne Area Convention and Visitors Bureau.

Platte Valley Shuttles and Tours runs standard tours of the Snowy Range or Battle Mountain scenic highways, statewide tours that take in the Oregon Trail, and custom tours for all of Wyoming. The company also provides shuttle service for snowmobilers, cross-country skiers, horseback riders, and anglers, or river float trips. They will shuttle you to a site or trailhead, or shuttle your vehicle (including pickups and horse or snowmobile trailers) to and from regional airports.

Large herds of wild horses range freely on public lands west of Baggs, and you can see the animals by taking a four-wheel-drive tour with Wild Horse Country Tours. Tours start at $200 for two people. Having grown up here, guides John and Esther Clark are very knowledgeable about the area.

Tour Operators **Cheyenne Trolley Ticket Sales** ⊠ Cheyenne Area Convention and Visitors Bureau, 309 W. Lincolnway ☎ 307/778-3133 ⊕ www.cheyenne.org ⊠ Wrangler shop, 16th and Capitol Sts. **Platte Valley Shuttles and Tours** Box 1652, Saratoga 82331 ☎ 307/326-5582 ⊕ www.plattevalleyshuttles.com. **Wild Horse Country Tours** Box 11, Baggs 82391 ☎ 307/383-6865 ⊕ www.wildhorsecountrytours.com

VISITOR INFORMATION

Tourist Information **Albany County Tourism Board (Laramie)** ⊠ 800 S. 3rd St., Laramie 82070 ☎ 307/745-7339 or 800/445-5303 ⊕ www.laramie-tourism.org. **Cheyenne Area Convention and Visitors Bureau** ⊠ 309 W. Lincolnway, Cheyenne 82001 ☎ 307/778-3133 or 800/426-5009 ⊕ www.cheyenne.org. **Evanston Chamber of Commerce** ⊠ 36 10th St., Evanston 82931 ☎ 307/783-0370 ⊕ www.etownchamber.com. **Green River Chamber of Commerce** ⊠ 1459 Uinta Dr., Green River 82935 ☎ 307/875-5711 or 800/354-6743 ⊕ www.grchamber.com. **Kemmerer Chamber of Commerce** ⊠ 800 Pine Ave., Kemmerer 83101 ☎ 307/877-9761 ⊕ www.kemmererchamber.com/. **Laramie Chamber of Commerce** ⊠ 800 S. 3rd St., Laramie 82070 ☎ 307/745-7339 or 866/876-1012 ⊕ www.laramie.org. **Medicine Bow-Routt National Forest** ⊠ 2468 Jackson St., Laramie 82070 ☎ 307/745-8971 ⊕ www.fs.fed.us/r2/mbr. **Rawlins-Carbon County Chamber of Commerce** ⊠ 519 W. Cedar St., Rawlins 82301 ☎ 307/324-4111 or 800/228-3547. **Rock Springs Chamber of Commerce** ⊠ 1897 Dewar Dr., Rock Springs 82902 ☎ 307/362-3771 or 800/463-8637 ⊕ www.tourwyoming.com. **Saratoga-Platte Valley Chamber of Commerce** Box 1095, Saratoga 82331 ☎ 307/326-8855 ⊕ www.saratogachamber.info. **Visitors Information Center/Depot Square** ⊠ 920 Front St., Evanston 82930 ☎ 307/789-1472.

NORTHEAST WYOMING

WITH THE SOUTH DAKOTA BLACK HILLS

FODOR'S CHOICE

Crazy Horse Memorial, *mountain carving in the Black Hills*
Deadwood, *historic Black Hills town*
Golden Phoenix, restaurant, Rapid City
Mount Rushmore National Memorial, *Black Hills*
National Historic Trails Interpretive Center, *Casper*
Sheridan Inn, *historic building in Sheridan*

HIGHLY RECOMMENDED

RESTAURANTS
Buffalo Dining Room, *near Mount Rushmore*
Deadwood Social Club, *Deadwood*
Colonel Bozeman's Restaurant and Tavern, *Buffalo*
Jakes, *Deadwood*

HOTELS
Alex Johnson Hotel and Landmark Restaurant, *Rapid City*
Audrie's Bed & Breakfast, *Rapid City*
Paradise Guest Ranch, *Buffalo*
Sylvan Lake Resort, *near Crazy Horse Memorial*

SIGHTS
Badlands National Park, *South Dakota*
Cave tours, *Wind Cave National Park*
Clear Creek Trail, *Buffalo*
Devils Tower National Monument, *butte near Gillette*
Fort Phil Kearny State Historic Site, *Buffalo*
Journey Museum, *Rapid City*
Nicolaysen Art Museum and Discovery Center, *Casper*
Reptile Gardens, *Rapid City*
Vore Buffalo Jump, *Sundance*
Wind Cave Canyon, *Wind Cave National Park*

By Tom Griffith

PINE-CARPETED HILLSIDES AND SNOWY MOUNTAIN SUMMITS give way to windswept prairies and clean-flowing rivers on the edge of the mighty Rockies, the backbone of America. Here, in the northeastern corner of Wyoming and in western South Dakota, just miles from the geographical center of the entire United States, the Great Plains meet the Rocky Mountains, marking the start of the American West. Although this is not a region wrought with the spouting geysers or alpine valleys many people expect of Wyoming, nor covered with the endless cornfields and red barns many associate with South Dakota, it is a distinctive and matchless landscape, where two unique parts of the country merge.

The rolling grasslands and rocky hillsides, although sparsely populated, are ripe with industry. Trains carrying coal by the ton stretch to the horizon near Sheridan. Hundreds upon hundreds of miles of pipeline connect the ever-widening web of oil and natural-gas wells outside Gillette with the power plants of the Midwest and the South. Lumber trucks regularly rumble past the ancient gold mines of Deadwood and Lead, hauling felled ponderosa pines away to mills.

But despite the intrusion of railroad tracks and open-pit mining, the land is, by and large, just as empty as it was more than a century ago when the first white people arrived here. Even though Europeans settled Wyoming as early as 1812, the state's population is the smallest in the nation at only 493,782 permanent residents. South Dakota, ranked 46th, is home to only 754,844 hardy souls. But the few that have dwelled in this place have been history-makers. This small part of these two states has a rich and storied past, from the gold rush begun by George Armstrong Custer and the Massacre at Wounded Knee to the Pony Express and Oregon Trail. Some of the most famous gunslingers, gamblers, miners, mule skinners, and warriors of the Old West have resided here (and some still do, among the historic cemeteries), including Buffalo Bill Cody, Wild Bill Hickok, Calamity Jane, Butch Cassidy, the Sundance Kid, Deadwood Dick, Sitting Bull, and Crazy Horse.

Exploring Northeast Wyoming

The territory of northeast Wyoming and western South Dakota is a point of convergence of all types. Here mountains meet prairies, forests meet ranches, and country towns meet Western cities. Most of the settlements have only a few hundred people or fewer; only four surpass 10,000 residents. Rapid City is on the eastern edge of the Black Hills in South Dakota and is the base from which many people launch their exploration of the Black Hills, which has the highest concentration of national parks, monuments, and memorials in the country. Casper, on the banks of the North Platte River in the center of Wyoming, is on or near five of the major pioneer trails of the mid-19th century, including the Oregon and Mormon trails. Gillette, in the Powder River basin near Devils Tower National Monument, and Sheridan, on the edge of the Bighorn Mountains 100 mi to the northwest, are both in Wyoming's energy country, although ranching (both dude and cattle) are mainstays of the communities.

About the Restaurants

Although not every community here has the eclectic mix of dining options common in more urban areas, there are plenty of small restaurants and local cafés with inimitable appeal. The larger cities of Wyoming and South Dakota often have several ethnic eateries from which to choose, serving everything from traditional Mexican and Native American specialties to old-world Italian and modern Korean dishes. The real strength of the region's dining, however, lies with the basics. In almost any small-town watering hole, you can order up some of the freshest and best-tasting beef and buffalo in the world. Whether it's prime rib and mashed potatoes with sunflower bread, or charred rib eye with corn on the cob, the area's best meals are simple yet filled with a flavor found only in the West.

About the Hotels

Just as diverse as the area's landscape, which fades from small Western cities into vast lengths of open prairie and forested mountains, are its accommodations. In the population centers, lodgings range from new chain hotels with in-room data ports to elegant and historic stone inns decorated with buffalo skins and Victorian furniture. Move beyond these cities, however, and everything changes. Campgrounds abound in the open countryside. On the prairie, expect sprawling guest ranches alongside cold mountain-fed creeks. In the higher elevations, look for charming bed-and-breakfasts on mountain slopes with broad alpine vistas. But no matter the type of accommodation, all kinds of amenities are available, from the ordinary to the unconventional, including saunas, hot tubs, horseback riding, fly-fishing lessons, and square dancing. Perhaps the greatest of all these amenities, however, is the isolation. In what some might call a welcome change in this era of information overload, many of the rural lodgings don't have in-room televisions or telephones, and some areas don't even have cell phone service.

WHAT IT COSTS

	$$$$	$$$	$$	$	¢
RESTAURANTS	over $22	$16–$22	$11–$16	$7–$11	under $7
HOTELS	over $220	$160–$220	$110–$160	$70–$110	under $70

Restaurant prices are for a main course at dinner, excluding sales tax of 4%–7%. Hotel prices are for two people in a standard double room in high season, excluding service charges and 5%–10% tax.

Timing

People come to experience Wyoming and South Dakota in all four seasons—sometimes all in the same week. The weather here is notoriously difficult to predict, as warm Chinook winds can shoot January temperatures into the 70s and freak storms can drop snow in July. On the whole, however, Mother Nature behaves herself and gives the area pleasantly warm summers and refreshingly snowy winters. Most travelers flock to the region between June and August, availing themselves of the higher temperatures optimal for outdoor activities. Many more come to ski or snowmobile the pristine powder of the Black Hills and Bighorn Mountains in the winter.

Temperatures in both seasons can be extreme, however. Thermometers often register a week of triple digits in August, especially in the badlands. Snow begins to blanket the mountain slopes in late September and begins to recede only in late May. Spring, especially in the mountains, is sometimes nothing more than a week or two of rain between the last winter snowfall and the warm sunshine of summer. Autumn, on the other hand, is full of pleasantly warm days, cooler nights, and vivid colors. Additionally, the only crowds to fight are small pockets of hunters, anglers, and local leaf peepers.

THE NORTH PLATTE RIVER VALLEY

Sweeping down from the Colorado Rockies into the very center of Wyoming, the North Platte River was a very important waterway for pioneers, since this was one of the few places where wagons could

Numbers in the text correspond to numbers in the margin and on the Northeast Wyoming and South Dakota Black Hills maps.

If you have 3 days

Northeastern Wyoming and the Black Hills cover a huge territory, as anyone who's made the 400-mi trip between Badlands National Park and Casper can tell you. If you have only three days to explore the region, consider sticking to one area, such as the Black Hills or the North Platte River Valley. For the whirlwind tour, begin your first day at the Ben Reifel Visitor Center in **Badlands National Park** 15 and proceed along Highway 240 as it loops through the park, ending up at Wall Drug Store for lunch, in the town of Wall. Follow I–90 west to **Rapid City** 11 and stop at the Journey Museum. If you have time, visit Reptile Gardens before dinner. Get up early on your second day and drive down U.S. 16 to **Mount Rushmore National Memorial** 12. Follow the Peter Norbeck National Scenic Byway through Custer State Park to **Crazy Horse Memorial** 13. Then head up U.S. 385 to **Deadwood** 10. Visit the Adams Museum and the Mount Moriah Cemetery; if you have time, try to squeeze in a visit to the Adams House Museum. After dinner, spend the evening in one of the many saloons or casinos that line Main Street. On your last day, head north on U.S. 14A through scenic Spearfish Canyon to I–90. Follow the interstate west to **Sundance** 9; then drive U.S. 14 north to **Devils Tower National Monument** 8. After a little hiking, follow U.S. 14 south and I–90 west to **Gillette** 7 for lunch. If you're not flying out of Gillette, continue along I–90 west until you reach **Sheridan** 4. You can break up the two-hour trip with a visit to the Fort Phil Kearny State Historic Site north of Buffalo.

If you have 5 days

If you have a couple more days and want to see central Wyoming, follow the suggested three-day itinerary above. On the fourth day, visit any sights you may have missed in **Sheridan** 4 before heading south on I–25 to **Casper** 3. Along the way, stop off in **Big Horn** 5 to see the Bradford Brinton Memorial. The drive south to Casper will take about 2½ hours, and there aren't many places to stop for lunch along the interstate; you may want to pack a lunch. Take in the sights of Casper, being sure to visit the National Historic Trails Interpretive Center. On the morning of the fifth day, get up early and drive southwest on Highway 220 to Independence Rock and Devil's Gate. If you need to return to Rapid City to catch a flight, follow I–25, U.S. 18, U.S. 385, and U.S. 16 northeast into the Black Hills. If you have time to spare, stop along the way in **Douglas** 2 to see Fort Fetterman State Historic Site and near **Lusk** 1 to see the Spanish Diggings.

If you have 7 days

If you have a full week, you can complete a loop of the region. Follow the above itinerary, but instead of heading back to Rapid City on the fifth day, overnight in **Lusk** 1. On the sixth day, head northwest via U.S. 85 and Highway 450 to explore Thunder Basin National Grasslands. After your appetite for the open range is satisfied, follow U.S. 16 east back into South Dakota. Have dinner and stay at the State Game Lodge and Resort or Sylvan Lake Resort in Custer State Park, not far from Crazy Horse Memorial. On the seventh day, head south on U.S. 385 to **Wind Cave National Park** 14 for hiking and a cave tour. Continue south on U.S. 385 to Hot Springs, where you can explore the Mammoth Site. Return to Rapid City by driving north for an hour on Highway 79.

safely cross the mountains. Several pioneer trails converged along the Platte and the Sweetwater rivers and through South Pass, the easiest pass in the Rockies for covered wagons to negotiate. The North Platte River valley is still one of Wyoming's important agricultural areas, but the real source of wealth for modern central Wyoming is based on its deposits of oil, uranium, and bentonite.

Much of this area is also cattle country, for one simple reason: it's flat and dry. Some of the last ranges of short grassland before the Rockies thrust up from the plains. The land here is relatively treeless, dominated by fences, livestock, a few small cow towns, and the bustling Western city of Casper.

Lusk

❶ *140 mi northeast of Cheyenne via I–25 and U.S. 18.*

The Cheyenne–Deadwood Stage Line, which operated between Wyoming's territorial capital and the Black Hills gold town after the discovery of gold in 1875, gave rise to a number of stations, including one at Silver Cliff. When the Wyoming Central Railroad started moving into the area, officials attempted to purchase land from Ellis Johnson, who had a store, saloon, and hotel at Silver Cliff. Thinking he had a sure deal, Johnson held out for a better price for his land, and nearby rancher Frank S. Lusk cut his own deal with the railroad. That meant the rail line bypassed Silver Cliff and instead went through the new area—named Lusk.

Once situated on a pioneering route that led to the development of the Black Hills, Lusk became a different sort of pioneering town in the 1990s, when it was wired. Town leaders led the state of Wyoming into the 21st century when they installed fiber-optic cable lines and subsequently obtained computers for schools, public facilities, and homes, making Lusk a "computer-literate" population on the cutting edge of technology when other small Wyoming towns had barely even heard of the Internet. The community of 1,500 was written up in national magazines and newspapers and was the subject of an advertising campaign conducted by Microsoft. It is still a very rural community, however: Niobrara County, of which Lusk is the seat, averages 524 acres per person. Townspeople often use this fact to poke gentle fun at themselves, emblazoning T-shirts with phrases such as "End of the world, 12 miles. Lusk, 15 miles."

Artifacts from early settlement days and the period when the Cheyenne–Deadwood Stage Line was in full swing are some of the displays at the **Stagecoach Museum.** You can also get information about the Texas Cattle Trail. ✉ *322 S. Main St.* ☎ *307/334–3444 or 800/223–5875* 💰 *$2* ⏲ *May–Aug., weekdays 10–6; Sept. and Oct., weekdays 10–4.*

You can still see the remains of one of the Cheyenne–Deadwood Stage Line stops at the **Historic Hat Creek Stage Station.** Also here are an old schoolhouse and post office out in the tallgrass plains. You can wander among the buildings whenever you like, but to see the insides you must call for a tour. ✉ *15 mi north of Lusk on U.S. 85, then 2 mi east on gravel road* ☎ *307/334–2950, 307/334–2134 for private tour* 💰 *Free* ⏲ *Daily.*

Where to Stay & Eat

$–$$$ ✕ **El Jarros.** At the center of town, this festive restaurant is filled with Ted DeGrazia prints, strung with lights, and decked in bright, warm col-

Dude Ranches & Pack Trips

Perhaps no state in the union exalts cowboy life as Wyoming does. The concept of the dude-ranch vacation—where urban folk learn to rope, ride, and rodeo with weathered ranchers and professional cattle drivers—started at Eaton's Guest Ranch just outside Sheridan. Numerous other guest ranches are strewn across the grassy plains here, from the alpine meadows of Wyoming's Bighorn Mountains to the ponderosa-pine-covered slopes of South Dakota's Black Hills. In almost all cases, dude ranching is supplemented by pack trips that take you into these high, rugged peaks, sometimes for days at a time. Even if you prefer a warm bed to sleeping under the stars, don't be deterred, and certainly don't leave either state without getting on a horse at least once. Try a shorter trail ride or a pack trip that ends at a furnished cabin.

Fishing

Casting lines into clear streams and placid blue lakes is popular all over Wyoming, with good reason: the waters of the entire state teem with trout, pike, whitefish, catfish, and bass of all kinds. Most fishing enthusiasts stick to the land near Yellowstone, leaving the blue-ribbon streams of northeast Wyoming and the Black Hills relatively untouched.

Fly-fishing is especially big here, and there's no shortage of outfitters willing to equip you, both in the larger cities and the wilderness. Anyone with a pole—be it an experienced fly-fisher or novice worm dangler—is respected out here. Anglers and suppliers at the tackle shops will often direct you to some good fishing spots, but you won't get to the choicest locations unless you find them yourself. Locals love to share their enthusiasm for the sport with anyone willing to listen, but grizzled veterans know to keep their favorite fishing holes to themselves.

Living History

Many towns here have a fascinating and storied past, filled with colorful characters such as Buffalo Bill Cody, Wild Bill Hickok, Calamity Jane, the Sundance Kid, Sitting Bull, and Crazy Horse. The personalities that defined the American West once walked the streets and slept in the beds of this fabled land—and some of them never left.

Deadwood is by far the best example of living history in the region. The brick-paved streets and Victorian facades of this gold camp turned gambling mecca have been restored to the point that the community looks much as it did at the end of the 19th century. Costumed locals wander the streets daily and reenact the city's important events. Other towns, such as Sundance, where Harry Longabaugh earned his "Sundance Kid" nickname, and Sheridan, where Buffalo Bill auditioned stars for his Wild West Show, are just as significant to the tales and legends of the West.

---

ors. Try the fajitas, barbecue ribs, or spicy shrimp stir-fry, and complement your meal with an icy margarita. Note that the restaurant closes between 2 and 5. ✉ *625 S. Main St.* ☎ *307/334–5004* ▭ *MC, V.*

¢–$ ✕ **Pizza Place.** A casual atmosphere and good food come together at this downtown eatery. Pizza, calzones, and sub sandwiches made with home-

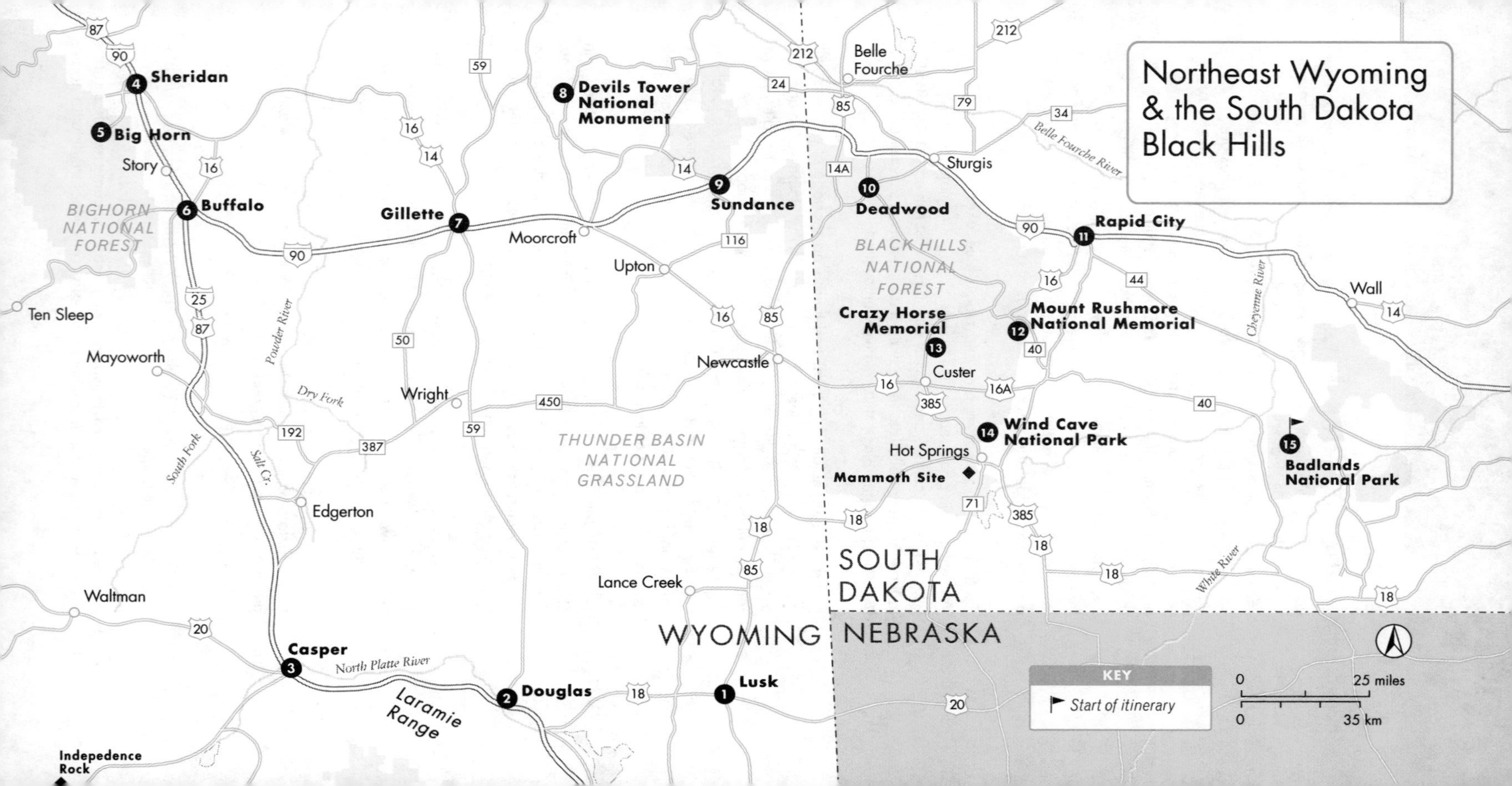

Northeast Wyoming & the South Dakota Black Hills
1 Lusk
2 Douglas
3 Casper
4 Sheridan
5 Big Horn
6 Buffalo
7 Gillette
8 Devils Tower National Monument
9 Sundance
10 Deadwood
11 Rapid City
12 Mount Rushmore National Memorial
13 Crazy Horse Memorial
14 Wind Cave National Park
15 Badlands National Park
Mammoth Site
Independence Rock
Story
Ten Sleep
Mayoworth
Edgerton
Waltman
Wright
Moorcroft
Upton
Newcastle
Lance Creek
Belle Fourche
Sturgis
Custer
Hot Springs
Wall
BIGHORN NATIONAL FOREST
BLACK HILLS NATIONAL FOREST
THUNDER BASIN NATIONAL GRASSLAND
Laramie Range
North Platte River
Powder River
Dry Fork
South Fork
Salt Cr.
Belle Fourche River
Cheyenne River
White River
WYOMING
SOUTH DAKOTA
NEBRASKA
KEY
Start of itinerary
0 25 miles
0 35 km

made bread are on the menu, and there's also a salad bar. ✉ *218 S. Main St.* ☎ *307/334–3000* ▭ *No credit cards.*

$ **Covered Wagon.** With a covered wagon on the front portico, an indoor pool, and an outdoor playground, this U-shape hotel is an inviting place for families with kids. ✉ *730 S. Main St., 82225* ☎ *307/334–2836 or 800/341–8000* 📠 *307/334–2977* *51 rooms* *Indoor pool, hot tub, sauna, playground, laundry facilities, meeting rooms* ▭ *AE, DC, MC, V* *CP.*

¢–$ **Best Western Pioneer Court.** Although the exterior of this motel near downtown and the Stagecoach Museum is unremarkable, the lobby is attractive, with a ceramic-tile floor, hardwood trim, and wrought-iron tables and lamps. There are some extra-large rooms that can accommodate up to eight people. ✉ *731 Main St., 82225* ☎ *307/334–2640* 📠 *307/334–2640* 🌐 *www.bestwestern.com* *30 rooms* *Restaurant, cable TV, pool, bar* ▭ *AE, D, DC, MC, V.*

¢ **Rawhide Motel.** The standard-size rooms are rustic but warm, and service is friendly at this affordable, locally owned motel in downtown Lusk. It's within walking distance of area restaurants. ✉ *805 S. Main St., 82225* ☎ *307/334–2440 or 888/679–2558* 📠 *307/334–2440* *19 rooms* *Cable TV, some pets allowed* ▭ *AE, D, MC, V.*

en route

Off U.S. 18 on the drive from Lusk to Douglas is **Glendo State Park,** which surrounds Glendo Reservoir, a human-made lake on the North Platte River. Rich in history, the park encompasses parts of the Oregon, Utah, and California trails (although much of the trails is now under water) and several prehistoric and historic Native American camps. In addition to a marina there are several hundred campsites at various places on the lakeshore. ✉ *State Rd. 319* ☎ *307/777–6323* 🌐 *wyoparks.state.wy.us/glendo1.htm* *$2 per vehicle* *Daily.*

A few miles east of Glendo State Park lies a vast stone quarry initially mistaken for the work of early Spanish explorers. Archaeologists later determined the site, known as the **Spanish Diggings,** to be the work of various indigenous tribes on and off for the past several thousand years. Tools and arrowheads carved from the stone quarried here, including quartzite, jasper, and agate, have been found as far away as the Ohio River valley. To see the diggings you'll have to drive through Glendo State Park.

Douglas

❷ *55 mi west of Lusk via U.S. 18 and I–25.*

Surveyors kept a step head of the Fremont, Elkhorn, and Missouri Valley Railroad as it laid tracks into this area in 1886. They plotted a town, but the railroad, which owned the townsite, refused to let anyone settle here before the rails themselves arrived. Some people, wanting to jump-start the town's development, pitched tentlike structures on Antelope Creek, outside the official boundaries. When the railroad arrived on August 22, they put their structures on wheels and moved them to the new city, named for Stephen A. Douglas, the presidential candidate who sparred with Abe Lincoln in the famous Lincoln-Douglas debates.

Now Douglas is best known for two things: the Wyoming State Fair, which has been held here annually since 1905, and the jackalope, a mythical animal that is a cross between a jackrabbit and an antelope. (A local taxidermist first put the creature together for display in a hotel here.) There's a large reproduction of the species in downtown Douglas, and many local businesses sell a smaller model.

The weeklong **Wyoming State Fair and Rodeo,** held in early August each year at the Wyoming State Fairgrounds, includes a carnival, livestock judging, commercial exhibits, and a Professional Rodeo Cowboys Association rodeo. ✉ *400 W. Center St.* ☎ *307/358–2398* 🌐 *www.wystatefair.com* 🎫 *$4* ⏲ *Early Aug.; call for exact dates.*

At the **Wyoming Pioneer Memorial Museum,** the emphasis is on the Wyoming pioneer settlers and overland emigrants, but this small state-operated museum on the state fairgrounds also has displays on Native Americans and the frontier military. ✉ *400 W. Center St.* ☎ *307/358–9288* 🌐 *wyoparks.state.wy.us* 🎫 *Free* ⏲ *June–Aug., weekdays 8–5, Sat. 1–5; Sept.–May, by appointment.*

Overland emigrants sometimes visited **Ayres Natural Bridge** (✉ Off I–25 ☎ 307/358–2950), a rock outcrop that spans LaPrele Creek. It's now a small but popular picnic area and campsite where you can wade in the creek or simply enjoy the quiet.

Built in 1867 to protect travelers headed west, the army post here is preserved today as the **Fort Fetterman State Historic Site.** Although the fort was never very large and had difficulty keeping its soldiers from deserting, its location on the fringes of the Great Sioux Indian Reservation made it an important outpost of civilization on the Western frontier. After white settlers overran the Black Hills and the government did away with the reservation, soldiers from here helped end armed Plains Indian resistance—and thus put an end to the fort's usefulness. Two buildings, the ordinance warehouse and officers' quarters, survived decades of abandonment and today house interpretive exhibits and artifacts related to the area's history and the fort's role in settling the West. The remains of other fort buildings can still be seen, as can the ruins of Fetterman City, which died out when Douglas was founded several miles to the south. ✉ *Hwy. 93* ☎ *307/358–2864 or 307/777–7629* 🌐 *wyoparks.state.wy.us* 🎫 *$1 residents, $2 nonresidents* ⏲ *Memorial Day–Labor Day, daily 9–5.*

The **Medicine Bow National Forest, Douglas District** (✉ Douglas Ranger District, 2250 E. Richards St. ☎ 307/358–4690 🌐 www.fs.fed.us/r2/mbr/), southwest of Douglas in the Laramie Peak area, includes four campgrounds ($5 for camping; campground closed in winter) and areas where you can fish and hike.

Where to Stay & Eat

$$–$$$ ✕ **Plains Trading Post.** Antique furnishings and portions of old bank buildings set the scene at this restaurant, where the menu is diverse but basic—chicken, burgers, steaks—and the portions are large. It's open 24 hours a day, a rarity even in the larger cities. ✉ *628 Richards St.* ☎ *307/358–4484* 💳 *MC, V.*

$–$$ ✕ **The Koop.** Serving breakfast and lunch, this place is known for its burgers and fries. The fries are unusual, since each curly fry is made from a whole potato. ✉ *108 N. 3rd St.* ☎ *307/358–3509* 💳 *MC, V* ⏲ *No dinner.*

$ ✕🏨 **Best Western Douglas Inn.** With its cathedral ceiling and fireplace, the atrium lobby is an impressive entranceway into this chain hotel. The location is convenient, next to I–25 on the north side of town and close to the Wyoming State Fairgrounds. The restaurant's menu ($$–$$$$) of mostly American dishes includes exotic choices such as ostrich and buffalo steak. ✉ *1450 Riverbend Dr., 82633* ☎ *307/358–9790* 📠 *307/358–6251* 🌐 *www.bestwestern.com* *117 rooms* *Restaurant, cable TV with movies, pool, gym, hot tub, sauna, video game room, laundry facilities, meeting rooms, some pets allowed (fee)* 💳 *AE, D, DC, MC, V.*

¢–$ **Morton Mansion.** The huge, covered wraparound porch of this inn on a quiet, residential street is perfect for relaxing. The mansion was built in 1903 in the Queen Anne style. Antiques and floral patterns decorate the guest rooms, and the attic suite has two bedrooms, a private living room, and a full kitchen. *425 E. Center St., 82633 307/358–2129 307/358–6590 www.mortonmansion.com 3 rooms, 1 suite Dining room; no room phones, no room TVs, no kids under 10, no smoking AE, D, MC, V CP.*

CAMPING **Esterbrook Campground.** Nestled among pine trees near Laramie Peak, 30 mi south of Douglas, Esterbrook is only a few miles from Black Mountain Lookout, one of the few staffed fire lookouts remaining in the country. During fire season (generally mid-June through September) be sure to ask the ranger-in-residence before exploring his or her home. *Pit toilets, drinking water, fire grates, picnic tables, ranger station 12 sites Forest Rd. 633 307/358–4690 or 307/358–1604 www.fs.fed.us/r2/mbr/rd-douglas/ $5 Reservations essential No credit cards Mid-May–mid-Oct.*

Casper

3 *50 mi west of Douglas via I–25.*

Casper, nearly in the center of Wyoming, is the state's second-largest city. It's also one of the oldest. Some of the first white Americans in Wyoming spent the winter here in 1811 on their way east from Fort Astoria in Oregon. Although they didn't stay, they helped to forge several pioneer trails that crossed the North Platte River near present-day Casper, which eventually led to the founding of a permanent settlement. The city is named for Lieutenant Caspar Collins—the spelling error occurred early in the town's development, and it stuck. The town has grown largely as a result of oil and gas exploration, although sheep and cattle ranchers run their stock on lands all around the city.

Fodor's Choice ★ Five major pioneer trails passed near or through Casper in the period between 1843 and 1870. The best known are the Oregon Trail and the Mormon Trail, both of which crossed the North Platte River in the vicinity of today's Casper. The **National Historic Trails Interpretive Center** examines the early history of the trails and the military's role in central Wyoming. Projected onto a series of screens 11 feet high and 55 feet wide, a film shows Wyoming trail sites and scenes of wagon travelers. You can climb into a wagon to see what it was like to cross the river, or learn about Mormon pioneers who traveled west with handcarts in 1856. *1501 N. Poplar 307/265–8030 www.wy.blm.gov/nhtic $6 Apr.–Oct., daily 8–7; Nov.–Mar., Tues.–Sat. 9–4:30.*

The **Fort Caspar Historic Site** re-creates the post at Platte Bridge, which became Fort Caspar after the July 1865 battle that claimed the lives of several soldiers, including Lieutenant Caspar Collins. A post depicts life at a frontier station in the 1860s, and sometimes soldier reenactors go about their tasks. Museum exhibits show the migration trails. *4001 Fort Caspar Rd. 307/235–8462 www.fortcasparwyoming.com May–Sept. $2, Oct.–Apr. $1 Museum June–Aug., Mon.–Sat. 8–7, Sun. noon–7; May and Sept., Mon.–Sat. 8–5, Sun. noon–5; Oct.–Apr., weekdays 8–5, Sun. 1–4. Fort buildings June–Aug., Mon.–Sat. 8:30–6:30, Sun. 12:30–6:30; May and Sept., Mon.–Sat. 8:30–4:30, Sun. 12:30–4:30.*

The **Casper Planetarium** has multimedia programs on astronomy. There are also interactive exhibits in the lobby and a gift shop. Public programs, which last an hour, are scheduled regularly in the summer. *904 N. Poplar St. 307/577–0310 www.trib.com/WYOMING/NCSD/*

PLANETARIUM/planetarium.html 🎫 *$2.50* ⏲ *Lobby exhibits weekdays 8–5. Public programs June–Aug., Mon.–Sat. 7 PM–8 PM; Sept.–May, Sat. 7 PM–8 PM; call to confirm.*

The **Werner Wildlife Museum,** near the Casper College campus, has displays of birds and animals from Wyoming and around the world. ✉ *405 E. 15th St.* ☎ *307/268–2676* 🌐 *www.caspercollege.edu* 🎫 *Free* ⏲ *Mid-May–Labor Day, daily 10–5; Labor Day–mid-May, weekdays 2–5.*

Casper College's **Tate Earth Science Center and Geological Museum** displays fossils, rocks, jade, and the fossilized remains of a brontosaurus, plus other dinosaur bones. ✉ *125 College Dr.* ☎ *307/268–3068* 🌐 *www.caspercollege.edu* 🎫 *Free* ⏲ *Weekdays 9–5, Sat. 10–4.*

★ A showcase for regional artists and mostly modern artwork, the **Nicolaysen Art Museum and Discovery Center** also exhibits works by national artists. The building's early-20th-century redbrick exterior and contemporary interior are an odd combination, but this makes the museum all the more interesting. There are hands-on activities, classes, children's programs, a research library, and a Discovery Center. ✉ *400 E. Collins Dr.* ☎ *307/235–5247* 🌐 *www.thenic.org* 🎫 *Donations accepted* ⏲ *Memorial Day–Labor Day, Tues.–Fri. 10–7, Sat. 10–5, Sun. noon–4; Labor Day–Memorial Day, Tues.–Sat. 10–5, Sun. noon–4.*

off the beaten path

INDEPENDENCE ROCK STATE HISTORIC SITE – This turtle-shape granite outcrop became an important site on the Oregon, California, and Mormon trails. Tradition dictated that travelers had to arrive at the rock by July 4 in order to reach the West Coast before winter set in. Many of these pioneers carved their names in the rock, and some are still legible more than a century later. The rock face looks steep but is relatively easy to climb without any special equipment. Midway between Casper and Rawlins, the site includes a rest stop with bathrooms and picnic tables. ✉ *Hwy. 220, 54 mi southwest of Casper* ☎ *307/777–6323* 🌐 *wyoparks.state.wy.us.*

DEVIL'S GATE – Local Shoshone and Arapaho tribes believed this deep cleft in the mountains through which the Sweetwater River flows was cut by a giant tusked beast in a fit of anger. Although Devil's Gate is only 30 feet wide at the base, the sheer walls of the ⅓-mi-long canyon rise more than 300 feet high. There are interpretive panels along the highway, and you can still see the ruts carved by the wagons that followed the pioneer trails nearby. Devil's Gate is less than 6 mi south of another pioneer-trail landmark, Independence Rock. ✉ *Hwy. 220, 59 mi southwest of Casper.*

HANDCART RANCH – The Martin's Cove Visitor Center, run by the Church of Jesus Christ of Latter-day Saints, has exhibits on the Sun family and their ranching operation, which took place here from 1872 until the church bought the Sun Ranch in 1997. The Oregon, California, and Mormon trails cross the ranch, which is particularly important to the Mormons because two groups of pioneers traveling with handcarts to Salt Lake City became stranded in the area by snowstorms in 1856. They had left the area along the Missouri River near Omaha, Nebraska, too late in the year to cross the mountains before winter set in. A 3½-mi trail leads to Martin's Cove, where the handcart pioneers found shelter from the cold. You can push one of 100 handcarts up the trail to get a feel for this mode of transportation. The carts are loaned for free on a first-come, first-served basis; none are loaned after 3:30 and none on Sunday.

✉ *Hwy. 220, 60 mi southwest of Casper* ☎ *307/328–2953* 🌐 *www.handcart.com* 🎫 *Free* ⏲ *Daily 8–7.*

Sports & the Outdoors

With thousands of acres of empty grassland and towering mountains only miles away, the landscape around Casper is full of possibilities for enjoying the outdoors. Casper Mountain rises 8,000 feet above the prairie 20 minutes from downtown, providing prime skiing and hiking trails.

Edness Kimball Wilkins State Park (✉ I–25, 6 mi east of Casper ☎ 307/577–5150) is a day-use area with picnicking, swimming, fishing, and a 3-mi walking path.

HIKING Much of Casper Mountain is taken up by private land, but there are some public trails, including mountain-bike routes and the Braille Trail, a simple hike with plaques (in braille) that describe the views and ecology of the mountain. The trails can get a little crowded in the summer. Contact the **Casper Convention and Visitors Bureau** (✉ 330 S. Center St. ☎ 307/234–5362 or 800/852–1889 🌐 www.casperwyoming.org) for more information.

The **Platte River Parkway** hiking trail runs adjacent to the North Platte River in downtown Casper. Access points are at Amoco Park at 1st and Poplar streets, or at Crosswinds Park, on North Poplar Street near the Casper Events Center.

SKIING Perched on Casper Mountain a few miles outside of town is **Hogadon Ski Area** (✉ Casper Mountain Rd. ☎ 307/235–8499), with a vertical drop of 600 feet. Less than a quarter of the runs are rated for beginners; the rest are evenly divided between intermediate and expert trails. Also here are a separate snowboard terrain park and a modest lodge. **Mountain Sports** (✉ 543 S. Center ☎ 307/266–1136) provides more than just ski and snowboard sales. It also runs Wyomaps, which sells personal Global Positioning System products and provides custom mapping services.

Where to Stay & Eat

$$–$$$$ ✕ **Armor's.** A quiet dining room with cozy booths and tables makes this a popular place for a special dinner. In addition to standards such as steaks and prime rib, the menu lists blackened and Cajun entrées. ✉ *3422 S. Energy La.* ☎ *307/235–3000* 💳 *AE, D, DC, MC, V.*

$$–$$$$ ✕ **Poor Boys Steakhouse.** Reminiscent of a frontier mining camp or Western town, this steak house has blue-and-white-check tablecloths and chair backs, quick service, and large portions of steak, seafood, and chicken. Salad comes in a bucket and is served with fresh, hot bread. Try the Moonshine Mama—grilled chicken breast smothered in mushrooms and Monterey Jack and cheddar cheeses—or enjoy a tantalizingly tender filet mignon with shrimp. For dessert try the Dutch apple pie or Ashley's Avalanche—a huge plate of ice cream, a white-chocolate brownie, cherry-pie filling, chocolate sauce, and whipped cream. ✉ *739 S. Center St.* ☎ *307/237–8325* 💳 *AE, D, DC, MC, V.*

$–$$$ ✕ **El Jarro.** Usually crowded and always noisy, this place serves hearty portions of Mexican cuisine. The beef fajitas are a favorite, second only to the fine margaritas, which come in glasses the size of bowls. The place is decorated with bright colors, which only seem to encourage the generally rowdy bunch at the bar. ✉ *500 W. F St.* ☎ *307/577–0538* 💳 *AE, MC, V.*

$–$$$ ✕ **Sanfords Grub and Pub.** This lively spot decorated with 20th-century memorabilia may be a brewery, but children are welcome here in the heart of downtown. The extensive menu includes pastas, pizzas, and calzones. If you're a vegetarian, this is your best bet in Casper for its variety of meatless dishes. ✉ *241 S. Center St.* ☎ *307/234–4555* ▭ *AE, D, DC, MC, V.*

$ **Hampton Inn.** The rooms in this clean and very quiet lodging have coffeemakers, large cable TVs, dark floral spreads, and an easy chair with an ottoman. The small restaurant, Cafe José's, serves authentic Mexican food, including enchiladas, flautas, and chimichangas. ✉ *400 W. F St., 82601* ☎ *307/235–6668* 🖷 *307/235–2027* 🌐 *www.hamptoninn.com* *122 rooms* *Restaurant, cable TV with movies, pool, sauna, meeting rooms* ▭ *AE, D, DC, MC, V* *CP.*

$ **Parkway Plaza.** With a large convention center, the Parkway is one of Casper's busiest motels. The rooms are quiet and large, with double vanities, one inside the bathroom and one outside. Furnishings are contemporary in the rooms but Western in the public areas. The pool has wading and diving sections. Attached to the hotel is Old Town, a small amusement park with an arcade, miniature-golf course, and a NASCAR-sanctioned go-kart track. ✉ *123 W. Center St., 82601* ☎ *307/235–1777 or 800/270–7829* 🖷 *307/235–8068* 🌐 *www.parkwayplaza.net* *295 rooms* *Restaurant, coffee shop, cable TV with movies, indoor-outdoor pool, gym, hair salon, hot tub, sauna, bar, video game room, playground, laundry facilities, business services, convention center, meeting rooms* ▭ *AE, D, MC, V.*

$ **Radisson.** This full-service location, off I–25, has everything under one roof, from dining options to business services. Muted blues, greens, and mauves decorate the large, contemporary rooms, some of which have whirlpool tubs. ✉ *800 N. Poplar St., 82601* ☎ *307/266–6000* 🖷 *307/473–1010* 🌐 *www.radisson.com* *229 rooms* *Restaurant, café, in-room data ports, some in-room hot tubs, cable TV with movies, indoor pool, hot tub, bar, business services, convention center, meeting rooms* ▭ *AE, D, DC, MC, V.*

The Arts

Both the Casper Symphony Orchestra and the Casper College Theater Department perform at the 465-seat **Gertrude Krampert Theater** (✉ Casper College, 125 College Dr. ☎ 307/268–2500). **Stage III Community Theater** (✉ 4080 S. Poplar St. ☎ 307/234–0946) presents plays and other dramatic performances at various times.

Shopping

The largest shopping center in a 175-mi radius, the **Eastridge Mall** (✉ 601 S.E. Wyoming Blvd. ☎ 307/265–9392), anchored by such standbys as Sears, JCPenney, Target, and Bon Marché, is popular and important to locals. There are also a few local stores here, including JAAG Racing, the largest NASCAR store in the state, and Corral West Ranchwear, which occasionally hosts roping competitions in the central court.

THE POWDER RIVER BASIN & THE WYOMING BLACK HILLS

A rolling grassland with rich mineral deposits, the Powder River basin, the ancestral homeland of the Lakota Sioux, is bounded by the Black Hills to the east, Montana to the north, the Bighorn Mountains to the west, and the North Platte River to the south. The mountains on the western edge are both a popular winter recreational area and a beautiful backdrop for the communities of Sheridan, Big Horn, and Buffalo. As you drive east, the mountains give way to coal mines (particularly around Gillette), oil wells, and family ranches, many of which were begun by the region's first settlers: Basque sheepherders.

Now one of the least-populated parts of America, the far northeastern corner of Wyoming was once settled by farmers from the East hoping to raise crops in the semiarid soil. Experienced only with the more humid conditions east of the Rockies, the farmers failed, and the region deteriorated into a dust bowl. Since then, most of the land, now known as the Thunder Basin National Grasslands, has reverted to its natural state, giving rise to millions of acres of grasslands and abundant wildlife, including one of the largest herds of pronghorn in the world (numbering approximately 26,000).

Although Black Hills National Forest is mostly contained within South Dakota, a couple of hundred thousand acres spill out onto the Wyoming plains. Thickly forested by pine, spruce, and fir trees, the rocky slopes stand in stark contrast to the prairie below. It was across this soil that some of the most famous characters of the American West roamed, including Wild Bill Hickok, Calamity Jane, and the Sundance Kid, who took his name from a local town.

Sheridan

4 *147 mi north of Casper via I–25 and I–90.*

Born from a simple trapper's cabin built along Little Goose Creek in 1873, Sheridan quickly became a regional center for the railroad. It wasn't long before cattle barons moved in and established their ranches, which remain the mainstay of this community of 15,804 residents. The area still has ties to the English nobility from which many of the barons came; in fact, Queen Elizabeth II herself has paid the town a visit. Sheridan also prospers from the Bighorn Mountains just to the west, which attract people looking to hike, mountain bike, ski, snowmobile, and fly-fish. Recently, however, the small city's prosperity has been linked to the coal mines and oil wells to the east, which give the entire region much-needed jobs and tax income.

Built in 1923 as a vaudeville theater called the Lotus, the **Wyo Theater** was closed and nearly demolished in the early 1980s. A strong show of support from the community saved the building, and now the refurbished art deco structure hosts everything from orchestras and ballets to lectures and Broadway revivals, especially in the summer. ✉ *42 N. Main St.* ☎ *307/672–9084* 🌐 *www.wyotheater.com.*

Local cowboy legend Don King owns **King's Saddlery and Ropes.** A saddle maker since the 1940s, King now lets his sons run the business. Besides selling high-quality equipment to area ranchers and professional rodeo performers, King's has crafted gear for many celebrities, including Queen Elizabeth II. Behind the store is a museum full of King's own collection, including saddles from the pre–Civil War era and medieval Japan. ✉ *184 N. Main St.* ☎ *307/672–2702* 🎟 *Free* ⏲ *Mon.–Sat. 8–5.*

A Flemish Revival mansion built in 1913 for John B. Kendrick, cattleman and one of Wyoming's first governors and senators, is now the **Trail End State Historic Site.** The furnishings and exhibits in the home are designed to depict early-20th-century ranching on the Plains. Highlights include elegant hand-carved woodwork and a third-floor ballroom. ✉ *400 Clarendon Ave.* ☎ *307/674–4589* 🌐 *www.trailend.org* 🎟 *$2* ⏲ *Mar.–May and Sept.–mid-Dec., daily 1–4; June–Aug., daily 9–6.*

Fodor's Choice ★ Evidence of the area's old-world ties can be found at the **Sheridan Inn,** just a few miles from downtown near the old railroad depot. Modeled after a hunting lodge in Scotland, the 1893 building sports 69 gables in a show of architectural splendor not often seen around these parts. On the National Register of Historic Places, the inn once lured the likes of Herbert Hoover, Will Rogers, and Ernest Hemingway, and Buffalo Bill auditioned performers here for his Wild West Show. The original Buffalo Bill Bar, an oak-and-mahogany monstrosity on the main floor, is said to have been a gift sent from England by Queen Victoria. Lunch and dinner are served all year, although patrons are no longer permitted to bring their horses inside. ✉ *856 Broadway* ☎ *307/674–5440* 🌐 *www.sheridaninn.com* 🎫 *Free, self-guided tour $2, guided tour $5* ⏲ *Hrs vary by season; call for current schedule.*

Sports & the Outdoors

Like every other community on the edge of the Bighorn National Forest, Sheridan abounds with opportunities for outdoor recreation. A love of sports seems to be a common thread among people here, whether they're visitors or locals, winter enthusiasts or sun seekers, thrill hunters or quiet naturalists. Because of Sheridan's proximity to U.S. 14, a mountain highway near hundreds of miles of snowmobile trails and alpine streams, the town is especially popular among sledders in the winter and fly-fishers in the summer and autumn.

FLY-FISHING More of a custom adventure company than an outfitter, **Angling Destinations** (✉ 151 Powder Horn Rd. ☎ 800/211–8530) arranges multiday fishing trips to some of the most remote locations of Wyoming, Montana, and Idaho, as well as international destinations. For the less experienced angler, **Big Horn Mountain Sports** (✉ 334 N. Main St. ☎ 307/672–6866) provides fly-fishing lessons and guided trips and rents and sells complete fly-fishing gear (including flies, rods, reels, waders, and hats). The full-service **Fly Shop of the Big Horns** (✉ 227 N. Main St. ☎ 800/253–5866) offers sales, rentals, guided trips, and a fly-fishing school, a 2½-day class covering everything from casting to landing and releasing. **World Flyfishing Journeys** (✉ 1349 Fort Rd. ☎ 307/673–1732) leads guided fishing trips in the Bighorns and Powder River country.

SKIING & SNOWMOBILING The expert runs at **Antelope Butte** (✉ 30 mi southwest of Dayton on U.S. 14 ☎ 307/655–9530 🌐 www.skiantelopebutte.com), about 40 mi southwest of Sheridan, aren't like the world-class ski slopes found elsewhere in Wyoming and Colorado, but the steep, rocky bluff and season-long snowpack provide more stable and more difficult skiing than that found farther east in the Black Hills. At the base of the mountain, there's also a trail popular with cross-country skiers and snowmobilers. Antelope Butte doesn't rent snowmobiles, but it does provide fuel and basic repair service. **Bear Lodge** (✉ Off U.S. 14A, Burgess Junction ☎ 307/752–2444), an hour northwest of Sheridan, rents Polaris snowmobiles by the half day or full day. Guided tours are available; reserve ahead. There's also a small service shop and parts store here.

Where to Stay & Eat

$–$$$$ ✕ **Oliver's Bar and Grill.** Soft yellows and greens decorate this modern restaurant with an open kitchen and paintings from local artists on the walls. The menu lists fairly typical salads, burgers, and chicken dishes year-round, but it also frequently includes seasonal items such as Copper River salmon from Alaska, which is available here for only three weeks in the early summer. You can watch your meal being prepared if you sit at the kitchen bar. ✉ *120 N. Main St.* ☎ *307/672–2838* 💳 *MC, V.*

¢–$$ ✕ **Silver Spur.** This hole-in-the-wall is sometimes mistaken for an abandoned building, but it's actually a popular breakfast spot serving bacon, hash browns, omelets, and other fried favorites. For lunch there are burgers and Philly cheesesteak sandwiches. Contractors often meet here to conduct business over breakfast and lunch. ✉ *832 N. Main St.* ☎ *307/673–7330* 💳 *No credit cards* ⏲ *No dinner.*

$ **Sheridan Holiday Inn.** The soaring atrium of this five-story lodging, which is five minutes from downtown by car, has a waterfall and is filled with overstuffed chairs and couches. The rooms are typical of chain hotels, but most have some Western-style touches, and some look out on the Bighorn Mountains. Two restaurants ($$), the Greenery and Scooter's Bar and Grill, serve burgers, steak, chicken, and pasta. Sunday brunch is an elegant and extensive buffet. *1809 Sugarland Dr., 82801 877/672–4011 307/672–6388 www.holidayinnrockies.com 212 rooms 2 restaurants, cable TV with movies and video games, putting green, indoor pool, gym, hair salon, hot tub, sauna, racquetball, bar, video game room, business services, convention center, meeting rooms, airport shuttle, some pets allowed (fee) AE, D, DC, MC, V.*

$$$ **Eaton's Guest Ranch.** This is the place credited with creating the dude ranch, back in the late 19th century, and it's still going strong as a working cattle ranch. Its location, west of Sheridan on the edge of the Bighorn National Forest, makes it ideal for horseback riding, fishing, cookouts, and pack trips. The ranch can accommodate 125 guests, and reservations for the summer should be made by March. The facilities are a collection of one-, two-, and three-bedroom cabins and the main lodge. There's a one-week minimum stay mid-June through August and a three-day minimum stay the rest of the season. *270 Eaton's Ranch Rd., Wolf 82844 307/655–9285 or 800/210–1049 307/655–9269 www.eatonsranch.com 51 cabins Dining room, pool, fishing, hiking, horseback riding, meeting rooms D, MC, V Closed Oct.–May FAP.*

$ **Best Western Sheridan Center Motor Inn.** The rooms at this lodging popular with tour groups are typical of chain motels, but some have lodgepole-pine furniture and blue and green tones. The motel consists of four buildings connected by a sky bridge over Main Street. *612 N. Main St., 82801 307/674–7421 307/672–3018 www.bestwestern.com 138 rooms 2 restaurants, cable TV, indoor pool, sauna, spa, bar, video game room, meeting rooms AE, D, DC, MC, V.*

$ **Mill Inn.** A former flour mill near a bridge has been converted into this motel on the east side of town. The building has six stories, but the top four floors are business offices. Furniture from a dude ranch fills much of the motel, giving it a definite Western style. *2161 Coffeen Ave., 82801 307/672–6401 or 888/357–6455 307/672–6401 www.sheridanmillinn.com 45 rooms Gym AE, D, MC, V.*

CAMPING **Big Horn Mountain KOA Campground.** On the banks of the Big Goose Creek minutes away from downtown Sheridan is this KOA, a well-developed campground with a basketball court, horseshoe pits, and a miniature-golf course. *Flush toilets, full hookups, drinking water, showers, food service, picnic tables, electricity, public telephone, play area, swimming (pool) 40 full hookups, 12 tent sites; 6 cabins 63 Decker Rd. 307/674–8766 www.koakampgrounds.com Full hookups $29, tent sites $21; cabins $29–$79 Reservations essential AE, D, MC, V.*

Foothills Motel and Campground. In the tiny town of Dayton, 20 mi west of Sheridan, this campground nestles in a cottonwood grove on the Tongue River, at the base of the Bighorns. In addition to tent and RV sites, there are cabins here. They are clean and well equipped with cable TV and showers, except for one: an aged and rustic log cabin heated by a woodstove. *Flush toilets, full hookups, partial hookups (electric and water), drinking water, guest laundry, showers, picnic tables, electricity, public telephone, play area, swimming (river) 12 full hookups, 10 partial hookups, 30 tent sites; 10 cabins 101 N. Main St., Dayton 307/655–2547 www.fiberpipe.net/~foothill/Home.*

htm 🎫 *Full hookups $18.50, partial hookups $16.50, tent sites $13.50; cabins $25–$40* 💳 *No credit cards.*

The Arts

A stronghold of frontier culture, the **Bozeman Trail Gallery** (✉ 190 N. Main St. ☎ 307/672–3928) has a varied collection of artifacts and art from the American West, ranging from vintage Colt revolvers and leather saddles to Cheyenne Sioux moccasins and Navajo rugs. The gallery also maintains a collection of significant Western paintings from artists such as Carl Rungius and Ernest Martin Hennings.

Shopping

The suburban malls that have drained so many downtowns are absent in Sheridan; instead, Main Street is lined with mostly homegrown—and sometimes quirky—shops.

In a break from typical gift stores stocked with rubber tomahawks, the **Best Out West Mall** (✉ 109 N. Main St. ☎ 307/674–5003) is a two-story bazaar of Western paraphernalia, with booths hawking everything from spurs to rare books. Some items are new, but most are antiques. For an excellent selection of both local and general-interest books, try the **Book Shop** (✉ 117 N. Main St. ☎ 307/672–6505). On occasion, local authors will spend several hours here signing their books. The **Crazy Woman Trading Company** (✉ 120 N. Main St. ☎ 307/672–3939) sells unique gifts and antiques, including deluxe coffees and T-shirts sporting a black bear doing yoga. Murphy McDougal, the store's CEO (and the owners' golden retriever), is usually sleeping near the front door.

Big Horn

❺ *10 mi south of Sheridan via Hwy. 335.*

Established on the Bozeman Trail, an emigrant trail that crossed the Bozeman Pass, in the mid-19th century, Big Horn City was a lawless frontier town of saloons and roadhouses until pioneers brought their families to the area in the late 1870s. The rowdy community quickly quieted down, and the tree-lined town with mountain views has stayed fairly calm ever since. It was never incorporated as an official Wyoming town, so although there are a post office, fire department, and school, there is no bona fide city government.

A hand-hewn-log blacksmith shop, built in 1879 to serve pioneers on their way to the goldfields of Montana, houses the **Bozeman Trail Museum,** the town's historical repository and interpretive center. The jewel of its collection is the Cloud Peak Boulder, a stone with names and dates apparently carved by military scouts just two days before the Battle of the Little Big Horn, which was fought less than 100 mi to the north in 1876. The staff is very friendly to children, and there are some old pipe organs that kids are encouraged to play. ✉ *335 Johnson St.* ☎ *307/672–5705 or 307/674–1600* 🎫 *Free* ⏲ *Memorial Day–Labor Day, weekends 11–6.*

If you're not staying at a ranch and you want to get a look at one of the West's finest, visit the **Bradford Brinton Memorial,** south of Big Horn on the old Quarter Circle A Ranch. The Brinton family didn't exactly rough it in this 20-room clapboard home, complete with libraries, fine furniture, and silver and china services. A reception gallery displays changing exhibits from the Brinton art collection, which includes such Western artists as Charles M. Russell and Frederic Remington. ✉ *239 Brinton Rd.* ☎ *307/672–3173* 🌐 *www.bradfordbrintonmemorial.com/* 🎫 *$3* ⏲ *Mid-May–Labor Day, daily 9:30–5.*

Sheridan and Big Horn are access points to the 1.1-million-acre **Bighorn National Forest,** which has lush grasslands, alpine meadows, rugged mountaintops, canyons, and deserts. There are numerous hiking trails and camping spots for use in the summer, and it's a popular snowmobiling area in the winter. ✉ *Ranger station, 1969 S. Sheridan Ave.* ☎ *307/672–0751* 🌐 *www.fs.fed.us/r2/bighorn.*

Sports & the Outdoors

Perhaps the most unexpected sport to be found in the outdoor playground of the Bighorn National Forest is polo. The game has been played at the **Big Horn Equestrian Center** (✉ Near state bird farm, on Hwy. 28, west of Big Horn ☎ 800/453–3650) ever since upper-class English and Scottish families settled the area in the 1890s. You can watch people at play for free on Sundays in the summer. The 65 acres here are also used for other events, including youth soccer and bronc riding.

Where to Stay & Eat

$–$$$ ✕ **Bozeman Trail Inn.** A wood-slat building with a false front and tin roof, this is the oldest operating bar in Wyoming, established in 1882. The inn's only sign is painted on a mock covered wagon that's perched above the door. The kitchen serves standard burgers and sandwiches for lunch, steak and seafood for dinner, and prime rib on the weekends. ✉ *158 Johnson St.* ☎ *307/672–9288* 💳 *MC, V* ⏲ *Closed Mon.*

$–$$ 🏨 **Spahn's Bighorn Mountain Bed and Breakfast.** Ron and Bobbie Spahn have guest rooms and cabins at their soaring log home in the Bighorn Mountains. The rooms have tongue-and-groove woodwork and peeled-log beams; ruffled curtains and peeled-log beds complete the look. You get more than a traditional B&B here: horseback riding, cookouts, and guided tours that include a wildlife-viewing trip. Family-style dinners, including fresh grilled steaks, are served by arrangement. ✉ *Hwy. 335, 7 mi south of Bighorn, Box 579, 82833* ☎ *307/674–8150* 📠 *307/674–8150* 🌐 *www.bighorn-wyoming.com* 🛏 *3 rooms, 2 cabins* 🖒 *No a/c, no room phones, no room TVs, no smoking* 💳 *No credit cards* 🍽 *BP.*

¢–$ 🏨 **Wagon Box Resort.** On the edge of the tiny town of Story, 14 mi south of Big Horn, the Wagon Box lies at the base of the Big Horn Mountains. The rooms and cabins are furnished modestly in Western style; the cabins have fireplaces and porches with swings. This is a great spot for outdoor recreation—from hiking and fishing to horseback riding and barbecuing—and your hosts are happy to help you plan whatever activity suits your fancy. There are even horse corrals at the campground next door, so planning a quick ride or a major expedition into neighboring Bighorn National Forest is a breeze. ✉ *108 N. Piney Rd., Story 82842* ☎ *307/683–2444* 🌐 *www.wilderwest.com/story/wagonbox* 🛏 *15 rooms, 6 cabins* 🖒 *Restaurant, some kitchens, some kitchenettes, hot tub, sauna, fishing, hiking, horseback riding, bar, some pets allowed; no a/c, no room phones, no room TVs* 💳 *AE, D, MC, V.*

Buffalo

❻ *25 mi south of Big Horn via I–90, U.S. 87, and Hwy. 335.*

Buffalo is a trove of history and a hospitable little town in the foothills below Big Horn Pass. This is the area where cattle barons who wanted free grazing and homesteaders who wanted to build fences fought it out in the Johnson County Invasion of 1892. Nearby are the sites of several skirmishes between the U.S. military and Native Americans along the Bozeman Trail.

The **Jim Gatchell Memorial Museum** is the kind of small-town museum that's worth stopping for if you're interested in the history of the region. It contains Native American, military, outlaw, and ranching artifacts collected by a local druggist who was a close friend of area Native Americans. ✉ *100 Fort St.* ☎ *307/684–9331* 🌐 *www.jimgatchell.com* 🎫 *$4* ⏲ *Mid-Apr.–Dec., Mon.–Sat. 9–8, Sun. noon–5.*

★ Signs bearing a buffalo symbol mark the **Clear Creek Trail** (☎ 307/684–5544 or 800/227–5122), which consists of about 11 mi of trails following Clear Creek through Buffalo and past historic areas. The trail has both paved and unpaved sections that you can traverse on foot or by bicycle. Along it you see the Occidental Hotel (made famous by Owen Wister's novel *The Virginian*), a brewery and mill site, and the site of Fort McKinney, now the Veterans' Home of Wyoming. You can also use the trail for wildlife viewing, photography, and access to fishing.

★ The frontier army occupied the military installation at **Fort Phil Kearny State Historic Site** for only a couple of years in the mid-1860s. Considered a hardship post by officers and enlisted men alike, the fort protected travelers headed to Montana's goldfields and later distracted Native Americans from the construction of the transcontinental railroad to the south. Eventually the constant attacks by the Plains Indians paid off, and the fort was abandoned in 1868 as part of the Fort Laramie Treaty. No original buildings remain at the site—they were likely burned by the Cheyenne as soon as the soldiers left—but fort buildings are marked and the visitor center has good details. The stockade around the fort was re-created after archaeological digs in 1999. ✉ *12 mi north of Buffalo on I–90* ☎ *307/684–7629 or 307/777–7014* 🌐 *www.philkearny.vcn.com* 🎫 *$1* ⏲ *Mid-May–Sept., daily 8–6.*

The **Fetterman Massacre Monument** (✉ 12 mi north of Buffalo, off I–90; obtain directions at Fort Phil Kearny) is a rock monolith dedicated to the memory of Lieutenant William J. Fetterman and his 80 men, who died in a December 21, 1866, battle against Lakota warriors led by Red Cloud.

Sports & the Outdoors

The forested canyons and pristine alpine meadows of the Bighorn Mountains teem with animal and plant life, making this an excellent area for hiking and pack trips by horseback. The quality and concentration of locals willing to outfit adventurers are high in Buffalo, making it a suitable base camp from which to launch an expedition.

The folks at **South Fork Mountain Outfitters** (✉ 16 mi west of Buffalo on U.S. 16 ☎ 307/267–2609 or 307/684–1225) can customize about any sort of adventure you'd like to undertake in the Bighorns, whether it's hiking, fishing, horseback riding, snowmobiling, or cross-country skiing. The company can arrange for all of your food and supplies and provide a guide, or render drop-camp services for the more experienced thrill seekers.

FLY-FISHING

The **Sports Lure** (✉ 66 S. Main St. ☎ 800/684–7682) stocks rods, reels, flies, books, and outdoor wear. You can also arrange for lessons and guided fishing trips.

HORSEBACK RIDING & PACK TRIPS

Located on a 24,000-acre working ranch, the **Powder River Experience** (✉ U.S. 14, Clearmont ☎ 307/758–4381 or 888/736–2402) gives you the chance to ride on the open range or to pack into the backcountry for an overnight stay at a log cabin. You're also encouraged to watch or personally experience as many ranch activities as you wish, whether it's branding, cattle driving, or calving.

Trails West Outfitters (✉ 259 Sunset Ave. ☎ 307/684–5233 or 888/283–9793 🌐 www.trailswestoutfitters.com) arranges multiday pack trips in the Bighorn and Shoshone national forests. The company also operates shorter wilderness excursions and drop camps for more independent adventurers.

Where to Stay & Eat

$$–$$$ ✕ **Winchester Steak House.** You can tie up your car in front of the hitch racks before this Western-style eatery in a false-front building. The Winchester has steak and more steak, plus a large rock fireplace and small bar. Locals rave about the place. ✉ *117 Hwy. 16 E* ☎ *307/684–8636* ▭ *MC, V.*

★ $–$$ ✕ **Colonel Bozeman's Restaurant and Tavern.** This eatery, which is literally on the Bozeman Trail, serves decent food amid Western memorabilia. Local favorites include buffalo steak and prime rib. You can dine outdoors on the deck. ✉ *675 E. Hart St.* ☎ *307/684–5555* ▭ *AE, D, MC, V.*

¢–$$ ✕ **Deerfield Boutique and Espresso Bar.** For a change from steak and potatoes, try this café in a renovated historic theater with high ceilings and old wallpaper. The place serves a wide selection of tortilla wraps and specialty sandwiches such as lemon-ginger chicken pita, and turkey and Swiss on focaccia. In summer there are chilled soups, such as tomato wine, cream of cantaloupe, and spinach cucumber. The Polynesian and mandarin orange salads are equally refreshing. Deerfield is next to Clear Creek, on a quiet side street in downtown Buffalo. ✉ *7 N. Main St.* ☎ *307/684–2788* ▭ *MC, V.*

¢–$ ✕ **Tom's Main Street Diner.** This tiny, clean place dishes up huge burgers and sandwiches in short order. A few mounted buck trophies line the walls above the tables, and you may notice a book or two lying on the counter about Gerry Spence, one of America's more-famous lawyers and the NBC legal consultant during the O. J. Simpson trial. If Tom is cooking, see if you can spot the family resemblance—Tom and Gerry are brothers. ✉ *41 N. Main St.* ☎ *307/684–7444* ▭ *AE, D, MC, V.*

★ $$$$ 🏨 **Paradise Guest Ranch.** Not only is this dude ranch—with a stunning location at the base of some of the tallest mountains in the range—one of the oldest (circa 1905), but it's also very progressive, as evidenced by its adults-only month (September) and a women-only week. The rest of the summer there are extensive children's programs, with everything from overnight pack trips to rodeo training. Adult programs involve sing-alongs, fancy barbecues, and square dances. The wranglers are very careful about matching riders to appropriate horses; multiday trips for veterans lead into Bighorn National Forest and the Cloud Peak Wilderness Area. Cabins are simple; some have fireplaces. There's a one-week minimum stay. ✉ *Hunter Creek Rd., off U.S. 16, Box 790, 82834* ☎ *307/684–7876* 📠 *307/684–9054* 🌐 *www.paradiseranch.com* *18 cabins* *Dining room, kitchenettes, pool, pond, hot tub, massage, fishing, basketball, hiking, horseback riding, horseshoes, bar, library, piano, recreation room, shops, children's programs (ages 6–18), playground, laundry facilities, meeting rooms, airport shuttle, travel services; no a/c, no room phones, no room TVs* ▭ *No credit cards* ⊙ *Closed Oct.–Apr.* *FAP.*

$ 🏨 **Comfort Inn.** Several blocks from downtown, this motel is close to Clear Creek Trail, the city's bike and walking path. Rooms have generic motel furnishings, including desks and coffeemakers. ✉ *65 U.S. 16 E, 82834* ☎ *307/684–9564 or 800/228–5150* 🌐 *www.comfortinn.com* *41 rooms* *Cable TV with movies, hot tub, some pets allowed (fee)* ▭ *AE, D, DC, MC, V* *CP.*

¢ 🏨 **Blue Gables Motel.** Old West collectibles and quilts add warmth to this highway-side motel's homey log cabins clustered in a U-shape. A few tent sites and a two-bedroom house are also available nearby. ✉ *662 N. Main St., 82834* ☎ *307/684–2574 or 800/684–2574* 🌐 *www.*

bluegables.com *17 rooms* *Microwaves, pool; no smoking* *D, MC, V.*

CAMPING **Deer Park Campground.** Although one section of this campground is quiet and relaxed, reserved for campers over 55, the main campsites are busy. In addition to a heated pool and a hot tub, Deer Park offers guided fishing excursions during the day (for a fee) and free ice-cream socials at night. Rates vary dramatically, depending on the number of site occupants. *Flush toilets, full hookups, partial hookups (electric and water), drinking water, showers, picnic tables, electricity, public telephone, swimming (pool)* *33 full hookups, 33 partial hookups, 34 tent sites* *146 U.S. 16* *307/684–5722 or 800/222–9960* *www.deerparkrv.com* *Full hookups $25–$37, partial hookups $22–$33, tent sites $16–$28* *Reservations essential* *MC, V* *May–Sept.*

Nightlife

Regulation pool tables and live country music and dancing every Friday and Saturday night (no cover charge) make the **White Buffalo Saloon** (106 U.S. 16 307/684–0101) a local favorite. The gift shop sells T-shirts, shot glasses, and other kitsch emblazoned with the White Buffalo logo.

Shopping

Cast-iron chandeliers with a Western flair are the signature products of ★ **Frontier Iron Works** (659 Trabing Rd. 307/684–5154 or 800/687–6952). They also craft distinctive furniture ranging from bar stools and patio sets to wall sconces and fireplace screens.

Gillette

7 *70 mi east of Buffalo on I–90.*

Gillette has worked hard to make itself presentable, but you don't have to go far to find a shovel bigger than a house at one of the giant strip mines nearby. Although the town started as a major livestock center from which ranchers could ship cattle and sheep to eastern markets, heavier industry has since claimed the community. Coal is now its primary commodity, and millions of tons are mined and shipped out each year to coal-fired power plants. In fact, if Gillette (and surrounding Campbell County) were its own nation, it would be the sixth-greatest producer of coal in the world. Currently the county is responsible for nearly a third of all American-mined coal.

Huge mines operate throughout the Powder River basin, and Gillette, with 19,646 residents, is the metropolis of the region. It's one of Wyoming's wealthiest cities as a result and therefore has an excellent community infrastructure ranging from the Campbell County Public Library to the Cam-Plex, a multiuse center for everything from crafts bazaars and indoor rodeos to concerts and fine-arts exhibits. Gillette is also a gateway town for Devils Tower National Monument, the volcanic plug that is one of the nation's most distinctive geological features and a hot spot for rock climbers. The community is a big fish in a small pond, however: Gillette is one of only two incorporated towns in Campbell County (the other is Wright, population 1,347).

Anything from a rodeo or crafts show to a concert or melodrama could be going on at the **Cam-Plex,** Gillette's multiuse facility. There's something scheduled almost every day; call or check the Web site for details. *1635 Reata Dr.* *307/682–0552, 307/682–8802 for tickets* *www.cam-plex.com* *$8–$13* *Call for schedule.*

You can fish, boat, swim, and camp at **Keyhole State Park.** Bird-watching is a favorite activity here, as up to 225 species can be seen on the grounds. ✉ *353 McKean Rd.* ☎ *307/756–3596, marina information 307/756–9529* 🌐 *wyoparks.state.wy.us/keyhole.htm* 🎫 *$2 resident vehicle, $5 nonresident vehicle; camping $4 resident vehicle, $9 nonresident vehicle.*

Local artifacts, including bits, brands, and rifles, make up the collection at the Campbell County–run **Rockpile Museum.** The museum's name comes from its location next to a natural rock-pile formation that served as a landmark for pioneers. ✉ *900 W. 2nd St.* ☎ *307/682–5723* 🌐 *www.gillettewyoming.com/rockpile/* 🎫 *Free* ⏲ *June–Aug., Mon.–Sat. 9–5; Sept.–May, Mon.–Sat. 9–7, Sun. 1–5.*

At the **Eagle Butte Coal Mine,** 17 mi south of Gillette, shovels and haul trucks dwarf anything you're likely to see in a science-fiction movie. There's a surprising amount of wildlife, from falcons to deer to bobcats, dwelling in and around the huge pits. You can register for the summer tours of the mine at the Gillette Visitors Center. ✉ *Gillette Visitors Center, Flying J Travel Plaza, 1810 S. Douglas Hwy.* ☎ *307/686–0040 or 800/544–6136* 🎫 *Free* ⏲ *Tours June–Aug., daily 9 AM–11 AM.*

off the beaten path

THUNDER BASIN NATIONAL GRASSLANDS – An 890-square-mi wilderness preserve that stretches from the edge of the Black Hills almost to the center of Wyoming, Thunder Basin truly is the outback of America. Except for a handful of tiny towns, deserted highways, and coal mines, it is entirely undeveloped. U.S. 116 and U.S. 450 are the best roads to use for access, although the grasslands are most impressive away from the highways. There are a few interior dirt roads navigable only in dry weather, but hiking allows you to get a real sense of the vast emptiness of this land. Pronghorn and prairie dogs are the most abundant form of animal life within the preserve. There are also many species of birds here, including burrowing owls, fist-size birds of prey that live in abandoned prairie-dog holes. ✉ *U.S. 450* ☎ *307/745–2300* 🌐 *www.fs.fed.us/r2/mbr/* 🎫 *Free* ⏲ *Daily, 24 hrs.*

Sports & the Outdoors

Although the town isn't on the slope of a mountain range or on the edge of a forest, there are plenty of sporting opportunities in Gillette—thanks largely to its own residents. The community as a whole is especially fitness conscious, and as a result, the town has many recreational facilities—including a multisport recreation center and two health clubs—that cities of a similar size lack. There are also more than 37 mi of developed walking trails within the city limits, including paths on the north end of town, off West Warlow Drive, in McManamen Park, a prime bird-watching spot.

An indoor track, gymnasium, five racquetball/handball courts, squash court, free-weight room, golf driving range, junior Olympic pool with a water slide, locker rooms, and steam rooms are all part of the **Campbell County Recreation Center and Pool** (✉ 1000 Douglas Hwy. ☎ 317/682–7406 🌐 www.ccprd.com). It costs $2.75 to use the recreation center and pool. Also here are the Campbell County Ice Arena, the Bell Nob golf course, and the Cam-Plex picnic area.

ICE-SKATING The **Campbell County Ice Arena** (✉ 121 S. 4J Rd. ☎ 307/687–1555), attached to the Campbell County Recreation Center and Pool, is open year-round for ice-skating. The arena accommodates public skating sessions, skating lessons, local hockey teams, and even figure skating.

Where to Stay & Eat

¢–$$ ✕ **Bailey's Bar and Grill.** With an interior that evokes an English pub, this handsome restaurant in an old brick building serves delicious sandwiches at lunch and has some Mexican dishes on the dinner menu. ✉ *301 S. Gillette Ave.* ☎ *307/686–7678* ▭ *AE, MC, V.*

¢–$$ ✕ **Hong Kong.** Lunches here are served fast and cheap (between $5 and $6) and include more than 30 different dishes, such as Mongolian beef and cashew chicken. They're popular with the business crowd, so you might want to avoid the noon lunch rush. ✉ *1612 W. 2nd St.* ☎ *307/682–5829* ▭ *AE, D, MC, V.*

¢–$$ ✕ **Packard's Grill.** Families are welcome at this large, airy, casual, no-smoking establishment—a cross between a brewpub and a sports bar, with team memorabilia on the walls. The favorites include prime rib and Southern-style dishes. There's a kids' menu. ✉ *408 S. Douglas Hwy.* ☎ *307/686–5149* ▭ *AE, D, DC, MC, V* ⊗ *No dinner Sun.*

$ **Best Western Tower West Lodge.** Shades of beige and teal decorate the large, comfortable rooms of this hotel on the west side of town. Among the public spaces are an outdoor courtyard and a lobby with leather couches and chairs grouped around the fireplace. ✉ *109 N. U.S. 14/16, 82716* ☎ *307/686–2210* *307/682–5105* ⊕ *www.bestwestern.com* *189 rooms* *Restaurant, indoor pool, gym, hot tub, bar* ▭ *AE, D, DC, MC, V.*

$ **Clarion Western Plaza.** Travelers with a yen for exercise appreciate the gym and a pool of lap-swimming proportions at this motel with everything under one roof. Rooms are decorated in soft teal and mauve. The on-site Sierra Café serves steak and seafood. ✉ *2009 S. Douglas Hwy., 82718* ☎ *307/686–3000 or 800/686–3368* *307/686–4018* ⊕ *www.westernplaza.com* *146 rooms, 13 suites* *Restaurant, cable TV, indoor pool, gym, hot tub, sauna, video game room, Internet, business services, meeting rooms* ▭ *AE, D, DC, MC, V.*

$ **Quality Inn.** This motel right off I–90 has large rooms but no frills, except for a free Continental breakfast. There's one other perk: antelope often graze nearby. ✉ *1004 E. U.S. 14/16, 82716* ☎ *307/682–2616 or 800/621–2182* *307/687–7002* ⊕ *www.qualityinn.com* *80 rooms* *Cable TV, no-smoking rooms* ▭ *AE, D, DC, MC, V* *CP.*

Nightlife & the Arts

NIGHTLIFE Pop and country performers make occasional appearances at Gillette's **Cam-Plex** (✉ 1635 Reata Dr. ☎ 307/682–0552, 307/682–8802 for tickets ⊕ www.cam-plex.com).

THE ARTS Founded in 1986, the **Powder River Symphony** (✉ 1635 Reata Dr. ☎ 307/660–0919) continues to perform on a regular basis at the Cam-Plex Heritage Center, a 960-seat auditorium within Cam-Plex. The orchestra is composed of area musicians of all ages, and they play everything from Beethoven to Andrew Lloyd Webber.

Shopping

The people of Campbell County take their gardening seriously, as any observer can tell by walking into the **Sunrise Greenhouse** (✉ U.S. 59, Wright, 38 mi south of Gillette ☎ 307/464–0889) in the springtime. A community institution, this greenhouse not only keeps local and exotic plants in stock but also carries an extensive selection of flowers for special occasions.

Devils Tower National Monument

★ 8 *65 mi northeast of Gillette via I–90 and U.S. 14.*

As you drive east from Gillette, the highways begin to rise into the forested slopes of the Black Hills. A detour north will take you to Devils Tower, a rocky, grooved butte that juts upward 1,280 feet above the plain of the Belle Fourche River. Native American legend has it that the tower was corrugated by the claws of a bear trying to reach some children on top, and some tribes still revere the site, which they call Bear Lodge. Geologists attribute the butte's strange existence to ancient volcanic activity. Rock climbers say it's one of the best crack-climbing areas on the continent. The tower was a tourist magnet long before a spaceship landed here in the movie *Close Encounters of the Third Kind.* Teddy Roosevelt made it the nation's first national monument in 1906, and it has attracted a steadily increasing throng of visitors ever since—up to nearly half a million people a year.

When you visit Devils Tower, take some time to stop at the **visitor center,** a few miles beyond the park entrance. Exhibits here explain the geology, history, and cultural significance of the monument, and a bookstore carries a wide selection of materials relating to the park. Park rangers can provide updated information on hiking and climbing conditions. ✉ *Hwy. 110* ☎ *307/467–5283* 🌐 *www.nps.gov/deto/* 🎫 *Cars $8; motorcycles, bicycles, and pedestrians $3* ⏲ *Butte daily 24 hrs; visitor center Apr. and May, daily 8:30–4:30; June–Aug., daily 8–8; Sept. and Oct., daily 9–5.*

At the **Prairie Dog Town** between Devils Tower and the Belle Fourche River, you can observe the rodents in their natural habitat. Prairie dogs were once plentiful on the Great Plains, but ranching and development have taken their toll; today, the only sizeable populations of the animal are found on protected federal lands. ✉ *Hwy. 110* ☎ *307/467–5283* 🌐 *www.nps.gov/deto/* 🎫 *Free* ⏲ *Daily 24 hrs.*

Sports & the Outdoors

HIKING Aside from affording excellent views of Devils Tower and the surrounding countryside, the hiking trails here are a good way to view some of the geology and wildlife of the Black Hills region. The terrain that surrounds the butte is relatively flat, so the popular **Tower Trail,** a paved 1⅓-mi path that circles the monument, is far from strenuous. It's the most popular trail in the park, though, so if you're looking for more isolation, try the 1½-mi **Joyner Ridge Trail** or the 3-mi **Red Beds Trail.** They're a bit more demanding, but the views from the top of Joyner Ridge and the banks of the Belle Fourche River are more than adequate rewards. Both the Tower and Red Beds trails start at the visitor center; Joyner Ridge Trail begins about a mile's drive north from there.

ROCK CLIMBING Climbing is the premier sporting activity at Devils Tower. Acclaimed as one of the best crack-climbing areas in North America, the monument has attracted both beginners and experts for more than a century. There are few restrictions when it comes to ascending the granite cone. Although climbing is technically allowed all year, there is generally a voluntary moratorium in June to allow for peaceful religious rites performed by local Native American tribes. Additionally, the west face of the formation is closed intermittently in the summer to protect the prairie falcons that nest there.

Before ascending Devils Tower you should sign in at the **visitor center** (✉ Hwy. 110 ☎ 307/467–5283) and discuss conditions with park officials. You can obtain a list of park-licensed guides here; courses are offered at all skill levels and sometimes include excursions into the Rockies or South Dakota. Some tour operators continue to guide climbs during the voluntary ban in June.

Camping

⛺ **Belle Fourche Campground.** Tucked away in a bend of the Belle Fourche River, this campground is small and spartan, but it is the only place in the park where camping is allowed. *Flush toilets, drinking water, picnic tables* *30 sites* *Hwy. 110* *307/467–5283* *307/467–5350* *www.nps.gov/deto/camp.htm* *$12* *Reservations not accepted* *No credit cards* *Apr.–Oct.*

Sundance

9 *31 mi southeast of Devils Tower National Monument via U.S. 14.*

Many Native American tribes, including the Crow, Cheyenne, and Lakota, congregated annually in June for their Sun Dance, an important ceremonial gathering. The event gave its name to the small town to the northeast of Sundance Mountain and south of the Bear Lodge Mountains. Both sites are sacred to Native Americans, including members of the Crow and Lakota tribes. The town in turn gave its name to the outlaw Harry Longabaugh, better known as the Sundance Kid, who spent time in the Sundance jail for stealing a horse. This town of 1,100, which had an Air Force installation during the 1950s, is surrounded by ranch country and the western portion of the Black Hills.

★ Thousands of buffalo bones are piled atop each other at the **Vore Buffalo Jump,** where Native Americans forced buffalos to plunge to their deaths in the era when hunting was done with spears rather than fast horses and guns. *Frontage Rd.* *307/283–1000* *www.sundancewyoming.com/vore.htm* *Free* *Daily.*

Projects by local young people are displayed at the **Crook County Fair and Rodeo** during the last week of July, from cooking and clothing to livestock projects. There also are live music shows, basketball tournaments, a Dutch oven cook-off, pig wrestling, and a rodeo with sheepdog trials and team roping events. *Fairgrounds Loop Rd.* *307/283–2644* *www.wyomingfairs.org* *Free.*

Where to Stay & Eat

¢–$$ **Aro Restaurant and Lounge.** This large family diner in downtown Sundance has a cowboys-and-Indians theme and an extensive, well-priced menu. Standards include burgers, prime rib, Southwestern smothered burritos, Reuben sandwiches, and a huge Devils Tower brownie sundae dessert. *205 Cleveland St.* *307/283–2000* *D, MC, V.*

¢–$$ **Country Cottage.** This one-stop shop in the center of town sells flowers, gifts, and simple meals, including submarine sandwiches. There's a modest seating area with some booths and small tables. *423 Cleveland St.* *307/283–2450* *MC, V.*

¢–$$ **Log Cabin Cafe.** Locals crowd this small log-cabin restaurant full of country crafts for burgers, steaks, and seafood. Because the place is always packed, service can be slow, but the staff is always friendly. *U.S. 14* *307/283–3393* *MC, V.*

$ **Sundance Mountain Inn.** Clean but basic rooms, friendly service, and a comfortable poolside area make this one-story ranch-style motor inn a nice place to stay. It is convenient to I–90 and across the street from area restaurants. *26 Hwy. 585, 82729* *307/283–3737 or 888/347–2794* *307/283–3738* *42 rooms* *Cable TV, indoor pool, hot tub, laundry facilities, some pets allowed (fee)* *AE, D, DC, MC, V* *CP.*

¢–$ **Best Western Inn at Sundance.** Dark-green carpeting and plum-color drapes decorate the spacious rooms of this hotel. With its inlaid cedar accents and comfortable deck chairs, the room housing the indoor pool is surprisingly stylish for a chain hotel. *2719 Cleveland St., 82729* *307/283–2800 or 800/238–0965* *307/283–2727* *www.bestwestern.com* *44 rooms* *Cable TV with movies, indoor pool, hot tub, shop, laundry facilities, meeting rooms, some pets allowed (fee)* *AE, D, DC, MC, V.* *CP.*

¢ **Bear Lodge Motel.** A cozy lobby, a stone fireplace, and wildlife mounts on the walls distinguish this downtown motel. Hardwood furniture and patterned bedspreads add a slightly Western touch to the spacious, simple bedrooms. ✉ *218 Cleveland St., 82729* ☎ *307/283–1611* 🖷 *307/283–2537* 🌐 *www.bearlodgemotel.com* *33 rooms* *Cable TV with movies, hot tub* 💳 *AE, D, DC, MC, V.*

en route

Carved into the northern edge of the Black Hills by a tiny creek over tens of millions of years, **Spearfish Canyon** (🌐 www.spearfishcanyon.com) surrounds U.S. 14A, a national scenic byway, as it meanders up into the rocky peaks, connecting I–90 with the historic mining camp of Deadwood. The canyon walls hug U.S. 14A so tightly that you sometimes have to lean your head out the car window and look up to see the tops of the cliffs. Pines, spruce, aspen, birch, and oak blanket the hillsides, occasionally growing straight out of the granite walls. Several waterfalls cascade down the sides of the canyon year-round, although they are most impressive in early summer. Autumn colors the entire area in deep hues of yellow, orange, pink, red, and brown, and people from miles around come here to go leaf hunting.

SOUTH DAKOTA BLACK HILLS & BADLANDS

Unlike the agricultural eastern half of the state, western South Dakota is a land of mountain meadows, pine forests, and desolate, rocky landscapes. It's also the major draw for most visitors to the state, who head for the magnificent scenery of the ancient, pine-covered Black Hills, with creek-carved canyons, sky-high granite spires, mountain meadows, and wandering wildlife. Capped by 17 peaks more than 7,000 feet high, this mountain range in the western part of the state covers an area roughly 50 mi wide and 120 mi long—about the size of the state of Delaware. Within the Black Hills are Deadwood, the 19th-century mining town turned gambling mecca; the mountain carving in progress known as Crazy Horse; and Mount Rushmore, whose giant stone carvings of four U.S. presidents have retained their stern grandeur for more than 60 years.

South of the Black Hills is another unique landscape, at Badlands National Park. Here you'll find some of the strangest formations in the state: towering spires, ragged ridgelines, and deep canyons.

Deadwood

10 *47 mi east of Sundance via I–90 and U.S. 85.*

Fodor's Choice ★

More than a decade after the legalization of gaming in modern-day South Dakota, the town of Deadwood stands as a testament to an unlikely benefactor. In 1989, South Dakota voters approved limited-stakes gaming for Deadwood—today the nation's third-largest gambling venue, behind Nevada and Atlantic City—on the condition that a portion of revenues be devoted to historic preservation. Since then, $170 million has gone into restoring and preserving this once infamous gold-mining boomtown, earning Deadwood a designation as a National Historic Landmark. Streets have been repaved with bricks, and old-time trolleys, period lighting, and original Victorian architecture add to the character of this town. Small gaming halls, good restaurants, and hotels occupy virtually every storefront on Main Street, just as they did back in Deadwood's heydey in the late 19th century. You can walk in the same footsteps as legendary

CloseUp

THE CUSTER EXPEDITION

"I **AM INCLINED TO THINK** *that the occupation of this region of the country is not necessary to the happiness and prosperity of the Indians, and as it is supposed to be rich in minerals and lumber it is deemed important to have it freed as early as possible from Indian occupancy.*

"I shall, therefore, not oppose any policy which looks first to a careful examination of the subject . . . If such an examination leads to the conclusion that country is not necessary or useful to Indians, I should then deem it advisable . . . to extinguish the claim of the Indians and open the territory to the occupation of the whites."

So stated a letter written in 1872 by Secretary of the Interior Columbus Delano. Although his job description included protection of Plains Indian territorial rights, Delano's statement was in direct contradiction to the Fort Laramie Treaty of 1868, which prevented white people from setting foot in the "country" he spoke of. Two years after Delano's letter, an army officer named George Armstrong Custer led an expedition out of Fort Abraham Lincoln in present-day North Dakota to make a survey of the protected Great Sioux Indian Reservation.

The illegal expedition arrived at the Belle Fourche River (in what would become Wyoming) before entering the Black Hills on their western edge. For two months the men of the Seventh Cavalry hiked through the pristine valleys and pine-covered canyons of the Black Hills, known to the Lakota as Paha Sapa, gathering animal specimens and writing reports about the clear mountain creeks and fields covered in wildflowers. These reports were rushed west to Fort Laramie, where they were telegraphed back east. One report in particular, written by Custer himself, forever changed the history of the nation:

". . . gold has been found at several places, and it is the belief of those who are giving their attention to this subject that it will be found in paying quantities. I have on my table forty or fifty small particles of pure gold . . . most of it obtained today from one panful of earth."

If the official military reports hadn't leaked out, the newspaper reporters Custer took with him would have informed the country anyway. Before the year was out, prospectors from all over the country were outfitting themselves in Sioux City, Helena, Bismarck, and Cheyenne, preparing to flood the forbidden Black Hills. The army was dispatched to keep the pioneers off the protected Sioux lands, but they were able to stem the tide for only a few short months.

The military all but gave up in 1875, and thousands of white settlers immediately flocked to the Black Hills, despite the threat of Native American attacks. Prospectors first headed to the French Creek area, where Custer had reported seeing the precious metal, and fittingly named their gold camp after the young officer. But rumors of bigger strikes drove the prospectors north. In a matter of months, as many as 5,000 people swarmed the hillsides of Deadwood Gulch, making it the largest settlement in the territory. The last great gold rush of the Western frontier had begun.

The various Sioux tribes, furious over the violation of the Laramie Treaty by the United States, consolidated their military strength and rebelled. They scored their largest victory in 1876 at the Battle of the Little Bighorn, where Custer and most of the men who were with him on the Black Hills expedition were killed.

Ultimately, however, the Sioux, along with their Cheyenne and Arapaho allies, were defeated and forced onto much smaller reservations. Their once-protected territory, land that ranged across the present-day states of Wyoming, Nebraska, and both of the Dakotas, was parceled out and sold to ranchers and prospectors. Although there were many contributing factors, Custer's expedition and the resulting Black Hills gold rush brought about the modern Native American reservation system.

lawman Wild Bill Hickok, cigar-smoking Poker Alice Tubbs, and the fabled Calamity Jane, who swore she could outdrink, outspit, and outswear any man—and usually did.

A heroic-scale bronze sculpture of three Native Americans on horseback driving 14 bison off a cliff is the centerpiece of **Tatanka: Story of the Bison,** on a ridge above Deadwood. The attraction, owned by *Dances with Wolves* star Kevin Costner, also includes an interpretive center with a Lakota Sioux encampment and Lakota guides who explain Plains Indian life circa 1840. ✉ *U.S. 85* ☎ *605/584–5678* 🌐 *www.storyofthebison.com* 🎫 *$6.50* ⏲ *Mid-May–Oct., daily 10–6.*

Scenes of Deadwood's turbulent years unfold at the **Ghosts of Deadwood Gulch Wax Museum.** A progressive audiovisual presentation depicts 19 episodes from the region's history, and a re-creation of the trial of Jack McCall for the murder of Wild Bill Hickok takes place daily in summer. ✉ *Old Town Hall, 12 Lee St.* ☎ *605/578–3583* 🌐 *www.deadwoodattractions.com* 🎫 *$5* ⏲ *Memorial Day–Labor Day, daily 9–5.*

You can pan for gold and join guides on a journey into the **Broken Boot Gold Mine,** a remnant of Deadwood's early days. You may not find any gold, but if nothing else, you'll leave with a souvenir stock certificate. ✉ *U.S. 14A* ☎ *605/578–9997* 🎫 *Tour $4.50, gold panning $4.50* ⏲ *May–Aug., daily 8–5:30; Sept., daily 9–4:30.*

The **Adams Museum,** between the massive stone-block post office and the old railroad depot, houses three floors of displays that include the first locomotive used in the area, photographs of the town's early days, and a reproduction of the largest gold nugget (7¾ troy ounces) ever discovered in the Black Hills (the original is in the museum vault). ✉ *54 Sherman St.* ☎ *605/578–1714* 🌐 *www.adamsmuseumandhouse.org* 🎫 *Donations accepted* ⏲ *Memorial Day–Labor Day, Mon.–Sat. 9–7, Sun. noon–5; Labor Day–Memorial Day, Mon.–Sat. 10–4.*

A tour of the restored **Adams House Museum** includes an explanation of the tragedies and triumphs of two of the community's founding families (the Franklins and the Adams) who lived here. The 1892 Queen Anne–style mansion was closed in the mid-1930s and sat empty for more than 50 years, preserving the original furniture and decor that you see today. ✉ *22 Van Buren St.* ☎ *605/578–3724* 🌐 *www.adamsmuseumandhouse.org* 🎫 *$4* ⏲ *Memorial Day–Labor Day, Mon.–Sat. 9–6, Sun. noon–4; Labor Day–Memorial Day, Mon.–Sat. 10–3.*

Mount Moriah Cemetery, also known as Boot Hill, is the final resting place of Wild Bill Hickok, Calamity Jane, and other notable Deadwood residents. The aging landmark was revitalized by extensive restoration work in 2003, including the addition of a visitor center that houses a leather Bible, stained-glass window, and pulpit chairs from the first and second Methodist churches of Deadwood that were destroyed in 1885 and 2003, respectively. From the top of the cemetery you'll have the best panoramic view of the town. ✉ *Top of Lincoln St.* ☎ *605/722–0837* 🎫 *$1* ⏲ *Memorial Day–Labor Day, daily 7 AM–8 PM; Labor Day–end of Sept., daily 9–5.*

The first week of August each year, the community of **Sturgis** becomes South Dakota's largest city when hundreds of thousands of motorcylists invade the region for the **Black Hills Motorcycle Rally** (✉ 13 mi east of Deadwood on U.S. 14 ☎ 605/347–2556 🌐 www.sturgis-sd.org). Begun in 1940 by a handful of bike owners, the event has grown into one of the largest gatherings of Harley-Davidson owners in the world.

Motorcycle shows, concerts, tours, and national racing events are just some of the activities that fill this 10-day festival. Most hotels within a 100-mi radius are totally booked for the festival up to a year in advance.

Sports & the Outdoors

Deadwood makes a good base for pursuing winter sports in the Black Hills, particularly snowmobiling and cross-country skiing. The surrounding Northern Hills are especially popular, both for their stunning scenery and heavy snows. The rocky peaks and deep canyons are the most dramatic here, and the snowfall is the heaviest. In some years the area around Deadwood can see as much as 180 inches of the white stuff, although the yearly average hovers around 150 inches. However, the climate here is more variable than in the Rockies, so snow won't blanket the region all winter. Often a spell of 50°F, 60°F, or even 70°F weather will hit the region for a week or so after a big snowfall, quickly melting the fresh powder. Before you make firm plans, be sure to check weather reports.

FISHING **Custom Caster** (✉ 21207 Thunder La., Lead, 8 mi southwest of Dead ☎ 605/584–2217) is a small one-man operation that specializes in hand-tied flies and custom-made rods. Owner Dale Peters also sells name-brand rods and reels.

HIKING & BICYCLING The railroad didn't reach Deadwood until 1891, in part because of the narrow canyons and sharp grades of the northern Black Hills. Although the old tracks have since outlived their usefulness for trains, they still help people get around thanks to a rails-to-trails program. Both the Mickelson Trail (a 111-mi trail that begins in Deadwood) and the Centennial Trail (a 116-mi trail that begins in nearby Sturgis) are great for hiking and biking amid stunning scenery.

Running the length of the Black Hills from north to south, the **Mickelson Trail** (🌐 www.mickelsontrail.com) incorporates more than 100 converted railroad bridges and four tunnels in its 111-mi-long course. Although the grade seldom exceeds 4%, parts of the trail are strenuous. A $2 day pass lets you hike or bike on the trail ($10 for an annual pass); passes are available at self-service stations along the trail, some state park offices, and through the South Dakota Game, Fish, and Parks Web site (🌐 www.state.sd.us/gfp/). A portion of the trail is open for snowmobiling in winter.

Deadwood Bicycles (✉ 180 Sherman St. ☎ 605/578–1345), in a restored engine house at the beginning of the Mickelson Trail, provides bike sales, service, and rentals, including bikes for men, women, and children, plus tandems. There's also a modest selection of rock-climbing equipment.

SKIING Heavy snowfalls and lovely views make the Black Hills prime cross-country skiing territory. Many trails are open to snowmobilers and skiers, although most skiers don't like the thought of being run over and stick to the quieter trails closed to motorized traffic. Many of these trails run along the rim or at the bottom of narrow canyons and gulches, affording outstanding views of some spectacular country. Depending on the freeze-thaw cycle, you may catch a glimpse of frozen waterfalls, particularly in Spearfish Canyon.

Although the Black Hills don't have the massive peaks that give Colorado, Wyoming, and Montana some of the best downhill skiing in the world, a couple of rocky slopes in the Northern Hills are both steep enough and snowy enough to support modest ski lodges, with runs of respectable intermediate level.

The groomed **Big Hill Trails** (✉ 7 mi south of Spearfish on Tinton Rd., 15 mi west of Deadwood ☎ 605/673–9200) travel all around Spearfish Canyon. The trees here are gorgeous, ranging from the ubiquitous ponderosa and Black Hills spruce to quaking aspen and paperbark birch. The towering canyon walls, abundant wildlife, and stark contrast between the evergreens and the bare trees make this a particularly outstanding trail.

The runs at **Deer Mountain Ski Area** (✉ 3 mi south of Lead on U.S. 85 ☎ 605/717–0422 🌐 www.skideermountain.com) aren't as challenging as those on nearby Terry Peak, but this slope has a massive beginner's area and the only night skiing in the Black Hills. There are also about 10 mi of groomed cross-country trails. Rentals, regular classes, and inexpensive personal lessons are available, and there's a modest lodge. Perched on the sides of a 7,076-foot mountain, **Terry Peak Ski Area** (✉ 2 mi south of Lead on U.S. 85 ☎ 605/584–2165 or 800/456–0524 🌐 www.terrypeak.com) claims the second-highest mountain summit in the Black Hills. The runs here are challenging for novice and intermediate skiers and should at least keep the experts entertained. The view from the top is spectacular; on a clear day you can see into Wyoming, Montana, and North Dakota.

SNOWMOBILING Trade and travel magazines consistently rank the Black Hills among the top snowmobiling destinations in the country for two simple reasons: dramatic scenery and an abundance of snow. You'll find both throughout the area, but especially in the Northern Hills.

One of the most popular places in the Black Hills for snowmobiling is **Deadwood Gulch Resort** (✉ 2 mi southwest of Deadwood on U.S. 85 ☎ 605/578–1294 or 800/695–1876 🌐 www.deadwoodgulch.com), which has a full-service hotel with gaming, a restaurant, and a convenient location right on the Mickelson Trail (which is open to snowmobiles during part of the winter). You can rent high-quality snowmobiles at reasonable rates here. **Trailshead Lodge** (✉ 21 mi southwest of Deadwood on U.S. 85 ☎ 605/584–3464 🌐 www.blackhillstravel.com), near the Wyoming border, has a small restaurant, a bar, gas, a repair shop, and dozens of brand-new snowmobiles for rent by the day. In summer (or during warm spells in winter when the snow melts) the lodge caters to bicyclists, horseback riders, and hikers.

Where to Stay & Eat

★ $$$–$$$$ ✕ **Jakes.** This restaurant owned by actor Kevin Costner may well be South Dakota's premier dining experience. Cherrywood pillars inlaid with etched-glass lights, white-brick fireplaces, and a pianist add to the elegance of the atrium dining room. Among the menu's eclectic offerings are buffalo roulade, Cajun seafood tortellini, filet mignon, and fresh fish. *✉ 677 Main St. ☎ 605/578–1555 ⚠ Reservations required 💳 AE, D, DC, MC, V.*

★ $–$$$ ✕ **Deadwood Social Club.** On the second floor of historic Saloon No. 10, this warm restaurant wraps you in wood and old-time photographs of Deadwood's past. The decor is clearly Western, but the food is northern Italian, a juxtaposition that keeps locals and visitors coming back time and again. The menu stretches from wild-mushroom pasta-and-seafood nest with basil cream to chicken piccata and melt-in-your-mouth rib eyes. The ever-growing wine list had nearly 200 selections at last count. Reservations are a good idea. *✉ 657 Main St. ☎ 605/578–3346 💳 AE, MC, V.*

¢–$ ✕ **Moonshine Gulch Saloon.** Although 25 mi south of Deadwood in the middle of a very empty section of the forest, the ghost town of Rochford is worth visiting. Once the site of a prosperous gold camp, the town now has about 15 residents and even fewer buildings. The saloon (in between the Rochford Mall, the self-proclaimed "Small of America," and the one-room Rochford University) stays quite busy in the summer despite its remote location. After you order your sarsaparilla (a carbonated beverage) and hamburger, look up and admire the collection of baseball caps and currency on the ceiling. ✉ *Rochford Rd., Rochford* ☎ *605/584–2528* 💳 *MC, V.*

$–$$ ✕🏨 **Bullock Hotel.** Built by Deadwood's first sheriff, Seth Bullock, in 1895, this pink granite hotel has been meticulously restored. Victorian reproduction furniture adorns the cozy lobby and bar, and the rooms are also decorated in a Victorian style. The suites have hot tubs. You can order a steak or hamburger at the casual and relaxed downstairs restaurant ($–$$$), complete with a period fireplace. ✉ *633 Main St., 57732* ☎ *605/578–1745 or 800/336–1876* 📠 *605/578–1382* ✉ *hub@mato.com* 🛏 *29 rooms, 7 suites* 🛎 *Restaurant, room service, some in-room hot tubs, cable TV with movies, bar, casino, business services, meeting rooms* 💳 *AE, D, MC, V.*

$ ✕🏨 **Deadwood Gulch Resort.** Perched on the banks of Whitewood Creek where it bubbles steadily down into Deadwood, this family-style resort has a deck with a view of the hills. Although the resort is about a mile from downtown, trolleys run frequently to other hotels, casinos, and attractions closer to the main drag. The resort also has a casino of its own. The Creekside Restaurant ($$–$$$) is decorated like an old saloon and serves hearty breakfasts and some of the best burgers in town. The giant salads here are also favorites, largely because of the side of sunflower bread and the homemade apricot dressing. ✉ *U.S. 85, 57732* ☎ *605/578–1294 or 800/695–1876* 📠 *605/578–2505* 🌐 *www.deadwoodgulch.com* 🛏 *98 rooms* 🛎 *Restaurant, cable TV with movies, pool, hot tub, snowmobiling, bar, casino, meeting rooms, some pets allowed (fee)* 💳 *AE, D, DC, MC, V.*

$ ✕🏨 **Franklin Hotel.** Built in 1903, the imposing Franklin Hotel has housed many famous guests in its time, including John Wayne, Teddy Roosevelt, and Kevin Costner. The original banisters, ceilings, and fireplace add character. The guest rooms are Victorian style, with reproduction furniture, lace on hardwood tables, and flowery bedspreads. A bar on the second floor spills out onto the veranda above the white-columned hotel entrance, affording a spectacular view down Main Street. The restaurant ($–$$$) serves charbroiled steaks, buffalo, pasta, and vegetarian dishes. ✉ *700 Main St., 57732* ☎ *605/578–2241 or 800/688–1876* 📠 *605/578–3452* 🌐 *www.historicfranklinhotel.com* 🛏 *81 rooms* 🛎 *Restaurant, room service, cable TV with movies, bar, casino, business services, meeting rooms, some pets allowed (fee)* 💳 *AE, D, DC, MC, V.*

$$–$$$ 🏨 **Holiday Inn Express.** Although this four-story building was built to resemble the much older brick facades of Deadwood's Main Street, the guest rooms have standard chain-hotel furnishings. Three suites have fireplaces and whirlpool tubs. ✉ *22 Lee St., 57732* ☎ *605/578–3330 or 888/777–4465* 📠 *605/578–3335* 🌐 *www.ichotelsgroup.com* 🛏 *78 rooms, 22 suites* 🛎 *Cable TV with movies and video games, indoor pool, gym, hot tub, casino, laundry facilities, meeting rooms, no-smoking rooms* 💳 *AE, D, DC, MC, V* 🍽 *CP.*

$$–$$$ 🏨 **Mineral Palace.** Like the other hotels built in town since gaming was reintroduced in 1989, the Mineral Palace was constructed to blend in with the architecture of historic Deadwood. The rooms have modern furnishings, but floral bedspreads, burgundy carpeting, and hardwood trim give them a slightly Victorian look. One deluxe suite has a hot tub and fireplace. ✉ *601 Main St., 57732* ☎ *605/578–2036 or 800/847–2522* 📠 *605/578–2037* 🌐 *www.mineralpalace.com* 🛏 *57 rooms, 6* *suites* ♿ *Restaurant, room service, some in-room hot tubs, cable TV with movies and video games, bar, laundry facilities, business services, meeting rooms; no smoking* ▭ *AE, D, MC, V.*

¢–$ **Calamity Rose.** This exquisite three-story Victorian B&B built in 1889 is furnished lavishly with antiques yet designed with understated elegance. You can stay in one of four suites or one single room. The house is five blocks away from downtown and the casinos. ✉ *21 Lincoln Ave., 57732* ☎ *605/578–1151 or 877/518–1151* 📠 *605/578–3193* 🌐 *www.calamityrose.com* *1 room, 4 suites* ♿ *Cable TV, laundry facilities; no smoking* ▭ *AE, MC, V* 🍽 *CP.*

Nightlife

There are more than 80 gaming establishments in Deadwood, most of them small and personal, with only a handful of blackjack and poker tables and slot machines. Most of these venues have other functions as well—restaurants, saloons, gift shops—meaning there are plenty of other activities to keep you occupied once you've dropped your last quarter.

In addition to gaming halls, you can expect live rock bands in the bars on weekends, actors portraying Wild West characters outside the hotels during the day, and comedians from time to time in the restaurants. The Deadwood City Limits complex, scheduled to open in 2005, will host national recording artists on a regular basis and operate several theme nightclubs.

Expect a family crowd in the day and a rowdier bunch at night at the **Bodega and Big Al's Buffalo Steakhouse Stockade** (✉ 658 Main St. ☎ 605/578–1300). The outdoor stockade section is only open in summer, when musicians entertain people who drop in for buffalo steak. At night there's live country or rock music. The Bodega has always had a rough past; from the 1890s up until 1980, the upper floors were used as a brothel. They now sit empty, although the secret buzzers and discreet back doors were only removed in the 1990s. Owned by actor Kevin Costner, the casino **Midnight Star** (✉ 677 Main St. ☎ 605/578–1555) is decorated throughout with props and costumes from his movies. The bar on the first floor is named for and modeled after the bar in the film *Silverado,* in which Costner starred. Wood accents, stained glass, and plush carpeting give the structure an elegant Victorian look.

★ Billed as the only museum in the world with a bar, the **Old Style Saloon No. 10** (✉ 657 Main St. ☎ 605/578–3346) is littered with thousands of artifacts, from vintage photos and antique lighting to a stuffed two-headed calf and Wild Bill Hickok's death chair (the chair in which he was supposedly shot). A reenactment of his murder takes place four times daily in the summer. At night, expect some of the region's best bands, lively blackjack tables, and quiet bartenders who cater to noisy customers. The **Silverado** (✉ 709 Main St. ☎ 605/578–1366 or 800/584–7005), at the top of Main Street and sprawling over half a city block, is among Deadwood's largest gaming establishments. Although the wood paneling and brass accents around the bars hark back to Deadwood's Wild West past, the red carpets, velvet ropes, and bow ties worn by the staff give the place an air of modern elegance. The prime-rib-and-crab buffet on Friday and Saturday nights attracts regulars from more than 100 mi away.

Shopping

Although most of the storefronts on **Main Street** are filled by gambling halls, saloons, restaurants, and hotels, a handful belong to souvenir shops. Some are typical tourist traps that hawk rubber tomahawks and plastic pistols, but some of the more upscale stores carry high-quality Western wear, Black Hills–gold jewelry, and fine art. Ice-cream parlors are never hard to find in summer.

Rapid City

11 *42 mi southeast of Deadwood via U.S. 14A and I–90.*

To locals, Rapid City is West River, meaning west of the Missouri. South Dakota's second-largest city (population 59,607), a cross between Western town and progressive community, is a good base from which to explore the Black Hills. Cowboy boots are common here, and business leaders often travel by pickup truck or four-wheel-drive vehicle. The city supports a convention center, a couple of museums, and a modern, acoustically advanced performance hall as well as numerous book, gift, and specialty shops downtown.

★ The **Journey Museum** combines the collections of the **Sioux Indian Museum,** the **Minnilusa Pioneer Museum,** the **Museum of Geology,** the **State Archaeological Research Center,** and a private collection of Native American artifacts into a sweeping pageant of the history and evolution of the Black Hills. A favorite among visitors is the tepee in the Sioux Indian Museum; you have to crouch down and peer inside to watch a holographic Lakota woman talk about the history and legends of her people. ✉ *222 New York St.* ☎ *605/394–6923* 🌐 *www.journeymuseum.org* 🎟 *$6* ⏲ *Memorial Day–Labor Day, daily 9–5; Labor Day–Memorial Day, Mon.–Sat. 10–5, Sun. 1–5.*

The **South Dakota Air & Space Museum** has a model of a Stealth bomber that's 60% actual size. Also here are General Dwight D. Eisenhower's Mitchell B-25 bomber and more than two dozen other planes, as well as a once-operational missile silo. The museum is open year-round, but tours are not available in winter. ✉ *2890 Davis Dr.* ☎ *605/385–5188* 🎟 *Free, tour $4.50* ⏲ *Mid-May–mid-Sept., daily 8:30–6; mid-Sept.–mid-May, daily 8:30–4:30.*

Although they were released in the early 1990s, the films *Dances with Wolves* and *Thunderheart* continue to generate interest and business in the Black Hills. The **Ft. Hays *Dances with Wolves* Movie Set** displays photos and shows a video taken during the making of the film. A chuck-wagon dinner show ($15) is offered Memorial Day through Labor Day. ✉ *Ft. Hays Dr. and U.S. 16* ☎ *605/394–9653* 🌐 *www.rushmoretours.com/forthays.htm* 🎟 *Free* ⏲ *Mid-May–mid-Sept., daily 7:30 AM–8 PM.*

On the west side of Rapid City is **Storybook Island,** a park on the banks of Rapid Creek that lets children romp through scenes from fairy tales and nursery rhymes. A children's theater troupe, sponsored by the Black Hills Community Theater, performs regular shows on a modest outdoor stage here and hosts workshops and acting programs. ✉ *1301 Sheridan Lake Rd.* ☎ *605/342–6357* 🌐 *www.storybookisland.org* 🎟 *Donations accepted* ⏲ *May–Sept., daily 9–7.*

★ **Reptile Gardens,** on the bottom of a valley between Rapid City and Mount Rushmore, is western South Dakota's answer to a zoo. In addition to the world's largest private reptile collection, the site also has a raptor rehabilitation center. Birds that cannot be rereleased into the wild are used in educational shows, as are many reptile species. No visit here is complete without watching some alligator wrestling or letting the kids ride the giant tortoises. ✉ *8955 S. U.S. 16* ☎ *605/342–5873* 🌐 *www.reptilegardens.com* 🎟 *$10* ⏲ *Apr.–Oct., daily 8–7.*

At the drive-through wildlife park **Bear Country U.S.A.,** you encounter black bears, wolves, and other North American wildlife. There's also a walk-through wildlife center with bear cubs, wolf pups, and other offspring. ✉ *13820 S. U.S. 16* ☎ *605/343–2290* 🌐 *www.bearcountryusa.com* *$12* ⏲ *May–Oct., daily 8–6.*

Sports & the Outdoors

The Black Hills are filled with tiny mountain creeks, especially on the wetter western and northern slopes, that are ideal for fly-fishing. Rapid Creek, which flows down from the Central Hills into Pactola Reservoir and finally into Rapid City, is a favorite fishing venue for the city's anglers, both because of its regularly stocked population of trout and for its easy accessibility (don't be surprised to see someone standing in the creek casting a line as you drive through the center of town on Highway 44). Also popular are nearby Spearfish, Whitewood, Spring, and French creeks, all within an hour's drive of Rapid City.

Although they'll take you on a guided fly-fishing trip any time of the year, the folks at **Dakota Angler and Outfitter** (✉ 513 7th St. ☎ 605/341–2450) recommend fishing between April and October. The guides lead individuals and groups on half- and full-day excursions, and they cater to all skill levels.

Where to Stay & Eat

$$–$$$$ ✕ **Firehouse Brewing Company.** Brass fixtures and firefighting equipment ornament the state's first brewpub, in a historic 1915 firehouse. The five house-brewed beers are the highlight of the menu, which also includes such hearty pub dishes as pastas, salads, and gumbo. Thursday nights buffalo prime rib is the specialty. Kids' menus are available. ✉ *610 Main St.* ☎ *605/348–1915* *Reservations not accepted* ▭ *AE, D, DC, MC, V* ⏲ *No lunch Sun.*

$$$ ✕ **Fireside Inn Restaurant & Lounge.** One of the two dining rooms here has tables arranged around a slate fireplace, and you can also dine on an outdoor deck, weather permitting. The large menu has 54 entrées, including prime rib, seafood, and Italian dishes. ✉ *Hwy. 44, 6½ mi west of town* ☎ *605/342–3900* ▭ *AE, D, DC, MC, V.*

$–$$$ ✕ **Botticelli Ristorante Italiano.** With a wide selection of delectable veal and chicken dishes as well as creamy pastas, this Italian eatery is a welcome respite from the traditional Midwestern meat and potatoes. The artwork and traditional Italian music in the background give the place a European air. ✉ *523 Main St.* ☎ *605/348–0089* ▭ *AE, MC, V.*

$–$$$ ✕ **Minerva's.** A pub and pool room complement this spacious restaurant next to hotels and the city's largest shopping mall. Specialties include linguine Minerva (chicken breast served on linguine with pesto, vegetables, pine nuts, and a cream sauce), rotisserie chicken, and a scrumptious rib eye with grilled onions and new potatoes. ✉ *2111 N. LaCrosse St.* ☎ *605/394–9505* ▭ *AE, D, DC, MC, V.*

$$ ✕ **Flying T Chuckwagon.** Ranch-style meals of barbecued beef, grilled chicken, potatoes, and baked beans are served on tin plates in this converted barn. Dinner, served between 5 and 6:30, is followed by a Western show with music and cowboy comedy. The prix fixe of $14 includes dinner and the show. For summer dining, it's a good idea to buy tickets in advance. ✉ *U.S. 16, 6 mi south of town* ☎ *605/342–1905 or 888/256–1905* ▭ *MC, V* ⏲ *Closed mid-Sept.–mid-May. No lunch.*

$ ✕ **Golden Phoenix.** Great food, low prices, convenient parking, and relaxed, friendly, and quick service make this one of South Dakota's best Chinese restaurants. The chef-owner, who often socializes with the locals who frequent his establishment, spices up traditional dishes from all over China with cooking elements from his native Taiwan. Try the Mongolian beef, sesame chicken, or Hunan shrimp. Local businesspeople crowd in for the daily lunch specials. ✉ *2421 W. Main St.* ☎ *605/348–4195* ▭ *AE, D, DC, MC, V.*

Fodor'sChoice ★

★ $–$$ **Alex Johnson Hotel and Landmark Restaurant.** Native American patterns and artwork predominate at this landmark hotel dedicated to the Lakota peoples. The hotel opened in 1928, and rooms have reproductions of their original furniture. A torch chandelier in the lobby is made of Lakota war lances. The Landmark Restaurant ($$$$) is popular for its lunch buffet and for such dinner specialties as prime rib, beef Wellington, freshwater fish, and wild game. *523 6th St., 57701 605/342–1210 or 800/888–2539 www.alexjohnson.com 143 rooms, 2 suites Restaurant, room service, cable TV with movies, bar, shop, business services, meeting rooms AE, D, DC, MC, V.*

$$$–$$$$ **Radisson Hotel Rapid City/Mount Rushmore.** Murals of the surrounding landscape and a large Mount Rushmore mosaic in the marble floor distinguish the lobby of this nine-floor hotel in the heart of downtown Rapid City. A popular accommodation, it's between the interstate and U.S. 16, the highway that leads into the southern Black Hills and Mount Rushmore. *445 Mt. Rushmore Rd., 57701 605/348–8300 605/348–3833 www.radissonrapidcity.com 176 rooms, 5 suites Cable TV with movies, indoor pool, gym, hair salon, shop, business services, meeting rooms AE, D, DC, MC, V.*

★ $$–$$$ **Audrie's Bed & Breakfast.** Victorian antiques and an air of romance greet you at this out-of-the-way B&B, set in a thickly wooded area 7 mi west of Rapid City. Suites, cottages, and creek-side cabins sleeping two come with old-world furnishings, fireplaces, private baths, hot tubs, and big-screen TVs. Bicycles and fishing poles can be obtained from the office. *23029 Thunderhead Falls Rd., 57702 605/342–7788 www.audriesbb.com 2 suites, 7 cottages and cabins Some in-room hot tubs, cable TV with movies, fishing, bicycles, shop; no kids, no smoking No credit cards BP.*

$–$$ **Holiday Inn Rushmore Plaza.** This eight-story hotel has a central lobby with an atrium, glass elevators, and a 60-foot waterfall. Located in the parking lot of the Rushmore Plaza Civic Center, it can be full during major events at the facility, such as the Black Hills Stock Show and Rodeo or the Black Hills Motorcycle Rally in Sturgis. Be sure to book ahead. *505 N. 5th St., 57701 605/348–4000 605/348–9777 www.holidayinnrapidcity.com 205 rooms, 1 suite Restaurant, room service, cable TV with movies, indoor pool, gym, hot tub, sauna, bar, business services, meeting rooms AE, D, DC, MC, V CP.*

CAMPING **Whispering Pines Campground and Lodging.** Block party–style cookouts are followed by movies every night here as long as the weather is good. Located 16 mi west of Rapid City in Black Hills National Forest, the campground is directly between Deadwood (22 mi to the north) and Mount Rushmore (22 mi to the south). In addition to RV and tent sites, cabins are available at a reasonable price. *Flush toilets, full hookups, partial hookups (electric and water), dump station, drinking water, guest laundry, showers, fire pits, food service, picnic tables, electricity, public telephone, general store, play area, swimming (lake) 26 full hookups, 2 partial hookups, 45 tent sites; 5 cabins 22700 Silver City Rd. 605/341–3667 605/341–3667 www.blackhillscampresort.com Full hookups $21.95, partial hookups $19.95, tent sites $14.95; cabins $32.95–$39.95 Reservations essential D, MC, V May–Sept.*

The Arts

At the **Dahl Fine Arts Center** (713 7th St. 605/394–4101), across from the downtown Rapid City Public Library, exhibits by local artists rotate regularly, but there is one permanent piece: a 180-foot oil-on-canvas mural depicting United States economic history from the colonization by the Europeans to the 1970s. The Black Hills Community Theater performs in the modest theater here on a regular basis.

Shopping

One of the world's top collections of Plains Indian artwork and crafts makes **Prairie Edge Trading Company and Galleries** (✉ 6th and Main Sts. ☎ 605/342–3086 or 800/541–2388) seem more like a museum than a store-gallery. With a collection ranging from books and CDs to artifact reproductions and artwork representing the Lakota, Crow, Cheyenne, Shoshone, Arapaho, and Assiniboin tribes of the Great Plains, Prairie Edge is one of the crown jewels of downtown Rapid City.

Mount Rushmore National Memorial

12 *24 mi southwest of Rapid City via U.S. 16 and U.S. 16A.*

Fodor's Choice ★

The carving of Mount Rushmore, one of the nation's most famous attractions, was begun by sculptor Gutzon Borglum in 1927, with the help of some 400 assistants, and finished in 1941. Borglum died in March of that year, leaving his son, Lincoln, to continue the work for a few months longer. The giant, 60-foot-high likenesses of Presidents George Washington, Thomas Jefferson, Abraham Lincoln, and Theodore Roosevelt grace a massive granite cliff, which, at an elevation of 5,725 feet, towers over the surrounding countryside and faces the sun most of the day. The memorial is equally spectacular at night, when a special lighting ceremony (June through mid-September) dramatically illuminates the carving. Admission is free, although an $8 charge is assessed for parking.

The **Mount Rushmore Information Center,** in a modest building between the entrance of the park and the Avenue of Flags, has a small exhibit with photographs of the presidents' faces as they were being carved. There's also an information desk here, staffed by rangers who can answer questions about the memorial or the surrounding Black Hills. A nearly identical building across from the information center houses rest rooms, telephones, and soda machines. ✉ *Beginning of Ave. of Flags* ☎ *605/574–3198* 🌐 *www.nps.gov/moru* 🎫 *Free* ⊙ *May–Sept., daily 8 AM–10 PM; Oct.–Apr., daily 8–5.*

The **Avenue of Flags,** which runs from the entrance of the memorial to the museum and amphitheater at the base of the mountain, represents each state, commonwealth, district, and territory of the United States. Waving from granite posts on both sides of the walkway, the flags are in alphabetical order and have engravings at their base listing the date of admittance to the Union.

Underneath the viewing platform and at the top of the amphitheater is the **Lincoln Borglum Museum,** a giant granite-and-glass structure with permanent exhibits on the carving of the mountain, its history, and its significance. Also here are a bookstore, a theater that shows an orientation film, and an area for temporary exhibits. ✉ *End of Ave. of Flags* ☎ *605/574–3165* 🎫 *Free* ⊙ *Apr. and May, daily 8–7; June–Sept., daily 8 AM–10 PM; Oct.–Mar., daily 8–5.*

Running around the museum toward the carving is the **Presidential Trail** (✉ near Lincoln Borglum Museum), an easy hike along a boardwalk and down some stairs to the very base of the mountain. Although the trail is thickly forested, you'll have more than ample opportunity to look straight up the noses of the four giant heads.

Built in 1939 as Gutzon Borglum's on-site workshop, the **Sculptor's Studio** displays tools used by the mountain carvers, a 1/12 scale model of the memorial, and a model depicting the unfinished Hall of Records. Borglum intended the Hall of Records to be a storehouse for documents that would explain the mountain carving to any future archaeologists. He died before he could complete the chamber, however. An incomplete version of the hall, behind the heads at the top of the mountain, was sealed in 1998. ✉ *¼ mi from Lincoln Borglum Museum* 🎫 *Free* ⏲ *May–Sept., daily 9–6.*

Founded in the 1880s by prospectors searching the central Black Hills for gold deposits, the small town of **Keystone** (✉ U.S. 16A ☎ 605/666–4896 or 800/456–3345) now survives on the 2½ million annual visitors who pass through here on their way to Mount Rushmore, 2 mi away. The touristy town has some 700 hotel rooms—more than twice the number of its permanent residents. Its 19th-century buildings house dozens of gift shops, restaurants, and attractions that range from wax museums and miniature golf to alpine slides and helicopter rides.

Where to Stay & Eat

$$–$$$$ ✕ **Creekside Dining.** This casual restaurant has not only a patio view of Mount Rushmore but also a strong menu of American cuisine. Chef Bear's finest dishes are the hearty meat platters of prime rib, buffalo, lamb, chicken, and fish. The desserts, which include bread pudding, crème brûlée, and peach cobbler, are also excellent. A kids' menu is available. ✉ *610 U.S. 16A, Keystone* ☎ *605/666–4904* 💳 *MC, V* ⏲ *Closed Nov.–May.*

★ ¢–$ ✕ **Buffalo Dining Room.** The only restaurant within the bounds of the memorial affords commanding views of Mount Rushmore and the surrounding ponderosa pine forest. The menu includes New England pot roast, buffalo stew, and homemade rhubarb pie. You can choose to end your meal with a "monumental bowl of ice cream." ✉ *Beginning of Ave. of Flags* ☎ *605/574–2515* 💳 *AE, D, MC, V* ⏲ *No dinner mid-Oct.–early Mar.*

$–$$$ 🏨 **Roosevelt Inn.** This midsize inn, less than 1 mi from the east entrance of Mount Rushmore, is one of the closest hotels to the"faces" (although you cannot see them from the inn itself). Standard motel-style furnishings fill the rooms, some of which have balconies. Mountain-view rooms are especially inviting in autumn. ✉ *206 Old Cemetery Rd., 57751* ☎ *605/666–4599 or 800/257–8923* 📠 *605/666–4535* 🌐 *www.rosyinn.com* 🛏 *21 rooms* 🛎 *Restaurant, cable TV, indoor pool, hot tub* 💳 *AE, MC, V.*

$$ 🏨 **Buffalo Rock Lodge B&B.** A large, native-rock fireplace surrounded by hefty logs adds to the rustic quality of this lodge decorated with Western artifacts. There's an extensive view of Mount Rushmore from an oversize deck surrounded by a plush pine forest filled with wildflowers. ✉ *Playhouse Rd., Box 641, 57751* ☎ *605/666–4781 or 888/564–5634* 🌐 *buffalorock.net* 🛏 *3 rooms* 🛎 *In-room hot tubs, hiking, fishing, some pets allowed* 💳 *DC, MC, V* 🍽 *CP.*

$–$$ 🏨 **Best Western Four Presidents.** In the shadow of Mount Rushmore in downtown Keystone, the hotel is within walking distance of the town's major attractions, including several restaurants. Short pack tours into the hills by horseback can be arranged next door. ✉ *250 Winter St., Keystone 57751* ☎ *605/666–4472* 📠 *605/666–4574* 🌐 *www.bestwestern.com* 🛏 *33 rooms, 1 suite* 🛎 *Room service, some in-room hot tubs, microwaves, cable TV with movies, indoor pool, gym, business services, laundry facilities* 💳 *AE, D, DC, MC, V* ⏲ *All but 3 rooms closed Nov.–Apr.* 🍽 *CP.*

Shopping

The **Mount Rushmore Bookstore** (✉ Lincoln Borglum Museum, end of Ave. of Flags ☎ 800/699–3142) carries a selection of books, CDs, and videos on the memorial, its history, and the entire Black Hills region. There are also some materials on geology and Native American history. The **Mount**

Rushmore Gift Shop (✉ Beginning of Ave. of Flags ☎ 605/574–2515), across from the Buffalo Dining Room, hawks any number of souvenirs, from shot glasses and magnets to T-shirts and baseball caps. You can also buy Black Hills–gold jewelry and Native American art.

en route

The fastest way to get from Mount Rushmore to Crazy Horse Memorial and the southern Black Hills is along Highway 244 and U.S. 16. This route, like all of the drives in the Black Hills, is full of beautiful mountain views, but the **Peter Norbeck National Scenic Byway** is an even more stunning, though meandering, route. The much longer road cuts south through Custer State Park, where buffalo, bighorn sheep, elk, antelope, and burros roam free, and comes back north through the Needles, towering granite spires that rise above the forest. A short drive off the highway yields access to 7,242-foot Harney Peak, the highest point in North America east of the Rockies. Because the scenic byway is challenging (with one-lane tunnels and switchbacks) and because you'll likely want to stop a few times to admire the scenery, plan on spending two to three hours on this drive.

4

Crazy Horse Memorial

13 Fodor'sChoice ★ *15 mi southwest of Mount Rushmore National Memorial via Hwy. 244 and U.S. 16.*

When finished, the mountain carving of Crazy Horse Memorial—depicting the legendary Lakota warrior who defeated General Custer at Little Bighorn—will be the world's largest sculpture (641 feet long by 563 feet high). Begun by self-taught sculptor Korczak Ziolkowski in 1948 as a memorial to Native American heritage, the carving work was taken over by the Ziolkowski family after Korczak's death in 1982. The project's completion date is unknown, as the work is limited by weather and funding. So far the head of Crazy Horse has been completed, and work is under way on the head of his horse. Expect frequent blasting at this work-in-progress. Also at the site are an impressive orientation and communications center, the Indian Museum of North America, the sculptor's studio home and workshop, indoor and outdoor sculpture galleries, and a restaurant. Admission is either $9 per adult or $20 per carload—whichever is lower. Native Americans and active military personnel are admitted free. ☎ *605/673–4681* 🌐 *www.crazyhorse.org* ⏲ *May–Sept., daily 8 AM–9 PM; Oct.–Apr., daily 8–4:30.*

When Ziolkowski agreed to carve Crazy Horse, he determined that he wouldn't stop with the mountain. He wanted an educational institution to sit at the base of the mountain, complete with a center showcasing examples of Native American culture and heritage. The construction in 1972 of the **Indian Museum of North America,** built from wood and stone blasted from the mountain, was the initial step in that direction. The permanent collection of paintings, clothing, photographs, and artifacts represents many of the continent's tribes. There is also a space for temporary exhibits that often showcases works by modern Native American artists. ✉ *Ave. of the Chiefs* ☎ *605/673–4681* 🎟 *Free* ⏲ *May–Sept., daily 8 AM–9 PM; Oct.–Apr., daily 8–4:30.*

Where to Stay & Eat

$–$$ ✕ **Laughing Water Restaurant.** This airy pine restaurant with windows facing the mountain sculpture is noted for its fry bread and buffalo burgers. There's a soup-and-salad bar, but you'd do well to stick to the Native American offerings; try the Indian taco or "buffaloski" (a Polish sausage made with Dakota buffalo). A kids' menu is available. ✉ *Ave. of the Chiefs* ☎ *605/673–4681* ▭ *AE, D, MC, V* ⊗ *Closed Nov.–Apr.*

$–$$$$ **State Game Lodge and Resort.** Once the summer White House for Presidents Coolidge and Eisenhower, this stately stone-and-wood lodge in nearby Custer State Park has well-appointed rooms and isolated pine-shaded cabins, many right on the banks of a creek. The cabins are simple and spartan, the motel rooms are comfortable, and the lodge rooms are almost stately, with elegant hardwood furniture and massive stone fireplaces. Jeep rides into the buffalo area are available. The menu at the excellent, upscale Pheasant Dining Room ($$–$$$$) is varied; the place is known for pheasant and buffalo specialties. In addition to a salad bar and lunch buffet, there's a kids' menu. ✉ *16 mi east of Custer on U.S. 16A (HCR 83, Box 74, Custer 57730)* ☎ *605/255–4541 or 800/658–3530* 🖷 *605/255–4706* ⊕ *www.custerresorts.com* *7 lodge rooms, 40 motel rooms, 33 cabins* *Restaurant, picnic area, some kitchenettes, bar, some pets allowed; no a/c in some rooms, no phones in some rooms, no TVs* ▭ *AE, D, MC, V* ⊗ *Closed Oct.–Mother's Day.*

★ **$–$$$** **Sylvan Lake Resort.** This spacious stone-and-wood lodge in Custer State Park affords fantastic views of pristine Sylvan Lake and Harney Peak beyond. The rooms in the lodge are large and modern, and there are rustic cabins, some with fireplaces, scattered along the cliff and in the forest. The Lakota Dining Room has an exceptional view of the lake, and the lovely veranda constructed of native stone is the perfect place to sip tea and watch the sunrise. On the menu are buffalo selections, including steaks, and rainbow trout. You can canoe, fish, and swim on the lake, and there are numerous hiking trails here. ✉ *16 mi east of Custer on U.S. 16A (HC 83, Box 74, Custer 57730)* ☎ *605/574–2561 or 800/658–3530* 🖷 *605/574–4943* ⊕ *www.custerresorts.com* *35 rooms, 31 cabins* *Restaurant, lake, boating, fishing, shops, meeting room* ▭ *AE, D, MC, V* ⊗ *Closed Oct.–Mother's Day.*

$–$$ **Strutton Inn B&B.** Set on 4 acres near the town of Custer and a few miles from Crazy Horse, this luxurious three-story Victorian home has a 140-foot veranda with a gazebo on each corner looking out over a lovely garden and the Black Hills beyond. Most of the guest rooms of this well-furnished retreat are decorated with pastels, frills, and floral patterns. The rooms have king-size beds but no TVs; there is, however, a 46-inch big-screen TV in the common room. Also within the house are antique-doll and crystal collections. ✉ *U.S. 16 (R.R. 1, Box 55 S, Custer 57730)* ☎ *605/673–4808 or 800/226–2611* 🖷 *605/673–2395* ⊕ *www.struttoninn.com* *9 rooms* *In-room hot tubs, outdoor hot tub; no room phones, no room TVs* ▭ *MC, V* *BP.*

Shopping

With handmade items representing the Lakota, Navajo, Huichol, Acoma, and other tribes, **Korczak's Heritage** (✉ Ave. of the Chiefs ☎ 605/673–4681) is more than a simple gift shop. In addition to crafted items such as jewelry and dream catchers, Korczak's carries sculpture and prints by Native American artists. The store also sells food, clothing, and gift items hewn from stones blasted from the mountain.

Wind Cave National Park

⓮ *28 mi southeast of Crazy Horse via U.S. 16 and Hwy. 87.*

There are more than 100 mi of mapped passageways in Wind Cave, and more than 44 square mi of wilderness preserve above and around it, giving you ample opportunity to go spelunking, discover curious underground speleothems (cave formations), and emerge to hike or watch wildlife all in one day. The cave holds a world of wonders: perfect examples of mineral boxwork (thin spikes of calcite that create a honeycomb pattern), gypsum beard that sways from the heat of a lamp, and delicate helicite balloons that would burst at the touch of a finger. Amazingly, 95% of Wind Cave has yet to be navigated. Aboveground, hundreds of bison, elk, deer, and pronghorn roam prairies, granite-walled canyons, and ponderosa pine forests in the wilderness surrounding the cave. Theodore Roosevelt made Wind Cave the country's seventh national park, and the first dedicated to preserving a cave, on January 3, 1903.

Besides being the primary place to get general park information, the **Wind Cave Visitor Center,** on top of the cave, has three exhibit rooms with displays on cave exploration, cave history, cave formations, the Civilian Conservation Corps, park wildlife, and resource management. ✉ *Off U.S. 385, 3 mi north of the park's southern border* ☎ *605/745–4600* 🌐 *www.nps.gov/wica* 🎟 *Free* 🕐 *May and Sept., daily 8–6; June–Aug., daily 8–7:30; Oct.–Apr., daily 8–4:30.*

★ You can choose among five different ranger-led **cave tours** (✉ Wind Cave Visitor Center, off U.S. 385 ☎ 605/745–4600) of Wind Cave if you visit from June through August; the rest of the year, only one or two tours are available. All tours depart from the visitor center, and on each you pass incredibly beautiful cave formations, including extremely well-developed boxwork. The least-crowded times to visit in summer are mornings and weekends. The cave is 53°F year-round, so bring a sweater, and be sure to wear comfortable, closed-toe shoes. Tour schedules, program times, and meeting points are subject to change, so call ahead.

The **Candlelight Cave Tour,** available twice daily from early June through Labor Day, lets you explore a section of the cave that lacks paved walks and lighting. Everyone on the tour carries a lantern similar to those used in expeditions in the 1890s. The $9 tour lasts two hours and covers 1 mi of the cave; reservations are essential. Children under 8 are not admitted.

On the **Fairgrounds Cave Tour,** available five times daily from early June through Labor Day, you visit some of the largest rooms in the cave, including the Fairgrounds room, which holds nearly every example of calcite formation found in the cave. There are some 450 steps, leading up and down, on this 1½-hour tour; the cost is $8.

You don't need to go far to see boxwork, popcorn, and flowstone formations. Just take the relatively easy, one-hour **Garden of Eden Cave Tour,** which covers only about ¼ mi and 150 stairs. It's available seven times daily early June through Labor Day, and three times daily October through early June; the cost is $6.

The popular, 1¼-hour **Natural Entrance Cave Tour** takes you ½ mi into the cave, over 300 stairs (most heading down), and out an elevator exit. It costs $8 and is available nine times daily from early June through Labor Day, and seven times daily for the rest of September.

For a serious caving experience, sign up for the challenging, extraordinary, four-hour **Wild Caving Tour.** After some basic training in spelunking, you crawl and climb through fissures and corridors, most lined with gypsum needles, frostwork, and boxwork. You'll also see artifacts left by early explorers. Expect to get dirty. Wear shoes with good traction, long pants, and a long-sleeve shirt. The park provides knee pads, gloves, and hard hats with headlamps. You must be at least 16 to take this tour; 16- and 17-year-olds must show signed consent from a parent or guardian. Tours cost $20 and are available at 1 PM daily early June through mid-August, and at 1 PM weekends mid-August through Labor Day. Reservations are essential.

★ One of the best birding areas in the park is **Wind Cave Canyon** (✉ About ½ mi east of visitor center). As you hike down the trail, the steep-sided canyon widens to a panoramic view east across the prairies.

Some of the best panoramic views of the park and surrounding hills can be seen from **Rankin Ridge Lookout Tower,** which at 5,013 feet is the highest point in the park. To get here you must hike the 1-mi Rankin Ridge loop, which starts 6 mi north of the visitor center on Highway 87.

off the beaten path

MAMMOTH SITE – It was during the construction of a housing development in the 1970s that earthmoving equipment uncovered this prehistoric sinkhole where giant mammoths came to drink, got trapped, and died more than 26,000 years ago. More than 50 of the fossilized woolly beasts have been unearthed since digging began, and many can still be seen in situ at the site. A structure was built on top of the sinkhole, allowing year-round access to the site for visitors and paleontologists. You can watch the excavation in progress and take guided tours of this unique discovery. ✉ *U.S. 18, Hot Springs, 15 mi south of Wind Cave National Park* ☎ *605/745–6017 or 800/325–6991* 🌐 *www.mammothsite.com* *$5* ⏲ *Daily; hrs vary, call ahead.*

Sports & the Outdoors

HIKING There are more than 30 mi of hiking trails within the park boundaries. Hiking into the wild, untouched backcountry is perfectly safe, provided you have a map (available from the visitor center) and a good sense of direction. Remember that wild animals, including coyotes and bison, are roaming the same territory that you are. Although bison may appear to be nothing more than big hairy cows, they are very wild. They can easily weigh a ton and if threatened can outrun a horse. Bison are especially unpredictable during the rut, or mating season, in late July and August. Admire their majestic power and typically peaceful nature from a distance.

If you want to get away from the crowds, head for the **Boland Ridge Trail.** It's a strenuous, 2⁷⁄₁₀-mi hike up to Boland Ridge, but the panorama from the top is well worth it—sunset from this remote point is absolutely spectacular. The trailhead is off Forest Service Road 6, 1 mi north of the junction with Forest Service Road 5.

Constructed to celebrate South Dakota's 100th birthday, the **Centennial Trail** bisects the Black Hills from north to south, covering 111 mi of territory. Designed for bikers, hikers, and horses, this trail is rugged but accommodating (note, however, that bicycling on the trail is not allowed within park boundaries). Pick up the trail off Highway 87, 2 mi north of the visitor center.

The difficult 8⅗-mi **Highland Creek Trail** is the longest and most diverse trail within the park, traversing mixed-grass prairies, ponderosa pine forests, and the riparian habitats of Highland Creek, Beaver Creek, and Wind Cave Canyon. The southern trailhead stems from Wind Cave Canyon trail 1 mi east of U.S. 385. The northern trailhead is on Forest Service Road 5.

From the Centennial trailhead on Highway 87, the 2⅕-mi **Lookout Point Trail** follows the prairie, traverses Lookout Point, and ends at Beaver Creek. Cross over to the Centennial Trail to make a 4⅘-mi loop.

SPELUNKING **Adventure Sport** (✉ 900 Jackson Blvd., Rapid City ☎ 605/341–6707) has a sizeable inventory of outdoor wear and climbing gear suitable for using in the cave.

Where to Stay & Eat

¢–$ ✕ **Alpine Inn.** With its rustic wood construction, pastoral paintings, lacy tablecloths, and beer steins, the Alpine Inn brings European charm to the Old West. The lunchtime menu changes daily but always has selections of healthful sandwiches and salads—and no fried food. Filet mignon is the only item on the dinner menu, but it's among the best steak available in the region. Lunch is served on the veranda overlooking Main Street. Beer and wine are the only alcoholic beverages served. ✉ *225 Main St., Hill City* ☎ *605/574–2749* *Reservations not accepted* ▭ *No credit cards* ⊗ *Closed Sun.*

¢–$ ✕ **Elk Horn Cafe.** With burgers and steaks that are hand-cut on the premises, this is a favorite among local ranchers. Also on the menu are homemade soups, chicken-fried steak, and a "death by chocolate" cake. You can eat on one of the two decks outside with a view of town. ✉ *310 S. Chicago St., Hot Springs* ☎ *605/745–6556* ▭ *AE, MC, V.*

$–$$ **Best Western Inn by the River.** Pleasant tones of blue and peach decorate the spacious rooms of this two-story hotel. It's three blocks from downtown Hot Springs and 10 mi south of Wind Cave. ✉ *602 W. River St., Hot Springs 57747* ☎ *605/745–4292 or 888/605–4292* 🖷 *605/745–3584* 🌐 *www.bestwestern.com* *32 rooms* *In-room data ports, cable TV with movies, pool, business services, meeting rooms* ▭ *AE, D, DC, MC, V* *CP.*

$–$$ **Comfort Inn Hot Springs.** Near U.S. 385, and three blocks from downtown Hot Springs, this hotel offers easy access to the Mueller Civic Center. Family suites are available, and some rooms have views of a little river. ✉ *737 S. 6th St., Hot Springs 57747* ☎ *605/745–7378 or 800/228–5150* 🖷 *605/745–3240* 🌐 *www.comfortinn.com* *32 rooms* *Some in-room hot tubs, microwaves, cable TV with movies, indoor pool, exercise equipment, hot tub, laundry facilities, business services, some pets allowed (fee)* ▭ *AE, D, MC, V* *CP.*

CAMPING **Elk Mountain Campground.** If you prefer a sculpted campsite and relative proximity to civilization, Elk Mountain is an excellent choice. You can experience the peaceful pine forests and wild creatures of the park without straying too far from the safety of the beaten path. There are only tent sites, and Sites 24 and 69 are reserved for campers with disabilities. *Flush toilets, running water (non-potable), fire grates, public telephone* *75 sites* ✉ *½ mi north of the visitor center* ☎ *605/745–4600* *$5–$10* ▭ *No credit cards* ⊗ *Apr.–late Oct.*

Shopping

The **Wind Cave Gift Shop** (✉ U.S. 385 ☎ 605/745–4600) at the visitor center carries a modest selection of books, videos, slides, and maps about the Black Hills, Wind Cave, and geology.

en route

Built on the "wall" of the South Dakota badlands, the town of **Wall** (✉ I–90, Exit 110 ☎ 605/279–2665 or 888/852–9255) was founded in 1907 as a railroad station for the Chicago and Northwestern Railroad. The town (population 818) borders Buffalo Gap National Grasslands and is only a few miles north of the Pinnacles entrance to Badlands National Park. For this reason, many visitors use Wall as a base to explore the two wildernesses.

Wall Drug Store (✉ 510 Main St. ☎ 605/279–2175), a South Dakota original, got its real boost when its owners decided to hand out free ice water to road-weary motorists en route to the Black Hills during the Great Depression. Today its four art-gallery dining rooms serve burgers and steaks, and its Western Mall has 14 shops. The place also has a life-size mechanical Cowboy Band and Chuckwagon Quartet. In the early morning, the restaurant fills with area ranchers who stop to talk weather and politics, grab a doughnut, and down a cup of black coffee before heading out to check the range. Copies of their brands line some of the walls. Wall Drug Store opens daily at 6:30 AM and closes at 7 PM.

Badlands National Park

★ ⚑ ⓯ *140 mi northeast of Wind Cave via Hwy. 87, U.S. 16, and I–90.*

So stark and isolated are the chiseled spires, ragged ridgelines, and deep ravines of South Dakota's badlands, that Lieutenant Colonel George Custer once described the area as "hell with the fires burned out." Although a bit more accessible and host to considerably more life than the depths of the underworld, the landscape of the badlands is easily the strangest in the state. Ruthlessly ravaged over the ages by wind and rain, the 380 square mi of wild terrain continue to erode and evolve, sometimes visibly changing shape in a few days. Despite harsh conditions, a community of prairie creatures, from bison and bald eagles to rattlesnakes and pronghorn, thrives on the untamed territory. Fossil evidence shows that mammals have roamed the area for more than 35 million years. In fact, there are more Oligocene fossil deposits in the badlands than anywhere else in the world. Paleontologists have detected within the ancient rock formations the evolution of such mammals as horses, cats, sheep, rhinoceroses, and pigs, plus traces of various birds and reptiles.

The park, first established as a national monument in 1939, then designated a national park in 1978, is divided into three units: the North Unit, which includes the Badlands Wilderness Area, and the southern Stronghold and Palmer units, which are within the Pine Ridge Indian Reservation. The National Park Service and the Oglala Sioux Tribe manage the southern units together. The North Unit is far more user-friendly and attracts the majority of visitors. Much of the southern two units is accessible only on foot, by four-wheel drive, or by a high-clearance recreational vehicle. ☎ *605/433–5361* 🌐 *www.nps.gov/badl* 🎫 *Cars $10; motorcycles, bicycles, and pedestrians $5* ⏲ *Daily, 24 hrs.*

Although the **Ben Reifel Visitor Center** is at the extreme eastern edge of the park, in the developed Cedar Pass area, it's a good idea to stop here first to pick up park brochures and maps. A lodge, campground, amphitheater, and six trails are less than 2 mi away. ✉ *Badlands Loop Rd. (Hwy. 240), Interior* ☎ *605/433–5361* 🎫 *Free* ⏲ *June 4–Aug. 19, daily 7 AM–8 PM; Aug. 20–Sept. 9, daily 8–6; Sept. 10–June 3, daily 9–4.*

From **Journey Overlook** (✉ 7 mi northwest of Ben Reifel Visitor Center on Hwy. 240) you can see Bigfoot Pass, where Sioux chief Big Foot and his band traveled through the badlands on their way to that fateful day at Wounded Knee, December 29, 1890, when U.S. troops killed more than 200 Sioux men, women, and children.

In a depression by the Conata Basin picnic area, paleontologists dig for fossils and field questions from curious visitors at the **Big Pig Dig** (✉ 17 mi northwest of Ben Reifel Visitor Center on Hwy. 240). This site was named for a large fossil originally thought to be the remainder of a prehistoric pig, although it actually turned out to be from a small, horn-

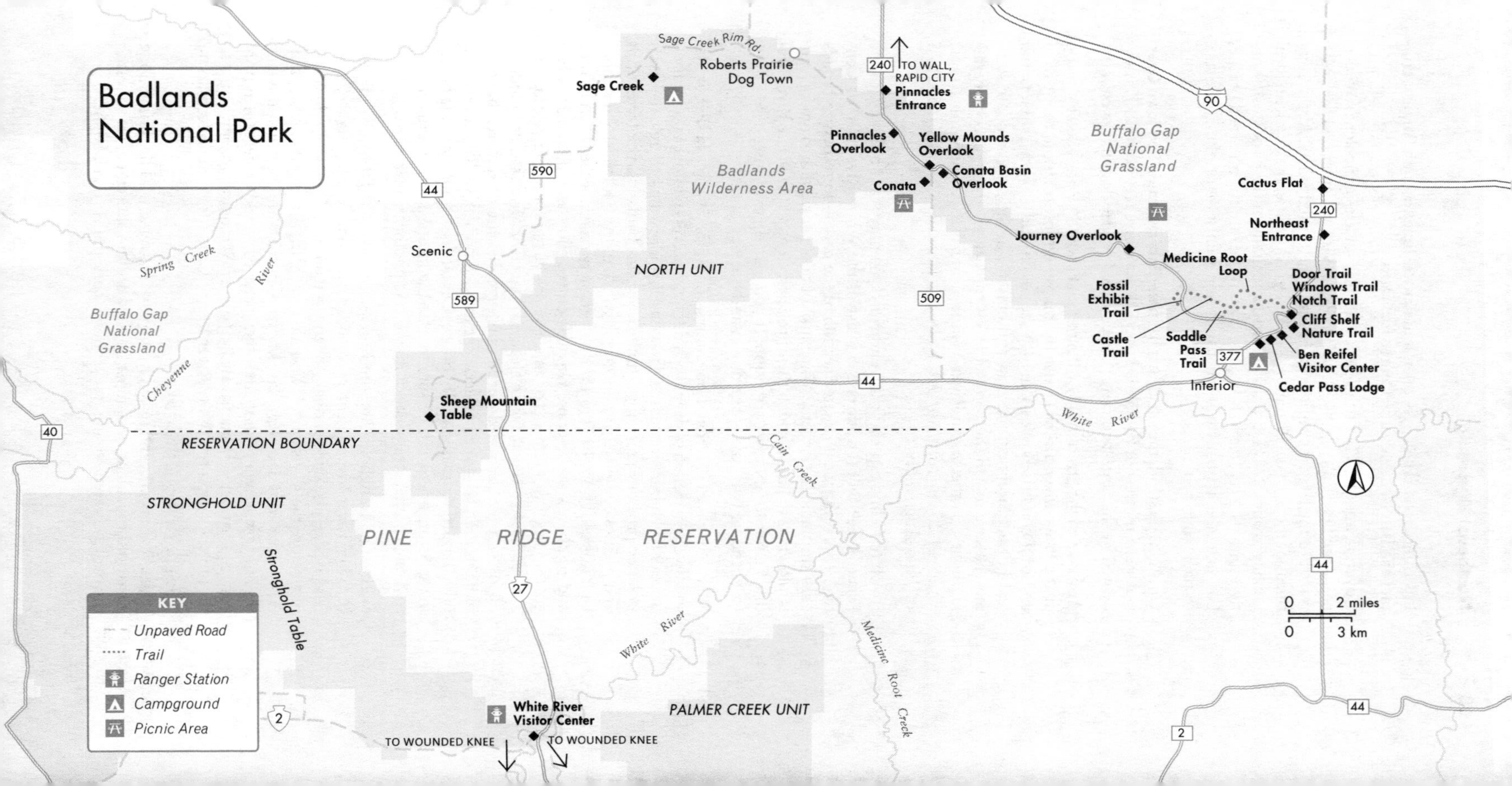
Badlands National Park
Sage Creek Rim Rd.
Roberts Prairie Dog Town
Sage Creek
240
TO WALL, RAPID CITY
Pinnacles Entrance
90
Buffalo Gap National Grassland
Pinnacles Overlook
Yellow Mounds Overlook
Conata Basin Overlook
Conata
590
44
Badlands Wilderness Area
Cactus Flat
Northeast Entrance
Journey Overlook
Medicine Root Loop
Door Trail
Windows Trail
Notch Trail
Cliff Shelf Nature Trail
Ben Reifel Visitor Center
Cedar Pass Lodge
Fossil Exhibit Trail
Castle Trail
Saddle Pass Trail
377
Interior
Scenic
NORTH UNIT
589
509
Spring Creek
Cheyenne River
Buffalo Gap National Grassland
Sheep Mountain Table
40
RESERVATION BOUNDARY
White River
Cain Creek
STRONGHOLD UNIT
PINE RIDGE RESERVATION
Stronghold Table
27
KEY
Unpaved Road
Trail
Ranger Station
Campground
Picnic Area
2
White River Visitor Center
TO WOUNDED KNEE
TO WOUNDED KNEE
PALMER CREEK UNIT
Medicine Root Creek
0 2 miles
0 3 km

less rhinoceros. The dig is open and staffed June through August; contact the Ben Reifel Visitor Center for hours.

Covering about 25% of the park, the 100-square-mi **Badlands Wilderness Area** (✉ 25 mi northwest of Ben Reifel Visitor Center on Hwy. 240) is part of the largest prairie wilderness in the United States. About two-thirds of the Sage Creek region is mixed-grass prairie, making it an ideal grazing ground for bison, pronghorn, and many of the park's other native animals. Feel free to hike your own route into the untamed prairie, but remember that any water in this region is unfit for drinking—be sure to pack your own.

Once a homestead, the site down from the **Roberts Prairie Dog Town Overlook** (✉ 5 mi west of Badlands Loop Rd. on Sage Creek Rim Rd.) is now owned by the largest colony of black-tailed prairie dogs in the country.

Any visit to the Stronghold or Palmer unit should be preceded by a stop at the **White River Visitor Center** for maps and information about road and trail conditions. You can also see fossils and Lakota artifacts and learn about Sioux culture past and present. In the early and late summer, be sure to call the Ben Reifel Visitor Center first to check operating hours, as the White River Visitor Center is open only for a short time. ✉ *25 mi south of Hwy. 44 via Hwy. 27* ☎ *605/455–2878* ⏲ *June–Aug., daily 10–4.*

If you're feeling especially adventurous, you may want to hike into the **Palmer Creek Unit** (✉ Starts 2 mi east of the White River Visitor Center). This is the most isolated section of the park—no recognized roads pass through its borders. You must obtain permission from private landowners to pass through their property. Contact the White River Visitor Center for more information. If you plan on exploring here, count on spending two days—one day in and one day out.

With few paved roads and no campgrounds, the **Stronghold Unit**, in the southwestern section of the park, is difficult to access without a four-wheel-drive or high-clearance vehicle. However, if you're willing to trek, the unit's isolation provides a rare opportunity to explore badlands rock formations and prairies completely undisturbed. Much of the Badlands' Stronghold Unit was used from 1942 to 1968 as a gunnery range for the U.S. Air Force and South Dakota National Guard. Bomber pilots would frequently target the large fossil remains of an elephant-size titanothere (an extinct relative of the rhinoceros), which gleamed bright white from the air. Hundreds of fossils were destroyed during this time. Beware of such remnants as old automobiles turned targets, unexploded bombs, shells, rockets, and other hazardous materials. If you see unexploded ordinance while hiking in the Stronghold Unit, be sure to note the location so you can report it to a ranger later, steer clear of it, and find another route.

Within the Stronghold Unit, the 3-mi-long **Stronghold Table** (✉ 7 mi west of White River Visitor Center) can be reached only by crossing a narrow land bridge just wide enough to let a wagon pass. It was here in 1890, just before the Massacre at Wounded Knee, that some 600 Sioux gathered to perform one of the last known Ghost Dances, a ritual in which the Sioux wore white shirts that they believed would protect them from bullets. Permission from private landowners is required to gain access to the table. Contact the White River Visitor Center for more information.

Sports & the Outdoors

BIRD-WATCHING & WILDLIFE VIEWING

If you're especially interested in the park's diverse wildlife, bring along a pair of binoculars, and, most notably around sunset, get set to watch the badlands come to life. Jackrabbits, bats, prairie dogs, gophers, porcupines, foxes, coyotes, skunks, bobcats, horned lizards, prairie rattlers, deer, pronghorn, bighorn sheep, and bison all call the badlands home. Although very rare, weasels, mountain lions, and the endangered black-footed ferret can also be spotted roaming the park. Additionally, more than 215 bird species have been recorded in the area, including herons, pelicans, cormorants, egrets, swans, geese, hawks, golden and bald eagles, falcons, vultures, cranes, doves, and cuckoos.

Scheels All Sport (✉ 2200 N. Maple Ave., Rapid City ☎ 605/342-9033), in Rapid City's Rushmore Mall, is one of the few places in the area to carry a wide selection of all-weather hiking clothes and binoculars suitable for wildlife viewing.

BICYCLING Bicycles are permitted only on designated roads, which may be paved or unpaved. They are prohibited on closed roads, trails, and the backcountry. Flat-resistant tires are recommended.

Forest City Adventures (✉ 107 Elm St., Hill City ☎ 605/574-3930 🌐 www.forestcityadv.com), a local outfitter based in the central Black Hills, rents mountain bikes by the day or half day, including comfort cruisers, standard mountain bikes, and high-end demo bikes. You can also rent a bike trailer for the 160-mi round-trip to the badlands, or you can have them dropped at your hotel for an extra fee. Guided bike tours of the park are also available.

In the southern unit on the Pine Ridge Indian Reservation, the 7-mi **Sheep Mountain Table Road** (✉ 14 mi north of White River Visitor Center on Hwy. 27) is ideal for mountain biking. At the top of this high, flat mesa you can take in great views of the entire Stronghold Unit. This is a dirt road and should be biked only when dry. The terrain is level for the first 3 mi; then it climbs the table and levels out again.

HIKING The isolation and otherworldliness of the badlands are best appreciated on a hike. Take time to examine the dusty rock beneath your feet, and be on the lookout for fossils and animals. Remember to bring at least 33 ounces of water per person.

The easy **Castle Trail** (✉ 5 mi north of Ben Reifel Visitor Center) stretches for 5½ mi one-way from the Fossil Exhibit trailhead on Badlands Loop Road to the parking area for the Door and Window trails. If you choose to follow the Medicine Root Loop, which detours off the Castle Trail, you'll add ½ mi to the trek.

The ½-mi **Cliff Shelf Nature Trail** (✉ 1 mi east of Ben Reifel Visitor Center) winds through a wooded prairie oasis in the middle of dry, rocky ridges and climbs 200 feet to a peak above the White River valley for an incomparable view. Look for chipmunks, squirrels, and red-wing blackbirds in the wet wood, and eagles, hawks, and vultures at hilltop.

The ¾-mi **Door Trail** (✉ 2 mi east of Ben Reifel Visitor Center) leads through a natural opening, or door, in a badlands rock wall. The eerie sandstone formations and passageways beckon, but it's recommended that you stay on the trail. The first 100 yards of the trail are on a boardwalk.

★ Fossils of early mammals are displayed under glass along the ¼-mi **Fossil Exhibit Trail** (✉ 5 mi west of Ben Reifel Visitor Center), which is accessible for people who use wheelchairs and is great for kids.

One of the park's more interesting hikes, the 1½-mi **Notch Trail** (✉ 2 mi north of Ben Reifel Visitor Center) takes you over moderately difficult terrain and up a ladder. Winds at the notch can be fierce, but it's worth lingering for the view of the White River valley and the Pine Ridge Indian Reservation.

The **Saddle Pass Trail** (✉ 2 mi west of Ben Reifel Visitor Center), which connects with Castle Trail and Medicine Root Loop, is a steep ¼-mi climb up the side of "The Wall," an impressive rock formation.

The 200-yard **Window Trail** (✉ 2 mi north of Ben Reifel Visitor Center) ends at a natural hole, or window, formation in a rock wall. Looking though, you'll see more of the distinctive badlands pinnacles and spires.

HORSEBACK RIDING The park has one of the largest and most beautiful territories in the state in which to ride a horse. Riding is allowed in most of the park except for some marked trails, roads, and developed areas. The mixed-grass prairie of the Badlands Wilderness Area is especially popular with riders.

Gunsel Horse Adventures (☎605/343–7608 ⊕www.gunselhorseadventures.com) arranges pack trips into the badlands and Buffalo Gap National Grasslands. The four-day trips are based in one central campsite and are all-inclusive, with the exception of sleeping bags and personal effects.

Where to Stay & Eat

¢–$ ✕ **Cedar Pass Lodge.** Each small white cabin at this lodging within the park has two beds and views of the badlands peaks. A gallery at the lodge displays the work of local artists, and the gift shop is well stocked with local crafts, including turquoise and beadwork. There are also hiking trails on the premises. Enjoy a hearty meal of steak, trout, or Indian tacos and fry bread within the restaurant ($–$$), with its dark, knotty-pine walls under an exposed-beam ceiling. ✉ *1 Cedar St. (Hwy. 240), Interior 57750* ☎ *605/433–5460* 🖷 *605/433–5560* ⊕ *www.cedarpasslodge.com* *24 cabins* *Restaurant, picnic area, hiking, some pets allowed; no room phones, no room TVs* *AE, DC, MC, V* *Closed Oct.–Apr.*

¢–$ **Badlands Ranch and Resort.** This 2,000-acre ranch lies outside the national park, and the ranch house and cabins have spectacular views of the badlands. The grounds—complete with gazebo, duck ponds, picnic areas, and a bonfire site—are ideal for summer family vacations and reunions. The ranch house has Jacuzzi tubs in wooden decks. ✉ *Hwy. 44 (HCR 53, Box 3, Interior 57750)* ☎ *605/433–5599* 🖷 *605/433–5598* ⊕ *www.badlandsranchandresort.com* *4 rooms, 7 cabins* *Picnic area, kitchenettes, cable TV with movies, pond, hot tub* *AE, D, MC, V.*

CAMPING There are no designated campgrounds in the Stronghold Unit, but you may pitch a tent anywhere that's ½ mi from a road or trail. Be careful of the remains of military gunning. Despite these historical reminders of civilization, camping in the Stronghold Unit emphasizes the sheer isolation of the badlands. Note that fires are not allowed anywhere within the park.

Badlands KOA. The green, shady sites spread over the 31 acres of this campground southeast of Interior are pleasant and cool after a day among the dry rocks of the national park. White River and a small creek border the property on two sides. *Flush toilets, full hookups, partial hookups (electric and water), dump station, drinking water, showers, fire grates, picnic tables, public telephone, general store, play area, swimming (pool)* *44 full hookups, 38 partial hookups, 62 tent sites* ✉ *4 mi south of Interior on Hwy. 44* ☎ *605/433–5337* ⊕ *www.koa.com* *Full hookups $30, partial hookups $23, tent sites $22* *MC, V* *May–early Oct.*

Cedar Pass Campground. Although it has only tent sites, this is the most developed campground within the park, and it's near the Ben Reifel Visitor Center, Cedar Pass Lodge, and a half-dozen hiking trails. You can buy $1 or $2 bags of ice at the lodge. *Flush toilets, pit toi-*

lets, dump station, drinking water, public telephone, ranger station 96 *sites* ✉ *Hwy. 377, ¼ mi south of Badlands Loop Rd.* ☎ *605/433–5361* 🌐 *www.nps.gov/badl* *$10* *Reservations not accepted* *No credit cards.*

Sage Creek Primitive Campground. The word to remember here is "primitive." If you want to get away from it all, this lovely, isolated spot surrounded by nothing but fields and crickets is the right camp for you. There are no designated campsites, and the only facilities are pit toilets and horse hitches. *Pit toilets* ✉ *25 mi west of Badlands Loop Rd. on Sage Creek Rim Rd.* ☎ *No phone* *Free.*

Shopping

The **Cedar Pass Gift Store** (✉ 1 Cedar St. ☎ 605/433–5460) at the Cedar Pass Lodge carries a small selection of handmade gifts and Native American crafts.

4

NORTHEAST WYOMING A TO Z

To research prices, get advice from other travelers, and book travel arrangements, visit www.fodors.com.

AIR TRAVEL

CARRIERS For the most part, airlines connect the region only to Denver, Minneapolis, or Salt Lake City, although some smaller carriers occasionally have routes to smaller cities such as Billings or Sioux Falls.

Delta Air/Skywest serves Casper and Rapid City from Salt Lake City. Northwest Airlines connects Rapid City and Minneapolis. United Airlines/United Express flies from Denver into Casper, Gillette, Rapid City, and Sheridan. Great Lakes Aviation connects Denver to Casper, Gillette, Rapid City, and Sheridan.

Airlines & Contacts **Delta Air/Skywest Airlines** ☎ 800/221-1212 or 800/453-9417 🌐 www.delta.com. **Great Lakes Aviation** ☎ 800/554-5111 🌐 www.greatlakesav.com. **Northwest Airlines** ☎ 800/225-2525 🌐 www.nwa.com. **United Airlines/United Express** ☎ 800/241-6522 🌐 www.ual.com.

AIRPORTS

The region's major airports are Casper's Natrona County International Airport, Gillette's Campbell County Airport, and Rapid City Regional Airport. Sheridan County Airport has one or two flights daily to and from Denver, plus charter service.

The Campbell County Airport is 6 mi north of Gillette and 106 mi east of Sheridan. Natrona County International Airport is 12 mi west of Casper. Rapid City Regional Airport is 11 mi east of town.

Airport Information **Campbell County Airport** ✉ 2000 Airport Rd., Gillette ☎ 307/686-1042 🌐 ccg.co.campbell.wy.us/airport/. **Natrona County International Airport** ✉ 8500 Airport Pkwy., Casper ☎ 307/472-6688 🌐 www.casperwyoming.org/airport/. **Rapid City Regional Airport** ✉ 4550 Terminal Rd., Rapid City ☎ 605/393-9924 🌐 www.rapairport.org. **Sheridan County Airport** ✉ 908 W. Brundage La. ☎ 307/674-4222.

BUS TRAVEL

Within the region, Greyhound Lines provides national service out of Rapid City only. Jack Rabbit Lines serves Wall and Rapid City. Casper, Gillette, Sheridan, and central Wyoming are well served by Powder River Transportation, which connects with Greyhound Lines in Rapid City and Cheyenne.

Gray Line of the Black Hills ☎ 605/342-4461. **Greyhound Lines** ☎ 307/634-7744 or 800/231-2222 🌐 www.greyhound.com. **Jack Rabbit Lines** ☎ 800/444-6287. **Powder River Transportation** ☎ 307/682-0960.

CAR RENTAL

The three major airports in the region are the best places to find car rentals. Make rental reservations early; Rapid City has many business travelers, and rental agencies are often booked.

Avis ☎ 800/831-2847 ⊕ www.avis.com. **Budget** ☎ 800/527-0700 ⊕ www.budget.com. **Casey's Auto Rental Service** ✉ 1318 5th St., Rapid City ☎ 605/343-2277 ⊕ www.caseyscorner.com. **Dollar** ☎ 800/527-0700 ⊕ www.dollar.com. **Hertz** ☎ 800/654-3131 ⊕ www.hertz.com. **National** ☎ 800/227-7368 ⊕ www.nationalcar.com.

CAR TRAVEL

Unless you're traveling with a package tour, a car is essential here. I–90 cuts directly through northeastern Wyoming, hitting the towns of Sheridan, Buffalo, Gillette, and Sundance, before going through Deadwood and bisecting South Dakota slightly south of its center. I–25 runs south from Buffalo through the Bighorns to Casper, Douglas, Cheyenne, and eventually Denver.

Within South Dakota, U.S. 14 leads from Rapid City to towns and attractions in the northern part of the Black Hills. U.S. 16 winds south of Rapid City toward Mount Rushmore and Crazy Horse Memorial. Highway 44 is an alternate route between the Black Hills and the badlands. The Black Hills area has seven tunnels with limited clearance; they are marked on state maps and in the state's tourism booklet.

Although it's fairly easy to find services within the Black Hills, the open range of northeastern Wyoming is a different story. There are few towns along the major routes here, including the interstates. It's rare to find a gas station open past the early evening unless you're in Gillette, Sheridan, or Casper. If you're driving in the remote regions of the badlands or Thunder Basin, it's wise to take along extra water. Although the communities here employ great fleets of snowplows in the winter, it can sometimes take them time to clear the upper elevations. Some passes in the Bighorns close entirely. Keep in mind, too, that residents are used to driving in a little snow and ice, so the plows will come out only if accumulations are substantial.

Contact the South Dakota and Wyoming state highway patrols for information on road conditions.

South Dakota State Highway Patrol ☎ 511 ⊕ hp.state.sd.us. **Wyoming State Highway Patrol** ☎ 888/996-7623 ⊕ whp.state.wy.us.

EMERGENCIES

Ambulance or Police **Emergencies** ☎ 911.

24-Hour Medical Care **Campbell County Memorial Hospital** ✉ 501 S. Burma St., Gillette ☎ 307/682-8811 ⊕ www.ccmh.net. **Rapid City Regional Hospital** ✉ 353 Fairmont Blvd., Rapid City ☎ 605/719-1000 ⊕ www.rcrh.org. **Sheridan County Memorial Hospital** ✉ 1401 W. 5th St., Sheridan ☎ 307/672-1000 ⊕ www.sheridanhospital.org. **Wyoming Medical Center** ✉ 1233 E. 2nd St., Casper ☎ 307/577-7201 ⊕ www.wmcnet.org.

LODGING

CAMPING The opportunities to camp in this region are almost limitless. There are countless campgrounds in the Black Hills, Bighorns, and the prairie in between. Most of the public land within the national forests and parks is open for camping, provided that you don't light any fires. Keep in mind when selecting your campsite that the majestic peaks of the Bighorns are home to black bears; the smaller peaks of the Black Hills are not.

LODGING RESERVATIONS Black Hills Central Reservations, also known as CenRes, handles reservations for hotels, campgrounds, lodges, ranches, and B&Bs in the Black Hills area.

Black Hills Central Reservations 800/529-0105 www.blackhillsvacations.com.

MEDIA

NEWSPAPERS Most small communities have their own newspapers that print at least once a week with local reports and weather forecasts, but the papers of the bigger communities tend to serve as the printed-news mainstays of the whole area. The *Rapid City Journal* and the *Casper Star-Tribune* are the largest and most comprehensive newspapers, although the *Gillette News-Record* and the *Sheridan Press* are also detailed and available every day. Some of the larger newsstands carry all four papers. Because most of the people here are staunchly conservative, most of the papers are as well.

TELEVISION & RADIO If you're not near Casper, Gillette, Rapid City, or Sheridan, chances are you won't pick up many stations, either on the television or radio. Many rural communities have cable just to get the regional affiliates. ABC/KOTA Channel 3, based in Rapid City, broadcasts across western South Dakota, western Nebraska, and much of northern Wyoming. Also available in Rapid City, the Black Hills, and parts of eastern Wyoming are CBS/KCLO Channel 15, FOX/KEVN Channel 7, NBC/KNBN Channel 21, PAX/KPAX Channel 24, and PBS/KBHE Channel 9. Stations out of Casper, including ABC/KFNB Channel 20, CBS/KGWC Channel 14, FOX/KWYF Channel 26, and NBC/KTWO Channel 2, cover some of the areas the Rapid City stations don't reach. These stations occasionally carry WB or UPN programming, although there are no local affiliates yet.

The radio waves, both AM and FM, are dominated largely by country- or Christian-music stations. In western South Dakota, KIQK 104.1 FM, KOUT 98.7 FM, and KIMM 1150 AM are popular country choices. Rock stations KDDX 101.1 FM and KSQY 95.1 FM, both based in the northern Black Hills, have a solid local following, mostly because of colorful radio personalities. In central Wyoming, KWYY 95.5 FM and KTWO 1030 AM play country, and KCSP 90.3 FM plays contemporary Christian music.

SPORTS & THE OUTDOORS

FISHING Besides the local chambers of commerce, the South Dakota Game, Fish, and Parks department and the Wyoming Game and Fish department are your best bet for updated information on the numerous fishing opportunities in this region. The countless local outfitters, guides, and community organizations can also provide information.

South Dakota Game, Fish, and Parks 523 E. Capitol Ave., Pierre 57501 605/773-3485 www.state.sd.us/gfp/. **Wyoming Game and Fish** 5400 Bishop Blvd., Cheyenne 82006 307/777-4600 gf.state.wy.us/.

SKIING & SNOWMOBILING Both the Bighorns and Black Hills receive a substantial amount of snow each year, turning the mountains into a winter playground. Even the flatter land between the two ranges is conducive to scenic sledding and cross-country skiing, and there are miles of groomed trails for that purpose. Because there is no one agency that keeps track of conditions in both states, your best sources of information on winter sports are local chambers of commerce.

TOURS

Gray Line of the Black Hills offers bus tours of the region, including trips to Mount Rushmore and Black Hills National Forest.

Gray Line of the Black Hills 605/342-4461 www.blackhillsgrayline.com.

VISITOR INFORMATION

There are plenty of publications, ranging from small booklets to thick magazines, geared to visitors to the area, especially for those headed to the Black Hills. Many of these publications can be found at hotels and restaurants, usually for free (although you should expect 75% of these magazines to be dedicated to advertisements).

South Dakota Tourist Information **Black Hills, Badlands and Lakes Association** ✉ 1851 Discovery Circle, Rapid City 57701 ☎ 605/355-3600 🌐 www.blackhillsbadlands.com. **Deadwood Area Chamber of Commerce & Visitor Bureau** ✉ 735 Main St., Deadwood 57732 ☎ 605/578-1876 or 800/999-1876 🌐 www.deadwood.org. **Rapid City Chamber of Commerce and Convention & Visitors Bureau** ✉ Civic Center, 444 N. Mt. Rushmore Rd. (Box 747, Rapid City 57709) ☎ 605/343-1744 or 800/487-3223 🌐 www.rapidcitycvb.com. **USDA Forest Service Buffalo Gap National Grasslands Visitor Center** ✉ 708 Main St. (Box 425, Wall 57790) ☎ 605/279-2125.

Wyoming Tourist Information **Buffalo Chamber of Commerce** ✉ 55 N. Main St., Buffalo 82834 ☎ 307/684-5544 or 800/227-5122 🌐 www.buffalowyo.com. **Campbell County Chamber of Commerce** ✉ 314 S. Gillette Ave., Gillette 82716 ☎ 307/682-3673 🌐 www.gillettechamber.com. **Casper Chamber of Commerce** ✉ 500 N. Center St., Casper 82601 ☎ 307/234-5311 or 800/852-1889 🌐 www.casperwyoming.org. **Casper Convention and Visitors Bureau** ✉ 330 S. Center St., Casper 82602 ☎ 307/234-5362 or 800/852-1889 🌐 www.casperwyoming.org. **Gillette Convention and Visitor's Bureau** ✉ 59 1810 S. Douglas Hwy., Gillette 82718 ☎ 307/686-0040 or 800/544-6136 🌐 www.visitgillette.net. **Sheridan Chamber of Commerce** 📫 Box 707, Sheridan 82801 ☎ 307/672-2485 🌐 www.sheridanwyomingchamber.org.

THE MONTANA PLAINS

GREAT FALLS, BILLINGS, LITTLE BIGHORN, THE BIG OPEN

5

FODOR'S CHOICE

C. M. Russell Museum Complex, *Great Falls*
Collins Mansion Bed and Breakfast, *Great Falls*
Juliano's, *restaurant in Billings*
Museum of the Upper Missouri, *Fort Benton*
Pictograph Cave State Monument, *Billings*
Pryor Mountain Wild Horse Range, *Bighorn Canyon*
Purple Cow, *restaurant in Hardin*

HIGHLY RECOMMENDED

RESTAURANT The Rex, *Billings*

HOTELS Charlie Russell Manor, *Great Falls*
Hotel Becker Bed and Breakfast, *Hardin*

SIGHTS Bucking Horse Sale, *Miles City*
Carter County Museum, *Ekalaka*
Charles Russell Chew-Choo, *scenic train tour in Lewistown*
Crow Fair and Rodeo, *near Hardin*
Crystal Lake, *Big Snowy Mountains*
Custer County Art Museum, *Miles City*
Devil's Canyon Overlook, *Bighorn Canyon*
Fort Assinniboine, *Havre*
Giant Springs State Park, *Great Falls*
Havre Beneath the Streets, *historic underground tour in Havre*
Indian Memorial, *Little Bighorn Battlefield*
Makoshika State Park
Medicine Rocks State Park, *near Ekalaka*
Museum of the Plains Indian, *Browning*
Slippery Ann Wildlife Viewing Area, *CMR Wildlife Refuge*

By Tom Griffith

SPACE IS THE HALLMARK of eastern Montana's gently rolling plains. Those who find crowds and urban sprawl stifling will do well in the wide-open reaches of Big Sky Country. The state as a whole averages six people per square mile, but some of its prairies measure in reverse: one person per six square miles. Although largely devoid of the epic snow-covered peaks of the towering Rockies, the eastern two-thirds of Montana have a beauty that stretches endlessly beyond the horizon, beckoning you to bask in the isolated serenity of one of the least-populated places in the country—in a land of almost too much sky.

That's not to say that eastern Montana is flat and boring. In fact, the grassy plains are often broken up by geographical oddities such as badlands, glacial lakes, ice caves, and even the occasional pine-covered foothills or snowcapped mountains looking strangely out of place rising from the surrounding prairie. And because of its topographical diversity, the region is a playground for lovers of the outdoors. Hiking, horseback riding, wrangling, boating, skiing, snowmobiling, caving, and some of the best fishing in the world are among the greatest attractions here, and the number of historic sites, state parks, museums, and archaeological digs reinforces the blessings nature has bestowed upon the state.

Ironically, the first- and third-largest cities in the state are in Montana's highly rural eastern region. The largest city in a 500-mi radius, Billings is a center for culture, shopping, entertainment, and medical care. Great Falls, straddling the Missouri River near a handful of thundering waterfalls, is one of Montana's greatest historical centers, with dozens of museums and interpretive centers that trace the state's varied forces of cultural influence. Scattered in between these two cities are more than 100 smaller communities, some with no more than two dozen inhabitants. Although small, sleepy, and dependent on the larger cities, each of these towns has its own distinct Western character, a taste that adds to the larger flavor of the region.

Exploring the Montana Plains

Most visitors to Montana neglect the eastern plains in their rush to get to the increasingly crowded forests and rocky peaks farther west, but the grassy prairies that roll ever onward into the Dakotas and Canada should not be overlooked simply because they lack the majesty of a mountain range. Those who stop here do so because of its isolation, its serenity, and its sky. Unbroken by human-made objects (or even the natural ones), the heavens don't just stretch upward—they stretch outward. At night the effect becomes even more intense, as millions of stars, unhindered by the lights of civilization, beam down from every direction on an otherwise pitch-black landscape.

Major roads are few and far between in this part of the state. I–94 sweeps westward from North Dakota to Billings, where it joins I–90, which comes up from Wyoming's Bighorn Mountains and snakes west through the Rockies into Idaho. The only other Interstate is I–15, which runs north out of Idaho and spills onto the plains outside Helena before looping around Great Falls and heading to Canada. In the vast stretches of prairie outside the interstates, the key thoroughfares are U.S. 2, also known as the Hi-Line, running east–west across the top of the state; U.S. 212, running southeast out of Billings into South Dakota; and U.S. 87, running north out of Billings.

Numbers in the text correspond to numbers in the margin and on Montana Plains, Great Falls, and Billings maps.

If you have 3 days

Spend the morning of the first day viewing the interpretive displays, memorials, and markers at **Little Bighorn Battlefield National Monument** 25. Afterward, head to **Hardin** 24 for lunch at the Purple Cow. An hour's drive west will bring you to **Billings** 12–23; spend the afternoon wandering through the town's lively downtown or sunning yourself at Lake Elmo State Park. After a pleasant dinner, check out one of the downtown nightclubs. Don't leave Billings right away on the second day; stick around and visit ZooMontana or Pictograph Cave State Monument first. After you've taken your time sightseeing in the morning, head northwest for **Great Falls** 1–8. Take a break halfway through your four-hour drive to stop for a short hike in the **Big Snowy Mountains** 11. Spend the night in Great Falls. On the third day explore the city, including the falls, Giant Springs State Park, and the Lewis and Clark National Historic Trail Interpretive Center.

If you have 5 days

Follow the three-day itinerary, and on the fourth day, leave Great Falls for **Fort Benton** 9. After you check out the Museum of the Upper Missouri and have lunch at the Union Grille in the Grand Union Hotel, continue up U.S. 87 to **Havre** 34. Take the Havre Beneath the Streets tour before dinner. Spend the night in Havre, and on your fifth day travel down the Hi-Line until you reach **Fort Peck** 31. You can spend the rest of the day either leisurely floating on Fort Peck Lake or driving through some of the vast Charles M. Russell National Wildlife Refuge. Camp overnight near Fort Peck Lake or stay at the Fort Peck Hotel.

If you have 7 days

Follow the five-day itinerary, and on the sixth day head for the Big Open, stopping in **Circle** 30 to have lunch and to check out the McCone County Museum. In the afternoon, drive south to **Miles City** 27, where you can walk through the Range Riders Museum or float down the Yellowstone River to Pirogue Island State Park before bedding down for the night. On the morning of the seventh day, drive southeast to **Ekalaka** 28, where you can visit Medicine Rocks State Park before you leave town. If you have time, also stop by the Carter County Museum, or drive south to Custer National Forest.

About the Restaurants

Showy dress and status symbols matter little to most Montanans. A cowboy in dusty blue jeans, flannel shirt, and worn boots leaning against his rust-eaten Chevy could be a millionaire rancher and stockbroker, and the ponytailed woman behind the counter of the general store might be the town mayor. Because of this, no matter where you go to eat—whether the food is extravagant or simple, the prices expensive or dirt cheap—dress is casual. But despite the universal informality in dining, eastern Montana has a surprising number of upscale, chic restaurants with sophisticated dishes. High-quality ethnic foods, with the possible exception of Mexican and Native American cuisine, are scarce, however. Classic steak houses and local ma-and-pa eateries are ubiquitous.

About the Hotels

The strength of eastern Montana's accommodations doesn't lie in luxury resorts, bustling lodges, or crowded dude ranches, which are confined almost entirely to the western third of the state. The crown jewels of lodging on the plains are the historic hotels and bed-and-breakfasts. Nearly every town with more than a few hundred residents has one of these properties, but no two are alike. From turreted Victorian mansions and rustic log ranch houses to Gothic manors and hulking sandstone inns with intricately carved facades, these lodgings have their own appeal and local flavor that set them apart from typical chain accommodations and commercial strip motels.

WHAT IT COSTS

	$$$$	$$$	$$	$	¢
RESTAURANTS	over $22	$16–$22	$11–$16	$7–$11	under $7
HOTELS	over $220	$160–$220	$110–$160	$70–$110	under $70

Restaurant prices are for a main course at dinner. Hotel prices are for two people in a standard double room in high season, excluding service charges and 4% tax.

Timing

Each season offers something different in Montana: summer brings warm, dry weather perfect for hiking, biking, and horseback riding; autumn yields throngs of wildlife for animal lovers and anglers; winter means plenty of snow for skiing, snowmobiling, and ice fishing. Although summer is the busiest season here—with good reason, since freezing temperatures can arrive as early as September and depart as late as May—many travelers are only passing through on their way farther west. The roads may be crowded, but the attractions, hotels, and restaurants are likely not. Winter can sometimes be just as busy as summer, as thousands of avid skiers rush through on their way to the slopes. Road conditions are generally poor as well in winter, especially when a heavy snowfall closes down entire sections of highway. Spring is a hard season to define, as snowstorms can strike well into May. Autumn weather, although not completely predictable, is usually the most stable of Montana's annual climate. Days are long and sunny, evenings are cool, and there are very few fellow travelers to contend with.

GREAT FALLS

With 56,690 residents, Great Falls isn't quite Montana's second-largest city. Ousted into third place by the burgeoning mountain town of Missoula and its 363 extra residents in the 2000 census, Great Falls is still one of Montana's commercial and social hubs. With its bi-level mall, thriving downtown district, bustling civic center, and near-boundless opportunities for outdoor recreation, the community attracts people from all over northern Montana and southern Alberta.

One of Great Falls' greatest resources, however, is its sense of history. Here, along the banks of the Missouri, where the plains meet the Rockies, Meriwether Lewis and William Clark encountered one of the more daunting obstacles of their expedition: the thundering waterfalls that gave the city its name. Although the interpretive center, guided boat trips, and paved trails that mark the passage of the two explorers here in 1805 are impressive, there are countless other museums and attractions that celebrate other chapters in the city's history. From prehistoric buffalo jumps and famous Western artists to pioneering cowboys and the Mis-

Museums Most of the land in the Montana plains didn't feel the footsteps of white settlers until the 19th century was well along—and in some cases nearly over. This makes the Montana plains extremely young in terms of documented history, even by American standards. Most communities here have barely more than a century's worth of written records. Perhaps that's why locals hang on dearly to what remnants of the past do exist. In any event, the tiny settlements and cow towns of the prairie are packed with museums. Although often small and modest, these museums are still critically important to preserving the character of America's last frontier. And they are true community fixtures, symbols of the great pride Montanans have in their homeland. Among the finest museums in the region are the C. M. Russell Museum Complex in Great Falls, the Museum of the Northern Great Plains and the Museum of the Upper Missouri in Fort Benton, and the Carter County Museum in Ekalaka.

Solitude & Reflection The total isolation afforded by this great and empty land is unique. Eastern Montana is one of the few places left in the world where you can go and feel truly alone. As any local will tell you, a stroll through a wildlife refuge or a drive along a quiet county road is an excellent way to take some time for yourself. You don't need to pull out your yoga mat to enjoy the solitude that exists here, but try to make time—even if it's for a few minutes—to take a walk by yourself. No kids, no spouse, not even the family dog—just you, the rocks, the grass, and the incredible sky that stretches endlessly into the distance.

You can enjoy the silence among the eerie rock formations of Medicine Rocks State Park or Makoshika State Park. Towering canyon walls make Bighorn Canyon National Recreation Area a good place to withdraw from civilization, so long as you're far enough away from the lake and its motorboats. The Big Snowy Mountains have miles of peaceful old-growth forest in which to wander, and the Charles M. Russell National Wildlife Refuge is so sprawling that it's easy to lose yourself—no kidding, so be sure to take a map with you, wherever you go.

---

souri River fur trade, Great Falls has a storied past rich enough to make its residents proud. And they are.

Exploring Great Falls

This is a beautiful city to drive through. Maple trees line the residential streets, the Missouri River slices through the center of town, and the Rockies sink their teeth into the distant horizon. Despite the curves of the river, most streets are straight and relatively easy to navigate, thanks largely to the flat terrain. However, with an air force base on the east side of town, a commercial airport on the west side, and only two bridges spanning the river in between, traffic can get heavy, especially late afternoons and on weekends. Pedestrian paths are far less congested. A gorgeous 24-mi-long riverside trail, ideal for walking and cycling, passes the city's largest park, Gibson Park, and one of the largest cold-water springs in the world.

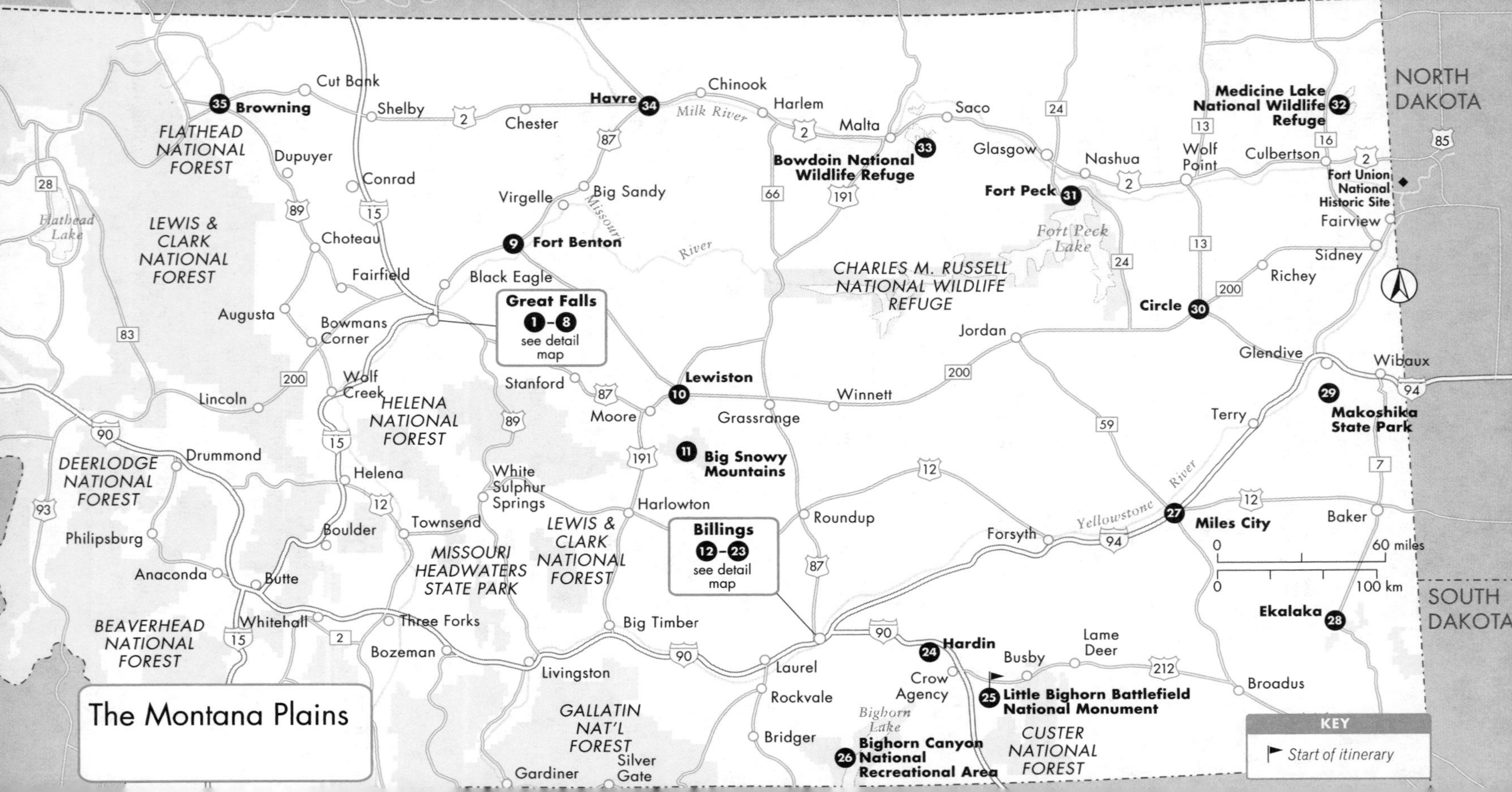
The Montana Plains
NORTH DAKOTA
SOUTH DAKOTA
KEY
Start of itinerary
0
60 miles
0
100 km
35 Browning
34 Havre
33 Bowdoin National Wildlife Refuge
32 Medicine Lake National Wildlife Refuge
31 Fort Peck
30 Circle
29 Makoshika State Park
28 Ekalaka
27 Miles City
26 Bighorn Canyon National Recreational Area
25 Little Bighorn Battlefield National Monument
24 Hardin
11 Big Snowy Mountains
10 Lewiston
9 Fort Benton
Great Falls
1–8
see detail map
Billings
12–23
see detail map
Fort Union National Historic Site
FLATHEAD NATIONAL FOREST
LEWIS & CLARK NATIONAL FOREST
HELENA NATIONAL FOREST
DEERLODGE NATIONAL FOREST
BEAVERHEAD NATIONAL FOREST
MISSOURI HEADWATERS STATE PARK
GALLATIN NAT'L FOREST
CUSTER NATIONAL FOREST
CHARLES M. RUSSELL NATIONAL WILDLIFE REFUGE
Flathead Lake
Fort Peck Lake
Bighorn Lake
Milk River
Missouri River
Yellowstone River
Cut Bank
Shelby
Chester
Chinook
Harlem
Malta
Saco
Glasgow
Nashua
Wolf Point
Culbertson
Fairview
Sidney
Richey
Glendive
Wibaux
Terry
Baker
Broadus
Lame Deer
Busby
Crow Agency
Jordan
Winnett
Grassrange
Roundup
Forsyth
Laurel
Rockvale
Bridger
Big Timber
Livingston
Gardiner
Silver Gate
Harlowton
Moore
Stanford
Black Eagle
Virgelle
Big Sandy
Dupuyer
Conrad
Choteau
Fairfield
Augusta
Bowmans Corner
Wolf Creek
Lincoln
Drummond
Helena
White Sulphur Springs
Townsend
Boulder
Butte
Anaconda
Philipsburg
Whitehall
Three Forks
Bozeman
2
7
12
13
15
16
24
28
59
66
83
85
87
89
90
93
94
191
200
212

a good tour

A good driving tour of Great Falls starts in the city's northeast corner along the southeastern banks of the Missouri. **Rainbow Falls** 1, one of the half dozen or so waterfalls in the area, is below Rainbow Dam. Follow Giant Springs Road west along the river for several miles and you will come across several sights of interest: **Giant Springs State Park** 2, where one of the largest freshwater springs in the world feeds a state fish hatchery before flowing into the tiny Roe River; the **Lewis and Clark National Historic Trail Interpretive Center** 3, which focuses on the explorers' relations with Native Americans; and another set of waterfalls, the **Black Eagle Falls** 4. After visiting Black Eagle Falls, turn left onto 25th Avenue and follow it south until you reach 1st Avenue North. Turn right and drive west to the **Paris Gibson Square Museum of Art** 5, at the center of the old town and housed in the city's first high school. Drive a couple of blocks farther west to 13th Street North, make a right, and drive to the **C. M. Russell Museum Complex** 6, which holds the world's most complete collection of art and personal effects of the famous cowboy artist. Drive west through the city's **historic district** 7 to view hundreds of beautiful Victorian homes; the streets here are laid out in a perfect grid, so there's little chance of getting lost. Once you reach Park Drive North, follow it north to **Gibson Park** 8, the city's largest.

TIMING Depending on how long you want to spend visiting the museums and wandering the historic district, this tour could keep you busy from sunrise to sunset. If you rush things, you might be able to finish this tour in five or six hours. The parks and waterfalls take on their own special beauty when the snow falls, but biting winds might keep you from enjoying them for very long; the warmth of summer and the colors of autumn make them the perfect seasons for this tour.

What to See

4 **Black Eagle Falls.** On the north side of the historic part of town is 40-foot-high, 500-foot-wide Black Eagle Falls, one of the places where the Missouri River takes a sharp dive on its 500-foot descent through town. The adjoining golf courses and baseball diamond give the area plenty of green space and a seminatural feel, although it's hard not to notice the concrete dam looming above the falls. ☒ *Intersection of U.S. 87 and 25th St. N.*

6 **C. M. Russell Museum Complex.** This 76,000-square-foot complex houses the largest collection of original art and personal objects of legendary cowboy artist Charlie Russell (1864–1926). Russell's more than 4,000 works of art—sculptures, watercolors, oil paintings—primarily portray the vanishing era of the Old West. His studio and log home, built at the turn of the 20th century, are adjacent to the main galleries. Also here are collections of paintings by other 19th-century and modern Western artists, interactive exhibits, and a research library. ☒ *400 13th St. N* ☎ *406/727–8787* ⊕ *www.cmrussell.org* 🎫 *$6* ⏲ *May–Sept., Mon.–Sat. 9–6, Sun. noon–5; Oct.–Apr., Tues.–Sat. 10–5, Sun. 1–5.*

Fodor'sChoice ★

★ 2 **Giant Springs State Park.** The freshwater springs here feed a state fish hatchery that covers 400 acres of parkland. According to residents, the waters that flow from the springs form the shortest river in the world, the 200-foot-long Roe River; Oregonians, however, hold that their D River is the shortest, at 120 feet (the length of both rivers can vary depending on factors like the tides). In addition to the hatchery, a visitor center, picnic grounds, a river drive, hiking and biking trails, and a playground are all on-site. You can also fish, attend educational programs, and take tours. ☒ *4600 Giant Springs Rd.* ☎ *406/454–5840* ⊕ *www.fwp.state.mt.us/parks/* 🎫 *$2* ⏲ *Daily sunrise–sunset.*

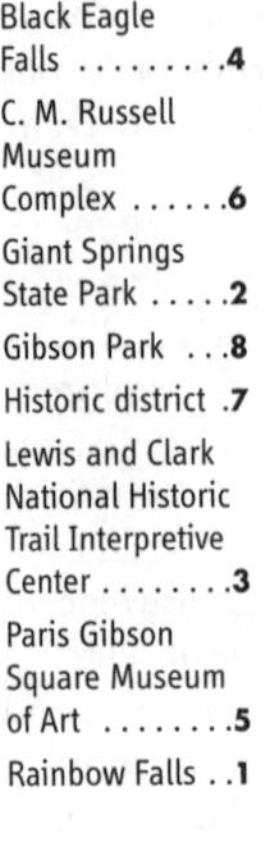

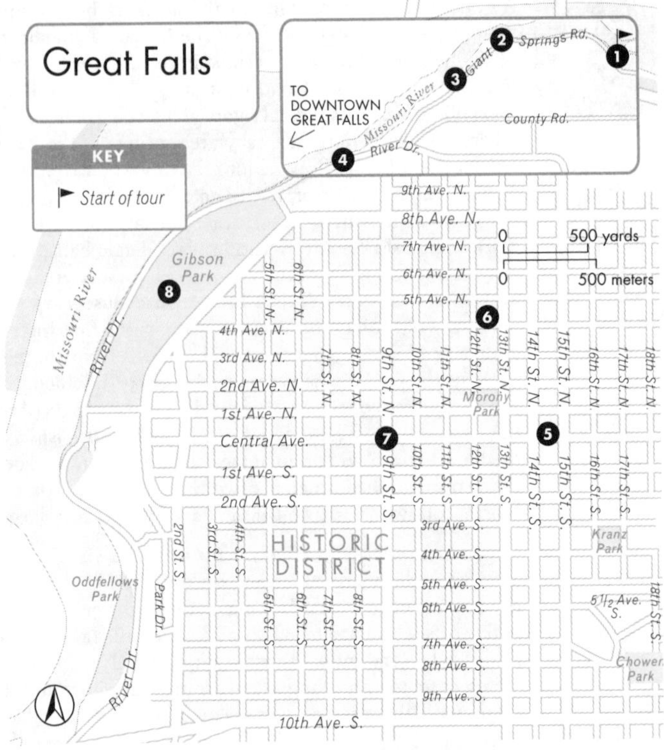

8 **Gibson Park.** This park, named for the insightful founder of Great Falls, is the crown jewel of the city's 400-acre park system. The most popular features are the duck pond, the extensive flower gardens, and a small café. There are also jogging paths, outdoor exercise equipment, basketball courts, rest rooms, a playground, a band shell, and prime picnicking spots. ✉ *Park Dr. N and 1st Ave. N* ☎ *406/771–1265* 🌐 *www.ci.great-falls.mt.us/people_offices/park_rec/* 🎫 *Free* ⏲ *Daily, 24 hrs.*

7 **Historic district.** There are more than 200 historic houses and small businesses here in the historic district, on the east bank of the Missouri River. The structures reflect various architectural styles, including bungalow, prairie, colonial, Queen Anne, Victorian, and Second Empire. You can obtain a brochure for a one-hour self-guided walking tour of the area from the **Great Falls Information Center** (✉ 15 Upper River Rd. ☎ 406/771–0885 or 800/735–8535). The area was laid out in a perfect grid pattern by city founder Paris Gibson, making it easy to navigate.

3 **Lewis and Clark National Historic Trail Interpretive Center.** At this interpretive center next to the Missouri River, you can trace the trail that the Corps of Discovery traveled from 1804 to 1806 while in search of an overland route to the Pacific Ocean. The center exhibits materials used by the travelers and the Native Americans they met on their journey. Films, a self-guided tour, and costumed interpreters who conduct daily demonstrations further illuminate the history. ✉ *4201 Giant Springs Rd.* ☎ *406/727–8733* 🌐 *www.fs.fed.us/r1/lewisclark/lcic.htm* 🎫 *$5* ⏲ *Memorial Day–Sept., daily 9–6; Oct.–Memorial Day, Tues.–Sat. 9–5, Sun. noon–5.*

5 **Paris Gibson Square Museum of Art.** Contemporary artwork of the northwest United States makes up the bulk of the collection here. In addition

MONTANA'S GREATEST SON

*C***HARLES M. RUSSELL.** *The name is legendary in Montana. It's found virtually everywhere you travel in this great state, including a massive national wildlife refuge that bears his name. But despite his near mythic status and the reverence his name evokes, people in these parts still prefer to call him simply "Charlie."*

Born to a wealthy St. Louis family in 1864, Charlie could have enjoyed any of the luxuries high society had to offer. In fact, his parents spent most of his childhood trying to force them down his throat. When he didn't take to a fine private education in St. Louis, he was shipped off to military school in New Jersey. After the first semester he was sent home with instructions not to return. His parents noticed that Charlie always seemed to be drawing, so they sent him to art school. He was kicked out in a matter of days.

Charlie wanted nothing more than to go west and draw, so for his 16th birthday, his parents sent him with a family friend to a ranch in Montana, figuring that roughing it in the real world would cure him of his authority problems and fantasies. They were wrong. But it was far from easy for Charlie at first. He was terrible at his first job, herding sheep. He'd draw on the job and become so preoccupied with sketching that he wouldn't notice the animals wandering off. Eventually he was taken under the wing of mountain man Jake Hoover, and after a couple of years helping him trade with miners and ranchers, Charlie finally got himself a respectable cowboy job—wrangling cattle.

He spent the next 11 years working as a wrangler and painting or drawing nearly every day. During this time he became friends with members of the Blood tribe, a branch of the Blackfeet Nation. For the rest of his life he would carry a deep respect for their culture and sympathy for their fate. "Those Indians have been living in heaven for a thousand years," he told a friend once, "and we took it away from 'em for forty dollars a month."

Eventually Charlie married. After a while, his wife, Nancy, persuaded him to work on his art full time, and in 1897 they moved to Great Falls, where Charlie built a studio. Within a few years Charlie was showing his work in New York galleries; not long after that he was traveling to Europe. He hated going east, and in a silent protest of the high-rises and smoke-spewing factories, he always wore his range clothes, including his trademark red sash.

Near the end of his life, health problems left Charlie tired and weak. The pain didn't bother him so much as the fact that he could no longer ride a horse. When he finally died in 1926, Charlie's home was handed over to the city of Great Falls as a memorial. Local Native American tribes thought so much of him that they raised money to maintain the house and eventually convert it into a museum. Although automobiles had been in use for years, Charlie's hearse was pulled by horses—one of his last requests.

Charlie's paintings and sculptures depict an era and a culture that were fading from the world during his lifetime. "The boosters say it's a better country than it ever was," he wrote to a friend in 1913 about the homesteading movement. "But it looks like hell to me. I liked it better when it belonged to God. It was sure his country when we knew it." Even his signature, which almost always included the symbol of a buffalo skull, reflected the end of the Western frontier. Some say that it was a tribute to his Native American friends, for whom the death of the buffalo meant the demise of their free-roaming way of life. But the West he loved is still documented and preserved today in his more than 4,500 oil paintings, watercolors, sculptures, and illustrated letters.

to several exhibition halls and a photography collection, the museum has a bistro, a gallery, and a store. Near the center of town, the massive sandstone building that houses the museum was built as a high school in 1896 and converted into a museum in 1977. ✉ *1400 1st Ave. N* ☎ *406/727–8255* 🌐 *www.the-square.org* 🎟 *$2* ⏲ *Memorial Day–Labor Day, Tues.–Fri. 10–5, weekends noon–5; Labor Day–Memorial Day, weekdays 10–5, Sat. noon–5.*

⚑ ❶ **Rainbow Falls.** One of the waterfalls that gives the city its name, 50-foot-high Rainbow Falls is below the Rainbow Dam, about 1½ mi east of Giant Springs State Park. The surrounding land is mostly owned by ranchers, although there are some trails cut into the hills near the falls. ✉ *Giant Springs Rd.*

off the beaten path

SMITH RIVER – Flowing out of the Helena National Forest in the heart of Montana is the 60-mi Smith River. Like most other waterways in the state, it fluctuates with the seasons, ranging from a trickle in September to a raging torrent in June (thanks to the melting mountain snowpack). Although the river is popular for numerous activities, including camping on its shores, fishing, and swimming, the most prevalent activity on the Smith is floating. Floating is so popular, in fact, that Montana Fish, Wildlife & Parks limits the number of groups boating down the river to 700 per year. Despite the river's popularity, this is still Montana, and the sense of serene isolation that comes from the sight of towering mountains and open prairie will far outweigh any annoyance at seeing a few other boats during your journey. ✉ *Between I–15 and U.S. 85* ☎ *406/454–5840* 🌐 *www.fwp.state.mt.us/parks/smith/* 🎟 *Charges for use permits vary; call for details.*

ULM PISHKUN STATE PARK – For centuries Native Americans hunted bison by stampeding them off a cliff at this park named after the Blackfoot words for "deep blood kettle." This is one of the largest buffalo jumps in the United States. The mile-long cliff affords a spectacular view of the Rocky Mountains, the Missouri River, and the plains. An interpretive center focuses on the culture of the Plains Indians before white settlement. ✉ *10 mi south of Great Falls on I–15 to the Ulm exit, then 3½ mi northwest* ☎ *406/866–2217* 🌐 *www.fwp.state.mt.us* 🎟 *$2* ⏲ *Memorial Day–Sept., daily 9–5; Oct.–Memorial Day, Wed.–Sat. 10–4, Sun. noon–4.*

Sports & the Outdoors

Although not at the base of world-class ski runs or sheer cliffs for rock climbing like some of Montana's more westerly cities, Great Falls is still popular with outdoor enthusiasts. One of the greatest resources the city has is its central location: the ski lodges and climbing trails are a short drive west, the pristine hunting grounds of the plains sit to the east, and stretching out north and south are Montana's famed blue-ribbon fishing streams. Not to be forgotten is the "Mighty Mo"—the Missouri River, a recreational playground that runs straight through the middle of the city.

The 24-mi **River's Edge Trail** (☎ 406/788–3313) follows the Missouri River through the city on both banks; four bridges connect the trail's two branches. The trail, which attracts bikers, joggers, and strollers, passes by Gibson Park, the West Gate Mall, Giant Springs State Park, and several waterfalls and dams. More than 13 mi of the path, which is still under development, are paved; the remaining 11 mi are gravel.

Six blocks from the River's Edge Trail in downtown Great Falls is **Bighorn Wilderness Equipment** (✉ 600 Central Ave. ☎ 406/453–2841), a sporting-goods superstore with everything from camping-stove fuel and freeze-dried food to ice-climbing equipment and kayaks. The store also rents bicycles and equipment.

Craig Madsen Montana River Outfitters (✉ 923 10th Ave. N ☎ 406/761–1677 or 800/800–8218), facing the river on the north side of town, is known among locals for its guided trips along the river by canoe or horseback. You can also rent bicycles here for use on the River's Edge Trail.

Where to Stay & Eat

$$$$ ✕ **Eddie's Supper Club.** Campfire steak, lobster, prime rib, and shrimp are the entrées of choice at this casual Great Falls mainstay. The large booths and tables may hark back to the 1950s, but Eddie's serves some of the best burgers and steaks in town. There's live piano music on the weekends. ✉ *3725 2nd Ave. N* ☎ *406/453–1616* ▭ *D, MC, V.*

$–$$$$ ✕ **Borrie's.** The atmosphere is casual and the dining family-style at this restaurant in Black Eagle, a small community that borders the northeast edge of Great Falls. Regulars favor the steaks, chicken, lobster, and burgers, although the huge portions of spaghetti, ravioli, and rigatoni are also popular. Historic photos of Great Falls line the walls, but the dim lighting makes all the furnishings look bland and dark. ✉ *1800 Smelter Ave., Black Eagle* ☎ *406/761–0300* ▭ *AE, D, MC, V* ⊗ *No lunch.*

$–$$$$ ✕ **Jaker's.** The menu at this restaurant, part of a regional chain of steak houses, ranges from simple chicken sandwiches and pot roast to more elaborate dishes such as pan-seared oysters and fillet à la Jaker's, a steak topped with crab, asparagus, and béarnaise sauce. Dress is casual, although the cherrywood interior adds a feeling of sophistication. ✉ *31501 10th Ave. S* ☎ *406/727–1033* ▭ *AE, D, DC, MC, V* ⊗ *No lunch weekends.*

$–$$$$ ✕ **The Lost Woodsman.** Western art and sculpture decorate this bucolic restaurant owned by local artist Rick Rowley. The menu mostly lists hearty fare such as steak, walleye, burgers, pasta, and chili. ✉ *1919 3rd St. NW* ☎ *406/761–1034* ▭ *AE, MC, V.*

★ **$–$$** **Charlie Russell Manor.** A local attorney has restored and lavishly furnished this 1916 home in the historic district of Great Falls. Antiques fill the spacious rooms. The house also contains a sunroom, a study, a large dining room, and an English-style ballroom. Breakfasts are hearty, and there is on-site catering for special parties. ✉ *825 4th Ave. N, 59401* ☎ *406/455–1400 or 877/207–6131* 📠 *406/727–3771* 🌐 *www.charlie-russell.com* *6 rooms* *Dining room, in-room data ports, meeting rooms; no smoking* ▭ *AE, MC, V* *BP.*

$ **Best Western Heritage Inn.** Amenities such as outdoor tennis courts, a courtyard garden, balconies that overlook the indoor pool, and poolside rooms distinguish this modern chain hotel in a suburban area 3 mi from the airport. ✉ *1700 Fox Farm Rd., 59404* ☎ *406/761–1900 or 800/548–8256* 📠 *406/761–0136* 🌐 *www.bestwestern.com* *239 rooms* *Restaurant, some microwaves, some refrigerators, cable TV with movies, tennis court, indoor pool, gym, hot tub, sauna, bar, casino, shop, laundry facilities, business services, meeting rooms, some pets allowed (fee)* ▭ *AE, D, DC, MC, V.*

$ **Collins Mansion Bed and Breakfast.** This gorgeous Victorian mansion, built in 1891, looks like a circular building from the outside, thanks to a massive wraparound porch. Oak chairs, wrought-iron beds, and miles of lace—on bedspreads, tables, and curtains—decorate the mansion. The spacious guest rooms all have baths, and the master suite has a fireplace.

Fodor's Choice ★

The B&B also has a gazebo, library, parlor, music room, and lounge. Breakfast is served in your room, on the veranda, or in the dining room. *⊠ 1003 2nd Ave. NW, 59404 ☎ 406/452–6798 or 877/452–6798 📠 406/452–6787 🌐 www.collinsmansion.com 5 rooms Cable TV, library, Internet; no room TVs, no smoking AE, MC, V BP.*

$ **Townhouse Inn.** Frequent travelers to Great Falls return again and again to this modern hotel for its low prices and well-furnished, spacious rooms. Shades of beige, green, red, and blue decorate the motel-style rooms. An indoor courtyard has plants, a swimming pool, and a large hot tub. A small casino also offers distraction for road-weary guests. *⊠ 1411 10th Ave. S, 59405 ☎ 406/761–4600 📠 406/761–7603 109 rooms Restaurant, cable TV with movies, indoor pool, hot tub, sauna, casino, video game room, shop, meeting rooms AE, D, DC, MC, V.*

¢ **Great Falls Inn.** Small but well appointed, this downtown hotel is accented by muted greens and reds, dark hardwood, and blazing white walls. Many of the guests of the inn stay here while using the services of the Great Falls Clinic and Benefis Healthcare Center next door. *⊠ 1400 28th St. S, 59405 ☎ 406/453–6000 📠 406/453–6078 60 rooms Some microwaves, some refrigerators, cable TV with movies, some pets allowed (fee) AE, D, MC, V CP.*

Camping

Fort Ponderosa Campground. Horseshoes, miniature golf, and helpful hosts are some of the attractions of this friendly campground nestled against the Little Belt Mountains, 20 mi south of Great Falls. A small store here stocks propane and some basic provisions, and larger stores are in the nearby town of Belt, a short drive—or tube ride down the creek—away. There's an extra $3 charge per night if you plan to use your RV's heater or air conditioner. *Flush toilets, full hookups, partial hookups (electric), drinking water, laundry facilities, showers, fire pits, food service, grills, picnic tables, electricity, public telephone, general store, play area, swimming (creek) 25 full hookups, 25 partial hookups, 25 tent sites, 1 cabin ⊠ 568 Armington Rd. ☎ 406/277–3232 📠 406/277–3309 🌐 www.fortponderosa.com Full hookups $20.75, partial hookups $18.75, tent sites $16.75, cabins $45 MC, V Apr.–Nov.*

Great Falls KOA. Regular evening entertainment at this campsite on the south edge of town includes bluegrass music, country humor, and a little cowboy poetry. The site is near three golf courses and has a large outdoor pool with a hot tub and sauna. *Flush toilets, full hookups, partial hookups (electric and water), drinking water, showers, food service, grills, picnic tables, electricity, public telephone, general store, pool 80 full hookups, 60 partial hookups, 30 tent sites, 25 cabins ⊠ 1500 51st St. S ☎ 406/727–3191 🌐 www.koa.com Full hookups $45, partial hookups $40, tent sites $30, cabins $50 AE, D, MC, V.*

Shopping

★ Thanks to insightful city planners, Great Falls is blessed with a beautiful and extensive **downtown shopping district** with the kind of old-fashioned stores that are rapidly vanishing in other parts of the country to make way for chain stores and shopping malls. Eat ice cream at a soda fountain, play with wooden cars at a toy store, and prepare for a trip down the Missouri with an outfitter here.

★ A co-op run by a dozen local artists, **Gallery 16** (⊠ 608 Central Ave. ☎ 406/453–6103) has creations from more than 100 craftspeople whose works include paintings, jewelry, furniture, pottery, and sculpture, among others. Gallery 16 also has a small gift shop at the Paris Gibson Square Museum of Art.

en route

Despite its name, the **Benton Lake National Wildlife Refuge** (✉ 922 Bootlegger Trail ☎ 406/727–7400), about 20 mi north of Great Falls, isn't really a lake. Dominated by prairie and seasonal wetlands, the 19-square-mi marsh shelters hundreds of thousands of birds representing more than 240 species. The most common birds are ducks, geese, and swans. There is limited hunting here, but most people come simply to watch, observe, and reflect.

CENTRAL MONTANA

Although central Montana consists mostly of rolling plains carpeted with golden grasses, the general flatness of the landscape is broken up by the occasional mountain range or swath of forest. There are other contrasts here as well, in this land where the pinnacles of the Rockies meet the ranches and farms of the prairie, and where old mining camps lie only a few miles from historic cow towns. Among the hallmarks of the region are its rivers: the Missouri, the Judith, and the Smith. They might not provide the kind of fishing found in Montana's famed Madison and Gallatin rivers, but they also aren't as crowded, and their rich history and stunning landscape make them the most popular Montana destinations you've probably never heard of.

Fort Benton

9 *40 mi northeast of Great Falls via U.S. 87.*

Lewis and Clark first camped at this site less than an hour downriver from Great Falls in 1805. The first steamboat arrived here in 1859, and Fort Benton was once the farthest inland port in the world. In 1866, 2½ tons of gold dust were shipped downriver from here. Today, the town of 1,594 people is the gateway to the wild and scenic Upper Missouri River, and reminders of its rich and rugged past are captured in the Museum of the Upper Missouri and the Museum of the Northern Great Plains.

The official museum of agriculture in Montana, the **Museum of the Northern Great Plains** tells the story of three generations of farmers from 1908 until 1980. The 30,000 square feet of exhibition space hold a village of businesses from the homestead era, a library, and the Hornaday-Smithsonian Bison. Taken from the Montana plains in 1886 amidst fears the species would become extinct, these six buffalo were stuffed and then exhibited in the Smithsonian for more than 70 years. ✉ *1205 20th St.* ☎ *406/622–5316* 🌐 *www.fortbenton.com/museums/agmuseum.htm* 🎫 *$4* ⏲ *May–Sept., daily 10–5; off-season by appointment only.*

Fodor'sChoice ★ Covering the era from 1800 to 1900, the **Museum of the Upper Missouri** highlights the importance of Fort Benton and the role it played as a trading post, military fort, and the head of steamboat navigation. Old Fort Benton is adjacent; considered the birthplace of Montana, with its 1846 blockhouse, this is the oldest standing structure in the state. ✉ *Old Fort Park* ☎ *406/622–5316* 🌐 *www.fortbenton.com/museums/muminfo.htm* 🎫 *$4* ⏲ *May–Sept., daily 10–5; off-season by appointment only.*

In 1805–06 Lewis and Clark explored the upper Missouri River and camped on its banks. Today the stretch designated the **Upper Missouri National Wild and Scenic River** runs 149 mi downriver from Fort Benton. Highlights include the scenic White Cliffs area, Citadel Rock, Hole in the Wall, Lewis and Clark Camp at Slaughter River, abandoned homesteads, and abundant wildlife. Commercial boat tours, shuttle service, and boat rentals—including rowboats, power boats, and canoes—are available at Fort Benton and Virgelle. ✉ *Visitor Center, 1718 Front*

St. ☎ 406/622–5185 🌐 www.mt.blm.gov/ldo/umnwsr.html 🎫 Free ⏲ Visitor center May–Oct., daily 8–5.

Sports & the Outdoors

As a quick and easy way to move people, the Missouri River was the lifeblood of 19th-century Fort Benton. The river still moves people today, although most of its passengers aren't traveling to seek their fortunes in the goldfields. Modern travelers of the Mighty Mo around Fort Benton paddle its placid waters for the peacefulness, serenity, and beauty of the surrounding country. Although sparsely inhabited, this calm stretch of the Missouri is becoming more and more popular with visitors. The benefit is no shortage of outfitters and guides offering their services at competitive prices.

★ The guided canoe trips offered by **Lewis and Clark Canoe Expeditions** (✉ 812 14th St. ☎ 406/622–3698 or 888/595–9151) last from one to seven days and can be altered to include horseback riding. You can also arrange for canoe rentals and a guide-only service, in which you provide transportation and food for your escort. The **Missouri River Canoe Company** (✉ 7485 Virgelle Ferry Rd. N, Loma ☎ 406/378–3110 or 800/426–2926), downriver from Fort Benton in the tiny town of Loma, provides canoe and kayak rentals by the day, outfitted excursions, and guided trips of one or four days. Also available are horseback-riding trips and lodging at Virgelle Merc, a restored homestead-era settlement with accommodations in cabins, B&B rooms, and even a sheepherder's wagon under the stars.

Where to Stay & Eat

$–$$ ✕🏨 **Grand Union Hotel.** Perhaps the oldest hotel in Montana, the Grand Union was built on the bank of the Missouri River in 1882 to serve steamboat and stage travelers. Filled with period pieces, the two-story building is as elegant as it ever was. Many of the spacious rooms have river views. With its dark-wood accents and Victorian-style lighting, the Union Grille Restaurant brings to mind the refined elegance of the Western frontier's elite. The menu includes seared sea scallops, charbroiled venison, and grilled buffalo tenderloin, and the wine list is populated by choices from California and Washington vineyards. Brunch is available on Sundays. *✉ 1 Grand Union Sq., 59442 ☎ 406/622–1882 or 888/838–1882 📠 406/622–5985 🌐 www.grandunionhotel.com 27 rooms Restaurant, some in-room hot tubs, cable TV, bar, shop, business services, meeting rooms; no smoking 💳 AE, D, MC, V ⏲ Restaurant closed Mon. in summer, Mon. and Tues. in winter. No lunch 🍽 CP.*

¢ 🏨 **Long's Landing Bed & Breakfast.** Western-style furnishings fill this homey, three-room B&B. You can enjoy breakfast—usually a simple plate of pancakes and fresh fruit—on one of two large decks at any time of the morning. *✉ 1011 17th St., 59442 ☎ 406/622–3461 📠 406/622–3455 3 rooms, 2 with shared bath Cable TV 💳 MC, V 🍽 BP ⏲ Closed Nov.–Apr.*

Shopping

There are thousands of bolts of quilting fabric at the **Quilting Hen** (✉ 1156 Buck Bridge Rd., Carter ☎ 406/734–5297), about halfway between Great Falls and Fort Benton. The store specializes in unusual patterns and kits, including one based on the Lewis and Clark expedition.

Lewistown

⑩ *90 mi southeast of Fort Benton via Hwys. 80 and 81.*

Begun as a small trading post in the shadow of the low-lying Moccasin Mountains, Lewistown has evolved into a pleasant small town of 5,813 residents. Self-guided-tour brochures are available for areas listed on the

National Register of Historic Places, including the Silk Stocking and Central Business districts, Courthouse Square, Judith Place, and Stone Quarry.

Nearly half the town—and several hundred visitors from across the country—turn out each year for the **Lewistown Chokecherry Festival.** Held the first Saturday after Labor Day, the annual harvest celebration includes contests, concerts, arts and crafts booths, a farmers' market, and a cook-off starring the wild-growing sour berry. ✉ *Main St.* ☎ *406/538–5436* 🌐 *www.lewistownchamber.com.*

Pioneer relics, blacksmith and cowboy tools, guns, and Native American artifacts are displayed at the **Central Montana Museum.** ✉ *408 Main St. NE* ☎ *406/538–5436* 🎟 *Free* 🕒 *Daily 10–6.*

Discover the vistas that inspired Western artist Charles Russell on the ★ **Charles Russell Chew-Choo,** a vintage 1950s-era train that travels through some of the most beautiful and remote landscapes in the state. The tour lasts 3½ hours and includes dinner. ✉ *211 E. Main St.* ☎ *406/538–5436* 🌐 *www.lewistownchamber.com/chewchoo.htm* 🎟 *$75, including dinner* 🕒 *May–Sept., Sat.; call for departure times.*

The regional **Lewistown Art Center** showcases artwork by local talent and hosts community art classes. ✉ *801 W. Broadway St.* ☎ *406/538–8278* 🌐 *www.lewistownchamber.com/Art/homepage.htm* 🎟 *Free* 🕒 *Tues.–Sat. 11:30–5:30.*

Ackley Lake State Park has a 23-site campground, two boat ramps, and great fishing. It's to the north of the Little Belt Mountains, about 26 mi southwest of Lewistown. ✉ *U.S. 87 to Hwy. 400, then 7 mi southwest* ☎ *406/454–5840* 🌐 *www.fwp.state.mt.us* 🎟 *Free* 🕒 *Daily.*

At the head of one of the purest cold-water springs in the world is the **Big Springs Trout Hatchery.** The state's largest cold-water production station nurtures several species of trout and kokanee salmon. ✉ *Hwy. 238, 5 mi south of Lewistown* ☎ *406/538–5588* 🎟 *Free* 🕒 *Daily sunrise–sunset.*

off the beaten path

JUDITH RIVER – The tame, deserted Judith flows more than 60 mi from the Lewis and Clark National Forest through arid plains and sandy mesas before emptying into the Missouri. The scenery is stunning, but the variably low water levels and stifling hot summer sun are not conducive to float trips. This is, however, excellent fossil-hunting ground, and the **Judith River Dinosaur Institute,** based in Malta, sponsors frequent digs here. Most of the land surrounding the river is private, though, so check before you start wandering the banks looking for bones. As always, remember to leave fossils where you find them, and report anything significant to the Dinosaur Institute. ✉ *North of Hwy. 200* ☎ *406/654–2323 for Dinosaur Institute* 🌐 *www.montanadinosaurdigs.com.*

WAR HORSE NATIONAL WILDLIFE REFUGE – In 1958, this 3,192-acre area was established as a refuge and breeding ground for migratory birds and other wildlife. The refuge comprises three units: War Horse Lake, Wild Horse Lake, and Yellow Water Reservoir. The three units are geographically separate, but all are part of the larger Charles M. Russell National Wildlife Refuge, which encompasses more than 1 million acres along the Missouri River. Note that it's necessary to take gravel roads to reach fishing and wildlife areas. The Charles M. Russell Complex Headquarters is in Lewistown (505 Airport Rd.), with substations at Fort Peck, Jordan, and Roy. ✉ *48 mi east of Lewistown on U.S. 87* ☎ *406/538–8706* 🌐 *refuges.fws.gov/* 🎟 *Free* 🕒 *Daily; headquarters weekdays 8–4.*

Sports & the Outdoors

Lewistown has access to water—and plenty of it. From alpine lakes to crystal-clear creeks fed by melting snow to natural springs, there are all kinds of ways to get wet within a few short miles of town. Although residents and visitors alike find plenty of uses for Lewistown's soggy natural resources, swimming is an especially dominant activity.

In a clearing outside Lewistown are the **Gigantic Warm Springs** (✉ north on U.S. 191, then west on Hwy. 81 for 5 mi), a small spring-fed lake that keeps a constant temperature of 68°F. One of the most popular places in Frank Day City Park is the **Lewistown Municipal Swimming Pool** (✉ 5th Ave. S ☎ 406/538–4503), a 13,000-square-foot water park with two large slides.

Where to Stay & Eat

¢–$$ ✕ **Whole Famdamily.** The home-style cooking on this menu includes dinner specials of stir-fries, Mexican dishes, beef, and chicken. The family-friendly restaurant is known for its soups, salads, and sandwiches, which are named after locals. There's also a children's menu. Save room for the famous cream puffs and other desserts. Wooden tables and chairs and pictures of the Old West lend homey touches. ✉ *206 W. Main St. (U.S. 87)* ☎ *406/538–5161* ▭ *AE, D, MC, V* ⊘ *No smoking* ⊗ *Closed Sun.*

¢–$ 🏨 **Yogo Inn of Lewistown.** This inn takes its name from the Yogo sapphires mined nearby. Rooms are contemporary, spacious, and well furnished; some have four-poster beds. Many rooms face an indoor courtyard with a swimming pool and hot tub. The outdoor Centermark Courtyard is named after surveyor documents buried here in 1912 proclaiming the spot the geographical center of Montana. You can pick up the Charlie Russell Chew-Choo dinner train at the inn, and you can also arrange for Western buggy rides and tours of historical ghost towns. ✉ *211 E. Main St., 59457* ☎ *406/538–8721 or 800/860–9646* 📠 *406/538–8969* 🌐 *www.yogoinn.com* *125 rooms* *Restaurant, cable TV with movies, indoor pool, hot tub, bar, video game room, meeting rooms, some pets allowed (fee)* ▭ *AE, D, MC, V.*

Big Snowy Mountains

⓫ *40 mi south of Lewistown via Red Hill Rd.*

South of Montana's geographical center, an island of rocky peaks rises more than 3,000 feet from the sea of windswept prairie. A combination of evergreen forests and barren tundra, much of the Big Snowy Mountains area is completely undeveloped. More than 80% of its 106,776 acres are designated federal wilderness areas, which means no homes, no commercial services, no industry, and very few roads. The result is almost total isolation for anyone who treks into the Big Snowies eager to explore their rocky pinnacles, icy caves, and tranquil forests. Few of the landmarks in the Big Snowies are marked, but you can pick up a map of the area from any of the Lewis and Clark National Forest ranger stations scattered around central Montana, including the **Musselshell Ranger Station** (✉ 809 2nd St. NW, Harlowton ☎ 406/632–4391 🌐 www.fs.fed.us/r1/lewisclark), 25 mi southwest of the mountains.

Greathouse Peak, named for a Forest Service ranger who died from wounds in World War I, is the tallest mountain in the Big Snowies at 8,681 feet. There are some two-tracks that lead off Forest Service roads partially up the peak where vehicle travel is permitted, but the simplest way up is to hike the 6 mi of unmarked trails that gradually zigzag up the slope from Halfmoon Canyon. The main trail, which is only mildly strenuous, doesn't quite make it to the top; in order to reach the summit, you'll need to hike a few yards off the main path. You'll know you've reached the highest point when you see the two stone cairns. ✉ *Pack Trail* ☎ *406/566–2292* ⏲ *Daily; automobile access June–Nov., other times by snowmobile only.*

The second-highest point in the mountain range is **Big Snowy,** also called Old Baldy. Just 41 feet shorter than Greathouse Peak, 8,640-foot-high Big Snowy still makes for an enjoyable climb. A two-track stretches almost to the summit, although fallen rocks block vehicle travel on the last stretch. The peak is a barren plateau with a small rocky outcropping marking the highest point. ✉ *Red Hill Rd.* ☎ *406/566–2292* ⏲ *Daily; automobile access June–Nov., other times by snowmobile only.*

★ In the higher reaches of the mountains is pristine **Crystal Lake.** There's excellent hiking along interpretive and wildflower trails as well as camping, fossil hunting, and ice-cave exploration. The ice cave is a 6-mi hike from the 28-site campground; June is the best time to see the 30-foot ice pillars formed over the winter. There's a cabin for snowmobilers. No motorized boats are allowed on the lake. ✉ *Crystal Lake Rd.* ☎ *406/566–2292* *Free* ⏲ *Daily; automobile access June—Nov., other times by snowmobile only.*

A 1909 limestone building in the town of Harlowton, 25 mi southwest of the mountains, houses the **Upper Musselshell Museum.** The collection primarily contains artifacts of the people who lived in, worked in, and developed the land around the Upper Musselshell River. There are also fossils of dinosaurs and bison. ✉ *11 S. Central St., Harlowton* ☎ *406/632–5519* *$1 suggested donation* ⏲ *May–Oct., Sun. and Mon. 1–5, Tues.–Sat. 10–5; Nov.–Apr., Sun. 1–5, Tues.–Sat. 10–5.*

Sports & the Outdoors

The evergreen forests and rocky slopes of the Big Snowies serve as a venue for numerous outdoor activities, including fishing, hiking, rock climbing, snowmobiling, and cross-country skiing, among others. The utter isolation of the region makes each a very peaceful experience but also means nearby outfitters are all but impossible to find. If you wish to take advantage of the Snowies' full recreational potential, it's best to get supplied in the larger communities of Lewistown, Great Falls, or Billings before making the trek out to the mountains.

A small local outfitter, **Don's Store** (✉ 120 2nd Ave. S, Lewistown ☎ 406/538–9408 or 800/879–8194) carries a wide selection of fishing gear and outdoor wear, plus some camera equipment. **High Plains Bike & Ski** (✉ 924 W. Water St., Lewistown ☎ 406/538–2902) sells many brands of alpine and bicycling equipment and can rush order cross-country-skiing equipment.

Where to Stay

¢ **Corral Motel.** Family units, some with two bedrooms, and a nearby restaurant are the hallmarks of this hotel filled with modern furniture. Most rooms afford unobstructed views of the Musselshell River as it flows out of the Little Belt Mountains 30 mi away; the Castle, Crazy, and Big Snowy mountains are also clearly visible. ✉ *U.S. 12 and U.S. 191, Box 721, Harlowton 59036* ☎ *406/632–4331 or 800/392–4723* *406/632–4748* *18 rooms, six 2-bedroom units* *Restaurant, some refrigerators, cable TV with movies, hot tub, bar* *MC, V.*

CAMPING **Crystal Lake Campground.** Tucked inside the lip of the crater that holds back the waters of Crystal Lake and surrounded by thick stands of trees, this primitive campground may be one of the most epic (and coldest) places to pitch a tent in the state. There are year-round ice caves nearby, and heavy snows force the campground to close autumn through late spring. There's plenty of space separating the campsites. Call to arrange to pay your fee in advance. *Pit toilets, drinking water, grills, picnic tables, swimming (lake) 28 sites Crystal Lake Rd., 22 mi west of U.S. 87 406/566–2292 406/566–2408 www.fs.fed.us/r1/lewisclark $8 MC, V Mid-May–late Sept. (call to verify).*

en route

Depending on how you entered and plan to leave the Big Snowy Mountains, any combination of U.S. 12, U.S. 191, U.S. 87, and I–90 will be your fastest route to Billings. However, if you have the time, try getting off the main roads. The square of land between these four highways is beautiful country and is home to **Halfbreed Lake National Wildlife Refuge** (Molt-Rapelje Rd. 406/538–8706), part of the Charles M. Russell National Wildlife Refuge. The several thousand acres of Halfbreed encompass a lake, wetlands, creeks, and grassy plains. Wildlife includes grouse, elk, deer, and antelope. This is a favorite spot for birders, who say Halfbreed is one of the best places in the state to see migratory species.

BILLINGS

When the Minnesota and Montana Land and Improvement Company founded the town of Billings along the Northwestern Railroad in the spring of 1882, three buildings marked the community: a home, a hotel, and a general store. Before six months had passed, 5,000 city lots had been sold and more than 200 homes and businesses had been erected. The city's immediate and consistent growth—spurred by the railroad, on the Yellowstone River, cattle barons, merchants, and miners headed to the gold fields farther west—earned it the nickname "the Magic City."

The population of Billings has doubled every 30 years since its founding, and today the metropolitan area has more than 120,000 residents, making it not only the largest city in Montana, but also the largest city for 500 mi in any direction. Midway between Minneapolis and Seattle, and Denver and Calgary, the community of Billings is one of the Northwest's premier trading centers. It's also an important regional center for medicine, education, culture, technology, and industry. Since the 1951 discovery of an oil field that stretches across Montana and the Dakotas into Canada, refining and energy production have played a key role in keeping the city vibrant, productive, and alive.

Exploring Billings

City planners have done a fine job of laying out the constantly growing community of Billings over the years. The primary residential districts are on the northern and western sides, the industrial parks are on the city's southern and eastern perimeters, and a lively downtown commercial district is sandwiched in between. There are plenty of major avenues to ease the flow of traffic between the sectors, and downtown streets are logically numbered, making navigation by car or foot relatively simple (note that some of the downtown streets are one-way only). Remember that Billings, like most other Western cities, sprawls; expect to do far more driving to reach your destination than walking. Also keep in mind that I–90, which runs along the southern and eastern edges of Billings, is the primary route many locals use to commute to work, so do your best to avoid it in the early morning and early evening.

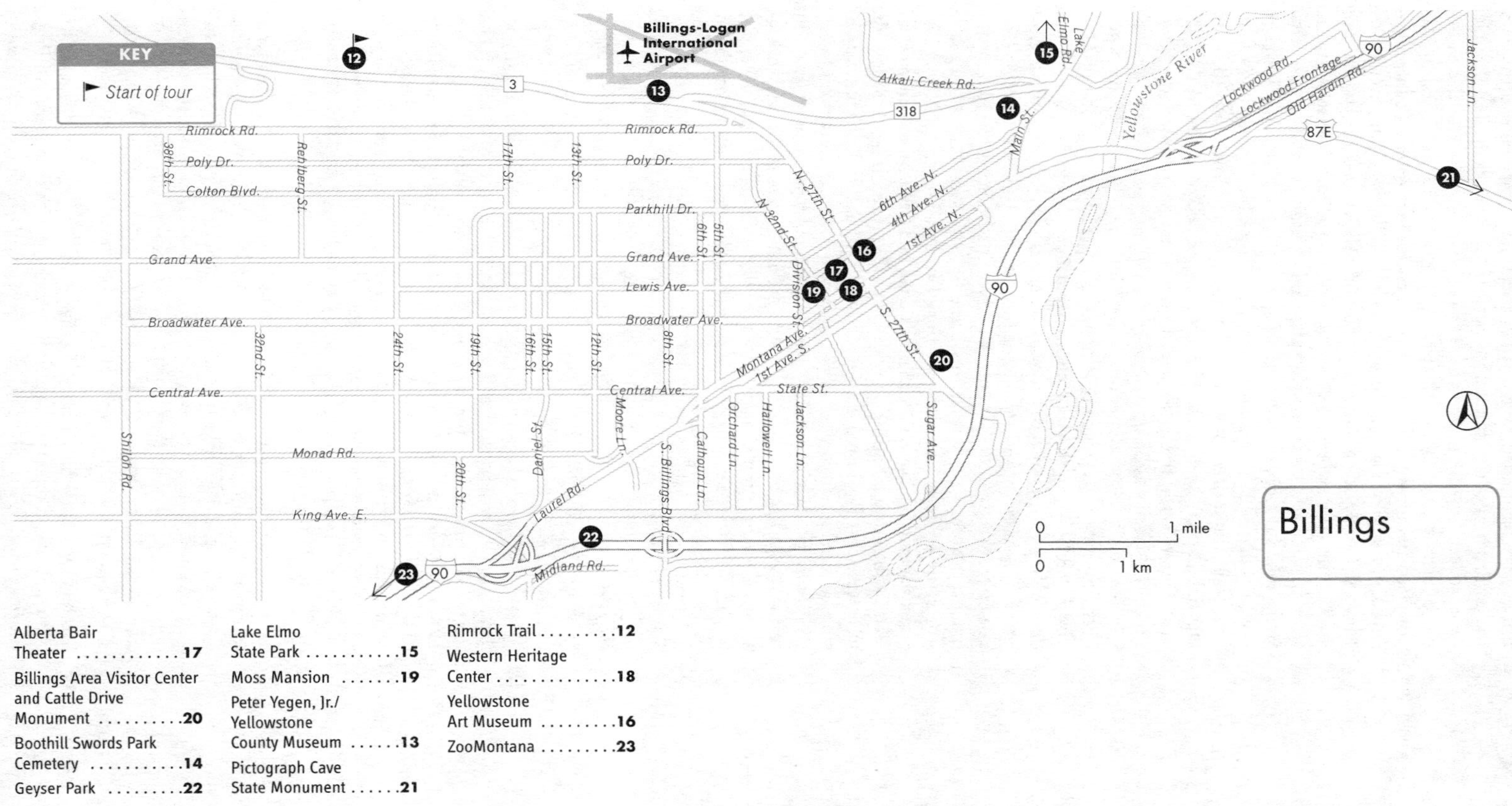

Alberta Bair Theater **17**
Billings Area Visitor Center and Cattle Drive Monument **20**
Boothill Swords Park Cemetery **14**
Geyser Park **22**
Lake Elmo State Park **15**
Moss Mansion **19**
Peter Yegen, Jr./ Yellowstone County Museum **13**
Pictograph Cave State Monument **21**
Rimrock Trail **12**
Western Heritage Center **18**
Yellowstone Art Museum **16**
ZooMontana **23**

a good tour

Billings is surrounded by a distinct rock wall, aptly named the Rimrocks. Running along part of the wall is the **Rimrock Trail** 12 ⚑, made up of several smaller trails, which has outstanding views and is a good place to start your tour of the city. After your hike, drive east on Airport Road/Highway 3 to the **Peter Yegen Jr./Yellowstone County Museum** 13, in a modest log building at the exit for Billings Logan International Airport. Get back on Airport Road and follow it to the intersection with Main Street, where you'll see **Boothill Swords Park Cemetery** 14, final resting place for both army scouts and frontier outlaws. **Lake Elmo State Park** 15, a popular recreational spot on the edge of town, is a short drive north on Main Street into Billings Heights. Head back down Main Street and then drive southwest on 6th Avenue North into the commercial district, where several sights are grouped together. Make a left onto North 27th Street and drive to 4th Avenue North for the **Yellowstone Art Museum** 16, displaying Western and contemporary art. Park your car in the area and continue on foot one block south on North 27th Street to 3rd Avenue North; make a right and walk one block to North 28th Street to reach the **Alberta Bair Theater** 17. Walk south down North 28th Street to Montana Avenue, where you'll find the **Western Heritage Center** 18. To reach the turn-of-the-20th-century **Moss Mansion** 19 from the center, head north on North 28th Street for two blocks; make a left onto 2nd Avenue North and follow it west for several blocks to Division Street. Return to your car and drive south on North 27th Street to reach the **Billings Area Visitor Center and Cattle Drive Monument** 20. Head south down South 27th Street until you reach I–90; follow the interstate east for 2 mi to Exit 452. Turn right and follow Highway 87 south a few miles to the border of the Crow Indian Reservation, where you'll find the fascinating **Pictograph Cave State Monument** 21. For a bit of fun, head back into Billings and take I–90 west to **Geyser Park** 22, an amusement complex with dozens of games and activities. Keep following I–90 to the edge of town to get to **ZooMontana** 23, one of a handful of zoos in the region.

TIMING You could easily spend one or even two days on this tour, depending on how much time you want to allocate to the sights and parks. In winter, this tour will take less time, as many of the outdoor sights close or are significantly less enjoyable.

What to See

17 **Alberta Bair Theater.** In the 1930s, 20th Century Fox built this art deco theater to screen movies on land homesteaded by a successful sheep-ranching family. Saved from the wrecking ball by community groups in the 1980s, it is now a cultural center for the region. Aside from being home to the Billings Symphony Orchestra, the Alberta Bair hosts dance companies, theater troupes, and national music acts. The interior of the theater can only be seen during performances and on free group tours for 15 or more (reserve in advance). ✉ *2801 3rd Ave. N* ☎ *406/256–6052 or 877/321–2074* 🌐 *www.albertabairtheater.org.*

20 **Billings Area Visitor Center and Cattle Drive Monument.** A hero-size bronze sculpture of a cattle drover commemorates the Great Montana Centennial Cattle Drive of 1989 (which commemorated the drive of 1889) at this visitor center. You can take guided tours of the center, study the exhibits on the region, and gather all the information you'll need on area attractions. ✉ *815 S. 27th St.* ☎ *406/252–4016 or 800/735–2635* 🌐 *billingscvb.visitmt.com* 🎫 *Free* 🕓 *Weekdays 8–5.*

14 **Boothill Swords Park Cemetery.** Many of the city's early residents are buried at this cemetery atop the Rimrocks, north of historic Billings. Among Boothill's residents are H. M. Muggins Taylor, the army scout

who carried word of Custer's defeat through 180 mi of hostile territory to Fort Ellis; Western explorer Yellowstone Kelly; and several outlaws executed in the territorial days. ✉ *Airport and Main Sts.* ☎ *406/252–4016.*

22 **Geyser Park.** A favorite diversion for area visitors with children, Geyser Park has bumper boats, go-carts, a climbing wall, laser tag, and a miniature golf course with waterfalls and geyser pools. Because each game operates on a ticket system and concessions are rather pricey, some families like to pack a cooler and eat in the picnic area. ✉ *4910 Southgate Dr.* ☎ *406/254–2510* *$3.75–$5 per game* ⏲ *Apr.–Oct., daily 11–11.*

15 **Lake Elmo State Park.** Surrounding a 64-acre reservoir in Billings Heights, this park is a popular spot for hiking, swimming, fishing, and nonmotorized boating. Although it's practically within the city limits, the park is still wild enough to seem miles away from civilization. It's a popular venue for concerts and sporting events such as triathlons and the Montana Games. ✉ *U.S. 87* ☎ *406/247–2940* 🌐 *www.fwp.state.mt.us* *$2* ⏲ *Daily sunrise–sunset.*

19 **Moss Mansion.** Dutch architect Henry Hardenbergh, who worked on the original Waldorf-Astoria and Plaza hotels in New York City, designed this house in 1903 for businessman P. B. Moss. The mansion still contains many of the elaborate original furnishings, ranging in style from Moorish to art nouveau. Guided tours are offered on the hour. ✉ *914 Division St.* ☎ *406/256–5100* 🌐 *www.mossmansion.com* *$6* ⏲ *Jan.–May, daily 1–4; June–Dec., Mon.–Sat. 9–5, Sun. 1–4.*

13 **Peter Yegen Jr./Yellowstone County Museum.** Although there isn't enough evidence to prove it, some documents suggest that this log cabin was built in 1877 as a trading post on the Yellowstone River by frontiersman Paul McCormick before it was moved to downtown Billings in 1893. In Billings it served as a gentlemen's club for many years, frequented by the likes of Teddy Roosevelt and Buffalo Bill Cody, before it was moved again, in 1949, to its present location at the entrance to the Billings Logan International Airport. The structure today serves as a small museum that interprets Montana's frontier history. Check out the chuck wagon, barbed-wire collection, and the creepy-looking tools from the city's first dentist office. A veranda here affords unparalleled views of the Bighorn, Pryor, and Beartooth mountains more than 100 mi to the south. ✉ *1950 Terminal Circle* ☎ *406/256–6811* 🌐 *www.pyjrycm.org* *Free* ⏲ *Feb.–Dec., weekdays 10:30–5, Sat. 10:30–3.*

21 **Pictograph Cave State Monument.** Once home to thousands of prehistoric hunters, this area has yielded more than 30,000 artifacts related to early human history. A paved trail affords good views of the 2,200-year-old cave paintings depicting animals and figures; if you bring binoculars, you'll be able to appreciate better the subtle detail of the artwork. Although there are three caves in the park, only one is open to the public. ✉ *Coburn Rd. (U.S. 87)* ☎ *406/247–2940* 🌐 *www.pictographcave.org* *$5 per vehicle* ⏲ *May–Sept., daily 8–8.*

Fodor's Choice ★

12 **Rimrock Trail.** Although its various routes may look straight and boring on a map, this trail system on the northern edge of Billings is actually a pleasant mix of paved urban paths and rugged dirt tracks, where elderly locals out for a Sunday stroll are just as welcome as extreme mountain bikers. Several individual trails make up the Rimrock system, which starts at Boothill Cemetery and winds past the airport up into the rocky formations that surround the city and give the trail its name. Expect fantastic views of the open plains and five distinct mountain ranges in some places, and the whir of jet engines and the sight of oil-refinery

smokestacks in others. *Airport Rd.* *406/245–4111* *www.billingschamber.com.*

18 **Western Heritage Center.** The permanent exhibits here include oral histories, artifacts, and kid-friendly interactive displays tracing the lives of Native Americans, ranchers, homesteaders, immigrants, and railroad workers living in the area between 1880 and 1940. Native American interpretive programs and tours to local cultural sites are available in summer. The impressive castlelike building that houses the center used to be the city's library and is just as interesting as the exhibits. *2822 Montana Ave.* *406/256–6809* *www.ywhc.org* *Donations accepted* *Tues.–Sat. 10–5, Sun. 1–5.*

16 **Yellowstone Art Museum.** One of the premier art museums in a four-state region, Yellowstone displays Western and contemporary art from nationally and internationally known artists. Among the artists whose works are on permanent display are Charles M. Russell and Will James. The museum also occasionally borrows works by artists such as Monet and Rodin. *401 North 27th St.* *406/256–6804* *yellowstone.artmuseum.org* *$7* *Tues.–Wed. and Fri.–Sat. 10–5, Thurs. 10–8, Sun. noon–5.*

23 **ZooMontana.** Although it specializes in native northern-latitude temperate species, ZooMontana has plenty of exotic plants and animals, making it a favorite destination for locals and visitors alike. There's a small children's zoo with kid-friendly exhibits and displays. Because this is one of the only zoos in the region, it can be extremely busy in summer. *2100 S. Shiloh Rd.* *406/652–8100* *www.zoomontana.org* *$6* *Daily 10–4.*

Sports & the Outdoors

The Rimrocks are easily the dominant feature of Billings. These 400-foot rock walls provide a scenic backdrop for numerous recreational pursuits. One of the most popular is mountain biking, as suitable terrain for beginners, experienced thrill seekers, and everyone in between can be found within a short driving distance.

Mountain Biking

The **Bike Shop** (1934 Grand Ave. 406/652–1202), owned by a local family since the 1970s, sells, rents, and services mountain bikes. **DVS Bikes** (520 Wicks La., Suite 12 406/256–3900) specializes in BMX and freestyle bikes but also sells mountain bikes and equipment. **Scheels All Sports** (Rimrock Mall, 1233 W. 24th St. 406/656–9220 300 S. 24th St. W 406/656–9220) sells mountain and street bikes, in addition to other sporting goods. Head to the **Spoke Shop** (1910 Broadwater Ave. 406/656–8342) for street bikes, mountain bikes, and equipment.

Golf

Perhaps in an attempt to reinforce its claim as a business-dealing, commercially active big city, or perhaps to make use of the state's vast tracts of undeveloped land, Billings has more than half a dozen golf courses. Ranging from quick 9-hole executives in the middle of town to grand 18-hole country-club courses set against the Rimrocks, the golfing venues around the city are diverse in design and often have exceptional views of the surrounding country.

Circle Inn Golf Links (1029 Main St. 406/248–4202), on top of the Rimrocks in Billings Heights, is a 9-hole public course that doesn't discriminate: men and women tee off from the same spot. A creek runs along three of the holes, and there's a bunker on one hole. Just below the Rimrocks near the airport is the 18-hole **Exchange City Golf Course** (✉ 19th St. W ☎ 406/652–2553), a casual course with a winding creek and plenty of hills on the front nine. A public 18-hole course near Lake Elmo State Park in Billings Heights, the **Lake Hills Golf Club** (✉ 1930 Clubhouse Way ☎ 406/252–9244) is in a wooded area frequented by grouse, antelope, and pheasant. Its two lakes and 444-yard final hole are its most famous features. The **Peter Yegen Jr. Golf Club** (✉ 3400 Grand Ave. ☎ 406/656–8099), an 18-hole public course, is set against the walls of the Rimrocks. Although not very wooded, the course has plenty of water hazards and bunkers.

Where to Stay & Eat

$$$–$$$$ ✕ **George Henry's.** With its stained glass and tearoom-style table settings, this restaurant in an 1882 Victorian house is elegant yet surprisingly laidback. It's popular with businesspeople, who come here for lunch and dinner meetings. Favorites include steak Oscar (steak with béarnaise sauce, crab, and asparagus), roasted crispy duck, quiche, and seafood pasta. ✉ *404 N. 30th St.* ☎ *406/245–4570* ▭ *AE, D, DC, MC, V* ⊙ *Closed Sun.*

$$$–$$$$ Fodor's Choice ★ ✕ **Juliano's.** Hawaiian-born chef Carl Kurokawa has won so many culinary awards, they'd probably fill a closet. But Carl isn't about trophies and plaques—he's about food. His menu changes monthly, but past entrées have included roasted ostrich, grilled elk, spicy watermelon salad, chicken with leeks and roasted tomato, and sea bass. Inspired by Pacific and European flavors, yet distinctly American, Carl's cooking is some of the best in the state. The building, with its tin ceiling, is almost as impressive, having once been a stable for the turn-of-the-20th-century sandstone mansion next door. Lunch is fast and inexpensive. Reservations are a good idea. ✉ *2912 7th Ave. N* ☎ *406/248–6400* ▭ *AE, D, MC, V* ⊙ *Closed Sun. No dinner Mon. or Tues.*

$$–$$$$ ✕ **The Granary.** A restored flour mill houses this restaurant, which ages its own beef. Seafood is also on the menu, and the salad bar is superb. Like the outdoor seating options at most Billings restaurants, the veranda here is very popular in the summer. ✉ *1500 Poly Dr.* ☎ *406/259–3488* ▭ *AE, D, DC, MC, V* ⊙ *Closed Sun.*

★ **$$–$$$$** ✕ **The Rex.** Built in 1910 by "Buffalo Bill" Cody's chef, this restaurant was saved from the wrecking ball and restored in 1975. Today it's one of the best steak houses in the city. The dining room and bar are big and airy, enhanced by wooden beams and an almost Southwestern look, but the outdoor patio is perhaps the most popular place to dine on such dishes as roasted buffalo, prime rib, Italian beef sandwiches, jerk steak with mango chutney, and Vietnamese noodle salad. The kitchen stays open until 11 PM, making the restaurant especially popular with the after-theater crowd. ✉ *2401 Montana Ave.* ☎ *406/245–7477* ▭ *AE, D, DC, MC, V.*

$–$$$ ✕ **Enzo Bistro.** People come to this attractive chalet-style building for European specialties such as the Mediterranean meat loaf with basil, cumin, and kalamata olives, and kids' favorites such as pizzas and pastas. ✉ *1502 Rehberg La., at Grand Ave.* ☎ *406/651–0999* ▭ *AE, DC, MC, V* ⊙ *No lunch.*

$–$$ ✕ **Thai Orchid.** When chef Lex Manraksa moved from Thailand to Billings, he brought with him authentic Thai cooking, incorporating spices Montana had never seen before. His downtown eatery is now a community fixture and gets especially popular with the business crowd around lunchtime. Manraksa is especially happy to talk with Thai-food connoisseurs and then serve them some superspicy traditional dishes, although he has plenty of milder dishes reminiscent of Chinese for the uninitiated. Expect plenty of beef, chicken, and pork, but also look for entrées highlighting shrimp, oyster, and duck. ✉ *2926 2nd Ave. N* ☎ *406/256–2206* ▭ *MC, V* ⊙ *Closed Sun.*

¢–$$ ✕ **Bruno's.** On the residential west side of town, this family-style Italian restaurant sits in the shadow of the Rimrocks. The building's exterior is unremarkable, but antique pasta machines, old olive-oil cans from Italy, traditional Italian music, and utensils the owners have picked up over their decades in the restaurant business create a warm dining environment. Locals come here for the homemade pasta, but the veal, made-from-scratch meatballs, and specialty pizzas are also delicious. There's a full bar, plus a modest selection of Italian wines and beers. Olive oils and pastas are for sale at the building's entrance. ✉ *2658 Grand Ave.* ☎ *406/652–4416* ▭ *D, MC, V* ⊙ *Closed Sun. No lunch.*

¢–$$ ✕ **Pug Mahon's.** Good Irish stews, pasties, and traditional fish-and-chips are the highlights of this authentic Irish pub, which serves dozens of imported beers and whiskies. The Sunday brunch is wildly popular. Be sure to try one of the 22 varieties of omelet. ✉ *3011 1st Ave. N* ☎ *406/259–4190* ▭ *MC, V* ⊙ *No dinner Sun.*

¢–$ ✕ **The Beanery Bar and Grill.** Located in Billings's 19th-century train depot downtown, the Beanery has a large outdoor patio that's a great spot for people-watching in summer. The bar inside is contemporary, but the old-fashioned signs and period light fixtures hark back to the building's railroad past. The menu has fewer than a dozen items, and the food here is simple. Especially noteworthy are the wraps (such as fajita or Caesar wraps), which are praised by downtown business folk out for a quick lunch, and the barbecue-pork sandwich, which is legendary. ✉ *2314 Montana Ave.* ☎ *406/896–9200* ▭ *AE, MC, V* ⊙ *Closed Sun.*

¢ ✕ **Poet Street Market.** The unique sandwiches include roast beef with blue cheese, turkey with cranberry-apple compote on pumpkin bread, and artichoke hearts with white cheddar cheese on olive bread. The soups, salads, and pizzas are equally creative. It's difficult to leave without ordering dessert: catching sight of fresh concoctions such as chocolate Bavarian torte, bourbon spice cake, or sour cream pear tart is enough to make you hungry again. ✉ *905 Poly Dr.* ☎ *406/245–9501* ▭ *MC, V* ⊙ *Closed Sun.*

$$–$$$ **Sheraton Billings.** The downtown location of this high-rise is convenient, and the contemporary rooms are spacious. Some rooms overlook the mountain ranges outside the city. The hotel encloses a pleasant and large central courtyard. The pool area is big and luxurious. ✉ *27 N. 27th St., 59101* ☎ *406/252–7400* 🖷 *406/252–2401* ⊕ *www.sheraton.com* *282 rooms* *Restaurant, in-room data ports, some in-room refrigerators, cable TV with movies, indoor pool, gym, hot tub, video game room, shop, business services, meeting rooms, some pets allowed (fee)* ▭ *AE, D, DC, MC, V.*

$–$$ **Historic Northern Hotel.** A fire in 1940 destroyed this 1905 building in downtown Billings. The hotel has since been rebuilt and remodeled, but it still provides a sense of the city's past. Rooms follow an American West theme, with woven rugs and bedspreads and a gaming table. Guest-room views—of the Pryor Mountains, rolling plains, or Rimrocks—are glorious. The massive fireplace centers the comfortable lobby—a common gathering place for guests and locals. The Golden Belle serves Continental cuisine in surroundings that are fancier than usual for Montana. ✉ *19 Broadway, at 28th St., 59101* ☎ *406/245–5121 or 800/542–5121* 🖷 *406/259–9862* ⊕ *www.northernhotel.com* *160 rooms* *Restaurant, gym, bar, shop, laundry facilities, meeting rooms* ▭ *AE, D, DC, MC, V* *CP.*

$–$$ **Josephine Bed and Breakfast.** Within walking distance of downtown is this lovely historic home with five theme rooms—such as the Garden

Room, with its floral fabrics. You're welcome to relax in the guest parlor, with a piano and TV and VCR, or in the library. Breakfast is served at your convenience; afterward, you can work off your meal with a free guest pass to the local YMCA. ✉ *514 N. 29th St., 59101* ☎ *406/248–5898 or 800/552–5898* 🌐 *www.thejosephine.com* *5 rooms* *Cable TV, some in-room data ports, some in-room hot tubs; no smoking* *AE, D, MC, V* *BP.*

¢–$$ **C'mon Inn.** Five hot tubs and an indoor pool attract families to this lodging near the major roads and the interstate. Even in winter, there's a garden inside the woodsy, tropical courtyard. There are wood-burning fireplaces in the lobby. ✉ *2020 Overland Ave., 59102* ☎ *406/655–1100 or 800/655–1170* *406/652–7672* 🌐 *www.cmoninn.com* *80 rooms, 8 suites* *Some in-room hot tubs, microwaves, refrigerators, indoor pool, gym, hot tubs, video game room, Internet, meeting rooms* *AE, D, DC, MC, V* *CP.*

¢–$$ **Dude Rancher Lodge.** As you might expect from the lodge's name, a Western theme pervades this downtown institution, right down to the lantern-style light fixtures, wood paneling, and custom-made carpet "branded" with the symbols of several area ranches. Breakfast, which costs extra, is full and hearty. ✉ *415 N. 29th St., 59101* ☎ *406/259–5561 or 800/221–3302* *406/259–0095* 🌐 *www.duderancherlodge.com* *57 rooms* *Restaurant, cable TV with movies, some microwaves, some refrigerators, some pets allowed (fee)* *AE, D, DC, MC, V.*

$ **Best Western Billings.** A round-the-clock restaurant next door and proximity to I–90 make this chain hotel a good stop for last-minute or late arrivals. It's also very close to a water park, making it a favorite among guests with children. ✉ *5610 S. Frontage Rd., 59101* ☎ *406/248–9800 or 800/528–1234* *406/248–2500* 🌐 *www.bestwestern.com* *80 rooms* *Some in-room hot tubs, cable TV with movies, indoor pool, hot tubs, laundry facilities, business services, meeting rooms, some pets allowed (fee)* *AE, D, DC, MC, V* *CP.*

$ **The Carlin Hotel.** Opened in 1910 for railroad passengers, the Carlin fell into disrepair, as did much of Billings's downtown district, with the demise of rail travel. It was luxuriously restored in 2002, however, and now has suites fully furnished for extended stays (there's a minimum one-week stay). The suites, decorated almost entirely in black, white, and bright primary colors, are distinctly modern. The bathrooms are tiled, and the kitchens have dishwashers and hardwood floors. There's a restaurant and martini bar on the first floor. ✉ *2501 Montana Ave., 59101* ☎ *406/245–7515* 🌐 *www.carlinhotel.com* *8 suites* *Restaurant, microwaves, refrigerators, cable TV with movies, bar, Internet* *AE, D, MC, V.*

$ **Quality Inn Homestead.** A delightful outdoor sundeck and an indoor swim center are the main attractions here. The rooms are contemporary in design and average in size, although the two-room suites are a favorite among families. The on-site car rentals are a bonus for business travelers. A complimentary full breakfast is made to order. ✉ *2036 Overland Ave., 59102* ☎ *406/652–1320* *406/652–1320* 🌐 *www.qualityinn.com* *140 rooms, 60 suites* *Restaurant, some microwaves, some refrigerators, cable TV with movies, indoor pool, hot tub, sauna, laundry facilities, business services* *AE, D, DC, MC, V* *BP.*

¢ **Riverstone Billings Inn.** Bright white walls stand out against curtains and furniture upholstered in dark red and green tones. Because of the inn's location on Billings's medical corridor and its squeaky-clean image, many people who come to town for a hospital visit stay here. ✉ *880 N. 29th St., 59101* ☎ *406/252–6800 or 800/231–7782* *406/252–6800* 🌐 *www.billingsinn.com* *60 rooms, 3 suites* *Some microwaves, some refrigerators, cable TV, laundry facilities* *AE, D, DC, MC, V* *CP.*

Nightlife & the Arts

Nightlife

★ The **Carlin Martini Bar and Nightclub** (✉ Carlin Hotel, 2501 Montana Ave. ☎ 406/245–2503) hosts an eclectic selection of entertainment most nights, ranging from rock and blues bands to comedians and DJs. **Casey's Golden Pheasant** (✉ 222 N. Broadway ☎ 406/256–5200) combines the Old West and the 1950s: the 1870s bar is solid mahogany, but the mural on the ceiling depicts 1950s rock stars, and neon signs hang from the walls. Bands play almost every night of the week; the music varies but usually falls somewhere among rock, blues, R&B, reggae, and jazz. A young crowd gathers at **Eleven: 11** (✉ 119 N. Broadway ☎ 406/238–0011) to play pinball, air hockey, and pool. The music is almost exclusively punk rock, and modern art by regional artists decorates the walls. No alcohol is served here.

The Arts

The **Alberta Bair Theater** (✉ 2801 3rd Ave. N ☎ 406/256–6052 or 877/321–2074 🌐 www.albertabairtheater.org) presents music, theater, dance, and other cultural events. It's the home theater for the Billings Symphony Orchestra.

Something of a community art center, the **Bill McIntosh Gallery** (✉ 2507 Montana Ave. ☎ 406/252–2010) displays the work of local and regional artists in all kinds of media. The gallery also offers art classes and sells a significant selection of art supplies. From paintings and etchings to sculpture and vintage rifles, the **Meadowlark Gallery** (✉ 118 N. 29th St. ☎ 406/294–8575 or 800/727–3949) showcases all kinds of Western artwork. The owners are experts on painter-etcher Hans Kleiber, and they love to talk with interested customers. Located in a four-story art ★ deco–style downtown building, **Nicholas Fine Art** (✉ 2814 2nd Ave. N ☎ 406/256–8607) presents itself as an upscale gallery. Most of the works here are by fashionable modern artists, but the owners like to keep paintings and sculptures from the 19th and 20th centuries on hand as well. The works of modern artists living in the region are shown at the downtown **Toucan Gallery** (✉ 2505 Montana Ave. ☎ 406/252–0122). The artwork varies from traditional paintings and sculptures to painted quilts, object collages, and dolls.

Shopping

The largest shopping destination for several hundred miles, the **Rimrock Mall** (✉ 300 S. 24th St. ☎ 406/656–3398) attracts people from all over Montana, Wyoming, Canada, and the Dakotas. There are almost 90 shops here, including several large department stores, national chains, and local retailers, plus a 10-screen movie theater.

Al's Bootery and Repair Shop (✉ 1820 1st Ave. N ☎ 406/245–4827) corrals your toes into fancy cowboy boots ranging from $50 to $1,800. Billing itself as "a deli for the mind," **Barjon's Books** (✉ 2718 3rd Ave. N ☎ 406/252–4398 or 800/788–4318) sells incense, Celtic statuary, Native American medicine wheels, books on Buddhism, and more. Regular guests to the store include New Age authors and Buddhist monks. A large downtown warehouse built in 1928 has been converted into the charming **Depot Antique Mall** (✉ 2223 Montana Ave. ☎ 406/245–5955 or 877/245–5955), which sells a varied collection that includes furniture, china, branding irons, and more. Unlike many other antiques shops, this one welcomes children. **Rand's Custom Hats** (✉ 2205 1st Ave. N ☎ 406/248–7688 or 800/346–9815) creates cowboy hats for working cowboys as well as the celluloid variety and will custom-fit a felt fur hat. Prices range from $300 to $2,000. Rand's also sells leather carrying cases.

en route

Although the route will take you slightly out of the way, take I–94 on your way to Hardin and stop at **Pompey's Pillar National Historic Landmark** (✉ I–94, 25 mi east of Billings ☎ 406/875–2233), the only physical evidence of the Lewis and Clark expedition. When William Clark saw this small sandstone mesa rising out of the prairie along the Yellowstone River on July 25, 1806, he climbed to the top to survey the area and then marked it with his signature and the date. His graffiti, along with other engravings by early-19th-century fur traders and homesteaders, is still visible. The interpretive center is open only in summer, but you can climb to the top of the mesa and view the signature year-round. The landmark was heavily publicized in 2002 when it was named one of America's 11 most endangered landmarks by the National Trust for Historic Preservation. Despite the national attention and concern, four massive grain elevators and a loading terminal for trucks and railcars were built less than a mile from the site. The view from the top is still well worth the 10-minute hike, despite the industrial intrusion. To get to Hardin, continue east on I–94 for a few miles and then head south on Highway 47.

SOUTHEAST MONTANA

As with most of eastern Montana, the word to keep in mind in the state's far southeastern reaches is "big." Characterized by badlands, shallow canyons, grassy hills, and, above all, treeless plains, the land here survives on annual rainfall that just barely exceeds that of a desert. Aside from the livestock, this land belongs to ranchers and Native Americans—specifically the Crow and Northern Cheyenne, who both have reservations here. Few settlements in the region have more than 1,000 people. When you find them, residents are friendly and almost always willing to show you around town—which typically consists of their home and the general store they run next door.

Hardin

24 *50 mi east of Billings via I–90.*

With 3,334 residents, Hardin is among the largest communities in southeast Montana. Although its roots are firmly planted in cattle ranching, the town gets a huge commercial boost from visitors to the Little Bighorn Battlefield National Monument just a few miles to the south. It's also a popular base camp for people looking to explore the several state parks and national recreation areas nearby, and a nice stop for people traveling to the western part of the state from South Dakota.

The **Arapooish State Fishing Access Site,** a mile north of Hardin, is a favorite spot among locals, who pack the family up, set up in a shaded picnic area, cast a line into the Bighorn River, and have a cookout. It's also a prime bird-watching venue. ✉ *Hwy. 47* ☎ *406/232–0900* 🌐 *www.fwp.state.mt.us* 🎫 *Free* 🕑 *Apr.–Oct., daily sunrise–sunset.*

Focusing on Native American and early homestead settlement, the 24-acre **Bighorn County Historical Museum and Visitor Information Center** complex comprises 20 historic buildings that have been relocated to the site, including a one-room schoolhouse, a barn, a smithy, teepees, and a log cabin. The center also serves as an official Montana State Visitor Center. ✉ *I–90, Exit 497* ☎ *406/665–1671* 🌐 *www.museumonthebighorn.org* 🎫 *Free* 🕑 *June–Aug., daily 8–8; Sept.–May, daily 8–5.*

During the third week in August, a stretch of land along the Bighorn ★ River becomes the "teepee capital of the world" when the **Crow Fair and Rodeo,** official fair of the Crow tribe, begins north of the town of Crow Agency. The fair focuses on traditional dances and activities, and the powwow is a central part of the gathering. Sports tournaments are nearly as important, and the events, ranging from archery and horse racing to basketball and softball, inspire a healthy rivalry among the various reservation communities. ✉ *Bighorn River north of Crow Agency, 14 mi south of Hardin on I–90* ☎ *406/638–2585* 🌐 *www.crowfair.com* *Free.*

Where to Stay & Eat

¢ ✕ **Purple Cow.** This family eatery with a friendly staff is a favorite among Fodor'sChoice ★ travelers, largely because it's one of the last restaurants east of Hardin until Belle Fourche, South Dakota, more than 200 mi away. The shakes and malts here are fantastic, as are the burgers and steaks. Chicken and simple salads are also on the menu. Portions are generous, so you might want to consider splitting some items, such as the delectable BLT. ✉ *I–90, Exit 495* ☎ *406/665–3601* ▭ *MC, V.*

¢–$$ **American Inn.** The massive waterslide that towers above the outdoor pool is the most noticeable feature of this lodging off I–90. Tans, browns, and dark reds decorate the guest rooms, differentiating the decor from the sterile whites and pastels of most chain hotels. ✉ *1324 N. Crawford Ave., 59034* ☎ *406/665–1870* 📠 *406/665–1615* *42 rooms* *Restaurant, some in-room hot tubs, some in-room refrigerators, cable TV, pool, hot tub, bar, laundry facilities, meeting rooms, some pets allowed (fee)* ▭ *AE, D, MC, V.*

★ ¢ **Hotel Becker Bed and Breakfast.** Built in 1908 for railroad passengers, this three-story brick hotel with yellow awnings is on the National Register of Historic Places. Depression-era items, such as handmade quilts, decorate the rooms. Owner Mary Slattery, a Hardin native, is more than happy to direct you to local points of interest—or, at the very least, to the chamber of commerce across the street in the old train depot. You can use the phone and TV in the living room, since the guest rooms don't have these amenities. ✉ *200 N. Center St., 59034* ☎ *406/665–2707* *7 rooms, 5 with bath* *Meeting room; no room phones, no room TVs* ▭ *No credit cards* *CP.*

CAMPING **Grandview Campground.** Cable TV, a copy machine, nightly ice-cream socials, movie rentals, and regular book swaps are some of the amenities available at this full-service campground on the edge of town, in the narrow corridor between downtown Hardin and I–90. The Hardin Community Activity Center is right next door, giving you access to an Olympic-size indoor pool and fitness facilities. The owner is a font of knowledge on Hardin and takes great pride in the community. The Grandview is open year-round, but only a few electric sites are available in winter. *Flush toilets, full hookups, dump station, drinking water, laundry facilities, showers, picnic tables, electricity, public telephone, play area, indoor pool* *50 full hookups, 30 tent sites* ✉ *1002 N. Mitchell* ☎ *406/665–2489 or 800/622–9890* 🌐 *www.grandviewcamp.com* *Full hookups $24.50, tent sites $13.50* ▭ *MC, V.*

Little Bighorn Battlefield National Monument

25 *17 mi south of Hardin via I–90.*

When the smoke cleared on June 25, 1876, neither Lieutenant Colonel George Armstrong Custer (1839–76) nor his 200 or so blue-shirted troopers were alive to tell the story of their battle against several thousand Northern Plains warriors, led by the likes of Sitting Bull (circa

1831–90) and Crazy Horse (1842–77), on this windswept prairie along the Little Bighorn River. It was a Pyrrhic victory for the tribes; the loss pushed the U.S. government to redouble its efforts to clear them off the plains. Now the Little Bighorn Battlefield, on the Crow Indian Reservation, has memorials to the warriors who took part in the conflict and an interpretive center. The land remains largely undeveloped. Note that there are rattlesnakes around the area, and also beware of touching the flesh-piercing yucca plants. ✉ *Battlefield Rd.* ☎ *406/638–3224* 🌐 *www.nps.gov/libi* 🎟 *$10 per vehicle* ⏲ *May–Aug., daily 8–9; Sept.–Apr., daily 8–4:30.*

The interpretive exhibits at the **Little Bighorn Battlefield Visitor Center** explain the events that led to and resulted from the battle, as well as the deeper issues regarding the historical conflict between white and Native American culture. You also can sign up for guided tours here, and perhaps listen to one of the special interpretive talks. ✉ *Battlefield Rd.* ☎ *406/638–3224* ⏲ *Late May–Aug., daily 8–8; Sept., daily 8–6; Oct.–Mar., daily 8–4:30.*

The old stone superintendent's house is now the **White Swan Memorial Library,** which has one of the most extensive collections of research material on the Battle of the Little Bighorn. You can view the material by appointment only; contact the visitor center for more information.

Among those interred at **Custer National Cemetery,** near the visitor center, are Custer's second-in-command, Marcus Reno; some of Custer's Native American scouts; and soldiers originally buried at frontier military posts that were abandoned as the West became settled. There are many soldiers from more modern wars buried here as well, from World Wars I and II to Korea and Vietnam. Note that you can visit the cemetery without having to pay the normal park entrance fee of $10.

For more than 120 years—until the opening of the Indian Memorial in 2003—the only memorial to those killed in the battle was the towering obelisk of the **7th Cavalry Monument.** The hike to the monument, at the top of Last Stand Hill, isn't difficult, but it can seem long on the inevitable scorching days of summer. Although the hill isn't particularly tall, it affords a good overall view of the battlefield site.

★ Until the **Indian Memorial** was unveiled in 2003, the only monument at the battlefield paid tribute to the immediate losers. Although they are meant to honor Native Americans who died on both sides (Custer had a few Crow and Arikara scouts), the three bronze riders of the memorial represent the united forces of the Lakota Sioux, Northern Cheyenne, and Arapahoe, who defeated the government troops. The wooden posts off to the side form a "spirit gate" welcoming the dead riders. The text, images, and pictographs are accounts of the battle from the perspective of the three united tribes.

Scattered around the battlefield are short white **markers** indicating the places where soldiers died. Although the markers may look like graves, the actual bodies are interred elsewhere, including that of Custer, whose remains rest at the military academy at West Point. One marker belongs to Custer's younger brother, Thomas, the most decorated soldier of the Civil War. Only three markers represent Native American warriors, in part because no one knows exactly where they fell: the Native American survivors buried their dead immediately after the battle in traditional fashion.

After Custer's defeat, two of his officers held their ground against the Native American forces at **Reno-Benteen Battlefield.** The seven companies lost only 53 men during the two-day siege, although more soldiers might have shared Custer's fate had the advance of several thousand fresh troops not caused the Native Americans to break camp and flee the region. The site is a 5-mi drive southeast along Battlefield Road.

off the beaten path

CHIEF TWO MOON MONUMENT – Although Lakota leaders Crazy Horse and Sitting Bull are the most well-known Native Americans associated with the Battle of the Little Bighorn, Cheyenne chief Two Moon was just as well respected among his people. The owner of the general store (and one of the only residents) in the nearby town of Busby became acquainted with the young and friendly chief and built a monument to him in the 1930s. A likeness of the chief, who served as the model for the head side of the buffalo nickel, adorns the memorial. ✉ *U.S. 212, 25 mi east of Crow Agency, Busby.*

ROSEBUD BATTLEFIELD STATE PARK – Eight days before Custer's defeat, 1,500 Lakota Sioux and Northern Cheyenne warriors met 1,000 troops under the command of General George Sherman along Rosebud Creek, 35 mi southeast of what would soon become the Little Bighorn Battlefield. For six hours the armies fought up and down a 10-square-mi patch of land. When the dust had cleared, neither side could claim victory. The very lack of a victor was enough proof for some that the Native Americans had become a dangerous fighting force. An officer with the Third Cavalry present at the battle later wrote that the Lakota "were the best cavalry soldiers on earth." A local rancher saved 3,000 acres of the battlefield from coal developers, and the area is now a state park. The land remains much the way it did in 1876, so enjoy the peaceful emptiness—and watch out for rattlesnakes. ✉ *25 mi east of Crow Agency on U.S. 212, 20 mi south on Hwy. 314, 3 mi west on county road* ☎ *406/232–0900* 🌐 *www.fwp.state.mt.us/parks/* 🎫 *Free* 🕒 *Daily, 24 hrs.*

Where to Eat

¢–$ ✕ **Custer Battlefield Trading Post and Cafe.** With its stock of T-shirts, inexpensive jewelry, and dreamcatchers, the trading post is touristy, but the small attached restaurant is a bit more respectable—as evidenced by the locals who regularly congregate here. Steak is the dish of choice, and there are no fewer than three ways to get it on a sandwich. The several variations of Indian taco made by the Crow cooks are especially popular. If tacos aren't your style, try a buffalo burger. ✉ *I–90 at U.S. 212* ☎ *406/638–2270* 💳 *D, MC, V.*

en route

North of Bighorn Canyon is the tiny settlement where Father Prando, a Jesuit missionary, founded the **St. Xavier Mission** (✉ Mission Ave. ☎ 406/784–4500) in 1887. This was the first mission for the Crow tribe and, as such, offered the people their first primary school. Although the town is barely inhabited, the church and school are still in use and may be visited. Now called Pretty Eagle School, after a Crow chief, the school provides a free primary and secondary education for 120 students from homes as far as 45 mi away.

Bighorn Canyon National Recreation Area

㉖ *40 mi southwest of Little Bighorn Battlefield National Monument via I–90 and Hwy. 313.*

Geological upheaval combined with natural forces of wind and water carved Bighorn Canyon, with steep walls too rugged for easy access.

Although early people in the area traveled and lived near the canyon, they spent little or no time on the river until the Yellowtail Dam was built. The post–World War II growth in population in America created a huge increase in demand for water and electricity. For the West, where an arid climate and mountainous terrain are conditions unsuitable for natural lakes, this translated into dams. Few rivers were left untouched by the Army Corps of Engineers, and the Bighorn River was no exception. Yellowtail Dam was completed in the 1960s, and shortly thereafter Congress declared the land around the 60-mi-long lake a national recreation area. The park, which stretches well into Wyoming between the Pryor and Bighorn mountains, is now a favorite destination for boaters, anglers, and people who come to admire the breathtaking views from the hills and cliffs above the lake. Note that the only way within the park to get directly from the northern unit, in Montana, to the southern unit, much of which is in Wyoming, is by boat—which is indeed how most people visit the park—so plan your trip well. Most of the major sights in the recreation area are accessible by boat, but you can also reach them by driving north from Wyoming on Highway 37. If you're visiting from Wyoming, Lovell makes a good base for exploring the area. ☎ *307/548–7326 or 406/666–2412* 🌐 *www.nps.gov/bical* 🎟 *$5 per vehicle* ⏲ *Daily, 24 hrs.*

The **Yellowtail Dam Visitor Center** in the northern unit is the starting point for guided tours of the dam named after a famous Crow chief. Note that the dam tour requires you to ascend three flights of short stairs. Exhibits within the center focus on the dam's construction, Chief Robert Yellowtail's life, the Crow people, the history of the Bighorn River, and the wildlife in the area. ✉ *Hwy. 313, Fort Smith* ☎ *406/666–3218* 🌐 *www.nps.gov/bical* 🎟 *Included in $5 admission to recreation area* ⏲ *Memorial Day–Labor Day, daily 9–5.*

The old **Hillsboro Dude Ranch** complex is probably the most well known and easiest to reach of the four ranch ruins within the recreation area. There are old log cabins, cellars, chicken coops, and other buildings that belonged to Grosvener W. Barry, one of the area's more colorful characters in the early 20th century. Barry attempted three gold-mining ventures, all of which failed, before opening a dude ranch here. Later on he attempted to turn the ranch into a town, built a post office, and had himself proclaimed postmaster in 1915. He died five years later. The town never really took off, however, and was completely abandoned during World War II. ✉ *Hwy. 37* 🌐 *www.nps.gov/bical* 🎟 *Included in $5 admission to recreation area.*

When Spanish explorers introduced horses to the Americas, certain animals inevitably escaped, wildly roaming the land and populating the two continents ahead of the settlers who would come centuries later. Some of the last descendants of these wild breeds can be seen in the **Pryor Mountain Wild Horse Range,** the first nationally designated refuge for the wild animals. Some 200 horses, generally broken into small family groupings, roam these arid slopes with bighorn sheep, elk, deer, and mountain lions. Coat variations such as grulla, blue roan, dun, and sabino indicate Spanish lineage, as do markings such as dorsal stripes, zebra stripes on the legs, and a stripe on the withers. The best way to view the herds is simply to drive along Highway 37 and look out your window. From the northern unit you'll have to reach the refuge by boat, or you can head to the town of Pryor (on the Crow Reservation in Montana) in a four-wheel-drive vehicle and take a gravel road through the range; the road eventually hooks back up with Highway 37 across the border in Wyoming. A road system circles the refuge, but, again, a four-

Fodor'sChoice ★

wheel-drive vehicle is necessary. ✉ *Hwy. 37* 🎫 *Included in $5 admission to recreation area.*

★ **Devil's Canyon Overlook,** a few miles north of the Wyoming border, affords breathtaking views of the point where narrow Devil's Canyon joins the sheer rock walls of Bighorn Canyon. The overlook itself is on a cliff 1,000 feet above the lake. Look for fossils in the colorful rock layers of the canyon walls. ✉ *Hwy. 37* 🌐 *www.nps.gov/bica/* 🎫 *Included in $5 admission to recreation area.*

The **Crooked Creek Ranger Station,** past the south entrance of the park in Wyoming, houses exhibits on four historic ranches located within the recreation area. A small shop sells books related to the history and geology of the area. ✉ *Hwy. 37* ☎ *307/548–7326* 🌐 *www.nps.gov/bica/* 🎫 *Included in $5 admission to recreation area* 🕒 *Daily; hrs vary by season.*

The main visitor center for the park, the **Bighorn Canyon Visitor Center** has geological and historical exhibits on the area, as well as a film about the canyon. Two shorter movies, one on the Pryor Mountain wild horses and the other about Medicine Wheel National Historic Landmark (east of Lovell), are shown on request. A small store sells books and other items related to the area. The center is in the town of Lovell, Wyoming, about 11 mi southwest of the recreation area's south entrance. ✉ *U.S. 310 at U.S. 14A, Lovell* ☎ *307/548–2251* 🌐 *www.nps.gov/bica/* 🎫 *Free* 🕒 *Memorial Day–Labor Day, daily 8–6; Labor Day–Memorial Day, daily 8–5.*

off the beaten path

CHIEF PLENTY COUPS STATE PARK – Although many Plains Indian tribes, notably the Cheyenne and Lakota Sioux, opposed the intrusion of whites into their lands, the Crow did not. Hoping that U.S. troops would keep the rival Cheyenne and Lakota off their lands, the Crow allied themselves with the U.S. government. Ultimately, the army protected Crow territory from the other tribes—but only so it could be settled by whites. Despite the betrayal, the last traditional chief of the Crow, Plenty Coups, strongly encouraged his people to adopt modern ways and cooperate with the U.S. government. At his request, his home and general store in the town of Pryor were preserved as a state park after his death. Note the blending of modern and traditional ways, such as the room of honor in the rear of his log home, meant to parallel the place of honor along the back wall of a teepee. The guides here are especially interested in helping children understand the site. ✉ *1 mi west of Pryor on county road, Pryor* ☎ *406/252–1289* 🌐 *www.fwp.state.mt.us/parks/* 🎫 *$2* 🕒 *May–Sept., daily 8–8.*

Sports & the Outdoors

When the Lewis and Clark expedition and fur traders encountered the Bighorn River, they avoided it at all costs. The narrow river, high canyon walls, and sharp rocks were dangerous. With the construction of the Yellowtail Dam in the 1960s, however, the water levels in the canyon rose dramatically, eliminating most rocky obstacles and creating new access points to the now tamed river. It wasn't long before boaters answered the call of the new lake that was created, which varies from wide basins to narrow passages through the canyon walls. The fishing here—for largemouth bass, rainbow and brown trout, walleye, yellow perch, and more—is excellent, both above and below the dam, although many come simply to rest on the water and enjoy the calm winds and pleasant views. An extended drought impaired both activities, however, when the lake's marinas and boat launches shut down in 2001 because of low water levels. The marinas reopened in summer 2003, but fishing and boating will likely be affected for several more years.

Because canyon walls create sharp turns and bottlenecks in the lake, there are some boating speed limits.

Boats can be docked or rented in the northern unit of the park at **Ok-A-Beh Marina** (✉ off Hwy. 313, on the north end of the lake ☎ 406/665–2216). The facilities here aren't luxurious, but you'll find a meager eatery, a few groceries, tackle, a swimming area, and reasonable rates.

One of the most popular boat launches in the southern unit is **Barry's Landing** (✉ Hwy. 37 ☎ No phone). There isn't much here—not even electricity—but the scenic campground, shaded picnic area, and central location in the canyon make it a favorite among the lake's more frequent guests. Many boats in the southern unit are based at **Horseshoe Bend Marina** (✉ Hwy. 37 ☎ 307/548–7230), which has boat rentals, a beach, a small general store, a modest restaurant, and the largest campground in the park. A nearby buildup of silt by the Shoshone and Bighorn rivers has made boat launching here a tricky business, and the facilities may one day move farther up the lakeshore.

Camping

Black Canyon Campground. This campground, about 5 mi south of the Ok-A-Beh Marina, up the small Black Canyon Creek, is accessible only by boat, and only during high water. Hiking in is impossible, both because of the terrain and because the private property that surrounds it is within Crow national boundaries. It's very primitive, but the isolation is unmatched. *Pit toilets, bear boxes, fire pits, picnic tables, swimming (lake) 17 sites ✉ Black Canyon Creek ☎ 406/666–3218 www.nps.gov/bica/ Included in $5 admission to recreation area Reservations not accepted.*

Horseshoe Bend Campground. The proximity to the marina in the southern unit makes this, the largest campground in the park, especially popular, although never very busy. It's open all year for tent and RV camping, but most services are unavailable in winter. *Flush toilets, dump station, drinking water, fire pits, food service, picnic tables, electricity, public telephone, general store, swimming (lake) 54 sites ✉ Hwy. 37 ☎ 307/548–7230 www.nps.gov/bica/ Included in $5 admission to recreation area Reservations not accepted.*

Medicine Creek Campground. The best way to get to this campground in the southern unit is by boat, although it's possible to hike in. Just north of Barry's Landing, this isolated site offers a good central location without the summer bustle of some other camping spots. *Pit toilets, grills, picnic tables, swimming (lake) 6 sites ✉ Medicine Creek ☎ 307/548–2251 www.nps.gov/bica/ Included in $5 admission to recreation area Reservations not accepted.*

Miles City

27 *160 mi northeast of Bighorn Canyon National Recreation Area via Hwy. 313 and I–94.*

The ranch town of Miles City (population 8,487), at the confluence of the cottonwood-lined Tongue and Yellowstone rivers, holds an attraction for history buffs. The federal Fort Laramie Treaty of 1868 stated that this area would be "Indian country as long as the grass is green and the sky is blue." The government reneged on its promise, however, when gold was found in the Black Hills of South Dakota to the southeast six years later, and white settlers streamed into this part of the world. This in turn led to the Battle of the Little Bighorn, which led to the construction of a new army post less than 2 mi from where Miles City would be founded. In time the ranchers took over, and in 1884, the last of the great herds of bison was slaughtered near here to make room for cattle. Ranching has been a way of life ever since.

★ During the third weekend in May, Miles City holds the **Bucking Horse Sale,** a three-day event with a rodeo and a giant block party. Rodeo-stock contractors come from all over the country to buy the spirited horses sold here. ✉ *Fairground Rd. at Main St.* ☎ *406/232–2890 or 877/632–2890* 🌐 *www.buckinghorsesale.com* 🎟 *$8.*

★ Although the holding tanks of an old water-treatment plant don't seem like the best location for fine art, the **Custer County Art Museum,** in the town's 1910 wastewater facility overlooking the Yellowstone River, is actually very attractive. The permanent exhibit reflects the town's Western heritage; the traveling shows that come here are usually a bit more varied. ✉ *Water Plant Rd.* ☎ *406/232–0635* 🌐 *www.ccac.milescity.org* 🎟 *Free* 🕒 *Feb.–Dec., Tues.–Sun. 9–5.*

The **Range Riders Museum,** built on the site of the 1877 Fort Keogh, is jammed to the rafters with saddles, chaps, spurs, guns, and other frontier artifacts. Some of the nine museum buildings of this complex were once part of the fort, which was abandoned in the 1920s after being used as a remount station during World War I. ✉ *Old Hwy. 10, across the Tongue River Bridge on west end of Main St., Exit 135 off I–94* ☎ *406/232–4483 or 406/232–6146* 🌐 *www.mcchamber.com/artmuseums.htm* 🎟 *$3.50* 🕒 *Apr.–Oct., daily 8–6.*

Pirogue Island State Park, a 269-acre chunk of land in the middle of the Yellowstone River, is completely undeveloped; the only way to access the park is by floating down the river or fording with a vehicle in low water. The cottonwood trees are an excellent habitat for waterfowl, raptors, and deer, and the geology of the area has made it prime agate-hunting ground. ✉ *1 mi north of Miles City on Hwy. 59, 2 mi east on Kinsey Rd., then 2 mi south on county road* ☎ *406/232–0900* 🌐 *www.fwp.state.mt.us/parks/* 🎟 *Free* 🕒 *Daily 5–10.*

More than 50,000 acres of the old 60,000-acre army post south of town belong to the **Fort Keogh Livestock and Range Research Laboratory,** administered by the U.S. Department of Agriculture and Montana State University. The facility conducts research on range ecology, beef-cattle genetics, range-animal nutrition, and livestock reproduction. There are no facilities specifically for the public, but if you're interested in science research, call ahead and try to arrange a tour with some of the scientists and ranchers who work here. ✉ *243 Fort Keough Rd.* ☎ *406/232–8200* 🌐 *larrl.ars.usda.gov.*

Where to Stay & Eat

¢–$$ ✕ **Mama Stella's Pizza.** You can always opt for pepperoni and a traditional red marinara sauce for your pizza, but you may want to try one of Mama Stella's imaginative creations, such as pizza topped with white Alfredo sauce. Unusual toppings include broccoli, sauerkraut, and asparagus. There are also several sandwiches, including the signature "paco," a thick tortilla stuffed with spicy taco goodies. Mama delivers and stays open until midnight on weekends—no small accomplishment in a town with fewer than 9,000 residents. It's in a bar and comedy club. ✉ *607 Main St.* ☎ *406/234–2922* 💳 *V.*

¢–$ 🏨 **Best Western War Bonnet Inn.** The two-room family suites and free admission to a nearby fitness facility make this chain hotel stand out. It's on the edge of town near I–94. ✉ *1015 S. Haynes Ave., 59301* ☎ *406/232–4560* 📠 *406/232–0363* 🌐 *www.bestwestern.com* 🛏 *51 rooms, 3* *suites* ♿ *Cable TV with movies, indoor pool, hot tub, laundry facilities, business services* ▭ *AE, D, DC, MC, V* 🍽 *CP.*

Nightlife & the Arts

NIGHTLIFE The downtown **Trail's Inn Bar and Comedy Club** (✉ 607 Main St. ☎ 406/234–2922) draws regional and national comedy acts. Mama Stella's Pizza restaurant is also here.

THE ARTS A pair of local artists (and part-time environmentalists) use scrap metal to create sculpture, furniture, and household items at the **Jabberwocky Studio** (✉ 811 S. Earling Ave. ☎ 406/232–2785). The **Wool House Gallery** (✉ 419 N. 7th St. ☎ 406/232–0769), located in a 1909 railroad building, showcases the work of Alice Walden, a talented local who does most of her work in painted steel. Her innovative pieces range from historical Western characters and animals to ornate birdbaths and benches. She also displays a few oil paintings.

Shopping

★ The craftspeople at **Miles City Saddlery** (✉ 808 Main St. ☎ 406/232–2512), in business since 1909, custom-design saddles of legendary quality. They also craft saddlebags, holsters, and other leather goods.

Ekalaka

28 *100 mi southeast of Miles City via U.S. 12, Ismay South Rd., and Miles City Cutoff.*

This isolated settlement of fewer than 500 people was named for a descendant of Sioux chief Sitting Bull, Ijkalaka, which means "swift one." But the name has little to do with the town's first raison d'être, namely parching the thirst of wanderers and drifters. The story of the town's founding, immortalized in legend, helps explain its location in the middle of nowhere. Buffalo hunter Claude Carter, journeying to build a saloon along the railroad tracks in Montana Territory, was driving his load full of logs when his wagon got stuck—or his horses refused to budge, depending on whom you ask—near the border with the Dakota Territory in the late 19th century. Claude looked around and spat, "Hell, anywhere in Montana is a good place for a saloon." Decades later Claude was still bartending at the Old Stand Saloon, which was now at the center of town. The original saloon has long since been torn down, but another saloon in town bears the same name.

★ Today Ekalaka is known for its county museum—the first in Montana and one of the most significant in the country. The collections at the **Carter County Museum** include fossils—and lots of them. More than 70 million years ago, this part of southeast Montana was marshland at the edge of a retreating sea. The marshes were prime habitat for many large dinosaurs, including tyrannosaurs and anatosaurs (duck-billed dinosaurs). Some complete skeletons have been unearthed in the area and are on display, along with skulls, smaller fossils, artifacts from early Native Americans, and tools used by the white settlers of Carter County. ✉ *100 Main St.* ☎ *406/775–6886* 🎟 *Free* ⏲ *Tues.–Fri. 9–5, weekends 1–5.*

★ Wind and water carved holes in the sandstone pillars north of Ekalaka, creating an eerie and barren landscape. Embracing the terrain's mystery, Native Americans used the site for rituals to conjure spirits centuries ago. Teddy Roosevelt was struck by the area's unique beauty when he visited in the late 19th century. In 1957 the area was designated **Medicine Rocks State Park.** The 320-acre park is largely undeveloped; aside from a few picnic tables, a short hiking trail, and a handful of unmarked campsites, the land is exactly how it was when Native Americans first performed their ceremonies here. ✉ *Hwy. 7* ☎ *406/232–0900* 🌐 *www.fwp.state.mt.us/parks/* 🎟 *Free* ⏲ *Daily, 24 hrs.*

off the beaten path

CUSTER NATIONAL FOREST, SIOUX RANGER DISTRICT – The name of these expansive federal lands is misleading: it should really be "Custer National Forests." Composed of dozens of discrete tracts dotting the land from Red Lodge (60 mi southwest of Billings, near Yellowstone National Park) all the way into South Dakota, Custer National Forest is one of the most ecologically diverse federally managed lands. The units in southeast Montana are called the Ekalaka Hills, and like their nearby neighbors in South Dakota, these pine-covered bluffs and mesas are often referred to as "an island of green in a sea of prairie," for good reason. Visible from miles away, the tiny forested ridges appear like mountains in the middle of the grassy plains. But when you finally reach them in a car, you barely have time to admire their short white cliffs and gnarled trees before they have passed, and soon they're nothing but a silhouette in the rearview mirror. Deer and turkey fill the woods, and many species of raptor are known to nest here. The area is completely undeveloped and offers no services. ✉ *11 mi southeast of Eklaka on Hwy. 323* ☎ *605/797–4432* 🌐 *www.fs.fed.us/r1/custer/.*

Where to Stay & Eat

¢–$$ ✕ **Deb's Coffee Shop.** This small downtown establishment has daily soup and sandwich specials for incredibly low prices. The food, although simple, is hearty and home-style. The pizzas are massive, and they can be delivered. Wash down your meal with a smoothie or a chai. ✉ *Main St.* ☎ *406/775–8718* 💳 *No credit cards* ⏲ *Closed weekends.*

CAMPING ⛺ **Medicine Rocks Campground.** Although these campsites are primitive—they aren't even marked—the weathered rocks here make an incredible backdrop for a night sleeping under the stars. And stars there will be; a benefit of the park's remote location is the absence of city lights to detract from the celestial gems. 👍 *Pit toilets, drinking water, grills, picnic tables* 🚐 *12 sites* ✉ *Off Hwy. 7* ☎ *406/232–0900* 🌐 *www.fwp.state.mt.us/parks/* 🎟 *Free* ✍ *Reservations not accepted.*

THE BIG OPEN

A great triangle bounded by the Yellowstone River to the south, the Missouri River to the north, and U.S. 87 to the west, the Big Open comprises nearly 10% of the state of Montana. Its residents, however, make up less than 1% of the state's total population, and the number is shrinking. This is a region with barely 1,000 people between the two largest towns (Jordan, with 364 residents, and Circle, with 644), where the livestock outnumbers the people a hundred to one, and where the tumbleweeds once clogged a highway so badly one winter that the state had to send out snowplows to clear the way. A visit here means forsaking resorts, fancy restaurants, and shopping centers, but the reward is wild grasslands, stark badlands, unhindered skylines, and spectacular sunsets—all of which you can enjoy without the rumble of jetliners, the roar of traffic, or the ringing of cell phones.

Makoshika State Park

★ 29 *115 mi north of Ekalaka via Hwy. 7, I–94, and N. Merrill Ave.*

Named after the Lakota word for "bad land," Makoshika State Park encompasses more than 11,000 acres of Montana's badlands, distinct rock formations also found in Wyoming and the Dakotas. The bare rock walls and mesas of the park create an eerie moonscape that is only occasionally broken by a crooked pine or juniper tree warped by the hard rock and lack of water. Practically a desert, the badlands are excellent fossil grounds, and the remains of tyrannosaurs and triceratops have been found here. Because it's south of the Yellowstone River, near the ranching town of Glendive (population 4,729), Makoshika is technically outside the boundaries of the Big Open. However, many people equate the barren rocks and empty sky of the park with the Big Open's dry and unpeopled plains, and Makoshika is usually considered part of the region. ⊠ *Makoshika State Park Rd.* ☎ *406/377–6256* 🌐 *www.fwp.state.mt.us/parks/* *$5 per vehicle* ⏲ *Daily, 24 hrs.*

At the entrance of the park is the small **Visitor Information Center,** with information on the history and geology of the park. There are also a few fossils on display, including a triceratops skull. ☎ *406/377–6256* ⏲ *Daily 9–5.*

Interpretive signs explain the geology of the rock layers visible on the ½-mi loop of the **Cap Rock Nature Trail,** which beings on Cains Coulee Road, a few miles from the park entrance. The trail affords excellent views of a natural rock bridge. Beginning at the campground, the 1½-mi **Diane Gabriel Trail** loops through both badlands and prairie terrain. At the halfway point a duck-billed-dinosaur fossil is embedded in a cliff. The ½-mi **Kinney Coulee Trail** starts about 4 mi south of the park entrance and leads 300 feet down a canyon. The terrain here is a bit more forested than elsewhere in the park, but the rock formations are the real stars.

Where to Stay

¢–$ **Charley Montana Bed & Breakfast.** Built by ranching mogul Charles Krug in 1907, this solid brick home appears like a fortress compared with its stick-built Victorian contemporaries. Indeed, with more than 25 rooms and 8,000 square feet, this place sometimes seems more like a castle than a B&B. The interior is decidedly soft, however, and much of the Krug family's period furniture is still in use. The local owners are more than happy to help you plan your itinerary. ⊠ *103 N. Douglas, Glendive 59330* ☎ *888/395–3207* 🌐 *charley-montana.com* *5 rooms* *Dining room, library; no room phones, no room TVs, no smoking* *AE, D, MC, V* *BP.*

CAMPING **Makoshika State Park Campground.** This small campground doesn't offer much in the way of amenities, but the views of the surrounding sheer cliffs and stone bluffs are incredible. There's a Frisbee-golf course nearby. Some facilities are at the nearby visitor center. *Flush toilets, drinking water, fire pits, grills, picnic tables, electricity, public telephone, ranger station* *22 sites* ⊠ *Makoshika State Park Rd.* ☎ *406/377–6256* 🌐 *www.fwp.state.mt.us/parks/* *$12* *No credit cards.*

Circle

30 *55 mi northwest of Makoshika State Park via Hwy. 200.*

Circle, the seat of McCone County and a community of barely 600 residents, is named after one of the great open-range cattle operations in the state, headquartered less than a mile from here. The town is best known for its county museum. The spacious facility houses the settlement's entire collection of history, from the age of the dinosaurs to modern ranching. Circle is also a good base for people planning to spend a day at nearby Fort Peck or the Charles M. Russell National Wildlife Refuge, both only a short drive away.

With more than 6,400 square feet of exhibit space, the **McCone County Museum** interprets the entire history of the local region, displaying everything from dinosaur and prehistoric plant fossils to sheep-ranching equipment and printing presses. Don't miss the blacksmith's shop and the lonely sheepherder's bunkhouse, and be sure to go behind the main building and walk through the old church, school, homestead house, small railroad station, and vintage caboose. *801 1st Ave. S* *406/485–2414* *www.circle.visitmt.com/museum.htm* *$3* *Weekdays 9–5.*

The only way that the small, redbrick **St. Francis Xavier Catholic Church,** built in 1954, can continue to operate today is by rotating visiting priests with two other churches in the nearby towns of Jordan and Richey. There is still daily mass and regular Sunday services at 11:30 AM. *1100 C Ave.* *406/485–3520* *www.frleo.org/circle/* *Daily, hrs vary.*

Where to Stay

$$$$ **Wolff Farms Vacation Home.** This family farming and ranching operation outside of Circle takes in only one group at a time, because it has only two guest rooms. This allows the family to cater exclusively to your needs, arranging everything from fishing trips and horseback-riding lessons to picnicking and sightseeing—all of which are included in the lodging price. On request and for an additional fee, they can also arrange boat rentals and tee times at a nearby golf course. Family antiques decorate the simple rooms. The home-cooked meals are hearty. *1073 North Rd., 59215* *406/485–2633 or 406/485–3523* *406/485–2736* *www.midrivers.com/~ajw1/* *2 rooms* *Some pets allowed; no room phones, no room TVs, no smoking* *No credit cards* *FAP.*

en route

The drive from Circle to Fort Peck will take you along the Hi-Line, otherwise known as U.S. 2, for a few miles through the **Fort Peck Indian Reservation** (U.S. 2 406/768–5155). Like most of Montana, much of the land here is empty; at nearly 2 million acres, the reservation is home to only 6,800 tribal members. However, the reservation does have a bustling industrial center, a community college, and a tribal cultural center and museum in Poplar. The diversity of the reservation is somewhat unusual: three bands of the Nakota Sioux and two bands of the Assiniboine live here. Two of the most important towns are Poplar and Wolf Point, both on U.S. 2.

Fort Peck

31 *100 mi northwest of Circle via Hwy. 13, U.S. 2, and Hwy. 117.*

In the middle of the Great Depression, the West was in poor condition, and desperate families in Montana struggled against drought and unemployment. President Franklin Roosevelt's answer was the New Deal, and among the largest New Deal projects was the Missouri River's Fort Peck Dam. In modern times, the environmental wisdom of Fort Peck and other dams that now tame the Mighty Mo has been called into question, but at the time, job-thirsty (and just plain thirsty) Montanans put up little resistance. Constructing the 250-foot-high, 4-mi-long dam required seven years and scores of workers, many of whom settled in the new government-built town, aptly named Fort Peck. Some built their own settlements nearby, with names like New Deal, Square Deal, and Wheeler. But when the dam was finished and work dried up by 1940, so did the settlements. Fort Peck itself is nearly a ghost town today, with 240 residents.

When the mayor of the nearby town of Glasgow learned of the government's plans to build what would become the largest dam on the Missouri, he was aghast. "Hell," he said, "a dam like that might cost a million dollars." In fact, it cost $156 million. Part of the money was used to build the **Fort Peck Visitor Center and Museum,** in the lobby of Power Plant No. 1, northeast of town. Interpretive displays recount the history and significance of the dam's construction, along with the larger history of the area. There are also some dinosaur fossils on display, including a triceratops skull. Guided tours of the dam and its power plants depart from here. ✉ *Lower Yellowstone Rd.* ☎ *406/526–3431 or 406/526–3421* 🌐 *www.nwo.usace.army.mil* 🎫 *Free* ⏲ *Memorial Day–Labor Day, daily 9–5.*

Nearly 11,000 workers gathered at Fort Peck during the peak construction of the dam; together with their families, they made up a thriving population center of 50,000. Government administrators saw a need to keep the populace entertained and in 1934 had the Army Corps of Engineers build what is now the **Fort Peck Summer Theater.** Initially a movie house, it was supposed to be a temporary structure. However, the chalet-style building was constructed so well that it stands today and continues to be a venue for live entertainment weekend nights in summer. ✉ *110 5th St.* ☎ *406/228–9219* 🎫 *$12* ⏲ *June–Aug., Fri.–Sun. 7–midnight.*

Sports & the Outdoors

Stretching 134 mi across the border between the Big Open and the Hi-Line, Fort Peck Lake is a prime destination for outdoor-adventure seekers. Fishing is especially popular here. Walleye are likely the lake's most well-known fish, but other species include northern pike, trout, perch, and salmon. Outfitters are hard to come by, so be sure to get most of your supplies before coming here. The lake is the venue for the annual **Governor's Cup Walleye Tournament** (☎ 406/228–2222) in July.

The **Fort Peck Dredge Cuts** (✉ Hwy. 117 ☎ no phone), also known as the Fort Peck Trout Pond, is a state fishing access site on the north shore of the lake. A boat launch permits access to the entire lake. The **Rock Creek Marina** (✉ 652 South Rock Creek Rd. ☎ 406/485–2560) has marina facilities, a boat launch, and a modern campground.

Where to Stay

¢–$ **Fort Peck Hotel.** Just about every piece of furniture in this wooden building that resembles a barn dates to the hotel's construction during the Great Depression. Inside, the hardwood floors, thick beams, sturdy rafters, and Western style transport you back to the 1930s. The computer in the lounge and cable TV, however, will bring you back into the 21st century. The rooms are small and modest. Most bathrooms have showers, but some have massive claw-foot bathtubs. The adjoining rustic dining room serves three square meals a day for an additional charge. This is a popular hotel with hunters. ✉ *175 S. Missouri St., 59223* ☎ *406/526–3266 or 800/560–4931* 📠 *406/526–3472* *37 rooms* *Dining room, cable TV, Internet, business services, meeting rooms; no room phones, no room TVs, no smoking* 💳 *AE, D, MC, V.*

CAMPING **Downstream Campground.** This large and wooded campground near the town of Fort Peck is one of a few developed camping facilities on the lake managed by the Army Corps of Engineers. *Flush toilets, pit toilets, partial hookups (electric), dump station, drinking water, showers, grills, picnic tables, electricity, public telephone, play area, swimming (lake)* *71 partial hookups, 3 tent sites* ✉ *Rd. 108* ☎ *406/526–3224* 📠 *406/526–3593* 🎫 *Partial hookups $12, tent sites $10* 💳 *AE, D, MC, V.*

Charles M. Russell National Wildlife Refuge

1 mi south of Fort Peck via Missouri Ave.

Bordering the shores of Fort Peck Lake—and even encompassing the town of Fort Peck itself—is the massive Charles M. Russell National Wildlife Refuge, a 1.1-million-acre preserve teeming with more than 200 species of birds, including bald eagles and game birds; 45 different mammals, including elk, antelope, prairie dogs, and deer; and a variety of fish and reptiles. But this is also a refuge for history: each year scientists from around the country march into the preserve, and each year they find something new, whether it's dinosaur bones, buffalo jumps, teepee rings, or an old homesteader's shack. Charlie Russell, whose wonderful paintings depicted a West about to be overrun by railroads, highways, and smokestacks, would surely be proud of the conservation being accomplished in his name—although he might not mind if there were a few more watering holes on the outskirts of this great tract of remote and undeveloped land. The refuge is open for hiking, horseback riding, fishing, boating, and other activities. Several access roads run through the area; most of these, aside from U.S. 191, which runs north–south through the western edge of the refuge, are unpaved. ☎ *406/538–8706* 🌐 *cmr.fws.gov* 🎫 *Free* ⏲ *Daily, 24 hrs.*

There are three staffed **field stations** (✉ U.S. 91, Hwy. 200, and Hwy. 24 ☎ 406/538–8706 🌐 cmr.fws.gov) in the refuge: the **Sand Creek Wildlife Station,** the **Jordan Wildlife Station,** and the **Fort Peck Wildlife Station.** Although they have no facilities open to the public, they are conveniently scattered around the park, and the rangers there will be more than happy to help you with directions or problems.

★ Hundreds of elk congregate evenings in fall at the **Slippery Ann Wildlife Viewing Area** (✉ U.S. 191). During the autumn mating season, the bulls violently lock horns over the herds of cows that come to watch. Be sure to bring binoculars and zoom lenses for your camera, because you don't want to get any closer than necessary to these massive animals.

A refuge within a refuge, the **UL Bend National Wildlife Refuge** consists of more than 20,000 acres of wilderness entirely within the boundaries of the Charles M. Russell National Wildlife Refuge. Its primary mission at the moment is to rescue one of the nation's most endangered animals: the black-footed ferret. The ferrets depend on the high concentration of prairie dog towns here for food. There are also plenty of grouse and burrowing owls, who use abandoned prairie dog tunnels for homes. ✉ *UL Bend National Wildlife Refuge Rd.* ☎ *406/538–8706* 🌐 *cmr.fws.gov* 🎫 *Free* ⏲ *Daily, 24 hrs.*

THE HI-LINE

The Hi-Line is named for U.S. 2, which connects Houlton, Maine, with Everett, Washington, making it the most northerly road you can use to travel east–west across the United States. The highway plows a path almost straight through northern Montana until it reaches the Rockies. It is the region's lifeline, connecting otherwise isolated communities with the rest of the country. From the descendants of wheat farmers and cattle ranchers to a half-dozen Native American tribes and two dozen German-speaking Hutterite colonies, the people of the Hi-Line are a hardy bunch, enduring the bone-chilling winters and poor economy for a quiet bit of land and a caring community. This is a place where you know your neighbors—all of them—and visitors often make the weekly paper. There may not be a Starbucks on every corner, or even a movie theater within 100 mi, but Hi-Line residents wouldn't have it any other way.

Medicine Lake National Wildlife Refuge Complex

32 *230 mi northeast of Charles M. Russell National Wildlife Refuge via Larb Creek Rd. and U.S. 2.*

Established in 1935, this refuge sandwiched between U.S. 2 and the Canadian border encompasses more than 30,000 acres of wetlands that provide ideal habitat for waterfowl and bird species migrating between the northern and southern parts of the continent. Dozens of mammal species, including bears and bobcats, and a variety of butterflies and moths make their home here. There are few facilities available, but as in any area seeking to preserve natural habitat, that is the point. ✉ *Hwy. 16* ☎ *406/789–2305* 🌐 *medicinelake.fws.gov* *Free* ⏱ *Daily sunrise–sunset.*

Winding through the central unit of the refuge is the **Auto Tour Route,** which is an excellent way to get a peek at the animals that call this pristine park home. Most of the route is open only during daylight hours.

The **Observation Tower,** adjacent to the refuge headquarters, provides a good overview of the lakes in the refuge and the surrounding terrain. Free from the trees and tall reeds, you can see the distinct lakes and ponds, as well as the sand hills around the borders. Birders often congregate in the **Grouse Observation Blind,** 2¼ mi east of the refuge headquarters, to take a good look at the resident bird species. The covered area is also good for watching other wildlife.

off the beaten path

FORT UNION TRADING POST NATIONAL HISTORIC SITE – Just across the border in North Dakota, near the confluence of the Missouri and Yellowstone rivers, is one of the most well-known fur-trading posts of the upper plains. Founded in 1828 by John Jacob Astor's American Fur Company, Fort Union bustled with activity well into the 1860s, despite its remote location and an outbreak of smallpox that wiped out up to 90% of some neighboring Native American tribes. By the conclusion of the Civil War, however, the fort had outlived its usefulness, and in 1867 it was dismantled, its pieces used to construct nearby Fort Buford. But no one ever forgot the site, and in 1941 the grounds of the old post were established as a state park; in 1966 this became a national historic site. The fort has been reconstructed, and you can wander through any number of interpretive exhibits relating to the fur trade and Native American life in the mid-19th century. ✉ *15550 Rte. 1804, Williston, ND* ☎ *701/572–9083* 🌐 *www.nps.gov/fous/* *Free* ⏱ *Sept.–May, daily 9–5:30; June–Aug., daily 8–8.*

Bowdoin National Wildlife Refuge

33 *200 mi west of Medicine Lake National Wildlife Refuge via U.S. 2.*

An oxbow of the Missouri River before the last ice age, Bowdoin National Wildlife Refuge is a massive series of lakes and wetlands a few miles east of Malta. Before the government started to administer the site, water levels would drastically vary by season, making it a poor breeding ground for birds—but an excellent breeding ground for disease. Since the construction of several dikes and water channels in the 1930s, however, the water levels of the lakes have remained fairly constant, and the 15,000-acre preserve now shelters numerous birds and mammals. Aside from typical prairie animals and field songbirds, there are sizeable populations of pelicans, gulls, and herons. Several protected species also may be seen here, including the piping plover, black-footed ferret, bald eagle, and peregrine falcon. ☎ *406/654–2863* 🌐 *bowdoin.fws.gov* 🎫 *Free* ⏲ *Daily during daylight hrs.*

As the main road through the refuge, the **Bowdoin Refuge Autotour Route** affords excellent views of the terrain and wildlife here. Old U.S. 2 is another main route, but it doesn't compare to the slower and far more scenic experience of the Autotour.

The **Bowdoin Wildlife Refuge Headquarters,** at the main entrance to Bowdoin, can provide information on the latest refuge conditions, species lists, and instructions for a drivable tour route. ✉ *Bowdoin Refuge Autotour Rte.* ☎ *406/654–2863* 🌐 *bowdoin.fws.gov* 🎫 *Free* ⏲ *Weekdays 8–5.*

Birders and wildlife photographers come to the **Pearce Waterfowl Production Area Bird Blind,** on the northeast edge of the refuge, for great views.

off the beaten path

PHILLIPS COUNTY HISTORICAL MUSEUM – This museum in the nearby town of Malta, a ranching community of about 2,000 people, is an official repository for fossils found in the Judith River basin. The highlight of the dinosaur display is a reconstructed albertosaur skeleton, which towers above the other collections. There also are some significant homesteading artifacts, including exhibits related to some outlaws who spent time here: Butch Cassidy, the Sundance Kid, Kid Curry, the Tall Texan, and other members of the Wild Bunch gang. ✉ *431 U.S. 2, Malta* ☎ *406/654–1037* 🌐 *www.montanadinosaurdigs.com/museum.htm* 🎫 *Free* ⏲ *May–Sept., Mon.–Sat. 10–5, Sun. 12:30–5; Oct.–Apr., by appointment only.*

Where to Stay

¢ **Maltana Hotel.** Easy to find, this downtown hotel is within walking distance of Malta's Amtrak station and a few blocks from the junction of U.S. 2 and 191. The rooms are modest but modern, with data ports and coffeemakers—unusual finds in a small, isolated town. ✉ *138 1st Ave. E, Malta 59538* ☎ *406/654–2610* 📠 *406/654–1663* *19 rooms* *In-room data ports, cable TV, airport shuttle* 💳 *AE, D, MC, V.*

Havre

34 *103 mi west of Bowdoin National Wildlife Refuge via U.S. 2.*

The trading center for a wide area of extreme north-central Montana and southern Alberta and Saskatchewan, the town of Havre (population 9,621) lies between the Milk River and Bear Paw Mountains. The town is the site of Northern Montana College, Fort Assinniboine and the H. Earl Clack Memorial Museum. There's also a preserve south of town where you can fish, picnic, or just enjoy the view.

Displays at the **H. Earl Clack Memorial Museum** include murals, artifacts, dioramas, and military and mining exhibits that explore the lives of Plains Indians and Havre's early settlers and ranchers. Many of the artifacts here come from nearby Fort Assinniboine and the Wahkpa Chu'gn Archaeological Site, a major buffalo jump; you can also arrange for tours of these sites through the museum. ✉ *306 3rd Ave.* ☎ *406/265–4000* 🎫 *$3* ⏲ *Labor Day–Memorial Day, Tues.–Sat. 1–5; Memorial Day–Labor Day, Tues.–Sat. 10–5.*

★ Once the largest military fort west of the Mississippi and known as the "West Point of the West," **Fort Assinniboine** was established in 1879 in the aftermath of the Battle of the Little Bighorn. At its peak, the fort had more than 100 brick and stone buildings and nearly 500 men. The soldiers that were stationed here brought their families with them, and because the fort was 6 mi southwest of Havre, a small ranching community still in the process of becoming a full-fledged town, the families lived on post. As a result, the Victorian-era fort became a cultural center as well as a military one, hosting plays and dances along with parades and training exercises. This was one of the more culturally diverse posts of its day, with Native American, black, and white soldiers, who were mostly charged with keeping indigenous tribes in check (there was some speculation, however, that the post's northern location reflected the ambitions of some U.S. senators to acquire Canada). The fort is now a museum, and many of the imposing buildings designed to accommodate the soldiers, officers, and their families still stand, although they appear eerily deserted. In fact, a few are storage or administrative facilities for the Northern Research Agricultural Center. Others are open to public tours, which begin at the H. Earl Clack Memorial Museum. ✉ *306 3rd Ave.* ☎ *406/265–8336* 🎫 *$3* ⏲ *May–Sept., hrs vary so call ahead.*

★ The **Havre Beneath the Streets** tour takes you to a bordello, opium den, bakery, and other stops in an underground business center dating from the early days of the frontier—the equivalent of a modern underground mall. ✉ *100 3rd Ave.* ☎ *406/265–8888* 🎫 *$6* ⏲ *Sept.–May, Mon.–Sat. 10–4; June–Aug., daily 9–5.*

Set in the ancient Bear Paw Mountains, about 10 mi south of town, is the 10,000-acre **Beaver Creek Park,** the largest county park in the country. It's a favorite spot for locals, who come here to fish in the two lakes, camp, picnic, and enjoy the scenery. ✉ *Hwy. 234* ☎ *406/395–4565* 🎫 *$5 per vehicle* ⏲ *Daily, 24 hrs.*

Where to Stay & Eat

$–$$ ✕ **Lunch Box.** There are daily specials of soup and sandwich at this family-style deli; two soups are made fresh daily. The menu lists a lot of healthful choices, with 70 sandwiches, as well as salads, nachos, baked potatoes, lattes, and espresso. ✉ *213 3rd Ave.* ☎ *406/265–6588* 💳 *No credit cards* ⏲ *Closed Sun.*

$ 🏨 **Best Western Great Northern Inn.** A clock tower, colorful flags, and off-white stones and bricks decorate the proud exterior of this spacious hotel. Contemporary furnishings fill the rooms, and a special annex separates the business suites from the rest of the hotel. ✉ *1345 1st St., 59501* ☎ *406/265–4200 or 888/530–4100* 📠 *406/265–3656* 🌐 *www.bestwestern.com* 🛏 *63 rooms, 12 suites* 👍 *Restaurant, some in-room hot tubs, cable TV with movies, indoor pool, hot tub, bar, laundry facilities, business services, airport shuttle, some pets allowed (fee)* 💳 *AE, D, DC, MC, V* 🍽 *CP.*

The Arts

Focusing on the pencil drawings of a local artist, the **Old Library Gallery** (✉ 439 4th Ave. ☎ 406/265–8165) also displays paintings and pottery; most have a connection with local history and culture.

Browning

35 *160 mi west of Havre via U.S. 2.*

Browning, east of the Continental Divide, is the center of the Blackfeet Nation, whose name is thought to have been derived from the color of their painted or dyed black moccasins. Until the late 19th century, the Blackfeet hunted the great northern buffalo, moving with them across the vast northern plains. At one time, the Blackfeet homeland stretched all the way from the Missouri River north to the Bow and Red Deer rivers in Canada, and from the Rocky Mountains 300 mi east. Rugged terrain and remoteness left Blackfeet territory some of the last Native American country in the contiguous United States to be opened to whites. The 1.5-million-acre reservation was established in 1851 and currently has about 13,000 enrolled tribal members. Outstanding fly-fishing opportunities exist on the reservation, which borders Glacier National Park.

★ The **Museum of the Plains Indian,** on the north end of town, houses a stunning collection of ancient artifacts from the Blackfeet, who have lived in the region for 7,000 years, and other Plains peoples. Among the exhibits are clothing, saddlebags, and artwork. ✉ *U.S. 2 at U.S. 89* ☎ *406/338–2230* 💲 *$4* ⏲ *June–Sept., daily 9–4:45; Oct.–May, weekdays 10–4:30.*

During the second weekend of July, the Blackfeet host the free **North American Indian Days** (✉ Agency Sq. ☎ 406/338–7276). This gathering of tribes is a pageant of drumming, chanting, traditional games, and teepees as far as the eye can see.

Sports & the Outdoors

The Blackfeet reservation has excellent fly-fishing. A tribal fishing permit is required and is available from tribal officials, outfitters in the area, and Browning's **Tribal Headquarters** (✉ Public Square ☎ 406/338–7521).

Where to Stay

¢–$ **Western Motel.** A central location and low rates are this small, modest hotel's highlights. There are few amenities, but the rooms do have microwaves and refrigerators, which make it easy to pack lunches for trips into Glacier National Park. The staff is knowledgeable and willing to answer questions about the reservation and the park. The hotel also accepts Canadian currency. ✉ *121 Central Ave. E, 59417* ☎ *406/338–7572* *15 rooms* *Microwaves, refrigerators; no room TVs, no smoking* *AE, D, MC, V.*

CAMPING **Aspenwood Campground and RV Park.** A nightly bonfire and teepee rentals are some of the fun, numerous extras at this campground 10 mi west of Browning and 2 mi from Glacier National Park. *Flush toilets, partial hookups (electric and water), dump station, drinking water, showers, fire pits, food service, picnic tables, electricity, public telephone, general store, play area.* *10 partial hookups, 9 tent sites; 3 teepees* ✉ *U.S. 89* ☎ *406/338–3009 or 858/945–1801* 🌐 *www.aspenwoodcamp.com* 💲 *Partial hookups $20, tent sites $15; tepees $35–$45* *MC, V* ⏲ *Open June–Sept.*

THE MONTANA PLAINS A TO Z

To research prices, get advice from other travelers, and book travel arrangements, visit www.fodors.com.

AIR TRAVEL

CARRIERS Within eastern Montana, commercial flights—generally via Salt Lake City, Seattle, Denver, or Phoenix—are available only to Billings and Great Falls, although small commuter and charter flights serve other towns in the region. Because the region is so isolated, flights here from anywhere in the country can be pricey—almost as much as (and sometimes more than) flights from New York to Los Angeles.

Airlines & Contacts **Big Sky** ☎ 800/237-7788 🌐 www.bigskyair.com. **Delta** ☎ 800/221-1212 🌐 www.delta.com. **Horizon** ☎ 800/252-7522 🌐 horizonair.alaskaair.com. **Northwest** ☎ 800/225-2525 🌐 www.nwa.com. **United** ☎ 800/864-8331 🌐 www.ual.com.

AIRPORTS

Both Billings Logan and Great Falls are international airports, but only because they have occasional service to and from Canada. Because Billings and Great Falls have direct service to only a few cities in the western part of the country, some residents of this region of Montana drive as far as Bismarck, North Dakota; Rapid City, South Dakota; or Gillette, Wyoming, to catch departing flights.

Airport Information **Billings Logan International Airport** ✉ 1901 Terminal Circle, Billings ☎ 406/238-3420 🌐 www.flybillings.com. **Great Falls International Airport** ✉ Airport Dr., Great Falls ☎ 406/727-3404 🌐 www.gtfairport.com.

BUS TRAVEL

Several bus companies connect most of the regional communities of 1,000 residents or more; smaller towns may not have service. Expect high ticket prices; depending on where you're going, taking the bus can be almost as expensive as flying, and because of the great expanse of Montana, it can take infinitely longer.

Bus Information **Greyhound Bus Lines** ☎ 406/245-5116 or 800/231-2222 🌐 www.greyhound.com. **Karst Stages** ☎ 406/586-8657 🌐 www.karststage.com. **Powder River Transportation** ☎ 307/674-6188. **Rimrock Stages** ☎ 406/245-5392 or 800/255-7655 🌐 www.rimrocktrailways.com. **Silver Eagle Shuttle Inc.** ☎ 800/625-4839 🌐 www.montanacustomtours.com.

CAR RENTAL

Rental cars are easily acquired in Billings and Great Falls; the airports are your best bet.

Avis ☎ 800/831-2847 🌐 www.avis.com. **Budget** ☎ 800/527-0700 🌐 www.budget.com. **Hertz** ☎ 800/654-3131 🌐 www.hertz.com. **National** ☎ 800/227-7368 🌐 www.nationalcar.com.

CAR TRAVEL

Having a car is critical to traveling around this region of Montana. One of the best things about driving here is not having to worry about traffic. Aside from a little bustle in Great Falls or Billings on weekdays in the late afternoon, gridlock and traffic jams are unheard of here. The largest driving hazards will be slow-moving farming or ranching equipment, wranglers on horseback, herds of grazing livestock that refuse to move off the highway, and deer bounding over ditches in the evening. Driving gets a little hairy in winter, but not because of the amount of snow that falls, which is generally very little. Whiteouts, when winds tearing across the plains whip up the tiniest bit of snow into ground blizzards, are the most common hazard. Large drifts and slick roads become more problematic at higher elevations.

For information on road conditions, contact the Montana Department of Transportation.

Montana Department of Transportation ☎ 800/226-7689 or 511 🌐 www.mdt.state.mt.us/travinfo/. **Montana Highway Patrol** ☎ 406/444-3780 🌐 www.doj.state.mt.us/department/.

EMERGENCIES

Ambulance or Police **Emergencies** ☎ 911 or 800/525-5555.

24-Hour Medical Care **Benefis Healthcare** 1101 26th St. S, Great Falls 406/455-5000 www.benefis.org. **Deaconess Billings Clinic** 2800 10th Ave. N, Billings 406/657-4000 www.billingsclinic.com. **St. Vincent Healthcare** 1233 N. 30th St., Billings 406/657-7000 www.stvincenthealthcare.org.

LODGING

The Montana Innkeepers Association's simple Web site searches a large database of lodgings throughout most of the state. The service is not without flaws, however, as many inns and motels in Montana's eastern reaches are small and may not have the resources available to join the association.

Montana Innkeepers Association 406/449-8408 visitmt.worldres.com.

CAMPING Camping in Montana is incredibly easy: many federal and state-owned lands allow camping for little or no charge, and you can often set up shop wherever you like, so long as you don't light a fire. In the more developed towns and cities, there is almost always a campground or two with some more modern conveniences, such as hot showers and flush toilets.

Contact Montana Fish, Wildlife & Parks for information on camping in state parks and the U.S. Forest Service for information on camping at national parks in the area.

Montana Fish, Wildlife & Parks 406/444-2535 www.fwp.state.mt.us/parks. **U.S. Forest Service** 406/329-3511 www.fs.fed.us/r1.

MEDIA

NEWSPAPERS & MAGAZINES The *Billings Gazette* is by far the most widely read newspaper in Montana; it even has a strong following among people in Wyoming and the Dakotas. Its only competitor in the immediate vicinity is the *Great Falls Tribune*. Whereas the *Gazette* tends to focus more on the plains of southern Montana and its neighbors, the *Tribune* finds its niche farther north.

TELEVISION & RADIO Radio and TV signals are few and far between in this incredibly vast region. Pushing the "seek" button on your car radio here does not always lead to the desired result—that is, actually finding a station. Many people subscribe to cable television simply so they can get two or three local stations. The major broadcasters are CBS/KTVQ Channel 2 and NBC/KULR Channel 8 in Billings, and ABC/KFBB Channel 5, CBS/KRTV Channel 3, and NBC/KTGF Channel 16 in Great Falls.

SPORTS & THE OUTDOORS

BOATING Although the plains are dry, man-made dams have tamed a few of the major rivers that run through the state, creating ideal venues for water sports. Motorized boating, including jet skiing, is usually not restricted, even in the massive Charles M. Russell National Wildlife Refuge. On Fort Peck Lake, Bighorn Lake, and a few of the other reservoirs scattered around the plains, there are marinas with boat rentals. Extended droughts can sometimes cause these marinas to go out of business—at least temporarily—or move to another location. If you're interested in boat rentals on a specific lake or river, call Travel Montana for information on a marina that serves that location.

Travel Montana 301 S. Park Ave., Helena 59620 406/841-2870 or 800/847-4868 www.visitmt.com.

FISHING Although the eastern two-thirds of Montana are decidedly drier than the western regions, small mountain-fed creeks and reservoirs on a few major rivers aren't hard to find on the plains. And unlike what you'll find at the blue-ribbon streams of the higher elevations, there are very few crowds to beat along the babbling brooks of the lowlands.

Montana Fish, Wildlife & Parks 1420 E. 6th Ave., Helena 59620 406/444-2535 www.fwp.state.mt.us.

TRAIN TRAVEL

Amtrak serves the isolated communities of the Hi-Line. The tracks run nearly parallel to U.S. 2 the entire distance of the state. Trains stop in the towns of Glasgow, Malta, Havre, Wolf Point, Cut Bank, and Browning, among others.

Train Information **Amtrak** ☎ 800/872-7245 🌐 www.amtrak.com.

VISITOR INFORMATION

Tourist Information **Billings Convention and Visitors Bureau** ✉ 815 S. 27th St., Billings 59107 ☎ 406/252-4016 or 800/735-2635 🌐 www.billingscvb.visitmt.com. **Great Falls Convention and Visitors Bureau** ✉ 710 1st Ave. N, Great Falls 59401 ☎ 406/761-4434 🌐 greatfallscvb.visitmt.com. **Travel Montana** ✉ 301 S. Park Ave., Helena 59620 ☎ 406/841-2870 or 800/847-4868 🌐 www.visitmt.com.

5

SOUTHWEST MONTANA

BOZEMAN, HELENA, NORTH OF YELLOWSTONE

6

FODOR'S CHOICE

The Big EZ, *hotel in Big Sky*
Fishing on the Gallatin River
Rainbow Ranch, *restaurant in Big Sky*
Scott Inn Bed and Breakfast, *Butte*

HIGHLY RECOMMENDED

RESTAURANTS
Chathams Livingston Bar and Grill, *Livingston*
Cross Ranch Cookhouse, *Dillon*
Historic Headwaters Restaurant, *Three Forks*
Last Chance Ranch, *Helena*
Windbag Saloon & Grill, *Helena*

HOTELS
B Bar Ranch, *Emigrant*
Canyon Ferry Mansion, *Townsend*
Chico Hot Springs Resort, *Pray*
Cottonwood Inn B&B, *Bozeman*
Grand Hotel, *Big Timber*
Pollard Hotel, *Red Lodge*
Potosi Hot Springs, *resort in Pony*
Sanders-Helena Bed and Breakfast, *Helena*
Summit at Big Sky, *Big Sky*
Voss Inn, *Bozeman*

SIGHTS
Arts Chateau Museum, *Butte*
Missouri Headwaters State Park, *Three Forks*
Nevada City Open Air Museum, *near Virginia City*

By Jean Arthur

GLISTENING, GLACIATED, AND GRAND, the Absarokas, Crazies, Gallatins, and other mountains send cooling summer winds to roil among the grasslands of southwest Montana. The south-central region of the state is known as Yellowstone Country, and it shares the topography, wildlife, river, and recreational opportunities of its namesake national park. To the west, in Montana's southwest corner, is Gold West Country, which includes the gold-rush towns of Helena, Virginia City, and Bannack. Sizeable ranches throughout the region, measured in the thousands of acres, are bordered by ranchettes of fewer than 20 acres around the towns of Bozeman, Big Timber, Red Lodge, and Dillon.

Southwest Montana is a wild place, with breeding populations of hundreds of species. Abundant wildlife is a daily sight, from the pronghorn sprinting across grasslands to the 17,000-strong northern elk herd in and north of Yellowstone National Park. Bald eagles and osprey perch in tall snags along the river, watching for fish. Mules and white-tailed deer spring over fences—and across roads, so watch out when driving. Golden eagles hunt over hay fields. Riparian areas come alive in spring with ducks, geese, pelicans, and great blue herons. Critters outnumber people here, which should come as no surprise when you consider that some counties have fewer than one person per square mile. Even the most densely populated area, Yellowstone County, still has only about 34 people per square mile. That leaves thousands of square miles in the region wide open for exploration.

Human history reaches back only about 12,000 years here, and non–Native American travel dates back only 200 years. Yet southwest Montana is a place full of exciting tales and trails, from the path followed by the Lewis and Clark expedition to the Bozeman and Nez Perce trails. Roadside historic signs along various routes in the region indicate the sites of battles, travels, and travails.

Exploring Southwest Montana

A private vehicle is far and away the best means of exploring southwest Montana, and it allows you to appreciate the grandeur of the area. Wide-open terrain affords startling vistas of mountains and prairies, where you're likely to see abundant wildlife. I–90 is the major east–west artery through the region; I–15 is the major north–south route. Most of the other routes here are paved and in good shape, but be prepared for gravel and dirt roads the farther off the beaten path you go. Driving through the mountains in winter can be challenging; a four-wheel-drive vehicle, available from most car-rental agencies, is best.

About the Restaurants

This is ranch country, so expect numerous Angus-steer steak houses. Many restaurants also serve bison meat and various vegetarian meals but few ethnic dishes. Restaurants here are decidedly casual: blue jeans, crisp shirts, and cowboy boots are dressy for the region.

About the Hotels

Lodging varies from national chain hotels to mom-and-pop motor inns. More and more elegant guest ranches are inviting lodgers, historic hotels are being restored, and new bed-and-breakfasts are opening their doors. In summer and during the ski season (December–mid-March), it's best to reserve rooms far in advance.

WHAT IT COSTS					
	$$$$	$$$	$$	$	¢
RESTAURANTS	over $22	$16–$22	$11–$16	$7–$11	under $7
HOTELS	over $220	$160–$220	$110–$160	$70–$110	under $70

Restaurant prices are for a main course at dinner. Hotel prices are for two people in a standard double room in high season, excluding service charges and a 7% bed tax.

Timing

With its cold, dry snow, December through March is the best time to visit for skiers, snowboarders, snowshoers, and people who just love winter. Summer draws even more visitors, especially in August. That's not to say that southwest Montana gets crowded, but you may find more peace and quiet in spring and fall, when warm days and cool nights offer pleasant vacationing under the Big Sky. September and October usually bring sunny days and cool to chilly nights but few visitors to the region.

Temperatures can drop below freezing in winter (and in fall and spring in the mountains) and jump into the 80s in summer. The weather can change quickly, particularly in the mountains and in the front range area north of Helena, and temperatures have been known to vary by as much as 70°F within a few hours, bringing winds, thunderstorms, and the like.

NORTH OF YELLOWSTONE

This mountainous stretch of land from the town of Red Lodge west to the resort region at Big Sky is mostly roadless, glaciated, and filled with craggy heights, including the state's tallest peak, Granite, at 12,799 feet. Winter often refuses to give up its grasp on this high alpine region until late spring. Snowpack assures that streams feeding the mighty Yellowstone River will flow throughout the hot summer, satiating the wildlife, native plants, and numerous wheat and other farms downstream.

Red Lodge

1 *60 mi southwest of Billings via U.S. 212.*

Nestled against the foot of the pine-draped Absaroka-Beartooth Wilderness and edged by the Limestone Palisades, Red Lodge was named for a band of Cheyenne who marked their tepee lodges with paintings of red earth. It became a town in the late 1880s when the Northern Pacific Railroad laid tracks here to take coal back to Billings. One of Red Lodge's most colorful characters from this time was former sheriff "Liver Eatin' " Jeremiah Johnson, the subject of much Western lore and an eponymous movie starring Robert Redford. Now the historic little burg is listed on the National Register of Historic Places and has become a full-blown resort town, complete with a ski area, trout fishing, access to backcountry hiking, horseback riding, and a golf course.

Each August, Red Lodge holds an eight-day **Festival of Nations** (☎ 406/446–1718 🌐 www.festivalofnations.us) to celebrate the numerous ethnic heritages of early settlers, many of whom worked in coal mines nearby. The festival includes music and dance.

When the snow flies in early March, the annual **Winter Carnival** (✉ 601 N. Broadway ☎ 888/281–0625 🌐 www.redlodge.com) draws skiers, snowboarders, and other fans of the cold to three days of events such as the zany Firehose Race, in which teams of skiing firefighters com-

Numbers in the text correspond to numbers in the margin and on the Southwest Montana, Bozeman, and Helena maps.

If you have 3 days

Begin in **Red Lodge** 1 with a drive up the Beartooth Pass; don't forget your camera, a picnic lunch, and drinking water. Plan a day hike on one of the trails that lead away from the highway. In winter, you can ski at Red Lodge Mountain Resort. The next day drive to **Big Timber** 2. En route, go white-water rafting on the Stillwater River if you're visiting in warm weather, or try fly-fishing the Yellowstone River with an outfitter once you get to Big Timber. On your third day, drive to **Livingston** 3 for a morning of museum and gallery hopping. After lunch, take a scenic drive through the Paradise Valley, and if you have time, join the dozens of folks fly-fishing the Yellowstone River. Consider overnighting at or at least visiting the Chico Hot Springs Resort, where you can unwind with a leisurely soak in the springs.

If you have 5 days

Follow the suggested three-day itinerary. On the fourth day, drive to historic **Bozeman** 6–11. In winter you could spend a day skiing at Bridger Bowl; at other times of the year, take in the sights on your own or on a walking tour of the historic downtown. If you've got kids in tow, don't miss the Museum of the Rockies, complete with dinosaur exhibits, a planetarium, and hands-on science activities. The next day, drive to **Big Sky and Gallatin Canyon** 5. In summer you can fish, play golf, or go rafting down the Gallatin River; in winter, you have a choice of cross-country skiing, downhill skiing, snowmobiling, or snowshoeing.

If you have 7 days

After your visit to Big Sky on the five-day itinerary, drive to **Virginia City** 28. Spend a few hours reliving the gold-rush days in this small historic town and neighboring Nevada City, which you can reach on a small steam train. On the drive to **Ennis** 29, be sure to keep your fly-fishing rod handy for fishing along the way. The tackle shops in town can give you tips on the best fishing spots, or you can hire a guide to find the big trout. If the fishing isn't good, take a trail ride through the mountains outside of Ennis. Drive to **Three Forks** 4 for a walk through the Lewis and Clark Caverns, Montana's oldest state park. Be sure to visit Missouri Headwaters State Park, where Lewis and Clark spent time two centuries ago. Wind up your day with dinner at the Historic Headwaters Restaurant.

---

pete while carrying a 50-foot hose. Other events include an obstacle ski course, the Snow Ball, a children's treasure hunt, and a snow-sculpture contest.

In addition to artifacts that once belonged to the famous Ridin' Greenoughs, a rodeo family, the **Peaks to Plains Museum** houses a historic gun collection, a reproduction of a coal mine, and Liver Eatin' Johnson exhibits. ✉ *224 N. Broadway* ☎ *406/446–3667* *$3* ⊙ *Mid-May–Sept., weekdays 10–5, weekends 1–5; Oct.–mid-May, Tues.–Fri. 10–5, Sat. 1–5.*

Sports & the Outdoors

DOWNHILL SKIING

In winter there are 69 ski trails on 1,600 acres at **Red Lodge Mountain Resort** (✉ 101 Ski Run Rd. ☎ 406/446–2610 or 800/444–8977 ⊕ www.

redlodgemountain.com). The family-friendly resort has a 2,400-foot vertical drop, a large beginner area, plenty of groomed intermediate terrain, and the Cole Creek area for powder-loving advanced and expert skiers. The best snow conditions are from February through April.

GOLF The surrounding mountains form a backdrop for the 18-hole **Red Lodge Mountain Golf Course** (✉ 828 Upper Continental St. ☎ 406/446–3344 or 800/444–8977 🌐 www.redlodgemountain.com/golf).

FISHING **Montana Trout Scout** (✉ 213 W. 9th St. ☎ 406/446–1951) conducts fly-fishing float trips and wade fishing on local streams and rivers such as the Yellowstone, Clark's Fork, Stillwater, and Rock Creek.

HORSEBACK RIDING Ride the Beartooth high country among 12,000-foot peaks with **Silver Run Outfitting & Guide Service** (✉ 303 W. Rosebud Rd., Fishtail ☎ 406/328–4412) on a horse or mule. You may see elk, bighorn sheep, birds of prey, and some of the 25 glacier-flanked peaks of the Absaroka-Beartooth Wilderness and along the West Rosebud River. You can also join in a cattle drive in summer.

WHITE-WATER RAFTING The Stillwater River's foaming white water flows from the Absaroka-Beartooth Wilderness, providing exhilarating rafting with **Adventure Whitewater** (✉ 1 mi north of Absarokee on Hwy. 78 ☎ 406/446–3061 or 800/897–3061 🌐 www.adventurewhitewater.com), which also has a combined rafting and horseback-riding trip.

Where to Stay & Eat

The friendly folks at **Red Lodge Reservations** (✉ 1119 S. Broadway, 59068 ☎ 406/446–3942 or 877/733–5634 📠 406/446–4701 🌐 www.redlodgereservations.com) can help you make lodging reservations in and around town—from snug cottages and cabins to historic B&Bs and hotels.

$–$$$ ✕ **Bridge Creek Backcountry Kitchen & Wine Bar.** This casual restaurant, often decorated with local artwork by schoolkids or professional artists, prepares fine dinners using naturally raised Montana beef. For lunch, try one of the three soups du jour, such as smoked turkey bisque, country Dijon vegetable chowder, or clam chowder. *✉ 116 S. Broadway ☎ 406/446–9900 ▭ AE, DC, MC, V.*

$–$$$ ✕ **Carbon County Steakhouse.** Saddles, saddle blankets, bridles, and other cowboy and ranch paraphernalia prepare you for the certified Angus beef from the grill, perhaps in the form of a hearty rib eye or even an appetizer of Rocky Mountain oysters (calf testicles). Vegetarian pasta dishes and seafood pasta are local favorites. *✉ 121 S. Broadway ☎ 406/446–4025 ▭ AE, DC, MC, V ⊙ Closed Mon. and Tues.*

★ **$$–$$$$** ✕🏨 **Pollard Hotel.** This 1893 landmark in the heart of Red Lodge's historic district has been restored to the charms of an earlier era, when the likes of Calamity Jane and Liver Eatin' Johnson frequented the hotel. Reproduction Victorian furniture throughout vivifies a fin de siècle feeling, and handsome oak paneling and green, brown, and gold flocked wallpapers decorate the public rooms. Arthur's restaurant specializes in steaks, chops, and exotic game such as ostrich. The sautéed steelhead trout is served with crayfish crème fraîche sauce and saffron-spinach rice. *✉ 2 N. Broadway, 59068 ☎ 406/446–0001 or 800/765–5273 📠 406/446–0002 🌐 www.pollardhotel.com ⇨ 39 rooms ♁ Restaurant, gym, hot tub, sauna, racquetball, bar; no smoking ▭ AE, D, MC, V 🍽 BP.*

$–$$$$ ✕🏨 **Rock Creek Resort.** After negotiating the cliff-hanging Beartooth Pass Highway between Red Lodge and Yellowstone National Park, this resort is a welcome respite. A Southwestern motif decorates the wood, log, and stone lodge, cabin, and condos, which perch along a babbling, boulder-strewn creek. Some of the rooms have hot tubs. A historic old cabin

Fishing

Montana has the best rainbow, brown, and brook trout fishing in the country. This is the land of *A River Runs Through It,* the acclaimed Norman Maclean novel that was made into a movie. Although the book was set in Missoula, the movie was filmed in the trout-fishing mecca of southwest Montana, with the Gallatin River playing the role of Maclean's beloved Big Blackfoot. Several rivers run through the region, notably the Madison, Gallatin, and Yellowstone (which run more or less parallel to one another flowing north of Yellowstone National Park), as well as the Big Hole River to the west. These are among the rivers that get the most recognition in the region, though it's hard to go wrong in these parts. All are easily accessible from major roads, which means that in summer you might have to drive a ways to find a hole to call your own. Stream fishing in these parts is a year-round enterprise. Even if you never catch a fish, your trip will be well spent: the mountain ranges that separate these rivers are among the most beautiful in the Rockies.

Skiing

It's called "cold smoke"—the exceedingly light, dry snow that falls on the mountains of southwest Montana—and it doesn't go to waste here. All told, the state has more than a dozen downhill ski areas/resorts and more than 950 km (600 mi) of cross-country trails. The ski season generally begins in late November or early December and runs through early to mid-April, though early and late storms can extend the season.

Downhill ski areas like Bridger Bowl, Discovery, and Red Lodge are family friendly, inexpensive, and relatively uncrowded. One of the country's largest resorts, Big Sky, not only rewards steep seekers with 500 or more consecutive turns on one slope but also caters to beginners and intermediate skiers out for leisure turns.

The famed cross-country ski tracks of Lone Mountain Ranch headline the trail systems of Montana. About 10 trails in southwest Montana are groomed daily or weekly and are track-set for both classic and skate skiing. Backcountry skiing has no limits, with hundreds of thousands of skiable acres among the millions of acres of public lands.

Hiking

Hundreds of hiking trails crisscross the state's mountains, forests, grasslands, and badlands. Many trails are marked and have corresponding trail maps available at sporting-goods shops and Forest Service and state-lands offices. Some trails are unmarked, however, and only partially maintained. These are often the trails that take you into the quietest, most remote regions of Montana. Wherever you choose to hike, bring sturdy hiking boots, food, water, and an eagerness for adventure.

Wildlife encounters are almost guaranteed. You are likely to see elk, deer, antelope, bighorn sheep, mountain goats, eagles, hawks, and herons. You may also come across unique natural features such as petrified wood, fossils, and evidence of early human existence like pictographs and arrowheads.

Follow some simple safety precautions when hiking: travel in groups, carry pepper spray (this is bear country), leave travel plans with someone, and be prepared for snow, even in August.

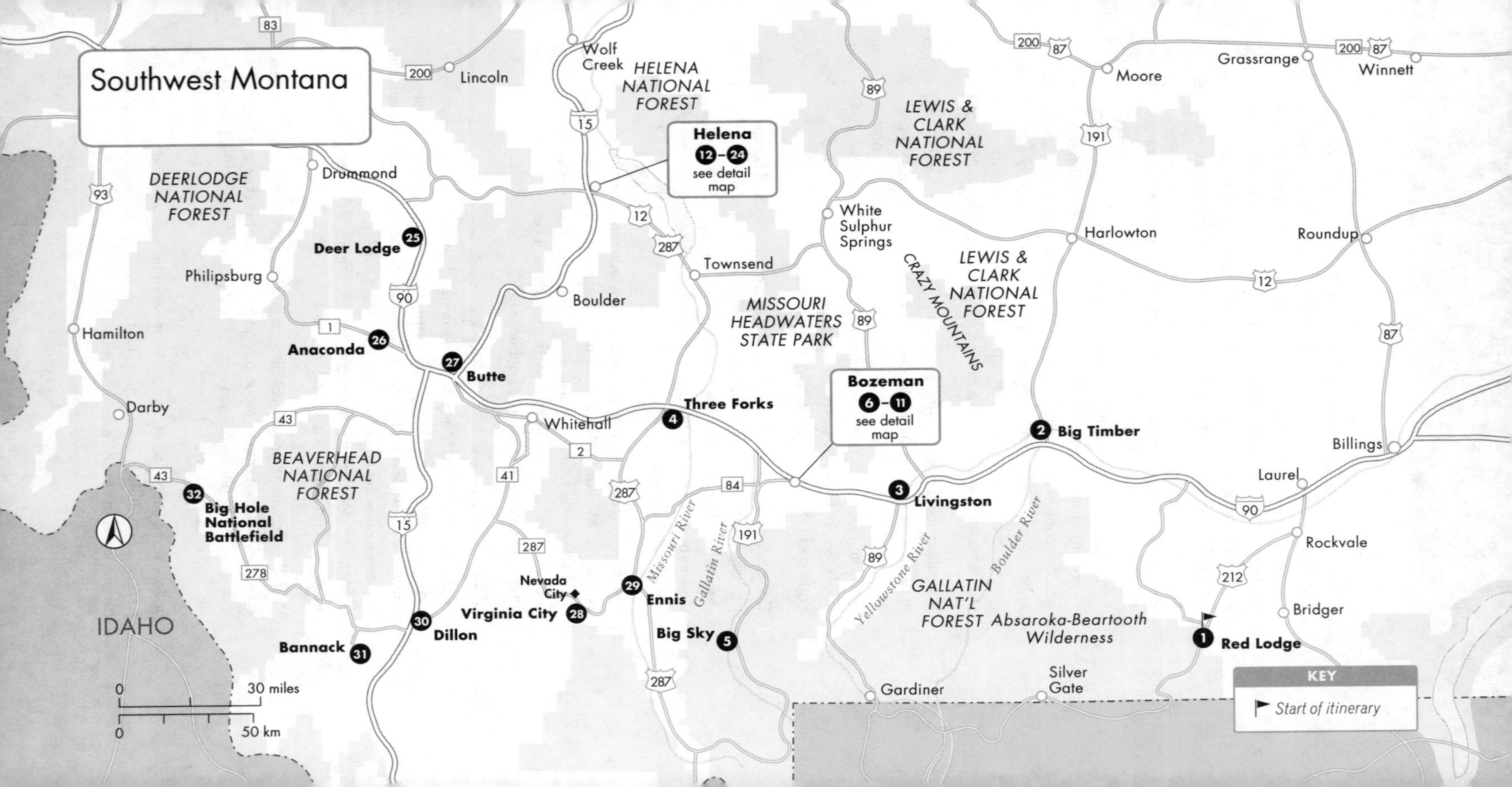
Southwest Montana
DEERLODGE NATIONAL FOREST
Drummond
Lincoln
Wolf Creek
HELENA NATIONAL FOREST
Helena 12–24 see detail map
LEWIS & CLARK NATIONAL FOREST
Moore
Grassrange
Winnett
White Sulphur Springs
Harlowton
Roundup
Deer Lodge
Philipsburg
Townsend
Boulder
MISSOURI HEADWATERS STATE PARK
CRAZY MOUNTAINS
LEWIS & CLARK NATIONAL FOREST
Hamilton
Anaconda
Butte
Three Forks
Bozeman 6–11 see detail map
Darby
Whitehall
Big Timber
Billings
BEAVERHEAD NATIONAL FOREST
Laurel
Livingston
Big Hole National Battlefield
Missouri River
Gallatin River
Yellowstone River
Boulder River
Rockvale
GALLATIN NAT'L FOREST
Absaroka-Beartooth Wilderness
Nevada City
Virginia City
Ennis
Bridger
IDAHO
Dillon
Big Sky
Red Lodge
Bannack
Gardiner
Silver Gate
0 30 miles
0 50 km
KEY
Start of itinerary

holds the wonderful Old Piney Dell restaurant ($$–$$$$), where locals go for intimate celebrations. The menu lists simple American, Mexican, and regional food. ✉ *6382 U.S. 212, on the Beartooth Hwy., Box 3500, 59068, 4½ mi south of Red Lodge* ☎ *406/446–1111 or 800/667–1119* 📠 *406/446–3688* 🌐 *www.rockcreekresort.com* *38 rooms, 48 condos, 1 cabin* *2 restaurants, in-room data ports, some in-room hot tubs, some kitchenettes, some microwaves, cable TV, 4 tennis courts, indoor pool, sauna, fishing, basketball, soccer, volleyball, cross-country skiing, 2 bars, shop, playground, laundry facilities, convention center, meeting rooms, airport shuttle, free parking; no smoking* 💳 *AE, D, DC, MC, V.*

$$$ **The Torgrimson Place.** A 1904 fully restored log home sits amid the 5,000 acres of the working Bench Ranch, a place of bald eagles, deer, elk, sheep, cattle, and peace. Part of the trout-rich West Rosebud River runs through the property. The house has five bedrooms (note that you must rent the entire house). The master bedroom, with its king-size lodgepole-pine bed and plump comforter, looks out upon glacier-sculpted peaks. The bunkhouse next door, available for rent separately, is ideal for kids. Other cabins are nestled in an aspen grove. The ranch can cater barbecues and also arranges summer horse-pack trips and other guided tours. ✉ *303 W. Rosebud Rd., Fishtail, 37 mi west of Red Lodge, 59028* ☎ *406/328–4412* 📠 *406/328–4416* 🌐 *www.benchranch.com* *1 house, 1 bunkhouse, 2 cabins* *Kitchens, fishing, mountain bikes, horseback riding, cross-country skiing, baby-sitting, laundry facilities; no TV in some rooms, no smoking* 💳 *No credit cards.*

CAMPING **Greenough Campground and Lake.** Pine trees, a small trout-stocked lake, and gentle hiking trails provide summer respite in Greenough, one of a dozen U.S. Forest Service campgrounds in the Red Lodge vicinity. *Pit toilets, drinking water, fire grates, picnic tables, swimming (lake)* *18 sites* ✉ *10½ mi south of Red Lodge on U.S. 212, then 1 mi west on Hwy. 421* ☎ *406/446–2103* 🌐 *www.fs.fed.us/r1/custer or www.reserveamerica.com* *$10* *Reservations essential* 💳 *AE, D, MC, V* *May–Sept.*

Red Lodge KOA. With its heated pool, playground, and trout-filled brook for fishing, this tidy campground is ideal for families. Sites are along the banks of small creeks and among shady willows and pine trees. The group site, popular for reunions, hosts up to 50 guests. *Flush toilets, full hookups, partial hookups (water), drinking water, laundry facilities, showers, fire grates, picnic tables, food service, electricity, public telephone, play area, pool* *13 full hookups, 35 partial hookups, 20 tent sites; 6 cabins* ✉ *7464 U.S. 212, 4 mi north of Red Lodge* ☎ *406/446–2364 or 800/562–7540* 📠 *406/446–2364* 🌐 *www.koa.com* *Full hookups $28, partial hookups and tent sites $20; cabins $40–$45* *Reservations essential* 💳 *D, MC, V* *Mid-May–mid-Sept.*

Nightlife & the Arts

NIGHTLIFE You can sit back with a beer and watch the Bearcreek Downs' Pig Races at the **Bear Creek Saloon** (✉ 108 W. Main St., Bearcreek, 7 mi east of Red Lodge on Hwy. 308 ☎ 406/446–3481), a bar and steak house. Piglets streak through the miniature race courses while patrons bet on favorite oinkers; the proceeds from the betting fund local scholarships. The races take place summer evenings at 7, from Friday through Sunday.

THE ARTS Internationally recognized painter Kevin Red Star, a Crow Indian, displays his oils, acrylics, lithographs, and etchings at **Kevin Red Star Studio & Gallery** (✉ 103 S. Main St., Roberts, 13 mi north of Red Lodge on U.S. 212 ☎ 406/445–2211 or 800/858–2584). His works are in the permanent collections of the Smithsonian Institution, the Institute of American Indian Art, and the Pierre Cardin Collection in Paris.

The historic **Round Barn Restaurant and Theater** (✉ 7193 U.S. 212 N, 2 mi north of Red Lodge ☎ 406/446–1197) hosts year-round plays, concerts, and comedy acts, mostly on weekends.

Shopping

Magpie Toymakers (✉ 115 N. Broadway ☎ 406/446–3044) sells a dizzying array of toys, some crafted locally. From hiking accessories to cross-country-skiing gear, **Sylvan Peak Mountain Shoppe** (✉ 9 S. Broadway ☎ 406/446–1770 or 800/249–2563) carries a large selection of top-quality mountain-country dry goods, locally made fleece jackets, hats, and kids' togs. Distinctive clothing, handmade jewelry, handcrafted furniture, and gifts are just some of the offerings at **Twin Elk** (✉ 6382 U.S. 212 ☎ 406/446–3121 or 877/894–6355), at the Rock Creek Resort.

en route

Driving south from Red Lodge on U.S. 212 will take you over the precipitous **Beartooth Pass,** which winds its way through lush alpine country to the "back door" of Yellowstone National Park in Wyoming. The highway is usually open from May to September, but wintery weather can close it at any time of the year. It's a good idea to fill the gas tank and cooler before you leave Red Lodge, because it's 64 mi to the next gas station. Several hiking trails lead off the highway; for hiking maps and more information, contact the **Beartooth Ranger District** (☎ 406/446–2103) in Red Lodge.

Absaroka-Beartooth Wilderness

12 mi south of Red Lodge via Beartooth Hwy.; 10 mi west of Red Lodge via Rock Creek Rd.

Although summer visitors swarm into Yellowstone National Park to the south, relatively few (except for dedicated backcountry travelers) come to the Absaroka-Beartooth Wilderness. One reason is that, unlike Yellowstone, the wilderness area has no paved roads leading into it, although a four-wheel-drive vehicle is not essential for access. Montana's highest mountains, including the 12,799-foot Granite Peak, are encompassed by the wilderness boundaries; because of that, the prime hiking season (August) is relatively short. Many of the 640 high-mountain lakes may remain partially frozen even into August, especially in the high plateau region. Perhaps the most popular hiking is in the East Fork–Rosebud Creek area (35 mi one-way), with its numerous lakes in alpine basins above 9,000 feet. Hikes are moderate to strenuous. Keep in mind that this is grizzly bear country. You can get information and permits from Custer National Forest in Billings, or Gallatin National Forest in Bozeman.

For information on the western half of the wilderness, contact **Gallatin National Forest** (✉ Federal Bldg., 3017 Fallon St., Suite C, Bozeman 59718 ☎ 406/522–2520 🌐 www.fs.fed.us/r1/gallatin). For information on the eastern half of the wilderness, contact **Custer National Forest** (✉ 1310 Main St., Billings 59105 ☎ 406/657–6200 🌐 www.fs.fed.us/r1/custer).

Sports & the Outdoors

Because the Beartooths are rugged and remote, it's best to hire a guide unless you are familiar with the backcountry. Climbing guides and horse-pack trail guides can lead trips to remarkable and scenic places, safely. Most important, know backcountry rules regarding travel in grizzly bear country.

HORSEBACK RIDING Ride the high alpine wilderness trails on one- to five-day pack trips with **Beartooth Plateau Outfitters** (✉ 819 Clear Creek Rd., Roberts, 14 mi north of Red Lodge on U.S. 212 ☎ 800/253–8545 🌐 www.beartoothoutfitters.com), which also runs fly-fishing expeditions.

MOUNTAIN CLIMBING Experienced climbers from **Beartooth Mountain Guides** (☎ 406/446–9874) lead outings to the top of Montana's tallest mountain, the challenging 12,799-foot Granite Peak. They also offer daylong and multi-day trips of rock climbing, alpine and ski mountaineering, and ice climbing for beginners and experts.

Camping

Beartooth Lake Campground. More than a dozen U.S. Forest Service campgrounds on the edge of the wilderness are open for summer car camping. Beartooth Lake, at a 9,000-foot elevation, allows for outstanding views, water sports, and alpine scenery. *Pit toilets, drinking water, swimming (creek) 20 sites ✉ U.S. 212, 31 mi south of Red Lodge ☎ 406/446–2103 or 877/444–6777 406/446–3918 🌐 www.fs.fed.us/r1/custer or www.reserveusa.com $9 D, MC, V July–early Sept.*

Big Timber & the Boulder River

2 *88 mi northwest of Red Lodge via Hwy. 78 north and I–90 west; 81 mi west of Billings via I–90.*

People come to Big Timber to shop at its galleries and antiques shops, fly-fish the blue-ribbon trout streams, float the Yellowstone River, or unwind in front of the Crazy Mountains (so called because supposedly a homesteader went crazy from living in such a remote setting). South of town you can follow the Boulder River in its mad dash out of the Absaroka-Beartooth Wilderness. This journey along Highway 298 will take you into wild country, with craggy peaks rising on either side of a lush, ranch-filled valley.

The **Sweet Grass Chamber of Commerce** (✉ I–90, Exit 367 ☎ 406/932–5131 🌐 www.bigtimber.com) can provide information about sightseeing in the region; of particular interest in the area are a prairie-dog park and a natural bridge.

Explore the Boulder Valley and drop by the **Yellowstone River Trout Hatchery** to gaze at cutthroat trout. The best time to visit the hatchery is in spring, when you can see the fingerlings. *✉ Fairgrounds Rd. ☎ 406/932–4434 ✉ Free Daily, 24 hrs.*

A beautiful building houses the **Crazy Mountain Museum,** with exhibits on Big Timber's history and people, as well as the Crazy Mountains. Highlights include the famous Cramer Rodeo, sheep and wool exhibits, and a room dedicated to pioneers that includes artifacts dating to the late 1890s. Also here are a detailed miniature model of Big Timber in 1907, the restored Sour Dough School House, and a reconstruction of a *stabbur* (a Norwegian-style grain storehouse). *✉ Cemetery Rd., Exit 367 off I–90 ☎ 406/932–5126 🌐 www.bigtimber.com Donations accepted Late May–early Sept., Tues.–Sun. 1–4:30 or by appointment.*

The comical critters at **Greycliff Prairie Dog Town State Park** pop out of their underground homes, sound their chirping alarms, and dash across the grassland to another hole. Explorers Meriwether Lewis and William Clark referred to these "barking squirrels" in their journals. At this large protected habitat, you can wander the trails for easy viewing. Watch out for rattlesnakes. *✉ I–90, Exit 377, Greycliff ☎ 406/247–2940 🌐 www.fwp.state.mt.us $1 May–Sept., daily dawn–dusk.*

At **Natural Bridge State Park,** the Boulder River disappears underground, creating a natural bridge, then reappears as roaring falls in the Boulder

River canyon. Hiking trails and interpretive signs explain how this geologic wonder occurred. ✉ *Hwy. 298, 22 mi south of Big Timber* ☎ *406/247–2940* 🌐 *www.fwp.state.mt.us* *Free* ⏲ *Daily.*

The annual one-day **"Running of the Sheep" Sheep Drive** (✉ I–90, Exit 392, Reed Point, 25 mi west of Big Timber ☎ 406/326–2288) in September celebrates the hundreds of sturdy Montana-bred sheep and the state's agriculture history with humor. In addition to the sheep run (the sheep are let loose down the main street, sort of like the bulls in Pamplona, Spain, only a lot tamer), you can see a precision draft-horse event (in which the handlers and horses maneuver together) and a contest for the ugliest sheep and the prettiest ewe.

off the beaten path

INDIAN CAVES PICTOGRAPHS – Native Americans lived in the area for more than 10,000 years, leaving evidence of their presence on cave walls here, including a depiction of a bison hunt. To get to the cave you'll have to hike 1½ mi along the Grouse Creek Trail, near the main Boulder Ranger Station on U.S. 298. The cave is always open and accessible, but in poor weather the trail can be difficult to hike. A flashlight is useful for visiting the cave, particularly on overcast days. ✉ *U.S. 298, 26 mi south of Big Timber on the Main Boulder River* ☎ *406/932–5155.*

Sports & the Outdoors

FISHING You're likely to see white pelicans, bald eagles, white-tailed deer, and cutthroat trout on float and fishing trips on the Yellowstone River with **Big Timber Guides and Rollin' Boulder Outfitters** (✉ 108 E. Boulder Rd., McLeod ☎ 406/932–4080 or 406/932–5836). The company also offers horseback riding and pack trips.

You can fish in private lakes or streams at the 2,300-acre **Burns Ranch** (✉ 333 Swamp Creek Rd. ☎ 406/932–4518, 406/932–4150, 406/220–6690, or 406/932–4891). The 40-acre Burns Lake, with rainbow, cutthroat, brown, and brook trout, is limited to a few anglers a day. The cost is $80 per rod, and reservations are required. The ranch is 4 mi north of Big Timber on U.S. 191 and then another 4 mi west on Swamp Creek Road.

HORSEBACK RIDING Ride the 11,000-acre range with cowboys on the **Range Riders Ranch** (✉ 238A Bridger Creek Rd., Reed Point ☎ 406/932–6538), a working cattle ranch. Trail rides take you to scenic spots with view of the Crazy and Beartooth mountains. You can also arrange for overnight campouts or a weeklong cattle drive.

Where to Stay & Eat

$–$$ ✕ **Prospector Pizza.** You can dine in or take out at this popular downtown pizza joint. Aside from basic pizzas, Prospector prepares deli sandwiches, burgers, ribs, and steaks. ✉ *121 McLeod St.* ☎ *406/932–4846* 💳 *D, MC, V* ⏲ *Closed Sun.*

¢–$ ✕ **Cole Drug.** Behind the historic brick-front facade of this pharmacy is an old-fashioned soda fountain, where friendly folks whip up Italian sodas, milk shakes, and the giant Big Timber, with nine scoops of ice cream and various toppings. ✉ *136 McLeod St.* ☎ *406/932–5316 or 888/836–4146* 💳 *AE, D, MC, V* ⏲ *Closed Sun. No dinner.*

★ **¢–$** ✕🏨 **Grand Hotel.** Fine dining and an 1890s saloon are two of the attractions of this classic Western hotel in the middle of downtown Big Timber. The romantic restaurant ($$$–$$$$) serves steaks, seafood, and lamb for lunch and dinner, plus decadent desserts. The antiques-furnished rooms are small, clean, and comfortable—the kind of accommodations you might find over the Longbranch Saloon in *Gunsmoke*. A full breakfast is included in the room rate. ✉ *139 McLeod St., 59011* ☎ *406/932–4459* 🖷 *406/932–4248* 🌐 *www.thegrand-hotel.com* *10 rooms, 4 with bath* *Restaurant, bar, meeting room; no smoking* ▭ *D, MC, V* *BP.*

$$ **Carriage House Ranch.** This ranch retreat, named for an 1886 Dutch carriage barn on the premises, has B&B rooms, trail rides, fishing, carriage rides, and a café. Events such as team steer roping and training for carriage driving are held in the ranch equestrian center, which also houses rare Holstein horses from Holland. There are even bed and barn facilities for the equines of the family. The B&B rooms have an eclectic Western style, with period furnishings and wallpaper. ✉ *771 U.S. 191 N, 59011* ☎ *406/932–5339 or 877/932–5339* 🖷 *406/932–5863* 🌐 *www.carriagehouseranch.com* *4 rooms* *Café, some kitchens, fishing, mountain bikes, horseback riding, shop, laundry facilities, meeting rooms, helipad, some pets allowed; no TVs in some rooms, no smoking* ▭ *AE, MC, V.*

CAMPING **Halfmoon Campground.** At the end of a dusty road leading into the remote and lovely Crazy Mountains, this respite with tent sites is ideal for scenic picnicking, hiking, and fishing. *Pit toilets. Drinking water. Some fire grates, picnic tables. Swimming (creek)* *12 sites* ✉ *11 mi north of Big Timber on U.S. 191, then 12 mi west on Big Timber Canyon Rd.* ☎ *406/932–5155* 🌐 *www.fs.fed.us/r1/gallatin* *$5* *Reservations not accepted* ▭ *No credit cards.*

Hicks Park Campground. On the Main Boulder River, this remote jewel is en route to one of the entrances to the Absaroka-Beartooth Wilderness and has good fishing access. *Pit toilets, drinking water, fire pits, picnic tables* *16 sites* ✉ *Rd. 212; head 25 mi south of Big Timber on U.S. 298, then 15½ mi south on Rd. 212* ☎ *406/932–5155* 🌐 *www.fs.fed.us/r1/gallatin* *$5* *Reservations not accepted* ▭ *No credit cards.*

West Boulder Campground and Cabin. Shady and cool, this remote setting is known for good fishing, access to the Absaroka-Beartooth Wilderness, and quiet camping. The cabin has electricity, a woodstove, a refrigerator, and water in summer. *Pit toilets, drinking water, fire pits, picnic tables* ✉ *West Boulder Rd.; head 16 mi south of Big Timber on U.S. 298 to McLeod, 6½ mi southwest on Rd. 30, and 8 mi southwest on West Boulder Rd.* ☎ *406/932–5155* 🌐 *www.fs.fed.us/r1/gallatin* *10 tent sites, 1 cabin* *Tent sites $5; cabin $35* *Reservations essential for cabin* ▭ *No credit cards.*

Nightlife & the Arts

NIGHTLIFE The name may evoke unsavory images, but that doesn't stop fly-fishing anglers, ranchers, and curious tourists from filling the **Road Kill Cafe and Bar** (✉ U.S. 298, McLeod, 14 mi south of Big Timber ☎ 406/932–6174). Beer, burgers, and Road Kill T-shirts are big sellers.

THE ARTS Cowboy music, poetry, and good humor spur the annual **Cowboy Poetry Wintercamp** (✉ 110 E. 3rd Ave. ☎ 406/932–4227), which takes place at the American Legion Hall in mid-January. Day shows are free; evening shows cost $12.

Livingston & the Yellowstone River

❸ *35 mi west of Big Timber via I–90; 116 mi west of Billings via I–90.*

The stunning mountain backdrop to the town of Livingston was once Crow territory, and a chief called Arapooish said about it: "The Crow country is good country. The Great Spirit has put it in exactly the right place. When you are in it, you fare well; when you go out of it, you fare worse."

The railroads brought white settlers, and Livingston, along the banks of the beautiful Yellowstone River, was built to serve the railroad. The railroad still runs through the town of 12,000, but now tourism is a leading business, and there are some 14 art galleries. Robert Redford chose the town, with its turn-of-the-20th-century flavor, to film parts of the movie *A River Runs Through It.*

Antique creels, fly rods, flies, and aquarium exhibits are among the displays at the Federation of Fly Fishers' **International Fly Fishing Center,** housed in a former school. The museum–education center hosts year-round classes, such as the free summer casting lesson every Tuesday and Thursday evening from 5 to 7. ✉ *At B and Lewis Sts.* ☎ *406/222–9369* 🌐 *www.fedflyfishers.org* 🎫 *$4* ⏲ *June–Sept., Mon.–Sat. 10–6, Sun. noon–5; Oct.–May, weekdays 10–4.*

The old **Livingston Depot Center in the Northern Pacific Depot** is now a museum with displays on Western and railroad history and works by artists from the region and across the country. The 1902 depot, an Italian villa–style structure, has mosaic trim, a terrazzo floor, and wrought-iron ticket windows. ✉ *200 W. Park St., Exit 333 off I–90 and turn right onto Park St.* ☎ *406/222–2300* 🎫 *$3* ⏲ *Mid-May–Oct., Mon.–Sat. 9–5, Sun. 1–5.*

The **Yellowstone Gateway Museum,** on the north side of town in a turn-of-the-20th-century schoolhouse, holds an eclectic collection, including items from a 10,000-year-old Native American dig site and a flag fragment associated with the Battle of the Little Bighorn. Outdoor displays include an old caboose, a sheep wagon, a stagecoach, and other pioneer memorabilia. ✉ *118 W. Chinook St.* ☎ *406/222–4184* 🎫 *$4* ⏲ *Late May–early Sept., daily 10–5; rest of Sept., daily noon–4; Oct.–late May, by appointment.*

Just south of Livingston and north of Yellowstone National Park, the **Yellowstone River** comes roaring down the Yellowstone Plateau and flows through Paradise Valley. Primitive public campsites (available on a first-come, first-served basis) and fishing access sites can be found at various places along the river, which is especially popular for trout fishing, rafting, and canoeing. U.S. 89 follows the west bank of the river, and East River Road runs along the east side.

Since the 1920s, cowboys and cowgirls have ridden and roped at the annual **Livingston Roundup Rodeo,** held on Independence Day weekend at the Park County Fairgrounds. A 3 PM parade, queen-selecting contest, and hoedown kick off the celebration. ✉ *46 View Vista Dr.* ☎ *406/222–6789 or 406/222–3199* 🌐 *www.yellowstone-chamber.com* 🎫 *$11* ⏲ *Independence Day weekend, 8 PM nightly.*

Since the 1950s the **Wilsall Rodeo** (✉ U.S. 89 N, east on Clark St. past grain elevator to rodeo grounds, Wilsall ☎ 406/578–2290) has been showcasing cowboy and cowgirl events in late June at this ranching community at the base of the Crazy Mountains.

off the beaten path

PARADISE VALLEY LOOP – A drive on this loop takes you along the spectacular Yellowstone River for a short ways and then past historic churches, schoolhouses, hot springs, and expansive ranches, all backed by the peaks of the Absaroka-Beartooth Wilderness. From Livingston head 3 mi south on U.S. 89, turn east onto East River Road, and follow it over the Yellowstone River and for 32 mi through the tiny towns of Pine Creek, Pray, Chico, and Emigrant. You'll eventually hit U.S. 89 again, where roadside historic markers detail early inhabitants' lives; follow it north to Livingston. ☎ *406/222–0850* 🌐 *www.yellowstone-chamber.com.*

Sports & the Outdoors

From the spring hatch of "Mother's Day" caddis flies through late-fall streamer fishing, the Yellowstone River and its tributary streams draw fly fishers from around the globe to the blue-ribbon streams for Yellowstone cutthroat, brown, and rainbow trout. Hiking trails lead into remote accesses of surrounding peaks, often snowcapped through June.

BOATING In late July, the annual three-day **Yellowstone Boat Float** (☎ 406/248–7182), a boating get-together with canoes, kayaks, and fishing and drift boats, begins at Livingston, with overnight stops in Big Timber and Reed Point, and ends at Laurel. Some people camp overnight; others stay in hotels or go home.

FISHING **George Anderson's Yellowstone Angler** (✉ 5256 U.S. 89 S ☎ 406/222–7130) specializes in catch-and-release fly-fishing trips floating on the Yellowstone River, wade trips on spring creeks, access to private lakes and streams, and fly-casting instruction.

The fishing experts at **Dan Bailey's** (✉ 209 W. Park St. ☎ 406/222–1673) can help you find the right fly, tackle, and outdoor clothing. Rental equipment, fly-fishing clinics, and float and wade trips are also available.

HORSEBACK RIDING **Bear Paw Outfitters** (✉ 136 Deep Creek Rd. ☎ 406/222–6642 or 406/222–5800) runs day rides and pack trips in Paradise Valley, the Absaroka-Beartooth Wilderness, and Yellowstone National Park; prices start at $25 per hour aboard horses or mules.

SCENIC FLIGHTS **Paradise Valley Flying Service** (✉ 3693 U.S. 89 S, 17 mi south of Livingston ☎ 406/333–4788) takes you soaring over the mountains and vales of Paradise Valley.

Where to Stay & Eat

★ $$–$$$$ ✕ **Chathams Livingston Bar and Grill.** The enlightened Continental cuisine and owner Russell Chatham's elegant drawings and lithographs of landscapes create a comfortable dining experience. The seasonal menu may include fresh blue-crab salad topped with avocado, or a tomato salad with Spanish anchovies. Fresh seafood is flown in daily and served with imported Italian pastas. The most popular dish is the filet mignon, topped with a port sauce or a bourbon-honey glaze. Chatham's work is also displayed down the block at Legends Fine Art. ✉ *130 N. Main St.* ☎ *406/222–7909* ▭ *DC, MC, V.*

$–$$$ ✕ **Montana's Rib & Chop House.** Here, in the middle of cattle country, you can expect the juiciest, most tender steaks—such as the flavorful hand-cut rib eye—all made from certified Angus beef. Jambalaya, baby back ribs, and catfish are also on the menu. ✉ *119 W. Park St.* ☎ *406/222–9200* ▭ *AE, D, MC, V.*

¢–$ ✕ **Paradise Valley Pop Stand & Grill.** You can dine in or order takeout from this 1950s-style burger and ice-cream joint. The ice cream is made locally. ✉ *5006 U.S. 89, 2 mi south of Livingston* ☎ *406/222–2006* ⏲ *Closed Mon.* ▭ *No credit cards.*

★ $$$$ 🏨 **B Bar Ranch.** In winter, this 20,000-acre working cattle ranch invites guests for spectacular winter adventures in cross-country skiing and wildlife tracking. The ranch shares a 6-mi boundary with Yellowstone National Park, in Tom Miner Basin, 36 mi south of Livingston. Some of the 24 mi of impeccably groomed trails are created by rare Suffolk Punch draft horses from the country's largest herd, here on the B Bar. Sleigh rides and naturalist-led trips into Yellowstone are some of the activities. Rates include meals and activities, and there's a two-night minimum stay. ✉ *818 Tom Miner Creek Rd., Emigrant 59027* ☎ *406/848–7523* 🖷 *406/847–7793* *6 cabins, 3 lodge rooms* *Dining room, outdoor hot tub, cross-country skiing, ice skating, piano, shop, meeting rooms; no room phones, no room TVs, no smoking* ▭ *No credit cards* *FAP* *Closed Mar.–mid-Dec.*

$$$$ **Mountain Sky Guest Ranch.** This full-service guest-ranch resort in the middle of scenic Paradise Valley and 30 mi north of Yellowstone National Park is a family favorite. The log cabins feel luxurious after a day in the saddle. The children's programs offer age-appropriate activities such as hiking, swimming, crafts, hayrides, campfires, and a talent show. Dinners range from Western barbecues to gourmet treats such as grilled lamb loin topped with fig-and-port-wine glaze. Everyone learns to dance the two-step to a local band. There's a seven-night minimum stay in summer only. ✉ *Big Creek Rd., Emigrant, U.S. 89 29 mi south of I–90, then west 4½ mi on Big Creek Rd.* *Box 1128, Bozeman 59715* ☎ *406/587–1244 or 800/548–3392* 🖷 *406/587–3977 or 406/333–4911* *www.mtnsky.com* *30 cabins* *Dining room, refrigerators, tennis court, pool, outdoor hot tub, sauna, fishing, mountain bikes, hiking, horseback riding, horseshoes, volleyball, bar, dance club, recreation room, shop, baby-sitting, children's programs (ages 1–18), playground, laundry facilities, laundry service, Internet, meeting rooms, airport shuttle; no room phones, no room TVs* ▭ *MC, V* *FAP.*

$$$ **63 Ranch.** Owned by the same family since 1929, this 2,000-acre working cattle ranch is one of Montana's oldest. Only weeklong packages are available, and they include a full range of activities, from horseback riding to fishing to pack trips. The eight rustic cabins are commodious yet comfortable, with log furniture and private baths. ✉ *Off Bruffey La.,12 mi southeast of Livingston* *Box MA979, 59047* ☎ *406/222–0570* 🖷 *406/222–9446 or 406/222–6363* *www.sixtythreeranch.com* *9 cabins* *Dining room, pond, fishing, horseback riding, laundry facilities* ▭ *No credit cards* *FAP* *Closed mid-Sept.–mid-June.*

★ ¢–$$$ **Chico Hot Springs Resort.** During the gold rush of the 1860s, a miner noted that he "washed [his] dirty duds" in the hot-springs water near the Yellowstone River. Soon, a series of bathhouses sprang up, attracting people to the medicinal waters. The Chico Warm Springs Hotel opened in 1900, drawing famous folks such as painter Charlie Russell (1864–1926) to the 104°F–107°F pools. The hotel is surrounded by large outdoor soak pools, a convention center, and upscale cottages that open to views of the 10,920-foot Emigrant Peak and the Absaroka-Beartooth Wilderness beyond. ✉ *1 Old Chico Rd., Pray 59065* ☎ *406/333–4933 or 800/468–9232* 🖷 *406/333–4694* *www.chicohotsprings.com* *82 rooms, 4 suites, 16 cottages* *Restaurant, pizzeria, snack bar, room service, in-room data ports, some in-room hot tubs, some kitchens, some refrigerators, massage, spa, fishing, hiking, horseback riding, cross-country skiing, 2 bars, piano, shop, business services, convention center, airstrip, free parking, some pets allowed, no-smoking rooms; no room TVs* ▭ *AE, D, MC, V.*

¢–$$ **The Murray Hotel.** Even cowboys love soft pillows, which is why they come to this 1904 town centerpiece, whose floors have seen silver-tipped cowboy boots, fly-fishing waders, and the sparkling heels of Hollywood celebrities. Antiques reflect a different theme in each guest room. Historic photos and stuffed game animals decorate the comfortable lobby and surround the antique elevator, which is still in use. ✉ *201 W. Park St., 59047* ☎ *406/222–1350* 🖷 *406/222–2752* *www.murrayhotel.com* *30 rooms* *In-room data ports, outdoor hot tub, bar, no-smoking floors* ▭ *AE, D, MC, V.*

CAMPING **Paradise Valley/Livingston KOA.** Set among willows, cottonwoods, and small evergreens, this full-service campground is well situated along the banks of the Yellowstone River, 50 mi north of Yellowstone National Park. It's popular with families, who enjoy the heated pool. It's a good idea to reserve ahead. *Flush toilets, full hookups, dump station, drinking water, laundry facilities, showers, fire grates, picnic tables, electricity, public telephone, general store, indoor pool* *82 RV sites, 27 tent sites, 22 cabins, 1 cottage* ✉ *163 Pine Creek Rd.; 10 mi south of Livingston on U.S. 89, then ½ mi east on Pine Creek Rd.* ☎ *406/222–0992 or 800/562–2805* 🌐 *www.koa.com* *Full hookups $30, tent sites $20; cabins $45–$55; cottage $130* *AE, D, MC, V* *May–Oct.*

Pine Creek Campground. A thick growth of pine trees surrounds this relatively flat campground at the base of the mountains. It's near the trailhead for challenging hikes to Pine Creek Waterfalls and the Absaroka-Beartooth Wilderness. *Pit toilets, drinking water, fire pits, picnic tables* *24 sites* ✉ *End of Pine Creek Rd.; 9 mi south of Livingston on U.S. 89, then 6 mi east on Pine Creek Rd.* ☎ *406/222–1892 or 877/444–6777* 🌐 *www.fs.fed.us/r1/gallatin* *$9* *AE, MC, V* *Late May–early Sept.*

Nightlife & the Arts

NIGHTLIFE With dancing and country music, microbrews, video poker, and keno, the **Buffalo Jump Steakhouse & Saloon** (✉ 5237 U.S. 89 S ☎ 406/222–2987) has livened up many a Saturday night in Livingston. Friday and Saturday evenings June through August, the **Pine Creek Cafe** (✉ 2496 East River Rd. ☎ 406/222–3628) serves up live bluegrass music, barbecue burgers, and beer under the stars. The fun starts at 7.

THE ARTS Livingston's beauty has inspired artists, as evidenced by the many fine art galleries in town. The **Danforth Gallery** (✉ 106 N. Main St. ☎ 406/222–6510) is a community art center that displays and sells works by local and regional artists. Subtle, moody images by Russell Chatham and ★ other artists line the walls of **Legends Fine Art** (✉ 120 N. Main St. ☎ 406/222–0317), and bronzes, oils, and lithographs fill the studio. **Visions West Gallery** (✉ 108 S. Main St. ☎ 406/222–0337) specializes in Western and wildlife art, including numerous works on the fly-fishing theme, from paintings and bronzes to hand-carved flies.

The historic district's **Blue Slipper Theatre** (✉ 113 E. Callender St. ☎ 406/222–7720) presents various full-length productions, including one-act plays, popular melodramas, and an annual Christmas variety show. The **Firehouse 5 Playhouse** (✉ Sleeping Giant Trade Center, 5237 U.S. 89 S ☎ 406/222–1420) stages comedies, dramas, and musicals year-round.

Shopping

The floorboards creak as you walk through **Sax and Fryer's** (✉ 109 W. Callender St. ☎ 406/222–1421), an old-time bookstore specializing in Western literature and especially books by Montana authors. It's the oldest store in Livingston and also sells newspapers, cards, and gifts.

In addition to selling outdoor clothing, boots, and bicycles, **Timber Trails** (✉ 309 W. Park St. ☎ 406/222–9550) helps mountain bikers, hikers, and cross-country skiers with trail maps, directions, and friendly advice.

Three Forks

❹ *51 mi west of Livingston via I–90; 29 mi west of Bozeman via I–90.*

Sacajawea (circa 1786–1812), famed for helping Lewis and Clark, traveled in the Three Forks area with her Shoshone family before she was kidnapped as a child by a rival tribe, the Hidatsas. Five years later she returned here as part of the Lewis and Clark expedition. In 1805 they arrived at the forks (of the Madison, Jefferson, and Gallatin rivers), now in Missouri Headwaters State Park, looking for the river that would lead them to the Continental Divide. A plaque in the city park commemorates her contribution to the expedition's success.

The Madison, Jefferson, and Gallatin rivers come together to form the ★ mighty Missouri River within **Missouri Headwaters State Park,** a National Historic Landmark. At 2,315 mi, the Missouri is the country's second-longest river, after the Mississippi. Lewis and Clark named the three forks after Secretary of the Treasury Albert Gallatin, Secretary of State James Madison, and President Thomas Jefferson. The park has historical exhibits, interpretive signs, picnic sites, hiking trails, and camping. ✉ *Trident Rd., 3 mi northeast of Three Forks on I–90, exit at the Three Forks off-ramp, then go east on 205, and 3 mi north on 286* ☎ *406/994–4042* 🌐 *www.fwp.state.mt.us* 🎫 *$5 per vehicle (includes admission to Madison Buffalo Jump)* ⏲ *Daily dawn–dusk.*

Within the **Madison Buffalo Jump** historic site is the cliff where Plains Indians stampeded bison to their deaths for more than 2,000 years until the arrival of Europeans' guns in the West. An interpretive center explains how the technique enabled Native Americans to gather food and hides. Picnic areas provide a restful break from touring. Be on the lookout for rattlesnakes here, and avoid wandering off the paths; do not turn over any rocks or logs, where the rattlers often hide. ✉ *Buffalo Jump Rd., 5 mi east of Three Forks on I–90, exiting at Logan, then 7 mi south on Buffalo Jump Rd.* ☎ *406/994–4042* 🌐 *www.fwp.state.mt.us* 🎫 *$5 per vehicle (includes admission to Missouri Headwaters State Park)* ⏲ *Daily dawn–dusk.*

The **Lewis and Clark Caverns,** Montana's oldest state park, hold some of the most beautiful underground landscape in the nation. Two-hour tours lead through narrow passages and vaulted chambers past colorful, intriguingly varied limestone formations. The temperature stays in the 50s year-round; jackets and rubber-sole shoes are recommended. Note that the hike to the cavern entrance is mildly strenuous and that the cave trip involves lots of bending and stooping. Each cave area is lighted during the tour, but it's still a good idea to bring a flashlight. A campground sits at the lower end of the park. ✉ *Hwy. 2, 19 mi west of Three Forks* ☎ *406/287–3541* 🎫 *$8* ⏲ *June–early Sept., daily 9–6:30; May and early Sept.–late Sept., daily 9–4:30.*

Thousands of local historical artifacts are on display in the **Headwaters Heritage Museum,** including a small anvil, all that is left of a trading post, Fort Three Forks, established in 1810. There's also an exhibit of a one-room schoolhouse. ✉ *Main and Cedar Sts.* ☎ *406/285–4778* 🎫 *Donations accepted* ⏲ *June–Sept., Mon.–Sat. 9–5, Sun. 1–5; Oct.–May by appointment.*

Sports & the Outdoors

BOATING In addition to arranging fly-fishing float trips, **Canoeing House and Guide Service** (✉ 11227 U.S. 287 ☎ 406/285–3488) rents canoes for trips down the Madison, Gallatin, and Jefferson rivers.

SCENIC FLIGHTS "Flightseeing" trips with **Bridger Aviation** (✉ 1680 Airport Rd. ☎ 406/285–4264) take you a thousand feet above the confluence of the Madison, Gallatin, and Jefferson rivers. The knowledgeable pilots can show you several otherwise-inaccessible historic sites from the air, including tepee rings, bison herds, and buffalo jumps.

Where to Stay & Eat

★ **$–$$$** ✕ **Historic Headwaters Restaurant.** This 1908 brick restaurant once served railroad passengers on their way to see Yellowstone National Park. The smoke-free dining area now includes a summertime dining patio surrounded

ON THE TRAIL OF LEWIS & CLARK

A **MERICA'S GREATEST ADVENTURE** *began with the stroke of a pen, when in 1803 President Thomas Jefferson purchased the vast Louisiana Territory from cash-strapped France, effectively doubling the size of the United States. The land, stretching from the Gulf of Mexico to Canada and from the Mississippi River to the Rockies, was unmapped and virtually unknown to outsiders. To understand what his $16 million had bought, Jefferson appointed a secret "Corps of Discovery" to venture west, make contact with native peoples, chart the landscape, and observe the growing British presence in the Pacific Northwest. The group would be headed by Jefferson's personal secretary, Meriwether Lewis, and another intrepid explorer, William Clark.*

On May 14, 1804, Lewis and Clark set out from St. Louis on their expedition with a party of 45 seasoned soldiers, scouts, interpreters, and others, poling up the Missouri River in well-stocked flatboats and keelboats. After wintering with the Mandans in North Dakota, the corps continued upriver in canoes and keelboats as soon as ice jams had cleared the waterway. They entered what is now Montana on April 27, 1805, and followed the Missouri to its Montana headwaters—the confluence of the Jefferson, Madison, and Gallatin rivers. After they reached the Continental Divide, Shoshone Indians helped them cross the Rockies. The party then followed the Snake, Clearwater, and Columbia rivers, reaching the Pacific Ocean that fall. On the return trip, the expedition split into two groups in Montana and explored several rivers, including the Yellowstone. The expedition arrived back in St. Louis on September 23, 1806, having traveled more than 8,000 mi. Over a quarter of the expedition was spent in Montana, where much of the land the explorers observed remains unchanged today.

If you want to retrace Lewis and Clark's footsteps, the best place to start is the Lewis and Clark National Historic Trail Interpretive Center in Great Falls, where the 200-year-old adventure unfolds before you. Nearby Giant Springs State Park marks the place where Clark discovered a large "fountain or spring" during an 18-mi portage around a series of waterfalls. Missouri Headwaters State Park near Three Forks preserves the spot where the explorers traced the river to its origin. The Lolo Pass Visitor Center, on U.S. 12 at the Montana-Idaho border, interprets the Lewis and Clark Expedition. Another means of Lewis and Clark discovery is a boat tour on the "Mighty Mo." Several operators offer tours at Gates of the Mountains, north of Helena off I–15, and also at the White Cliffs area of the Upper Missouri National Wild and Scenic River below Fort Benton. A canoe rental and shuttle service on the Missouri near Loma gives you a self-guided option. And look for Lewis and Clark Trail signs along state, U.S., and interstate highways that follow the expedition's route.

---

by native plants, flowers, and a stream. Today diners eat better than Lewis and Clark: the Culinary Institute of America–trained chef-owner prepares such dishes as buffalo-chorizo enchiladas with black-bean sauce and smoked-corn salsa, and melt-in-your-mouth barbecue beef. ✉ *105 S. Main St.* ☎ *406/285–4511* ▭ *MC, V* ⊗ *Closed Mon. and Tues.*

¢–$ ✕ **Wheat Montana.** A local ranching family grows and grinds its wheat, then bakes it into sandwich bread and bakery items for one of the best lunch meals in the state. Try the gigantic cinnamon rolls. Also for sale is grind-your-own flour from several kinds of wheat, including Prairie Gold Whole Wheat and Bronze Chief Hard Red Spring Wheat. Note that the shop closes at 7 PM. ✉ *I–90 at Exit 274* ☎ *406/285–3614 or 800/535–2798* ▭ *MC, V.*

$ 🏨 **Sacajawea Hotel.** The original portion of this hotel, built in 1910 by the Old Milwaukee Railroad, was rolled on logs to its current location, where it became a railroad hotel for travelers heading to Yellowstone National Park. The lofty lobby and cozy rooms retain their period style, and the front porch has rockers where you can relax with a book or watch the sunset. The restaurant prepares basic steak and fish, and the bar serves lighter fare. ✉ *5 N. Main St., 59752* ☎ *406/285–6515 or 888/722–2529* 🖷 *406/285–4210* 🌐 *www.sacajaweahotel.com* *30 rooms, 1 suite* *Restaurant, in-room data ports, cable TV, fishing, bar, piano, meeting rooms, some pets allowed (fee); no smoking.* 💳 *AE, D, DC, MC, V.*

CAMPING **Missouri Headwaters State Park.** Tent sites are strewn among the cottonwood trees of the campground at this park. An interpretive kiosk details the Lewis and Clark adventure through the area. Be prepared for mosquitoes and rattlesnakes along the 4 mi of hiking trails. Reservations are taken only for groups. *Flush toilets, pit toilets, drinking water, fire grates, picnic tables* *23 sites* ✉ *Hwy. 286; 4 mi northeast of Three Forks on Hwy. 205, then north on Hwy. 286* ☎ *406/994–6934* 🌐 *www.fwp.state.mt.us* *$12–$15* 💳 *No credit cards* *May–Sept.*

Big Sky & Gallatin Canyon

❺ *75 mi southeast of Three Forks via I–90 and then U.S. 191; 43 mi south of Bozeman via U.S. 191 and west on Big Sky Rd.*

Lone Peak, the mountain that looms over the isolated community beneath Big Sky, is an appropriate metaphor for the **Big Sky Ski and Summer Resort,** conceived in the 1970s by the renowned TV newscaster Chet Huntley. Three village areas make up a solitary node of civilization in otherwise undeveloped country, between Bozeman and West Yellowstone. One is in the Gallatin Canyon area along the Gallatin River and U.S. 191, and another, the Meadow Village, radiates from the 18-hole Big Sky Golf Course. The third enclave, 9 mi west of U.S. 191, is the full-service ski resort itself, overlooking rugged wilderness areas and Yellowstone National Park. The 1,220 locals are used to driving nearly 50 mi to Bozeman for such simple pleasures as a fresh head of lettuce.

This is not to suggest that Big Sky is uncivilized. Indeed, being just a few decades old and still growing, the resort is quite modern in its design and amenities. It's not as if you can't get a daily newspaper, cable TV, or a substantial, well-prepared meal. Still, Big Sky is one of the most remote major ski resorts in the country. Getting here invariably means at least one plane change en route to Bozeman and about an hour's drive to the resort through Gallatin Canyon, a narrow gorge of rock walls, the frothing Gallatin River, and the occasional snow-glazed grass benchland. However, once you're here, a true wilderness awaits you. Yellowstone National Park is visible from the upper mountain ski runs, as are 11 mountain ranges in three states. The park's western entrance at West Yellowstone is 40 mi from the town of Big Sky along a route frequented by elk, moose, and bison (use caution when driving U.S. 191).

There's a lack of crowds amongst all this rugged nature, but you don't even have to give up the creature comforts of a warm bed and a good meal. Major real-estate developments around Big Sky have started to impinge upon that resort-in-the-wild atmosphere, though. In addition to skiing, golfing, hiking, horseback riding, and other activities, Big Sky hosts many festivals, musical events, races, and tournaments. ✉ *1 Lone Mountain Trail, Box 160100, Big Sky 59716* ☎ *406/995–5000 or 800/548–4486* 🌐 *www.bigskyresort.com.*

A restored early-20th-century homestead and cattle ranch, **Historic Crail Ranch** makes a pleasant picnic spot in the midst of Big Sky's Meadow

Village area. To get here drive west on Big Sky Spur Road, make a right on Little Coyote, go past the chapel, and make a left onto Spotted Elk Road in Meadow Village. ✉ *Spotted Elk Rd.* ☎ *406/995–3000* 🌐 *www.bigskychamber.com* 🎟 *Free* ⏲ *Memorial Day–Labor Day, daily sunrise–sunset.*

Sports & the Outdoors

FISHING Fodor'sChoice ★ Rivers such as the **Gallatin,** which runs along U.S. 191, the Madison (one valley west), and the Yellowstone (one valley east) have made southwest Montana famous among fly fishers, most of whom visit during the nonwinter months. However, that's not to say the trout stop biting in winter; on almost any day of the winter, no matter how bitter or nasty the weather, usually a dozen or more die-hard anglers lay out lines in the Gallatin River.

East Slope Anglers (✉ 47855 Gallatin Rd. ☎ 406/995–4369 or 888/359–3974 🌐 www.eastslopeanglers.com) arranges guides for winter and summer fly-fishing. You can also rent or buy flies, rods and reels, clothing, and gifts here. Flies, rods and reels, clothing, and equipment rentals are available at **Gallatin Riverguides** (✉ U.S. 191 ☎ 406/995–2290 or 888/707–1505 🌐 www.montanaflyfishing.com), ½ mi south of the Big Sky entrance. Rental equipment and guide service is offered through **Lone Mountain Ranch** (✉ 4 mi west of U.S. 191, 6 mi from Big Sky resort, and ½ mi down gravel ranch road ☎ 406/995–4644 or 800/514–4644).

GOLF The 18-hole Arnold Palmer–designed **Big Sky Golf Course** (✉ Black Otter Rd., Meadow Village ☎ 406/995–5780 or 800/548–4486) has challenging holes along the fork of the Gallatin River, cooling breezes from snowy Lone Peak, and the occasional moose, elk, or deer on the green.

HORSEBACK RIDING **Jake's Horses & Outfitting** (✉ U.S. 191 and Beaver Creek Rd., 3 mi south of Big Sky ☎ 406/995–4630 or 800/352–5956) will take you riding through mountainous trails on Forest Service lands for one- and two-hour rides year-round. Weeklong pack trips inside Yellowstone National Park are also available.

KIDS' ACTIVITIES The kids-only Outdoor Youth Adventures program at **Lone Mountain Ranch** (✉ 4 mi west of U.S. 191 on Westfork Meadows and ½ mi down gravel ranch road ☎ 406/995–4734) includes building snow caves, tubing, snowshoeing, playing snow kick ball, and cross-country skiing.

RAFTING **Geyser Whitewater Expeditions** (✉ 46651 Gallatin Rd. ☎ 406/995–4989 or 800/914–9031) has guided raft trips on the Gallatin River. Since 1978, ★ **Yellowstone Raft Company** (✉ 55265 Gallatin Rd. ☎ 406/995–4613 or 800/348–4376) has been arranging guided raft trips and kayak lessons on the Gallatin and Yellowstone rivers.

SNOWMOBILING Far and away the most popular nonskiing activity in the region is snowmobiling into and around Yellowstone National Park. West Yellowstone, 50 mi south of Big Sky on U.S. 191, prides itself on being the "Snowmobile Capital of the World," and in winter there are more snowmobiles in town than cars. The most popular excursion is the 60-mi round-trip between West Yellowstone and Old Faithful.

SNOWSHOEING You can rent snowshoes through **Big Sky Rentals** (✉ Snowcrest Lodge, Plaza Area ☎ 406/995–5841) for use on the resort's 2-mi Moose Tracks trail, which wends through aspen groves. Quiet and picturesque snowshoe trails lead through the woods and meadows of **Lone Mountain Ranch** (✉ 4 mi west of U.S. 191 on Westfork Meadows and ½ mi down gravel ranch road ☎ 406/995–4644 or 800/514–4644), where you can get a trail map and rent snowshoes and poles. **Montana Backcountry Adventures** (✉ Big Sky Spur Rd.; 1 mi outside Mountain Village ☎ 406/995–

3880 or 866/766–9622 🌐 www.skimba.com) offers guided half-day snowshoe tours through the Lee Metcalf Wilderness, where naturalists discuss fire ecology and native flora and fauna.

Downhill Skiing & Snowboarding

For many years, the attitude of more advanced skiers toward Big Sky was "big deal." There wasn't nearly enough challenging skiing to keep expert skiers interested for long, and certainly not for an entire ski week. As a remedy, the Big Sky people strung up the Challenger chairlift, one of the steepest in the country, and then installed a tram to the summit of Lone Peak, providing access to an array of steep chutes, open bowls, and at least one scary-steep couloir. The tram also gave Big Sky the right to claim the greatest vertical drop—4,350 feet—of any resort in the country. Those changes now provide big action for experts.

None of that, however, has diminished Big Sky's otherwise easy-skiing reputation. There is, indeed, a good deal of intermediate and lower-intermediate terrain, a combination of wide-open bowl skiing higher up and trail skiing lower down. And as on the Challenger terrain, the skiing on these slopes is fairly unpopulated. Additionally, there are 75 km (47 mi) of groomed cross-country skiing trails nearby at Lone Mountain Ranch.

The other plus about skiing Big Sky is its wide variety of exposures. Many of the ski areas here are built on north-facing slopes, where snow usually stays fresher longer, protected from the sun. In addition to these, Big Sky also has plenty of runs facing south and east, and the differing snow textures that result make for more interesting skiing.

FACILITIES 4,350-foot vertical drop; 3,600 skiable acres; 100 runs; 10% beginner, 47% intermediate, 43% advanced; 1 aerial tram, one 4-passenger gondola, 3 high-speed quads, 1 quad chair, 4 triple chairs, 5 double chairs, 4 surface lifts.

LESSONS & PROGRAMS Half-day group-lesson rates at the **ski school** (☎ 406/995–5743 or 800/548–4486) are $38; a learn-to-ski package (half-day lesson, equipment rentals, and restricted lift ticket) is $63. Racing, powder, mogul, and snowboarding clinics are also available. There's also a ski school just for kids—whether they're first-timers or speedsters—with enthusiastic instructors and a day camp.

LIFT TICKETS Lift tickets cost $59. Multiday tickets (up to six of seven days) are available, with savings of up to $5 per day. Kids 10 and under ski free with an adult who has purchased a lift ticket.

RENTALS The resort's **Big Sky Ski Rentals** (☎ 406/995–5841) at the base of the mountain offers rental packages for $27, and performance ski packages for $40. Moderate rental packages (starting at $16 per day) are available from **Mad Wolf Ski & Sport** (✉ U.S. 191, 8 mi from ski area ☎ 406/995–4369).

OUTSIDE OF BIG SKY Although the Big Sky resort dominates downhill skiing in the area, the 2003–2004 ski season saw the debut of a new resort at **Moonlight Basin** (✉ 2 mi east of Big Sky resort on Big Sky Spur Rd. ☎ 406/993–6000 🌐 www.moonlightbasin.com), with north-facing slopes overlooking the Lee Metcalf Wilderness Area. The runs here may not be as lengthy as they are next door at Big Sky, but the terrain offers some unique knolls, chutes, and glades. Best of all, tickets are competitively priced at $39 a day for the four chairlifts. Lifts access 1,300 acres of skiing, with 1,850 feet of lift-served descent and an additional 1,200 feet of hike-to terrain.

Nordic Skiing

BACKCOUNTRY SKIING **Lone Mountain Ranch** (☎ 406/995–4644 or 800/514–4644 🌐 www.lmranch.com) offers guided cross-country ski and snowshoe tours in the nearby backcountry as well as in Yellowstone National Park. Ski tours near Big Sky are best for experienced skiers; they tend to cover steeper terrain, with opportunities for telemarking, backcountry skiing, and snowboarding. Tours in Yellowstone generally cover flat or gently rolling terrain, for which little or no cross-country skiing experience is necessary. In some cases, snow "coaches" (essentially, over-the-snow buses and vans) take skiers from West Yellowstone to scenic parts of the park for skiing.

Cat-ski adventures from Big Sky in the nearby yet remote Moonlight Basin run daily in winter by **Montana Backcountry Adventures** (✉ 1020 Big Sky Spur Rd. [Hwy. 64], 1 mi west of resort at Moonlight Basin Ranch ☎ 406/995–3880 or 866/766–9622 🌐 www.skimba.com); you'll have access to 1,800 acres of untracked powder ski terrain with views into the Lee Metcalf Wilderness Area.

Using snowmobile or helicopter services, **Montana Powder Guides** (✉ 15792 Bridger Canyon Rd. ☎ 406/587–3096) leads backcountry expeditions into several mountain ranges for untracked powder skiing and snowboarding. The best conditions are late February through late April.

TRACK SKIING ★ **Lone Mountain Ranch** (☎ 406/995–4644 or 800/514–4644 🌐 www.lmranch.com) is a rare bird in cross-country circles. Not only are there 75 km (47 mi) of groomed trails, but the network is superb, with everything from a flat, open, golf-course layout to tree-lined trails with as much as 1,600 feet of elevation gain (and loss). Much of the trail network provides a genuine sense of woodsy mountain seclusion. If there is a drawback, it's that moose sometimes wander onto the trails, causing pockmarked tracks and occasional moose-skier confrontations.

Mountain Meadows Guest Ranch (☎ 406/995–4997 or 888/644–6647 🌐 www.mountainmeadowsranch.com) has 24 km (15 mi) of groomed cross-country and snowshoe trails for lodging guests in a beautiful log facility on a mountaintop above Big Sky.

Where to Stay & Eat

$$$$ ✕ **Moonlight Dinners by Montana Backcountry Adventures.** For a unique dining experience, ride a Sno-Cat into the pristine Moonlight Basin for a moonlighted meal. While the chef prepares French onion soup, filet mignon, and garlic mashed potatoes on a woodstove, you can sled on hills under the light of the moon and tiki lamps. Yurt dining is accompanied by acoustic music and candlelight. ✉ *1020 Big Sky Spur Rd. (Hwy. 64); 1 mi outside Mountain Village* ☎ *406/995–3880* ✍ *Reservations essential* ▭ *AE, MC, V* ⊗ *Closed mid-Apr.–late Nov.*

$$$–$$$$ ✕ **Buck's T-4 Lodge and Restaurant.** Within a historic log lodge and bar, this restaurant is known for its dinners of wild game (try the antelope satay) and steaks. There's live jitterbug music after dark. ✉ *U.S. 191, 1½ mi south of Big Sky entrance* ☎ *406/995–4111* ▭ *MC, V* ⊗ *Closed mid-Apr.–May.*

$$$–$$$$ ✕ **Cafe Edelweiss.** Stepping into this cozy post-and-beam lodge is a bit like wandering into the Tirol. Among the traditional Austrian and German dishes on the menu are schnitzel, bratwurst, and *schweinebrater* (pork roast with homemade sauerkraut). ✉ *Meadow Village, Big Sky Spur Rd.* ☎ *406/995–4665* ▭ *AE, D, MC, V* ⊗ *Closed late Apr.–mid-June.*

$$–$$$ ✕ **By Word of Mouth.** By day this café is filled by sunlight, and by night, by noise, particularly Friday nights, when the after-ski crowd gathers for an all-you-can-eat fish fry. The menu includes Thai chicken strips

served with soba, and *opa* (a Hawaiian sunfish) sautéed in teriyaki sauce and served with organic vegetables and rice. The wine list is lengthy, and there are several local beers on tap. ✉ *2815 Aspen Dr., in West Fork Meadow* ☎ *406/995–2992* ▭ *AE, D, MC, V.*

$–$$$ ✕ **Big Horn Cafe.** This spacious café, possibly the best value in the area, serves contemporary fare, with starters such as hummus with roasted garlic, olives, peppers, and pita chips. The real treat is the wonton lasagna: layers of wontons, spinach, peppers, and portobello mushrooms. ✉ *Big Horn Center, U.S. 191, 1 block north of Big Sky entrance* ☎ *406/995–3880* ▭ *MC, V* ⊗ *Closed Mon.*

$–$$$ ✕ **The Corral.** Trucker-size portions of everything from steak and eggs to burgers and local brews feed cowboys and skiers at this local hangout. Stuffed elk, moose, and deer heads watch over diners from walls lined with posters and humorous photos. ✉ *42895 Gallatin Rd., 5 mi south of Big Sky entrance* ☎ *406/995–4249* ▭ *AE, D, MC, V* ⊗ *Closed 2 wks in late Nov. and late Apr.–mid-May.*

$$$$ ✕ **Lone Mountain Ranch.** Four-night to one-week packages include seasonal activities such as naturalist-guided trips to Yellowstone, cross-country ski lessons, downhill skiing, and kids' camps. The ranch maintains 75 km (47 mi) of groomed trails for classic and skate cross-country skiing. An additional four trails totaling 10 km (6 mi) are for snowshoers only. Some activities cost extra, such as fly-fishing with world-renowned, Orvis-endorsed guides. Lodging ranges from rustic, historic cabins to elegant log homes. Nonguests fill the log-lodge dining room (try the bison steak) or partake of a night of backcountry sleigh rides, dinner, and entertainment. *Box 160069, 59716* ✉ *4 mi west of U.S. 191, 6 mi from Big Sky resort, and ½ mi down gravel ranch road* ☎ *406/995–4644 or 800/514–4644* *406/995–4670* *www.lmranch.com* *23 cabins, 7 rooms* *Restaurant, hot tub, fishing, hiking, horseback riding, cross-country skiing, sleigh rides, bar, recreation room, shop, children's programs (all ages), airport shuttle, travel services; no smoking* ▭ *D, MC, V* ⊗ *Closed Oct., Nov., Apr., and May* *FAP.*

$$$–$$$$ Fodor's Choice ★ ✕ **Rainbow Ranch.** Lovely log-accented cabins and a historic and fully updated 1919 log lodge perch alongside the Gallatin River. A fishing motif decorates the spacious rooms in the cabins, which have fireplaces, lodgepole-pine beds, and down comforters. The exceptional restaurant, decorated with Western paintings, has the state's largest collection of wines, 6,500 bottles, displayed in the Bacchus Room, where groups of up to 14 can dine. Fresh fish is flown in daily. Among the game dishes are pistachio-crusted antelope and bison rib eye prepared with *chimichurri* herbs. ✉ *42950 Gallatin Rd., 5 mi south of Big Sky entrance, 59716* ☎ *406/995–4132 or 800/937–4132* *406/995–2861* *www.rainbowranch.com* *16 rooms* *Restaurant, in-room data ports, cable TV, in-room VCRs, outdoor hot tub, fishing, cross-country skiing, bar, shop, meeting rooms; no smoking* ▭ *AE, D, MC, V.*

$$$$ Fodor's Choice ★ **The Big EZ.** Atop a mountain at a 7,500-foot elevation, the Big EZ lodge overlooks other mountains and the Gallatin River drainage. Each luxury suite is appointed with Western-style furnishings, an eclectic collection of fine art, and state-of-the-art technology, including laptops and Internet access. The property includes an 18-hole, par-72 championship putting course and one of the state's largest outdoor hot tubs. Dinners are unusual, elegant, and savory: try pan-roasted caribou loin or African pheasant, and save room for Tasmanian-honey crème brûlée. ✉ *7000 Beaver Creek Rd., 59716* ☎ *406/995–7000 or 877/244–3299* *406/995–7007* *www.bigezlodge.com* *13 suites* *Restaurant, in-room data ports, cable TV, in-room VCRs, putting green, exercise equipment, outdoor hot tub, fishing, bar, shop, laundry service, concierge, Inter-*

net, business services, meeting rooms, airport shuttle; no smoking ☐ *AE, MC, V* ☐ *FAP.*

$$$$ **Big Sky Resort Condominiums.** These comfortable on-mountain units—with one, two, or three bedrooms—have large kitchens, dining rooms, fireplaces, and underground parking. Stone and wood accents give the otherwise utilitarian decor some mountain character. Many of the units are ski-in, ski-out properties. ☒ *1 Lone Mountain Trail, 59716* ☎ *406/995–5000 or 800/548–4486* ☐ *406/995–8095* ⊕ *www.bigskyresort.com* ☐ *600 condos* ☐ *6 restaurants, kitchens, minibars, microwaves, refrigerators, cable TV, golf privileges, 3 indoor-outdoor pools, gym, massage, spa, mountain bikes, horseback riding, cross-country skiing, downhill skiing, ski shop, ski storage, 5 bars, shops, baby-sitting, children's programs (ages 2–12), laundry facilities, business services, convention center, meeting rooms, airport shuttle, no-smoking rooms* ☐ *AE, D, MC, V* ☐ *Closed late Apr.–early June and late Oct.–mid-Nov.*

★ $$$$ **Summit at Big Sky.** The rooms of this slope-side, full-service hotel take in the full view of Lone Mountain and several ski runs. A Euro-Western flavor decorates the spacious rooms and suites, which are ideal for discriminating business travelers and families looking to be at the center of the mountain action. The best things about the Summit just may be the underground, heated parking garage, unusual in Montana, and the outdoor, year-round soaking pool. ☒ *1 Lone Mountain Trail, 59716* ☎ *406/995–5000 or 800/548–4486* ☐ *406/995–8095* ⊕ *www.bigskyresort.com* ☐ *213 rooms, 8 suites* ☐ *2 restaurants, room service, in-room data ports, kitchenettes, minibars, refrigerators, golf privileges, indoor-outdoor pool, gym, massage, spa, mountain bikes, downhill skiing, ski shop, ski storage, bar, shops, baby-sitting, children's programs (ages 2–12), concierge, business services, meeting rooms, airport shuttle, no-smoking rooms* ☐ *AE, D, MC, V.*

¢–$$ **Comfort Inn of Big Sky.** This is a family-friendly, affordable lodging option, sitting right along the Gallatin River, less than 1 mi south of the Big Sky entrance. A Southwestern theme permeates the simple, comfortable, clean rooms, which have pine accents and queen-size beds. Kids love the 90-foot waterslide that spills into the pool. ☒ *47214 Gallatin Rd., 59716* ☎ *406/995–2333 or 800/228–5150* ☐ *406/995–2277* ⊕ *www.comfortinnbigsky.com* ☐ *62 rooms* ☐ *Some kitchens, some microwaves, cable TV, indoor pool, gym, hot tub, ski storage, laundry facilities, some pets allowed (fee), no-smoking floors* ☐ *AE, D, MC, V.*

CAMPING **Greek Creek.** Squeezed into the narrow Gallatin Canyon, this Forest Service campground with tent sites snuggles up to the Gallatin River under a canopy of tall evergreens. ☐ *Pit toilets, drinking water, fire grates, picnic tables, swimming (river)* ☐ *14 sites* ☒ *U.S. 191, 13 mi south of Bozeman* ☎ *406/522–2520 or 877/444–6777* ⊕ *www.fs.fed.us/r1/gallatin or www.reserveusa.com* ☐ *$10* ☐ *AE, D, MC, V* ☐ *Mid-May–mid-Sept.*

Nightlife & the Arts

NIGHTLIFE There's live rock music at **Dante's Inferno** (☒ Mountain Mall, 1 Lone Mountain Trail ☎ 406/995–3999), where the dancing often spills out onto the deck for a boogie in ski boots. Some weekends the **Corral** (☒ 42895 Gallatin Rd., 5 mi south of Big Sky entrance ☎ 406/995–4249) rocks to the house band, Montana Rose. Other entertainment comes from quirky bartenders, pool-table bets, and legions of skiers, snowmobilers, and locals in for the Montana brews.

THE ARTS ★ Every July and August, the **Music in the Mountains** (☒ Meadow Village Pavilion ☎ 406/995–2742 or 877/995–2742) summer concert series showcases headliners such as Taj Mahal, Willie Nelson, and the Bozeman Symphony Orchestra in outdoor venues.

Gallatin River Gallery (✉ 50 Meadow Village Dr., No. 102, in the Ringston Bldg., Meadow Village ☎ 406/995–2909), the only contemporary gallery in Big Sky, showcases one-of-a-kind jewelry, paintings, sculptures, and more from international, national, and local artists.

Shopping

Top-of-the-line ski and snowboard equipment and outerwear are sold at **Big Sky Sports** (✉ Mountain Mall, 1 Lone Mountain Trail ☎ 406/995–5840). **Lone Mountain Ranch Outdoor Shop** (✉ 4 mi west of U.S. 191, 6 mi from Big Sky resort, and ½ mi down gravel ranch road ☎ 406/995–4644) sells beautiful Nordic sweaters, cross-country-skiing and snowshoeing accessories, summer outdoor wear, fly-fishing gear, and unique gifts.

BOZEMAN

In 1864, a trader named John Bozeman led his wagon train through this valley en route to the booming goldfields of Virginia City and southwest Montana. For several years it was the site of Fort Ellis, established to protect settlers making their way west along the Bozeman Trail, which extended into Montana Territory. Nowadays the city is a recreation capital for everything from trout fishing to white-water river rafting to backcountry mountain biking. The arts have flowered here, in the home of Montana State University, and cowboys, professors, students, and skiers make Bozeman one of the more diverse communities of the northern Rockies.

Bozeman has a strong Western heritage, as displayed at local museums, downtown galleries, and even the airport.

Exploring Bozeman

You can easily maneuver downtown Bozeman's mix of Old West bars, saddle shops, upscale stores and restaurants, and espresso cafés on foot or by bicycle. A vehicle is necessary—in winter, a four-wheel-drive vehicle is best—to explore surrounding parks, trails, and recreation areas among the mountain ranges surrounding Bozeman.

Historic walking tours from the Pioneer Museum, on Main Street, take you through three areas of town: Main Street, historic neighborhoods, and Sunset Hills Cemetery and parks.

a good tour

Main Street, the original Bozeman Trail, running east–west through town, leads to some 700 homes and buildings listed on the National Register of Historic Places. Many have signs detailing their history. Begin a walking tour at the former Gallatin County Jail, now the **Pioneer Museum** 6 ►, at Main Street and 4th Avenue. Head east on Main Street, noting the former **Gallatin County High School** 7 complex, comprising two distinct buildings, across the street. Turn left onto Grand Avenue and walk north one block to the elegant Victorian **Ketterer Building** 8. Walk south on Grand Avenue for two blocks (you'll cross Main Street) to the Gothic Revival **Emerson Cultural Center** 9, a former school and now a center for the arts. Return to Main Street, turn right, and continue east for a leisurely stroll past several notable historic buildings that now house shops, offices, and apartments. Once your feet wear down, hop in the car and drive to the south side of town to the **Museum of the Rockies** 10. Another option is a visit to the **American Computer Museum** 11 on North 7th Avenue.

TIMING This tour should take about three hours, including time for visiting the museums. Note that some of the downtown businesses close on Sun-

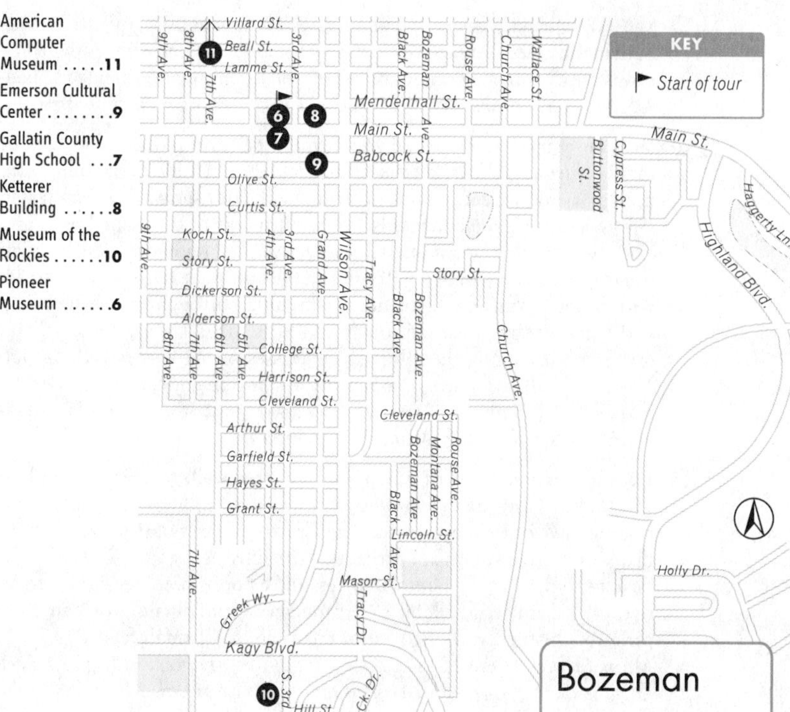

days. It's a good idea to carry a jacket around, even on warm days, in case of sudden changes in the weather.

What to See

11 **American Computer Museum.** This museum takes you through the Information Age, from ancient items—such as a 4,000-year-old clay tablet with cuneiform writing, an abacus, and an astrolabe—to some of the most modern technology of the 21st century. ✉ *2304 N. 7th Ave.* ☎ *406/582–1280* 🌐 *www.compustory.com* *$3* *Daily 9–5.*

Bozeman Hot Springs. You can soak for an hour or a day at Bozeman Hot Springs, with nine indoor pools, one outdoor pool, a sauna, spa, gym, and juice bar. ✉ *81123 Gallatin Rd., 5 mi west of Bozeman at Four Corners Junction of Huffine La. (Main St.) and U.S. 191* ☎ *406/586–6492* *$6.50* *Mon.–Thurs. 7 AM–10 PM, Fri. 7 AM–7:15 PM, Sat. 8:15 PM–midnight, Sun. 8 AM–10 PM.*

9 **Emerson Cultural Center.** A school until 1990, this 1918 Gothic Revival brick building now houses 37 galleries, studios, and classrooms, plus a performing-arts hall. You can watch craftspeople at work, purchase artwork, take a class, or catch a performance here. ✉ *111 S. Grand Ave.* ☎ *406/587–9797* 🌐 *www.theemerson.org* *Free* *Daily 10–5 and for scheduled evening performances.*

7 **Gallatin County High School.** In the 1920s, actor Gary Cooper was a student at this high school. The original structure, constructed in 1901–02, includes neoclassical and Romanesque elements. An art deco addition was built in the 1930s. This is the only school building still standing in town that was built before the Great Depression. Today it houses offices. ✉ *404 W. Main St.* ☎ *406/586–5421* 🌐 *www.bozemanchamber.com.*

8 **Ketterer Building.** This 1901 building, which now houses law offices, was built in the Queen Anne style, with some colonial touches. It was the home of Emil Ketterer, a German immigrant, blacksmith, and carriage maker. ✉ *35 N. Grand Ave.* ☎ *406/586–5421* 🌐 *www.bozemanchamber.com.*

10 **Museum of the Rockies.** Here you'll find a celebration of the history of the Rockies region, with eclectic exhibits that include everything from prehistory to pioneers to a planetarium with laser shows. You can watch workers clean dinosaur fossils and see displays of dinosaur bones and eggs excavated in Montana. Children love the hands-on science activities in the Martin Discovery Room and the outdoors Tensley Homestead, with home-crafts demonstrations, including butter churning, weaving, and blacksmithing. May through mid-September, sheep, donkeys, and horses graze among the tall pasture grasses of the homestead. ✉ *600 W. Kagy Blvd., south end of university campus* ☎ *406/994–3466 or 406/994–2251* 🌐 *www.museumoftherockies.org* *$8 museum, $3 planetarium laser shows* ⏲ *Mon.–Sat. 9–5, Sun. 12:30–5.*

6 **Pioneer Museum.** West of downtown, this redbrick former jail, built in 1911 in the Gothic Revival style, serves as a reminder of the rough-and-tumble days of the past. Inside, the Gallatin County Historical Society displays Native American artifacts, Fort Ellis items, an 1870s authentic log cabin, a library, photo archives, and a bookstore. Free guided tours of the museum are available by arrangement, and outside you can often pick up a historic walking tour of the town (for a small fee). ✉ *317 W. Main St.* ☎ *406/522–8122* 🌐 *www.pioneermuseum.org* *Free* ⏲ *June–Sept., Mon.–Sat. 10–4; Oct.–May, Tues.–Fri. 11–4, Sat. 1–4.*

Sports & the Outdoors

Bicycling

Austin Lehman Adventures (✉ 1106 S. 29th St. W ☎ 406/655–4591 or 800/575–1540) offers bike and multisport tours in the Gallatin Valley and all over the state.

Fishing

The **Bozeman Angler** (✉ 23 E. Main St. ☎ 406/587–9111) sells fly rods and gear and arranges guided trips on several lakes, streams, and rivers, including the Gallatin and Yellowstone rivers.

Rafting

★ **Yellowstone Raft Company** (✉ 55265 Gallatin Rd. ☎ 406/995–4613 or 800/348–4376) provides guided scenic and white-water raft trips and kayak instruction on the Gallatin and Yellowstone rivers.

Skiing

Bridger Bowl (✉ 15795 Bridger Canyon Rd. ☎ 406/587–2111 or 800/223–9609 🌐 www.bridgerbowl.com) is known for the "cold smoke," light, dry-powder skiing. The terrain, from steep, rocky chutes to gentle slopes and meadows, is the headline act at this city-owned mountain, where lift tickets are half the price of those at upscale resorts. In late September, the ski area hosts the Bridger Raptor Festival to celebrate the golden-eagle flyway along the mountain-range crest. Some days, more than 200 goldens are spotted gliding the thermals.

Using Sno-Cat or helicopter services, **Montana Powder Guides** (✉ 15792 Bridger Canyon Rd. ☎ 406/587–3096) leads expeditions into the snowy backcountry for untracked powder skiing and snowboarding.

Where to Stay & Eat

$$$–$$$$ ✕ **The Savory Olive.** Rib-eye steak, vegetarian dishes, duck, and two fresh seafood specials nightly are served at this elegant restaurant in the historic Baxter Hotel. Many of the side dishes incorporate local ingredients, such as the salad of tomatoes, basil, and mozzarella. The pan-seared diver scallops and pan-seared Alaskan halibut, available seasonally, are delicious. There's patio dining in summer. ⊠ *105 W. Main St.* ☎ *406/586–8320* *Reservations essential* ▭ *AE, D, MC, V* ⊗ *Closed Sun.*

$$–$$$$ ✕ **Cafe International.** This classic white-tablecloth restaurant inside the Emerson Cultural Center attracts the business crowd for lunch with a large selection of hot and cold salads and sandwiches. The elegant presentation of specials such as the Portobello-mushroom lobster chowder draws oohs and ahs. ⊠ *111 S. Grand Ave.* ☎ *406/586–4242* ▭ *AE, D, MC, V.*

$$–$$$$ ✕ **Montana Ale Works.** A cavernous brick building, the former Northern Pacific Railroad depot houses a brewery and restaurant with outdoor dining in summer. In addition to the 42 beers on tap, the Ale Works serves bison burgers, wild game, baked pasta dishes, and nightly specials such as fresh grilled yellowfin tuna. ⊠ *611 E. Main St.* ☎ *406/587–7700* ▭ *AE, D, MC, V* ⊗ *No lunch.*

$$–$$$$ ✕ **Sophia's Restaurant and Looie's Downunder.** Two eateries are packed under one roof in the historic downtown area. Upstairs, Sophia's serves Italian specialties such as the penne Looie, with mushrooms, chicken, and Gorgonzola cream sauce. Downstairs, Looie's is popular for both the atmosphere (casual and intimate) and the food; try the nightly specials such as curried halibut with sushi and seaweed salad. ⊠ *101 E. Main St.* ☎ *406/582–0393 or 406/522–8814* ▭ *AE, D, MC, V.*

¢–$ ✕ **La Parrilla.** At this cottage turned café, you choose the ingredients and watch the crew build your burrito wrap. The Bombay wrap includes beans, rice, chicken, ginger, and chutney. Dining is indoors or outside on the flower-draped deck. ⊠ *1533 W. Babcock St.* ☎ *406/582–9511* ▭ *No credit cards.*

$–$$$ ✕ **Gallatin Gateway Inn.** The Milwaukee Railroad built this sumptuous inn 10 mi from town on U.S. 191 as a stopping-off point for visitors to Yellowstone National Park. After a stint as a seedy bar, the inn has recaptured its reputation. A modern, Western style decorates the uniquely furnished rooms painted in soothing pastels. The bathrooms, with original tile work and brass fixtures, exude simple elegance. Crisp white linens and candlelight set the formal tone in the wonderful restaurant, which serves regional cuisine. The Baggage Room Pub's casual fare complements a day of recreation. ⊠ *U.S. 191, Box 376, Gallatin Gateway 59730* ☎ *406/763–4672 or 800/676–3522* *406/763–4672* *www.gallatingatewayinn.com* *33 rooms* *Restaurant, tennis court, pool, pub* ▭ *AE, MC, V.*

$$$$ **Gallatin River Lodge.** On the property of a 350-acre ranch, this full-service, year-round fly-fishing lodge perches on the famed fly-fishing river for which it is named. Packages include guided fishing. The elegant country inn has six suites, with rustic furnishings and views of the river. ⊠ *9105 Thorpe Rd., 59718* ☎ *406/388–0148 or 888/387–0148* *406/388–6766* *www.grlodge.com* *6 suites* *Dining room, cable TV, fishing, bar, library, business services, meeting rooms, airport shuttle, free parking* ▭ *MC, V* *BP.*

★ **$–$$** **Cottonwood Inn B&B.** Stained-glass windows, a fireplace, and a baby grand greet you at this country-style home at the base of the Gallatin Mountains. Each guest room is named for a local river; pine furnishings and fishing accents decorate the Gallatin Room. The honeymoon suite has a large bathroom with an antique claw-foot tub. The full breakfast includes fresh fruit, a Southwestern soufflé, and banana-walnut French toast topped with fresh berries. ✉ *13515 Cottonwood Canyon Dr., 10 mi south of Bozeman, 59718* ☎ *406/763–5452 or 888/879–4667* 📠 *406/763–5639* 🌐 *www.cottonwood-inn.com* *5 rooms* *Dining room, outdoor hot tub, massage, cross-country skiing, library, piano, shop, Internet, free parking; no TVs in some rooms, no kids under 12, no smoking* 💳 *AE, MC, V* 🍽 *BP.*

★ $–$$ **Voss Inn.** This B&B occupies an elegant 1883 Victorian house and is lavishly furnished with antiques and knickknacks. Stop by the parlor to enjoy afternoon tea or to catch up on the news with other guests who drop in to watch TV or to chat. Huge breakfasts are served in rooms or in the parlor. The lovely English garden makes a great spot for a quiet conversation. ✉ *319 S. Willson Ave., 59715* ☎ *406/587–0982* 📠 *406/585–2964* 🌐 *www.bozeman-vossinn.com* *6 rooms* 💳 *AE, D, MC, V* 🍽 *BP.*

Nightlife & the Arts

Nightlife

On weekends, young professionals, university professors, and tourists head to the **Robin** (✉ 105 W. Main St. ☎ 406/522–0362), a smoke-free bar at the Baxtor Hotel, for live jazz, drink specials, and casual socializing. A smoke-free downtown saloon, the **Rocking R Bar** (✉ 211 E. Main St. ☎ 406/587–9355) draws a young crowd with its classic-rock bands and original local acts, suds, and dancing. Pool tables, a jukebox, a poker room, and foosball fill one side of the **Zebra Cocktail Lounge** (✉ 321 E. Main St. ☎ 406/585–8851), a downtown basement hangout. The other side has a dance floor, couches, and live music on weekends, all in swanky surroundings.

The Arts

The **Bozeman Symphony Society** (✉ 404 W. Main St. ☎ 406/585–9774) runs a year-round concert series, often featuring talented university students and traveling artists. Performances take place at the Willson Auditorium, and there's one outdoor summer concert each year in Big Sky.

Shopping

Antiques, collectibles, and more fill the 12,000-square-foot **Antique Barn** (✉ 5 Wheeler Mountain Way, ½ mi north of Gallatin Gateway Inn ☎ 406/763–4676). Among the more unique items are antler light fixtures and animal hides. Outdoor wear, cross-country-skiing equipment, and boating gear are sold at **Northern Lights Trading Co.** (✉ 1716 W. Babcock St. ☎ 406/586–2225). Don't be surprised to see any of the helpful staff members out on the trails, tracks, or rivers beside you.

HELENA

This jewel of a town, where the prairie meets the mountains, started as a rowdy mining camp in 1864 and became a banking and commerce center in the Montana Territory. At the turn of the 20th century, Helena had more millionaires per capita than any other town in the country. Some of that wealth came from Helena's present-day main street, called Last Chance Gulch, the site of the first of several gulches that yielded more than $15 million in gold during the late 1800s. With statehood came a fight between the towns of Anaconda and Helena over which would be the capital. In a notoriously corrupt campaign in which both sides bought votes, Helena won. Today, Helena is a city of

28,000, with 25 city parks, several museums, a thriving arts community, and its own minor-league baseball team. In the southern part of the city, the area near the State Capitol Building and neighboring museums, mansions, and parks is hilly and thick with lush greenery in summer. The iron ball of urban renewal robbed the town of much of its history, but Helena still has ornate brick and granite historic buildings along Last Chance Gulch.

Exploring Helena

The downtown historic area has a pedestrian-only mall on Last Chance Gulch with shops, coffeehouses, and restaurants. There are several historic sights here that you can see on foot, but other sights are spread out in the city and best accessed by automobile.

The **Downtown Helena Office** (✉ 121 N. Last Chance Gulch ☎ 406/442–9869 🌐 www.downtownhelena.com) in the center of Helena's historic downtown can provide a brochure for a self-guided walking tour.

a good tour

Start your tour on foot at the brick-road **Reeder's Alley** 12 ⚑, lined with miners' houses and shops built between 1872 and 1884. Note the 1880 Morelli Bridge spanning a gulch here. One block east, the gold-rush-era **Pioneer Cabin** 13 is among the oldest structures in town. Head northeast on Park Avenue, then one block east on Wong Street to the famed **Last Chance Gulch** 14. Walking north on the pedestrian mall on Last Chance Gulch, closed to traffic between Wong Street and 6th Avenue, is like stepping back through time into gold-mining history. Note the statue of Atlas on top of the 19th-century **Atlas Building** 15 at No. 7 Last Chance Gulch. Farther on at No. 15 is the elegant 1913 **Placer Hotel** 16, now an apartment building. Stop for a meal at the former bordello at No. 19, the Windbag Saloon, or for candy at the Parrot Confectionery at No. 42, the Lalonde building. You'll pass several historic buildings as you walk to the 300 block of Last Chance Gulch and the 1931 art deco **First National Bank Building** 17. At the north end of the block, step inside the **Wells Fargo Bank** 18, which houses a collection of gold nuggets. Walk one block east of Last Chance Gulch on Lawrence Avenue to the **Holter Museum of Art** 19, showcasing contemporary and historic art.

From here, hop in your car and drive east on 6th Avenue to the **Montana Governor's Mansion** 20. Continue east on 6th Avenue to Montana Avenue and the **State Capitol Building** 21. Note the spectacular 19th-century mansions in the area, many restored to their early glory. After a tour of the capitol's elegant rotunda and grounds, walk one block east to Roberts Street and the **Montana Historical Society Museum** 22. Get back in your car and drive west on 6th Avenue and north on Ewing Street to the **Cathedral of St. Helena** 23. End the day at the **Great Northern Carousel** 24; to get here drive north on Ewing Street and west on 14th Avenue.

TIMING If you wish to hit all of the major sights in town, set aside an entire day for this tour. Plan on spending at least two hours strolling around the historic district and another two hours visiting the capitol, Montana Historical Society Museum, and the Governor's Mansion.

What to See

15 **Atlas Building.** A statue of Atlas himself and two lizards and a salamander crown this building, symbols of insurance protection offered by the company housed in this 1887 neo-Romanesque structure. ✉ *7 Last Chance Gulch* ☎ *406/442–9869* 🎟 *Free* ⏲ *Mon.–Sat. 9–5, Sun. noon–5.*

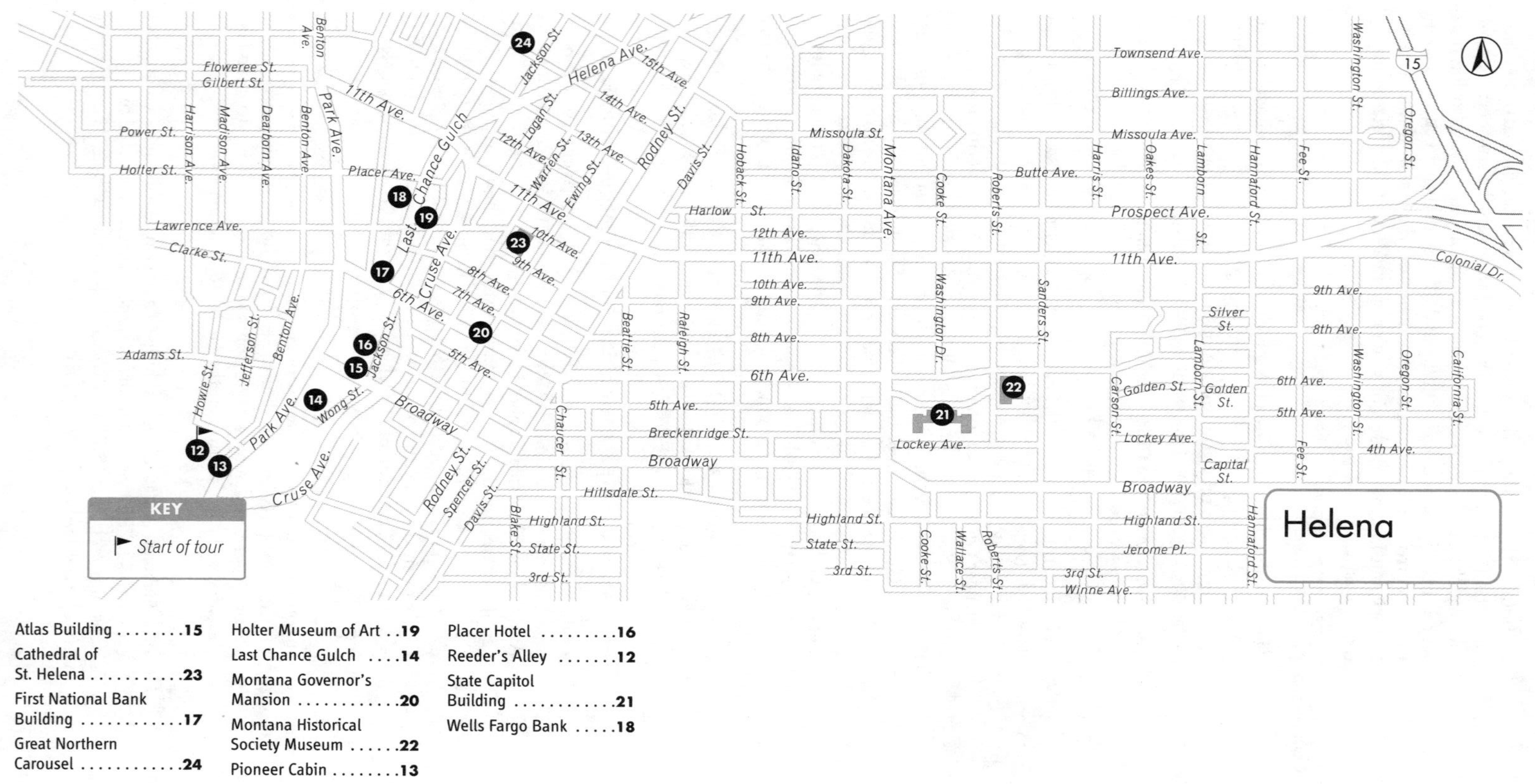
Helena
KEY
Start of tour
Atlas Building 15
Cathedral of St. Helena 23
First National Bank Building 17
Great Northern Carousel 24
Holter Museum of Art . .19
Last Chance Gulch 14
Montana Governor's Mansion 20
Montana Historical Society Museum 22
Pioneer Cabin 13
Placer Hotel 16
Reeder's Alley 12
State Capitol Building 21
Wells Fargo Bank 18
15
Colonial Dr.
California St.
Oregon St.
Washington St.
Fee St.
Hannaford St.
Lamborn St.
Oakes St.
Harris St.
Sanders St.
Roberts St.
Cooke St.
Wallace St.
Washington Dr.
Montana Ave.
Dakota St.
Idaho St.
Hoback St.
Raleigh St.
Beattie St.
Chaucer St.
Blake St.
Townsend Ave.
Billings Ave.
Missoula Ave.
Prospect Ave.
11th Ave.
9th Ave.
8th Ave.
6th Ave.
5th Ave.
4th Ave.
Silver St.
Golden St.
Capital St.
Lockey Ave.
Carson St.
Broadway
Highland St.
Jerome Pl.
3rd St.
Winne Ave.
Butte Ave.
Missoula St.
12th Ave.
10th Ave.
State St.
Harlow St.
Breckenridge St.
Hillsdale St.
Davis St.
Rodney St.
Ewing St.
Warren St.
Logan St.
Jackson St.
15th Ave.
14th Ave.
13th Ave.
Helena Ave.
7th Ave.
Spencer St.
Last Chance Gulch
Cruse Ave.
Placer Ave.
Wong St.
Park Ave.
Benton Ave.
Dearborn Ave.
Madison Ave.
Harrison Ave.
Jefferson St.
Howie St.
Floweree St.
Gilbert St.
Power St.
Holter St.
Lawrence Ave.
Clarke St.
Adams St.

need a break?

For an old-fashioned sweet treat, pull up a stool at the **Parrot Confectionery** (✉ 42 N. Last Chance Gulch ☎ 406/442–1470), a soda fountain and candy store built in the 1920s that sells everything from chocolate malts with homemade ice cream to hand-dipped chocolates and a regional favorite, a cherry phosphate. The building's ornate facade resembles a wedding cake.

23 **Cathedral of St. Helena.** Modeled after the cathedral in Cologne, Germany, this Gothic Revival building has stained-glass windows from Bavaria and 230-foot-tall twin spires that are visible from most places in the city. Construction began in 1908 and was completed 16 years later. Note the white marble altars, statues of Carrara marble, and gold leaf decorating the sanctuary. Guided tours are available with one day's advance notice. ✉ *530 N. Ewing St.* ☎ *406/442–5825* *Donations accepted* *Daily 10–4.*

17 **First National Bank Building.** This art deco building was constructed in 1931 to replace a late-19th-century structure on the same spot. Note the low-relief, stylized patterning on this building, common to the art deco style. ✉ *302–306 N. Last Chance Gulch.*

24 **Great Northern Carousel.** Hand-carved ponies gallop through the center of town on this carousel, open 365 days a year. You can buy homemade Painted Pony ice cream and fudge here. ✉ *924 Bicentennial Plaza, at 14th Ave. W* ☎ *406/457–5353* *$1* *Sept.–May, daily 11:30–8; June–Aug., Sun.–Thurs. 10–9, Fri. and Sat. 10–10.*

19 **Holter Museum of Art.** Displays at this museum not far from Last Chance Gulch include folk art, crafts, photography, painting, and sculpture, with an emphasis on homegrown Montana artists. ✉ *12 E. Lawrence Ave.* ☎ *406/442–6400* *www.holtermuseum.org* *Donations accepted* *Memorial Day–Labor Day, Mon.–Sat. 10–5, Sun. noon–5; Labor Day–Memorial Day, Tues.–Fri. 11:30–5, weekends noon–5.*

14 **Last Chance Gulch.** Four down-and-out prospectors designated this spot their "last chance" after they'd followed played-out gold strikes across the West. Their perseverance paid off when they discovered the first of several gold deposits here, which propelled Helena to the ranks of Montana's leading gold producers. Many of the mansions and businesses that resulted from the discovery of gold still stand on this historic route, also known as Main Street.

20 **Montana Governor's Mansion.** Governors lived in this Victorian mansion between 1913 and 1959. You can take a scheduled guided tour, but call ahead, because some tours are unexpectedly canceled. ✉ *304 N. Ewing St.* ☎ *406/444–4789* *www.montanahistoricalsociety.org* *$2* *Tours June–Aug., Wed. and Sat. at noon, 1, 2, 3, and 4; call for tour times Apr. and May.*

22 **Montana Historical Society Museum.** Highlights here include the MacKay Gallery, which displays one of the most important collections of artist Charlie Russell's work, and early black-and-white photos of Yellowstone National Park taken by F. Jay Haynes on display in the Haynes Gallery. The expansive Montana Homeland exhibit, which contains nearly 2,000 historical artifacts, documents, and photographs, takes a thorough look at Montana from the time of the first native settlers to the present. The venue also hosts special events and family days during the summer, including programs on folk music, Native American culture, and cowboys. Call ahead for information on upcoming events. Out in front of the Historical Society Museum, catch the **Last Chance Train Tour** (☎ 406/442–1023 or 888/432–1023 www.lctours.com) for an hour-long tour that

threads through Helena's historic neighborhoods of miners' mansions on the west side to the site where four miners made their first gold discovery on the gulch. Train tours cost $6.50 and take place daily on the hour, 10–6 in July and August, and 10–3 in May, June, and September. ✉ *225 N. Roberts St., across from the State Capitol* ☎ *406/444–2694 or 800/243–9900* 🌐 *www.montanahistoricalsociety.org* 🎫 *Donations accepted* ⏰ *Memorial Day–Labor Day, weekdays 9–6, weekends 9–5; Labor Day–Memorial Day, weekdays 9–5, Sat. 9–5.*

15 **Pioneer Cabin.** This 1864 hand-hewn log structure now houses a museum of the gold-rush days of the 1860s. This is Helena's oldest extant home. ✉ *200 S. Park Ave.* ☎ *406/443–7641* 🎫 *$1* ⏰ *May–Labor Day, daily 9–5; Labor Day–Memorial Day by appointment only.*

16 **Placer Hotel.** Now housing apartments, this 1913 building is one of only two historic hotels that remain in downtown Helena. Early on in its history, the hotel was a favorite after-hours gathering place for prominent state politicians; it was the site of closed-door lobbying by powerful companies. Note the statue of the bullwhacker (a man using a stick to urge cattle along the trails), symbol of the making of Montana, at the corner of the Placer Hotel. ✉ *15-27 N. Last Chance Gulch.*

12 **Reeder's Alley.** Miners' houses and distinctive shops built between 1872 and 1884 line this carefully restored area of old Helena. Also here are some restaurants and a visitor center. Note the stone pillars and wooden stringers of the Morelli Bridge, spanning a dry gulch. ✉ *Near south end of Last Chance Gulch.*

21 **State Capitol Building.** The Greek Renaissance capitol is topped by a dome of Montana copper and holds Charlie Russell's largest painting, a 12- by 25-foot depiction of Lewis and Clark. Self-guided-tour booklets are available. ✉ *6th Ave. and Montana Ave.* ☎ *406/444–2511 or 800/243–9900* 🎫 *Free* ⏰ *Mon.–Sat. 9–5, Sun. noon–5.*

18 **Wells Fargo Bank.** The lobby of this bank on the corner of Last Chance Gulch and Lawrence Street displays a collection of gold nuggets, including one nugget worth $600,000, taken from area diggings. ✉ *350 N. Last Chance Gulch* ☎ *406/447–2000* 🎫 *Free* ⏰ *Weekdays 9–4.*

Sports & the Outdoors

To stretch your legs, consider taking an hour-long hike to the top of Mt. Helena, which towers over the Last Chance Gulch pedestrian mall on the west edge of town. From the summit, you'll have panoramic views of Helena, the Helena Valley, and the Rocky Mountains to the west.

Bicycling

Old logging roads such as the McDonald Pass area, 20 mi west of town on the Continental Divide, offer challenging mountain biking. Other trails closer to town, such as the Mount Helena Ridge Trail, the Birdseye Loop, and the Helena Valley Loop, lead to mining towns and thick forests. To find out more about routes, check the Web site of the **Helena Bicycle Club** (🌐 www.helenabicycleclub.org). The **Helena National Forest** (☎ 406/449–5201) can be of help over the phone with bike route information.

Boating

The more than 75 mi of shoreline of the **Canyon Ferry Recreation Area** (✉ Hwy. 284, Townsend, near Helena ☎ 406/475–3310) give you a great place to fish, boat, sail, camp, and watch wildlife. The Missouri River once flowed freely here, though now the water is a dammed lake. You can rent canoes, Jet Skis, and pontoon, fishing, and pedal boats from

Kim's Marina, RV Park and Store (✉ 8015 Canyon Ferry Rd., 2 mi east of dam on Hwy. 284 ☎ 406/475–3723).

★ In their travels on the Missouri River, Lewis and Clark recorded passing towering limestone cliffs. **Gates of the Mountains** (✉ Off I–15, 20 mi north of Helena ☎ 406/458–5241 🌐 www.gatesofthemountains.com) boat tours take you past these same great stone walls, which rise 1,200 feet above the river.

Fishing

High Plains Outfitters of Helena (✉ 31 Division St. ☎ 406/442–9671) offers guided trips on various rivers in Montana, including the Missouri, the Big Hole, and the Blackfoot, and wading on smaller rivers and streams.

Where to Stay & Eat

★ **$$$$** ✕ **Last Chance Ranch.** After a wagon ride, which is included in the price, there's dinner, usually prime rib, salads, potatoes, and huckleberry cheesecake. Dinner is served family style at 7 PM in Montana's largest tepee, with seating for 50, and is accompanied by singing and storytelling. *✉ 2884 Grizzly Gulch, 8 mi southwest of Helena ☎ 406/442–2884 or 800/505–2884 ▭ MC, V ⊗ Closed Oct.–May.*

$$–$$$$ ✕ **On Broadway.** Wooden booths, discreet lighting, and brick walls contribute to the comfortable ambience at this Italian restaurant. Popular dishes include New York strip steak and pasta *puttanesca* (sautéed Greek olives, artichoke hearts, red bell peppers, red onions, capers, and pine nuts). When the state legislature is in session, members of Congress make this a boisterous place. *✉ 106 Broadway ☎ 406/443–1929 ✍ Reservations not accepted ▭ AE, D, DC, MC, V ⊗ No lunch. Closed Sun.*

★ **$$–$$$** ✕ **Windbag Saloon & Grill.** This historic restaurant in the heart of downtown was called Big Dorothy's until 1973, when a crusading county attorney forced Dorothy to shut down her house of ill repute. Now it's a family restaurant, named for the political debates you're likely to hear while dining on burgers, quiche, salads, and sandwiches. It also has a large selection of imported beer, on tap and in bottles. Old photos of Helena characters and a bounty of cherrywood give the place a warm, comfortable feel. *✉ 19 S. Last Chance Gulch ☎ 406/443–9669 ▭ AE, D, MC, V ⊗ Closed Sun.*

¢–$ ✕ **The Staggering Ox.** The unique deli sandwiches here have even more unique names, often political, and humorous descriptions. Try the Capitol Complex (loaded with different deli meats and cheese) or the Clinton Shuffle (with chicken, ham, Swiss cheese, and guacamole). The sandwiches are served on specialty breads shaped like a can of beans. Zany decor ranges from old records dangling from the ceiling to wildlife oil paintings. *✉ Lundy Center, 400 Euclid St. ☎ 406/443–1729 ▭ MC, V.*

★ **$–$$$** 🏨 **Canyon Ferry Mansion.** Saved from drowning in 1954 when the Canyon Ferry Reservoir was created, this former cattle baron's home was relocated to a premier perch above the lake. Antiques, many of which are for sale, accent the frilly modern furnishings and lovingly restored woodwork throughout the B&B. In addition to several private rooms, there's a dorm-style bunkhouse that sleeps seven. Outdoorsy types come here for summer water sports and winter ice boating. In summer there are lots of weddings and outdoor events. *✉ 7408 U.S. 287, Townsend, 20 mi southeast of Helena at mi marker 74, 59644 ☎ 406/266–3591 or 888/732–5583 🖷 406/266–4003 🌐 www.canyonferrymansion.com ⇨ 7 rooms, 3 with bath; 1 bunkhouse ♖ Dining room, in-room data* *ports, lake, outdoor hot tub, spa, beach, boating, fishing, mountain bikes, concierge, meeting rooms, free parking, no-smoking rooms* ▭ *AE, D, MC, V* 🍽 *BP.*

★ $ **Sanders-Helena Bed and Breakfast.** Colonel Wilbur Sanders, one of the first senators of Montana, built this three-story Victorian mansion in 1875. The colonel's rock collection is still in the front hall, and the B&B has retained his furnishings. Most of the rooms overlook mountain-ringed downtown Helena. Breakfasts are a work of art: Grand Marnier French toast, orange soufflé, or gingerbread waffles. ✉ *328 N. Ewing St., 59601* ☎ *406/442–3309* 📠 *406/443–2361* 🌐 *www.sandersbb.com* *7 rooms, 6 with bath* ▭ *AE, MC, V* 🍽 *BP.*

Camping

Cromwell-Dixon Campground. High above Helena on MacDonald Pass at 6,320 feet, this forested spot is frequented by migrating birds in spring and fall. *Pit toilets, drinking water, fire grates, grills, picnic tables* *15 sites* ✉ *MacDonald Pass, U.S. 12* ☎ *406/449–5490* 🌐 *www.fs.fed.us/r1/gallatin or www.reserveusa.com* *$8* ▭ *AE, D, MC, V* ⏲ *Early June–early Oct.*

Nightlife & the Arts

Late May through mid-September there's live music Wednesday evenings from 5 to 9 as part of the **Alive at Five** (☎ 406/447–1535 🌐 www.downtownhelena.com) series. The type of music and the venues vary, but it's always free and fun for the whole family.

In a remodeled historic stone jail, the **Myrna Loy Center for the Performing Arts** (✉ 15 N. Ewing St. ☎ 406/443–0287 🌐 www.myrnaloycenter.com)—named after the Montana-born actress—hosts live performances by nationally and internationally recognized musicians and dance troupes. Two theaters show foreign and independent films, usually two films per night.

Shopping

★ Since 1951, many of the nation's best ceramic artists have come to work in residency at the **Archie Bray Foundation** (✉ 2915 Country Club Ave. ☎ 406/443–3502 🌐 www.archiebray.org). Wander near the five antiquated, 8-foot-high, dome-shape brick kilns on a self-guided walking tour, and visit the gift shop, which sells work produced by foundation artists. It's open Monday–Saturday 9–5 and Sunday 1–5.

The **Made in Montana Store and Gallery** (✉ 21 N. Last Chance Gulch ☎ 406/442–3136 or 800/700–3136 🌐 www.madeinmontanastore.com) stocks the largest selection of Montana-made foods and gifts, including huckleberry and chokecherry treats, T-shirts, and books. There's also an Old West photo studio. A refreshing stop among the historic center of town, the independent **Montana Book and Toy Company** (✉ 331 N. Last Chance Gulch ☎ 406/443–0260 🌐 www.mtbookco.com) lines its shelves with regional and hard-to-find books, unique toys, games, and gifts.

en route

At the turn of the 20th century, radon health mines were considered cure-alls. Several of these underground mines still operate outside of Helena, including the **Merry Widow Health Mine,** where you sit in lighted chambers and breathe radon gas. ✉ *93 Basin Rd., at Basin exit off I–15, Basin, 40 mi south of Helena* ☎ *406/225–3220* 🌐 *www.merrywidowmine.com* *$3.50* ⏲ *Mar.–mid-Nov., daily 8–7.*

THE SOUTHWEST CORNER

This remote area of Montana is blessed with plenty of snowfall in winter to coat the mountains and feed the lush valleys, where ranching and forestry are the main industries and where remnants of the mining era abound. Early towns in the Montana Territory days were filled with hard-drinking miners, bordellos, thieves, and the people who became rich on it all.

Deer Lodge

25 *60 mi southwest of Helena via U.S. 12 and I–90.*

Ranching entered the 55-mi-long Deer Lodge Valley in 1862, when John Grant built the area's first cabin and began a cattle operation, selling beef to miners. The town that developed here is rooted in the cattle industry. The name Deer Lodge derives from a 40-foot-high geothermal mound, where steam once exited from the top, resembling a large Native American medicine lodge. The minerals and water attracted deer, thus earning the name Deer Lodge from the Native Americans. The mound is hidden behind trees and buildings at the Warm Springs State Hospital. Today, Deer Lodge is a quiet community of 3,400 residents, many of whom still ranch.

Built in 1871, the old Montana Territorial Prison was still in use until 1979. It's now the **Old Montana Prison Museum,** where you can enter cells and learn about early Montana law. Also on display is the gallows tree taken from town to town in territorial days to hang convicted prisoners. Admission here grants you access to the Montana Automobile Museum, Frontier Montana Museum, and Yesterday's Playthings. ☒ *1106 Main St.* ☎ *406/846–3111* 🎟 *$9* ⏲ *June–Aug., daily 8–8; Sept.–May, daily 8:30–5.*

The **Montana Automobile Museum,** part of a complex of museums based around the old penitentiary, is a car buff's delight. Displays include more than 100 vintage Fords and Lincolns dating from 1903 to the 1970s, including such rarities as a Fordson tractor and a Model A snowmobile. Admission here also grants you entrance to the Old Montana Prison Museum, the Frontier Montana Museum, and Yesterday's Playthings doll and toy museum. ☒ *1106 Main St.* ☎ *406/846–3111* 🎟 *$9* ⏲ *Late May–early Sept., daily 8–8; early Sept.–Oct. and Apr.–late May, daily 8:30–5:30. Call for hrs rest of yr.*

The **Frontier Montana Museum** displays hats, saddles, spurs, chaps, and all things cowboy. Also here are Civil War items, Native American artifacts, and Desert John's Saloon, complete with whiskey memorabilia. Admission here also grants you entrance to the Old Montana Prison Museum, the Montana Automobile Museum, and Yesterday's Playthings doll and toy museum. ☒ *1106 Main St.* ☎ *406/846–0026* 🎟 *$9* ⏲ *Mid-May–Sept., daily 10:30–5:30.*

Whimsical old toys and dolls and a large, excellent clown collection inhabit **Yesterday's Playthings** in an 1880s print shop on the National Register of Historic Places. Admission here grants you access to the Montana Automobile Museum, Frontier Montana Museum, and the Old Montana Prison Museum. ☒ *1017 Main St.* ☎ *406/846–1480* 🎟 *$9* ⏲ *Mid-May–Sept., daily 9–5.*

The **Powell County Museum** focuses on local history; it includes an antique gun collection, photographs, and a 1926 Model T Ford. ☒ *1193 Main*

St. ☎ 406/846–3111 Free ⏲ June–Sept., daily 8:30–5:15; Oct.–May, daily noon–5.

Daily tours of the 1,600-acre **Grant-Kohrs Ranch National Historic Site,** a working cattle ranch run by the National Park Service, give insight into ranching life in the 1850s. You can learn about roping steers, watch blacksmith demonstrations, and enjoy a hayride. The annual Western Heritage Days Celebration, with demonstrations and kids' programs, takes place in mid-July. ✉ *Grant Circle, ½ mi off I–90* ☎ *406/846–2070* 🌐 *www.nps.gov/grko* *Free* ⏲ *June–Aug., daily 8–5:30; Sept.–May, daily 9–4:30.*

Where to Stay & Eat

¢–$ ✕ **The Coffee House.** Remember to save room for one of the 40 different milk shakes and malts at this Western-front eatery, which serves a bit of everything: pizza, calzones, cold and grilled sandwiches, salads, and baked potatoes. ✉ *200 Main St.* ☎ *406/846–1750* *Reservations not accepted* *AE, MC, V* ⏲ *Closed Sun.*

$ **Deer Lodge Super 8.** This cookie-cutter motel is clean and convenient to the interstate, historic sights, and restaurants. ✉ *1150 N. Main St., 59722* ☎ *406/846–2370 or 800/800–8000* *406/846–2373* 🌐 *www.super8.com* *57 rooms* *Restaurant, cable TV, some pets allowed, no-smoking rooms* *AE, D, DC, MC, V.*

CAMPING **Indian Creek Campground.** Set among brush and flats, this campground along tiny Indian Creek has large campsites, plus cable TV hookups. For a small fee you can use the Internet at the office. It's a good idea to make reservations. *Flush toilets, full hookups, drinking water, guest laundry, showers, picnic tables, electricity, public telephone, general store* *55 full hookups, 20 tent sites* ✉ *745 Maverick La.,* ☎ *406/846–3848 or 800/294–0726* 🌐 *www.indiancreekcampground.net* *$19 full hookups, $14 tent sites* *MC, V* ⏲ *Mid-Apr.–Oct.*

Nightlife & the Arts

Bluegrass bands perform outdoors (weather permitting) at the three-day **Prison Breakout Bluegrass Festival** (☎ 800/255–1318) in late June. Barbecues, vendors, and concessions are set up at this annual event 10 mi west of town at Garrison Junction's Riverfront RV Park.

Anaconda

26 *22 mi south of Deer Lodge via I–90.*

Nicknamed the Smelter City, Anaconda still bears remnants of the copper-smelting operations around which the town was built in the form of a dormant 585-foot smokestack, visible for miles. Although copper is no longer the town's chief industry, Anaconda's rough-and-tumble past offers history buffs a look at the copper barons' work. It's also an ideal spot for fishing, hiking, and even golfing—there's a Jack Nicklaus–designed golf course that uses smelter-tailings slag for sand traps. The town sits at the base of the rugged Pintlar Mountains, popular for cross-country skiing, downhill skiing, and backcountry adventures.

The **Anaconda Visitor Center,** in the old railroad depot, displays memorabilia of the town's railroad and copper history. It also hosts tours, performances, and exhibits. You can even buy a pen with ink made from slag. A 1931 **Vintage Bus** departs from the visitor center for a tour of historic Anaconda. ✉ *306 E. Park Ave.* ☎ *406/563–2400* 🌐 *www.anacondamt.org* *Visitor center free, bus $5* ⏲ *Visitor center June–Sept., daily 9–5; Oct.–May, weekdays 9–5. Bus mid-May–mid-Sept., Mon.–Sat. at 10 and 2.*

The **Copper Village Museum and Arts Center** houses displays on the area's history along with video presentations and local artwork. The center also hosts musical performances and special events. ✉ *401 E. Commercial St.* ☎ *406/563–2422* 🎫 *Free* ⏲ *May–Sept., daily 10–4; Oct.–Apr., Tues.–Sat. 10–4.*

The classic art deco **Washoe Theatre** (✉ 305 Main St. ☎ 406/563–6161), built in 1931, was ranked by the Smithsonian as the fifth-most-beautiful theater in the nation. Murals and ornamentation in silver, copper, and gold leaf are some of the highlights of this theater, which is open nightly for movies and other events.

At 585 feet tall, "the Stack" at **Anaconda Smoke Stack State Park** is a solid reminder of the important role the Anaconda Copper Company played in the area's development. Smelting operations ceased in 1980. Built in 1919, the stack, one of the tallest freestanding brick structures in the world, is listed on the National Register of Historic Places. There's a viewing and interpretive area with displays and historical information, but you cannot access the smokestack itself. ✉ *Hwy. 1* ☎ *406/542–5500* 🌐 *www.state.mt.us* 🎫 *Free* ⏲ *Daily, sunrise–sunset.*

off the beaten path

ANACONDA-PINTLAR WILDERNESS – Shared by three ranger districts of the Beaverhead-Deerlodge National Forest, the 159,000-acre Anaconda-Pintlar wilderness area extends more than 30 mi along the Continental Divide to the southwest of Anaconda. Elevations range from 5,400 feet near the Bitterroot River to 10,793 feet at the summit of West Goat Peak. Glaciation formed many spectacular cirques, U-shape valleys, and glacial moraines in the foothills. About 280 mi of Forest Service trails cross the area. If you hike or ride horseback along the Continental Divide, at times you can view the Mission Mountains to the northwest and the mountains marking the Idaho-Montana border to the southwest. The habitat supports mountain lions, deer, elk, moose, bears, and many smaller animals and birds. If you want to explore the wilderness, you must obtain a detailed map and register your plans with a Forest Service office. Stock forage is scarce, so if you're riding a horse, you're encouraged to bring concentrated feed pellets. Note that no motorized travel is permitted in the wilderness area. There are more than 20 access points to the area, including popular ones at Moose Lake, Georgetown Lake, and the East Fork of the Bitterroot River. ✉ *Access to East Fork of Bitterroot River via U.S. 93* ☎ *406/821–3201* 🎫 *Free* ⏲ *Daily, 24 hrs.*

PINTLAR SCENIC HIGHWAY – The 63 mi of mountain road on this highway pass a ghost town, historic burgs, and Georgetown Lake. The road begins in Anaconda and ends on I–90 at Drummond, backdropped by the 159,000-acre Anaconda-Pintlar Wilderness. ☎ *406/563–2400 for information on highway.*

Sports & the Outdoors

Need a mountain bike or just some suggested bike routes? Check with **Sven's Bicycles of Anaconda** (✉ 220 Hickory St. ☎ 406/563–7988) for local advice, including the best mountain-biking routes, from back roads to challenging mile-high trails. In winter, Sven's rents ice skates and cross-country-skiing equipment and can provide ski-trail maps and telemarking suggestions.

CROSS-COUNTRY SKIING

Beautifully groomed skate and classic-ski trails climb nearly to the Continental Divide at the **Mt. Haggin Cross-Country Ski Trails** area, the state's largest wildlife management area, with more than 54,000 acres. There's a warming hut but no services. Ski rentals and information are available at Sven's Bicycles on Hickory Street. To get to the area from Anaconda, head southwest on Highway 1, cross the railroad tracks, and look for the sign to Wisdom; from here, make a left onto Highway 274 and follow it for 11 mi to the parking area.

GOLF The public, 18-hole, Jack Nicklaus–designed **Old Works Golf Course** (✉ 1205 Pizzini Way ☎ 406/563–5989), on the site of Anaconda's historic Old Works copper smelter, uses smelter-tailings slag for sand traps.

DOWNHILL SKIING Powder skiing at **Discovery Ski Area** (✉ Hwy. 1, 23 mi northwest of Anaconda at Georgetown Lake ☎ 406/563–2184 🌐 www.skidiscovery.com), an inexpensive family resort, includes thrills on the extreme steeps and extensive beginner and intermediate runs.

Where to Stay & Eat

$$–$$$ ✕ **Barclay II.** This supper club and lounge is known for its steak, and folks come especially for the huge set meal of tenderloin served with salad, a relish tray, spaghetti, salami and cheese, and ice cream. Dim lighting, white tablecloths, mirrors, and historic photos of Anaconda decorate the restaurant. ✉ *1300 E. Commercial St.* ☎ *406/563–5541* 💳 *AE, D, MC, V* 🕐 *Closed Mon.*

¢ ✕🏨 **Seven Gables Resort.** At Georgetown Lake, this simple, clean lodge has views of the Pintlar Mountains and is 4 mi from skiing and across the road from fishing. The restaurant ($–$$) serves simple fare such as pressure-fried chicken and burgers; there's also a salad bar. ✉ *20 Southern Cross Rd., 59711* ☎📠 *406/563–5052* 🌐 *www.sevengablesmontana.com* ⇨ *9 rooms* 👍 *Restaurant, cable TV, lake, beach, dock, boating, fishing, cross-country skiing, downhill skiing, bar, casino, no-smoking rooms* 💳 *AE, D, MC, V.*

$$–$$$$ 🏨 **Fairmont Hot Springs.** This resort between Anaconda and Butte is a great lodging option if you have children. Although not much to look at, the Fairmont has naturally heated indoor and outdoor swimming pools, a 350-foot waterslide, a playground, and a wildlife zoo in a beautiful setting. There's also an 18-hole golf course on the grounds. ✉ *1500 Fairmont Rd., Fairmont 59711* ☎ *406/797–3241 or 800/332–3272* 📠 *406/797–3337* 🌐 *www.fairmontmontana.com* ⇨ *129 rooms, 23 suites* 👍 *Restaurant, coffee shop, 18-hole golf course, 2 tennis courts, 2 pools (1 indoor), massage, volleyball, bar, playground* 💳 *AE, D, DC, MC, V.*

$$ 🏨 **Lodge at Old Works.** This resort hotel, scheduled to open in 2004, reflects a mountain-lodge style, with timber accents, large windows, and spacious rooms. The resort overlooks the Old Works Golf Course and is convenient to alpine skiing and fly-fishing. ✉ *1005 Pizzini Way, 59711* ☎ *406/563–5827 or 866/653–9757* 📠 *406/563–7737* 🌐 *www.lodgeatoldworks.com* ⇨ *68 rooms* 👍 *Restaurant, golf privileges, pool, hot tub, lounge, business center, meeting rooms, no-smoking rooms* 💳 *AE, D, MC, V.*

CAMPING ⛺ **Lost Creek State Park.** A short trail at this scenic recreation area leads to the Lost Creek Falls. Views of limestone cliffs rising 1,200 feet above the canyon floor, and frequent sightings of bighorn sheep and mountain goats are some of the attractions of this park. The campground has hiking trails and creek fishing. 👍 *Pit toilets, drinking water, fire grates, picnic tables, swimming (creek)* ⇨ *25 sites* ✉ *1½ mi east of Anaconda on Hwy. 1, then 2 mi north on Hwy. 273, then 6 mi west* ☎ *406/542–5500* 🌐 *www.state.mt.us* 🎫 *Free* ✍ *Reservations not accepted* 💳 *No credit cards* 🕐 *May–Oct.*

The Arts

Washoe Park, with its flower gardens, tennis courts, picnic areas, an outdoor swimming pool, and the Montana State Fish Hatchery, hosts **Art in Washoe Park** (☎ 406/563–2422 ✉ Park St.). This three-day celebration in July includes juried art and crafts booths, ethnic foods, and professional entertainment.

The art deco **Washoe Theatre** (✉ 305 Main St. ☎ 406/563–6161) presents movies, concerts, and other kinds of performances.

Butte

27 *30 mi east of Anaconda via Hwy. 1 and I–90; 79 mi northwest of Virginia City via Hwy. 287 and Hwy. 55.*

Dubbed the "Richest Hill on Earth," Butte was once a wealthy and rollicking copper-, gold-, and silver-mining town, which during its heyday had an international population of 100,000 and, by 1880, had generated about $22 billion in mineral wealth. Today about 34,000 people live in the Butte–Silver Bow County area and cheer on a revival of the historic district. Uptown Butte, a National Historic Landmark area, has numerous ornate buildings reminiscent of the Old West days, and several museums in town preserve Butte's past. The city maintains a strong Irish flavor, and its St. Patrick's Day Parade celebration is one of the region's finest.

Changing exhibits at the **Butte Chamber of Commerce** include historic photographs, artifacts, and artwork related to Butte. ✉ *1000 George St.* ☎ *406/723–3177 or 800/735–6814* *Free* *June–Labor Day, daily 8–8; Labor Day–May, daily 8–5.*

Keeping watch over Butte—as seen from the east ridge of the Rocky Mountains—is **Our Lady of the Rockies,** a 90-foot-tall, 80-ton statue of the Virgin Mary on the Continental Divide; it's lighted at night. For a 2½-hour bus tour, stop by the visitor center, a nonprofit, nondenominational organization. ✉ *3100 Harrison Ave., at the Butte Plaza Mall* ☎ *406/782–1221 or 800/800–5239* *www.ourladyoftherockies.org* *Bus tour $10* *June–Sept., Mon.–Sat. at 10 and 2, Sun. at 11 and 2, weather permitting.*

Butte has the dubious distinction of containing the largest toxic-waste site in the country—thanks to the old mining wastes. The underground copper mines were dug up in the 1950s, creating the **Berkeley Open Pit Mine,** which stretches 1½ by 1 mi, reaches 1,800 feet deep, and is filled with toxic water some 800 feet deep. A viewing platform allows you to look into the now-abandoned, mammoth pit where more than 20 billion pounds of copper, 704 million ounces of silver, and 3 million ounces of gold were extracted from the Butte mining district. ✉ *Continental Dr. at Park St.* ☎ *406/723–3177 or 800/735–6814* *Free* *Daily 8–dusk, weather permitting.*

William Clark, one of Butte's richest copper barons, built the **Copper King Mansion** between 1884 and 1888. Tours of the house take in the hand-carved oak paneling, nine original fireplaces, antiques, a lavish ballroom, and frescoes. ✉ *219 W. Granite St.* ☎ *406/782–7580* *www.copperkingmansion.com* *$5* *May–Sept., daily 9–4; Oct. and Apr., weekends 9–4; Nov.–Mar., by appointment.*

Built in 1890 as a sporting house, the **Dumas Brothel Museum** was America's longest-running house of ill repute: it was shut down in 1982 and reopened as a museum. Tours are available of the building and of Butte's red-light district, Venus Alley. ✉ *45 E. Mercury St.* ☎ *406/494–6908* 🌐 *www.thedumasbrothel.com* 🎟 *$5* ⏲ *May–Aug., daily 10–5.*

More than 1,300 mineral specimens are displayed at Montana Tech University's **Mineral Museum,** including a 27½-troy-ounce gold nugget and a 400-pound smoky quartz crystal. ✉ *1300 W. Park St.* ☎ *406/496–4414* 🌐 *www.mbmg.mtech.edu* 🎟 *Free* ⏲ *Late May–early Sept., daily 9–6; early May–late May and mid-Sept.–Oct., weekdays 9–4, weekends 1–5.*

The **Mai Wah Museum** contains exhibits on the history of the Chinese and other Asian settlers of Butte. The museum comprises two restored historic buildings constructed to house Chinese-owned businesses: the Wah Chong Tai Company building and the Mai Wah Noodle Parlor. ✉ *17 W. Mercury St.* ☎ *406/723–6731* 🌐 *www.maiwah.org* 🎟 *Donations accepted* ⏲ *Tues.–Sat. 11–5.*

★ The **Arts Chateau Museum,** an elegant 1898 four-story Victorian mansion, now serves as a gallery space and an interactive youth center. The collection includes 18th- and 19th-century furniture, textiles, and collectibles as well as artwork. ✉ *321 W. Broadway* ☎ *406/723–7600* 🌐 *www.artschateau.org* 🎟 *$3* ⏲ *Tues.–Sat. 11–4.*

A classic 1900 fire station, on the National Register of Historic Places, houses the **Butte Silver Bow Archives,** with historical documents, photographs, and artifacts related to Butte. ✉ *17 W. Quartz St.* ☎ *406/497–6226* 🎟 *Free* ⏲ *Weekdays 9–5.*

off the beaten path

SHEEPSHEAD MOUNTAIN RECREATION AREA – At this designated Wildlife Viewing Area, you might glimpse elk, deer, moose, and birds of prey. There's a picnic area and drinking water. ✉ *13 mi north of Butte on I–15 to Exit 138 (Elk Park), west on Forest Service Rd. 442, follow signs for 6 mi* ☎ *406/494–2147* 🌐 *www.fs.fed.us/r1/bdnf* 🎟 *Free* ⏲ *Memorial Day–Labor Day, daily.*

Sports & the Outdoors

FISHING **Tom's Fishing and Bird Hunting Guide Service** (✉ 3460 St. Ann St. ☎ 406/723–4753 or 800/487–0296) arranges float and wade trips for blue-ribbon trout fishing.

HORSEBACK RIDING **Cargill Outfitters** (✉ 40 Cedar Hills Rd., Whitehall ☎ 406/494–2960), which is just over the Continental Divide, 20 minutes east of Butte, offers two-hour to full-day horseback riding into the Highland Mountain range.

ICE-SKATING You can speed skate on ice at the **U.S. High Altitude Sports Center** (✉ 5155 Continental Dr. ☎ 406/494–7570) with international speed-skaters or beginners. The ice track is open for general ice-skating as well; call for times. Skate rentals are available.

Where to Stay & Eat

$$–$$$$ ✕ **Acoma.** Renovations haven't altered the authentic art deco decor of this restaurant on the National Historic Register. Dine on game hen chasseur, hunter-style with tomatoes, mushrooms, and duchess potatoes, or veal Acoma sautéed with artichoke hearts and mushrooms and finished with white-wine cream sauce. ✉ *60 E. Broadway* ☎ *406/728–7001* 💳 *AE, D, MC, V.*

$$–$$$$ ✕ **Uptown Café.** Fresh seafood, steaks (try the Cajun prime rib), poultry, and pasta are served in this informal, smoke-free café. Try the artichoke ravioli or the chicken *zingara,* a boneless breast sautéed with Italian ham, olives, and onions. Rotating paintings by local artists line the walls. ✉ *47 E. Broadway* ☎ *406/723–4735* 💳 *AE, D, MC, V.*

$–$$$ ✕ **Spaghettini's.** In the historic district, this Italian trattoria squeezes a bit of the Mediterranean into a narrow brick building with thick ferns and murals of Old Italy. Seafood and pasta marry into wonders such as shrimp spaghettini, with shrimp, asparagus, prosciutto, and artichoke bottoms, sautéed in pesto sauce and served over pasta. ✉ *26 N. Main St.* ☎ *406/782–8855* ▭ *No credit cards.*

¢–$ ✕ **Broadway Café.** This turn-of-the-20th-century building is the place for pizzas and salads. Try the ginger tahini salad or the "madhouse" pizza, with red onions, sun-dried tomatoes, olives, artichokes, feta, and mozzarella cheese. Thursday and Friday nights there's live music, usually contemporary jazz. It's right near the Berkeley Open Pit Mine. ✉ *302 E. Broadway* ☎ *406/723–8711* ✍ *Reservations essential* ▭ *AE, D, MC, V* ⊗ *Closed Sun.*

¢ ✕ **Town Talk Bakery.** No visit to Butte is complete without trying a famous Butte pasty, a traditional miner's dinner of meat, potatoes, and onion baked inside a pastry shell. This bakery is one of the best of several eateries that serve these pocket-size meals, generally to go. There are two tables for dining here, but most people order takeout. ✉ *611 E. Front St.* ☎ *406/782–4985* ▭ *No credit cards* ⊗ *Closed Mon.*

$–$$ **Best Western Butte Plaza Inn.** Butte's largest facility is convenient to shopping, sports events, and the interstates. The rooms are clean and comfortable, if somewhat bland. ✉ *2900 Harrison Ave., 59701* ☎ *406/494–3500 or 800/543–5814* *406/494–7611* 🌐 *www.bestwestern.com* *134 rooms* *Restaurant, in-room data ports, cable TV, indoor pool, sauna, steam room, bar, laundry facilities, meeting rooms, airport shuttle, free parking, some pets allowed, no-smoking rooms* ▭ *AE, D, MC, V.*

$ **Scott Inn Bed and Breakfast.** Built in 1897 as a boardinghouse for miners, this three-story, redbrick building has undergone artful renovation: the woodwork, doors, banisters, and many windows have been left intact, yet the baths and furnishings are new. This elegant, affordable B&B is Butte's oldest accommodation, and it's within walking distance of historic attractions, museums, and antiques and bookshops. Rooms have extraordinary views of the historic district, the Rockies, and the Highland Mountains. Early-20th-century boarders probably didn't get to appreciate the views, however—they slept three to a room for an eight-hour stay. ✉ *15 W. Copper Ave., 59701* ☎ *406/723–7030 or 800/844–2952* *406/782–1415* 🌐 *www.scottinn.com* *7 rooms* *In-room VCRs, lounge* ▭ *AE, D, MC, V* *BP.*

Fodor's Choice ★

CAMPING **Butte KOA.** This large and grassy campsite with cottonwood trees has a playground and allows fishing and swimming in the on-site Silver Bow Creek. It's next to a tourism office and is easily accessed from the interstate. It's a good idea to reserve ahead. *Flush toilets, full hookups, partial hookups (water), dump station, drinking water, laundry facilities, showers, food service, picnic tables, electricity, public telephone, general store, pool, swimming (creek)* *100 RV sites (full or partial hookups), 20 tent sites; 4 cabins* ✉ *1601 Kaw Ave., off I–90 at Exit 126* ☎ *406/782–0663 or 800/562–8089* 🌐 *www.koa.com* *Full hookups $28, partial hookups $25, tent sites $22; cabins $35* ▭ *D, MC, V* ⊗ *Mid-Apr.–Oct.*

Nightlife & the Arts

Every August, the Montana Gaelic Cultural Society hosts the **An Ri Ra, Montana Irish Festival** (✉ Park St. between Main and Montana Sts. ☎ 800/735–6814), with an art show, a film festival, children's activities, and the Pipers' Parade in Uptown Butte. On March 17, the annual **St. Patrick's Day Parade** (✉ Uptown Butte ☎ 406/782–0742 🌐 www.butteamerica.com) celebrates Butte's Irish heritage.

Community and children's theater productions at the **Mother Lode** (✉ 316 W. Park St. ☎ 406/723–3602) include Broadway shows and concerts. This 1922 grand theater is the last of several that once embellished Uptown.

Shopping

Find everything from Butte collectibles to fine porcelain and antique furniture at **D&G Antiques** (✉ 16 N. Montana St. ☎ 406/723–4552), one of eight antiques shops in the historic district. Montana's largest bookstore, **Second Edition Books** (✉ 112 S. Montana St. ☎ 406/723–5108 or 800/298–5108), buys, sells, and trades books on many different subjects but specializes in hard-to-find regional tomes. While visiting the historic district, stop at the **Uptown Butte Farmers' Market** (✉ Main St. between Park St. and Broadway ☎ 406/723–3177 or 800/735–6814) for fresh garden produce, fruit, flowers, baked goods, and local crafts. It's open Saturday in summer from 9 to 1.

Virginia City

28 *72 mi southeast of Butte via Hwys. 2, 41, and 287.*

Remnants of Montana's frontier days, Virginia City and its smaller neighbor Nevada City are two of the most unusual attractions in the state, with partially restored historic buildings, a boardwalk, and stores stocked with 19th-century goods. When miners stampeded into the state after the discovery of gold on May 26, 1863, many headed to Virginia City's Alder Gulch, where the diggings were rich; the city prospered and eventually became the capital of Montana Territory. The success of the city enticed criminals, who held up miners. In turn, vigilance committees—eager to maintain order—grew, held lightning-fast trials, and strung up the bad guys. Some of the graves of those hanged by vigilantes remain atop Boot Hill, overlooking town.

Begin a visit at the **Virginia City Depot Visitor Center,** where you can get information on theater, historic accommodations, and gold panning. There's also a gift shop. ✉ *Lower Wallace St.* ☎ *406/843–5239* 🎟 *Free* ⏲ *May–Oct., daily 9–5.*

The eclectic collection at the **Thompson-Hickman Memorial Museum** includes a petrified wedding cake, the clubfoot of "Club Foot" George Lane, rifles, and numerous photographs. This historic collection, with items dating from between 1860 and 1900, is made up of heirlooms of three local families. The local library is upstairs. ✉ *Wallace St.* ☎ *406/843–5238* 🎟 *Donations accepted* ⏲ *May–Sept., daily 10–5.*

An old-time narrow-gauge steam train, the **Baldwin Locomotive No. 12,** Montana's only operating steam locomotive run by volunteer crews, travels between Virginia City and Nevada City on weekends. On weekdays, a smaller locomotive, the **Alder Gulch Shortline Railroad,** makes the same journey. ☎ *406/843–5247* 🌐 *www.virginiacitychamber.com/train* 🎟 *$10 round-trip* ⏲ *Memorial Day–Labor Day, 5 trips daily (on either Baldwin or Alder Gulch); select weekends rest of yr.*

The annual **Heritage Days** festival celebrates the Victorian West, with historical reenactments, activities along the boardwalk, and the evening **Victorian Ball,** with authentic music, dancing, and costumes. The event lasts for two days in mid-August. ✉ *Victorian Ball: Virginia City Gymnasium, Van Buren and Idaho Sts.* ☎ *406/843–5314 or 800/829–2969* 🌐 *www.virginiacitychamber.com* 🎟 *Festival free; $30 for ball and dinner, $5 to observe ball from balcony.*

★ The living-history **Nevada City Open Air Museum,** next door to Virginia City, preserves the town as it was at the turn of the 20th century, with restored buildings, thousands of artifacts from the gold-rush era, and demonstrations. New to the collection is the **Frontier House Museum,** from the PBS television series of the same name. ✉ *U.S. 287, 1½ mi west of Virginia City* ☎ *406/843–5247* 🌐 *www.virginiacitychamber.com* 🎫 *$6* 🕘 *Mid-May–mid-Sept., daily sunrise–sunset.*

After they were hanged by vigilantes, the notorious criminals who preyed on miners were buried at **Boot Hill** cemetery. The hill affords a good view of the town and surrounding mountains. ✉ *From Wallace St. turn north on Spencer St. and follow signs for ROAD AGENTS' GRAVES* ☎ *406/843–5555 or 800/829–2969* 🌐 *www.virginiacitychamber.com.*

Sports & the Outdoors

Spend a day moving cattle from high in the saddle with **Upper Canyon Outfitters/Tate Ranch** (✉ 2149 Upper Ruby Rd., 35 mi southwest of Virginia City ☎ 800/735–3973). You can also sleep under the stars on the six-day cattle drive on the ranch and into the Gravelly Range.

Where to Stay & Eat

¢ ✕ **City Bakery.** Fresh pastries and gingerbread keep people coming back for more at this bakery. Wash your order down with a huckleberry iced tea. There's no seating in the bakery, but there are benches on the sidewalk outside. ✉ *325 W. Wallace St.* ☎ *406/843–5227* *Reservations not accepted* 💳 *MC, V* 🕘 *Closed Oct., Nov., and Jan.–May.*

$ **Stonehouse Inn Bed & Breakfast.** Period charm pervades this 1884 Gothic Revival home with antiques, brass beds, 12-foot ceilings, and a teddy-bear collection. The full breakfast might include strawberry French toast with cream cheese and fresh fruit. ✉ *306 E. Idaho St., 59755* ☎ *406/843–5504* 🌐 *www.stonehouseinnbb.com* *5 rooms* *Dining room, fishing, piano, baby-sitting, laundry facilities, meeting room; no room phones, no room TVs, no smoking* 💳 *MC, V* *BP.*

¢–$ **Fairweather Inn and the Nevada City Hotel and Cabins.** Virginia City's Fairweather Inn is a classic Western-Victorian hotel with balconies in the heart of the area's gold-mining country. The two-story 1864 Nevada City Hotel is 1½ mi away in Nevada City; there are Victorian-style hotel rooms, plus rustic miners' cabins. ✉ *305 W. Wallace St., 59755* ☎ *406/843–5377 or 800/829–2969* 📠 *406/843–5235* *Fairweather Inn: 15 rooms, 5 with bath. Nevada City Hotel: 11 rooms, 2 suites, 17 cabins* *No room phones, no room TVs, no smoking* 💳 *D, MC, V* 🕘 *Closed Oct.–mid-May.*

CAMPING **Virginia City Campground & RV Park.** The large grassy campsites here are close to miniature golf, horseshoes, volleyball, and a recreation field. It's a good idea to reserve ahead. *Flush toilets, full hookups, partial hookups (some electric, some electric and water), dump station, drinking water, showers, fire pits, picnic tables, electricity, public telephone* *10 full hookups, 8 partial hookups, 24 tent sites* ✉ *Hwy. 287, ¼ mi east of Virginia City* ☎ *406/843–5493 or 888/833–5493* 🌐 *www.virginiacitycampground.com* 🎫 *Full hookups $28, partial hookups $24, tent sites $15* 💳 *MC, V* 🕘 *Mid-May–mid-Sept.*

Nightlife & the Arts

NIGHTLIFE Weekend evenings in summer there's often live rock music at **Banditos** (✉ 320 Wallace St. ☎ 406/843–5556), in the historic Wells Fargo building. The **Brewery Follies** (✉ H. S. Gilbert Brewery building, Cover St. ☎ 406/843–5218 or 800/829–2969) are contemporary comedies (ages 12 and up); shows take place Wednesday through Monday evenings from late May through August.

THE ARTS ★ The historic **Opera House** (✉ 338 W. Wallace St. ☎ 406/843–5314 or 800/829–2969 🌐 vcplayers.com) is the oldest continuously operating summer theater in the West, in operation since 1949. Early June through early September, the theater hosts an amusing vaudeville show by the Virginia City Players. The cost is $15.

Shopping

Opened in 1864, **Rank's Mercantile** (✉ 211 Wallace St. ☎ 406/843–5454 or 800/494–5442) is Montana's oldest continuously operating store. Period clothing, books, toys, gifts, and groceries are for sale here.

Ennis

29 *14 mi east of Virginia City via Hwy. 287.*

In addition to being a hub of ranching in the area, this tiny town sits among some of the best trout streams in the West. People come from around the world for the area's blue-ribbon trout fishing. You'll even be welcomed into town by a sign that reads 600 PEOPLE, 11,000,000 TROUT.

Consistently rated among the most exciting and challenging rodeos in Montana, the Independence Day **Ennis Rodeo** (☎ 406/682–4700) attracts top cowpokes and rodeo stock to the evening shows.

At the **Ennis National Fish Hatchery,** six strains of rainbow trout produce 23 million eggs per year for stocking streams throughout the United States. Blaine Springs provides the fresh, clean spring water at a constant temperature of 54°F, ideal for nurturing trout. Note that the 10-mi access road leading here is bumpy. ✉ *180 Fish Hatchery Rd.* ☎ *406/682–4847 or 800/344–9453* 🌐 *ennis.fws.gov* *Free* *Daily 8–5.*

For a bit of relaxation, nothing beats soaking in the natural hot water of the **Norris Hot Springs** pool. Note that no kids are allowed in the pool after 7:30 PM. ✉ *Hwy. 84, 16 mi north of Ennis on U.S. 287, then west through town, Norris* ☎ *406/685–3303* *$5* *Daily noon–9.*

off the beaten path

BEARTRAP CANYON – In this part of the Lee Metcalf Wilderness northeast of Ennis, you can hike, fish, and go white-water rafting on the Madison River. A picnic area and access to Trail Creek are at the head of the canyon below Ennis Lake. To get here, drive north out of Ennis on U.S. 287 to the town of McAllister and turn right down a bumpy dirt road (no number), which takes you around to the north side of the lake across the dam. Turn left after the dam onto an unmarked road and drive across the river to the Trail Creek access point. ☎ *406/683–2337* *Free* *Daily.*

Sports & the Outdoors

FISHING The fly-fishing specialists of **Eaton Outfitters** (✉ 307 Jeffers Rd. ☎ 800/755–3474) lead trips on the Madison, Beaverhead, Big Hole, and Ruby rivers. The **Tackle Shop** (✉ 127 E. Main St. ☎ 406/682–4263 or 800/808–2832) offers guided float and wade fishing on the Madison, Big Hole, and other rivers. The full-service Orvis fly shop also sells luggage, clothing, and fishing accessories.

HORSEBACK RIDING Ride the dusty trails with **Bar 88 Horses** (☎ 406/682–4827) on half- and full-day adventures in the Beaverhead National Forest.

Where to Stay & Eat

$$$–$$$$ ✕ **Continental Divide.** This bistro-style restaurant is a pleasant surprise among the numerous steak houses in the area. Among the specials are local free-range chicken roasted with tomatoes and vegetables, and lobster ravioli. In summer there's live jazz music during Sunday brunch.

✉ 311 E. Main St. ☎ 406/682–7600 ▭ AE, D, MC, V ⏲ Closed Oct.–May.

$$$ ✕ **Diamond J Guest Ranch.** Fishing, horseback riding, supervised kids' activities, weekly square dances, and steak cookouts are all part of the fun at this family-run 1930s ranch bordering the Lee Metcalf Wilderness. The lodgepole-pine cabins have stone fireplaces, hardwood floors, hickory furniture, and private baths. There's a seven-day minimum stay. *✉ 800 Jack Creek Rd., 59747 ☎ 406/682–4867 or 877/929–4867 ℻ 406/682–4106 ⊕ www.ranchweb.com/diamondj ⇨ 8 cabins ♁ Dining room, tennis court, pool, hot tub, fishing, hiking, horseback riding, horseshoes, Ping-Pong, volleyball, lobby lounge, library, shop, baby-sitting, airport shuttle; no room phones, no room TVs, no smoking ▭ AE, MC, V ⏲ Closed mid-Sept.–mid-June ♈ FAP.*

★ $$$$ **Potosi Hot Springs.** Western and fishing accents decorate the private cabins at this hot-springs resort. Soak pools vary in size and temperature; the 20- by 50-foot Big Pool is at the base of a mossy granite cliff. You can join in numerous outdoor activities on the resort's 75 acres or in the Tabacco Root Mountains. Dinner, perhaps oven-roasted pheasant or grilled elk tenderloin, is served in your cabin in front of the fireplace. *✉ S. Willow Creek Rd., Pony, 35 mi northwest of Ennis, 59747 ☎ 406/685–3330 or 888/685–1695 ℻ 406/685–3390 ⊕ www.potosiresort.com ⇨ 4 cabins ♁ Restaurant, room service, kitchens, refrigerators, sauna, fishing, mountain bikes, horseback riding, cross-country skiing, lobby lounge, piano, shop, meeting room, some pets allowed; no room phones, no room TVs, no kids under 13, no smoking ▭ AE, MC, V ♈ BP, FAP.*

¢ **Fan Mountain Inn.** This simple but clean family motel has wonderful views of the Madison Range and is within walking distance of downtown shops and galleries. *✉ 204 N. Main St., 59729 ☎ 406/682–5200 or 877/682–5200 ℻ 406/682–5266 ⊕ www.fanmountaininn.com ⇨ 27 rooms ♁ Some microwaves, some refrigerators, cable TV, shop, meeting rooms, some pets allowed (fee), no-smoking rooms ▭ AE, D, MC, V.*

CAMPING **Ennis RV Village.** Hiking trails wend past a small stream at this 8-acre park with views of the Madison, Gravelly, and Tabacco Roots ranges. Reservations are recommended. *♁ Flush toilets, full hookups, partial hookups, dump station, drinking water, laundry facilities, showers, fire pits, grills, picnic tables, electricity, public telephone, general store ⇨ 41 full hookups, 10 partial hookups, 4 tent sites ✉ 5034 N. U.S. 287, 1 mi north of Ennis ☎ 406/682–5272, 866/682–5272, or 888/519–5879 ℻ 406/682–5245 ⊕ www.ennisrvvillage.com ✉ Full hookups $23, partial hookups $19, tent sites $15 ▭ AE, MC, V ⏲ May–Oct.*

Nightlife & the Arts

NIGHTLIFE Live music Friday and Saturday night at the **Claim Jumper Saloon** (✉ 305 Main St. ☎ 406/682–5558) ranges from blues to classic rock. The patio has outdoor seating and horseshoes.

THE ARTS The **River Stone Gallery** (✉ 219 E. Main St. ☎ 406/682–5768) displays original paintings, sculptures, pottery, and contemporary jewelry by Western artists. Local stones are often used in the jewelry. One-of-a-kind abstract sculptures are made of copper and brass at the **Trudi Gilliam Metal Sculpture Studio and Gallery** (✉ 212 E. Main St. ☎ 406/682–7772).

Dillon

❸⓪ *65 mi south of Butte via I–90 west and I–15 south.*

Dillon is a capital of southwest Montana's ranch country and the seat of the state's largest county, Beaverhead. The town began as a shipping point between Utah and the goldfields of Montana. Later, the Union Pacific Railroad shipped cattle and sheep from here to processing. Hiking and mountain biking lead into the nearby Ruby and Tendoy mountains. Blue-ribbon trout fishing on the Beaverhead River attracts thousands of flies and anglers year-round.

The **Beaverhead County Museum** exhibits Native American artifacts, ranching and mining memorabilia, a homesteader's cabin, mining equipment and agricultural artifacts, and a boardwalk imprinted with the area's ranch brands. ✉ *15 S. Montana St.* ☎ *406/683–5027* *Donations accepted* ⏲ *Memorial Day–Labor Day, weekdays 8:30–8, Sat. noon–4; Labor Day–Memorial Day, weekdays 8:30–5.*

The annual weeklong **Lewis and Clark Festival** (☎ 406/683–5511 🌐 www.beaverheadchamber.com) in August highlights the explorers' travels through the area. Historic reenactments, presentations, and a buffalo and beef barbecue are all part of the fun. Events take place at various sites around town.

Everyone is a cowboy for the annual **Dillon Jaycee Labor Day Rodeo and Parade** (✉ Fairgrounds, Railroad St. ☎ 406/683–5511), which has been staged here since 1914. Among the activities that take place at this festival running late August through early September are a fair, rodeo, and concert.

Within **Beaverhead Rock State Park** there is a historical landmark—a rock shaped like the head of a beaver that was used as a marker by Native Americans traveling from western valleys to hunt bison on Montana's plains. On the Lewis and Clark expedition in 1805, Sacajawea recognized and pointed out the rock along the Beaverhead River as part of the route across the mountains. Most people view the massive rock from an overlook because the primitive park is not developed, lacks signs, and has lots of rattlesnakes. ✉ *15 mi north of Dillon on Hwy. 41* ☎ *406/834–3413* 🌐 *www.fwp.state.mt.us* *Free* ⏲ *Daily dawn–dusk.*

off the beaten path

RED ROCK LAKES NATIONAL WILDLIFE REFUGE – In the undeveloped and remote Centennial Valley, this 43,500-acre refuge shelters moose, deer, and antelope but is primarily a sanctuary for 230 species of birds, including trumpeter swans. Once threatened with extinction, these elegant birds have survived thanks to refuge protection; today, they build their nests and winter here among the 14,000 acres of lakes and marshes. ✉ *27820 Southside Centennial Rd.; 60 mi south of Dillion on I–15 to Monida; follow signs east 28 mi on gravel and dirt road, Lima* ☎ *406/276–3536* 🌐 *redrocks.fws.gov* *Free* ⏲ *Daily 7:30–4.*

Sports & the Outdoors

FISHING

Whether they're discussing nymphs, caddis flies, or crane flies, the guides of **Backcountry Angler** (✉ 426 S. Atlantic St. ☎ 406/683–3462) know the art of fly-fishing. They lead overnight fishing-lodging trips, plus wade- and float-fishing day adventures. **Watershed Fly Fishing Adventures** (✉ 11 Pierce Dr. ☎ 406/683–6660 or 800/753–6660) arranges float- and wade-fishing trips on private creeks and ponds and the Beaverhead, Big Hole, Jefferson, and Ruby rivers.

HORSEBACK RIDING

Horse and mule day rides and pack trips traverse the Continental Divide and the Lima Peaks with **Centennial Outfitters** (✉ 2 Steel Bridge La., 45 mi south of Dillon via I–15, Lima ☎ 406/276–3463). **Diamond Hitch Outfitters** (✉ 3405 Ten Mile Rd., 4 mi west of Dillon ☎ 406/683–5494 or 800/368–5494) takes you by horse or mule to high rocky summits, past endless flowery meadows, and along trout fisheries on hourly rides, cookout rides, and overnight pack trips.

SKIING A fun family attraction, **Maverick Mountain Ski Area** (✉ Hwy. 278 [Maverick Mountain Rd.], 40 mi west of Dillon ☎ 406/834–3454) has a top elevation of 8,620 feet, a vertical drop of 1,927 feet, and 24 runs. Lessons and ski and snowboard rentals and sales are available for kids and adults.

Where to Stay & Eat

★ $$–$$$$ ✕ **Cross Ranch Cookhouse.** Dine in a cookhouse with some of the ranch hands of a working cattle ranch. In addition to salads, bread, and dessert, there's "pitchfork fondue"—Angus beef sirloin, skewered and then deep-fried in a cauldron via pitchfork. A local fiddle, banjo, and guitar band plays country music. To get here from Dillon, head south on I–15 to Exit 44, drive 12 mi west on Highway 324 to the Bannack turnoff, and then turn right and follow the dirt road for 2 mi. ✉ *12775 Bannack Rd.; south on I–15, Exit 44, on Hwy. 324 12 mi to Bannack turnoff, right 2 mi ahead on right* ☎ *406/681–3133* *Reservations essential* *No credit cards* *Closed Sun.*

¢–$ ✕ **The Grasshopper Inn.** In the spectacular Pioneer Mountains, this wilderness lodge is ideally situated for snowmobiling, hiking, and fishing. The tidy, colorful rooms have log beds and views of the mountains. The restaurant's back bar dates to the 1800s. The simple yet filling meals (¢–$$) include burgers, steak, and fish. You can rent snowmobiles here in winter and four-wheel drives in summer. ✉ *460505 Polaris Rd., 45 mi west of Dillon, Polaris 59746* ☎ *406/834–3456 or 866/468–6386* *406/834–3507* *www.pioneermountainrecreation.com* *10 rooms* *Restaurant, cable TV, cross-country skiing, snowmobiling, bar, shop, meeting rooms, some pets allowed, no-smoking rooms; no room phones* *MC, V* *Closed weekdays Apr. and May.*

$$ **Goose Down Ranch.** Darling cabins, one log and one clapboard, have front-porch views of the Blacktail Mountains and are near the famed Poindexter Slough blue-ribbon fly-fishing spot on the Beaverhead River. The cabins both have two bedrooms, fireplaces, and cozy couches. ✉ *710 S. Pacific St., 59725* ☎ *406/683–6704 or 406/683–3590* *406/683–8390* *www.goosedownranch.com* *2 cabins* *Kitchens, microwaves, in-room VCRs, fishing, laundry facilities; no room phones, no smoking* *MC, V.*

$ **Centennial Inn B&B.** Period furnishings, claw-foot tubs, and a turreted sitting area are the highlights of this Victorian-theme B&B on Montana's last frontier. The 1905 Queen Anne home is within walking distance of downtown. High tea, foreign-film nights, workshops, and Victorian-arts demonstrations might be part of your stay. ✉ *122 S. Washington St., 59725* ☎ *406/683–4454* *406/683–4454* *www.bmt.net/~centenn* *4 rooms* *Dining room, in-room data ports, shop, baby-sitting, laundry facilities; no room TVs, no smoking* *AE, DC, MC, V* *BP.*

$ **Guest House Inn & Suites.** This hotel is affordable, clean, and quiet and has an outdoor sundeck off the indoor pool. The staff can direct you to interesting local sights, scenic viewpoints, and perhaps even a good local fishing hole. ✉ *580 Sinclair St., 59725* ☎ *406/683–3636 or 800/214–8378* *406/683–3637* *www.guesthouseintl.com* *58 rooms* *In-room data ports, some kitchens, microwaves, refrigerators, cable TV, in-room VCRs, pool, hot tub, some pets allowed, no-smoking rooms* *AE, D, MC, V* *CP.*

CAMPING **Dillon KOA.** Pine, aspen, and birch trees shade this campground on the banks of the Beaverhead River. The campground, which is on the edge of Dillon, has views of the Pioneer Mountains and other peaks. *Flush toilets, full hookups, dump station, drinking water, laundry facilities, showers, picnic tables, electricity, public telephone, general store, play area, pool* *68 full hookups, 30 tent sites; 4 cabins* ✉ *735 W.*

Park St. ☎ 406/683–2749 or 800/562–2751 🌐 www.koa.com 🎫 Full hookups $29, tent sites $22; cabins $37 ▭ D, MC, V.

Shopping

Watercolor originals of flowers, dragonflies, and other scenes from nature are for sale as posters and cards at the **Cathy Weber–Artmaker** (✉ 26 N. Idaho St. ☎ 406/683–5493) studio. Antiques and collectibles are for sale in **P & L Antiques** (✉ 236 N. Idaho St. ☎ 406/683–9863).

Bannack

31 *24 mi west of Dillon via I–15 and U.S. 278.*

Bannack was Montana's first territorial capital and the site of the state's first major gold strike, in 1862, at Grasshopper Creek. Now **Bannack State Historic Park,** this frontier boomtown has historic structures lining the main street, and picnic and camping spots. It was here that the notorious renegade Sheriff Henry Plummer and several of his gang members were caught and executed by vigilantes for murder and robbery. The gallows on which Plummer was hanged still stands. Rumors persist that Plummer's stash of stolen gold was hidden somewhere in the mountains near here and never found. To get to Bannack from Dillon, follow Highway 278 24 mi west and watch for a sign just before Badger Pass; take the well-maintained gravel road for 3 mi. *☎ 406/834–3413 🎫 $4 per vehicle ⏲ Park daily dawn–dusk. Visitor center late May–early Sept., daily 10–6; early Sept.–late May, daily 8–5.*

Lectures, an old-fashioned school day, demonstrations of historical log-cabin construction, and guided tours are all part of **Dale Tash Montana History Day** (☎ 406/843–3548 🌐 www.bannack.org) at Bannack State Historic Park. It takes place in mid-July.

For two days in mid-July, **Bannack Days** (☎ 406/834–3413 🌐 www.bannack.org) celebrates life in Montana's first territorial capital with stagecoach rides, a main-street gunfight, old-time music and dancing, and pioneer-crafts demonstrations.

off the beaten path

PIONEER MOUNTAIN SCENIC BYWAY – Mountains, meadows, lodgepole-pine forests, and willow-edged streams line this road, which runs north–south between U.S. 278 (west of Bannack) and Highway 43. As it runs north, the byway skirts the Maverick Mountain Ski Area and Elkhorn Hot Springs and ends at the town of Wise River on the Big Hole River. *☎ 406/683–5511.*

Camping

Bannack Campgrounds. Grasshopper Creek, where gold was discovered in 1862, flows not far from this rustic campground, which has few amenities but is close to Bannack. Grocery stores and restaurants are in nearby Dillon. It's a good idea to reserve ahead for the single tepee. *Pit toilets, drinking water, fire pits, picnic tables 28 tent sites, 1 tepee ✉ 4200 Bannack St. ☎ 406/834–3413 🌐 www.fwp.state.mt.us 🎫 $12 tent sites, $15 tepee ▭ No credit cards.*

Big Hole National Battlefield

32 *60 mi northwest of Bannock via Hwy. 278 northwest and Hwy. 43 west; 87 mi southwest of Butte via I–90 west, I–15 south, and Hwy. 43 west.*

One of the West's greatest and most tragic stories played out on Big Hole National Battlefield. In 1877, Nez Perce warriors in central Idaho killed some white settlers as retribution for earlier killings by whites. Several hundred Nez Perce, knowing the U.S. Army would make no distinction between the guilty and innocent, fled—the beginning of a 1,500-mi, five-month odyssey that has come to be known as the Nez Perce Trail. They engaged 10 separate U.S. commands in 13 battles and skirmishes. One of the fiercest of these was here at Big Hole Battlefield, where both sides suffered serious losses. From here, the Nez Perce headed toward Yellowstone. A visitor center overlooks the meadows of Big Hole, which remain as they were at the time of the battle. Tepee poles erected by the park service mark the site of a Nez Perce village and serve as haunting reminders of what transpired here. Ranger-led programs for groups or individuals can be arranged with advance request. The park stays open for winter snowshoeing and cross-country skiing on a groomed trail through the battlefield's sites. Big Hole National Battlefield is one of 38 sites in four states that make up the **Nez Perce National Historic Park** (☎ 406/689–3155 🌐 www.nps.gov/nepe), which follows the historic Nez Perce Trail. ✉ *Hwy. 43, 10 mi west of Wisdom* ☎ *406/689–3155* 🌐 *www.nps.gov/biho* 🎫 *$5 per vehicle Memorial Day–Labor Day; free rest of yr* ⏲ *May–Labor Day, daily 8:30–6; Labor Day–Apr., daily 9–5.*

The annual **Commemoration of the Battle of Big Hole** (☎ 406/689–3155 🌐 www.nps.gov/nepe), in early August, includes traditional Nez Perce music, ceremonies, and demonstrations, along with cavalry exhibitions.

Sports & the Outdoors

You can cross-country ski (with your own equipment) or snowshoe through the historic trails of **Big Hole Battlefield** (✉ Hwy. 43, 10 mi west of Wisdom ☎ 406/689–3155 🌐 www.nps.gov/biho). A few pairs of snowshoes are available for use for free at the visitor center.

Where to Stay & Eat

¢–$ ✕🏨 **Jackson Hot Springs Lodge.** Lewis and Clark cooked their dinner in the hot springs near this spacious log lodge decorated with elk antlers, a stuffed mountain lion, and other critters. Lodging is in cabins, many with fireplaces, and there's also tent and RV camping. The Olympic-size outdoor pool is filled with artesian hot water that averages 103°F year-round. The dining room ($$–$$$$) specializes in wild game dishes such as pheasant, bison, and elk steaks. ✉ *Main St., Box 808, Jackson 59736, 30 mi northwest of Big Hole* ☎ *406/834–3151 or 888/438–6938* 📠 *406/834–3157* 🌐 *www.jacksonhotsprings.com* 🛏 *20 cabins* 🛎 *Restaurant, pool, fishing, bar, piano, meeting rooms, some pets allowed (fee); no room phones, no room TVs* 💳 *MC, V.*

CAMPING ⛺ **Miner Lake Campground.** Campsites have a view of the Bitterroot Mountains at this quiet, out-of-the-way lakeside spot. You can fish in 30-acre Miner Lake, which is also popular for nomotorized boats. 🛎 *Pit toilets, drinking water, fire grates, picnic tables, swimming (lake)* 🛏 *18 RV or tent sites* ✉ *Forest Rd. 182, Jackson* ☎ *406/689–3243* 📠 *406/689–3245* 🌐 *www.fs.fed.us/r1/ or www.reserveamerica.com* 🎫 *$6* 💳 *No credit cards* ⏲ *June–mid-Sept.*

SOUTHWEST MONTANA A TO Z

To research prices, get advice from other travelers, and book travel arrangements, visit www.fodors.com.

AIR TRAVEL

CARRIERS Several daily flights are scheduled in and out of Bozeman's Gallatin Field Airport to Butte, Denver, Minneapolis, Salt Lake City, and Seattle. Butte Airport has service from Bozeman, Salt Lake City, and Seattle. Helena

Airport has service from Billings, Great Falls, Minneapolis, and Salt Lake City. Note that major air carriers tend to use smaller planes to serve the area.

Airlines & Contacts **Delta** 800/221-1212 www.delta-air.com. **Horizon** 800/547-9308 www.horizonair.com. **Northwest** 800/225-2525 www.nwa.com. **Skywest** 800/453-9417 www.skywest.com. **United/United Express** 800/241-6522 www.unitedairlines.com.

AIRPORTS

Butte Airport is 7 mi south of downtown. Gallatin Field Airport is 16 mi west of Bozeman. Helena Airport is 3 mi from downtown.

Butte Airport 101 Airport Rd., Butte 406/494-3771 www.butteairport.com. **Gallatin Field Airport** 850 Gallatin Field Rd., Belgrade 406/388-6632 www.gallatinfield.com. **Helena Airport** 2850 Skyway Dr., Helena 406/442-2821 www.helenaairport.com.

BUS TRAVEL

Greyhound Lines serves several communities along I–90, including Billings, Livingston, Bozeman, and Butte. Karst Stage/4X4 Stage has regional service in the Bozeman area, plus service from Bozeman to Big Sky. Rimrock Trailways, which is based in Billings, serves major communities in the state.

Greyhound Lines 800/231-2222 www.greyhound.com. **Karst Stage/4x4 Stage** 800/287-4759 www.karststage.com. **Rimrock Trailways** 800/255-7655 www.rimrocktrailways.com.

CAR RENTAL

Vehicle rentals in Bozeman and Butte vary from economy cars to four-wheel-drive vehicles, which may be necessary for some winter travel.

Avis 406/388-6414 or 800/831-2847 www.avis.com. **Budget** 406/388-4091 or 800/952-8343 www.budget.com. **Hertz** 406/388-6939 or 800/654-3131 www.hertz.com. **National** 406/388-9994 or 800/227-7368 www.nationalcar.com. **Thrifty** 406/388-3484 or 800/344-1705 www.thrifty.com.

CAR TRAVEL

Major routes are paved and well maintained, but there are many gravel and dirt roads off the beaten track. When heading into remote regions, be sure to fill up the gas tank, and check road reports for construction delays or passes that may close in severe winter weather. Always carry a flashlight, drinking water and some food, a first-aid kit, and emergency overnight gear (a sleeping bag and extra, warm clothing). Most important, make sure someone is aware of your travel plans. While driving, be prepared for animals crossing roads, livestock on open ranges off the highway, and other hazards such as high winds and dust- or snowstorms.

When driving in the mountains in winter, make sure you have tire chains, studs, or snow tires.

Montana Highway Patrol 406/388-3190 or 800/525-5555 www.doj.state.mt.us/department/highwaypatroldivision.asp or www.mdt.state.mt.us. **Statewide Road Report** 800/226-7623 www.mdt.state.mt.us.

EMERGENCIES

Ambulance or Police **Emergencies** 911.

24-Hour Medical Care **Barrett Hospital** 1260 S. Atlantic St., Dillon 406/683-3000. **Beartooth Hospital** 600 W. 21st St., Red Lodge 406/446-2345. **Bozeman Deaconess Hospital** 915 Highland Blvd., Bozeman 406/585-5000. **Livingston Memorial Hospital** 504 S. 13th St., Livingston 406/222-3541. **St. James Healthcare** 400 S. Clark St., Butte 406/723-2500.

LODGING

Montana Bed & Breakfast Association 800/453-8870 www.mtbba.com. **Montana Dude Ranch Association** 406/284-9933 www.montanadra.com. **Montana Innkeepers Association** 406/449-8408 www.montanainnkeepers.com. **Mountain Home-Montana Vacation Rentals** 406/586-4589 or 800/550-4589 www.mountain-home.com.

CAMPING There are numerous campsites throughout the region, and they vary from rustic (with pit toilets) to relatively plush (with cabins and heated swimming pools). When camping, ask about bears in the area and whether or not food must be stored inside a hard-side vehicle (not a tent). Avoid bringing pets to campgrounds—it can lead to confrontations with the wildlife, and it's against the rules at most campgrounds.

Contact Montana Fish, Wildlife & Parks for information on camping in state parks and the U.S. Forest Service for information on camping at national parks in the area.

Montana Fish, Wildlife & Parks 406/444-2535 www.fwp.state.mt.us/parks. **U.S. Forest Service** 406/329-3511 www.fs.fed.us/r1.

MEDIA

NEWSPAPERS & MAGAZINES The largest daily newspapers in the region are the *Billings Gazette,* the *Bozeman Chronicle,* the *Missoulian,* and the *Great Falls Tribune.*

TELEVISION & RADIO Two National Public Radio affiliates' broadcasts cover most of the state: Yellowstone Public Radio, KEMC 91.7 FM, Billings, and Montana Public Radio, KUMF 89.1 FM, Missoula. When driving near mountain passes or other road hazards, look for a sign along your route indicating which radio station to check for road information.

Billings and Bozeman have national-affiliate television stations: Fox/KHMT Channel 4 and CBS/KBZK Channel 7, respectively. KUSM Channel 9 is the public television station based in Bozeman.

SPORTS & THE OUTDOORS

When you are heading into the backcountry, it's best to hire a guide or outfitter who knows the local trails, weather patterns, and unique features of the region.

BICYCLING Adventure Cycling can create route maps and provide other resources for cycling in the region.

Adventure Cycling 150 E. Pine St., Missoula 59807 406/721-1776 www.adventurecycling.org.

FISHING Fishing Outfitters Association of Montana and Montana Outfitters and Guides Association can help you find outfitters who lead fishing excursions throughout the state.

Fishing Outfitters Association of Montana Box 67, Gallatin Gateway 59730 406/763-5436 www.foam-montana.org. **Montana Outfitters and Guides Association** Box 1248, Helena 59624 406/449-3578 www.moga-montana.org.

SKIING The best information for downhill and cross-country skiing is available through the state tourism bureau, Travel Montana. There's detailed information on the Web site, and you can order a free winter guide.

Travel Montana 301 S. Park Ave., Helena 59620 406/841-2870 or 800/847-4868 www.visitmt.com.

TOURS

Adventure Cycling specializes in bicycling tours of Montana and other regions of the United States and Canada. Using trains and buses, Montana Rockies Rail Tours follows the path of the Lewis and Clark expedition and visits Glacier and Yellowstone national parks. Accomplished guides lead Off the Beaten Path outdoor journeys in Montana and the

Rockies. Swan River Tours conducts tours that focus on the Lewis and Clark expedition, Glacier and Yellowstone national parks, fall foliage, and more.

Tour Operators **Adventure Cycling** ✉ 150 E. Pine St., Missoula 59807 ☎ 406/721-1776 🌐 www.adventurecycling.org. **Montana Rockies Rail Tours** ☎ 800/519-7245 🌐 www.montanarailtours.com. **Off the Beaten Path** ✉ 7 E. Beall St., Bozeman 59715 ☎ 800/445-2995 🌐 www.offthebeatenpath.com. **Swan River Tours** ✉ Box 1010, Condon 59826 ☎ 877/696-1666 🌐 www.swanrivertours.com.

VISITOR INFORMATION

Travel Montana is the state's tourism bureau.

Tourist Information **Beaverhead Chamber of Commerce** ✉ 125 S. Montana, Box 425, Dillon 59725 ☎ 406/683-5511 🌐 www.beaverheadchamber.com. **Big Sky Chamber of Commerce** ✉ Box 160100, Big Sky 59716 ☎ 406/995-3000 or 800/943-4111 🌐 www.bigskychamber.com. **Bozeman Chamber of Commerce** ✉ 2000 Commerce Way, Bozeman 59715 ☎ 406/586-5421 or 800/228-4224 🌐 www.bozemanchamber.com. **Gold West Country** ✉ 1155 Main St., Deer Lodge 59722 ☎ 406/846-1943 or 800/879-1159 🌐 www.goldwest.visitmt.com. **Helena Chamber of Commerce** ✉ 225 Cruse Ave., Helena 59601 ☎ 406/447-1530 or 800/743-5362 🌐 www.helenachamber.com. **Red Lodge Chamber of Commerce** ✉ 601 N. Broadway, Red Lodge 59068 ☎ 888/281-0625 🌐 www.redlodge.com. **Travel Montana** ✉ 301 S. Park Ave. Helena 59620 ☎ 406/841-2870 or 800/847-4868 🌐 www.visitmt.com. **Yellowstone Country** ✉ 1822 W. Lincoln, Bozeman 59715 ☎ 800/736-5276 🌐 www.yellowstone.visitmt.com.

NORTHWEST MONTANA

MISSOULA, MISSION & FLATHEAD VALLEYS, GLACIER NATIONAL PARK

FODOR'S CHOICE

Boat outings from Flathead Lake Lodge, *Bigfork*

Buffalo Cafe, *Whitefish*

Hiking on the Highline Trail, *Glacier National Park*

Jewel Basin Hiking Area, *Flathead Lake*

National Bison Range, *Flathead Indian Reservation*

Seven Lazy P Guest Ranch, *Bob Marshall Wilderness Area*

HIGHLY RECOMMENDED

RESTAURANTS

Bernice's Bakery, *Missoula*

Guy's Lolo Creek Steakhouse, *near Missoula*

La Provence, *Bigfork*

Showthyme!, *Bigfork*

The Bridge, *Missoula*

The Shack Cafe, *Missoula*

The Staggering Ox Downtown, *Missoula*

HOTELS

Garden Wall Inn B&B, *Whitefish*

Goldsmith's Bed and Breakfast, *Missoula*

Hidden Moose Lodge B&B, *Whitefish*

Mountain Lake Lodge, *Bigfork*

Spotted Bear Ranch, *Bob Marshall Wilderness Area*

SIGHTS

Art Museum of Missoula

Daly Mansion, *Hamilton*

Glacier Park Boat Tours

Logan Pass, *Glacier National Park*

Many Glacier, *Glacier National Park*

Sqelix'u/Aqfsmakni-k Cultural Center, *Flathead Indian Reservation*

Sun Tours, *Glacier National Park*

By Jean Arthur

NORTHWEST MONTANA'S SEEMINGLY ENDLESS mountain ranges shimmer under the Big Sky, reflecting the state's motto, *Oro y Plata* (gold and silver). When the Lewis and Clark expedition traveled through the region, they found lush forests surrounding glaciated valleys teeming with wildlife. In the 200 years since their famed exploration, the statewide population has grown to 902,000, with much of it concentrated in the northwestern Bitterroot, Missoula, Mission, and Flathead valleys.

For about 12,000 years, native peoples lived in the region and traveled through it to reach bison herds east of the Rockies. Today the Flathead Indian Reservation spreads out in the Mission and Flathead valleys; it's home to the Confederated Salish and Kootenai tribes. Fur trappers, miners, and settlers followed Lewis and Clark. Many of the frontier communities they founded are only now celebrating centennial anniversaries.

The largest city in the area, with a population of approximately 57,000, Missoula is the business and shopping center of northwest Montana and home to the University of Montana and many arts and cultural attractions. Hamilton, Stevensville, Kalispell, Polson, and Whitefish are friendly towns perched on the edge of millions of acres of wild lands, including the 2.7 million acres of roadless wilderness among the northern Rockies.

People visit this part of the world for the water, wildlife, and wild lands; favored activities include scenic driving, bird-watching, fishing, golfing, bicycling, and skiing. You'll also find here well-preserved historical sites, small yet resourceful museums, and entertaining activities, from theater to Native American festivals.

At the top of a must-see list are the 1.2-million-acre Glacier National Park and the millions of additional acres of roadless wilderness, portions of which are visible from scenic drives. Glacier remains open year-round, though most visit in summer when they can drive the Going-to-the-Sun Road. In winter, the cross-country skiing and snowshoeing trails lead to turquoise waterfalls and cedar forests where, if trekkers are lucky, they just might hear the howling of wolves.

Exploring Northwest Montana

Rivers, streams, lakes, and mountains dominate landscapes here and attract boaters, fly fishers, and outdoor adventurers. Once here, they discover playhouses, art galleries, and summer festivals and rodeos. In winter, visitors seek out northwest Montana's seven ski areas and scores of miles of cross-country ski trails. Spring and fall, the quiet seasons, are blessed with temperate weather and wildlife sightings.

About the Restaurants

Although Montana generally isn't known for elegant dining, several sophisticated restaurants are tucked away among the tamaracks and cedars, where professionally trained chefs bring herbed nuances and wide-ranging cultural influences to their menus. More typical of the region are steak houses featuring certified Angus beef; in recent years, particularly in resort communities, these institutions have diversified their menus to include bison meat, fresh fish, and a few token vegetarian options. Small cafés offer hearty, inexpensive meals, and you can pick up on local history through photographs and artwork on walls and conversation with the local denizens. Attire everywhere is decidedly casual: blue jeans, a clean shirt, and cowboy boots are dress-up for most Montana restaurants.

Numbers in the text correspond to numbers in the margin and on The Northwest Montana, Missoula, and Glacier National Park maps.

If you have 3 days

Begin a tour in **Glacier National Park** 20–28 at West Glacier, by driving over the Going-to-the-Sun Road and Logan Pass. Stop at the Trail of the Cedars for a short walk, and stop again at Logan Pass to hike up to the Hidden Lake Overlook. Proceed to St. Mary for dinner, or at least an ice cream cone. Return to West Glacier by the same route or via U.S. 2, where you can see mountain goats at Goat Lick. If there's time, take a raft trip down the Middle Fork of the Flathead River. Overnight in West Glacier. The next day, drive south and east to **Whitefish** 18, where numerous restaurants and shops line downtown. On a summer day, golf, bike, or simply lounge at Whitefish City Beach on Whitefish Lake. Drive north 8 mi to the Big Mountain Ski and Summer Resort to ski in winter or hike to the mountaintop in summer. There's also a summer gondola and chairlift that takes you to the 7,000-foot summit for outstanding views of Glacier Park peaks and the Canadian Rockies. Overnight in Whitefish. Drive to **Kalispell** 17 for museums and art galleries, then to Bigfork on **Flathead Lake** 16 for shopping in boutiques. Plan on dining in Bigfork, followed by a show at the Bigfork Playhouse, or enjoy the lake with a sailboat excursion on the historic *Questa* sloop.

If you have 5 days

Follow the suggested three-day itinerary and on Day 4, drive to Polson, where you can golf, swim in Flathead Lake, or go white-water rafting on the lower Flathead River. Drive south on U.S. 93 to **Flathead Indian Reservation** 15 and the People's Center, which has exhibits concerning the Salish, Kootenai, and Pend d'Oreille Indians. Continue south, stopping to fish at the Ninepipe National Wildlife Refuge; then drive through the National Bison Range. Overnight in **Missoula** 1–11 and spend the next day exploring the city.

If you have 7 days

Follow the suggested five-day itinerary; then on Day 6 continue south on U.S. 93 to the Lewis and Clark campsite at Travelers' Rest State Park. After looking around, drive south to **Stevensville** 12 in the Bitterroot Valley, where you can explore the historic sites or spend the afternoon trout fishing in the area. Spend the night in the valley, and on the next day head for **Hamilton** 13 to visit the Daly Mansion, other museums, art galleries, and shops. Wrap up your trip with by trail riding into the Bitterroot Mountains or mountain biking near **Darby** 14.

About the Hotels

From massive log lodges to historic bed-and-breakfasts to chain hotels, you'll find the range of lodging options here that you'd expect from a region that makes a business of catering to tourists. During ski season and the summer vacation months, reservations are necessary. Some hotels, such as those inside Glacier National Park, are open only in summer and early fall.

WHAT IT COSTS					
	$$$$	**$$$**	**$$**	**$**	**¢**
RESTAURANTS	over $22	$16–$22	$11–$16	$7–$11	under $7
HOTELS	over $220	$160–$220	$110–$160	$70–$110	under $70

Restaurant prices are for a main course at dinner, excluding sales tax of 2%–4% in some resort communities. Hotel prices are for two people in a standard double room in high season, excluding service charges and 7% bed tax.

Timing

Most visitors to northwest Montana come in summer, enticed by lakes, rivers, golf courses, and fresh mountain air. Arts festivals, rodeos, powwows, fairs, farmers' markets, and outdoor concerts fill the summer calendar. Even during this busiest season, though, you're unlikely to feel cramped among Montana's wide open spaces. Winter is the second peak season; deep snows attract snowboarders and skiers to the region's seven alpine ski areas and some 250 named alpine ski runs. It's also an excellent time to explore mountain trails amid the light, fluffy snow.

Spring and fall are the quiet seasons, but they're becoming increasingly popular. In spring, wildlife sightings include newborn elk calves, fawns, and an occasional bear cub. Snowmelt cools the nights, and the occasional late-spring storm can cloak the region in snow, if only for a day. Fall's dry, warm days and blessedly cool nights offer the best of weather; there are few other tourists, and most attractions are still open. No matter the time of year, keep in mind that weather in this part of the world can change rapidly. Be prepared with extra clothing.

MISSOULA

Located in a fertile valley hemmed in by mountains, Missoula is aptly nicknamed the Garden City. Now the largest metropolis in western Montana, with a population of 57,000, it began as the Hell Gate trading settlement in 1860, more than 50 years after the Lewis and Clark expedition traveled through the area. The town's name comes from Salish Indians' word for "near the cold, chilling waters." Gold speculators, homesteaders, and the coming of the Northern Pacific Railroad in 1883 all helped establish Missoula as a travel stop and business center in the region.

Maple trees line the residential streets, the Clark Fork River slices through the center of town, and the University of Montana cozies up against the slopes of Mt. Sentinel. A 6-mi-long riverside trail passing the university en route to Hell Gate Canyon is ideal for walking and cycling. Missoula is the cultural center of northwest Montana—it's the home to numerous writers and artists—and it's also a good base for regional exploration by way of Interstate 90 east–west, U.S. 93 north–south, and numerous byways and back roads leading in all directions.

Exploring Missoula

Missoula is home to the Adventure Cycling Association (formerly Bike Centennial), so it's no surprise that the city has more bicycles than people. Exploring by bicycle is popular and easy: downtown and the university district are relatively flat and have bike paths and bike traffic lanes; many storefronts are adorned with bike racks. Within the center of the city, walking is a good option, too, particularly given that parking is at a premium and that the university itself is a car-free zone. The Missoula Valley and sights on the outskirts of town are best explored by car.

Bicycling Hill climbing, single track, dirt road, or easy cruising bike paths—whatever your favorite bicycle terrain might be, the region is flush with cycling opportunities. Bicycle trail maps, available at local sports shops and U.S. Forest Service offices, lead mountain bikers into the backcountry, where other travelers are seldom seen and wildlife abounds. Remember that in bear country it's best to travel in groups of four or more, make plenty of noise, and carry pepper spray. Note that bicycles are not allowed in designated wilderness areas and backcountry trails of national parks.

Hiking Hiking trails lace mountains and meadows, cross streams, and skirt lakes all over northwest Montana. Before lacing up hiking boots, it's best to determine where you want to go, what you want to bring, and what you're likely to encounter on the trail. The book *Hiking Montana* by Bill Schneider has useful, basic hiking safety information and offers route details from several trailheads. *The Hiker's Guide to Glacier National Park,* by the Glacier Natural History Association, lists 25 hikes with tips for hiking in the park. U.S. Forest Service offices have local maps, trail guides, and safety information. If you're new to hiking, you may want to employ one of the several outfitters that offer guided hikes in Glacier National Park and the surrounding wild areas.

Wilderness An immense chunk of northwest Montana is a continuous block of wild lands. Most notable of these areas is the spectacular 1.2-million-acre Glacier National Park. If you really want to get away from it all, plan a trip to the roadless 1.5 million acres of the Bob Marshall, Great Bear, and Scapegoat wilderness areas. Access is limited, although once you penetrate this huge wilderness tract, there are trails such as the 120-mi-long Chinese Wall, a reeflike stretch of cliffs in the Bob Marshall Wilderness. Outfitters offer rafting, hiking, and horse-pack trips into these remote mountains.

Skiing Winter in northwest Montana is ski season, and the region's seven alpine ski areas are among the best in the state, highlighted by Big Mountain Ski Resort near Whitefish. Novices to the slopes will be in good hands at the area's well-established ski schools. There are scores of cross-country trails cutting through the lovely snow-blanketed landscape.

---

a good tour From Northern Pacific Railroad Depot to the Clark Fork River, a walking tour of Missoula passes historic buildings that now house shops, restaurants, and offices. Begin on the north edge of downtown at the **Northern Pacific Railroad Depot** 1, and if you're there in the morning or a Tuesday evening in summer, check out the produce and local crafts at the farmers' market and the nearby people's market. As you walk south on Higgins, stop in for a deli sandwich in the historic Worden's Market, named for Francis L. Worden, who established an 1860 Hell Gate Trading Post about 4 mi west of here. Walk one block east to Pattee Street to find the **Art Museum of Missoula** 2. Returning to Higgins, you'll pass the **Higgins Block** 3, commissioned by a cofounder of Missoula, C. P. Higgins, who was a member of the first Territorial Legislature. Before crossing the Higgins Bridge over the Clark Fork River, stop at **A Carousel**

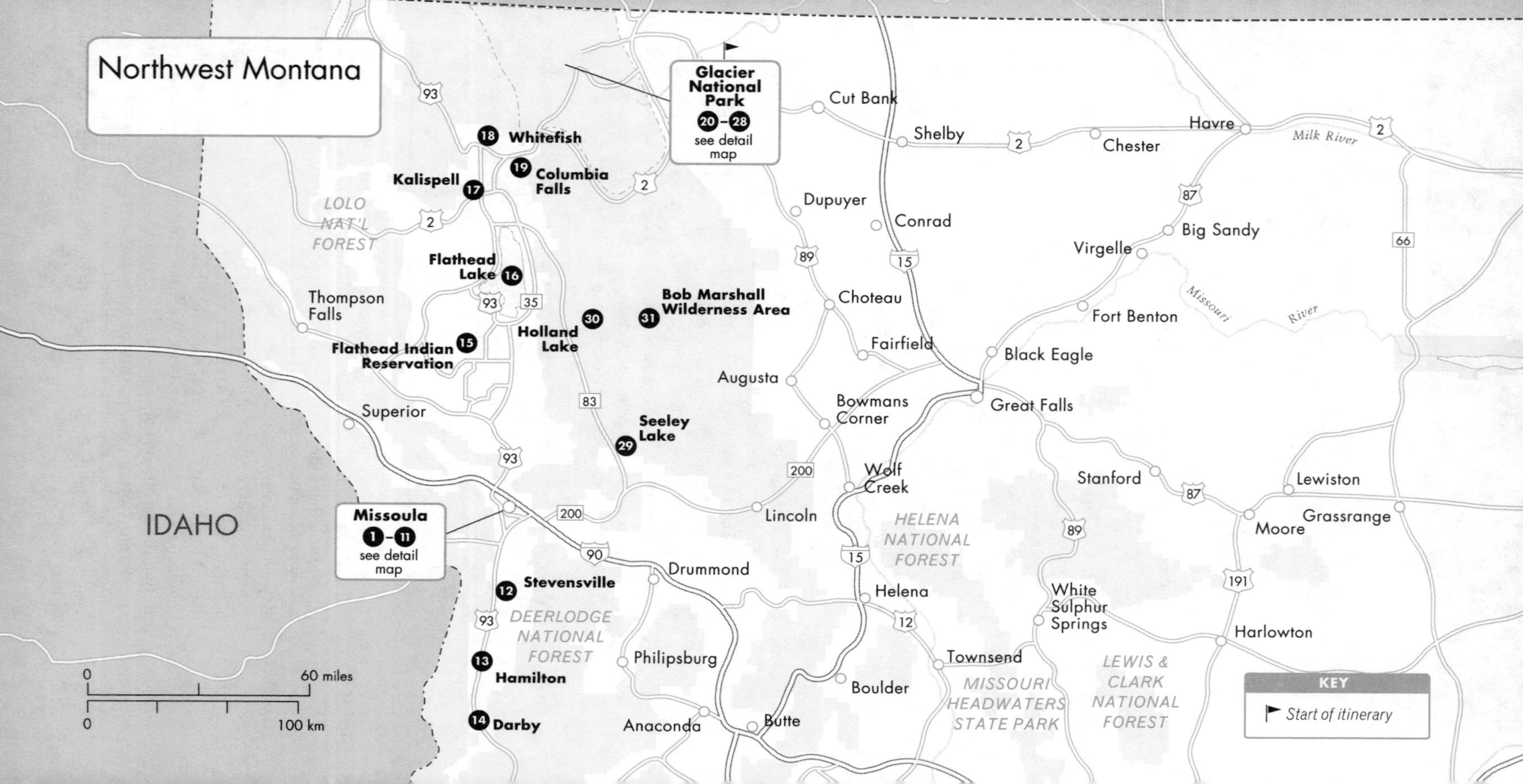
Northwest Montana
Glacier National Park
20–28
see detail map
Missoula
1–11
see detail map
IDAHO
Cut Bank
Shelby
Chester
Havre
Milk River
Dupuyer
Conrad
Big Sandy
Virgelle
Fort Benton
Missouri River
Choteau
Fairfield
Black Eagle
Great Falls
Augusta
Bowmans Corner
Wolf Creek
Lincoln
Stanford
Lewiston
Moore
Grassrange
Harlowton
White Sulphur Springs
Helena
Townsend
Boulder
Butte
Anaconda
Philipsburg
Drummond
Superior
Thompson Falls
18 Whitefish
19 Columbia Falls
17 Kalispell
16 Flathead Lake
15 Flathead Indian Reservation
30 Holland Lake
31 Bob Marshall Wilderness Area
29 Seeley Lake
12 Stevensville
13 Hamilton
14 Darby
LOLO NAT'L FOREST
DEERLODGE NATIONAL FOREST
HELENA NATIONAL FOREST
MISSOURI HEADWATERS STATE PARK
LEWIS & CLARK NATIONAL FOREST
93
2
35
83
200
90
15
89
87
191
12
66
0
60 miles
0
100 km
KEY
Start of itinerary

for Missoula ❹ for a ride on hand-carved horses, and perhaps catch lunchtime entertainment in **Caras Park** ❺. From there you can easily spot the **Milwaukee Railroad Depot** ❻ just across the **Clark Fork River** ❼.

Other worthwhile spots require a vehicle. The University of Montana campus itself offers a lovely stroll past tall pines and leafy maple trees. A visit to the **Montana Museum of Art and Culture at the University of Montana** ❽, located in the Performing Arts and Radio-TV Center, can present some frustrations because of the highly restricted campus parking; consider parking north of campus, across the Clark Fork River at Front Street and Van Buren, and walking across the footbridge. A drive west on Broadway takes you to the **Rocky Mountain Elk Foundation Wildlife Visitor Center** ❾, which houses the conservation group's wildlife artwork, a theater, and many taxidermy displays. Farther west on U.S. 10, near the airport, is the **Smokejumper Visitor Center** ❿. Another worthwhile detour takes you southwest of downtown via Reserve Street and South Avenue, to the **Historical Museum at Fort Missoula** ⓫.

TIMING A Missoula tour will take a full day if you include a morning at the farmers' market, the walking tour, and time at the museums on the campus and the outskirts of town.

What to See

★ ❷ **Art Museum of Missoula.** A dozen changing exhibits each year of contemporary work join a small permanent collection featuring works by E. S. Paxson, Walter Hook, and Rudy and Lela Autio in this 1903 Carnegie Library building. ✉ *335 N. Pattee St., 1 block from the intersection with W. Broadway* ☎ *406/728–0447* 🌐 *www.artmissoula.org* 🎫 *Donations accepted* ⏲ *Tues. 10–7, Wed.–Fri. 10–6, Sat. 10–4.*

❺ **Caras Park.** Downtown's favorite green space, the park has a walking path paralleling the Clark Fork River and a pavilion that's the site of musical acts. ✉ *Front and Ryman Sts.* ☎ *406/721–7275* 🌐 *www.ci.missoula.mt.us/parksrec* 🎫 *Free* ⏲ *Daily 6 AM–11 PM.*

❹ **A Carousel for Missoula.** In downtown Caras Park along the Clark Fork River, kids saddle up to hand-carved steeds on this carousel. The horses and chariots ride on a lovingly restored 1918 frame, accompanied by tunes from the largest band organ in continuous use in the United States. The Dragon Hollow play area next to the carousel features a dragon, a castle, and many play structures. ✉ *1 Caras Park* ☎ *406/549–8382* 🌐 *www.carrousel.com* 🎫 *$1 per ride, play area free* ⏲ *Memorial Day–Labor Day, daily 11–7; Labor Day–Memorial Day, daily 11–5:30.*

❼ **Clark Fork River.** The heart of Missoula is defined by the Clark Fork River, which comes down from Mt. Sentinel, cuts through downtown, and passes by the university. A 6-mi-long riverside trail and the connecting 2½-mi Kim Williams trail make for easy, pleasant walks, with picnic spots and benches along the way where you can watch the river. Take note: the powerful currents of the Clark Fork are dangerous—they've taken many lives over the years.

Council Grove State Park. History buffs appreciate this park's significance as the place where Isaac Stevens and the Pend d'Oreille and Flathead Kootenai Indians signed the Hell Gate Treaty in 1855 to establish the Flathead Indian Reservation. The park occupies 87 primitive acres; it has interpretive signs, a picnic area, fishing access, and a hiking trail. To get here, travel west from downtown on Interstate 90, exit at Reserve Street, then drive 2 mi south on Reserve and 10 mi west on Mullan Road. ✉ *Off Mullan Rd.* ☎ *406/542–5500* 🌐 *www.state.mt.us* 🎫 *Free* ⏲ *Daily dawn–dusk.*

❸ **Higgins Block.** This lovely, ornate Queen Anne commercial building, occupying a block in the heart of downtown, is on the National Register of Historic Places. It's now home to a coffeehouse, toy store, bookstore, and other shops. ✉ *202 N. Higgins Ave.* 🌐 *www.missouladowntown.com* 🎫 *Free* ⏲ *Tues. noon–8, Wed.–Sat. noon–6.*

⓫ **Historical Museum at Fort Missoula.** Fort Missoula, at the western edge of town, was established in 1877 at the height of the U.S. Army's conflict with the Nez Perce, led by Chief Joseph. The museum's indoor and outdoor exhibits, including 13 historic structures relocated from nearby sites, depict and explain the early development of Missoula County. The black 25th Infantry of bicycle soldiers arrived in 1888 to test bicycles for military use; near-life-size photos depict the soldiers during an expedition to Yellowstone National Park's Mammoth Terraces, and uniforms and artifacts are also on display. They ultimately rode one-speed bicycles from Missoula to St. Louis. Guided tours are available by appointment. ✉ *Fort Missoula, Bldg. 32* ☎ *406/728–3476* 🌐 *www.fortmissoulamuseum.org* 🎫 *$3* ⏲ *Memorial Day–Labor Day, Mon.–Sat. 10–5, Sun. noon–5; Labor Day–Memorial Day, Tues.–Sat. noon–5.*

❻ **Milwaukee Railroad Depot.** A Missoula landmark along the river, this 1910 passenger depot, with Romanesque windows, a Spanish-style roof, two towers, and mission-style parapet walls, is on the National Register of Historic Places. It's now the site of the Boone and Crockett Club, an organization founded in 1887 by Theodore Roosevelt to establish conservation of wild habitats. Open to the public are a gun collection, a library, and a display of a world-record-size taxidermied elk. ✉ *250 Station Dr.* ☎ *406/542–1888* 🌐 *www.boone-crockett.org* 🎫 *Free* ⏲ *Weekdays 8–5:30.*

❽ **Montana Museum of Art and Culture at the University of Montana.** The university's art museum, divided into the Paxson Gallery and the Henry Meloy Gallery, has a permanent collection of more than 9,500 works, with an emphasis on contemporary art from the West. A highlight is the magnificent tapestry titled *Montana Horses* by Missoulian Rudy Autio. ✉ *Performing Arts and Radio/Television Center, University of Montana* ☎ *406/243–2019* 🌐 *www.umt.edu/partv/famus* 🎫 *Free* ⏲ *Weekdays 1–5.*

❶ **Northern Pacific Railroad Depot.** The construction of the Northern Pacific Railroad was instrumental in opening up the West to settlers, and the arrival of the line in Missoula is a key point in the city's history. The depot, opened in 1901, is an example of the Renaissance Revival architecture that dominates this end of downtown. Today the depot is the site of private offices, but you can still look around inside. ✉ *N. Higgins St.* ☎ *406/543–4238* 🌐 *www.missouladowntown.com* 🎫 *Free* ⏲ *Weekdays 9–5.*

❾ **Rocky Mountain Elk Foundation Wildlife Visitor Center.** The visitor center features natural-history displays (including hands-on displays for kids), films, art, taxidermied animals, and a world-record-size pair of elk antlers. The foundation works to preserve wild lands for elk and other wildlife; in its 20-year existence, it has saved more than 2 million acres from development. ✉ *2291 W. Broadway* ☎ *406/523–4545 or 800/225–5355* 🌐 *www.rmef.org* 🎫 *Donations accepted* ⏲ *Memorial Day–Labor Day, weekdays 8–6; Labor Day–Memorial Day, weekdays 8–5, weekends 10–4.*

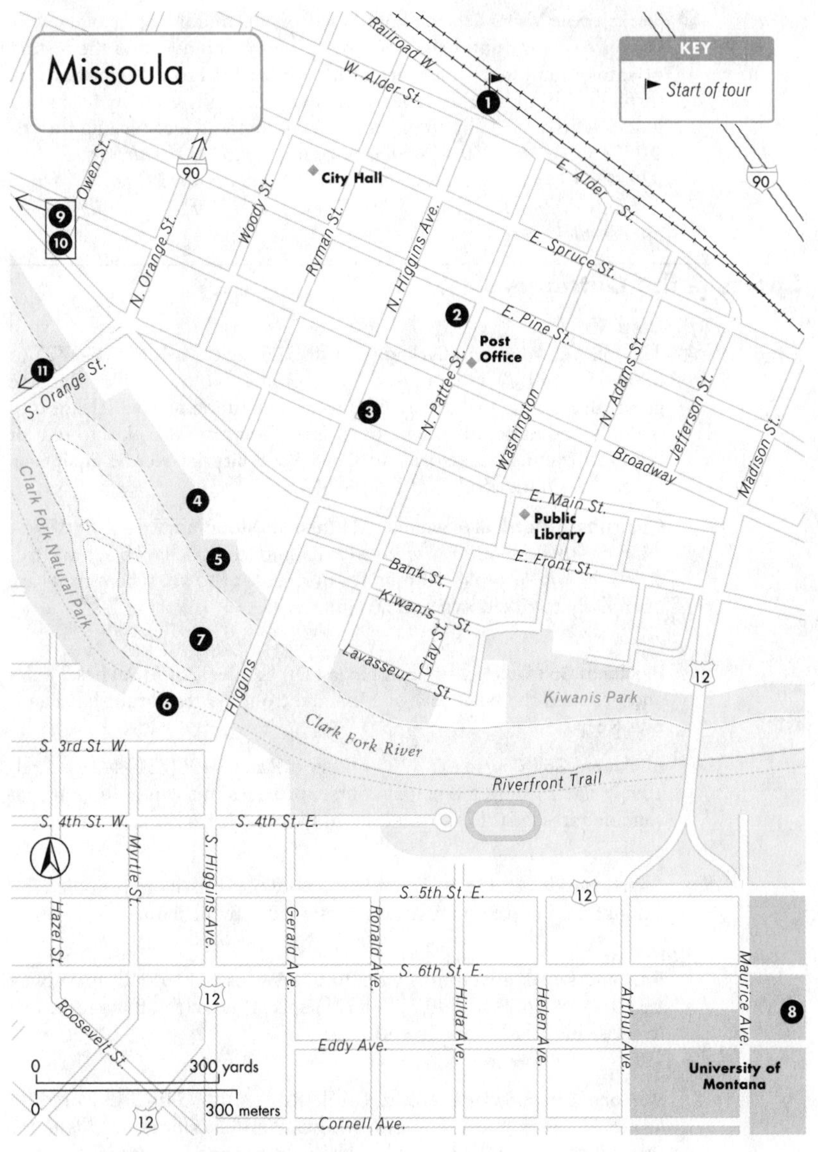

Art Museum of Missoula **2**
Caras Park **5**
A Carousel for Missoula .**4**
Clark Fork River **7**
Higgins Block **3**
Historical Museum of Fort Missoula **11**
Milwaukee Railroad Depot **6**
Montana Museum of Art and Culture at the University of Montana . . .**8**
Northern Pacific Railroad Depot **1**
Rocky Mountain Elk Foundation Wildlife Visitor Center **9**
Smokejumper Visitor Center **10**

10 **Smokejumper Visitor Center.** Exhibits, videos, and murals here explain wildland fire ecology and behavior, fire-fighting technique, and the history of smoke jumping, which began here in 1942. From Memorial Day through Labor Day, the center offers five tours daily given by firefighter guides who provide firsthand accounts of jumping into blazing forests. ✉ *5765 Old Hwy. 10 W, 6 mi west of town, next to the airport* ☎ *406/329–4934* 🌐 *www.smokejumpers.com* *Donations accepted* ⏲ *Memorial Day–Labor Day, daily 8:30–5, tours on the hr 10–11 and 2–4; by appointment rest of yr.*

Sports & the Outdoors

Bicycling

★ The folks at **Adventure Cycling** (✉ 150 E. Pine St. ☎ 406/721–1776 or 880/755–2453 🌐 www.adv-cycling.org) in downtown Missoula have good suggestions for nearby bike routes and an extensive selection of regional and national bike maps for sale. You can find bikes to rent or buy and cycling accessories at **Open Road Bicycles Nordic Equipment** (✉ 517 S. Orange St. ☎ 406/549–2453).

Chairlifts at **Marshall Mountain** (✉ Marshall Mountain Rd. ☎ 880/755–2453 or 406/258–6000 🌐 www.marshallmtn.com) deliver bikes and riders to the top of peaks 10 minutes northeast of town, where trails are open daily to ride down and around.

Golf

Highlands Golf Club (✉ 102 Ben Hogan Dr. ☎ 406/728–7360) has 9 holes and provides the best view of Missoula from the restaurant-bar Shadows Keep.

Larchmont Golf Course (✉ 3200 Old Fort Rd. ☎ 406/721–4416), a relatively flat 18-hole municipal course, provides in-town golfing at reasonable rates ($20 for a round in midweek).

Fishing

Grizzly Hackle (✉ 215 W. Front St. ☎ 406/721–8996) offers guided fly-fishing, float trips, and instruction and has a retail shop.

Rafting

Raft and kayak adventures with **10,000 Waves** (✉ 1311 E. Broadway ☎ 406/549–6670 or 800/537–8315) splash down the Blackfoot, Bitterroot, and Clark Fork rivers.

Skiing

Montana Snowbowl (✉ Grant Creek Rd. ☎ 406/549–9696 or 406/549–9777 🌐 www.montanasnowbowl.com) has slopes for advanced skiers who are hooked on steep, challenging runs and powdery views of nearby Rattlesnake Wilderness. Telemarkers and geländesprung alpine ski jumpers are a colorful element of the local ski scene. New skiers aren't neglected: groomed beginner and intermediate runs make up more than half the trails on the 950 acres here, 12 mi northwest of Missoula. Services include a restaurant, bar, and Geländesprung Lodge in the base area.

Where to Stay & Eat

★ **$–$$$$** ✕ **Guy's Lolo Creek Steakhouse.** For a real taste of Montana, head for this steak house in a rustic log structure 8 mi south of Missoula, in Lolo. The dining room has a hunting-lodge atmosphere, replete with taxidermied wildlife on the walls. Although most diners opt for one of Guy's signature sirloins—cooked over a crackling open-pit barbecue and available in three sizes—there are other well-prepared meat, chicken, and seafood

"HOWDY"

Driving through Montana's western valleys, you'll notice that folks wave. Don't be alarmed. It's just a "howdy" and a courtesy along remote roads where fellow travelers are few and far between. Wave back and you'll have a new friend.

You'll also see white crosses along the highways here. These are markers where someone has died on the highway. The somber reminders are messages telling you to slow down and enjoy the West, like Norman McLean describes it, in A River Runs Through It. *McLean and numerous writers before and after describe life under the Big Sky as one of independence and hardtack survival in what Bill Kitteredge called "The Last Best Place." And it truly is.*

---

dishes from which to choose. ✉ *6600 U.S. 12 W, Lolo* ☎ *406/273–2622* ▭ *AE, D, MC, V* ⊙ *Closed Mon. No lunch.*

$$–$$$ ✕ **Zimorino's Red Pies over Montana.** Some of the best pizza ever tossed under the Big Sky is served here. The pasta and bruschetta are top-notch, too. Eat in, take out, or call for a delivery. Beer and wine are served. ✉ *424 N. Higgins Ave.* ☎ *406/721–7757* ▭ *AE, D, MC, V* ⊙ *No lunch.*

★ **$–$$$** ✕ **The Bridge.** Snug inside an old dime-a-dance hall, this great find is known for its vegetarian dishes, Gorgonzola burger, and scallops and chanterelles over angel hair pasta. You can sit at forest-green tables or an antique bar from Butte and wash everything down with one of 10 local microbrews. ✉ *515 S. Higgins* ☎ *406/542–0638* ▭ *AE, D, MC, V.*

★ **$–$$$** ✕ **The Shack Cafe.** A longtime Missoula favorite for any meal, this elegant restaurant isn't in a shack but rather in a tastefully remodeled auto dealership. Swinging doors take you into the saloon, where there's an oak bar that arrived in Montana via steamship up the Missouri River a century ago. For dinner, try broiled lamb chops with rosemary butter or one of the specials. Breakfasts of elegant pastries and hearty omelets are popular with the locals. ✉ *222 W. Main* ☎ *406/549–9903* ▭ *AE, MC, V.*

¢–$$ ✕ **Food For Thought.** Locals, professors, and students hang out, study, and eat wholesome food at this restaurant next to the university. Sandwiches to go and bakery goods fill backpacks of day hikers and bikers en route to trailheads. ✉ *540 Daly Ave.* ☎ *406/721–6033* ✍ *Reservations not accepted* ▭ *AE, D, MC, V* ⊙ *No dinner June–Aug.*

★ **¢–$** ✕ **The Staggering Ox Downtown.** Reading the menu here is as much fun as eating the deli sandwiches, which are served on specialty breads shaped like a tin can. Evocative sandwich names include the Headbanger's Hoagie (with ham, salami, pepperoni, cream cheese, cheddar, Swiss, mozzarella, lettuce, and Italian dressing) and Chernobyl Melt Down (with turkey, salami, Swiss, sharp cheddar, cream cheese, veggies, and salsa). Like its sister restaurant in Helena, this Staggering Ox is decorated with thrift-store artifacts hung from the ceiling and walls. ✉ *123 E. Main* ☎ *406/327–9400* ✍ *Reservations not accepted* ▭ *MC, V.*

¢–$ ✕ **Worden's Market & Deli.** Floorboards creak beneath you as you explore this old-fashioned market, which spills over with deli delicacies. There's a huge selection of imported beer and groceries. With 150 cheeses to choose from, the sandwich possibilities are endless; have them pile on Black Forest ham and horseradish for a creation that will get you down the trail. There's limited seating both inside and outside. ✉ *451*

N. Higgins Ave. ☎ 406/549–1223 ⚠ Reservations not accepted ▭ AE, D, MC, V.

¢–$ ✕ **Tipus.** One of the few Indian restaurants in the northern Rockies, vegetarian-only Tipus serves such delectables as traditional samosas, dals, chapatis, and fresh chutneys. Try the appetizer spicy yam fries with tamarind chili chutney. You can sit at the stainless-steel counter or a cozy table, or order takeout. ✉ *115½ S. 4th W* ☎ *406/542–0622 or 877/705–9843* ⚠ *Reservations not accepted* ▭ *AE, D, MC, V.*

★ ¢ ✕ **Bernice's Bakery.** Missoula's best bakery sells buttery croissants, muffins, scones, quiche, and other treats plus a tempting array of desserts, breads, and coffee from 6 AM to 10 PM. There's seating inside and outside, or you can eat alongside the nearby river. ✉ *190 S. 3rd W* ☎ *406/728–1358* ⚠ *Reservations not accepted* ▭ *No credit cards.*

$–$$$ **Wingate Inn.** Oversize guest rooms and a 24-hour self-service business center here are designed with the business traveler in mind, but two waterslides at the pool please kids as well. Rooms have cordless phones, lounge chairs, and large TVs; a few have Jacuzzis. The inn has a pleasant lobby that includes a breakfast area, and it's convenient to restaurants, historic sites, and the airport. ✉ *5252 Airway Blvd., 59808* ☎ *406/541–8000 or 866/832–8000* 📠 *406/541–8008* 🌐 *www.wingateinn.com* *100 rooms* *Dining room, in-room data ports, refrigerators, cable TV, indoor pool, gym, hot tub, laundry facilities, Internet, business services, meeting rooms, airport shuttle, no-smoking rooms* ▭ *AE, D, DC, MC, V* *BP.*

$$ **C'mon Inn.** This hotel at the bottom of Grant Creek, near the Snowbowl ski area, is family-friendly and has easy access to recreation and business in Missoula. It features a spacious, tree-filled indoor courtyard with a pool, baby pool, five hot tubs, and a waterfall. The large guest rooms open onto the pool on the first floor and have balconies on the second. Some rooms have kitchens. ✉ *2775 Expo Pkwy., off I–90, 59808* ☎ *406/543–4600, 888/989–5569* 📠 *406/543–4664* 🌐 *www.cmoninn.com* *119 rooms* *Indoor pool, gym, hot tubs, business services* ▭ *AE, DC, MC, V* *CP.*

★ $–$$ **Goldsmith's Bed and Breakfast.** Built in 1911 for the first president of the University of Montana, this lodging is on the shore of the Clark Fork River, at the end of a footbridge that leads to the campus. Within the prairie-style building, with big white eaves and a huge porch, are period furnishings, wool carpets, and fresh flowers. Each private room is unique, and public rooms include a library and TV sitting area. Breakfast offerings include French toast and crepes, served in the dining room or on the deck overlooking the Clark Fork River. ✉ *809 E. Front St., 59801* ☎ *406/728–1585* 📠 *406/543–0045* 🌐 *www.goldsmithsinn.com* *3 rooms, 4 suites* *Library* ▭ *D, MC, V* *BP.*

$–$$ **Holiday Inn Missoula–Parkside.** The Missoula member of the Holiday Inn chain is a large, comfortable hotel with a lush atrium in the center and modern rooms. The property's greatest asset is its location in Missoula's riverfront park, a stone's throw from the Clark Fork River and across the river from the university. Sunday brunch is served in the atrium. ✉ *200 S. Pattee St., 59802* ☎ *406/721–8550 or 800/399–0408* 📠 *406/728–3472* 🌐 *www.park-side.com* *200 rooms* *Restaurant, indoor pool, gym, hot tub, bar* ▭ *AE, D, DC, MC, V.*

Camping

⛺ **Jellystone RV Park.** On the outskirts of town, this lively park is popular with families for the playground, miniature golf, swimming pools, and, a kid favorite, pictures with Yogi Bear. *Flush toilets. Full hookups, partial hookups, dump station. Drinking water, guest laundry, showers. Food service, grills, picnic tables. Electricity, public telephone. Gen-*

eral store. Swimming (pool) 🚐 110 full hookups, 10 tent sites; 3 cabins ✉ I–90, Exit 96, ½ mi north ☎ 406/543–9400 or 800/318–9644 🌐 www.campjellystonemt.com 💵 Full hookups $28, partial hookups $25, tent sites $21; cabins $39 ▭ MC, V ⏲ May–Oct.

⛺ **Missoula KOA.** This lovely campsite in the Montana-born KOA chain is easy to reach from the interstate. It has two hot tubs, a game center, miniature golf, bike rentals, space for kids to play, and a petting zoo with miniature goats, peacocks, llamas, and more. ♿ *Flush toilets. Full hookups, dump station. Drinking water, guest laundry, showers. Food service, grills, picnic tables. Electricity, public telephone. General store. Swimming (pool) 🚐 134 full hookups, 36 tent sites; 19 cabins ✉ 3450 Tina Ave., I–90, Exit 101, 1½ mi south ☎ 406/549–0881 or 800/562–5366 📠 406/541–0884 🌐 www.missoulakoa.com 💵 Full hookups $33–$37, partial hookups $28, tent sites $23; cabins $40–$45 ✍ Reservations essential ▭ AE, D, MC, V.*

Nightlife & the Arts

The wildest film stars in the world are up on the big screen at the weeklong **International Wildlife Film Festival** (✉ 718 S. Higgins Ave., 59802 ☎ 406/728–9380 🌐 www.wildlifefilms.org), which shows animal documentaries in early May at the Wilma and Roxy theaters in downtown Missoula. Seminars, panel discussions, a parade, and artwork are also part of the event.

At the **Missoula Children's Theatre** (✉ 200 N. Adams ☎ 406/728–1911 or 406/728–7529 🌐 www.mctinc.org), year-round productions vary from Broadway musicals to community theater for and by children of all ages. From October to June, you can see local talent and guest artists (usually professionals) perform family favorites like *Fiddler on the Roof*. In summer, there's a theater camp where kids are the stars of the productions.

The University of Montana's Department of Drama and Dance manages the **Montana Repertory Theater** (✉ University of Montana campus ☎ 406/243–5288), a professional company that provides the region with a steady diet of popular Broadway shows.

Shopping

Take a break while touring downtown Missoula and have a cappuccino or a glass of fresh-squeezed orange juice at **Butterfly Herbs** (✉ 232 N. Higgins Ave. ☎ 406/728–8780), or try the Butterfly Coffee Soda—a cold drink with multiple layers of sweetness. The shop also sells baked goods, candies, soaps, candles, china, and other odds and ends.

Montana authors' work, a fine selection of regional books, and gift items are found at **Fact and Fiction** (✉ 220 N. Higgins St. ☎ 406/721–2881). Readings, signings, and other literary events are scheduled year-round at this comfortably shop, where you're likely to rub elbows with an author browsing through the shelves.

At the outdoor **Missoula Farmers' Market** (✉ N. Higgins Ave. on Circle Square between Railroad and Alder Sts. ☎ 406/543–4238 🌐 www.missouladowntown.com) you can buy flowers, fresh fruits and vegetables, and unique handmade goods. It's held on Market Plaza, a two-block area downtown, every morning from mid-May to mid-October and Tuesday evenings from July through mid-September.

For locally made crafts, come to the **People's Market** (✉ Pine St. between Higgins Ave. and Pattee St. ☎406/543–4238 🌐www.missouladowntown.com), open mornings from mid-May to mid-October.

BITTERROOT VALLEY

This historic valley south of Missoula, flanked by the Bitterroot and Sapphire mountains, was home to Nez Perce who helped Lewis and Clark find their way through the mountains. It's named for the state flower, the delicate pink rosette-shape bitterroot, which blooms in late spring and was a staple for Salish Indians, who ate its roots. Early settlers founded the towns of Stevensville, Hamilton, and Darby, attracted by temperate weather and fertile soil for farming. U.S. 93 leads through the heart of this lush valley and alongside the Bitterroot River, where fly fishers flock. Back roads lead to many remote trailheads for biking and hiking. Other sights worth seeing include wildlife refuges, Lewis and Clark campsites, and historic mansions and missions.

Stevensville

⓬ *25 mi south of Missoula via U.S. 93.*

Stevensville, population 1,550, sits on the site of the state's first non–Native American settlement, St. Mary's Mission, a restored treasure that dates back to 1841. Nearby Fort Owen is a partially restored 1850s trading post. The town itself is named for General Isaac Stevens, who was in charge of the Northwest Territory's military posts and Indian affairs. Today it's a mix of beautiful old homes and haphazard modern construction. The Stevensville Museum provides an overview of the area's original inhabitants—Salish, Nez Perce, and Lemhi Shoshone—Lewis and Clark's two visits, early settlers, subsequent orchard farmers, and today's cybercommuters. The Lee Metcalf National Wildlife Refuge, on the edge of town, is nearly as pristine as it was before development encroached upon the wilds here.

Major John Owen established **Fort Owen** as a trading post 1850. The property also served as the headquarters of the Flathead Agency until 1860. On display in restored barracks are see artifacts and original furnishings. ✉ *Rte. 269, ½ mi east of U.S. 93 at Stevensville* ☎ *406/542–5500* 🌐 *www.fwp.state.mt.us/parks* 🎫 *$3* 🕒 *Daily dawn–dusk.*

Within the 2,800 acres of the **Lee Metcalf National Wildlife Refuge** reside 235 species of birds, 41 species of mammals, and 17 species of reptiles and amphibians. Bald eagles, osprey, deer, and muskrats are frequently seen along the preserve's 2 mi of nature trails and in the wildlife-viewing area. Note that fishing is permitted in the refuge. ✉ *115 W. 3rd St., 2 mi north of Stevensville* ☎ *406/777–5552* 🌐 *leemetcalf.fws.gov* 🎫 *Free* 🕒 *Daily dawn–dusk.*

St. Mary's Mission, established by Father Pierre DeSmet in 1841, was the first Catholic mission in the Northwest and the site of the first permanent non–Native American settlement in Montana. It was the home of Father Anthony Ravalli, an Italian priest recruited to the mission by Father DeSmet in 1845 who, besides his religious function, was also Montana's first physician and pharmacist. On the site are a chapel, a priest's quarters, a pharmacy, Father Ravalli's log house, and the cabin of Chief Victor, a Salish Indian who refused to sign the Hell Gate Treaty and move his people onto the Flathead Reservation. A burial plot has headstones bearing the names of both Native Americans and white settlers. ✉ *4th St., from Main St., turn west at 4th and drive 3 blocks* ☎ *406/777–5734* 🌐 *www.saintmarysmission.org* 🎫 *$3* 🕒 *Mid-May–mid-Oct., daily 10–4.*

Historical items in the **Stevensville Museum** include the belongings of early settlers, particularly the missionaries who came to convert the Indians of the West. ✉ *517 Main St.* ☎ *406/777–3201* *Donations accepted* ⊙ *Memorial Day–Labor Day, Thurs.–Sat. 11–4, Sun. 1–4.*

off the beaten path

TRAVELER'S REST STATE PARK – This park includes a Lewis and Clark camp on a floodplain overlooking Lolo Creek. The explorers stayed here from September 9 to 11, 1805, and again from June 30 to July 3, 1806. Archaeologists in 2002 found evidence of a latrine and a fire hearth, making this one of only a few locations with a physical record of the expedition's camp. Tepee rings suggest that Native Americans used the riverside location, too. Self-guided tours meander through cottonwoods and the historic campsite. Daily interpretive presentations and guided tours run during the summer, on the hour between 11 and 3. ✉ *6550 Mormon Creek Rd., south of Lolo, ¼ mi west of U.S. 93, Lolo 59847* ☎ *406/273–4253* 🌐 *www.travelersrest.org* *$2* ⊙ *Memorial Day weekend–Labor Day, daily 8–8.*

Sports & the Outdoors

FISHING **Anglers Afloat, Inc.** (✉ 2742 Alpenglow Rd. ☎ 406/777–3421) leads trophy trout trips on the Bitterroot and Blackfoot rivers. During the mayfly caddis, and salmon fly hatches, fish with **Backdoor Outfitters** (✉ 227 Bell Crossing E ☎ 406/777–3861), along spring creeks, in private ponds, or on river float trips. You can find all your fishing needs and a bit of advice, too, at the **Bitterroot Angler's Fly Shop** (✉ 4039 U.S. 93 N ☎ 406/777–5667), which specializes in fly-fishing and gifts.

Where to Stay & Eat

$–$$ ✕ **Frontier Cafe.** For a bit of town gossip and great burgers, stop in this classic small-town café, a dressed-down spot where the locals love to hang out. ✉ *3954 U.S. 93 N* ☎ *406/777–4228* *Reservations not accepted* *AE, MC, V.*

¢–$$ ✕ **Food Fetish Cafe and Catering.** Dine to live music on Friday evening and at Sunday brunch in the historic Old Bank Building. The menu tends toward Western standards given a French accent, along with several good seafood selections—oysters on the half shell and steamed mussels are favorites. Rotating exhibits of local art add color to the dining room. ✉ *308 Main* ☎ *406/777–2133* *Reservations not accepted* *AE, MC, V* ⊙ *Closed Sun. and Mon.*

$ **Big Creek Pines B&B.** Spacious, airy rooms in this B&B along Big Creek have views of the Bitterroot and Sapphire mountains and come equipped with armoires and comfortable duvets. The innkeepers know the region; after a breakfast of fruit smoothies, vegetable frittatas, or Danish pancakes, they can help with the day's itinerary. ✉ *2986 U.S. 93 N, 59870* ☎ *406/642–6475 or 888/300–6475* *406/642–6482* 🌐 *www.bigcreekpines.com* *4 rooms* *Dining room, some refrigerators, fishing, shop, meeting room, free parking; no room TVs, no smoking* *MC, V* *BP.*

CAMPING **Charles Waters Campground.** Located in the historical area of Stevensville, this is an access point to the Selway-Bitterroot Wilderness. Trails, fishing, picnic spots, and a bicycle campsite are sheltered among trees, affording glimpses of the surrounding mountains. *Pit toilets. Drinking water. Fire grates, picnic tables* *22 sites* ✉ *2 mi west of U.S. 93 on County Rd. 22, then 1 mi northwest on Forest Rd. 1316* ☎ *406/777–5461* *406/777–7423* 🌐 *www.fs.fed.us/r1* *$9* *AE, D, MC, V* ⊙ *Late May–early Sept.*

en route

A refreshing stop for wildlife viewing is the **Teller Wildlife Refuge** (✉ Quast La., Corvallis ☎ 406/961–3507), a 1,200-acre private preserve dedicated to conservation, education, and research. Situated along 3 mi of the Bitterroot River, about 8 mi north of Hamilton, the refuge is home to otters, beavers, spotted frogs, and salamanders, as well as pileated woodpeckers, birds of prey, waterfowl, deer, and many native plants. An education center conducts numerous courses, including teachers' workshops, fly-fishing classes, and lectures. To get to the refuge, take Route 269 to Quast Lane and follow the signs.

Hamilton

13 *36 mi south of Stevensville via U.S. 93.*

Nineteenth-century industrialist Marcus Daly made a fortune mining copper in Montana. He spent some of his wealth on thoroughbred race horses that he raised in this area on the 22,000-acre Bitterroot Stock Farm. It was a high-maintenance venture, so Daly developed the town of Hamilton as a place for his employees to live. His own home here, the Daly Mansion, is open for tours. The town of 5,000 is also home to the Ravalli County Museum and is a gateway to the Selway-Bitterroot Wilderness.

★ Copper king Marcus Daly's 56-room **Daly Mansion,** with 24 bedrooms, 15 baths, and five Italian marble fireplaces, is the showplace of Hamilton. Daly's heirs opened the Georgian Revival–style house to the public, and today tours run on the hour. There's also a printed walking guide available to the extensive grounds. Call the local **chamber of commerce** (☎ 406/363–2400) or the mansion to learn about events held here, such as Missoula Symphony productions. ✉ *251 Eastside Hwy.* ☎ *406/363–6004* 🌐 *www.dalymansion.org* 🎫 *$6* ⏲ *Mid-Apr.–mid-Oct., daily 11–4.*

The **Ravalli County Museum,** in the former courthouse, is the site of exhibits on Native Americans, Lewis and Clark, and other subjects related to the region. During the weekly Chautauqua series (Sunday, 2 PM), speakers share local history and lore. ✉ *205 Bedford* ☎ *406/363–3338* 🌐 *www.cybernet1.com/rcmuseum* 🎫 *Donations accepted* ⏲ *Mon., Thurs., and Fri. 10–4, Sat. 10–2.*

Hamilton is situated in the midst of the 1.6-million-acre **Selway-Bitterroot National Forest.** It includes the Bitterroot and Sapphire mountains and parts of the Selway-Bitterroot, Anaconda-Pintler, and Frank Church–River of No Return wildernesses; it's traversed by the Salmon and Selway rivers. More than 1,600 mi of trails wend through the forest, where visitors may encounter bears, elk, moose, deer, and bighorn sheep. There are also songbirds and birds of prey such as eagles and owls. The forest has three historically significant trails: the Continental Divide Scenic Trail, the Lewis and Clark Trail, and the Nez Perce Trail; some parts of the trails are open to hikers, other parts to bikes and vehicles. Wildfires of 2000 scorched parts of the forest; hikers should be alert to the danger of falling trees in the burnt-out areas. ✉ *1801 North Ave.* ☎ *406/363–3131 or 406/777–5461* 🌐 *www.fs.fed.us/r1* 🎫 *Free* ⏲ *Daily.*

off the beaten path

SKALKAHO HIGHWAY – Three miles south of Hamilton, turn east onto Route 38, also known as the Skalkaho Highway, and you'll find yourself on a beautiful, seldom-traveled route leading into the Sapphire Mountains and on to the Georgetown Lake area near Anaconda. This fair-weather road is best traveled in summer, since 20 mi of it are gravel. Mountain bikers tour here, and there are plenty of hiking trails through the 23,000-acre Skalkaho Wildlife Preserve. Note that Forest Road 1352 into the preserve is closed October 15 to December 1, making that a fine time for nonmotorized travel. Only

10 mi of the Skalkaho Highway are plowed in winter, which means the area is excellent for cross-country skiing and snowshoeing.

Sports & the Outdoors

RODEO See more than 300 of the country's top senior rodeo cowboys and cowgirls rope and ride at the **Senior Pro Rodeo** (☒ Ravalli County Fairgrounds ☎ 406/375–1400) in mid-July. There are also cowboy poetry readings, arts and crafts booths, and live music.

FISHING There are two good options for fishing excursions in the area. You can float and fish with **Fly Fishing Adventures** (☒ 112 Freezout La. ☎ 406/363–2398) on the Bitterroot River. Fishing trips with **Fly Fishing Always** (☒ 1 Fisherman La. ☎ 406/363–0943) amble down the Bitterroot River looking for brown trout and west slope cutthroat. Scenic float trips are also available.

TRAIL RIDES Take a horse trip into the Selway-Bitterroot Wilderness with **Lightning Creek Outfitters** (☒ 1424 Skalkaho Hwy. ☎ 406/363–0320), which also offers cowboy dinner rides and pack trips. Spend an hour, half day, or full day in the saddle with **Iron Horse Outfitters** (☒ Box 1346, 59840 ☎ 406/821–4474), which offers cookouts, too.

Where to Stay & Eat

¢–$$ ✕ **Spice of Life.** The romantic atmosphere inside this historic building is enhanced with live music on Wednesday night. Eclectic fare includes pasta, seafood, steak, and Thai and Japanese specials. ☒ *163 2nd Ave. S* ☎ *406/363–4433* ▭ *AE, MC, V* ⊙ *No dinner Sun.–Tues.*

¢ ✕ **A Place to Ponder Bakery and Cafe.** Excellent baked goods available here include croissants, cookies, and cheesecake. You can get a packed lunch for the trail—particularly good is the chicken salad on outfitters bread, similar to croissant dough with cheese baked inside. There's also pizza. A couple of seats are available, but business is primarily takeout. ☒ *166 S. 2nd St.* ☎ *406/363–0080* ▭ *No credit cards* ⊙ *No dinner. Closed Sun. and Mon.*

$–$$ ✕ **Deer Crossing B&B.** The two deluxe rooms, two luxury suites, and two cabins at this historic homestead are set on 25 acres of property surrounded by pastureland, pines, the Sapphire Mountains, and Como Peak. You find here fireplaces, hot tubs, and Western furnishings. The hearty ranch breakfast consists of French bread custard, smoked ham, and a fruit platter, served on the deck in summers. ☒ *396 Hayes Creek Rd., 59840* ☎ *406/363–2232 or 800/763–2232* 🖷 *406/375–0771* ⊕ *www.deercrossingmontana.com* *2 rooms, 2 suites, 2 cabins* *Dining room, fishing, hiking, horseback riding, baby-sitting, free parking, some pets allowed; no a/c, no room phones, no room TVs, no smoking* ▭ *AE, MC, V* *BP.*

¢–$ **Best Western Hamilton Inn.** This clean and convenient hotel is typical of the chain. It's within walking distance of many of the town's sites and restaurants. A Continental breakfast and newspaper are available in the lobby each morning. ☒ *409 S. 1st St., 59840* ☎ *406/363–2142 or 800/426–4586* 🖷 *406/363–2142* ⊕ *www.bestwestern.com* *36 rooms* *Dining room, in-room data ports, some microwaves, some refrigerators, cable TV, hot tub, laundry facilities, business services, meeting rooms, no-smoking rooms* ▭ *AE, D, DC, MC, V* *CP.*

CAMPING **Blodgett Canyon Campground.** From this undeveloped campsite along a canyon creek you have easy access to hiking and biking trails, fishing, and rock climbing. *Pit toilets. Drinking water. Fire grates, picnic tables. Swimming (creek)* *6 sites* ☒ *Blodgett Canyon, 5 mi northwest of Hamilton* ☎ *406/363–3131* ⊕ *www.fs.fed.us/r1* *Free* *Reservations essential* ▭ *No credit cards.*

The Arts

The annual **Bluegrass Festival** (✉ Hamilton Fairgrounds ☎ 406/363–1250 🌐 www.bluegrassfestival.org) draws musicians from around the West for three days in mid-July. The outdoor event also includes arts and crafts vendors and food stands.

The **Good Nations Powwow** (✉ Daly Mansion grounds ☎ 406/363–5383, 406/726–3701, or 406/363–2400) takes place over three days in late July. It attracts tribes from all over the country to take part in drumming, singing, and dancing.

Summer comedies and spring Shakespeare are standard parts of the year-round schedule put on by the **Hamilton Players** (✉ 100 Ricketts Rd. ☎ 406/375–9050) at the Hamilton Playhouse.

Shopping

You'll find all kinds of gifts and gear for the cabin in the **Bitterroot Trading Co.** (✉ 206 W. Main ☎ 406/363–2782), including Western-style lodgepole-pine and hickory furniture, and regional jewelry.

Original Western art, including oils, watercolors, and prints, is available at the **Ponderosa Art Gallery** (✉ 944 Springhill Rd. ☎ 406/375–1212 🌐 www.ponderosaartgallery.com), which hosts special guest artists' shows.

Darby

⓮ *14 mi south of Hamilton via U.S. 93.*

This town of 900 in the Bitterroot Valley is home to the U.S. Department of Agriculture's first Forest Service station, the Alta Ranger Station, as well as Painted Rocks State Park and the Darby Pioneer Memorial Museum. Visitors often stop here for a break, a meal, and some shopping while driving through the Bitterroot Valley.

The one-room, lodgepole-pine cabin **Alta Ranger Station** was constructed in 1899 by early forest rangers as the first ranger station in the country. Bicyclists often access forest roads from here. Rangers have maps and knowledge of the backcountry in surrounding mountains. ✉ *6735 West Fork Rd.* ☎ *406/821–3269 or 406/821–3913* 🌐 *www.fs.fed.us/r1* *Free* *Daily dawn–dusk.*

One of the area's first hand-hewn log homesteads is now the **Darby Pioneer Memorial Museum,** a repository for pioneer artifacts, photographs, and memorabilia. ✉ *334 Bunkhouse Rd.* ☎ *406/821–4503* 🌐 *www.visitmt.com* *Donations accepted* *June–Aug., weekdays 1–5.*

The **Painted Rocks State Park** reservoir is a great place to cool off. Boating, camping, and fishing are popular here with the locals. ✉ *Rte. 473, 23 mi southwest of U.S. 93* ☎ *406/542–5500* 🌐 *www.fwp.state.mt.us* *Donations accepted.*

Sports & the Outdoors

BICYCLING Seemingly endless miles of mountain-biking terrain open up in the Bitterroot National Forest, where several loop routes challenge riders along dirt roads. Within the 16 mountainous miles of the **Railroad–Daly Loop** you may see moose, deer, elk, or livestock. Remember that bicycles are forbidden in designated wilderness areas. For maps, directions, and other loop routes, stop in at the Darby Ranger Station (✉ 721 Main ☎ 406/821–3913 🌐 www.fs.fed.us/r1/bitterroot).

CROSS-COUNTRY SKIING Groomed trails for skate and classic skiing on the **Chief Joseph Cross-Country Ski Trails** (✉ 1 mi east of U.S. 93 on Rte. 43 ☎ 406/821–3201) cover more than 25 km (15 mi) over hills and through meadows.

DOWNHILL SKIING Ten feet of snow can accumulate at **Lost Trail Powder Mountain** (✉ 7674 U.S. 93 S, Sula ☎ 406/821–3211 or 406/821–3742), which straddles the Montana–Idaho border. There are 40 runs, and lift tickets are inexpensive ($22).

FISHING **Joe Biner's Rainbow Guide Service** (✉ 5424 West Fork Rd. ☎ 406/821–4643 or 406/239–1192) will show you the ropes of trout fishing in the area. They also offer float trips.

LOGGING The annual **Darby Logger Days** (✉ at U.S. 93, just after Tin Cup Rd. ☎ 406/821–4981 🌐 www.visitmt.com), held in mid-July in a field at the south end of town, celebrates forests and logging, which began in the region in the 1880s. Contests include log rolling, speed cutting, speed chopping, and ax throwing.

TRAIL RIDES See the Bitterroots from horseback with **Circle KBL Outfitters** (✉ 171 Bunkhouse Rd. ☎ 406/821–0017 or 800/946–6778), who will take you on hour- or daylong trail rides and wilderness pack trips into the Bitterroot or Selway wilderness.

Where to Stay & Eat

$–$$$ ✕ **The Rocky Knob.** This 1940s log lodge and former brothel is now a delightful eatery that specializes in hickory-smoked ribs and prime rib. Dine by one of the two fireplaces, or hang out in the lounge, where pool and fishing stories are popular. ✉ *6065 U.S. 93 S, Conner, 13 mi south of Darby* ☎ *406/821–3520* ▭ *AE, MC, V.*

$$$$ 🏨 **Pepperbox Ranch.** Bring your cowboy hat for a relaxing stay on this working cattle ranch in the Bitterroot Mountains. From your log cabin (or tepee and covered wagon), you can step outside to fish, trail ride, photograph moose and elk, and hike, and kids can take archery and roping lessons. In the evening, cowboy entertainment, campfires, and wagon and buggy rides are offered. In winter, there's downhill and cross-country skiing. Meals, which are part of the all-inclusive package, are served family style in the main lodge and include fried chicken and ranch-raised beef; each ends with homemade pie. Private log cabins have spacious porches and handmade quilts. ✉ *9959 West Fork Rd., 59829* ☎ *406/349–2920* 📠 *406/349–2039* 🌐 *www.pepperbox.com* *4 cabins, 1 tepee, 1 wagon* *Dining room, refrigerators, outdoor hot tub, mountain bikes, horseback riding, cross-country skiing, downhill skiing, shop, free parking, no-smoking rooms; no room phones, no room TVs* ▭ *MC, V* 🍽 *FAP.*

$$$$ 🏨 **Triple Creek Ranch.** This ranch is definitely off the beaten path, but it's well worth the effort for those seeking utter seclusion and indulgence. Luxurious log cabins tucked into ponderosa-pine forest offer the kind of privacy and pampering that attract celebrities to this year-round, adults-only resort. The humblest accommodations share a hot tub amid the trees, and the others (mostly one-bedroom suites) have roomy indoor Jacuzzis or hot tubs on decks overlooking the Bitterroot Range. Massive log beds, fireplaces, and his-and-her bathroom suites with steam showers will change your concept of what it means to stay in a "cabin." All meals and drinks are included in the per-couple rate, as are on-ranch trail rides, fly-casting instruction, snowshoeing, and cross-country skiing. The staff has that rare blend of friendliness and discretion. ✉ *5551 West Fork Rd., 59829* ☎ *406/821–4600* 📠 *406/821–4666* 🌐 *www.triplecreekranch.com* *19 cabins* *Restaurant, in-room data ports, kitchenettes, minibars, in-room VCRs, putting green, tennis court, pool, hot tubs, massage, fishing, hiking, horseback riding, cross-country skiing, snowmobiling, bar, library, laundry service, business services, meeting room, airport shuttle* ▭ *AE, D, MC, V* 🍽 *FAP.*

$$–$$$$ **Tin Cup Lodge B&B.** On a clear day, you can see 80 mi of mountains and valley from this pleasant log lodge in the foothills of the Bitterroot Range. Lodge rooms and cabins are appointed with Western flair, featuring log furniture and comforters; cabins have private hot tubs. ✉ *582 Tin Cup Rd., 59829* ☎ *406/821–1620* 📠 *406/821–3046* 🌐 *www.tincuplodge.com* *4 rooms, 2 cabins* *Dining room, room service, some in-room phones, some microwaves, some refrigerators, in-room VCRs, pond, hot tub, sauna, bicycles, billiards, recreation room, shop, laundry facilities, business services, meeting room, free parking; no kids, no smoking* *AE, MC, V* *BP.*

CAMPING **Lake Como Lower Campground.** This lakeside site among the tall pines is popular with campers—spaces fill up fast during July and August. There's also an upper campground available when there's no vacancy here. *Pit toilets. Drinking water. Fire grates, picnic tables. Swimming (lake)* *12 sites* ✉ *County Rd. 82, 4 mi north of Darby on U.S. 93, then 4.8 mi west on County Rd. 82* ☎ *406/821–3269 or 406/821–3913* 🌐 *www.fs.fed.us/r1* *$14* *AE, D, MC, V* *Late May–early Sept.*

Shopping

Old West Gallery and Antiques (✉ 202 S. Main ☎ 406/821–4076) is a huge shop selling gifts, collectibles, Native American and Western art, and furniture. The kids are likely to be enamored of the Old West Candy Store inside, which features fudge and hand-dipped chocolates.

MISSION & FLATHEAD VALLEYS

Glaciated valleys, scoured out by ice sheets some 12,000 years ago, are dappled with tree-lined lakes and snowy peaks. Between Missoula and the Canadian border, several fertile vales, including the Mission and Flathead valleys, are home to ranching, farming, and a growing number of recreational outlets for golfing, boating, and skiing.

Flathead Indian Reservation

15 *20 mi north of Missoula via U.S. 93.*

Home to the Salish and Kootenai tribes, this 1.2-million-acre reservation is patchworked with non-Indian ranches and other property. Archaeological evidence indicates that Native Americans were here some 14,000 years ago, but it wasn't until the 1700s that the Kootenai, Salish, and Pend d'Oreille shared common hunting grounds in this area. The Kootenai hunted bison, descendants of which can be seen at the National Bison Range. When Catholic "Black Robes" arrived to convert the Indians, they built the St. Ignatius Mission. Both tribes celebrate their cultures during the annual July Powwow, and at the Sqelix'u/Aqfsmakni-k Cultural Center (The People's Center). Of the approximately 6,950 enrolled tribal members of the **Confederated Salish and Kootenai Tribes,** about 4,500 live on the reservation. For visitors, the main attractions are the bison range, the People's Center, Flathead Lake, numerous lakes and streams (such as Nine Pipes) for fishing and water recreation, and bird-watching opportunities. ✉ *Box 278, Pablo, 59855* ☎ *406/675–2700* 🌐 *tlc.wtp.net/salish.htm* *Free* *Weekdays 9–5.*

Established in 1846 as a Hudson's Bay Company trading post, **Fort Connah** was used by fur traders until 1871. Of the original three buildings, one remains today; it's believed to be the oldest building still standing in Montana. You can't go inside, but a historical marker details events and inhabitants. ✉ *U.S. 93 at Post Creek, between St. Ignatius and Charlo* ☎ *406/549–4431* *Free* *Dawn–dusk.*

Fodor'sChoice ★ The Red Sleep Mountain Drive, a 19-mi loop road at the **National Bison Range,** allows close-up views of bison, elk, pronghorn, deer, and mountain sheep. The gravel road rises 2,000 feet and takes about two hours to complete; you're required to begin the drive no later than 6 PM and to finish before the gate closes at dark. The 19,000-acre refuge at the foot of the Mission Mountains was established in 1908 by Theodore Roosevelt. Today the U.S. Fish and Wildlife Service ranches a herd of 400 bison. A visitor center explains the history, habits, and habitat of the bison. To reach the bison range, follow the signs west, then north from the junction of U.S. 93 and Route 200 in Ravalli. ✉ *132 Bison Range Rd., Moiese* ☎ *406/644–2211* 🌐 *bisonrange.fws.gov* 🎫 *$4 per vehicle* ⏲ *Mid-May–Sept., daily 7–9; Oct.–mid-May, weekdays 8–4:30.*

The **St. Ignatius Mission**—a church, cabin, and collection of other buildings—was built in the 1890s with bricks made of local clay by missionaries and Native Americans. The 58 murals on the walls and ceilings of the church were used to teach Bible stories to the natives. In the St. Ignatius Mission Museum (an old log cabin) there's an exhibit of early artifacts and arts and crafts. To reach the mission from St. Ignatius, take Main Street south to Mission Drive. ✉ *1 Catholic Mission Dr.* ☎ *406/745–2768* 🎫 *Donations accepted* ⏲ *Mid-Mar.–mid-Oct., daily 9–9; mid-Oct.–mid-Mar., daily 9–5; Sun. Mass 9:15.*

Sprawling **Ninepipe National Wildlife Refuge** is *the* place for bird-watchers. This 2,000-acre wetland complex in the shadow of the Mission Mountains is home to everything from marsh hawks to kestrels to red-winged blackbirds. It features rookeries for double-crested cormorants and great blue herons; bald eagles fish here in the winter. Roads through the center of the refuge are closed March through mid-July during nesting season, but you can drive along the periphery throughout the year. Maps are available from the nearby National Bison Range, which manages Ninepipe. ✉ *U.S. 93* ☎ *406/644–2211* 🌐 *bisonrange.fws.gov/Ninepipe.*

★ The **Sqelix'u/Aqfsmakni-k Cultural Center (The People's Center)** exhibits artifacts, photographs, and recordings concerning the Salish, Kootenai, and Pend d'Oreille people. The People's Center oversees educational programs, guided interpretive tours, outdoor traditional lodges, and annual festivals. A gift shop sells both traditional and nontraditional work by local artists and craftspeople. ✉ *53253 U.S. 93 W, Pablo, 6 mi south of Polson* ☎ *406/883–5344 or 800/883–5344* 🌐 *www.peoplescenter.org* 🎫 *$3* ⏲ *Weekdays 9–5, weekends 10–5.*

off the beaten path

SYMES HOT SPRINGS HOTEL AND MINERAL BATHS – Truly a unique find on the western edge of the Flathead Indian Reservation, this rustic 1928 hotel has hot mineral pools from continuously flowing springs, spa treatments, massage, live music on weekends, and organic food in its restaurant. The hotel itself isn't a standout, though the rates ($45–$80 for a room) are reasonable. Several historic hot springs in the area attracted Native Americans for centuries. ✉ *209 Wall St., Hot Springs* ☎ *406/741–2361 or 888/305–3106* 🌐 *www.symeshotsprings.com* 🎫 *Baths $6* ⏲ *Daily 8 AM–11 PM.*

Where to Stay & Eat

$$ ✕ **Dinner Bell.** Chicken, roast beef, meat loaf, mashed potatoes, and vegetables—all organically raised or grown—are the staples at this restaurant run by a local Amish family. Meals are brought to the table family style by servers in traditional Amish dress. At dessert, fresh pies and ice cream are accompanied by the a cappella voices of the family's children.

Note that the restaurant is open only on Tuesday and Thursday nights for one 6 PM sitting. ✉ *14281 Watson Rd., St. Ignatius* ☎ *406/745–3202* *Reservations essential* *No credit cards* *Closed Fri.–Mon. and Wed. No lunch.*

$–$$$$ **Cheff's Guest Ranch.** This 10,000-acre working cattle ranch at the base of the Mission Mountains lets you take part in ranching life in the summer and conducts pack trips from September through November. Hearty breakfasts start off days of trail rides, fishing for trout, bass, bullhead, and perch, and exploration on the nearby National Wildlife Refuge, Ninepipes, and Kicking Horse Reservoir in the valley below. Guests can join in duties such as milking cows, moving stock, and bucking bales of hay. A full range of package options is available, from lodging with no services to all-inclusive packages. ✉ *4274 Eagle Pass Trail, Charlo 59824* ☎ *406/644–2557* *406/644–2611* *www.gordonsguide.com/cheffranch* *7 rooms, 3 with bath; 2 cabins* *Dining room, some kitchens, some microwaves, some room TVs, pond, hot tub, fishing, mountain bikes, badminton, basketball, hiking, horseback riding, horseshoes, Ping-Pong, volleyball, library, piano, recreation room, shop, laundry facilities, meeting rooms, airport shuttle; no a/c, no room phones, no smoking* *AE, MC, V* *Closed Dec.–May* *FAP.*

¢–$$ **Twin Creek B&B.** The setting is first-rate at this contemporary B&B: two creeks meander through the property, located under the spectacular Mission Mountains, with views of Mission Valley farmland. Two tepees and the resident St. Bernard dogs are popular with kids. Breakfast consists of homemade biscuits and huckleberry jam, ham, and eggs any way you like them. ✉ *2295 Twin Creek Rd., Ronan 59864* ☎ *406/676–8800 or 877/524–8946* *406/676–2662* *www.twincreeksbb.com* *7 rooms* *Dining room, room service, in-room data ports, in-room VCRs, hot tub, massage, spa, fishing, shop, baby-sitting, laundry facilities, business services, meeting rooms, free parking, some pets allowed; no smoking* *AE, MC, V* *BP.*

CAMPING **Mission Meadows RV.** This grassy meadow near the highway is conveniently located near the bison range and fishing. *Flush toilets. Full hookups, dump station. Drinking water, guest laundry, showers. Fire pits, food service, picnic tables. Electricity, public telephone. General store* *20 full hookups, 70 partial hookups, 30 tent sites* ✉ *205-102 Mud Creek La., 2 mi north of Ronan* ☎ *406/676–5182* *406/676–5182* *Full hookups $23, partial hookups $19, tent sites $12* *D, MC.*

The Arts

For more than a century, the four-day powwow during the **Arlee 4th of July Celebration** (✉ Pow-Wow Rd., ½ mi east of U.S. 93, Arlee ☎ 406/745–4984 www.go.to/Arlee_powwow) has drawn Native Americans from all over the West. Highlights are drumming, dancing, and singing contests; the parade; the traditional encampment; and arts, crafts, and food vendors.

Shopping

The **Flathead Indian Museum and Trading Post** (✉ 1 Museum La., St. Ignatius ☎ 406/745–2951) has an extensive collection of authentic artifacts from local Native American tribes. On sale are arts, crafts, books, maps, and gifts.

Flathead Lake

16 *12 mi north of Ronan via U.S. 93.*

The 370-foot-deep Flathead Lake, with 180 mi of shoreline, is the largest natural freshwater lake in the western United States. It's a wonderful—and popular—place for sailing, fishing, and swimming. Wild-horse Island State Park, located in the lake, is home to bighorn sheep and other wildlife; the 2,165-acre island can be reached only by private boat. Cherry groves line the lake's shores, and toward the end of July, farmers harvest them and sell cherries at roadside stands along the two highways that encircle the lake.

Polson, a quiet community of 4,000 on the southern edge of Flathead Lake, sits under the morning shadow of the jagged Mission Mountains. It's the largest town on the Flathead Indian Reservation. Picnic spots, lake access, and playgrounds are found at Boettcher, Sacajawea, and Riverside parks. Some other parks are for tribal members only; signs identify picnic areas that are closed to the public.

The Swan River empties into Flathead Lake at the small, idyllic resort community of **Bigfork.** The small town is filled with shops, galleries, restaurants, and a cultural center. Many summer events are so popular that you should make dinner and playhouse reservations a month in advance. This is a great spot to browse after you're finished with your outdoor activities. The rotating exhibits at **Bigfork Art and Cultural Center** (✉ 525 Electric Ave. ☎ 406/837–6927) display bronzes, paintings, and other media works by Montana artists.

off the beaten path

MISSION MOUNTAINS WILDERNESS COMPLEX – From much of the Mission Valley and Flathead Indian Reservation you can see the Mission Mountains, on which there's a 73,877-acre wilderness area full of hiking, camping, and fishing opportunities. The area is probably best known for the 1,000-foot drops of Elizabeth and Mission falls. Glorious McDonald Peak looms at 9,280 feet; it's a favorite of grizzly bears, who gather on the snow fields to eat swarms of cutworm moths and ladybugs. Those who aren't tribal members must obtain a recreation permit to hike, fish, and camp here among the mountain lions, lynx, wolverines, black bears, and grizzlies. Recreational permits are available at local grocery and sporting-goods stores and most gas stations. Call the Flathead National Forest at the number below for camping permits and information on the recreation permits. ✉ *Mission Reservoir Rd., off U.S. 93* ☎ *406/758–5200* 🎟 *Recreational permit $25* ⏲ *Daily.*

Sports & the Outdoors

BOATING

Flathead Lake Boat Rentals (✉ 303 U.S. 93, Polson ☎ 406/883–5900 or 800/358–8046) has everything from canoes and sea kayaks to deck boats and fishing boats. At **Dayton Yacht Harbor** (✉ 299 C St., Dayton ☎ 406/849–5423 or 800/775–2990) you can rent a sailboat, go on an excursion, take sailing lessons, or moor your own sailboat near Wild Horse and Cromwell islands.

Fodor's Choice ★

One of the most pleasant ways to see the lake is to take a two-hour sail on the historic *Questa* or the *Nor'Easter,* both 51-foot Q-class racing sloops built in the 1920s. They depart from **Flathead Lake Lodge** (✉ 150 Flathead Lake Lodge Rd., Bigfork ☎ 406/837–4391).

FISHING

Take a charter trip on Flathead Lake with **A-Able Fishing Charters & Tours** (✉ 63 Twin Acres Dr., Kalispell ☎ 406/257–5214) to fish for lake trout and mackinaw. Fly-fish with **Two River Gear and Outfitter** (✉ 603 Electric Ave., Bigfork ☎ 406/837–3474) on local streams, rivers, and lakes.

GOLF

★ Wonderful views of mountains and Flathead Lake from **Eagle Bend** (✉ 279 Eagle Bend Dr., Bigfork ☎ 406/837–7310 or 800/255–5641) are matched by the golfing on the 27-hole course. Each of the 27 holes of the **Polson Country Club** (✉ 111 Bayview Dr. ☎ 406/883–8230 or 800/

392–9795 www.golfmontana.net) has a view of the Mission and Swan mountain ranges and the lake.

HIKING Fodor'sChoice ★ **Jewel Basin Hiking Area** (✉ 10 mi east of Bigfork via Rte. 83 and Echo Lake Rd.) provides 35 mi of well-maintained trails among 27 trout-filled alpine lakes. You'll find the nearest phone and hearty to-go trail lunches at the Echo Lake Cafe at the junction of Route 83 and Echo Lake Road. The **U.S. Forest Service** (✉ 200 Ranger Station Rd. ☎ 406/837–7500) in Bigfork sells hiking maps.

MOUNTAIN BIKING Hundred of miles of unpaved roads are perfect for biking. Rentals and maps are available at **Mountain Mike's Rental Bikes** (✉ 417 Bridge St., Bigfork ☎ 406/837–2453).

RAFTING Eight white-water miles of the lower Flathead River are covered by **Flathead Raft Co.** (✉ 1501 U.S. 93 S ☎ 406/883–5838 or 800/654–4359 www.flatheadraftco.com). From June through September it provides wild rafting adventures, kayaking, and Native American interpretive trips between Kerr Dam and Buffalo Bridge.

SKIING As you schuss runs of **Blacktail Mountain Ski Area** (✉ Blacktail Mountain Rd., Lakeside ☎ 406/844–0999), you'll glimpse Flathead Lake and surrounding peaks. This family-friendly mountain is known for inexpensive lift tickets; uncrowded, mostly intermediate slopes; a lovely new lodge; and friendly staff.

Where to Stay & Eat

★ **$$$** ✕ **La Provence.** The garden dining here offers a flower-studded view down Bigfork's main street. Local artists' work decorates the whitewashed walls. The owner-chef specializes in French onion soup with Gruyère cheese served inside a large onion, and venison tenderloin with figs and Bordeaux sauce. An international wine list and a traditional chocolate soufflé round out the Mediterranean meals. *✉ 408 Bridge St., Bigfork ☎ 406/837–2923 ▭ AE, MC, V ⊗ Closed Sun.*

★ **$$–$$$** ✕ **Showthyme!** In Bigfork's former bank building, built in 1908, diners opt for street- or bay-side seating, or a table in the snug bank vault. Signature dishes include fresh ahi tuna with sweet soy ginger and wasabi over jasmine rice. Save room for Benedictine chocolate truffle pie. *✉ 548 Electric Ave., Bigfork ☎ 406/837–0707 ▭ AE, DC, MC, V ⊗ No lunch.*

$$–$$$ ✕ **Swan River Café and Dinner House.** This relaxed yet elegant eatery serves dishes such as rack of lamb, pork tenderloin, pastas, and fondues (which require advance reservation) inside or on the terrace overlooking Bigfork Bay. The Sunday brunch and dinner buffets are popular with locals. *✉ 360 Grand Ave., Bigfork ☎ 406/837–2220 ▭ AE, D, MC, V.*

$$$$ **Averill's Flathead Lake Lodge.** Since 1945 Averill's has been providing families a wholesome and active Western getaway. The beautiful green grounds are on the shore of the lake, where beach fires, canoeing, and sailing take place. The lodge, accommodations, and other buildings are all log-and-stone structures. Horseback rides set out both in the morning and evening, and you can learn to rope in the rodeo arena. Many activities such as rafting and guided fishing trips are available for an extra cost. It's BYOB at the bar. *✉ 150 Flathead Lake Lodge Rd., Flathead 59911 ☎ 406/837–4391 406/837–6977 www.averills.com 20 rooms, 20 cottages Dining room, 4 tennis courts, pool, lake, beach, boating, waterskiing, fishing, hiking, horseback riding, horseshoes, volleyball, children's programs (ages 3 and up), airport shuttle ▭ AE, MC, V ⊗ Closed Oct.–May FAP.*

$$–$$$$ **Marina Cay Resort and Conference Center.** Most of the large, plainly decorated rooms here have views of the waterfront of Bigfork Bay. Luxury suites have private hot tubs, balconies, or patios. Nearby golf courses get lots of use from the guests, and you can park your boat next to the outdoor bar, which is a popular spot in summer. ✉ *180 Vista La., Bigfork 59911* ☎ *406/837–5861 or 800/433–6516* 🖷 *406/837–1118* 🌐 *www.marinacay.com* *125 rooms* *Restaurant, café, snack bar, in-room data ports, some kitchens, cable TV, pool, hot tub, dock, boating, jet skiing, marina, waterskiing, fishing, bicycles, bar, casino, shop, baby-sitting, laundry facilities, business services, convention center, no-smoking rooms* ▭ *AE, D, MC, V.*

★ $$–$$$$ **Mountain Lake Lodge.** This resort perched above crystalline Flathead Lake offers 30 well-appointed suites surrounding an outdoor pool. Guests enjoy sweeping views of the lake and surrounding mountains from their rooms. The hotel is well situated for hiking, golfing, rafting, and lake cruising. The log-accented dining room is designed to let you watch the sunset while enjoying smoked pheasant and other delicacies. The dining room is open seasonally; the bar serves light dinners year-round. ✉ *1950 Sylvan Dr. at Hwy. 35 mile marker 26.5, Bigfork 59911* ☎ *406/837–3800 or 877/823–4923* 🖷 *406/837–3861* 🌐 *www.mountainlakelodge.com* *30 suites* *Restaurant, pool, hot tub, bar* ▭ *AE, DC, MC, V.*

$ **O'Duach'ain Country Inn Bed & Breakfast.** In a quiet lodgepole-pine forest outside of Bigfork, this cozy and comfy B&B consists of two log cabins. The main house is light filled and has two stone fireplaces and a wraparound terrace; horses graze next door. Each room is individually decorated in Old West style. The room in the main house has a step-up Queen Ann bed. Full breakfasts are served at a long dining room table. ✉ *675 Ferndale Dr., Bigfork 59911* ☎ *406/837–6851* 🖷 *406/837–0778* 🌐 *www.montanainn.com* *4 rooms, 1 suite* *Dining room, hot tub, hiking* ▭ *AE, MC, V* *BP.*

CAMPING **Polson/Flathead KOA.** Perched above Flathead Lake with incredible views of the Mission and Swan mountains, this grassy spot is convenient to the lake and town, and hosts can direct you to fossil and arrowhead hunting. Cabins have front porch swings. *Flush toilets. Full hookups, dump station. Drinking water, guest laundry, showers. Fire pits, picnic tables. Electricity, public telephone. General store. Play area, swimming (pool)* *31 full hookups, 23 partial hookups, 21 tent sites; 12 cabins* ✉ *200 Irving Flat Rd., Polson* ☎ *406/883–2151 or 800/562–2130* 🖷 *406/883–0151* 🌐 *www.flatheadlakekoa.com* *RV sites $31, tent sites $19; cabins $42* ▭ *D, MC, V* *May–Sept.*

Flathead Lake state parks. Five lakeside parks are scattered around Flathead, offering quiet camping, boat launches, and good views. Bigfork's Wayfarers, Lakeside's West Shore, and Polson's Big Arm, Finley Point, and Yellow Bay parks are all owned by Montana Fish, Wildlife and Parks. Reservations are a good idea in summer, as spots fill up fast. *Pit toilets. Drinking water. Fire grates, picnic tables. Swimming (lake)* *273 tent sites* ✉ *490 N. Meridian Rd., Kalispell* ☎ *406/752–5501* 🖷 *406/257–0349* 🌐 *www.fwp.state.mt.us* *$15* *May–Sept.*

The Arts

From late June through Labor Day, the repertory group **Bigfork Summer Playhouse** (✉ 526 Electric Ave., 59911 ☎ 406/837–4886) presents Broadway musicals and comedies every night except Sunday in the Bigfork Center for the Performing Arts. Phone orders for tickets are available from mid-May to the end of August, or by mail beginning in April. Children's workshops and theater are held in the same facility.

Enjoy summer theater with the **Port Polson Players** (✉ Boetcher Park, U.S. 93 ☎ 406/883–9212). The high-quality amateur troupe puts on musicals, comedies, and dramas.

Summer Sundays at Bigfork's Everit L. Sliter Memorial Park find live music performed by local musicians and regionally known bands at the **River Bend Stage** (✉ Bridge St. ☎ 406/837–4400).

Shopping

Bigfork's Electric Avenue is lined with galleries and eclectic gift shops and is recognized for unparalleled dining and sweets. Try the soft cookies and hot-out-of-the-oven cinnamon rolls baked daily and shipped nationwide from **Brookies Cookies** (✉ 191 Mill St. ☎ 406/837–2447).

Filled to the brim with Montana history, regional travel, and other unique books, **Electric Avenue Books** (✉ 490 Electric Ave. ☎ 406/837–6072) is a comfortable setting in which to browse. The shopkeeper offers tips on local events, restaurants, and out-of-the-way places.

Electric Avenue Gifts (✉ 459 Electric Ave. ☎ 406/837–4994) carries folk-art gifts and souvenirs.

See award-winning sculptor Eric Thorsen at work during daily tours of his studio, across the street from **Eric Thorsen Fine Art Gallery** (✉ 547 Electric Ave. ☎ 406/837–4366).

You can pick up a tiny jar of huckleberry jam or honey at **Eva Gates Homemade Preserves** (✉ 456 Electric Ave. ☎ 406/837–4356) or have one of the family-size jars of various berry flavors shipped back home.

The not-for-profit **Sandpiper Gallery** (✉ 2 1st Ave., Polson ☎ 406/883–5956), located inside the Polson public library, shows the work of local and regional artists and presents an annual art show on the courthouse lawn the first Saturday in August.

en route

Two scenic routes (one to Creston and the other to Kalispell) lead north from Bigfork, over the Flathead River (look for osprey nests atop poles), past fields of mint, seed potatoes, hay, and tree nurseries. When the last glacier receded 10,000 years ago it left a 100-foot depth of fertile soil called glacier loam. The route to Creston leads to the **Gatiss Gardens** (✉ 4790 Hwy. 35, at Broeder Loop Rd., Creston, 8 mi north of Bigfork ☎ 406/755–2418), which has a gentle 1¼-mi trail past hundreds of perennials, bulbs, and shrubs.

Kalispell

17 *20 mi northwest of Bigfork via Rte. 35.*

Two major highways, U.S. 2 and U.S. 93, meet at a busy downtown intersection in this century-old city. Kalispell is the Flathead County seat and a regional business and shopping center for folks around northwest Montana. Main Street (U.S. 93) is lined with galleries, jewelry stores, boutiques, and restaurants. The Great Northern Depot is a historic spot where you can pick up visitor information. An Andrew Carnegie library is now home to the Hockaday Museum of Art, and just a few blocks away, Kalispell's first school building has been turned into the Central School Museum.

You can ring the old school bell at the **Central School Museum,** an 1894 Romanesque building. In the museum are galleries, activities, and displays concerning regional heritage and history. You'll also find a café, museum store, conference rooms, and reference library. ✉ *124 2nd Ave. E* ☎ *406/756–8381* 🌐 *www.visitmt.com* *$4* *May–Sept., Mon.–Sat. 10–4; Oct.–Apr., Tues.–Sat. 11–3.*

A town highlight is the **Conrad Mansion National Historic Site Museum,** a 26-room Norman-style mansion that was the home of C. E. Conrad, the manager of a freighter on the Missouri River and the founder of Kalispell. Come Christmas, the mansion is lavishly decorated and filled with the wares of local artisans. ✉ *4th St. between 6th and Woodland* ☎ *406/755–2166* 🎫 *$7* ⏲ *Guided tours mid-May–mid-June and mid-Sept.–mid-Oct., daily 10–5:30; mid-June–mid-Sept., daily 9–8.*

The **Hockaday Museum of Art,** housed in the renovated Carnegie library, presents contemporary art exhibits. The museum hosts the annual Hockaday Arts in the Park in late July at Depot Park, where vendors from around the Northwest sell fine art and crafts. ✉ *302 2nd Ave. E, at 3rd St.* ☎ *406/755–5268* 🌐 *www.hockadayartmuseum.org* 🎫 *Free* ⏲ *June–Sept., Mon.–Wed., Fri., and Sat. 10–6, Thurs. 10–8; Oct.–May, Tues.–Sat. 10–5.*

One of 20 city green spaces, **Woodland Park** has a popular swimming pool, a playground, ball fields, and a picnic area. Geese, ducks, peacocks, and black swans flutter to the pond, which in winter opens for ice skating; there's a warming hut nearby. ✉ *Conrad Dr. and Woodland Dr.* ☎ *406/758–7718 or 406/758–2800* 🌐 *www.kalispellchamber.com* 🎫 *Free* ⏲ *Daily dawn–dusk.*

Inside the historic **Great Northern Depot** is visitor information from the Kalispell Chamber of Commerce and the Flathead Convention and Visitors Bureau. Outside is the lovely Depot Park, where live music, arts shows, a gazebo, picnicking, and a playground attract both locals and travelers. ✉ *15 Depot Park* ☎ *406/758–2800 or 800/543–3105* 🌐 *www.kalispellchamber.com or www.fcvb.org* 🎫 *Free* ⏲ *Weekdays 8–5.*

off the beaten path

LONE PINE STATE PARK – At an elevation of 2,959 feet, you can view Kalispell, Flathead Lake, and the Whitefish Mountain Range from this 186-acre park. Features include a self-guided nature trail, a visitor center, nature interpretive programs, picnic areas, horse trails, and an archery range. ✉ *4 mi southwest of Kalispell on Foyes Lake Rd., then 1 mi east on Lone Pine Rd.* ☎ *406/755–2706* 🌐 *www.fwp.state.mt.us* 🎫 *$4 per vehicle* ⏲ *Mid-Apr.–Oct., daily dawn–dusk.*

Sports & the Outdoors

HIKING Every year from May through October, the **Montana Wilderness Association** (✉ 43 Woodland Park Dr., No. 9 ☎ 406/755–6304) organizes free guided hikes in the backcountry. They vary from short wildflower walks to strenuous climbs.

GOLF At one time, a private herd of bison grazed on what's now **Buffalo Hill Golf Club** (✉ 116 N. Main ☎ 406/756–4530 or 888/342–1619) in the heart of Kalispell. This municipal 27-hole course, built in 1936, has tree-lined fairways along the Stillwater River.

At **Northern Pines Golf Club** (✉ 3230 U.S. 93 N ☎ 406/751–1950 or 800/255–5641), the challenging 18-hole links-style course has rolling fairways lined with native grasses and giant pine trees along the Stillwater River.

SKYDIVING Learn the fun of parachuting with **Skydive Lost Prairie** (✉ Lost Prairie Rd.; 40 mi west of Kalispell on U.S. 2 to milepost 87, 4 mi north on Lost Prairie Rd. ☎ 406/858–2493 or 888/833–5867), where annually nearly 500 skydivers make about 7,000 jumps, some at the annual July Boogie event.

TRAIL RIDING Ride on an 800-acre ranch with **High Country Trails** (✉ 2800 Foy's Lake Rd. ☎ 406/755–1283 or 406/755–4711), which also offers evening rides with an old-fashioned steak cookout.

Big Sky Rides (✉ 750 Foy's Lake Rd. ☎ 406/755–7433) leads horse trips along lovely Ashley Creek and conducts old-fashioned hay and carriage rides.

Where to Stay & Eat

$$$–$$$$ ✕ **Cafe Max.** The menu changes frequently in this cozy Main Street café; appetizers, such as Camembert fritters with brandied apricots, are likely to have a French influence, whereas entrées have a Montana twist. Try the buffalo osso buco or fresh wild salmon coated with black-and-white sesame seeds, broiled, and topped with huckleberry chutney. *✉ 121 Main St. ☎ 406/755–7687 ▭ AE, MC, V ⊗ Closed Mon.*

$$–$$$$ ✕ **Painted Horse Grill.** Though the decor here is unusually bland, what's delivered to your table is likely to grab your attention. The calamari tempura is wonderfully tender, and cumin in the chiles rellenos gives the Southwestern appetizer an Indian twist. You can catch up on your vegetable intake here, as the salad greens are the freshest in the area and the cooked vegetables are nicely steamed. You can't go wrong with the creative entrées, including the roast curried duck. *✉ 110 Main St. ☎ 406/257–7035 ▭ AE, MC, V ⊗ Closed Sun. No lunch Sat.*

$–$$ ✕ **The Knead Cafe.** The café's baked goods, including croissants, fresh baguettes, and chocolate cakes, will entice you in, but it's worth your while to stay for a meal—try the curry shrimp or the New Orleans gumbo with shrimp and chicken. The funky, mismatched dining tables and chairs are surrounded by local artwork. *✉ 25 2nd Ave. W ☎ 406/755–7510 ▭ MC, V ⊗ Closed Sun. and Mon.*

$$ **Hampton Inn Kalispell.** This hotel 1 mi west of downtown features an indoor 24-hour guest pool and free extended buffet breakfast. The spacious rooms, Western decor, and river-rock fireplace in the lobby give the place a homey feel. *✉ 1140 U.S. 2 W, 59901 ☎ 406/755–7900 or 800/426–7866 🖷 406/755–5056 ⊕ www.northwestinns.com ⇨ 120 rooms ♢ Refrigerators, in-room VCRs, indoor pool ▭ AE, D, DC, MC, V ꟾ○ꟾ BP.*

$–$$ **Cottonwood Hill Farm Inn.** In this renovated farmhouse, the three elegantly appointed guest rooms have views of the valley and surrounding peaks. Breakfasts, which can be taken outside on the deck, include panfried lake trout, fruits grown on the farm, and fresh baked goods with homemade jams and jellies; you can opt to take lunch and dinner here as well. The location is convenient to golf and water sports. *✉ 2928 Whitefish Stage Rd., 59901 ☎ 406/756–6404 or 800/458–0893 🖷 406/756–8507 ⊕ www.cottonwoodhillfarm.com ⇨ 3 rooms ♢ Dining room, room service, in-room data ports, in-room VCRs, bicycles, badminton, croquet, business services; no a/c, no kids under 12, no smoking ▭ AE, MC, V.*

$–$$ **WestCoast Kalispell Center Hotel.** Attached to the downtown Kalispell Center Mall, this hotel has large, modern rooms and a solarium pool. The restaurant is well lighted by an atrium ceiling. *✉ 20 N. Main St., 59901 ☎ 406/751–5050 or 800/325–4000 🖷 406/751–5051 ⊕ www.westcoasthotels.com ⇨ 132 rooms ♢ Restaurant, indoor pool, lounge, casino, business services, meeting rooms, free parking ▭ AE, D, DC, MC, V.*

CAMPING ⛺ **Glacier Pines RV Park.** This spacious campground set among pines has paved roads and no maximum size limit or time limit. There are no tent sites. *♢ Flush toilets. Full hookups, dump station. Drinking water, guest laundry, showers. Fire pits, picnic tables. Electricity, public telephone. General store, play area, swimming (pool) ⇨ 75 full hookups ✉ 1850 Rte. 35 E, 1 mi east of Kalispell ☎ 406/752–2760 or 800/533–4029 Full hookups $24 ▭ MC, V ⊗ Mid-Apr.–Oct.*

Nightlife & the Arts

THE ARTS Live performances take place each Tuesday and Wednesday from 11:30 to 1:30 at **Depot Park** (✉ 1 Depot Park ☎ 406/758–7718). Performers vary from a one-man blues band to Montana mytho-poet entertainer Jack Gladstone.

Every October, the **Glacier Jazz Stampede** (✉ 1705 E. 2nd St., Whitefish 59937 ☎ 406/863–3812 or 888/888–2308 🌐 www.kalispellchamber.com/jazz) brings 15 toe-tapping jazz bands to several venues around downtown Kalispell for four days of live music.

Voices of the mountains blend at concerts by the **Glacier Orchestra and Chorale** (✉ 140 Main St. ☎ 406/257–3241), held in several venues around Kalispell and Whitefish.

NIGHTLIFE Cowboy boots and sneakers shift the sawdust on the floor at **Moose's Saloon** (✉ 173 N. Main ☎ 406/755–2337), where tunes from the jukebox get the raucous crowd moving. You can order pizza to go with your beer.

Shopping

Browse through the large selection of Montana authors in **Books West** (✉ 101 Main St. ☎ 406/752–6900 or 800/471–2270), where you will find Western Americana, gifts, and U.S. Geological Survey maps.

Noice Studio and Gallery (✉ 127 Main St. ☎ 406/755–5321) features ongoing exhibits of paintings, sculpture, fiber arts, and photography by Montana artists such as Rudy Autio, Russell Chatham, and Marshall Noice, in a lovingly restored turn-of-the-20th-century building.

Sportsman Ski Haus (✉ U.S. 2 and U.S. 93 ☎ 406/755–6484 or 406/862–3111) is a good place to pick up skis, outdoor gear, clothing, and fishing tackle. It also has a store in Whitefish's Mountain Mall.

A scenic drive between Kalispell and Whitefish is the **Whitefish Stage Rd.** (✉ 1 mi east of U.S. 93). The two-lane route passes forested hills and farmland and makes a fine bike ride, although shoulders are not especially large. If you're driving, expect to go slowly, as farm traffic and bicyclers share the road.

Whitefish

18 *15 mi north of Kalispell via U.S. 93.*

The sporty resort town of 5,000 is recognized as a mecca for golfing, lake recreation, hiking, mountain biking, and skiing. Early settlers came a century ago to farm or join the timber or railroad industries. Named for the 2- by 7-mi Whitefish Lake where Native Americans caught and dried whitefish, the town sits at the base of Big Mountain Ski and Summer Resort. Nine lifts serve 3,000 acres of powder skiing and provide outstanding winter and summer views into Glacier National Park and the Canadian Rockies.

Summer on the **Big Mountain** attracts hikers for the Danny On Trail to the mountain summit, which can be accessed on the Glacier Chaser chairlift. Numerous other activities, including a kids' bike academy, art treks, and nighttime stargazing events, have become popular. Additionally, you can rent mountain scooters, try a 9-hole folf (Frisbee golf) course, and walk in the trees along an 800-foot path in the treetops, 60 feet above the forest floor. Mountain-bike trails, a nature center, and a few gift shops and restaurants remain open June–September. 📭 *Box 1400, Whitefish*

59937 ☎ 406/862–1900 or 800/858–4152 📠 406/862–2922 🌐 www.skiwhitefish.com ⏲ Mid-June–mid-Sept., daily 9–4:30.

If you want to check out a cross section of American life, drop by the Whitefish train station at 6 AM as a sleepy collection of farmers, cowboys, and skiers awaits the arrival of Amtrak's *Empire Builder*, en route from Seattle to Chicago. Next to the half-timber depot is the **Stumptown Historical Society's Museum.** The focus here is the Great Northern Railway, the nation's first unsubsidized transcontinental railway that passed through Whitefish. On display are lanterns, old posters, and crockery, as well as reminders of local history, such as the books of author Dorothy M. Johnson and photos of the Whitefish football team from 1922 through 1954. You can pick up a walking-tour map of Whitefish's historic district here. *✉ 500 Depot St. ☎ 406/862–0067 🎟 Donations accepted ⏲ June–Sept., Mon.–Sat. 10–4; Oct.–May, Mon.–Sat. 11–3.*

Sports & the Outdoors

BICYCLING Of the 2,000 mi of county roads in the area, only 400 mi are paved, leaving dirt and gravel roads and innumerable trails open for discovery. You can rent bikes suitable to the terrain at **Glacier Cyclery** (✉ 326 E. 2nd St. ☎ 406/862–6446 🌐 www.glaciercyclery.com). Monday-night group rides begin at the shop courtyard and lead to a variety of trails of varying degrees of difficulty. Bike maps, gear, and free air are available at this full-service shop.

CANOEING You can paddle the Whitefish River Canoe Trail in your own boat or rent one from **Ski Mountain Sports** (✉238 Central Ave. ☎406/862–7541). The trail begins at Whitefish lake and ends at a take-out spot at the Highway 40 bridge. Be sure to arrange a shuttle back to town if you don't want to return upstream.

DOGSLEDDING The dogs are raring to run at **Dog Sled Adventures** (✉U.S. 93, 20 mi north of Whitefish, 2 mi north of Olney ☎ 406/881–2275 🌐 www.dogsledadventuresmt.com). Your friendly musher will take care to make the ride suit anyone from kids to senior citizens; bundled up in a sled, you'll be whisked through Stillwater State Forest on a 1½-hour ride over a 12-mi trail.

GOLF The 27-hole **Whitefish Lake Golf Club** (✉ 1200 U.S. 93 W ☎ 406/862–4000 or 406/862–5960) had its modest beginning as an airstrip. Reservations are required for the championship course.

FISHING Toss a fly on one of the region's trout streams or lakes and you might snag a west slope cutthroat, rainbow trout, or grayling. By winter, you can dangle a line through a sawed hole in the ice of Whitefish Lake. The best place for fishing gear in Whitefish is **Lakestream Fly Fishing Shop** (✉334 Central Ave. ☎ 406/862–1298). Guided trips to secluded private lakes, equipment, and fly-fishing gear are sold at the shop. Advice is free. The **Tally Lake Ranger District** (☎ 406/863–5400) can recommend good fishing spots.

SNOWMOBILING There are more than 200 groomed snowmobile trails in the Flathead region. Unless you are an experienced snowmobiler and expert at avalanche forecasting, you should take a guided trip. **Extreme Motorsports** (✉ 803 Spokane Ave. ☎ 406/862–8594) rents machines and clothing and leads guided tours.

Downhill Skiing & Snowboarding

The **Big Mountain Ski and Summer Resort** has been one of Montana's top ski areas dating back to 1930s—so why hasn't it grown much in all that time? Perhaps for lack of a sexy name, for starters: the Big Mountain, near Whitefish, on Flathead National Forest—how enticing does that sound? The ski resort is 8 mi from Whitefish and remains comfortably small; it's popular among train travelers from the Pacific Northwest and the upper Midwest.

The mountain's most distinctive features are its widely spaced trees, which—when encased in snow—are known as snow ghosts. With 3,000 skiable acres, plus out-of-bounds areas for Sno-Cat skiing, the Big Mountain offers a lot of terrain to explore and many different lines to discover among those widely spaced trees. The pleasure of exploration and discovery—such as finding a fresh cache of powder many days after a snowstorm—is perhaps the main reason to ski the Big Mountain. Easy discovery comes with the help of free mountain tours by mountain ambassadors. They meet intermediate skiers near the bottom of the main quad chair, Glacier Chaser, at 10:30 AM and 1:30 PM daily.

In general, the pitch is in the intermediate to advanced-intermediate range; there's not a whole lot of super-steep or super-easy skiing. A sameness in pitch, however, doesn't mean a sameness in skiing. With trails falling away on all sides of the mountain, there is a tremendous variation in exposure and hence in snow texture; also take into consideration the number of trees to deal with and the views (the best being northeast toward Glacier National Park).

One of the Big Mountain's best features is its long high-speed quad, the Glacier Chaser, meaning that runs using most of the mountain's 2,300-foot vertical are interrupted by less than 10 minutes of lift-riding time. A negative is weather. Foggy days are not uncommon; at those times you're thankful that those snow ghosts are around as points of reference. *Box 1400, 59937 ☎ 406/862–1900 or 800/858–4152 📠 406/862–2922 🌐 www.skiwhitefish.com 🕒 Thanksgiving–early Apr., daily 9–4:30.*

FACILITIES 2,500-foot vertical drop; 3,000 skiable acres; 25% beginner, 50% intermediate, 25% advanced; 2 high-speed quad chairs, 1 quad chair, 4 triple chairs, 1 double chair, 3 surface lifts. Snow report (☎ 406/862–7669 or 800/847–4868).

LESSONS & PROGRAMS Group instruction in downhill is offered for $30 for a half day (plus a lift ticket); cross-country, telemark skiing, and snowboarding lessons are also available. Specialty clinics such as racing, mogul, and telemark techniques are provided, as well as children's programs. For information call the **Ski and Snowboard School** (☎ 406/862–2909).

LIFT TICKETS $47. $14 night skiing (mid-December–March, Wednesday–Saturday 4:30–9).

RENTALS Full rental packages (skis, boots, and poles) start at $22 per day. Snowboard rentals start at $28 per day.

Nordic Skiing

BACKCOUNTRY SKIING Because of an unusually liberal policy regarding skiing out-of-bounds, backcountry tours are possible from the top of the Big Mountain. For the most part, the Big Mountain ski patrol does not prevent skiers from crossing ski-area boundary ropes, although if you do so and get into trouble, you're responsible for paying rescue costs. Although the avalanche danger (*very* relatively speaking) is usually not high around the Big Mountain, the chances of getting lost are. It is easy to ski too far down the wrong drainage, creating the prospect of a tiring and excruciating bushwhack back to the base. For an introduction to the nearby backcountry, you might want to try the Big Mountain's Sno-Cat-skiing operation, in the **Ski and Snowboard School** (☎ 406/862–2909), which takes skiers for as little as $60 per person plus a lift ticket on a four-hour off-piste adventure.

TRACK SKIING There are two machine-groomed track systems in the Whitefish area: both systems serve their purpose well enough, but don't expect inspiring views or a sense of wilderness seclusion. One advantage that **Glacier Nordic Touring Center** (✉ 1200 U.S. 93 W ☎ 406/881–4230 for snow report) on Whitefish Lake Golf Course has is that 2.8 km (1.6 mi) of its 12 km (7 mi) of groomed trail is for night skiing. A $3-per-person donation is suggested. Rentals, lessons, and trail maps are available at the **Outback Ski Shack** (☎ 406/862–9498). The **Big Mountain Nordic Center** (☎ 406/862–2946) has its own 16 km (9.6 mi) of groomed trails; the daily fee is $5. Rentals and trail maps are available at **Outpost on Big Mountain lodge** (☎ 406/862–2946). Arrangements for cross-country lessons can be made through the **Ski and Snowboard School** (☎ 406/862–2909).

Where to Stay & Eat

For lodging at the base of the Big Mountain Ski and Summer Resort, contact **central reservations** (☎ 800/858–4152), which handles everything from upscale Kandahar Lodge to dormitorylike Alpinglow Inn and various condominiums.

$$–$$$$ ✕ **Tupelo Grille.** In homage to Louisiana, native son and chef-owner Pat Carloss cooks up fine dishes such as crawfish cakes, fried catfish, Acadian-style orange roughy, and creole chicken and dumplings. Carloss rotates his well-chosen art collection in the dining room and further enlivens the atmosphere with piped-in New Orleans jazz, Dixieland, or zydeco music. *✉ 17 Central Ave. ☎ 406/862–6136 ▭ AE, MC, V ⊙ No lunch.*

$–$$$$ ✕ **Whitefish Lake Golf Club Restaurant.** In the historic clubhouse on the municipal golf course, dine on such fresh fish dishes as halibut steak wrapped in herbs and phyllo dough, baked and served with garlic mashed potatoes. Hand-cut steaks, prime rib, and vegetarian pasta dishes are prepared with flair. You can also get a burger at the bar. *✉ 1200 U.S. 93 N ☎ 406/862–5285 ⚠ Reservations essential ▭ AE, D, DC, MC, V ⊙ No lunch.*

$–$$$ ✕ **Truby's.** Individual-size, wood-fired gourmet pizzas are the specialty here, but there are also options such as a Gorgonzola burger and hickory-smoked baby back ribs. On a warm evening, diners fill the patio garden area. The smoke-free bar has seven beers on tap, from the local Black Star brews to Guinness. *✉ 15 Central Ave. ☎ 406/862–4979 ⊙ No lunch Sun.*

$–$$$ ✕ **Wasabi Sushi Bar.** Not your typical Western ski-town eatery, Wasabi is an East-meets-West experience, serving Japanese cuisine in a relaxed, irreverent setting with pale green walls, a salmon-egg-orange ceiling, and rock and roll and reggae on the sound system. The fish may not be up to Tokyo standards, but it's more than passable for the northern Rockies, and there are other good options if you prefer your meal cooked, including tempura-fried soft-shell crab and chicken teriyaki with rice. *✉ 419 E. 2nd St. ☎ 406/863–9283 ▭ AE, MC, V ⊙ No lunch. Closed Mon.*

¢–$ ✕ **Buffalo Cafe.** For the classic small-town café experience, this is the place.
Fodor's Choice ★ Locals and visitors happily coexist in a casual, friendly atmosphere as they dig into well-prepared breakfasts and lunches. (There's no dinner served.) You can start your day with pancakes ("bigger than bowling balls," the menu brags, but considerably lighter), biscuits and gravy, or any of a dozen egg dishes. At lunchtime, it's burgers, salads, grilled sandwiches, and Tex-Mex-style burritos and tacos. This is comfort food at its best—familiar, filling, delicious, and served with a smile. *✉ 516*

Third St. ☎ *406/862–2833* ⚠ *Reservations not accepted* ▭ *AE, MC, V* ⊙ *No dinner.*

¢ ✕ **Montana Coffee Traders.** Coffees, fresh roasted locally, pastries, and homemade gelato are favorites at this downtown hangout. Unique hand-painted furniture, gifts, and bulk coffees and teas line the brick walls. Browse through the Saddest Pleasure Bookstore in the back of the café for local works, used tomes, and cards. ✉ *110 Central Ave.* ☎ *406/862–7667* ⚠ *Reservations not accepted* ▭ *AE, MC, V.*

$$$–$$$$ ✕ **Kandahar–The Lodge at Big Mountain.** Cafe Kandahar, the small, rustic dining room in this lovely mountain lodge, serves the finest meals on the mountain. In addition to dressed-up standards such as tournedos of beef and New York strip steak, you can choose from game dishes such as roast quail and elk rib chops, all prepared with a French provincial touch. In the rest of the lodge, the massive lobby fireplace and the Snug Bar are attractive public spaces, and the wood-accented guest rooms feature down comforters and cut velvet duvets. You can catch a free two-minute shuttle to the slopes, then ski back to the lodge. ✉ *3824 Big Mountain Rd.* ☎ *406/862–6247 (café) or 800/862–6094* 📠 *406/862–6095* 🌐 *www.kandaharlodge.com* ⇐ *49 rooms* ♨ *Restaurant, in-room data ports, some kitchens, hot tub, mountain bikes, hiking, cross-country skiing, downhill skiing, ski storage, sleigh rides, bar, shop, laundry facilities, meeting rooms, airport shuttle, free parking; no smoking* ▭ *AE, D, MC, V* 🍽 *BP* ⊙ *No lunch. Closed mid-Apr.–May and Oct.–late Nov.*

$$$$ **Kintla Lodge.** This deluxe condo at the base of Big Mountain's beginner runs is reminiscent of the grand lodges of Glacier Park—in fact, it's named for one of the park's lakes. Wood accents, slate and carpeted floors, rustic decor, and ski-in, ski-out access make Kintla a top property on the mountain. Fireplaces, pine furniture, down comforters, and large windows all give the lodge a cozy feel. There's underground parking, and you'll be within walking distance of restaurants. ✉ *3910 Big Mountain Rd., 59937* ☎ *406/862–2900 or 800/858–3830* 📠 *406/862–1969* 🌐 *www.stayatbigmountain.com* ⇐ *20 rooms* ♨ *Kitchens, microwaves, refrigerators, cable TV, outdoor hot tub, sauna, mountain bikes, cross-country skiing, downhill skiing, ski storage, shop, laundry facilities, airport shuttle; no smoking.*

$$–$$$ **Grouse Mountain Lodge.** On the edge of Whitefish, people check in here and then go out and do something, whatever the season. Public tennis courts and cross-country trails border the lodge, and there's a 36-hole golf course right next door. Off-season you can book some bargain activity packages. The thoroughly modern lodge has a sunny lounge area with a lacquered slate floor, elk-horn chandeliers, soft-cushioned furniture, and a tall fireplace. Guest rooms are less refined but have standard modern furnishings, cable TV, and coffeemakers. The loft units with kitchenettes are good choices for families. ✉ *2 Fairway Dr., 59937* ☎ *406/862–3000 or 800/321–8822* 📠 *406/862–0326* 🌐 *www.grmtlodge.com* ⇐ *133 rooms, 12 suites* ♨ *Restaurant, indoor pool, outdoor hot tubs, bicycles, cross-country skiing, downhill skiing, ski storage, bar, lounge, recreation room, baby-sitting, business services, meeting rooms, airport shuttle, car rental* ▭ *AE, D, DC, MC, V.*

★ $$–$$$ **Hidden Moose Lodge B&B.** At the foot of the road that climbs to Big Mountain, this two-story log lodge makes a great place for unwinding among the ski memorabilia. Some of the rooms have their own Jacuzzis, and there's one outdoors as well. Rooms are individually decorated with rough-hewn pine furniture and ironwork, and each has its own entrance off a small deck. The living room's vaulted ceiling creates space for plenty of light and a 20-foot-high fireplace. In the evening, a glass of wine or bottle of locally brewed beer is on the house, which can be quite social, especially in summer. ✉ *1735 E. Lakeshore Dr., 59937* ☎ *406/862–6516* 📠 *406/862–6514* 🌐 *www.hiddenmooselodge.com* *8 rooms* *Refrigerators, in-room VCRs, hot tub, bicycles, meeting rooms; no smoking* 💳 *AE, D, MC, V* *BP.*

★ $–$$$ **Garden Wall Inn B&B.** Most of what you see in this 1923 home is antique, from first-edition books about Glacier National Park to bed linens with lace borders. All rooms are individually decorated and have down duvets. Special extras include a wake-up coffee tray delivered to your room and afternoon beverages and hors d'oeuvres in front of the fireplace. The three-course breakfast in the dining room is served on china from a Glacier National Park lodge. The innkeeper lives on the premises and shares cooking duties with the vivacious owner. The snow bus to the ski resort stops one block away. ✉ *504 Spokane Ave., 59937* ☎ *406/862–3440 or 888/530–1700* 🌐 *www.gardenwallinn.com* *3 rooms, 1 suite* *Dining room, bicycles, cross-country skiing, library, free parking; no room phones, no room TVs, no smoking* 💳 *AE, D, MC, V* *BP.*

CAMPING **Whitefish Lake State Park.** On Whitefish Lake in a shady grove of tall pines, this clean campground is very popular and fills early. It has a shallow bay for swimming, a boat launch, and views of the Whitefish Range. One downside is that trains rumble through at all hours. *Flush toilets, pit toilets. Drinking water. Fire grates, picnic tables. Swimming (lake)* *25 sites* ✉ *State Park Rd.* ☎ *406/752–5501* 📠 *406/257–0349* 🌐 *www.fwp.state.mt.us* *$15* 💳 *AE, D, MC, V* *May–mid-Oct.*

Nightlife & the Arts

THE ARTS The **O'Shaughnessy Cultural Arts Center** (✉ 1 Central Ave. ☎ 406/862–5371) hosts a variety of year-round performances in an intimate theater setting.

Every June the founders-day celebration, **Stumptown Days** (✉ Downtown Whitefish ☎ 406/862–3501 or 877/862–3548 🌐 www.whitefishchamber.org) includes vintage window displays, historical walking tours, fiddlers, and the Stumptown Social.

The wild and the woolly show up in mid-January for the annual **Whitefish Winter Carnival** (✉ Box 1120, 59937 ☎ 406/862–3501 or 877/862–3548 🌐 www.whitefishchamber.org), where you may be chased by a yeti or kissed by a mountain man at the parade. There are activities on the Big Mountain, including a torchlight parade and the Spirit of Winter show by the Ski School. In town, events include snow-sculpting contests and skijoring races (skiers pulled by horse and riders).

Ride your favorite La-Z-Boy or just bring your camera to the **Annual Furniture Race** (✉ 3910 Big Mountain Rd., 59937 ☎ 406/862–2900 🌐 www.bigmtn.com) on Big Mountain Ski and Summer Resort on the last day of skiing every April.

NIGHTLIFE Regional microbrews, herb-crusted pizza, and live funk and reggae most weekends draw a younger crowd to the **Dire Wolf Pub** (✉ 845 Wisconsin Ave. ☎ 406/862–4500). The microbrewery **Great Northern Brewing** (✉ 2 Central Ave. ☎ 406/863–1000) is open for free tastings of seven different beers, including the Black Star Wild Huckleberry. In winter it's open Monday–Saturday 3–7 and in summer Monday–Saturday noon–6.

Shopping

From local history to best sellers, you'll find it at **Bookworks** (✉ 244 Spokane ☎ 406/862–4980), which has a fine selection of kids' books and handmade pottery.

The largest toy shop in northwest Montana, **Imagination Station** (✉ 221 Central Ave. ☎ 406/862–5668) has fun, educational, and creative toys and gifts in all price ranges. It also has a downtown Kalispell location.

Sage and Cedar (✉ 214 Central Ave. ☎ 406/862–9411) sells lotions, potions, massage products, and perfumes.

Columbia Falls

19 *8 mi east of Whitefish via U.S. 93 and Rte. 40.*

Many roadside attractions open during summer between the hard-working lumber town of Columbia Falls and Glacier National Park. Hands down, the most popular place on hot summer days is the **Big Sky Waterpark and Miniature Golf.** Besides the 10 waterslides and golf course, there are arcade games, bumper cars, a carousel, barbecue grills, a picnic area, and food service. ✉ *7211 Hwy. 2 E, junction of U.S. 2 and Rte. 206* ☎ *406/892–5025 or 406/892–2139* 🌐 *www.bigskywaterpark.com* *$18* *Memorial Day–Labor Day, daily 10–8.*

Get lost in the maze at the **Amazing Fun Center**—a circuitous outdoor route made of plywood walls and ladders, with viewing areas where parents can watch their kids (and give directions when necessary). Other attractions include Bankshot Basketball, go-carts, 18 holes of miniature golf, bumper boats in a pond, and a picnic area. ✉ *10265 U.S. 2 E, Coram* ☎ *406/387–5902* *$5* *Memorial Day–mid-Sept., daily 9:30–8:30.*

You've found the vortex of Montana at the **House of Mystery,** a wacky roadside attraction where the laws of physics don't apply and other mystifying phenomena prevail. ✉ *7800 U.S. 2 E, Columbia Falls* ☎ *406/892–1210* *$5* *Apr.–Oct., daily 9–8.*

Sports & the Outdoors

GOLF Flowers and tall pines line the greens of **Meadow Lake Golf Course** (✉ 100 St. Andrew's Dr. ☎ 406/892–8700 or 800/321–4653), where you'll find 18 holes, a pro shop, lodging, a restaurant, and a lounge.

LLAMA HIKES Lead your own llama with **Great Northern Llama Co.** (✉ 600 Blackmer La. ☎ 406/755–9044) on a day trip, overnight trek, or fishing expedition.

Where to Stay & Eat

$$$–$$$$ **Meadow Lake Golf Resort.** As the name indicates, Meadow Lake Golf Course is front and center here. The inn is just a few steps from the pro shop, and the veranda has views of the course, as well as the surrounding mountains and a pond. Condos and vacation homes, with private decks, barbecue grills, fireplaces, and simple, comfortable furnishings, line the fairways. The Sunset Grill specializes in New Zealand rack of lamb. You can dine outside in summer. ✉ *100 St. Andrew's Dr., 59912* ☎ *406/892–8700 or 800/321–4653* *406/892–0330* 🌐 *www.meadowlake.com* *24 rooms, 100 condos, 20 vacation homes* *Restaurant, in-room data ports, some kitchens, some microwaves, some refrigerators, 18-hole golf course, putting green, pro shop, 2 pools, (1 indoor), hot tub, massage, sauna, mountain bikes, billiards, Ping-Pong, cross-country skiing, bar, shop, laundry facilities, concierge, business services, meeting rooms, airport shuttle, no-smoking rooms* *AE, D, DC, MC, V.*

CAMPING **Columbia Falls RV Park.** The in-town location, with tall trees to shelter against the breeze, is convenient to the Big Sky Waterpark, shopping, and the Flathead River. Pull-through spaces are adequate for large RVs.

Flush toilets. Full hookups. Picnic tables. Electricity, public telephone. General store *40 full hookups, 10 tent sites* *1000 3rd Ave. E, on U.S. 2* *406/892–1122 or 888/401–7268* *406/892–2055* *www.visitmt.com* *RV sites $22, tent sites $10* *D, MC, V* *June–Oct.*

Nightlife & the Arts

THE ARTS Rodeos, a parade, sports events, a crafts fair, and local color are all part of the late-July **Columbia Falls Heritage Days** (Nucleus Ave. 406/892–7111 or 406/892–2072 www.columbiafallschamber.com).

The outdoors echoes with the **Summer Concert Series** (Marantette Park on U.S. 2 E 406/892–2072) in the Don Lawrence Amphitheater from mid-June through late July. Types of music vary but are aimed to a broad audience; the Don Lawrence Big Band has a performance every year.

NIGHTLIFE Whether the owner's band is playing on the stage or cowboys are serenading a sparse crowd of locals during karaoke, the **Blue Moon Nite Club, Casino and Grill** (Hwy. 40 and Hwy. 2, Columbia Falls 406/892–9925) is a hoot. The wooden dance floor gets a good scuffing on Western dance and country-swing nights. Two stuffed grizzly bears rear up near the entrance, and other species decorate the large saloon as well.

Shopping

Huckleberry Patch Restaurant & Gift Shop (8868 U.S. 2 E, Hungry Horse 406/387–5000) has been the huckleberry headquarters of the state for 50 years, selling the purple wild berry native to the region in all sorts of varieties, from jams to fudge-encased fruit.

en route

Enter Glacier National Park through the back door by driving the **North Fork Road** (From Nucleus Ave. drive north to the T, turn east and follow North Fork Rd. [Rte. 486]). It's a rutted, bumpy, dusty gravel road that's teeming with wildlife along the North Fork of the Flathead River. The 40 mi to the Polebridge entrance station pass thick forests, some of which burned during fires of 2001. You can opt out early and enter Glacier at the Camas Creek entrance gate and avoid rough roads.

GLACIER NATIONAL PARK

The massive peaks of the Continental Divide are the backbone of Glacier National Park and its sister park across the border, Canada's Waterton Lakes National Park. From their slopes, melting snow and alpine glaciers yield streaming ribbons of clear, frigid water, the headwaters of rivers that flow west to the Pacific Ocean, north to the Arctic, and southeast to the Atlantic via the Gulf of Mexico. The parks embody the essence of the Rocky Mountains, where raw nature dominates. Coniferous forests, thickly vegetated stream bottoms, and green-carpeted meadows and basins provide homes and sustenance for all kinds of wildlife. In the backcountry you can see some of the Rockies' oldest geological formations and numerous rare species of mammals, plants, and birds. The Going-to-the-Sun Road, which snakes through the precipitous center of Glacier, is one of the most dizzying rides on the continent.

In the rocky northwest corner of America's fourth-largest state, Glacier encompasses more than 1 million acres (1,563 square mi) of untrammeled wilds. It came into being under the aegis of President William Howard Taft in 1910. Great Northern Railway baron Louis Hill's "See

America First" campaign drew wealthy Easterners to the new park, where he'd built lodges, chalets, roads, and trails, many of which are still in use today. Along the 720 mi of trails are 37 named glaciers, 200 lakes, and 1,000 mi of streams. Neighboring Waterton Lakes National Park, across the border in Alberta, Canada, covers another 130,000 acres. In 1932, the parks were symbolically unified to form the Waterton-Glacier International Peace Park in recognition of the two nations' friendship and dedication to peace. Both parks continue to be maintained by their respective park's services.

Exploring Glacier

Motorized access to the park is limited, but the few roads can take you through a range of settings—from densely forested lowlands to craggy heights. Going-to-the-Sun Road is the main thoroughfare, snaking through the precipitous center of the park. As you navigate the narrow, curving highway, built from 1922 to 1932, you'll understand why access is restricted. Vehicles more than 21 feet long and 8 feet wide (including mirrors) are not allowed to drive over Logan Pass—a restriction that is enforced at checkpoints at the east and west entrances. Touring cars can take you over the Going-to-the-Sun Road while a driver interprets. Shuttle services will drop off and pick up hikers—useful, since parking at many trailheads is limited. Most development and services are concentrated around St. Mary Lake, on the east side of the park, and Lake McDonald, on the west side. Other islands of development occur in Many Glacier, in the northeastern part of the park; Logan Pass Visitor Center; Apgar Village; and West Glacier. Remember that weather in the mountains can change quickly; snow can fall even in August. Be prepared with extra layers, a hat, and rain gear. If you intend to travel to Canada, be sure that everyone in your vehicle has proper identification. A U.S. driver's license will do for adults; kids traveling with one parent need a notarized letter from the other parent giving permission to enter Canada. If you are traveling with pets, you need proof of immunizations to cross the border into Canada. ✉ *Glacier National Park Headquarters, West Glacier 59936* ☎ *406/888–7800* 🌐 *www.nps.gov/glac* 🎟 *$10 per vehicle for a 7-day permit* ⏲ *Park year-round. Going-to-the-Sun Road's center section closed over Logan Pass Oct.–June. Limited services in winter. Visitor centers: St. Mary mid-May–late Oct.; Logan Pass mid-June–late Oct.; Apgar mid-May–late Oct.; Many Glacier late May–late Sept.; headquarters weekdays year-round.*

A Good Tour

Begin in West Glacier at the entrance station, where you'll receive a free park map, newspaper, and wildlife safety information. Drive to **Apgar** ⑳ ⚑, and enjoy some time on the rocky beach or rent a canoe and paddle on **Lake McDonald** ㉑. Continue driving along Going-to-the-Sun Road on the lake's east shore, making sure to stop at Avalanche Creek, which is the trailhead for the **Trail of the Cedars** ㉒. As you drive farther, **The Garden Wall** ㉓ looms ahead as an impassible rock fortress. The road climbs below its crest to the summit at **Logan Pass** ㉔, where you'll want to take photos of the wildflowers, peaks, and mountain goats that graze here. If you have time, climb to the **Hidden Lake Overlook** ㉕. Continuing your drive east, you'll find several pull-outs, including the **Jackson Glacier Overlook** ㉖. As you drive alongside **St. Mary Lake** ㉗, you'll see the lake campgrounds, visitor center, and the end of the Going-to-the-Sun Road where it meets U.S. 89. Turn south on U.S. 89 for the return trip to West Glacier. Along the way, take a short detour to the **Goat Lick Overlook** ㉘ to catch a glimpse of the white-bearded mountain goats.

If you don't want to drive the Going-to-the-Sun Road, consider making the ride in a Jammer, an antique red bus operated by **Glacier Park, Inc.** (☎ 406/892–2525 🌐 www.glacierparkinc.com). The drivers double as guides, and they can roll back the tops of the vehicles to give you improved views and the sensation of wind on your face. Reservations are required.

TIMING A drive along Going-to-the-Sun Road is a satisfying day trip, though you can easily devote days and even weeks to visiting the park; the more time you have to explore in depth, the more rewarding your experience will be. Watch for weather alerts, as snow can fall in any season. The Going-to-the-Sun Road is generally closed from mid-October through late May.

What to See

⚑ 20 **Apgar.** Entering Glacier National Park at the west entrance, you come to a stop sign about a mile inside the park. If you turn left, you will reach Apgar, on the southwest end of Lake McDonald. Apgar is a tiny hamlet with a few shops, motels, ranger buildings, a campground, a historic schoolhouse, and lake access for swimming, fishing, and boating. In summer, Apgar is the hub of activity for the west side of the park. From November to mid-May, no services remain open, except the weekend-only visitor center. ✉ *2 mi north of the west entrance.*

The small **Apgar Visitor Center** is a great first stop if you're entering the park from the west. You can get all kinds of park information, maps, permits, and books here. The large relief map inside is a model of the park; you can plan your route and get a glimpse of where you're going. ☎ *406/888–7800 or 406/888–7939* 🌐 *www.nps.gov/glac* ⏲ *Mid-May–Sept., daily 8–8; Oct., daily 8–4:30; Nov.–mid-May, weekends 9–4.*

The **Apgar Education Cabin,** next to the visitor center, is filled with animal posters, kids' activities, and maps. ☎ *406/888–7939* ⏲ *Mid-June–Labor Day, daily 2:30–4.*

Baring Falls. For an easy family hike, try the 1³⁄₁₀-mi path from the Sun Point parking area. It leads to a spruce and Douglas fir wood; cross a log bridge over Baring Creek and you arrive at the base of gushing Baring Falls. ✉ *11 mi east of Logan Pass on Going-to-the-Sun Rd.*

Belly River Country. Trailing through both parks, this valley has lovely low meadows and large alpine lakes. Waters from Belly River eventually drain into Hudson Bay. Backcountry camp spots see few human footprints and lots of bear tracks. One trailhead is south of the Chief Mountain Customs Station on Route 17. Another trailhead lies 2 mi north of the station on Canada Route 6, at the Belly River campground. The trails from the campground provide the only access to Cracker (12 mi round-trip), Cosley (15 mi), Glenns (18 mi), Helen (25 mi), and Elizabeth (16 mi) backcountry lakes. ✉ *Rte. 17 to Canada Rte. 6* ☎ *406/888–7800.*

23 **The Garden Wall.** An abrupt and jagged wall of rock juts above Going-to-the-Sun Road and is visible from the road as it follows Logan Creek from just past Avalanche Creek Campground for about 10 mi to Logan Pass. The knife-edge wall, called an arête, was created by massive glaciers moving down the valleys on either side of it. ✉ *Going-to-the-Sun Rd.*

Goat Haunt. Reached only by foot trail or tour boat from Waterton Townsite, this spot on the U.S. end of Waterton Lake is the stomping ground for mountain goats, moose, grizzlies, and black bears. The ranger posted at this remote station gives thrice-daily dock talks, free 10-minute

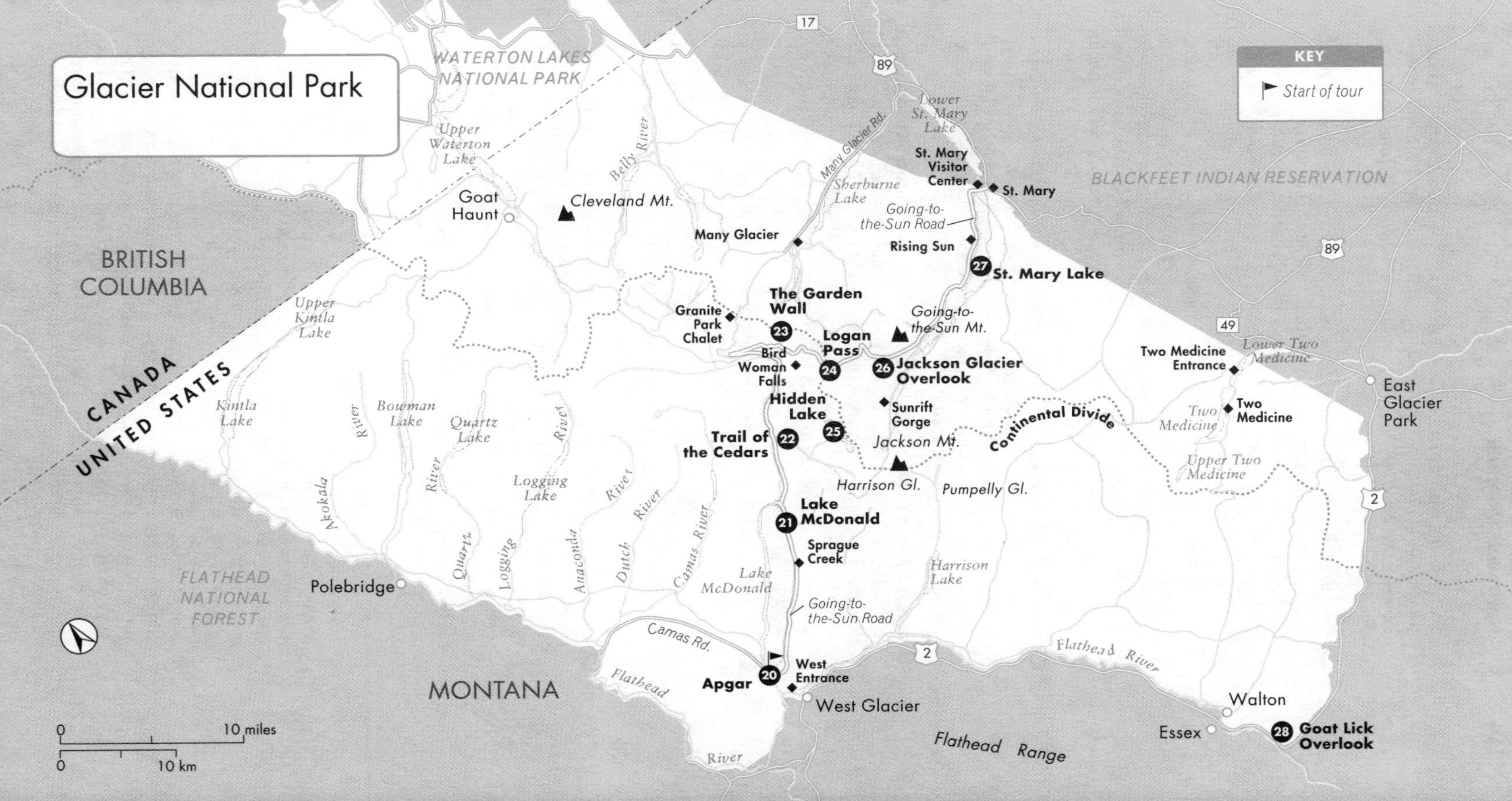

Glacier National Park
KEY
Start of tour
WATERTON LAKES NATIONAL PARK
Upper Waterton Lake
Goat Haunt
Cleveland Mt.
Belly River
BRITISH COLUMBIA
CANADA
UNITED STATES
Upper Kintla Lake
Kintla Lake
Bowman Lake
Quartz Lake
Logging Lake
Akokala
River
Quartz
Logging
Anaconda
Dutch
Camas River
FLATHEAD NATIONAL FOREST
Polebridge
MONTANA
Many Glacier Rd.
Sherburne Lake
Lower St. Mary Lake
St. Mary Visitor Center
St. Mary
Going-to-the-Sun Road
Rising Sun
Many Glacier
27 St. Mary Lake
BLACKFEET INDIAN RESERVATION
The Garden Wall
Granite Park Chalet
23
Logan Pass
24
Going-to-the-Sun Mt.
Bird Woman Falls
26 Jackson Glacier Overlook
Sunrift Gorge
Hidden Lake
25
Jackson Mt.
Trail of the Cedars
22
Continental Divide
Harrison Gl.
Pumpelly Gl.
Lake McDonald
21
Sprague Creek
Harrison Lake
Lake McDonald
Going-to-the-Sun Road
Camas Rd.
Apgar
20
West Entrance
West Glacier
Flathead
River
Flathead River
Flathead Range
Two Medicine Entrance
Lower Two Medicine
Two Medicine
Upper Two Medicine
East Glacier Park
Walton
Essex
28 Goat Lick Overlook
17
89
49
2
0
10 miles
10 km

overviews of natural and human history in Waterton Valley. You can see exhibits in the ranger station, camp, and picnic. ✉ *South end of Waterton Lake* ☎ *406/888–7800 or 403/859–2362* *Tour boat $22* ⏲ *Mid-May–Oct.*

28 **Goat Lick Overlook.** From this highway pull-out, you may see more than a dozen mountain goats at a natural salt lick on a cliff above the Middle Fork of the Flathead River. Take a short, paved trail from the parking lot to the observation point. ✉ *2½ mi east of Walton Ranger Station on U.S. 2.*

Grinnell and Salamander Glaciers. Formed only about 4,000 years ago, these glaciers were one ice mass until 1926, and they continue to shrink. Icebergs often float in Grinnell Lake across from the glaciers. The best viewpoint is reached by the 5½-mi Grinnell Glacier Trail from Many Glacier. ✉ *5½ mi from Swiftcurrent campground on Grinnell Glacier Trail.*

25 **Hidden Lake Overlook.** Take a walk from Logan Pass up to see the crystalline Hidden Lake, which often still has ice clinging to it in early July. It's a 1½-mi hike on an uphill grade, partially on a boardwalk that protects the abundant wildflowers. You'll meet lots of others along the way. ✉ *Logan Pass, Going-to-the-Sun Rd.*

26 **Jackson Glacier Overlook.** As you descend Going-to-the-Sun Road on the east side of the Continental Divide, you come into view of Jackson Glacier looming in a rocky pass across the upper St. Mary River valley. If it isn't covered with snow, you'll see sharp peaks of ice. The glacier is shrinking and may disappear in another 100 years. ✉ *Going-to-the-Sun Rd., 5 mi east of Logan Pass.*

21 **Lake McDonald.** From one end to the other, beautiful Lake McDonald is 10 mi long and accessible year-round on Going-to-the-Sun Road. Take a boat ride to the middle for a unique view of the surrounding glacier-clad mountains. You can go fishing and horseback riding at either end of the lake. Three drive-in campgrounds are along the shore at Apgar, Fish Creek, and Sprague Creek. ✉ *2 mi from the west entrance at Apgar.*

★ 24 **Logan Pass.** At 6,660 feet, Logan Pass, the highest point in the park accessible by motor vehicle, presents unparalleled views of both sides of the Continental Divide. It's the apex of Going-to-the-Sun Road, and a must-see. The pass is frequented by mountain goats, bighorn sheep, and grizzly bears—trailheads spread out from the visitor center to wildlife-viewing points. There are no phones or food services here, so be sure to bring along enough water and provisions for the round-trip. The road and the pass are both extremely crowded in July and August. ✉ *34 mi from West Glacier, 18 mi from St. Mary.*

Built of stone, the **Logan Pass Visitor Center** stands sturdy against the severe weather that forces it to close in winter. Snow often dapples the high alpine terrain around the visitor center late into spring, providing moisture for the summer wildflowers. Park information, books, and maps are stocked inside. Rangers staff the center and give 10-minute talks on the alpine environment. ☎ *406/888–7800* ⏲ *Mid-June–Oct., daily 8–4:30.*

★ **Many Glacier.** On the shore of Swiftcurrent Lake, the historic, Swiss-style Many Glacier Lodge has a restaurant, a bar, a gift shop, and a lovely foyer. You can enjoy the quiet deck overlooking Swiftcurrent Lake. The view of jagged peaks over the lake is worth packing a camera. You can book boat rentals and cruises. Also in the area are a campground, camp store, ranger station, horseback riding outfitter, and several trailheads.

12 mi west of Babb on Many Glacier Rd. *406/888–7800 or 406/732–7741* *June–late Sept., daily.*

Running Eagle Falls. This falls, sometimes called Trick Falls, cascades near Two Medicine and is actually two different waterfalls from two different sources. In spring, when the water level is high, the upper falls join the lower falls for a 40-foot drop into Two Medicine River; in summer, the upper falls dry up, revealing the lower, 20-foot falls that start midway down the precipice. *2 mi east of the Two Medicine entrance.*

27 **St. Mary Lake.** When the breezes calm, the lake acts as a reflecting pool mirroring the snowcapped granite peaks that line the St. Mary Valley. The Sun Point Nature Trail follows the lake's shore 1 mi each way. You can buy an interpretive brochure for 50¢ at the trailhead on the north side of the lake, about halfway between the Logan Pass and the St. Mary Visitor Center. Use it and drop it at the box at the other end of the trail so that it may be recycled. *1 mi from St. Mary on Going-to-the-Sun Rd.*

The park's largest visitor complex, the **St. Mary Visitor Center** has a huge relief map of the park's peaks and valleys. Rangers can answer your questions, and they host a 45-minute slide show program each evening at 8. Traditional Blackfeet dancing and drumming performances are held weekly. The center has books and maps for sale, and there are large viewing windows facing 10-mi-long St. Mary Lake. *Going-to-the-Sun Rd. off Rte. 89* *406/732–7750* *Mid-May–mid-Oct., daily 8 AM–4:30 PM and 8 PM–9 PM.*

★ **Sun Tours.** Ride with Blackfeet interpreters to get a historical perspective on the park and region as seen by the Native American community. Tours depart daily from East Glacier and St. Mary in 24-passenger, air-conditioned coaches. *29 Glacier Ave., East Glacier* *406/226–9220 or 800/786–9220* *www.glacierinfo.com* *Mid-May–Sept., daily.*

22 **Trail of the Cedars.** This ½-mi-long handicap-accessible boardwalk meanders through the westernmost western red-cedar rain forest. The ancient trees are home to numerous small animals, such as chipmunks. Interpretive signs detail the cedars' resistance to fires and other information about the habitat. *15 mi north of Apgar on Going-to-the-Sun Rd.*

Two Medicine Valley. Rugged, often windy, and always beautiful, the valley is a remote 9-mi drive from Route 49 and is surrounded by some of the park's most stark, rocky peaks. On and around the valley's lake you can rent a canoe, take a narrated boat tour, camp, and hike. Be aware that bears frequent the area. You'll find a camp store, a gift shop, and a picnic area here, but no formal lodging. The road is closed from late October through late May. *Two Medicine entrance, 9 mi east of Rte. 49* *406/888–7800, 406/257–2426 boat tours.*

Waterton Information Centre. If you make your way up to Canada, stop here on the eastern edge of Waterton Townsite to orient yourself in Canada's Waterton Lakes National Park. You can pick up brochures and buy maps and books. Rangers are on hand to answer questions and give directions. *Waterton Rd.* *403/859–5133 or 403/859–2224* *403/859–2650* *www.parkscanada.pch.gc.ca/waterton* *Mid-May–mid-June, daily 8–6; mid-June–early Sept., daily 8–8; early Sept.–Oct. 8, daily 9–6.*

Sports & the Outdoors

The **Glacier Institute** (Box 7457, Kalispell 59901 406/755–1211 www.glacierinstitute.org), based inside the park near West Glacier at the Field Camp and on the remote western boundary at the Big Creek Outdoor Education Center, offers year-round field courses for kids and adults. Experts in wildlife biology, native plants, and river ecology lead educational treks into Glacier's backcountry on daylong and multiday programs.

A nearly all-purpose outfitter for the park is **Glacier Wilderness Guides and Montana Raft Company** (✉ 11970 U.S. 2 E, 1 mi south of West Glacier ☎ 406/387–5555 or 800/521–7238 🌐 www.glacierguides.com), which operates daylong to weeklong trips that can combine hiking, rafting, and horseback expeditions.

Boating

★ See the park's larger lakes with **Glacier Park Boat Tours** (☎ 406/257–2426 🌐 www.montanaweb.com/gpboats), which offers cruises on Lake McDonald, Swiftcurrent Lake, Lake Josephine, Two Medicine Lake, and St. Mary Lake. Tours last 45 minutes to 1½ hours. You can also rent rowboats and small motorboats.

Tour by boat with **Waterton Inter-Nation Shoreline Cruise Co.** (✉ Waterton Townsite Marina ☎ 403/859–2362 🌐 www.watertoninfo.ab.ca/m/cruise) on a two-hour trip from Waterton Townsite in Canada, along Upper Waterton Lake to Goat Haunt, Montana. The narrated tour passes scenic bays, sheer cliffs, and snow-clad peaks.

Fishing

Within Glacier National Park there's an almost unlimited range of fishing possibilities, with a catch-and-release policy encouraged. The sportfishing species include burbot (ling); northern pike; whitefish; kokanee salmon; grayling; and cutthroat, rainbow, lake (mackinaw), and brook trout. You can fish in most waters of the park, but the best fishing is generally in the least-accessible spots. A fishing license is free, but it is expected that you familiarize yourself with all park fishing regulations before you use any facilities. Stop by a park office to pick up a copy of the regulations and speak with a ranger. If you want a guide for fly-fishing or hiking, contact **Glacier Wilderness Guides and Montana Raft Company** (✉ 11970 U.S. 2 E, 1 mi south of West Glacier ☎ 406/387–5555 or 800/521–7238 🌐 www.glacierguides.com).

Golf

Glacier Park Lodge (☎ 406/226–9311), in East Glacier, has a 9-hole, par-36 course, as well as a 9-hole pitch-and-putt course. **Glacier View Golf Course** (☎ 406/888–5471), in West Glacier, is an 18-hole course. On the Canadian side of the park, you can play 9 holes at the **Waterton Golf Course** (☎ 403/859–2114), just outside Waterton Townsite. Don't be surprised if you see moose, elk, deer, bighorn sheep, and other wildlife on the course.

Hiking & Backpacking

Maps for hiking are available at the **Apgar Visitor Center** (☎ 406/888–5441) near the western entrance of Glacier. If you want to backpack, you must pick up a backcountry permit there. Cross-country skiers and snowshoers can pick up maps here, too.

Hiking trails of various lengths and levels are well marked within the park. Novices and those who want the help of an experienced guide can sign up with **Glacier Wilderness Guides and Montana Raft Company** (✉ 11970 U.S. 2 E, 1 mi south of West Glacier ☎ 406/387–5555 or 800/521–7238 🌐 www.glacierguides.com). The most spectacular hiking-and-lodging adventure in the state is the gentle 7-mi **Highline Trail** (Fodor's Choice ★) from Logan Pass to Granite Park Chalet, a National Historic Landmark, which is open for rustic lodging from late July to mid-September. Built in 1914 by the Great Northern Railway, the chalet was one of nine backcountry lodges of which only two remain, the other being Sperry Chalet.

Horseback Riding

Mule Shoe Outfitters (☎ 406/888–5121 or 406/888–5010 ⊕ www.muleshoe.com) runs the horseback riding concession in Glacier from early June to September 15, as the weather allows. Stables are at Lake McDonald and Many Glacier. Trips for beginning to advanced riders cover country both flat and mountainous; all are led by guides who provide information on the park. Rates run from $27 for an hour to $120 for a full day.

Rafting

Glacier Wilderness Guides and Montana Raft Company (✉ 11970 U.S. 2 E, 1 mi south of West Glacier ☎ 406/387–5555 or 800/521–7238 ⊕ www.glacierguides.com) will take you on raft trips through the stomach-churning white water of the Middle Fork of the Flathead and combine it with a hike or horseback ride.

Glacier Raft Company (✉ 11957 U.S. 2 E, West Glacier ☎ 406/888–5454 or 800/235–6781 ⊕ www.glacierraftco.com) is a river outfitter that also rents bikes, snowshoes, and cabins and has a full-service fly-fishing shop. **Great Northern Whitewater** (✉ 12127 U.S. 2 E, 1 mi south of West Glacier ☎ 406/387–5340 or 800/735–7897 ⊕ www.gnwhitewater.com) offers daily white-water, kayaking, and fishing trips and rents Swiss-style chalets with views of Glacier's peaks. **Wild River Rafting** (✉ 12900 U.S. 2 E, 1 mi south of West Glacier ☎ 406/387–9453 or 800/700–7056 ⊕ www.RiverWild.com) offers rafting, trail rides, and scenic fishing trips on rivers around Glacier Park.

Skiing

Cross-country ski excursions reveal mountain views, frozen lakes and streams, and wildlife such as moose, deer, and bald eagles. Glacier National Park distributes a free pamphlet titled "Ski Trails of Glacier National Park," which describes 16 ski trails. On scenic trails such as Autumn Creek near the Continental Divide, **Glacier Park Ski Tours** (☎ 800/646–6043 Ext. 3724) guides custom day trips and winter camping in snow huts or tents.

The 19 mi of groomed track at **Izaak Walton Inn** (✉ U.S. 2, Essex ☎ 406/888–5700 ⊕ www.izaakwaltoninn.com), at the edge of Glacier National Park, nicely combine the pleasures of groomed-trail skiing with the spirit of backcountry skiing with views into the park and the Great Bear Wilderness. Because it's alongside the railroad tracks, it is also accessible from Whitefish by train. Track, touring, and telemark rentals and multiday packages including skiing, lodging, and meals are available. Be careful when crossing the highway between trails.

Where to Stay & Eat

$$–$$$$ ✕ **Lake McDonald Lodge Dining Room.** Pasta, steak, and salmon are standards on the menu here. Don't miss the apple bread pudding with caramel-cinnamon sauce for dessert. The adjoining coffee shop, a cheaper alternative, serves an enormous Indian taco—layers of chili, cheese, onions, tomatoes, sour cream, guacamole, and olives on *bannik,* a flat, fried Native American bread. ✉ *10 mi north of Apgar on Going-to-the-Sun Rd.* ☎ *406/888–5431* ▭ *D, MC, V* ⊙ *Closed late Sept.–early June.*

$$–$$$$ ✕ **Many Glacier Dining Room.** Sophisticated cuisine is served in this early-20th-century chalet. Each night there's a chef's special such as smoked salmon and pasta with a pink marinara sauce or the pork prime rib with a huckleberry demi-glace. For a true Montana creation, have a huckleberry daiquiri. ✉ *Many Glacier Rd.* ☎ *406/732–4411* ▭ *D, MC, V* ⊗ *Closed late Sept.–early June.*

$$–$$$$ ✕ **Prince of Wales Lodge Dining Room.** Enjoy upmarket cuisine before a dazzling view of Waterton Lake in this century-old chalet high on a hill overlooking the lake. Choose from a fine selection of wines to accompany your meal. Every afternoon a British high tea is served in Valerie's Tea Room (with the same great view); true to form, tea includes finger sandwiches, scones and other pastries, and chocolate-dipped fruits. ✉ *Waterton Townsite* ☎ *403/859–2231* ▭ *D, MC, V* ⊗ *Closed Oct.–May.*

¢–$$ ✕ **Curly Bear Cafe & Pizza Co.** Dine outside on the deck, where you can see Glacier's peaks. Buffalo burgers, rotisserie chicken, and pizza are on the menu. Save room for baked goodies or head to the ice cream parlor next door. ✉ *U.S. 89 and Going-to-the-Sun Rd., St. Mary* ☎ *406/732–4431* ✍ *Reservations not accepted* ▭ *AE, D, MC, V* ⊗ *Closed Oct.–May.*

$$$$ 🏨 **Sperry Chalet.** This elegant backcountry lodge, built in 1913 by the Great Northern Railway, is accessible only by trail—either hike in or arrive on horseback. Guest rooms have no electricity, heat, or running water, but who cares when the view includes Glacier's Gunsite peak, Mt. Edwards, Lake McDonald, and mountain goats in wildflowers. Informal meals, such as turkey with the trimmings, are simple yet filling. ✉ *Box 188, Going-to-the-Sun Rd., West Glacier 59936* ☎ *406/387–5654 or 888/345–2649* 🌐 *www.sperrychalet.com* ⇨ *17 rooms* 👍 *Dining room, kitchens, hiking, horseback riding, shop; no a/c, no room phones, no room TVs, no smoking* 🍽 *FAP* ⊗ *Closed mid-Sept.–early July.*

$$–$$$$ 🏨 **Belton Chalet.** This fully restored historic 1910 railroad hotel was the original winter headquarters for the park, just outside the West Glacier entrance. Rooms are cozy and bright, with original woodwork around the windows and period furnishings. Cottages are snug up to the evergreen forest behind the lodge. ✉ *12575 U.S. 2 E, West Glacier 59936* ☎ *406/888–5000 or 888/235–8665* 📠 *406/888–5005* 🌐 *www.beltonchalet.com* ⇨ *27 rooms* 👍 *Dining room, massage, spa, bicycles, cross-country skiing, bar; no room phones, no room TVs, no smoking* ▭ *AE, MC, V* ⊗ *Closed mid-Oct.–Nov. and Jan.–late May* 🍽 *BP.*

$$–$$$$ 🏨 **Glacier Park Lodge.** On the east side of the park, across from the Amtrak station, you'll find this beautiful hotel built in 1913. The full-service lodge is supported by 500- to 800-year-old fir and 3-foot-thick cedar logs. Rooms are sparsely decorated, but there are historic posters on the walls in the halls. Cottages and a house are also available on the ground next to the golf course. If you golf on the spectacular course, watch out for moose. ✉ *Off U.S. 2, East Glacier* 📫 *Box 2025, Columbia Falls 59912* ☎ *406/892–2525 or 406/226–9311* 🌐 *www.glacierparkinc.com* 📠 *406/226–9152* ⇨ *154 rooms* 👍 *Restaurant, snack bar, 9-hole golf course, pool, bar, playground.*

$$–$$$ 🏨 **Izaak Walton Inn.** This historic lodge sits on the southern edge of Glacier and under the shadow of the Great Bear Wilderness. You can ride Amtrak to the back door and stay either in quaint lodge rooms or in unique train cabooses, refurbished for guests. Lodge rooms have knotty-pine paneling, lacy curtains, and simple furnishings. Caboose Cottages (three-night minimum for $575) sleep up to four people and have kitchenettes. In winter, you can ski or snowshoe from the door or head into Glacier with a guide from the inn. ✉ *290 Izaak Walton Inn Rd. (off U.S. 2), Essex 59916* ☎ *406/888–5700* 🌐 *www.izaakwaltoninn.com* ⇨ *33 rooms, 4 caboose cottages* 👍 *Restaurant, mountain biking, cross-coun-*

try skiing, bar, shop, meeting rooms; no room phones, no room TVs, no smoking.

$$–$$$ **Many Glacier Hotel.** The most isolated of the grand hotels—it's on Swiftcurrent Lake on the northeast side of the park—this is also one of the most scenic, especially if you nab one of the balcony rooms. There are several hiking trails nearby, and a large fireplace in the lobby where guests gather on chilly mornings. *Many Glacier Rd., 12 mi west of Babb Box 2025, Columbia Falls 59912 406/892–2525 or 406/732–4411 406/732–5522 www.glacierparkinc.com 211 rooms Restaurant, ice cream parlor, hiking, bar.*

$$ **Granite Park Chalet.** This 1914 stone hut perched on a knoll below the Continental Divide and Garden Wall is reachable only by hiking trail or horseback ride. The 7.4-mi trek is fully worth the effort, because from the balcony, you see Heaven's Peak and Logan Pass and may even watch grizzly bears digging for glacier lily bulbs in a meadow nearby. You pack in your own food and bedding (there's optional linen service for a fee). The innkeeper will help you organize in the kitchen, find a good hiking trail, and watch for wildlife. Guided hut hikes can be arranged through Glacier Wilderness Guides. *Going-to-the-Sun Rd. Box 330, West Glacier 59936 406/387–5555 or 800/521–7238 www.glacierguides.com 406/387–5656 12 rooms Dining room, kitchens, horseback riding, library, shop; no a/c, no room phones, no room TVs, no smoking Closed Labor Day–June.*

$$ **The Great Bear Lodge and Resort at Glacier.** Just outside the park boundary, this full-service resort is a good base for a few days of fishing, hiking, and boating. All rooms have decks, wet bars, sitting areas, and spectacular views of Glacier's peaks. Sparse decor doesn't distract from the view outside. Nearby, the Pinnacle Cottages have river-rock fireplaces, private decks, and barbecue grills. *U.S. 89 and Going-to-the-Sun Rd. Resort at Glacier, St. Mary 59417 406/732–4431 or 800/368–3689 www.glcpark.com 48 rooms Restaurant, café, coffee shop, pizzeria, in-room data ports, some kitchens, cable TV, lake, fishing, mountain bikes, bar, shops, laundry facilities, business services, meeting rooms, no-smoking rooms AE, D, MC, V Closed mid-Oct.–Apr.*

$–$$ **Lake McDonald Complex.** This former hunting lodge on the shore of lovely Lake McDonald offers cabins, which sleep up to four and don't have kitchens, motel rooms outside the lodge, and rooms in the lodge itself. The lobby is decorated with stuffed wild animals. *Going-to-the-Sun Rd. Box 2025, Columbia Falls 59912 406/892–2525 or 406/888–5431 www.glacierparkinc.com 30 rooms, 13 cabins Restaurant, coffee shop, boating, fishing, hiking, bar.*

$–$$ **Village Inn.** On Lake McDonald at Apgar Village, this motel could use some updating but is very popular and offers a view of the lake and surrounding peaks. It's near the lake outlet and good fishing. A restaurant, bar, and coffee shop are nearby. *Apgar Village Box 2025, Columbia Falls 59912 406/756–2444 www.glacierparkinc.com 36 rooms Boating, fishing, hiking.*

Camping

Apgar Campground. On the southern shore of Lake McDonald, this popular and large campground has many activities and services. From here you can hike; boat, fish, or swim in the lake; and sign up for trail rides. Stores and the visitor center are a short walk from the campground. *Flush toilets, pit toilets. Dump station. Drinking water. Bear boxes, fire grates, food service, picnic tables. Public telephone. General store, ranger station. Swimming (lake) 194 sites Apgar Rd. 406/888–7800 or 800/365–2267 www.nps.gov/glac $15 AE, D, MC, V May–Oct.*

Avalanche Creek Campground. Sheltered by huge red cedars and bordered by Avalanche Creek, this campground sits at trailheads and along the Going-to-the-Sun Road. *Flush toilets. Drinking water. Fire grates, picnic tables* *87 sites* *Going-to-the-Sun Rd.* *406/888–7800 or 800/365–2267* *406/888–7808* *www.nps.gov/glac* *$15* *AE, D, MC, V* *May–Oct.*

Bowman Lake Campground. In the remote northwestern corner of the park, this quiet camping spot is a fishermen's favorite for the lake and stream fishing. Mosquitoes can be bothersome here, as can the potholes and ruts in the one-lane drive in from Polebridge. *Pit toilets. Drinking water. Bear boxes, fire grates, picnic tables. Ranger station. Swimming (lake)* *48 sites* *Bowman Lake Rd.* *406/888–7800 or 800/365–2267* *406/888–7808* *www.nps.gov/glac* *$12* *AE, D, MC, V* *May–Sept.*

Many Glacier Campground. One of the most beautiful spots in the park is also a favorite for bears. Several hiking trails take off from here, and often ranger-led hikes climb to Grinnell Glacier. Scenic boat tours and a lovely lodge are nearby. *Flush toilets, pit toilets. Drinking water, showers. Bear boxes, fire grates, food service, picnic tables. Public telephone. Ranger station. Swimming (lake)* *110 sites* *Many Glacier Rd.* *406/888–7800 or 800/365–2267* *406/888–7808* *www.nps.gov/glac* *$14* *AE, D, MC, V* *May–Sept.*

Rising Sun Campground. As the name says, you can watch the sun rise from your camp, across the peaks and grassy knolls here. The campground is near St. Mary Lake and many hiking trails. *Flush toilets, pit toilets. Drinking water, showers. Bear boxes, fire grates, food service, picnic tables. Public telephone. Swimming (lake)* *83 sites* *Going-to-the-Sun Rd.* *406/888–7800 or 800/365–2267* *406/888–7808* *www.nps.gov/glac* *$14* *AE, D, MC, V* *May–Sept.*

St. Mary Campground. This large, grassy spot alongside the lake and stream has mountain views and cool breezes. It's within walking distance of the St. Mary Visitor Center. *Flush toilets, pit toilets. Drinking water, showers. Bear boxes, fire grates, food service, picnic tables. Public telephone. Swimming (lake)* *173 sites* *Going-to-the-Sun Rd.* *406/888–7800 or 800/365–2267* *406/888–7808* *www.nps.gov/glac* *$14* *AE, D, MC, V* *May–Sept.*

St. Mary KOA. Just outside the park boundary, this full-service campground 1 mi west of St. Mary offers everything from hot tubs to canoe rentals, and there's lots for kids to do. There are barbecue dinners nightly. *Flush toilets. Full hookups, dump station. Drinking water, guest laundry, showers. Food service, picnic tables. Electricity, public telephone. General store. Swimming (pool)* *91 full hookups, 72 partial hookups; 27 cabins* *106 W. Shore Rd.* *406/732–4122 or 800/562–1504* *406/732–4327* *www.koa.com* *Full hookups $37, partial hookups $22; cabins $54–$150* *D, MC, V* *Mid-May–Sept.*

Two Medicine Campground. Situated next to Two Medicine Lake in the remote southeastern side of the park, this is often the last campground to fill during the height of summer. It's not near a town, but a general store, snack bar, and boat rentals are available. *Flush toilets, pit toilets. Drinking water, showers. Bear boxes, fire grates, food service, picnic tables. Public telephone. General store. Swimming (lake)* *112 sites* *Two Medicine Rd.* *406/888–7800 or 800/365–2267* *406/888–7808* *www.nps.gov/glac* *$14* *AE, D, MC, V* *May–Sept.*

Nightlife & the Arts

The annual **Days of Peace and Friendship** (406/888–7800 or 403/859–5133) in early July are filled with special programs, including hikes with rangers and historical presentations celebrating the International Peace Park theme on both sides of the border.

Most campgrounds within Glacier offer **Ranger-Led Evening Programs** (☒ Apgar Rd. ☎ 406/888–7800) nightly or several evenings a week at campground amphitheaters. Check the free *Nature with a Naturalist* newspaper, available at the Apgar Ranger Station.

Shopping

Paintings, photographs, and sculptures by regional artists are available at the **Cedar Tree** (☒ Apgar Rd. ☎ 406/888–5232).

The **Glacier Natural History Association Bookstore** (☒ U.S. 2, West Glacier ☎ 406/888–5756 🌐 www.glacierassociation.org) sells guidebooks, maps, and historical publications at its shop inside the Historic Belton Depot, within the visitor centers of the park, and on its Web site.

Gift shops in the park lodges such as the **Lake McDonald Lodge** (☒ Going-to-the-Sun Rd. ☎ 406/888–5431) sell keepsakes, postcards, books, T-shirts, and sweatshirts.

Montana House of Gifts (☒ Apgar Rd. ☎ 406/888–5393) displays weavings and other works of art by local and regional artisans.

Schoolhouse Gifts (☒ Apgar Rd. ☎ 406/888–5235) sells clothing and high-quality artists' work.

SEELEY–SWAN VALLEY

Squeezed between two magnificent mountain ranges—the Missions on the west and the Swan Range on the east—the glacially formed Swan Valley is littered with lakes, sprinkled with homesteads, and frosted with snow for five months of the year. One road, U.S. 83, winds along an 80-mi course that follows the Clearwater and Swan rivers, popular for boating and fishing—both winter ice fishing and summer trout fishing. Several trailheads lead into the Bob Marshall Wilderness from the Swan Valley. Modern amenities are as sparse as the population. Only about a thousand people reside here year-round, so you are much more likely to encounter a dozen deer than a dozen humans. With that in mind, it's imperative that drivers be on the lookout for deer and elk on the road, day and night. Summer visitors fill campgrounds and the few guest lodges. Winters are quiet aside from snowmobiling and cross-country skiing.

Seeley Lake

㉙ *120 mi south of Glacier National Park via U.S. 2, Rte. 206, and Rte. 83.*

A recreation hub, this community of 1,400 is bordered by a lake, campgrounds, hiking trails, and wildlife-viewing opportunities. Lovely Seeley Lake is the center point of town. The major industry, logging, which began in 1892, is evident on some hillsides. Norman McLean, author of *A River Runs Through It,* wrote about family and fishing on the Big Blackfoot River near here. In winter 350 mi of snowmobile trails rip through the woods. The Seeley Creek Nordic Ski Trails roll across hills and meadows, playing host to races and recreational outings.

Paddling on the **Clearwater Canoe Trail,** along an isolated portion of the Clearwater River, you may see moose and will likely see songbirds, great blue herons, and belted kingfishers. The Seeley Lake Ranger Station has maps and directions to the put-in for the two-hour paddle. ☒ *Rte. 83* ☎ *406/677–2233* 🌐 *www.fs.fed.us/r1* 🎫 *Free* ⊙ *May–Oct.*

Ten days of events celebrate winter during the January **Seeley Lake Area Winterfest,** including a snow-sculpture contest, parade, kids' games, cross-country ski events, snowmobile fun runs, and more. ✉ *Rte. 83 S* ☎ *406/677–2880* 🌐 *www.seeleylakechamber.com* ⏲ *Mid- to late Jan., daily.*

Logging's colorful past is displayed at the **Seeley Lake Museum and Visitors Center,** along with tools of the trade and visitor information. ✉ *Downtown Seeley Lake at mile marker 14.5* ☎ *406/677–2880* 🌐 *www.seeleylakechamber.com* 🎫 *Free* ⏲ *June–Aug., daily 9–5; Sept.–May, by appointment.*

off the beaten path

MORRELL FALLS NATIONAL RECREATION – A 2-mi hike leads to the lovely cascades of Morrell Falls. It is actually a series of falls, with the longest about a 100-foot drop. This is a moderately difficult family hike, perfect for a picnic (although it's wise to remember this is bear country). Maps and travel information are available at the Seeley Lake Ranger District office. ✉ *From Rte. 83, turn east on Morrell Creek Rd. and follow signs* ☎ *406/677–2233* 🌐 *www.fs.fed.us/r1* 🎫 *Free* ⏲ *Daily.*

Sports & the Outdoors

★ You can romp in deep snows on the **Seeley Creek Nordic Ski Trails** at the edge of town. Trails are groomed for skate and classic skiing. Nearby are dogsled trails. The trail systems share a parking lot and covered picnic area where you can join a campfire to warm your toes. ✉ *Forest Rd. 477; from Rte. 83, turn east on Morrell Creek Rd., aka Cottonwood Lakes Rd., and drive 1 mi to trailhead* ☎ *406/677–2233* 🌐 *www.seeleylakechamber.com* 🎫 *$4* ⏲ *Dec.–Mar., daily.*

CROSS-COUNTRY SKIING

You can ski a few kilometers on the **Double Arrow Resort** (✉ Rte. 83 at milepost 12, 2 mi south of Seeley Lake ☎ 406/677–2777 or 800/468–0777), where you may see moose in the willows.

Ski-touring equipment and maps from **Seeley Lake Fun Center** (✉ Rte. 83 N ☎ 406/677–2287) will take you to the winter trails. You can also rent snowshoes here.

DOGSLED RACING

Mushers and their dogs join the late-January **Seeley–Lincoln 100/200 Dog Sled Race** (✉ Forest Rd. 477 ☎ 406/677–3016 🌐 www.seeleylakechamber.com), which dashes through the snowy wooded trails from a dogsled trailhead at Seeley Creek. Spectators are welcome. To get there from Route 83, turn east on Morrell Creek Road (aka Cottonwood Lakes Road) and drive 1 mi to the trailhead.

SNOWMOBILING

Rent snowmobiles or take a guided snowmobile tour with the **Seeley Lake Fun Center** (✉ Rte. 83 N ☎ 406/677–2287), where you can pick up winter maps.

Where to Stay & Eat

$$$–$$$$ ✕ **Lindey's Steak House.** Locals will send you here to watch the sun set over the lake while dining on the only thing on the menu: steak. Select cuts of prime rib, all 16 oz. portions, are served with potatoes, garlic bread, and pickled watermelon rind served family style. ✉ *Rte. 83, downtown Seeley Lake* ☎ *406/677–9229* 💳 *AE, MC, V.*

¢–$$ **The Filling Station.** Friendly folks fill up on the simple food at this diner, which doubles as a bar and casino. Old standards are burgers with fries, porterhouse steaks, and huckleberry barbecue ribs served with baked beans and coleslaw. ✉ *Rte. 83, downtown Seeley Lake* ☎ *406/677–2080* ✍ *Reservations not accepted* 💳 *AE, D, MC, V.*

$$–$$$$ **Double Arrow Resort.** The handsome, 60-year-old log main lodge combines European grace and Western trimmings on a 200-acre spread. The great room's stone fireplace is a guest gathering spot; nearby in the dining room, the sophisticated menu features foie gras salad, lobster and butternut squash ravioli, and rib-eye steak rubbed with cumin and charbroiled. Guest rooms and log cabins are simply furnished with a few antiques and fluffy comforters on brass beds. Historic log homes with antiques, knotty-pine interiors, and modern kitchens are popular with families. *Rte. 83, milepost 12, 2 mi south of Seeley Lake 59868 Box 747, Seeley Lake, 59868 406/677–2777 or 800/468–0777 406/677–2922 www.doublearrowresort.com 3 rooms, 12 cabins, 6 homes Restaurant, in-room data ports, some kitchens, cable TV, driving range, 18-hole golf course, tennis courts, pro shop, indoor pool, hot tub, massage, fishing, mountain bikes, horseback riding, cross-country skiing, sleigh rides, bar, piano, recreation room, shop, playground, laundry facilities, concierge, business services, convention center, meeting rooms, no-smoking rooms D, MC, V.*

CAMPING **Big Larch.** Giant larch trees shade the large site, where fishing and boating are popular. There's a swimming area near the beach, a horseshoes pit, handicapped-accessible picnicking, and marked nature trails. Shopping, laundry, and services are nearby. *Flush toilets. Dump station. Drinking water. Fire grates, picnic tables. Ranger station. Swimming (lake) 50 sites Forest Rd. 2199; 1 mi north of Seeley Lake on Rte. 83, and ½ mi west on Forest Rd. 2199 406/677–2233 406/677–3902 www.fs.fed.us/r1 $10 AE, D, MC, V Mid-May–Sept.*

Seeley Lake Forest Service Campground. This busy campground among tall pines is on the lake, so mosquitoes can be pesky. Groceries, sports rentals, and restaurants are about 4 mi away. Reservations are recommended. *Flush toilets. Dump station. Drinking water. Fire grates, picnic tables. Ranger station. Swimming (lake). 29 sites Boy Scout Rd. 406/677–2233 406/677–3902 www.fs.fed.us/r1 $10 AE, D, MC, V Late May–Labor Day.*

Shopping

Find country fabrics in **Deer Country Quilts** (Rte. 83 406/677–2730), as well as thousands of bolts of flannels, batiks, and cotton in the store's lovely log lodge studio. Ask about receptions for quilters and the annual mid-July quilt show.

Beaver pelts, furs, blankets, and painted buffalo and elk hides hang from walls in the **Grizzly Claw Trading Company** (Rte. 83 406/677–0008 or 888/551–0008). Other one-of-a-kind items also are available, including pottery, jewelry, clothing, wood carvings, and furniture.

Holland Lake

30 *19 mi north of Seeley Lake via Rte. 83.*

This 400-acre lake is home to kokanee salmon, rainbow trout, and bull trout—kept company by the handful of people who run Holland Lake Lodge. There's a campground, and numerous trails depart from the lake area—maps are available at Holland Lake Lodge or through the Forest Service office. Some routes climb the Swan Range into the Bob Marshall Wilderness. Popular for cross-country skiing and snowmobiling, the lake is also an ice-fishing spot in winter.

The hike to **Holland Falls** is about 1½ mi from the lodge. The last bit is a steep climb, but it's well worth it for the view. *Holland Lake Rd.;*

from Rte. 83, turn east on Forest Rd. 44 for 3 mi to Holland Lake Rd. ☎ *406/837–7500* 🌐 *www.fs.fed.us/r1* 🎫 *Free* ⏲ *Daily.*

Where to Stay & Eat

$ **Holland Lake Lodge.** When the snow flies, this lodge is nearly buried, which makes for cozy fireside dining and relaxing. The log lodge sits on the lakeshore, where you can ski or snowshoe from the door. In summer, step off the cabin porch for a hike or a swim. Cabins are updated yet rustic. You can dine on trout in the restaurant ($–$$) while watching the wild fish jumping outside. ✉ *1947 Holland Lake Rd., Swan Valley 59826* ☎ *406/754–2282 or 877/925–6343* 📠 *406/754–2208* 🌐 *www.hollandlakelodge.com* *9 rooms, 6 cabins* *Restaurant, snack bar, room service, lake, sauna, boating, fishing, mountain bikes, horseback riding, cross-country skiing, ski shop, lobby lounge, shop, business services, meeting rooms; no room phones, no room TVs, no smoking* 💳 *AE, D, MC, V.*

CAMPING **Holland Lake Campground.** Large trees provide lots of shade for campers near the lake. The spot is popular with outfitters who pack horses into the nearby Bob Marshall Wilderness. Food service is available nearby at Holland Lake Lodge. *Pit toilets. Dump station. Drinking water. Bear boxes, fire grates, picnic tables. Swimming (lake)* *40 sites* ✉ *Holland Lake Rd.* ☎ *406/837–7500 or 406/837–3577* 📠 *406/837–7503* 🌐 *www.fs.fed.us/r1* 🎫 *$12* 💳 *AE, D, MC, V* ⏲ *Mid-May–Sept.*

Bob Marshall Wilderness Area

31 *5 mi east of Rte. 83 via Pyramid Pass Trail, Lion Creek Pass Trail, or Smith Creek Pass Trail.*

The Bob Marshall, Scapegoat, and Great Bear wilderness areas take up 1.5 million rugged, roadless, remote acres within the Flathead National Forest. Preservation pioneer, forester, and cofounder of the Wilderness Society, Bob Marshall pushed Congress in 1964 to create the wilderness area that bears his name. Since then, little has altered the landscape, which runs 60 mi along the Continental Divide. More than 1,000 mi of trails enter the wilderness from near Seeley Lake at Pyramid Pass Trail and Holland Lake at Pyramid Pass, Condon's Lion Creek Pass, and Smith Creek Pass, where hikers are sure to meet outfitters and packhorses. An old airstrip at Shafer Meadows is used for float parties on the wild whitewater Middle Fork of the Flathead.

Information on the Bob Marshall Wilderness is available through the **Flathead National Forest,** which has maps, listings of outfitters and access points, and safety information regarding travel in bear country. ✉ *1935 3rd Ave. E, Kalispell 59901* ☎ *406/758–5200* 🌐 *www.fs.fed.us/r1* 🎫 *Free* ⏲ *Weekdays 8–4.*

A complete list of trails, elevations, and backcountry campsites can be found in the book *Hiking Montana's Bob Marshall Wilderness* by Erik Molvar, available at **Books West** (✉ 101 Main, Kalispell 59901 ☎ 406/752–6900).

off the beaten path

SPOTTED BEAR – At the end of a long gravel road, Spotted Bear is a remote entrance into the Bob Marshall Wilderness. You'll find there a ranger station, outfitter's ranch, campground, swimming, and boating down the South Fork of the Flathead River to the Hungry Horse Dam. ✉ *Forest Service Rd. 38; 55 mi from Hungry Horse on either E. or W. Hungry Horse Reservoir Rd.* ☎ *406/387–3800* 🌐 *www.fs.fed.us/r1* 🎫 *Free* ⏲ *Apr.–Oct.*

Sports & the Outdoors

FISHING Five-day pack and float trips with **Bob Marshall Wilderness Horse Pack and Float Expeditions** (✉ 55 mi from Hungry Horse on either E. or W. Hungry Horse Reservoir Rd. toward Spotted Bear Ranger Station ☎ 406/755–7337 or 800/223–4333) go deep into the backcountry for fly-fishing in the wilderness. This Orvis-endorsed expedition is limited to 12 people per trip.

Wilderness Lodge (✉ West Side Reservoir Rd., 55 mi east of Hungry Horse ☎ 406/387–4051 or 800/256–0580) conducts three-day float and fishing trips in the wilderness area.

TRAIL RIDES Take a day ride or an overnight pack trip into the wilderness with **Diamond R Guest Ranch** (✉ Eastside Hungry Horse Reservoir Rd., 55 mi from Hungry Horse ☎ 406/756–1573 or 800/597–9465). Multiday pack trips with **Glacier Raft Company** (✉ 11957 U.S. 2 E, West Glacier ☎ 406/888–5454 or 800/235–6781) follow trails into the wilderness for campouts, fishing, and observing nature.

Where to Stay & Eat

$$$$ Fodor's Choice ★ **Seven Lazy P Guest Ranch.** A snug haven in a rugged landscape, this 1,200-acre ranch is surrounded by pines and aspens deep in Teton Canyon, an eastern gateway to the Bob Marshall Wilderness. The duplex cabins feel like a second home, with comfortable furniture, wood-paneled ceilings, rough-hewn wainscoting, and picture windows; enveloping sofas and chairs, a large stone fireplace, and more golden wood fill the main lodge. Three meals daily (included in the room rate) are served family-style, and the food is memorable: a sausage-egg-and-cheese bake with homemade muffins for breakfast, grilled lemon-glazed salmon for dinner, and pies just out of the oven. They'll fortify you for a day of hiking, wildlife viewing, or guided horseback-riding (also included in the room rate). In summer, multiday pack trips into the Bob Marshall give riders a glimpse of the Rockies as Lewis and Clark saw them. ✉ *Box 178, Choteau, MT 59422* ☎ *406/466–2044* 🌐 *www.sevenlazyp.com* *3 rooms, 3 duplex cabins* *Dining room, fans, refrigerators, billiards, hiking, horseback riding, piano, airport shuttle, no-smoking; no a/c, no room phones, no room TVs* *V.* *Closed Nov.–Apr.* *FAP.*

★ **$$$$** **Spotted Bear Ranch.** Remote yet upscale, the two-bedroom log cabins here among the evergreens are cozy yet have generator power, flush toilets, showers, fireplaces, and views into the million-plus-acre wilderness. The ranch specializes in fly-fishing expeditions. Dinners are served family style in the historic main lodge, which overlooks the South Fork of the Flathead River. Hearty home-style meals vary from prime rib to grilled salmon. ✉ *55 mi from Hungry Horse on either E. or W. Hungry Horse Reservoir Rd. toward Spotted Bear Ranger Station; winter address 115 Lake Blaine Dr., Kalispell 59901* ☎ *406/755–7337 or 800/223–4333* *406/755–7336* 🌐 *www.spottedbear.com* *5 cabins* *Restaurant, snack bar, boating, fishing, horseback riding, shop, meeting rooms; no room phones, no room TVs, no smoking* *MC, V* *Closed mid-Sept.–mid-June* *FAP.*

CAMPING **Spotted Bear Campground.** Alongside the South Fork of the Flathead River, this remote campground is clean and shaded by tall pines. Grizzly bears frequent the area, so a clean camp is imperative. Trailheads lead into both the Bob Marshall and the Great Bear wilderness areas. *Pit toilets. Dump station. Drinking water. Bear boxes, fire grates, picnic tables. Ranger station. Swimming (river)* *13 sites* ✉ *Forest Service Rd. 38, 55 mi southeast of U.S. 2 at Hungry Horse* ☎ *406/756–5376* *406/758–5390* 🌐 *www.fs.fed.us/r1* *$10* *AE, D, MC, V* *Late June–early Sept.*

NORTHWEST MONTANA A TO Z

To research prices, get advice from other travelers, and book travel arrangements, visit www.fodors.com.

AIR TRAVEL

The region has two principal airports: Missoula International, on U.S. 93 just west of Missoula, and Glacier Park International, 8 mi northeast of Kalispell and 11 mi southeast of Whitefish on U.S. 2. Both are serviced by major airlines; if you're coming from outside the Rockies area, the odds are that you'll have a connecting flight through a larger hub such as Denver, Salt Lake City, or Minneapolis/St. Paul.

Airlines & Contacts **Big Sky** ☎ 800/237-7788 🌐 www.bigskyair.com. **Delta** ☎ 800/221-1212 🌐 www.delta-air.com. **Horizon** ☎ 800/547-9308 🌐 www.horizonair.com. **Northwest** ☎ 800/225-2525 🌐 www.nwa.com. **SkyXpress** ☎ 866/354-8677 🌐 www.skyxpress.ca. **Skywest** ☎ 800/453-9417 🌐 www.skywest.com. **United/United Express** ☎ 800/241-6522 🌐 www.united.com.

Airport Information **Glacier Park International Airport** ✉ 4170 U.S. 2 E, Kalispell ☎ 406/257-5994 🌐 www.glacierairport.com.

Missoula International Airport ✉ 5225 U.S. 10, Missoula ☎ 406/728-4381 🌐 www.msoairport.org.

BUS TRAVEL

Commercial buses that travel along U.S. 93 between Missoula and Whitefish depart daily and stop at several small towns en route.

Bus Information **Rimrock/Trailways** ☎ 800/255-7655 🌐 www.rimrocktrailways.com.

CAR RENTAL

Car rentals are available in East and West Glacier, Hamilton, Kalispell, Missoula, and Whitefish.

Avis Rent-a-Car ☎ 406/257-2727 or 800/331-1212 🌐 www.avis.com. **Budget Rent-a-Car** ☎ 406/755-7500 or 800/527-0700 🌐 www.budget.com. **Hertz Rent-a-Car** ☎ 406/758-2220 or 800/654-3131 🌐 www.hertz.com. **National Car Rental** ☎ 406/257-7144 or 800/227-7368 🌐 www.nationalcar.com. **Thrifty Car Rental** ☎ 406/549-2277 or 800/344-1705 🌐 www.thrifty.com.

CAR TRAVEL

There are certainly more gravel and dirt roads in Montana than paved. Many of the unpaved routes are in good shape, yet you'll need to slow down and, as on any Montana road, be on the lookout for wildlife, open-range livestock, farm equipment, unexpected hazards such as cattle crossing guards, and changing weather and road conditions. Snow can fall any month of the year. In more remote areas, carry an emergency kit with water, snacks, extra clothing, and flashlights. Gasoline is available along most paved roads. However, if you are traveling in more remote areas, be sure to gas up before leaving town. Note that cell phone coverage has increased in the state recently, yet in mountainous terrain, it's unlikely that you will have cell reception.

Statewide Road Report ☎ 800/226-7623 🌐 www.mdt.state.mt.us.

Montana Highway Patrol ☎ 911, 406/388-3190, or 800/525-5555 🌐 www.doj.state.mt.us/department/highwaypatroldivision.asp or www.mdt.state.mt.us.

EMERGENCIES

Ambulance or Police **Emergencies** ☎ 911.

24-Hour Medical Care **Kalispell Regional Medical Center** ✉ 310 Sunnyview La., Kalispell ☎ 406/752-5111 🌐 www.krmc.org. **Marcus Daly Memorial Hospital** ✉ 1200 Westwood Dr., Hamilton ☎ 406/363-2211 🌐 www.mdmh.org. **North Valley Hospital**

✉ 6575 U.S. 93 S, Whitefish ☎ 406/863-3500 🌐 www.nvhosp.org. **St. Joseph Hospital** ✉ 6 13th Ave. E, Polson ☎ 406/883-5377 🌐 www.saintjoes.org. **St. Patrick Hospital** ✉ 500 W. Broadway, Missoula ☎ 406/543-7271 🌐 www.saintpatrick.org.

LODGING

Montana Bed & Breakfast Association ☎ 800/453-8870 🌐 www.mtbba.com. **Montana Dude Ranchers' Association** ✉ 1627 W. Main, Suite 434, Bozeman, MT 59715 ☎ 406/284-9933 🌐 www.montanadra.com. **Montana Innkeepers Association** ☎ 406/449-8408 🌐 www.montanainnkeepers.com.

CAMPING Campgrounds across the region vary from no-services, remote state or federal campsites to upscale commercial operations. During July and August, it's best to reserve a camp spot. Ask locally about bears and whether or not food must be stored inside a hard-side vehicle (not a tent). Avoid leaving pets alone at campgrounds because of wildlife confrontations, and because it's against the rules at most campgrounds.

Montana Fish, Wildlife and Parks ☎ 406/444-2535 🌐 www.fwp.state.mt.us/parks. **U.S. Forest Service** ☎ 406/329-3511 🌐 www.fs.fed.us/r1. **KOA, Kamprounds of America** 🌐 www.koa.com.

MEDIA

NEWSPAPERS & MAGAZINES The only regional newspaper is the *Missoulian,* based in Missoula. Each community has a daily or weekly publication. The statewide magazine of recreation and travel, *Montana Magazine,* is published six times a year.

TELEVISION & RADIO National television affiliates are based in Missoula and Kalispell. Most lodging facilities offer cable TV. You can tune in to local radio stations from most places in northwest Montana. Public radio, KUMF, is based at the University of Montana in Missoula and broadcasts throughout the region. Near mountain passes and other road hazards you'll often see a sign identifying a radio station that broadcasts road information.

SPORTS & THE OUTDOORS

GUIDES & OUTFITTERS When heading into the backcountry, it's best to hire a guide or outfitter who knows the local trails, weather patterns, and unique features.

Fishing Outfitters Association of Montana ✉ Box 67, Gallatin Gateway 59730 ☎ 406/763-5436 🌐 www.foam-montana.org. **Montana Outfitters and Guides Association** ✉ Box 1248, Helena 59624 ☎ 406/449-3578 🌐 www.moga-montana.org.

SKIING Although there is a statewide ski areas' association, the best information for both downhill and cross-country skiing is available through the state tourism bureau. A free winter guide booklet is available as well as detailed information on the Web. For descriptions of many cross-country ski trails throughout the state, pick up a copy of the book *Winter Trails Montana,* by Jean Arthur, which details 40 trail systems in Montana's snowy regions.

Travel Montana ✉ 301 S. Park, Helena 59620 ☎ 406/841-2870 or 800/847-4868 🌐 www.wintermt.com or www.visitmt.com.

TOURS

Some out-of-state tour operators offer Montana trips. Local tour operators, including those listed below, provide a variety of options, including custom trips.

Tour Operators **Adventure Cycling** ✉ 150 E. Pine, Missoula 59807 ☎ 406/721-1776 🌐 www.adventurecycling.com. **Off the Beaten Path** ✉ 7 E. Beall St., Bozeman 59715 ☎ 800/445-2995 🌐 www.offthebeatenpath.com. **Swan River Tours** ✉ Box 1010, Condon 59826 ☎ 877/696-1666 🌐 www.swanrivertours.com.

TRAIN TRAVEL

Amtrak chugs across the Highline and the northwest part of the state, stopping in East Glacier, West Glacier, and Whitefish daily. Specialty tours offer localized trips.

Train Information **Amtrak** ☎ 800/872-7245 🌐 www.amtrak.com. **Montana Rockies Rail Tours** ☎ 800/519-7245 🌐 www.montanarailtours.com.

VISITOR INFORMATION

Glacier Country ✉ Box 1035, Bigfork 59911-1035 ☎ 406/837-6211 or 800/338-5072 🌐 www.glacier.visitmt.com. **Travel Montana** ✉ 301 S. Park, Helena 59620 ☎ 406/841-2870 or 800/847-4868 🌐 www.visitmt.com.**Bigfork Chamber of Commerce** ✉ 8155 Rte. 35, Bigfork 59911 ☎ 406/837-5888 🌐 www.bigfork.org.**Bitterroot Valley Chamber of Commerce** ✉ 105 E. Main St., Hamilton 59840 ☎ 406/363-2400 🌐 www.bvchamber.com. **Missoula Chamber of Commerce** ✉ Box 7577, Missoula 59807 ☎ 406/543-6623 or 800/526-3465 🌐 www.missoulachamber.com.**Whitefish Chamber of Commerce** ✉ 520 E. 2nd St., Whitefish 59937 ☎ 406/862-3501 or 877/862-3548 🌐 www.whitefishchamber.org.

SOUTHERN IDAHO

SUN VALLEY, BOISE, THE CENTRAL MOUNTAINS, THE SNAKE RIVER VALLEY

FODOR'S CHOICE

Anniversary Inn, *Boise*
Burgdorf Hot Springs, *McCall*
Idaho Shakespeare Festival, *Boise*
National Oldtime Fiddlers' Contest, *Weiser*
Rafting on the Payette River, *northeast of Boise*
Sun Valley Ski Resort
Twin Peaks Ranch, *Salmon*

HIGHLY RECOMMENDED

ESTAURANTS

Bardenay, *Boise*
Bistro Off Broadway, *Idaho Falls*
Buffalo Café, *Twin Falls*
Gino's Gelato & Pizzeria, *Boise*
Michel's Christiania, *Ketchum*
Pennay's at River Run, *Sun Valley/Ketchum*
Pines Motel Guest Haus, *Driggs/Grand Targhee Ski Resort*
Pioneer Saloon, *Ketchum*

HOTELS

Billingsley Creek Lodge & Retreat, *Hagerman*
Idaho Heritage Inn, *Boise*
Idaho Rocky Mountain Ranch, *Stanley*
Pennay's at River Run, *Sun Valley/Ketchum*

SIGHTS

Land of the Yankee Fork Interpretive Center, *Challis*
Minnetonka Cave, *Bear Lake*
Morrison-Knudsen Nature Center, *Boise*
World Center for Birds of Prey, *Boise*

By Jo Deurbrouck

SOUTHERN IDAHO IS HOME to the majority of Idahoans. In fact, about a quarter of the entire population lives in and around Boise, the state capital. Most of the rest are clustered in southeastern Idaho between Pocatello and Idaho Falls. What has contributed most to southern Idaho's growth is agriculture, and a big reason for agriculture's success in this semi-arid climate is the massive Snake River. One of the largest rivers in the country, it swings out of Wyoming to arch across the bottom third of the state—dammed, diverted, and drained again and again along the way. Every major town in the state, from Idaho Falls in the east to Nampa in the west, sits on the Snake River or a major tributary.

North and south of the Snake River Plain, Idaho becomes parched and crumpled. The mountain ranges in the southern and central parts of the state can be so dry that sage fares better on the south-facing flanks than do pine trees, and peaks are seldom cloaked in anything more than last winter's snow. But the Owyhees, Lemhis, Centennials, White Clouds, and Sawtooths are perhaps even more lovely in their jagged severity than are the lusher, but far less imposing, mountains of the north.

Exploring Southern Idaho

Southern Idaho is bisected by several interstates. I–84 and I–86 run east–west between Pocatello and Boise, and I–15 passes through Pocatello and Idaho Falls on its north–south trajectory. Head off the interstate in any direction and you leave behind the population centers. You also move into more mountainous country, where winding roads and more unpredictable weather are the norm. This pattern is most noticeable in the central part of the state, where the Snake River Plain gives rise to Idaho's other defining geologic feature, a massive granite structure called the Idaho Batholith, solidified beneath the earth's surface and rammed upward to form the famous Sawtooth Mountains. Here you'll discover much of the state's highest elevations, including its tallest mountain, 12,662-foot Mt. Borah. You can hardly say you've seen southern Idaho if you haven't spent time in both the sage-covered flats of the Snake River Plain and the massive mountains found nearly everywhere else.

Good bets for mountain travel are Highway 55, which heads north out of Boise along the North Fork of the Payette River, through the pretty ski town of McCall and on to parts north; and Highways 75 and 93, which part ways north of I–84, cross paths briefly in Shoshone, and are reunited once again at the struggling mining and ranching town of Challis before veering northeast up the course of the Salmon River and on to the border of Montana. A final bit of southern Idaho to explore is the state's corner of Yellowstone National Park, which it shares with Montana and Wyoming. Idaho's ragged edge of the nation's first national park is completely roadless beyond the end of Cave Falls Road, where you'll find hiking trails, a campground, and a ranger station.

About the Restaurants

The state's larger cities teem with enough chain restaurants and fast-food joints to satisfy the take-no-chances traveler; they're easy to find, usually lined up next to strip malls and clustered near highway exits. Places such as Pocatello, Idaho Falls, Twin Falls, and most particularly Boise also have their share of local favorites. Despite their small size, tourist centers such as Ketchum and McCall are full of international restaurants serving everything from Thai and Indian to Italian and French. In less tourist-focused towns such as Challis and Caldwell expect glass-front cafés and dark-paneled steak houses, with fair prices, generous portions, and, more often than not, made-from-scratch goodness.

Numbers in the text correspond to numbers in the margin and on the Southern Idaho and Boise maps.

If you have 3 days

The giant loop tour connecting Boise to Wood River valley takes in a diverse mix of terrain, from arid desert to alpine forest. On your first day, head east from Boise on Interstate 84 for the two-hour drive to **Twin Falls** 23. Check out Shoshone Falls along the way, and then enjoy lunch in the town's charmingly retro downtown district. In the afternoon you can drive north on scenic Highway 75 to **Sun Valley/Ketchum** 8. Prowl Sun Valley's pedestrian mall, browse in the shops and galleries along Ketchum's trendy main street, or take a ride along the paved bike path that runs north and south of Ketchum. Take advantage of one of the area's fine restaurants, and then sample the nightlife in Ketchum.

On Day 2, drive north on Highway 75 for about 25 mi to Galena Pass, where you can enjoy the view of the jagged Sawtooth Mountains and the meandering Upper Salmon River far below. All along Highway 75 and Highway 21 gravel roads lead to trailheads, so it would be a shame not to go for a hike through this stunning wilderness. End the day in the tiny town of **Stanley** 9, with its awe-inspiring backdrop.

On Day 3, head out on Highway 21, yet another gorgeous mountain road. It takes you through the former gold-mining town of **Idaho City** 12 and back to **Boise** 16–22. The trip takes about three hours, leaving plenty of time to sample some of the capital city's offerings, including the Morrison-Knudsen Nature Center, a virtual tour of the area's ecosystems.

If you have 5 days

If you have a few more days, you can see a lot more of southern Idaho. Start by following the three-day itinerary outlined above. On Day 4 head north on what is one of the loveliest stretches of Highway 55. Join a one-day whitewater raft trip on the Payette River, which ranges from fast to furious. You can spend the night back in Boise. On your last day, head up Highway 55 again, this time all the way to **McCall** 13. On your way, make sure to stop off at pretty Gold Fork Hot Springs for a soak in waters said to have healing properties. Arrive in time to enjoy one of the town's restaurants.

If you have 7 days

With seven days to spend in southern Idaho, you can see most of the region. Start in Boise as described in the three-day tour, heading for **Twin Falls** 23. After spending the night, continue on to **Pocatello** 4, making sure to visit the Museum of Natural History. Head north on I–15 to **Idaho Falls** 3, a good place to stop for your second night. The next day, continue north on I–15 and then northwest on Highway 28, which parallels the Lemhi Mountains, until you reach the intersection of Highway 93 near the town of **Salmon** 15. Plan on spending the night here. On Day 4, head south on Highway 93, perhaps the prettiest drive in the southern part of the state because it runs along the Salmon River, the fabled "River of No Return." When you reach **Stanley** 9, join the above itineraries.

About the Hotels

Southern Idaho is studded with popular sights and crisscrossed by major highways, which means there are plenty of motels. Except in tourist towns such as Sun Valley or Stanley, advance reservations are usually not necessary unless you're looking for a room in a cozy bed-and-breakfast or a few nights in that uniquely Western lodging option, the dude ranch. In general, you can expect all the standard amenities, from cable televisions to coffeemakers. Be aware, however, that hotels using the word "rustic" means all bets are off. Check to make sure that cabin in the woods has electricity and running water.

WHAT IT COSTS

	$$$$	$$$	$$	$	¢
RESTAURANTS	over $22	$16–$22	$11–$16	$7–$11	under $7
HOTELS	over $220	$160–$220	$110–$160	$70–$110	under $70

Restaurant prices are for a main course at dinner, excluding sales tax of 5%. Hotel prices are for two people in a standard double room in high season, excluding service charges and 11% tax.

Timing

Southern Idaho is a land of extremes, with some of the warmest and certainly the coldest climates in the state. Daytime temperatures in Boise can top 100°F in the summer, but there's seldom a lasting snow in the winter. Tiny Stanley, tucked below the jagged Sawtooth Mountains, disappears under its frozen blanket as early as November and doesn't emerge until March or April. Its nighttime temperatures often drop below zero. To a large extent, when you visit depends on where you visit.

If you're traveling throughout the region, the best times to visit this part of the state are summer and fall. In summer, the wildflower-covered mountains make this area extremely popular, whereas the bright-starred nights of autumn see fewer tourists. At lower elevations, summers are hot and dry, but even though the heat begins to fade in September, that parched feeling continues until October and sometimes beyond.

Although many ski resorts open as early as Thanksgiving, snow lovers begin to crowd the towns of Driggs, Sun Valley, and McCall around Christmas. January to early March sees the worst weather but the best skiing. April through early June is the muddy season, and many back roads are closed to prevent them from being damaged by four-wheel-drive vehicles. And one additional detail to keep in mind in this region of extremes: for every 1,000 feet of elevation, the air temperature can change 3 degrees. It adds up fast.

EASTERN IDAHO

Most of the cities and towns in southern Idaho were founded by Mormon pioneers moving up from recently settled Utah before the turn of the last century. Even in the places where the Mormons didn't arrive first, they managed to stick around after others had abandoned this hardscrabble land. They initially hung on by their fingernails as dryland farmers but then, as irrigation projects were completed, found life much easier. To this day, many small east Idaho towns have one large modern building: their Mormon church.

To the east of the Snake River valley, deep in the heavily forested terrain, tiny towns that are little more than crossroads are chock-full of lore about trappers and mountain men. Bear Lake and other sparkling

Getting Into Hot Water

Scientists theorize that the "hot spot" responsible for the geysers of Yellowstone National Park was once positioned beneath what is now Idaho. The entire region is still geothermically active, creating plenty of opportunities for that popular pastime, soaking in hot springs. Quaint little resorts are scattered around the state, including one near McCall and several between Hagerman and Twin Falls. Those in the know favor the less-developed hot springs, places where the hot water bubbling up from the earth is captured in shallow pools or narrow gullies (sometimes with a little assistance from a sheet of plastic or some carefully stacked rocks). If you're interested in hot potting, as some call soaking in these natural pools, ask the locals. It's great to find a pool where you can soak in complete solitude.

Riding the Rapids

Idaho has more white water than any other state in the country, and much of it runs through parts of southern Idaho that are not accessible by road. If you want to challenge these waters, all you have to do is grab your camera. The dozens of outfitters will handle the rest, leaving you to enjoy this once-in-a-lifetime experience. The Main Salmon, Lower Salmon, Owyhee, Jarbidge, and Bruneau rivers are all wilderness white water. Plan on spending three to six days running the rapids.

---

waters attract anglers for blue-ribbon fishing. Hot springs, a spurting geyser, and meandering caves are among the geologic phenomena luring visitors to Lava Hot Springs, Soda Springs, and other small towns tucked in this corner of the state. To the west are eerie remains of spatter cones, lava flows, and other volcanic features that pockmark the arid Snake River plateau.

If you're coming from Wyoming, or you just want to see some of the state's most beautiful countryside, a good place to start a tour of eastern Idaho is on U.S. 20 in West Yellowstone, Montana, which dips down to Island Park, Idaho. Pristine Lower and Upper Mesa Falls are the main attractions along the Mesa Falls Scenic Byway, otherwise known as Highway 47. Continue south until you reach the Teton Scenic Byway (Highway 32); then turn onto Highway 31 as it ambles through Tetonia, Driggs, and Victor. Strictly a farming and ranching region until the Grand Targhee ski resort was built just across the Wyoming border in 1969, it now has something of a split personality. Continue south on Highway 31 through the Snake River valley, one of the state's most beautiful drives in any season. In winter, hoofprints of elk, deer, and smaller animals zigzag across the hills. In spring and summer, wildflowers coat the gentle slopes. At Swan Valley, you'll meet up with U.S. 26, which crosses the Snake River and continues into Idaho Falls.

Island Park

❶ *20 mi south of the Montana border via Hwy. 20.*

Full of woodsy cabins, Island Park is a weekend playground for residents of Idaho Falls and, to a lesser extent, Salt Lake City. Snowmobiles are a popular means of transportation in winter, and off-road vehicles and powerboats are everywhere in summer. More a series of

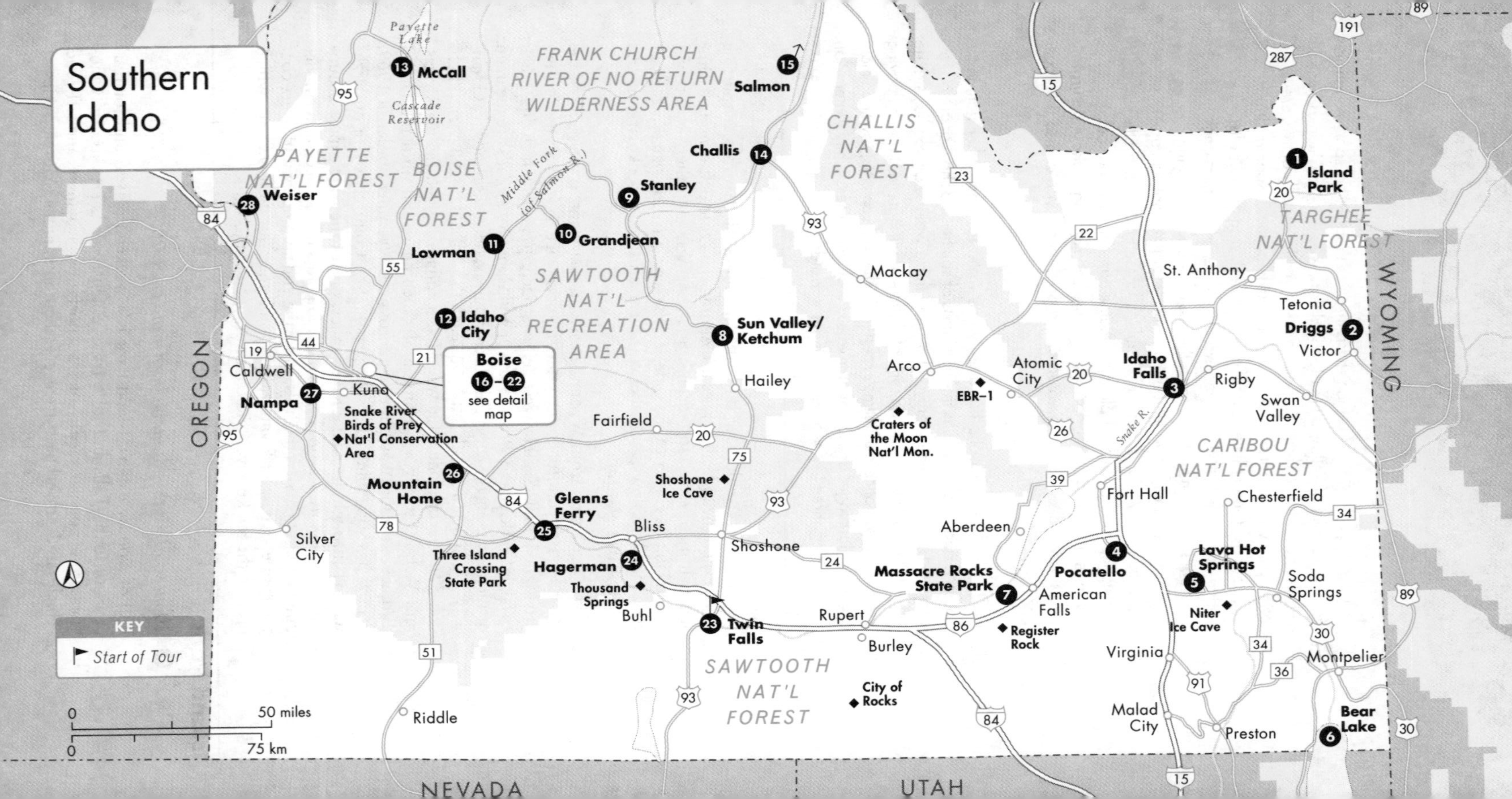
Southern Idaho
KEY
Start of Tour
0 50 miles
0 75 km
FRANK CHURCH RIVER OF NO RETURN WILDERNESS AREA
PAYETTE NAT'L FOREST
BOISE NAT'L FOREST
SAWTOOTH NAT'L RECREATION AREA
CHALLIS NAT'L FOREST
TARGHEE NAT'L FOREST
CARIBOU NAT'L FOREST
SAWTOOTH NAT'L FOREST
OREGON
NEVADA
UTAH
WYOMING
Payette Lake
Cascade Reservoir
Middle Fork (of Salmon R.)
Snake R.
1 Island Park
2 Driggs
3 Idaho Falls
4 Pocatello
5 Lava Hot Springs
6 Bear Lake
7 Massacre Rocks State Park
8 Sun Valley/ Ketchum
9 Stanley
10 Grandjean
11 Lowman
12 Idaho City
13 McCall
14 Challis
15 Salmon
Boise 16–22 see detail map
23 Twin Falls
24 Hagerman
25 Glenns Ferry
26 Mountain Home
27 Nampa
28 Weiser
Caldwell
Kuna
Snake River Birds of Prey Nat'l Conservation Area
Fairfield
Silver City
Three Island Crossing State Park
Thousand Springs
Buhl
Riddle
Bliss
Shoshone
Shoshone Ice Cave
Hailey
Mackay
Arco
Craters of the Moon Nat'l Mon.
EBR-1
Atomic City
St. Anthony
Tetonia
Victor
Rigby
Swan Valley
Fort Hall
Chesterfield
Aberdeen
American Falls
Register Rock
Rupert
Burley
City of Rocks
Soda Springs
Niter Ice Cave
Virginia
Malad City
Preston
Montpelier
15
20
22
23
24
26
39
75
93
21
44
19
55
95
84
78
51
86
34
36
91
30
89
191
287

tourist service centers than a town, Island Park stretches for some 20 mi along Highway 20, roughly paralleling the world-famous trout fishing waters of Henry's Fork.

Henry's Fork of the Snake River empties into a prehistoric collapsed volcano now known as the **Island Park Caldera.** The former cone is 18 mi long and 23 mi wide, which means that it's impossible to see all at once. It is marked by a 1,200-foot cliff on the southern and western rims. U.S. 20 climbs the scarp at Big Bend Ridge. ✉ *25 mi south of Ashton off U.S. 20* ☎ *208/374–5476.*

Sports & the Outdoors

BIRD-WATCHING Bird-watchers should flock to **Harriman State Park,** about 80 mi north of Idaho Falls and 33 mi southwest of West Yellowstone, Montana. In this 16,000-acre wildlife refuge you'll glimpse Canada geese, osprey, bald eagles, prehistoric-looking sandhill cranes, and other waterfowl year-round. In winter, some 300 to 400 Rocky Mountain trumpeter swans, the world's heaviest flying bird, lay over here. Winter bird-watching can be paired with Nordic skiing on the park's groomed trails. ✉ *3489 E. Hwy. 20* ☎ *208/558–7368* 🌐 *www.idahoparks.org* *$3 per car.*

FLY-FISHING It's strictly catch-and-release at Henry's Fork in the Snake River, but this regulation doesn't seem to bother anyone. In fact, sometimes it seems that every fisherman in the country can be found standing midstream. Cutthroats and cutbows, natural (and potentially massive) hybrids between non-native rainbows and native cutthroat trouts, throng in these waters. But that doesn't make the fishing easy: way too many of these fish know an artificial lure when they see one. **Henry's Fork Anglers** (✉ 3340 Hwy. 20, Last Chance ☎ 208/558–7525 🌐 www.henrysforkanglers.com) offers guide services from a convenient location adjacent to the river. The company also guides fishing excursions to other area rivers, as well as Island Park Reservoir and Henry's Lake. A full-service fly shop is on the premises.

SNOWMOBILING Island Park is eastern Idaho's snowmobile mecca, thanks in part to its generally high altitude. Most of the area sits at about 6,000 feet. By February, snow depths of 6 feet or more are typical. Island Park has more than 400 mi of groomed main trail on top of some 200 mi of irregularly groomed backcountry routes. This maze of trails connects to an even larger system that includes trails around West Yellowstone, Montana, and Yellowstone National Park. **Action Motor Sports** (✉ 1355 E. Lincoln Rd., Idaho Falls ☎ 208/522–3050) rents snowmobiles and trailers. It has trail maps for snowmobile routes across the region, including Island Park.

Where to Stay

¢–$$ **Ponds Lodge.** Built in 1935, the lodge huddles around a massive log structure where you'll find a café, a small grocery, and the Buffalo River Saloon. A half ring of cabins reaches behind it. Most of the pine-paneled cabins are basic, with simple furnishings and carpeted floors. Most have been winterized, so you can use them year-round. Camping is also available. A restaurant serves a standard and plentiful breakfast, lunch, and dinner. ✉ *3757 N. Hwy. 20, 83429* ☎ *208/558–7221* *25 cabins* *Restaurant, some kitchens, lounge, laundry facilities; no a/c, no room phones, no room TVs* *MC, V.*

CAMPING **Island Park Ranger District Campgrounds.** Among the prettier Forest Service campgrounds of the seven in the area are McCrea's Bridge, on a lightly wooded hillside on the shores of Island Park Reservoir, and tiny Coffee Pot, with an idyllic location on the banks of Henry's Fork. Coffee Pot is 1½ mi from Highway 20, making it easy to get here. Big Springs Campground is near the headwaters of Henry's Fork. *Most camp-*

grounds with pit toilets, drinking water, fire pits, picnic tables ✉ *3726 Hwy. 20, 83429* ☎ *208/558–7301* 🌐 *www.fs.fed.us* *Free–$12* *No credit cards* ⏲ *May–Sept.*

en route

The **Mesa Falls Scenic Byway** is only a slight detour if you're en route to Teton Valley. From Highway 20 south of Island Park, take Forest Road 294 and then Highway 47 on into Ashton. You'll drive through lodgepole-pine forests along Henry's Fork (invisible in its deep canyon) past Upper and Lower Mesa Falls, the only major waterfalls in Idaho not harnessed for hydroelectricity or drained for irrigation. You can drive the byway in an hour, but hiking trails in the area of the upper falls beckon. From Ashton, jump on the **Teton Scenic Byway** by taking Highway 32 to Tetonia and 33 on into Driggs. This route runs toward and then along the western flanks of the Tetons, the youngest mountains in the Rocky Mountain range.

Driggs

❷ *66 mi south and east of Island Park via Hwys. 20, 32, and 31.*

Two Mormons from Salt Lake City were so impressed with the potential for farming the Teton Valley that they persuaded an attorney named B. W. Driggs to invest in property here as well. In 1889 the first wagon train of Salt Lake emigrants arrived. Undeterred by the harsh winters, the settlers harvested wild hay and dug irrigation ditches, and soon the farming community of Driggs was established. But long before there was a Driggs, fur traders regularly met about 1 mi south of town, in the valley then known as Pierre's Hole (a hole is any deep, steep-sided mountain valley), for about 20 years until 1840. The most famous gathering was the 1832 Rendezvous, by all accounts a raucous event that brought together 200 mountain men and 200 lodges of Nez Perce and Flathead Indians to trade over several days.

Alongside the less tourist-oriented towns of Victor and Tetonia, Driggs sits on the western flanks of the Tetons. The valley is also home to a ski resort called Grand Targhee, known for its champagne powder. It is nearly as lovely but more subdued than Jackson, Wyoming, the world-famous resort on the east side of the range.

Learn about the Targhee National Forest and Teton Basin Ranger District at the **Teton Basin Ranger Station.** The district offers some of the nicest hiking in the region, especially in the Alaska Basin and Table Mountains. Locals return again and again for the spectacular views of the Tetons. ✉ *515 S. Main St.* ☎ *208/354–2312* 🌐 *www.fs.fed.us* ⏲ *Weekdays.*

Sports & the Outdoors

FLYING **Teton Valley Aviation** (✉ 675 Airport Rd. ☎ 208/354–3100 or 800/472–6382) takes you aloft for aerial views of the western flanks of the Tetons. Take an engineless glider or, if you prefer, one of the small airplanes. The cost is about $199 for a one-hour flight. Flights leave from Driggs-Reade Memorial Airport. The on-site restaurant, Warbirds Café, serves breakfast, lunch, and dinner and offers a surprisingly varied menu, from bison to elk to Thai dishes.

DOWNHILL SKIING The **Grand Targhee Ski & Summer Resort** is nicknamed "Grand Foggy" by locals because the mountain is regularly socked in with heavy fog. Nobody complains much, though: the same weather helps account for those signature powder dumps, averaging 43 cumulative feet per year. One detachable high-speed quad, three other lifts, and a rope tow take you to 3,000 total skiable acres, much of it left ungroomed for die-hard powder hounds. There are also plenty of trails for cross-country skiers.

Facilities include a bar with live music on weekends, a ski school, rentals, on-site lodging, and restaurants. ✉ *Ski Hill Rd., Alta, WY 83422* ☎ *307/353–2300 or 800/827–4433* 🌐 *www.grandtarghee.com* ⏲ *Skiing mid-Nov.–mid-Apr.*

SNOWMOBILING In the Teton Valley and spreading out into the Big Holes Mountains to the west are 240 mi of groomed, mapped trails used almost exclusively by snowmobilers. There are between 200 and 300 riders per day, on average. **Racin' Station** (✉ 225 S. Main St. ☎ 208/354–2777) rents a limited number of snowmobiles and trailers, as well as helmets and other equipment. Call a week in advance to reserve so the company can have your machine in tip-top shape. Big Holes Trails maps are available at the Teton Basin Ranger Station.

NORDIC SKIING A gently rolling cross-country ski trail begins at the end of the plowed section of Teton Canyon Road, on the way up to Grand Targhee, and continues for more than 4 mi up Teton Canyon. **Yöstmark Mountain Equipment** (✉ 12 E. Little Ave. ☎ 208/354–2828) rents cross-country gear and can point you toward the area's best ski trails. The company also offers guided ski tours in the Tetons.

Where to Stay & Eat

$–$$ ✕ **The Royal Wolf.** Housed in a charming building dating from 1916, this restaurant is loved by locals for its casual atmosphere. If you're in the mood for home cooking, this is the place. The french fries are hand-cut and the burgers hand-shaped. Everything from the dinner rolls to the salad dressings is made fresh in the kitchen. There are 10 beers on tap, mostly microbrews. In good weather, the deck out front is a popular hangout. ✉ *63 Depot St.* ☎ *208/354–8365* 💳 *AE, DC, MC, V.*

$–$$ **Teewinot Lodge.** Western-inspired furnishings enliven the otherwise conventional rooms at this mountainside lodge. Grand Targhee is laid out like a tiny village, so all of the resort's amenities are within a short stroll of Teewinot Lodge, including the hot tub and the heated outdoor pool (both open in winter). If you're staying for more than a few days, ask about a discount. The lodge is about 12 mi east of Driggs. ✉ *Ski Hill Rd., Alta, WY 83422* ☎ *307/353–2300 or 800/827–4433* 🖷 *307/353–8148* 🌐 *www.grandtarghee.com* *48 rooms* *3 restaurants, coffee shop, in-room VCRs, tennis court, pool, exercise equipment, hot tub, massage, spa, horseback riding, cross-country skiing, downhill skiing, bar, laundry facilities, business services* 💳 *AE, D, MC, V* ⏲ *Closed Apr.–June, and Sept.–mid-Nov.*

$ **Best Western Teton West.** Only 30 mi from Grand Targhee, this budget lodging is a good alternative to the higher-priced accommodations in the resort. Rooms are furnished with dark-rose floral spreads and carpet and dark-wood furniture. Most have distant views of the Tetons. There's a ski-wax room right on the premises. ✉ *476 N. Main St., 83422* ☎ *208/354–2363* 🖷 *208/354–2962* 🌐 *www.bestwestern.com* *40 rooms* *Cable TV, indoor pool, hot tub, ski shop, some pets allowed* 💳 *AE, D, DC, MC, V* ⏲ *Closed Oct.–Dec.* *CP.*

$ **Intermountain Lodge.** These modern little cabins nestled in a grove of cottonwood trees have basic, comfortable furnishings. Kitchenettes make them popular with families. Only 10 mi from Grand Targhee and 2 mi outside of Driggs, the location is quiet without being inconvenient. ✉ *34 Ski Hill Rd., 83422* ☎ *208/354–8153* 🖷 *208/354–2998* *14 rooms* *Kitchenettes, outdoor hot tub, laundry facilities; no a/c, no smoking* 💳 *AE, D, MC, V* *CP.*

★ ¢ **Pines Motel Guest Haus.** The cedar-shingled cottage looks as though it would be right at home in the Bavarian Alps. The guesthouse is surrounded by an acre of shady lawns with a grill that makes you want to have a picnic. Guest rooms are simple and comfortable, with country-style furnishings and homemade quilts. You're about a block from the center of town and 12 mi from Grand Targhee. ✉ *105 S. Main St., 83422* ☎ *208/354–2774 or 800/354–2778* *7 rooms* *Hot tub, some pets allowed (fee).* *AE, D, DC, MC, V.*

CAMPING **Teton Basin Ranger District Campgrounds.** The district maintains six campgrounds, perhaps the prettiest of which is Teton Canyon, at the end of Teton Canyon Road and literally in the shadows of the Tetons. Most of these campgrounds are surprisingly quiet except for busy holiday weekends. *Most campgrounds have pit toilets, drinking water, fire pits, picnic tables* ✉ *515 S. Main St., 83429* ☎ *208/354–2312* *www.fs.fed.us/* *Free–$12* *No credit cards* *May–Sept.*

Idaho Falls

3 *67 mi west and south of Teton Valley via Hwys. 31 and 26.*

Idaho Falls sits at the edge of the Snake River plain, which arcs across southern Idaho. This town of nearly 50,000 sprouted up when an industrious stagecoach driver figured a bridge across a narrow section of the Snake River would be much faster than the ferry upstream. He completed the bridge in 1866, and around it grew a community called Eagle Rock. Later the name was changed to Idaho Falls, despite the lack of any waterfalls. In 1911 a weir, or low dam, was built across the river to generate power, lending some legitimacy to the name.

The 1916 Andrew Carnegie Library that was the original home of the **Museum of Idaho** is now joined to the former Masonic temple next door with an imposing three-story-high glass arc. The new exhibition space is devoted to frequently changing shows. Permanent exhibits in the older building include an extensive selection of Shoshone-Bannock artifacts and a re-creation of early Eagle Rock. The faux street is complete with a dentist's office, dry-goods store, and other facades. ✉ *200 N. Eastern Ave.* ☎ *208/522–1400* *www.museumofidaho.org* *$5* *Weekdays 10–5, Sat. 1–5.*

Learn about the Targhee National Forest's hiking trail, and other recreation opportunities, at the **Eastern Idaho Visitor Information Center** (✉ 505 Lindsay Blvd., Idaho Falls 83402 ☎ 208/523–1010 or 800/634–3246 www.fs.fed.us/r4/caribou-targhee). A Forest Service representative is on hand to answer your questions.

off the beaten path

CRATERS OF THE MOON NATIONAL MONUMENT – Every 2,000 to 3,000 years, starting about 15,000 years ago, the ground north of here has split open and poured molten rock over the landscape. Basalt flows have pushed the Snake River south and left this plain an otherworldly landscape of lava tubes and jagged rock. The visitor center, off Highway 26, provides an introduction to the area, but if you want to see it up close, you can drive a 7-mi self-guided loop. In winter the loop is groomed for cross-country skiing. The park's hiking trails, most of which are short and well signed, also lead to weird and wonderful rock formations. The national monument is 65 mi west of Idaho Falls and 18 mi west of Arco. ✉ *Hwy. 26,* ☎ *208/527–3257* *$5 per vehicle.*

EBR-1 – Idaho Falls is home to the Idaho National Engineering and Environmental Laboratory, set on 890 square mi of sage desert northwest of town. It's off U.S. 20 near the aptly named small town of Atomic City. When you're driving on to "the site," as locals call the nuclear facility, it's easy to understand why the writers of B movies thought odd things might crawl out of the desert at night.

Here, back in 1951, EBR-1 became the nation's first nuclear reactor to generate usable amounts of electricity. It is now a National Historic Landmark and houses a museum that tells the story of nuclear power. ✉ *785 DOE Pl.* ☎ *208/526–2029* 🎫 *Free* ⏲ *Memorial Day–Labor Day, daily 8–4.*

Sports & the Outdoors

If the weather is warm and the skies are blue, take a break on the 2⅓-mi **Greenbelt,** spread along both sides of the Snake River from south of Broadway Bridge to John's Hole Bridge. Locals bike, run, or in-line skate along the paved paths. Picnic tables set up at intervals are perfect for lunch breaks. Freeman, the largest park in town, is on the Greenbelt. For bike and skate rentals, call **Idaho Mountain Trading** (✉ 474 Shoup Rd. ☎ 208/523–6679). These folks also rent Frisbees for use on Freeman Park's disc golf course.

FISHING The South Fork of the Snake River flows out of the Palisades Reservoir past stands of cottonwoods and beneath basalt bluffs. Its waters above the mouth of Henry's Fork are touted as a great spot for catching cutthroats. (These fish are wary of anglers, however.) Although roads run along much of its length, the South Fork is most easily (and effectively) fished by boat. Outfitters use drift boats (rowboats designed for moving water) and outboard powerboats, but many people prefer to fish from rafts and canoes. The Snake River flows (and pools in a reservoir called Gem Lake) through town, and fishing from shore for rainbow and brown trout is a popular pastime. For all the gear you'll need to catch cutthroats, visit **Jimmy's All Season Angler** (✉ 275 A St. ☎ 208/524–7160), a family-owned business catering to fly-fishing fans. They'll also point you toward the best fishing spots. To rent canoes or inflatable rafts, try **Canyon Whitewater Supply** (✉ 450 S. Yellowstone Hwy. ☎ 208/522–3932).

Where to Stay & Eat

$$–$$$ ✕ **Sandpiper.** Although the owners may have gone a little overboard with the nautical theme, there's no doubt that the fresh seafood makes this one of the better dining spots in town. Meat eaters can also order delicious steaks. Because it sits on the bank of the Snake River, there are lovely views from the back windows. Diners often indulge in after-dinner strolls along the river. ✉ *750 Lindsay Blvd.* ☎ *208/524–3344* 💳 *AE, D, DC, MC, V.*

★ **$–$$** ✕ **Bistro Off Broadway.** With a menu featuring such unique salads as the "strawberry fields," made with jicama, bitter greens, and, of course, strawberries, you'll have trouble saving room for this restaurant's signature dessert, a softball-size cream puff filled with locally made Reed's Dairy ice cream and topped with hot fudge sauce. You might even opt for just the ice cream, which is incredibly creamy because of its butterfat content. Steaks, pork, chicken, and trout round out the menu. The atmosphere manages to be both elegant and minimal, with sponge-painted concrete floors, faux marble pillars, and adobe-colored walls. Idaho's wineries are featured on the wine lists. ✉ *325 River Pkwy.* ☎ *208/524–0011* 💳 *AE, DC, MC, V* ⏲ *Closed Sun.*

$–$$ ✕ **Smitty's Pancake House Restaurant.** The waitresses still call you "honey" in this cross between a diner and a roadhouse. This is the type of place where breakfast is served all day. Weekend mornings you should expect a wait. The list of pancakes almost certainly includes versions you haven't encountered before. If you don't want anything too fancy, the burgers are reliable. ✉ *645 W. Broadway* ☎ *208/523–6450* 💳 *MC, V.*

$–$$ ✕ **Snakebite.** This casual eatery dishes out everything from steaks to pasta in an atmosphere that the management proudly calls "southwestern eclectic." Vegetarians will be pleased to find veggie burgers and other meat-free items in the menu. Snakebite has a wide selection of microbrews. ✉ *425 River Pkwy.* ☎ *208/525–2522* ▭ *MC, V* ⊙ *Closed Sun. No dinner Mon.*

$–$$ **Best Western Driftwood Inn.** Six rooms in an area called the Overhang are your best choice here, as each has views of the waterfalls on the Snake River. Four with oversize kitchenettes are particularly nice for families. Traditional light-pine furnishings give the rooms an airy feel. The park is just steps away, and you can take a seat on one of the benches to appreciate the lush gardens. ✉ *575 River Pkwy., 83402* ☎ *208/523–2242 or 800/528–1234* 🖷 *208/523–0316* 🌐 *www.bestwestern.com* *74 rooms* *Some kitchenettes, microwaves, refrigerators, laundry facilities* ▭ *AE, D, MC, V.*

$ **AmeriTel Inn.** With speaker phones and computer connections, the rooms at this hotel let you get right to work. But you don't always want to feel like you're at the office, which is why it's handsomely decorated in deep colors. Some units let you relax after that meeting in front of a fireplace or in a whirlpool tub. There is a comfortable lounge with plump sofas and a health club with the latest equipment. ✉ *645 Lindsay Blvd., 83402* ☎ *208/523–1400 or 800/528–1234* 🖷 *208/523–0004* *126 rooms* *In-room data ports, kitchenettes, indoor pool, gym, hot tub, lounge, business services, meeting room* ▭ *AE, D, DC, MC, V* *CP.*

$ **Red Lion Hotel on the Falls.** The wedge-shaped rooms in an eight-story-tall cylindrical tower are the choicest accommodations in this local landmark. Those facing the Snake River have private balconies and floor-to-ceiling windows where you can enjoy the view. Standard rooms wrap around the restaurant and the large outdoor pool area. The park is across the road. ✉ *475 River Pkwy., 83402* ☎ *208/523–8000 or 800/432–1005* 🌐 *www.redlion.com* *138 rooms, 1 suite* *Restaurant, some refrigerators, pool, exercise equipment, hot tub, lounge, laundry facilities, business services, meeting rooms* ▭ *AE, DC, MC, V.*

Pocatello

❹ *51 mi south of Idaho Falls via I–15.*

Trains, trails, and travelers have all figured in the history of Pocatello, the state's second-largest city. Spread out along the Snake River in a fertile valley ringed by softly sculpted mountains, Pocatello was once the largest rail center west of the Mississippi. It's perhaps the only town to have an ordinance (passed in 1948) making frowns and grimaces unlawful. Stroll downtown through the shady streets of Old Town Pocatello, a renovated shopping and commercial district, and glimpse the historic Oregon Short Line Depot and turn-of-the-last-century houses with turrets and lovely brick and stone work and trimmed with gingerbread. Nine buildings and five districts are listed on the National Register, including the Idaho State University administration building. Getting around town is a breeze. Both transportation and entertainment, two trolleys ply the main streets.

The **Idaho Museum of Natural History,** on the campus of historic Idaho State University, has a fine collection of more than 400,000 artifacts. Here you'll find Ice Age specimens of mammoths, mastodons, and other previous residents of what is now Idaho. The Discovery Room gives kids hands-on encounters with fossils. From I–15, take U.S. 91 to Yellowstone Avenue and follow the signs to the campus. ✉ *S. 5th Ave. and E. Dillon St.,* ☎ *208/236–3168 or 208/236–3317* *$3* ⊙ *Mon.–Sat. 10–4.*

Fort Hall was a major pioneer outpost northeast of Pocatello, and it is now within the ½-million-acre Fort Hall Native American Reservation. Massive wooden gates open to a museum complex, the **Fort Hall Replica,** representing a historic trading post once near here on the Portneuf River and serving as an important stop along the Oregon Trail. ✉ *Upper Ross Park, Ave. of the Chiefs, off 4th St.* ☎ *208/234–1795* 🎫 *$2* ⏲ *Apr. and May, Tues.–Sat. 10–2; June–Sept. 1, daily 10–6; Sept. 2–30, Tues.–Sat. 10–2.*

Where to Stay & Eat

$–$$ ✕ **Oliver's.** An extensive menu stretching from pastrami sandwiches to liver and onions to pot roast, a solid selection of vegetarian dishes, and the fact that it delivers all contribute to this little restaurant's popularity. Even when it is slammed during weekday lunches, there is often counter seating available. You're welcome to bring your own bottle of wine, and there's no corkage fee. ✉ *130 S. 5th* ☎ *208/234–0672* ▭ *MC, V.*

$ ✕ **Chang's Garden.** Locals say Chinese food can't get more authentic or tastier than at Chang's Garden. Signature dishes at this family-owned restaurant include lightly breaded shrimp topped with walnuts and white sauce and served over steamed broccoli. Any dish can be made hot and spicy on request. The extensive menu includes vegetarian options and a few American dishes for those in your party who don't enjoy Chinese. ✉ *1000 Pocatello Creek Rd.* ☎ *208/234–1475* ▭ *AE, DC, MC, V.*

¢–$ ✕ **Buddy's.** A few blocks from the campus of Idaho State University, this bustling family-owned restaurant has been packing them in for more than 30 years with tasty Italian food. Even better, the prices are reasonable. The garlic salad dressing is so good that they bottle it to sell all over the state. Takeout is available. ✉ *626 E. Lewis St.* ☎ *208/333–1172* ▭ *MC, V.*

$$–$$$$ 🏨 **Black Swan Inn.** Theme rooms such as the Jungle Falls Suite, with its waterfall and faux-stone grotto, or the Sea Cave Suite, where you sleep in a giant clamshell shimmering with fiber-optic lights, await in this renovated old church in downtown Pocatello. The Black Swan Garden Suite, one of the most popular accommodations, has an in-room sauna. Weekday rates are significantly cheaper than those listed above. A Continental breakfast is included in the rate. ✉ *746 E. Center, 83201* ☎ *208/233–3051* 🌐 *www.blackswaninn.com* *14 suites* *In-room hot tubs, microwaves, refrigerators, in-room VCRs; no kids, no smoking.* ▭ *AE, DC, MC, V* 🍽 *CP.*

$ 🏨 **Best Western Cotton Tree Inn.** This efficient motel is off I–15. Take Exit 71, which leads to Pocatello Creek Road. Rooms were recently remodeled, so they all look like new. Some have whirlpool tubs and kitchenettes. ✉ *1415 Bench Rd., 83201* ☎ *208/237–7650 or 800/662–6886* 📠 *208/238–1355* 🌐 *www.bestwestern.com* *149 rooms* *Restaurant, hot tub, racquetball, bar, laundry facilities* ▭ *AE, D, DC, MC, V.*

CAMPING ⛺ **Pocatello KOA.** Some of the campsites are dotted by tall locusts and elms at this RV park. The biggest, shadiest sites cost a bit more. Here you can rent movies and access the Internet. *Flush toilets. Full hookups, partial hookups, dump station. Drinking water, guest laundry, showers. Grills, picnic tables. Public telephone. General store* *22 full hookups, 24 partial hookups, 12 tent sites* ✉ *9815 W. Pocatello Creek Rd., 83201* ☎ *208/233–6851* 🎫 *Full hookups $27–$31, partial hookups $27, tent sites $12–$23* ▭ *AE, DC, MC, V.*

Nightlife & the Arts

NIGHTLIFE ★ Dinner theater shows and full-scale productions are showcased at **Mystique** (✉ 158 E. Chubbuck Rd. ☎ 208/238–8001), owned by Terry and Melanie Commons. At smaller productions, held in either of two private dining rooms, Terry, a former Las Vegas magician, delights the crowds as ghosts speak from mirrors, skeletons rise out of the dining table, and, at the end, he—poof!—literally disappears. Halloween-season shows are particularly popular. Larger-scale productions held in the main hall include classic Broadway plays.

This bar looks like the set for the bar scene from *Urban Cowboy*, complete with a mechanical bull, several pool tables, three main bars at which to belly up, and a stage for the live acts that play most weekends. The only thing you'll find a little askew at the **Green Triangle** (✉ 4010 Yellowstone ☎ 208/237–0354) are the busloads of Japanese tourists having their pictures taken on the bull.

Lava Hot Springs

★ ❺ *35 mi southeast of Pocatello via I–15 and Hwy. 30.*

One of the funkiest little towns in Idaho, Lava Hot Springs has one claim to fame: hot water. Ownership of the steamy springs passed from Native Americans to the U.S. Army to the state of Idaho. They are now in the hands of a foundation that has turned the area around the pools into a lush garden. The springs have almost no sulfur or chlorine but are rich in other minerals, which attracts people who believe in the healing properties of the waters as well as those who simply want to relax. Area motels tap into the springs, piping the bubbling brew into hot tubs.

Lava Hot Springs, population 400, also has a tiny downtown. There is one main street and some turn-of-the-last-century brick buildings clustered right to the edges of the narrow Portneuf River.

The **World Famous Hot Pools** lets you choose between five pools with temperatures ranging from 104°F to 112°F. Two swimming pools, one covering ⅓ acre, are on each end of the 25-acre landscaped property and are open only in summer. Suits, towels, and lockers are available. ✉ *430 E. Main St.* ☎ *208/776–5221 or 800/423–8597* 🌐 *www.lavahotsprings.com* 🎫 *$6* ⏲ *Hot pools Apr.–Sept., daily 8 AM–11 PM; Oct.–Mar., daily 9 AM–10 PM.*

off the beaten path

CHESTERFIELD – Virtually a ghost town, Chesterfield was founded in 1880 by Mormons, who laid down the traditional grid pattern for the streets. Many of the original buildings stand forlornly, as if waiting for the original inhabitants to return. Chesterfield, 20 mi from Lava Hot Springs via U.S. 30 east to Bancroft and Chesterfield Road north, is listed on the National Register of Historic Places.

Where to Stay & Eat

$–$$ ✕ **Johnny's.** This pleasant little place gets quite a bit of the local traffic, owing to its hearty breakfasts. For lunch there are burgers, and dinner selections include steaks and seafood. The homemade soups are particularly tasty. ✉ *78 E. Main St.* ☎ *208/776–5562* 💳 *AE, D, MC, V.*

$–$$ 🏨 **Lava Hot Springs Inn.** This grand old building began as a hospital and is now a European-style B&B. The rooms, decorated in shades of pink and purple, are neat and well appointed. Suites have private baths with whirlpool tubs. A hot mineral pool, steps away from the back door, overlooks the Portneuf River. A buffet breakfast is included. ✉ *94 E. Portneuf Ave., Box 670, 83246* ☎ *208/776–5830 or 800/527–5830* 🌐 *www.lavahotspringsinn.com* 🛏 *19 rooms, 2 with bath; 12 suites* ♨ *Dining room, library* 💳 *AE, D, MC, V* 🍽 *BP.*

Bear Lake

❻ *75 mi southeast of Lava Hot Springs via Hwys. 30 and 89.*

One of the state's most distinctive bodies of water, 120-square-mi Bear Lake runs from bright turquoise to robin's-egg blue. The vivid colors are caused by high concentrations of minerals dissolved in the water. The shoreline, although not particularly memorable, is largely undeveloped and has some sandy beaches. The lake, which begins about 20 mi south of Montpelier, is particularly appealing when viewed from the 7,800-foot summit of U.S. 89 as it passes through Garden City, Utah.

Bear Lake National Wildlife Refuge runs along the lake's northern shore. The 17,600 acres of marsh and grasslands provide nesting habitat for several species of ducks, such as mallard, pintail, and canvasback, as well as sandhill cranes, herons, egrets, Canada geese, and white pelicans. ✉ *U.S. 89, Montpelier* ☎ *208/847–1757.*

Covering about 966 acres, **Bear Lake State Park** sits in the mountains at an elevation of about 6,000 feet. The gradual slope of the lake bottom makes it a perfect place for swimming. Some 5 mi of shoreline allows access for water sports. Boat ramps are available for powerboating, waterskiing, sailing, and fishing. You can catch native cutthroat or lake trout in the summer. In winter when the Bonneville cisco run, bring your buckets and nets; this species is found nowhere else. There is a campground in the park. ✉ *2661 U.S. 89* ☎ *208/847–1045* 🌐 *www.idahoparks.org* 🎫 *$3 per car.*

★ In 1907, a grouse hunter discovered the **Minnetonka Cave,** a series of caverns filled with fascinating formations. It opened to the public in 1947. Guided tours take you to soda-straw formations, banded travertine, and helicites in nine chambers. The hour-long tours of the state's largest developed limestone cave climb more than 400 steps and travel 1,800 feet into the cave, which is at a constant, chilly 48°F. ✉ *St. Charles Canyon* ☎ *208/847–0375* 🎫 *$6* ⏲ *Guided tours mid-June–Labor Day.*

This majestic Mormon tabernacle was built of red sandstone blocks in 1889, all hauled by sled through the snow from a quarry 18 mi away. The Romanesque-styled temple has intricately carved woodwork and a soaring sanctuary with balconies above. A small museum at the **Paris Tabernacle Historical Site** houses heirlooms and artwork left behind by the homesteaders. Free guided tours are available daily. ✉ *U.S. 89, Paris* ☎ *435/946–2760* 🎫 *Donations accepted* ⏲ *Memorial Day–Labor Day, daily 10–5.*

off the beaten path

THE NATIONAL OREGON/CALIFORNIA TRAIL CENTER – Ever wondered what it would be like to be a pioneer traveling on the Oregon Trail? Tours that let you do just that start every hour in the wagon shop, where costumed guides teach you how to purchase and maintain your wagon. In the mercantile you find out what supplies you'll need, and then you climb on a replica of a covered wagon for a ride over the rocks and ruts along the famous route. A museum houses artifacts from the pioneers who settled in the Bear Valley. ✉ *320 N. 4th St., at Hwys. 30 and 89, Montpelier* ☎ *208/847–3800 or 800/448–2327* 🌐 *www.oregontrailcenter.org* 🎫 *$6* ⏲ *May–Oct., daily 10–5.*

Massacre Rocks State Park

❼ *40 mi from Pocatello via I–15 and I–86.*

"Devil's Gate" was the name given by travelers on the Oregon Trail to an intimidatingly narrow break in the tumble of basalt buttresses that heave through the soil in this part of the state. The original name reflected their fear of an ambush, although that never occurred at this particular spot. A bloody skirmish between three wagon trains and local tribes did take place not far away in 1862, hence the current name.

A 900-acre desert plateau overlooking the Snake River, Massacre Rocks State Park is heaven for hikers. There are several short hiking trails. The longest, just over 1 mi, takes you along the old Oregon Trail, where wagon ruts are still visible. It is also a haven for almost 300 species of desert plants and 200 species of birds. The visitor center has exhibits on the Oregon Trail, the Shoshone people, local geology, and fur trapping. From Memorial Day through Labor Day, costumed performers tell you about life in pioneer days. ✉ *Hwy. 78* ☎ *208/366–7919* 🌐 *www.idahoparks.org* 🎫 *$3 per car.*

Wagons on their way west often stopped to camp at 20-foot-high **Register Rock,** 2½ mi from the park. During the night, pioneers left proof of their passage by painting or carving their names into the stone. Some of these date back to the 1860s. Take I–86 west from Pocatello 8 mi past its junction with Highway 37. Signs lead you to the ¼-mi trail to the rock and surrounding picnic area.

Camping

⛺ **Massacre Rocks State Park Campground.** Many campsites here have a tucked-away feeling because of the low, scrubby juniper trees and knobs of basalt that dot the area. What they don't have is shade, which on summer mornings gets you up and out in a hurry. Many sites in the lower loop and a few in the upper have nice views of the placid Snake River and its basalt canyon wall. Small cabins with air-conditioning and outdoor grills are available all year. ♿ *Flush toilets. Partial hookups, dump station. Drinking water, showers. Grills, picnic tables. Ranger station* *34 partial hookups, 6 tent sites* ✉ *3592 N. Park La., I–86, Exit 28* ☎ *208/548–2672* 🌐 *www.idahoparks.org* 🎫 *Partial hookups $16–$22, tent sites $12* 💳 *MC, V* ⏲ *Lower loop closed Sept.–Apr.*

SUN VALLEY/KETCHUM

8 W. Averell Harriman, chairman of the Union Pacific Railroad in the 1930s, decided that the railroad needed some attractions to lure travelers out west. He wasn't thinking small; what he had in mind was a Saint Moritz rising out of the Rockies. The location he chose was an old mining town in the Wood River valley, which was quickly changed to the much more marketable Sun Valley. In 1936 he flew in a host of Hollywood stars for the 1936 opening, and since that glittery event Sun Valley has remained a top ski destination. A model for later resorts, it helped to convince people that the ski slopes could also be used in the summer for hiking, biking, and other outdoor pursuits.

Today Sun Valley and neighboring Ketchum are gold-plated resort towns. Down the road in Hailey, which hasn't been quite so gentrified, a charming Idaho town peeks through the perfect storefronts that line Main Street. These three towns are so small that locals don't know the major cross streets by name or, often, their own addresses. They don't need them: directions like "turn left at the Pioneer and watch for a sign on your right" work fine. The entire area is a haven for outdoor activities such as hiking, biking, alpine and cross-country skiing, snowshoeing, and fishing, which residents and visitors alike pursue with fervor.

Sightseeing around Sun Valley is largely limited to admiring the beauty of the surrounding mountains. But literary types make a pilgrimage to the region to visit the Ketchum Cemetery, the site of **Ernest Hemingway's Grave** (✉ Hwy. 75 near 10th St.). A small memorial to the author of *The Sun Also Rises* and *The Old Man and the Sea* sits north of Sun Valley Resort on Sun Valley Road.

Sports & the Outdoors

A paved public path popular with runners, bikers, and in-line skaters runs most of the length of Wood River valley. It's possible to take the trail all the way from Carey, a small town below Hailey, to a point about 2 mi north of Sun Valley Resort, a distance of about 20 mi. Maps are available from the **Blaine County Recreation District** (308 N. Main St., Hailey 208/788–2117). In Ketchum, **Sturtevants Mountain Sports** (340 N. Main St. 208/726–4501) has bike and skate rentals by the hour or the day. There are plenty of other shops in Sun Valley, Ketchum, and Hailey.

FISHING The cold-spring-fed Silver Creek is known far and wide for dry fly–fishing. About 18 mi south and east of Hailey, it's a slow-moving, easy-to-wade, yet extremely challenging fishery with huge browns and native rainbows. Longtime dry-flying aficionados are quick to compare fishing Silver Creek to golfing at Augusta National, which may explain why more than 12,000 anglers find their way here each year. Only catch-and-release fishing is allowed. The high-desert **Silver Creek Preserve** (Silver Creek Preserve Rd., Box 624, Picabo 208/788–2203) is protected by the Nature Conservancy.

Silver Creek Outfitters (500 N. Main St., Ketchum 208/726–5282 or 800/732–5687) is Wood River valley's biggest fly-fishing outfitter. Professional guides know every ripple of Hemingway's beloved Silver Creek and Big Wood River.

GOLF Without question, one of Idaho's most popular golf courses is at Sun Valley. Designed by the legendary Robert Trent Jones Jr., the **Sun Valley Golf Course** (Trail Creek Rd., Sun Valley 208/622–2251 www.sunvalley.com) makes great use of its spectacular alpine setting and challenging terrain along pretty Trail Creek. Greens fees are steep (more than $100), but a bit cheaper for resort guests. About 1 mi southwest of Ketchum, **Warm Springs Golf Course** (Warm Springs Rd. 208/726–3715) is a reasonably priced 9-hole course.

ICE-SKATING Many resorts have a skating rink or two, but this one at Sun Valley Resort is something special. The original rink dates back to 1937 and has been a training and performance spot for stars ranging from Sonja Henie to Kristi Yamaguchi. Katarina Witt has reportedly named this one of her favorite places to skate. Shows featuring some of the world's great skaters are staged here regularly, mainly in the summer. When they aren't on the ice, you can be. Contact the **Ice Center** (Dollar Loop Rd. 208/622–2194).

PARAGLIDING With some help from **Fly Sun Valley** (208/726–3332 www.flysunvalley.com), you can soar above Bald Mountain. Winter and summer, tandem paraglider flights launch from the side of the mountain to float over the valleys and make slow, soft landings, usually on the River Run side of Bald Mountain. You can also try out air kites—sort of like the kites you played with as a kid except you wear a harness because the kite is big enough to pull you up a mountain on a snowboard or even lift you into the air.

SLEIGH RIDES Bundle up and take a half-hour moonlight ride aboard a horse-drawn sleigh to dinner at a log cabin on the northern end of the Sun Valley Golf Course. Leave around 5 PM, to catch the alpenglow on the way out and the stars on the way back. A blast from Sun Valley's past, **Trail Creek Cabin** (208/622–2135 Sun Valley Reservations) was built in 1937 and hosted many a party of Union Pacific bigwig W. Averell Harriman and his movie-star cronies. Today, it maintains its original hunting-lodge decor with stuffed pheasants perched overhead and vintage pictures lining the walls. Warm yourself by the fire; then settle in for sumptuous prime rib, Idaho trout, and barbecued ribs. Although a bit schmaltzy, this is one of those must-do activities while in Sun Valley. Make reservations well ahead; these rides fill up fast, particularly during the Christmas holidays.

Downhill Skiing & Snowboarding

Fodor'sChoice ★ The **Sun Valley** ski area is a well-proportioned mix of trail and open-bowl skiing, easy glides and the tough stuff. It tends toward steep and continuous runs. The unfortunate rap on Sun Valley has been a lack of snow. Because it's not in a natural snowbelt and parts of the mountain are exposed to too much sun, the ski area has been more likely than most other western resorts to suffer snow shortages.

Dollar Mountain is Sun Valley's original ski hill, but when you compare it with the newer Bald Mountain—"Baldy" for short—you get a good idea of how far skiing has come in almost 60 years. Dollar Mountain alone was enough to lure celebrities in the '30s and '40s, but it's a beginner's hill by today's standards, utterly dwarfed by Baldy's 3,400 vertical feet. Together they have 75 runs. On-hill amenities include three restaurants, and the children's program is among the best at any ski resort. Some purists might find Baldy a little crowded with glittery lodge sitters. ✉ *Sun Valley Rd., Sun Valley 83353* ☎ *208/622–6151* 🌐 *www.sunvalley.com* ⏲ *Thanksgiving–early Apr., daily 9–4.*

FACILITIES 3,400-foot vertical drop; 2,054 skiable acres; 36% beginner, 42% intermediate, 22% advanced/expert; 7 high-speed quad chairs, 4 triple chairs, 5 double chairs, 3 T-bars.

LESSONS & PROGRAMS Half-day general ski clinics run $45; all-day children's group lessons are $87. Daylong child-care programs are available. Race clinics are $65 for three hours of instruction. Throughout the season, masters racing, snowboarding, and women's clinics are also offered. For more information, call the **Sun Valley Ski School** (☎ 208/622–2248).

LIFT TICKETS The base lift ticket price is $66. Various discounts are available, starting with multiday tickets valid, for instance, for three of four consecutive days.

RENTALS You can rent all the gear you need at a number of shops in Ketchum, Hailey, and Warm Springs, as well as at the base lodges of Sun Valley. **Elephant's Perch** (✉ 280 N. East Ave., Ketchum ☎ 208/726–3497) has good deals on standard ski packages (skis, boots, and poles). The company also rents expert gear. **Backwoods Mountain Sports** (✉ 711 N. Main St., Ketchum ☎ 208/726–8818) also rents skis and other equipment.

Nordic Skiing

An extensive system of cross-country trails runs along Wood River valley. Dogs are allowed on designated trails. For maps and information about these and other trails throughout the valley, talk to the **Sun Valley/Ketchum Chamber of Commerce** (✉ 4th and Main Sts., Sun Valley 83353 ☎ 208/726–3423 or 800/634–3347).

BACKCOUNTRY SKIING Backcountry tours for skiers of all abilities, from first-time tourers to seasoned telemarkers, can be arranged through **Sun Valley Trekking** (✉ Box 2200, Sun Valley 93353 ☎ 208/726–1002). Among Sun Valley Trekking's highlight trips are hut-to-hut tours and a strenuous "haute route" tour, comparable to similarly named high-mountain journeys in the French Alps.

RENTALS At the northern tip of the Harriman Trail is **Galena Lodge** (☎ 208/726–4010), a log lodge with a huge fireplace that makes it a good place to relax after a morning of cross-country skiing. There's a ski shop with rental packages and a snack bar that serves tasty lunches. The lodge is about 22 mi from Ketchum.

A good place to rent cross-country gear is the **Elephant's Perch** (✉ 280 N. East Ave., Ketchum ☎ 208/726–3497). These folks pride themselves on their in-depth knowledge of outdoor activities in the area, especially skiing.

Where to Stay & Eat

In Wood River valley, eating alfresco when weather permits is a passion, and most restaurants offer outdoor seating. Make sure to call ahead if you want a table on the rail.

$$$$ ✕ **A Winter's Feast.** No doubt about it, this restaurant is distinctive. After a snowy sleigh ride, step into this authentic Mongolian yurt—or a modern alternative, if you prefer—and indulge in a luscious five-course meal. The illusion of dining in the wilds is a bit marred by lights blazing in the million-dollar homes on the hill, but the candles and wood-burning stove inside the simple structures provide a more enjoyable light. Entrées include house-smoked salmon, beef tenderloin, and rack of lamb. ✉ *Warm Springs Golf Course, Warm Springs Rd., Ketchum* ☎ *208/788–7655* *Reservations essential* ▭ *MC, V.*

★ **$$$–$$$$** ✕ **Michel's Christiania.** This is as old-fashioned as you can get in Sun Valley. Hemingway had cocktails here when it was a hangout for the smart set. Michel Rudigoz, a former U.S. ski-team coach, took over the chalet-style restaurant in 1994, reinvigorating the menu with traditional French cuisine. The dining room blends white-linen elegance with old timbers and gigantic wrought-iron chandeliers. Elk, duckling, and trout are paired with delicious sauces and dramatic presentations. ✉ *303 Walnut Ave., Ketchum* ☎ *208/726–3388* ▭ *AE, D, MC, V.*

$$–$$$ ✕ **Globus.** The menu borrows from all over the continent, with inventive fare spanning the culinary corridor from China to Thailand to India. Diners dive into huge white porcelain bowls piled high with steaming chunks of chili beef, sizzling twice-cooked pork, and pungent vegetarian green curry. Homemade desserts such as five-spice ice cream cool down the palate after all that fire. ✉ *291 6th St., Ketchum* ☎ *208/726–1301* ▭ *AE, D, MC, V* ⊙ *No lunch.*

$–$$$ ✕ **Gretchen's.** This rustic restaurant offers breakfast, lunch, and dinner from its perch overlooking the famous ice rink at Sun Valley Resort. The menu features well-prepared entrées such as fresh salmon and trout, as well as more casual sandwich-and-salad fare. The hamburgers are enormous, and the pasta dishes are zingy. The young staff is very enthusiastic. ✉ *Sun Valley Rd., Sun Valley* ☎ *208/622–2144* ▭ *AE, MC, V.*

★ **$–$$$** ✕ **Pioneer Saloon.** A local institution, the Pioneer Saloon is known for its sizzling steaks—not surprising, as the place sells about a ton of beef each week. And don't pass up one of the big Idaho bakers, never less than a pound each and some nearly twice that big, which is so ridiculously huge they merit mention in national publications such as *USA Today.* The atmosphere manages to be dark and smoky, even though nobody is smoking. Paneled walls are decorated with interesting artifacts and mounted animal heads. During the dinner rush, you can wait an hour for a table. ✉ *308 N. Main St., Ketchum* ☎ *208/726–3139* ▭ *AE, MC, V* ⊙ *No lunch.*

$–$$ ✕ **Desperado's.** For well-prepared south-of-the-border fare, head to this informal cantina in the heart of Ketchum. Huge fish burritos, big bowls of black beans, and four kinds of fiery salsa headline the menu. For those watching their weight, there are low-fat options. The restaurant also has a steady carry-out business. ✉ *4th St. and Washington Ave., Ketchum* ☎ *208/726–3068* ▭ *AE, D, MC, V.*

$ ✕ **Viva Taqueria.** A renovated private home, its walls painted green and yellow and hung with ristras of dried chiles, provides nearly as tempting a fiesta atmosphere as the sunny patio outside. The tortillas, chips, and salsa are made daily, so you know they're fresh. The recipe for the margaritas is a closely guarded secret. The bar stocks 22 brands of tequila, so you can organize your own tasting. ✉ *411 N. Main St., Hailey* ☎ *208/788–4247* *Reservations not accepted* ▭ *AE, DC, MC, V* ⏲ *Closed Sun.*

¢–$ ✕ **Perry's.** The Belgian waffles in this cozy café are favorites of local skiers looking for a carbohydrate and sugar rush. Hot oatmeal, crunchy cereals, yogurt parfaits, and legendary cakelike muffins round out the breakfast menu. Hot and cold sandwiches, soups, and a selection of crunchy salads are offered for lunch, which lasts until 5:30 PM. Take-out service is available. ✉ *131 W. 4th St., Ketchum* ☎ *208/726–7703* ▭ *MC, V* ⏲ *No dinner.*

$$$$ ✕ **Knob Hill Inn.** With lots of wood and log furnishings, the interior of this exclusive inn suits Ketchum's Western character. Since this is a new building, everything inside is decidedly modern. All rooms have nice touches such as wet bars and balconies with mountain views. The suites all have fireplaces. The intimate Place Restaurant ($$–$$$$) serves "seasonal comfort food" paired with stellar wines. A full buffet breakfast, afternoon refreshments, and fresh baked goods are included in the rate. ✉ *960 N. Main St., Box 800, Ketchum 83340* ☎ *208/726–8010 or 800/526–8010* *208/726–2712* *www.knobhillinn.com/info.html* *20 rooms, 4 suites* *2 restaurants, indoor-outdoor pool, gym, sauna* ▭ *AE, MC, V* *BP.*

$$–$$$$ ✕ **Sun Valley Lodge.** Since it opened for business in 1936, this has been the most complete year-round resort in Idaho. The "mall" is patterned after an Austrian village, with a lawn and ponds where white swans float across the waters. In winter, with a thick frosting of snow, the place takes on the look of a toy town. Rooms are charming, with beds made of solid oak. The dramatic Lodge Dining Room, a circular, two-level room, serves old standards such as fresh trout. The standout is a Caesar salad prepared tableside. The resort also has four other restaurants. ✉ *1 Sun Valley Rd., Sun Valley 83353* ☎ *800/786–8259* *208/622–3700* *www.sunvalley.com* *234 rooms, 301 suites* *5 restaurants, tennis court, 3 pools, sauna, bowling, horseback riding, cross-country skiing, ice-skating, cinema, nightclub* ▭ *AE, D, DC, MC, V.*

★ **$$$–$$$$** **Pennay's at River Run.** An owner-operated cluster of well-maintained, homey condos in a parklike setting provides easy access to the paved bike path and, in winter, to Nordic skiing. Sun Valley Resort's quieter secondary base area, River Run, is a quick, complimentary snowmobile ride away. This place is small and its owner and staff pride themselves on personal attention. They are happy, for instance, to suggest and arrange activities. ✉ *300 Wood River Dr., Ketchum 83340* ☎ *208/726–9086* *www.pennays-sunvalley.com* *17 condos* *Hot tub, cross-country skiing; no smoking.* ▭ *AE, MC, V.*

$$$ **Clarion Inn of Sun Valley.** A five-minute shuttle ride from the lifts and steps from downtown shops and restaurants, this hotel would seem to have an enviable location. The disadvantage, though, is that noise leaks into rooms that face Bald Mountain and Highway 75. One of the valley's few outdoor pools (heated year-round) is tucked among the buildings away from the road. The Rustic Moose, a casual restaurant with outdoor seating in summer, sits poolside. During the shoulder seasons, when the ski hill is closed, rates are cut almost in half. ✉ *600 N. Main St., Ketchum 83340* ☎ *208/726–5900 or 800/262–4833* *57 rooms, 1 suite* *Microwaves, refrigerators, pool, exercise equipment, hot tub* ▭ *AE, D, DC, MC, V.*

$ **Wood River Inn.** Hailey's nicest lodging has a stacked-sandstone facade leading to an elegant lobby with subdued lighting. The sunny pool room is enjoyed by a lucky few who have discovered this little gem. The suites in the back face Wood River valley's buttressed western slope. *603 N. Main St., Hailey 83333 208/578–0600 or 877/542–0600 208/578–0700 www.woodriverinn.com 58 rooms, 12 suites Some in-room hot tubs, kitchens, microwaves, refrigerators, pool, hot tub, meeting room, some pets allowed. AE, D, DC, MC, V CP.*

¢–$ **Lift Tower Lodge.** Don't let the old-fashioned lift tower and chair outside the front door confuse you; it's just for show—think of it as Western-style lawn art. Half the rooms at this little lodge look toward the ski mountain; the other seven face Highway 75 (also known in town as Main Street). A Continental breakfast is included. *703 S. Main St., Box 185, Ketchum 83340 208/726–5163 or 800/462–8646 208/726–2614 14 rooms Refrigerators, cable TV in some rooms, outdoor hot tub AE, D, DC, MC, V CP.*

CAMPING **Sawtooth National Recreation Area Campgrounds.** From Ketchum to Stanley is a cornucopia of campgrounds. You'll find nine within 20 mi of Ketchum, either on the Sawtooth National Recreation Area north of Ketchum, or in the Challis National Forest to the northeast and southeast. Of the nine, the Wood River Campground, 10 mi north of Ketchum on Highway 75, is the largest, with 30 sites and an outdoor amphitheater for lectures. Most are much smaller and, being slightly off the beaten path, see relatively few travelers for such a major travel corridor. *Most campgrounds have pit toilets, drinking water, fire pits, picnic tables Hwy. 75, north of Ketchum 208/727–5013 Free–$12 No credit cards May–Sept.*

CONDOMINIUMS **Premier Resorts at Sun Valley** has a collection of condominiums and town houses throughout Wood River valley for short- and long-term stays. The company prides itself on representing top-notch properties, from in-town condominiums for families to ski-to-your-door luxury homes at the base of the ski mountain. *Box 659, Sun Valley 83353 208/727–4000 or 800/635–4444 208/727–4040 www.sunvalley-realestate.com.*

Nightlife & the Arts

Nightlife

The area's most happening nightspot for more than a decade has been **Whiskey Jacques** (Main St. and Sun Valley Rd., Ketchum 208/726–3200). It's a cross between a trendy nightclub and a cowboy bar. Live music, Western dancing, and lots of drinking help to create a rowdy crowd and a few red eyes on ski slopes the next day. The food is popular, too—everything from burgers to hand-tossed pizzas. You'll think you've stepped into an English country pub when you walk in the door of the **Cellar Pub** (400 Sun Valley Rd., Ketchum 208/622–3832). Sip from an authentically shaped pint glass of Bass, Harp, or Bodington Pub Ale and enjoy fish-and-chips or bangers and mash (they're sausages soaked in lager and grilled, served with mashed potatoes and gravy). Other pub grub is equally good. Enjoy live blues and rock once a week or so at the **Red Elephant Saloon** (107 Main St., Hailey 208/788–6047). You can have a good dinner here, too. The management prides itself on its Black Angus beef but also serves seafood, pork, and chicken.

The Arts

Hailey's **Liberty Theatre and Company of Fools** (116 N. Main St., Hailey 208/788–6520) presents everything from the sublime (*The Pied Piper*) to the intentionally ridiculous (*Waiting for Godot*). The total audience for the company's first show was 30 back in 1997. Now about 14,000 turn out every season. When live shows aren't on the boards, films are screened in this intimate, 250-seat theater.

Shopping

Downtown Ketchum is packed with small shops, galleries, and cafés. Everything from Ralph Lauren designs to Native American beadwork beckons from shop windows. For more information on gallery tours, or a map, contact **Sun Valley Gallery Association** (Box 1241, Sun Valley 83353 ☎ 208/726–2602). In the famous resort's pedestrian mall, **Sun Valley Village** (✉ Sun Valley Rd., Sun Valley ☎ 208/622–2194) is the home to a baker's dozen of mostly upscale specialty shops ranging from Bill Mason Outfitters to Towne and Park Jewelers.

CENTRAL IDAHO MOUNTAINS

In sharp contrast to the low, hot Snake River plain that dominates much of southern Idaho, this is a region of tree-covered mountains divided by rushing rivers. Towns are small and seldom prosperous, subsisting on a thin soup of seasonal tourism, ranching, and the remains of once-dynamic logging and mining industries. Roads are slow and winding, lined with breathtaking vistas but a bit low on gas stations. At the center of this region are the Sawtooth National Recreation Area and the jagged Sawtooth Mountains. Four nature preserves—the Boise, Challis, Targhee, and Sawtooth national forests—contain, between them, most of the land in the region and practically all of it outside the valleys.

Stanley

9 *61 mi northwest of Ketchum via Hwy. 75.*

Deep in the heart of south-central Idaho, the Sawtooth Range assembles more than 40 needlelike spires that reach up at least 10,000 feet and march across the valley floor for more than 35 mi. The 8,700-foot Galena Pass overlook, about 25 mi north of Ketchum on Highway 75, marks the southern end of the Sawtooths and the White Cloud Range, which faces the Sawtooths on the eastern side of the valley. The renowned Salmon River, powerful enough to carve one of the deepest gorges in North America a couple of hundred miles downstream, is a shallow, laughing river as it passes Stanley. In the summer, Stanley hosts a swarm of hikers, bikers, campers, rafters, and kayakers.

Sports & the Outdoors

HIKING At one time, the Sawtooths were in line to become a national park, but it didn't happen: Congress instead divvied the land up into two parcels—a wilderness area and a national recreation area, each with different regulations. This has not, however, detracted significantly from the beauty of the landscape of rough-edged peaks. And perhaps *because* this is not a national park, much of the backcountry here is barely visited, even in summer. There are 180 lakes, but only two or three of the most accessible receive much traffic. The time to trek is between July and September, when trails are generally clear of snow. A good source of official information are the rangers of the **Sawtooth National Forest** (✉ 2647 Kimberly Rd. E, Twin Falls, ID 83301 ☎ 208/737–3200). If your desired trail is in the recreation area portion of the Sawtooths, check in with the **Sawtooth National Recreation Area** (✉ Star Rte., Ketchum 83340 ☎ 208/726–7672).

Fishhook Trail is a gentle trek of less than 5 mi round-trip (sturdy sneakers suffice) along Fishhook Creek, with spectacular views of meadows, beaver ponds, and snowcapped peaks. The trailhead parking area is near Redfish Lake, about 2 mi south of Stanley on Highway 75.

KAYAKING & RAFTING Daylong rafting trips on the Salmon River in the Sawtooth Valley are available through several area outfitters. One good local guide is the **River Company** (✉ Hwy. 21 ☎ 208/774–2244 🌐 therivercompany.com).

As far as kayakers and rafters are concerned, however, the two sections of the Salmon River of greatest interest are the long wilderness runs on the Middle Fork and the Main. Most Middle Fork trips launch from the Stanley area, and runs on the Main Salmon start downstream near the town of Salmon. Trips are offered by a host of outfitters, but one that does it a little differently is **OARS-Dories** (☎ 208/423–7201). Instead of the more typical inflatable rafts, the company runs its five- and six-day trips in dories, which are graceful rowing craft designed to handle well in white water.

Where to Stay & Eat

$$–$$$ ✕ **Kasino Club Bar & Restaurant.** The pine-paneled walls are hung with rafting and fishing photos at this small-town bar and grill. The menu, although heavy on standards such as steaks and ribs, offers interesting alternatives such as garlic lime pork and the popular "black-and-blue beef" (prime rib rubbed with Cajun spices and Gorgonzola). The salad bar is ample and extensive. ✉ *21 Ace of Diamonds St.* ☎ *208/774–3516* ▭ *AE, DC, MC, V* ⊙ *May–mid-Oct., open daily; Jan.–Mar. weekends only; no lunch.*

¢ ✕ **Stanley Baking Company.** The tables in the sunny little dining room are full most summer mornings. So are those on the deck. Breakfasts at this coffeehouse and deli range from oatmeal to fritatas; lunches are mostly sandwiches and wraps (feel free to design your own). Everything can be packaged to take with you on your hike. ✉ *Wall St.* ☎ *208/774–2981* ▭ *AE, MC, V* ⊙ *Open mid-Apr.–mid-Oct. No dinner.*

★ **$$$$** **Idaho Rocky Mountain Ranch.** Constructed in the 1930s by a New York business executive as an invitation-only guest ranch, the 8,000-square-foot chinked log lodge with its massive rock fireplace remains much the same, decorated with period photographs and deer and elk heads on the walls. Even the original monogrammed white china is still in use. Lodge rooms and most of the duplex cabins have stone showers and handcrafted log furniture. A natural hot springs pool is a short walk away. On weekends, barbecue dinners are given on the wide front porch, where musicians entertain with toe-tapping acoustic Western music and spin yarns about Idaho cowboys and local ghosts. ✉ *Off U.S. 75, 9 mi south of Stanley, 83278* ☎ *208/774–3544* 📠 *208/774–3477* *4 lodge rooms, 17 duplex cabin units* *Dining room, pool, hiking, horseback riding, horseshoes, volleyball* ▭ *D, MC, V* ⊙ *Open mid-June–mid-Sept.* *FAP.*

$–$$ **Redfish Lake Lodge.** A bustling community in the woods, Redfish Lake Lodge offers accommodations, dining, and recreation under one roof. Your options range from simple, small rooms under the eaves of the log lodge, built in 1926, to more modern apartments with stone fireplaces and kitchens. The cafeteria-style restaurant has great views of Redfish Lake. It serves a standard breakfast with more eclectic offerings for lunch and dinner. A marina has lake rides and boat rentals. Hiking and other outdoor opportunities abound. *Box 9, Stanley 83278* ☎ *208/774–3536* 🌐 *www.redfishlake.com* *9 rooms with shared bath, 32 cabins* *Restaurant, snack bar, lake, marina, hiking, lounge; no a/c, no room phones, no room TVs, no smoking* ▭ *AE, DC, MC, V* ⊙ *Open mid-May–late Sept.*

$ **Mountain Village Resort.** The biggest motel in Stanley is across the road from the only grocery store and has a restaurant that serves breakfast, lunch, and dinner seven days a week. A ½-mi walk from the motel takes you to an enclosed hot tub fed by a natural spring. Ask about rooms in the newer building in the rear, where you'll have high ceilings and views are of the Sawtooth Mountains and the valley floor. In winter, a section of snowmobile trail runs right past the property. *Box 150, Stanley 83278 208/774–3661 208/774–3761 www.mountainvillage.com 57 rooms, 3 suites Restaurant, lounge, in-room VCRs, laundry facilities, some pets allowed, no-smoking rooms; no a/c AE, DC, MC, V.*

¢ **Jerry's Country Store & Motel.** This pleasant, easygoing motel offers clean, comfortable rooms and an excellent view of the Sawtooth Mountains. There's a VCR in your room, and there are movies for rent in the lobby. It's about 1 mi north of Stanley. *Box 300, Stanley 83278 208/774–3566 208/774–3518 9 rooms Kitchenettes, in-room VCRs AE, D, MC, V.*

Sawtooth National Recreation Area Campgrounds. Scattered along the Sawtooth Valley from Galena Summit to Stanley, down the Salmon River, and near Highway 21 is a delightful range of developed campgrounds. The best are the eight small campgrounds west of Stanley. The most remote, undoubtedly, is the Grandjean Campground, 35 mi from Stanley with trail access into the Sawtooth Wilderness. *Most campgrounds with pit toilets, drinking water, fire pits, picnic tables 208/727–5013 Free–$12 No credit cards May–Sept.*

off the beaten path

CUSTER MOTORWAY ADVENTURE ROAD – This 35-mi driving tour follows Forest Road 070 between Stanley and Challis. It begins at the Sunbeam Dam, about 10 mi east of Stanley. The narrow dirt road is suitable for all but low-clearance vehicles and large RVs. The route had its start when miners were in a hurry to get to the gold mines near Challis in the 1870s. By 1879 an enterprising young man had built a toll road to the optimistically named community of Bonanza, now a ghost town. The old road was reconstructed by the Civilian Conservation Corps in 1933 and designated the Custer Motorway. Along the way are the remains of the original tollgate; the Bonanza Cemetery; and the mammoth 112-foot-long Yankee Fork Dredge, where the riverbed was dug up to recover gold. A brochure and map are available from the **Yankee Fork Ranger District** (HC 67, Box 650, Clayton 83227 208/838–2201).

Grandjean

10 *103 mi west of Ketchum via Hwy. 75 and Grandjean Rd.*

Tucked into the western flanks of the jagged Sawtooth Range and perched at the edge of the Sawtooth Wilderness Area, Grandjean is less a town than the abrupt end of a dirt road. The place gets its name from Emil Grandjean, who hunted and trapped here in the late 19th century and later became forest supervisor of the Boise National Forest. Grandjean Road follows the South Fork Payette River upstream, away from the highway. The river is packed with smaller rainbows, cutthroats, and brook trout. Natural hot springs bubble from the ground here and there along the way. Grandjean Road provides good trail access to the wilderness. Sawtooth Lodge, the only source of food and shelter in the area, was at one time a Forest Service ranger station.

Where to Stay

¢–$ **Sawtooth Lodge.** Accommodations here are as rustic as they come: most cabins have beds and bedding, handmade log furniture, and enamel wood-fired stoves for heating and cooking. There is electricity for lights, but

OF DUDES & RANCHES

*B***Y THE LATE 1800S,** *stories of the jagged peaks and roaring rivers in the Rocky Mountains had caught the nation's imagination. Travelers headed west to see these wonders firsthand, riding on the recently completed transcontinental railroads. But when they arrived, they found that the frontier was exactly what they had heard it was—a rough-and-tumble wilderness. The lodging these Easterners were accustomed to did not yet exist.*

So these early travelers stayed where they could, which was often at rustic ranches. It worked out well, because ranchers, starved for fresh faces and news from back home, were pleased to have the company. Travelers found that staying on these ranches gave them a taste of life in the West. Often they came back the following year, and the year after that. Soon ranches began hosting paying guests. These "dudes" stayed for weeks or months and participated in the day-to-day operations of the ranch, often mending fences and driving cattle. By 1940, more than 300 dude ranches were operating in the United States and Canada.

Today, you'd be hard pressed to find one of these places calling itself a dude ranch—"guest ranch" sounds better. And monthlong stays are a thing of the past. The typical stay is about a week. Activities include trail rides, barbecues, hoedowns, and sometimes opportunities to work with the livestock. The week often culminates in a gymkhana, a series of competitive horseback events.

not enough power to run other appliances. The oldest cabins, built in 1927, don't have interior plumbing, although drinking water and hot showers are available nearby. In the cozy, low-ceilinged main lodge you can buy a few supplies and catch a home-cooked meal. A swimming pool, heated by underground springs, averages between 78°F and 88°F. Reservations are a must. ✉ *636 Grandjean Rd., 83637* ☎ *208/259–3331* 🌐 *www.sawtoothlodge.com* *11 cabins* *Restaurant, pool, some pets allowed (fee); no a/c, no room phones, no room TVs* 💳 *AE, MC, V* ⏲ *Open late May–mid-Oct.*

Lowman

⓫ *119 mi west of Ketchum via Hwy. 75.*

Soak in natural hot water beside the pretty South Fork of the Payette River at **Kirkwood Hot Springs.** The U.S. Forest Service has improved the area with stairs and a hiking trail but otherwise left it as pleasantly funky as it has long been—part natural depressions catching the hot water that runs down the steep slope, part haphazardly constructed walls and blockages. There are several pools, none larger than a hot tub. A Forest Service campground is here as well, if you like it so much you want to spend the night. ✉ *Hwy. 21, 2 mi east of Lowman.*

There's plenty to do in the **Boise National Forest,** with its more than 2 million acres chock-full of hiking, fishing, camping, and white-water rafting opportunities. Elevations in the forest range from 2,600 feet to 9,800 feet, where you'll have a dramatic view of the rugged mountains in almost every direction. The Boise and Payette river systems are found in this forest, along with parts of the Middle Fork of the Salmon and its lesser-known but lovely cousin, the South Fork of the Salmon. For information, visit the **Lowman Ranger Station** (✉ Hwy. 21 ☎ 208/259–3361 🌐 www.fs.fed.us).

Where to Eat

$–$$ ✕ **Sourdough Lodge.** The breakfasts here are so good that people drive up from Garden Valley to chow down on the plate-size sourdough pancakes. Like everything else on the breakfast menu, they are served all day. The lunch menu has an extensive list of sandwiches, including a tasty hamburger. Dinners also offer a good variety, from homemade pizza to spaghetti and meatballs to strip steak. ✉ *8406 Hwy. 21, Milepost 84* ☎ *208/259–3326* 💳 *AE, DC, MC, V* 🕓 *Closed Mon. Oct.–Apr.*

Idaho City

⓬ *30 mi west of Lowman via Hwy. 21.*

Gold was discovered here in 1862, and the massive migration to the Boise Basin was the biggest since California's gold rush more than a decade earlier. In 1863, at the height of the mining boom, Idaho City was the state's largest community, with a population topping 6,275. At one time more than 200 buildings stood along the town's dusty streets. In 1898, the mining area surrounding the frontier town of Idaho City was overrun with dredging operations; the scars from these giant machines that stripped mile after mile of the landscape can still be seen when you drive through the countryside.

Today the town is part ghost town, part thriving community at the confluence of More's Creek and Elk Creek. You can see weathered wood-frame buildings and other reminders of the town's heyday, including the oldest Masonic Hall west of the Mississippi still in use, the Independent Order of Odd Fellows Hall, the former county courthouse, and a Catholic church. The town publishes a walking-tour map that points out these and other sights.

The **Boise Basin Museum,** originally a post office, was constructed when this was a bustling boomtown in 1867. It later was used as a stop along the stagecoach route. It also served at times as a private residence before it was turned into a museum. Mining techniques are illustrated in several exhibits, and there is also a short movie on the gold rush. ✉ *501 Montgomery St.* ☎ *208/392–4550* 🌐 *www.idahocitychamber.com* 🎟 *$2* 🕓 *Memorial Day–Labor Day, daily 11–4.*

Men carried guns in the town's rough gold-mining days, and they didn't hesitate to use them when challenged. The losers are buried at **Pioneer Cemetery,** along with many other people caught in the cross fire. The cemetery, ¼ mi northwest of town, provides a fascinating look at the area's colorful history. ☎ *208/392–4550* 🌐 *www.idahocitychamber.com* 🎟 *Free.*

McCall

⓭ *98 mi west and north of Lowman via South Fork Rd. and Hwy. 55.*

Although it falls within the state capital's sphere of influence, the town of McCall has the alpine feel of the northern half of the state. The 108-mi drive north from Boise on Highway 55 is one of the most beautiful in Idaho, if not the country. The road, choked by recreational vehicles in summer, runs along the shore of the Payette River as it rollicks down the mountains, over boulders, and through alpine forests. The arid plains of the Snake River give way to higher and higher mountains covered by increasingly dense stands of pine.

McCall traces its beginnings to a wagon train carrying Tom McCall and his family, who liked the area so much that they decided to stay. Laid out in 1901, the town blossomed a few years later with the arrival of the Union Pacific Railroad. The area's first ski slope, Little Ski Hill, opened in 1937. Today it's overshadowed by Brundage Mountain, which is still considered modest compared with other ski resorts in the West, with 1,400 acres of skiable terrain. Currently developers are working to transform nearby **Lake Cascade** into a major ski destination.

During the 1980s, the area was discovered by Californians. Espresso shops and tourist-friendly stores line the streets. Locals are a little ambivalent about all this, but there's no doubt the changes have made McCall one of the most popular resort destinations in the state. The town hosts a popular Winter Carnival each January with massive, intricately detailed ice sculptures.

McCall sits on the south shore of pretty **Payette Lake,** so close that as you enter town proper headed north on Highway 55, it looks like you are going to drive straight into the water. A combination of paved and unpaved road encircles the lake, which is full of cabins and vacation homes. Lake access points include a small public park on East Lake Street, called Rotary Park, and the more tranquil North Beach off Eastside Drive on the north shore of the lake.

The **Payette National Forest** encompasses 2.3 million acres in west-central Idaho. To the east it's bounded by the wild and lovely Frank Church–River of No Return Wilderness, at 2.4 million acres the largest designated wilderness in the lower 48 states, and to the west by the Hells Canyon National Recreation Area. In the forest there are 2,100-odd mi of trail, and 2,500 mi of back roads leading to 30 campgrounds. Snowmobilers will find 600 mi of groomed winter terrain. For information about Payette National Forest, contact the McCall Ranger Station ✉ *102 W. Lake St.* ☎ *208/634–0400* 🌐 *www.fs.fed.us.*

Fodor'sChoice ★ About 30 mi from McCall, the funky little resort of **Burgdorf Hot Springs** consists mostly of a gravel-bottom, log-side pool with 150 gallons per minute of naturally hot water pumping through it and a smaller hot tub fed by the same spring. There's also a scattering of old cabins (available for $25 per person per night) in various stages of repair, although none have electricity, running water, or even sheets and towels. Heat is provided by woodstoves, light by kerosene lamps. Nothing else is out here but the surrounding mountains. In summer, cow elk keep an eye on their calves on the meadow across the dirt road. In fall, bull elk whistle and bugle from the forest. ✉ *Forest Rd. 246 off Warren Wagon Rd.* ☎ *208/636–3036* *$5* ⏲ *Daily 10–dusk.*

Sports & the Outdoors

BOATING Boating is a popular pastime on pretty Payette Lake. You can rent canoes and other paddle-propelled vehicles at North Beach from a company called **Silver Pig** (✉ off Warren Wagon Rd. ☎ 208/634–4562).

GOLF In operation since the first 9 holes were built back in 1926, **McCall Golf Course** (✉ 1000 Reedy La., ☎ 208/634–7200) is one of the oldest links in the state. It now has 27 holes in three 9-hole segments that can be played in any order. The course is characterized by undulating greens and natural hazards such as wetlands and tall pines. Some fairways, especially on the oldest 9, are quite narrow.

CROSS-COUNTRY SKIING & SNOWSHOEING South of McCall, **Little Ski Hill** (✉ Hwy. 55 ☎ 208/634–5691) still serves some downhill skiers, primarily those who want to make a few telemark turns. But most people heading to McCall's original ski area go to enjoy the more than 30 mi of groomed Nordic skating and touring trails. One short loop is reserved for dogs and their owners.

Ponderosa State Park (✉ Scenic Dr. off Eastside Dr. ☎ 208/634–2164 🌐 www.idahoparks.org) maintains about 14 mi of cross-country trails, of which a little more than 1 mi is lighted for night skiing. Lovely views of Payette Lake are your reward.

DOWNHILL SKIING & SNOWBOARDING

Brundage Mountain might be a small ski area as far as chairlifts and tows are concerned, but the area has ample tree-lined terrain and lots of powder. Although the runs are a little short, Brundage does have enough of a challenge to keep intermediates and beginners interested. Advanced skiers find solace in the powder glades. On top of the hill are spectacular views of the Seven Devils Peaks and jewel-like Payette Lake. With a vertical drop of 1,800 feet and 38 runs, Brundage has one quad, two triple chairs, a platter tow, and a handle tow. Brundage is off Highway 55, about 8 mi north of the center of town. ✉ *3890 Goose Lake Rd., McCall* ☎ *208/634–4151* 🎫 *$34* 🕒 *Late Nov.–Apr., daily 9:30–4:30.*

Where to Stay & Eat

$$–$$$$ ✕ **The Mill.** With heavy wooden beams above and antiques scattered about, this longtime favorite couldn't be more atmospheric. The place is also a carnivore's dream, dishing out huge portions of steak and prime rib accompanied by a steaming spud. There are also plenty of seafood dishes for those who want to go against the flow. The food is as good as it could be, and so is the service. ✉ *324 N. 3rd St.* ☎ *208/634–7683* 💳 *AE, D, MC, V.*

$$–$$$ ✕ **Romano's Ristorante & Lounge.** Locals favor this place for the accompaniments at dinner: fresh-baked bread hot from the oven and a bottomless salad bowl with rarely seen items such as garbanzo beans and pepperoncini. Top it all off with the homemade Italian dressing. You'll want to grab a table outdoors, because the deck faces stunning Payette Lake. If you've had your fill of spaghetti and meatballs, entrées such as liver and onions and rib-eye steak are also popular. There's also a short children's menu. ✉ *203 E. Lake St.* ☎ *208/634–4396* 💳 *MC, V* 🕒 *Closed Sun. and Mon. Sept.–May. No lunch.*

$–$$$ ✕ **Pancake House.** At the south edge of town, this breakfast spot has long been a skiers' favorite, thanks to its massive platters of pancakes. Now it also serves old-fashioned dinners such as hearty meat loaf and chicken and dumplings, as well as lighter fare such as burgers and sandwiches. Wash it all down with a beer or glass of wine. Despite the recent move to an almost monolithic log building, you may have a short wait to get in the door, as everybody in McCall seems to eat here. ✉ *209 N. 3rd St.* ☎ *208/634–5849* 💳 *MC, V.*

¢–$ ✕ **Bistro 45.** The most pleasant outdoor dining spot in McCall is hidden on a private courtyard behind Hotel McCall. The fare is simple, mostly salads, soups, quiches, and sandwiches. There's a wide range of coffees and espressos to give you a jolt of caffeine, and beer, wine, and mimosas when you're ready to relax. The wine list changes weekly. If you prefer to bring your own, there's a $5 corkage fee. Locals turn out for the simple breakfast served only on weekends. ✉ *1101 N. 3rd St.* ☎ *208/634–4515* 💳 *MC, V.*

$$$$ 🏨 **Whitetail.** A $50 million renovation transformed the Shore Lodge, once a local landmark, into a resort so posh that it doesn't seem to belong in laid-back Idaho. There's a bit of whimsical log trim here and there to remind you that this once was the frontier, but you dine on crisp linen and relax on overstuffed and richly upholstered chairs and sofas. Most suites have lake views through massive windows, and those on the first floor are steps from the narrow beach. Here you'll find a crescent-shape

hot tub extending for 20 feet. Unlike at many other resorts, the 18-hole golf course is lined with trees instead of mansions. ✉ *501 W. Lake St., 83638* ☎ *208/634–2244 or 800/657–6464* 📠 *208/634–7504* 🌐 *www.whitetailclub.com* *77 suites* *2 restaurants, refrigerators, 18-hole golf course, tennis court, pool, gym, massage, beach, marina, bar, lounge, business services, meeting rooms, no-smoking rooms* 💳 *AE, DC, MC, V.*

$–$$$ **Hotel McCall.** Right in the center of town, this historic hotel has many of the characteristics of the best B&Bs, such as afternoon tea in the library and cookies with milk when you're ready to turn in. Constructed in 1904, the building faces McCall's main drag, so it's near plenty of shops. A pleasant, private courtyard is surrounded by several dining establishments. Avoid the small, dark rooms with shared bath, as others are almost grand and have lots of light streaming in through the windows. The best choices have views of photogenic Payette Lake. A Continental breakfast is included. ✉ *1101 N. 3rd St., 83638* ☎ *208/634–8105* 📠 *208/634–8755* *16 rooms, 10 with bath, 6 suites* *Restaurant, dining room, some in-room hot tubs, some in-room VCRs, business services, meeting room; no a/c in some rooms* 💳 *AE, MC, V* *CP.*

$–$$ **Hartland Inn & Motel.** Located about 10 mi from Brundage in the tiny town of New Meadows, this historic house dates back to 1911. The owners have furnished it with pleasant antiques. The stairs creak quietly, which adds to the charm, as does the lace at the windows and the silver service in the dining room. Two smaller rooms have just water closets, whereas the other three have full baths. A claw-foot tub graces one third-floor room. There are also inexpensive motel rooms and oversize suites with kitchens and gas fireplaces. The grounds are so large there's even room to board your horses. ✉ *Hwy. 95, New Meadows 83654* ☎ *208/347–2114 or 888/509–7400* 📠 *208/347–2535* *5 B&B rooms, 13 motel rooms, 4 suites* *Some kitchenettes, hot tub, meeting room; no a/c in some rooms, no phones in some rooms, no TV in some rooms* 💳 *AC, DC, MC, V.*

¢–$ **Brundage Inn.** The motel closest to the ski area is also one of the area's most family-friendly. The grassy area behind the main building, complete with a picnic table and a barbecue grill, is narrow but long enough for a game of flag football. Many rooms have sleeping lofts that are a big hit with the kids. One of the largest rooms sleeps seven and has a full kitchen, including a dishwasher. If you're looking for even bigger quarters, ask these folks about their vacation bungalows. ✉ *1005 W. Lake St., 83638* ☎ *208/634–2344 or 800/643–2009* 📠 *208/634–4331* 🌐 *www.brundagevacations.com* *16 rooms, 7 suites* *Refrigerators, microwaves, some kitchens, some pets allowed (fee)* 💳 *AE, DC, MC, V.*

CAMPING **Lake Cascade State Park Campgrounds.** The 4,400-acre state park contains 10 locations scattered along the western and southern edges of the lake. Many of the 300 campsites have pretty water views. Small and quiet, Curlew Campground is a tent-only area with minimal facilities. Poison Creek, Van Wyck, and Blue Heron campgrounds stay open year-round. *Drinking water. Grills, picnic tables. Swimming (lake)* ✉ *Lake Cascade, Cascade* ☎ *208/382–4258* 🌐 *www.idahoparks.org* *$11–$13* 💳 *MC, V* *Some campgrounds open year-round.*

Southwestern Idaho Senior Citizen Recreational Association. It takes longer to say the name than to realize you've found one of the most pleasant RV parks in Idaho. The park is on 60 acres of heavily forested land along Lake Cascade, where you'll find a boat ramp and fishing dock. Activities include games in the recreation hall, walks on the nearby trails, and even twice-daily coffee. Best of all are the low prices. If you plan on spending a lot of time in the area, ask about becoming a member and saving even more. The campground is 3 mi off Highway 55: watch for the signs. *Flush toilets, partial hookups, dump station. Drinking water, showers. Grills, picnic tables. Public phone. 200 partial hookups, 26 tent sites ✉ 12991 SISCRA Rd., Donnelly ☎ 208/325–8130 Partial hookups $10, tent sites $5 Reservations not accepted No credit cards June–Sept.*

Nightlife & the Arts

NIGHTLIFE The **Yacht Club** (✉ 203 E. Lake St. ☎ 208/634–5649) draws a mixed crowd of tourists and locals. During ski season and the middle summer, bands play everything from oldies to alternative rock on the weekends. On sunny afternoons, the big draw is the view of sparkling Lake Payette. You can even wander downstairs and out onto the dock for a closer inspection.

The **Pub** (✉ 807 N. 3rd St. ☎ 208/634–1010) serves handcrafted brews and finger food in a cabin with rough paneling, bare rafters, and hardwood floors. Bands often play during the week, making the place popular with locals. There are always at least six house selections on tap, making choosing just one a bit difficult. Brewmaster Gregg Eames likes to put a rich, malty accent even on traditionally dry brews such as stouts.

en route

Highway 55 reaches its peak a few miles outside McCall and then gradually snakes its way downhill. Near Donnelly, you'll soon pass the turnoff to **Gold Fork Hot Springs** (✉ 1026 Gold Fork Rd., near Donnelly ☎ 208/890–8730). This is a pretty 6½-mi drive, although 4 mi of it is dirt that can be muddy in some spots in wet weather. Follow the signs carefully: there are sudden turns, but all are well marked. At the end of the road you'll find a series of concrete pools, each cascading downhill into the next. One is sand-bottomed, another is boulder-walled, and all are pretty. These are soaking pools, not swimming pools: the hottest runs as much as 108°F. At the town of New Meadows, Highway 55 joins U.S. 95 and the Little Salmon River and heads into mining territory, where gold and silver, and rumors of both, drew hundreds of mostly disappointed men.

Challis

14 *187 mi east of McCall via Hwy. 55, South Fork Rd., and Hwys. 21, 75, and 93.*

Challis is not a destination itself, although many people stop here to stock up as they head north into the Salmon National Forest or south into the Challis National Forest, the Sawtooth National Recreation Area, or the Centennials, a mountain range that contains Idaho's highest peak, 12,662-foot Mt. Borah. The area's two main attractions are Challis Hot Springs and the Land of the Yankee Fork Interpretive Center.

At the turn of the last century, **Challis Hot Springs** offered soothing soaks to tired miners. Today you'll find an outdoor cool pool and a pebble-floored hot pool enclosed in a garage-size building. Both are supplied by naturally heated water from the nearby springs. The resort, with some accommodations available, is along the Salmon River. *✉ Hot Springs Rd., 4 ½ mi off Hwy. 93, south of Challis ☎ 208/879–4442 $5.*

If you want to know what daily life was like for gold miners, head to ★ the **Land of the Yankee Fork Interpretive Center.** Displays are informative and attractive, explaining not only how miners lived, but why gold formed in this region, how it was discovered, and the reasons gold towns became ghost towns. A short interpretive trail leads to the Bison Jump, a spot from which local tribes once herded bison to their deaths. ✉ *Hwy. 93 and Hwy. 75* ☎ *208/879–5244* 🌐 *www.idahoparks.org* ⏲ *May–Sept., daily 9–5; Oct.–Apr., weekdays 9–5.*

Salmon

15 *49 mi north of Challis via Hwy. 93.*

Once people came this way looking for a way to cross the Salmon River on their way to gold-colored dreams in the mines of Leesburg. First a ferry was built, then a wagon-size toll bridge. The river still splits the isolated ranching and farming town of Salmon, laid out in 1867, into two parts. Few Idaho towns have retained more of their pioneer feel or have been changed so little by the lure of tourist dollars. Structures dating from the town's earliest years still stand downtown, clustered mostly along Main Street, including the **Shoup Building** (completed in 1885) and the old **Odd Fellows Lodge** (1871). A self-guided walking tour takes you past 19 historic buildings.

Today, many people find themselves in Salmon because Highway 93, the only north–south route through mountainous central Idaho, brings them here on their way to Montana. Or they come, as miners once did, because of the river, only now they want to run it, not cross it. Daylong white-water rafting trips and extended wilderness journeys begin not far from town in the Frank Church–River of No Return Wilderness. Trips on the wild and scenic Middle Fork of the Salmon end just north of Salmon.

Built to celebrate the bicentennial of Meriwether Lewis and William Clark's journey through the region in 1804 and 1805, the **Sacajawea Interpretive Cultural & Education Center** shows how the native Shoshone (or Agai Dika) people helped the explorers survive their mission. The tale is told through the eyes of a Shoshone named Sacajawea, wife of a trapper, who traveled with the pair. The facility has a visitor center, gift shop, and a 1-mi trail with picnic facilities. ✉ *200 Main St.* ☎ *208/756–1188* 🌐 *www.sacajaweacenter.org* 🎫 *$3* ⏲ *May, Sept., and Oct., Tues.–Sat. 9–5; June–Aug., daily 9–5.*

The massive **Salmon-Challis National Forest** contains more than 4.3 million acres of mostly remote country in east-central Idaho, including 1.3 million acres of the Frank Church–River of No Return Wilderness, the largest wilderness area in the lower 48 states. The forest is also home to Borah Peak, the state's tallest mountain, and the Main Salmon River. For information in the Salmon-Challis National Forest, contact the **Salmon-Challis Forest Supervisor's Office** (✉ 50 Hwy. 93 ☎ 208/756–5100 🌐 www.fs.fed.us ⏲ Weekdays 7:45–4:30).

The **Salmon River** was called the "River of No Return" because at one time huge wooden "sweep boats" were launched at the town of Salmon, taking the extremely difficult but most direct route to the miners and settlers in western Idaho. It was a one-way trip, as the giant rafts were dismantled at the other end, their lumber sold to the traders. The Salmon River is still a one-way trip for most, five or more days of white-water-interspersed calm and idyllic riverside camping through busy but roadless wilderness.

Sports & the Outdoors

Permits for those wanting to tackle the river on their own are available through a lottery system, but the easiest way to get on the Salmon River is with an outfitter. Local companies offer daylong excursions as well as journeys lasting five days or even longer. For wilderness trips on the Main Salmon, a small company that will work with you to design the perfect trip is **Cascade Adventures** (☎ 208/634–4909 🌐 www.cascadeadventures.com).

Where to Stay & Eat

$$–$$$ ✕ **Bertram's Brewery & Restaurant.** An extensive menu ranging from Mexican fajitas to Thai curries makes this a pleasant stop along your journey. The pub atmosphere and eclectic salad bar bring old-timers and newcomers in droves. The only downside is that, particularly on summer evenings, the place is so packed that the otherwise good service suffers. Of the handcrafted brews, the India Pale Ale is particularly tasty. ✉ *101 S. Andrews St.* ☎ *208/756–3391* 💳 *MC, V.*

$$$$ **Twin Peaks Ranch.** Established as a dude ranch in the middle of the last century, this 2,900-acre spread about 18 mi south of Salmon is isolated in a mile-high valley between the Salmon River and the Frank Church–River of No Return Wilderness. A pleasant lodge, a few cabins, and a pool are set on 2 acres of well-tended lawn. Activities include fishing, horseback riding, and white-water rafting. You can even practice your marksmanship on the shooting range or, if you're in the frontier spirit, help to herd the cattle. Rates include all meals and activities. There is a three-night minimum in high season. *Box 774, Salmon 83467* ☎ *208/894–2290 or 800/659–4899* *208/894–2429* 🌐 *www.twinpeaksranch.com* *13 cabins* *Dining room, pool, hot tub, boating, fishing, horseback riding* 💳 *MC, V* *Closed Nov.–Apr.* *FAP.*

Fodor's Choice ★

¢–$ **Syringa Lodge Bed & Breakfast Inn.** Pretty views of the town of Salmon and the nearby river make the decks surrounding this three-story lodge even more inviting. The lodge has an open, airy floor plan, so the comfortable great room merges with the bright breakfast room. Interior floors of knotty pine, buffed to a shine, look great with the exterior walls made of bark-covered logs. The main house was built from fire-killed spruce salvaged out of the mountains. The building sits on nearly 20 acres, so you won't look out your bedroom window at another house. ✉ *13 Gott La., 83467* ☎ *208/756–4424 or 877/580–6482* *8 rooms, 6 with bath* *Breakfast room, some pets allowed; no a/c, no room phones, no room TVs, no smoking* 💳 *MC, V* *BP.*

CAMPING **Heald's Haven RV & Campground.** With only 20 campsites on a tree-covered lot surrounded by the sage-covered hills marking the Salmon River's route, this is one of the most peaceful RV parks in the area. It's 12 mi south of Salmon, meaning that traffic noise is nonexistent. The bathroom facilities are unusually clean and pleasant. If you should need anything, the owners live in the campground. You have easy access to the Salmon River from here. *Flush toilets. Full hookups, partial hook-ups. Drinking water, showers* *12 full hookups, 8 partial hookups, 10 tent sites* ✉ *22 Heald's Haven Dr., off Hwy. 93* ☎ *208/756–3929* *Full hookups $15, partial hookups $14, tent sites $12* 💳 *No credit cards* *May–Oct.*

BOISE

"It's tough to be the object of so much swooning, so much rosy wooing . . . ," wrote *Idaho Statesman* reporter Marianne Flagg in 1992. "Now please stop writing about us." Nestled against foothills and riverbanks, with a desert to the south and alpine forests to the north, Boise is worried that its "discovery" is bringing an end to the very quality of life that attracts new transplants. On summer weekends, Highway 55, the major northern route into and out of the Treasure Valley, is bogged down with RVs and SUVs festooned with mountain bikes, kayaks, canoes, and powerboats. In the foothills lining the northern reaches of town, joggers now easily outnumber the deer. New subdivisions sprawl ever wider, blurring the boundaries of towns such as Eagle and Meridian.

Make no mistake, though: even with 185,000 people (and 350,000 in the metro area), the City of Trees can still feel like a small town, especially around its pedestrian-friendly, thoughtfully restored downtown. People exchange waves as they whiz by on their in-line skates or mountain bikes. Traffic stops without complaint for pedestrians. As the only urban center for 300 mi in any direction, Boise gets to lay claim to the title of "most remote urban area in the United States." That and the fact that it's the state's capital and the home to a major university explain why it has cultural attractions, shopping opportunities, and dining variety rare in communities its size.

a good tour

The best place to start your exploration of Boise is at the **Idaho State Capitol** ⚑. The rest of the city fans out from the capitol steps. From here, walk northwest to 8th Street, the heart of downtown Boise. Streets on both sides of this major artery are lined with shops, restaurants, and cafés. When you have seen the area, get into your car and drive south on South Capitol Boulevard. Head east on West Myrtle Street until you reach South 3rd Street, which leads south into leafy Julia Davis Park. Here you'll find the **Idaho Historical Museum** 17. Back on West Myrtle Street about a block east is **Discovery Center of Idaho** 18, a popular stop for kids of all ages. Continue on West Myrtle Street to Walnut Street, where you'll find the **Morrison-Knudsen Nature Center** 19.

After exploring the downtown area, get into your car and drive east on **Warm Springs Avenue** 20 past mansions heated by underground hot springs. About 2½ mi east you'll reach Old Penitentiary Road. Head north to the fortresslike **Old Idaho Penitentiary** 21, one of only three territorial prisons still standing. Here you'll shiver to tales of notorious criminals, as well as evidence of the cruel treatment they received here.

If you're into eagles and falcons, drive west on I–84 to Exit 50. Head south for 6 mi on South Cole Road until you reach West Flying Hawk Lane on the right, where you'll find the **World Center for Birds of Prey** 22.

What to See

18 **Discovery Center of Idaho.** On the northern edge of Julia Davis Park, this hands-on science museum is popular with children, as well as their parents. Almost every exhibit moves, talks, or otherwise acts up. ✉ *131 W. Myrtle St.* ☎ *208/343–9895* 🌐 *www.scidaho.org* 🎫 *$4* 🕒 *Tues.–Sat. 10–5, Sun. noon–5.*

17 **Idaho Historical Museum.** Exhibits on Idaho's past and present include very detailed reconstructions of buildings that make accompanying text about the pioneer days come to life. The museum is in lovely Julia Davis Park. ✉ *610 Julia Davis Dr., off Capitol Blvd.* ☎ *208/334–2120* 🌐 *www.idahohistory.net* 🎫 *Free* 🕒 *May–Sept., Tues.–Fri. 9–5, Sun. 1–5; Oct.–Apr., Tues.–Fri. 9–5, Sat. 11–5.*

16 **Idaho State Capitol.** A replica of the U.S. Capitol in Washington, D.C., this landmark is notable for its graceful dome. You can explore the main rotunda on your own, and in the summer you can join a twice-daily guided tour of the rest of the building. Otherwise, call ahead to schedule a tour. The legislature met in various buildings around town until they finally persuaded the territorial governor to fund a small capitol building and insane asylum in 1885. After the state's population grew, the first capitol was deemed too small, and the current capitol was built in 1912. Sandstone from the Table Rock Quarry east of the city was cut by inmates of the nearby Idaho Penitentiary. ✉ *Capitol Blvd. and Jefferson*

Discovery Center of Idaho **18**
Idaho Historical Museum **17**
Idaho State Capitol **16**
Morrison-Knudsen Nature Center **19**
Old Idaho Penitentiary . . **21**
Warm Springs Avenue **20**
World Center for Birds of Prey . . **22**

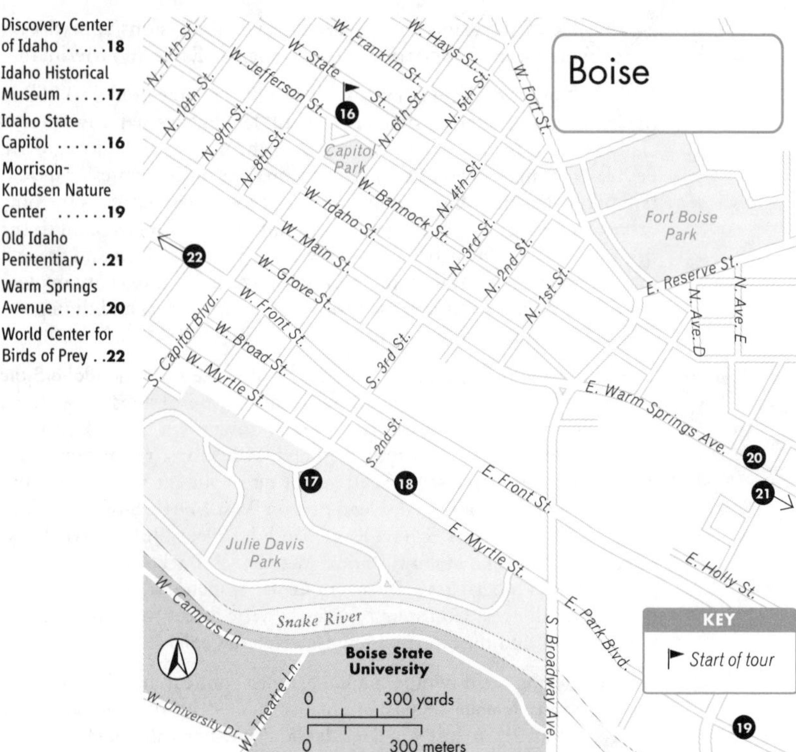

St. ☎ *208/334–5174* *Free* *Weekdays 9–5; tours June–Aug., daily 10 and 1:30 and by appointment year-round.*

★ 19 **Morrison-Knudsen Nature Center.** Behind the Idaho Department of Fish and Game headquarters you'll find an artificial stream, constructed so that you can view trout and salmon from above and below the water's surface. Walking trails pass a sampling of local ecosystems, from a wetlands pond to a high-desert plain. ✉ *600 S. Walnut Ave., at East Park Blvd.* ☎ *208/334–2225* *www.ohwy.com/id/m/mknatctr.htm* *Donations accepted* *Daily sunrise–sunset.*

21 **Old Idaho Penitentiary.** Built in 1870, the prison was used until 1974 without much improvement in conditions. Things became so intolerable by the '60s and '70s that prisoners staged a series of rebellions. The final revolt, in 1973, triggered the move to a more modern facility. The cell blocks have been left exactly as they were after the riot. Scorched stone walls, tiny cells hung with calendars marking the days, and metal bunks evoke the spirit of the place. A self-guided tour, replete with tales of such colorful inmates as Lady Bluebeard and Diamondfield Jack, takes at least 90 minutes. The Idaho Botanical Gardens next door offers an attractive change of scenery. ✉ *2445 Old Penitentiary Rd., off Warm Springs Ave.* ☎ *208/368–6080 or 208/334–2844* *www.ohwy.com/id/o/oldidpen.html* *$4* *Labor Day–Memorial Day, daily noon–5; Memorial Day–Labor Day, daily 10–5.*

20 **Warm Springs Avenue.** Many of the graceful old mansions along this street date back to the late 1800s. The oldest home still standing, built in 1868, is at 1035 Warm Springs Avenue. Many of these houses were heated by underground hot springs. The first in the nation to be heated in this manner is at 1109 Warm Springs Avenue. ✉ *1 mi east of South Capitol Blvd.*

★ 22 **World Center for Birds of Prey.** The headquarters for a conservation and educational program run by the Peregrine Fund, this center houses rare species such as the harpy eagle and peregrine falcon. Live cameras in the nesting areas allow viewing of actual nesting pairs without disturbing them. Displays focus on biology, ecology, and preservation. The highlight of guided visitor center tours is often the appearance of a peregrine falcon "on the glove." ✉ *5666 W. Flying Hawk La.* ☎ *208/362–8687* *$4* *Mar.–Oct., daily 9–5; Nov.–Feb., daily 10–4.*

Sports & the Outdoors

Julia Davis Park is the spot to catch the Boise Tours train but is even more notable as a key gateway to the pleasant **Boise River Greenbelt,** which runs for 25 mi along one and sometimes both banks of the river, linking parks and other attractions all the way from Lucky Peak Reservoir to below the Glenwood Bridge. The trails are favorites of in-line skaters, bikers, and joggers.

Bicycling

The Greenbelt, paved and mostly level, is a great place for cycling. Mountain biking is popular on the hills just outside central Boise. Some of the best trails include the 8th Street Extension (north on 8th Street to where the pavement ends) and Cartwright Road (Harrison Boulevard north to Hill Road, to Bogus Basin Road, then left on Cartwright Road). **Bikes 2 Boards** (✉ 3525 W. State St. ☎ 208/343–0208) rents everything from road bikes to recumbent bikes. The company also rents mountain boards (picture an off-road skateboard and scooter hybrid) and snowboards. For those who like long downhill runs, the staff will shuttle you 3,500 feet up into the mountains for a 7-mi-long, intermediate- or expert-level ride back to the city. Best of all, they'll deliver and pick up their rental equipment anywhere within the city limits.

Golf

With spectacular scenery and gently rolling terrain, it's no surprise that Boise attracts golfers. **Quail Hollow Golf Course** (✉4520 N. 36th St. ☎208/344–7807) has 18 holes and matchless views from Stewart Gulch. Local golfers have rated **Shadow Valley Golf Course** (✉ 15711 Hwy. 55 ☎ 208/939–6699) the best public golf course for four years in a row. Its 18 holes were laid out with an eye for protecting the local wildlife. **Warm Springs Golf Course** (✉ 2495 Warm Springs Ave. ☎ 208/343–5661), closest to downtown, is in the midst of a $4 million face-lift.

Skiing

Only 16 mi north of town, **Bogus Basin Mountain Resort** (✉ 2405 Bogus Basin Rd., 83702 ☎ 208/332–5151 or 800/367–4397) is Boise's backyard ski area, better known for its proximity to town than its reliable snow. The vertical drop is 1,800 feet; six double chairs and four rope tows serve 48 runs, 17 of which are lighted for night skiing.

Tubing

In summer, thousands of people discover the easygoing attractions of tubing—basically, it's just plopping down in an inner tube and floating down a sedate stretch of the Boise River. A special shuttle service from **Ann Morrison Park** (✉ Americana Blvd. between Owyhee St. and Capitol Blvd.) carries tubers to Barber Park, about 6 mi to the east. From there, you drift back to Ann Morrison Park. Inner tubes can be rented at Barber Park.

Water Park

It's easy to be cool at **Roaring Springs** (✉ I–84 at Exit 44 ☎ 208/884–8842 or 877/420–7529). Tot-friendly rides include Endless River, a ¼ mi of canals that circle through the water park. More daring kids can try The Avalanche, which looks like a giant, water-slick half pipe, or Mammoth Canyon, a giant tube slide nearly big enough to drive a Volkswagen through. Lines for popular rides get frustratingly long, especially on summer weekends.

White-Water Rafting

Fodor'sChoice ★ About 45 minutes northeast of Boise on Highway 55, dozens of rafting companies run half-day, full-day, and overnight trips on three forks of the **Payette River.** The various routes range from peaceful and pretty to white-knuckled and wild. Dam releases allow strong flows long after most of the state's white water is gone. Companies can run trips from March to October. Most companies specialize in paddleboats, where you're the passenger as well as the crew. **Cascade Raft Company** (✉ 7050 Hwy. 55, Horseshoe Bend ☎ 208/793–2221 or 800/292–7238) is the biggest outfitter on the Payette River and one of the most conveniently located.

Where to Stay & Eat

$$–$$$ ✕ **Cottonwood Grille.** Dine at linen-covered tables as you gaze down at the Boise River and the surrounding strips of green. Rough sandstone walls and vaulted ceilings create the feeling of a country manor. Chef Peter Blatt prides himself on using the freshest ingredients, so herbs, fruits and vegetables, and seafood are flown in from around the region. The top-quality beef is aged and cut right at the restaurant. Although the place is often packed, extra seating on the patio means you can sometimes walk in without a reservation. ✉ *913 W. River St.* ☎ *208/333–9800* 🌐 *cottonwoodgrille.com* ✍ *Reservations essential* 💳 *AE, MC, V.*

★ **$–$$** ✕ **Bardenay.** Billed as "possibly the nation's first distillery pub," this spacious, wood-trimmed restaurant and bar on Boise's "Basque Block" proudly produces its own gin, vodka, and rum. From great pastrami sandwiches to delectable salmon dishes, Bardenay offers well-prepared meals with creative touches. The place is noisy and vibrant on weekday evenings, when it is filled to overflowing with the after-work crowd. ✉ *610 Grove St.* ☎ *208/426–0538* 💳 *AE, DC, MC, V.*

$ ✕ **Gernika Basque Pub & Eatery.** This popular downtown bar and café is a window on the city's Basque culture. Many people come here for Basque-style finger food such as pimiento sandwiches and spicy sausages, and others opt for the tasty burgers. You may have to squeeze yourself into this narrow corner café if you decide to go on a weekend evening. ✉ *202 S. Capitol Blvd., at Grove St.* ☎ *208/344–2175* 💳 *AE, MC, V* ⏲ *Closed Sun.*

$ ✕ **Goldy's Breakfast Bistro.** There are lines out the door for a table at this breakfast bistro beloved by Boiseans. Create your own breakfast, choosing from offbeat meat selections such as salmon cakes, pesto-chicken sausage, and even Spam. Some of the most popular offerings include fritatas and several variations on the classic eggs Benedict. For lunch the restaurant adds a variety of salads and sandwiches to the menu. A second location, called Goldy's of Hyde Park, has similar offerings but adds steak and salmon dishes for dinner. ✉ *108 S. Capitol Blvd.* ☎ *208/345–4100* ✍ *Reservations not accepted* 💳 *AE, MC, V* ⏲ *No dinner* ✉ *1513 N. 13th St.* ☎ *208/368–0027.*

$ ✕ **Highlands Hollow Brewhouse.** This pub, which brews up its own half-dozen ales, is a favorite stop for skiers and snowboarders heading to or returning from Bogus Basin. The building's massive timbers are matched by the huge portions of everything from overstuffed sandwiches to heaping helpings of red beans and rice. A central fireplace adds to the ski-lodge atmosphere, and speakers pour forth blues and R&B. ✉ *2455 Harrison Hollow Rd.* ☎ *208/343–6820* ▭ *AE, DC, MC, V.*

$ ✕ **Tablerock Brew Pub & Grill.** This microbrewery is responsible for some of the best beer in Idaho, which is what draws huge crowds, especially on weekend nights. Long tables where you can sit with a dozen of your closest friends, an energetic staff that never seems to take a break, and music ranging from pop to jazz create a kinetic atmosphere. The casual menu offers hearty portions of varied fare that goes well with beer—from fiery Cajun dishes to British bangers and mash. ✉ *705 Fulton St.* ☎ *208/342–0944* ▭ *AE, D, DC, MC, V.*

★ ¢–$ ✕ **Gino's Gelato & Pizzeria.** Tony Vuolo is your gracious host, as well as the chef, at this popular pizza place. The upscale atmosphere, the down-home prices, and thin-crust pizzas that make you think you're in Rome are the irresistible draws. Some of Tony's most creative pizzas dispense with the tomato sauce, relying instead on bases of sun-dried tomatoes or caramelized onions. For dessert, try the refreshing gelatos (like ice milk but better), all of it made fresh daily. An extensive wine list and a small selection of domestic, microbrewed, and imported beers round out the menu. The restaurant is upstairs in the Capitol Terrace Building. ✉ *150 N. 8th St.* ☎ *208/331–0475* ✍ *Reservations not accepted* ▭ *AE, MC, V* ⊙ *Closed Sun.*

¢ ✕ **Rockies Diner.** Nothing surprises about the food here, as it's standard diner fare. But the roller-skating waitresses, the over-the-top vinyl-and-linoleum '50s decor, and the exuberant DJ in his glass booth in the evenings are definitely out of the ordinary. At night the volume goes way up and crowd participation is encouraged, so if you're not looking for a party atmosphere, go elsewhere. Rockies opens at 6 AM for more subdued breakfasts. ✉ *3900 Overland Rd.* ☎ *208/336–2878* ▭ *AE, D, DC, MC, V.*

$$–$$$$ Fodor's Choice ★ **Anniversary Inn.** As tastefully luxurious on the outside as it is startling on the inside, the inn never fails to surprise newcomers. Rooms here are decorated according to theme, and some are pretty outrageous. The Biker Roadhouse Room, for instance, comes complete with a cave for a breakfast nook, a dartboard and darts, and, of course, a Harley. Among 25 other options are the Jungle Safari Room and the Sultan's Palace Room. If you like your room so much you don't want to leave, the Continental breakfast is delivered to your door. Weekdays the room rate is about $29 cheaper. The hotel is adjacent to Anne Morrison Park. ✉ *1517 S. Lusk St., 83706* ☎ *208/387–4900 or 800/324–4152* 🖷 *208/331–7022* 🌐 *www.anniversaryinn.com* *41 rooms* *In-room hot tubs, refrigerators, in-room VCRs; no kids, no smoking* ▭ *AE, DC, MC, V* *CP.*

$$ **Doubletree Riverside.** Freshly baked chocolate chip cookies are your reward when you check into this attractive hotel. It occupies a prime location just off the the highway but is sheltered from road noise and is adjacent to the Boise River Greenbelt. The grounds, covered with roses, are beautifully manicured. Rooms are clean and comfortable, with nice touches such as coffeemakers. ✉ *2900 Chinden Blvd., 83714* ☎ *208/343–1871* 🖷 *208/344–1079* 🌐 *www.doubletree.com* *304 rooms, 34 suites* *Restaurant, cable TV, pool, gym, sauna, spa, bar, business services, meeting rooms* ▭ *AE, D, DC, MC, V.*

$–$$$ **Owyhee Plaza.** Several Hawaiians who traveled the Idaho wilderness in the 1800s became local legends. One old spelling for Hawaii is Owyhee, now the name of this hotel. Built in 1910, it lost a little of its charm during renovations in the 1950s, but a bit of its old glory can still be seen in its giant light fixtures and dark-wood paneling. The Gamekeeper restaurant specializes in elegant presentations of lamb and duck. ✉ *1109 Main St., 83702* ☎ *208/343–4611 or 800/233–4611* 🖷 *208/*

381–0695 www.owyheeplaza.com 98 rooms, 2 suites 2 restaurants, pool, hair salon, bar, business services, meeting rooms AE, D, DC, MC, V.

$$ **The Grove Hotel.** Impeccable service makes this luxury hotel a cut above the rest. The unbeatable location doesn't hurt, either. In the heart of downtown, the hotel sits adjacent to its namesake, a block-long plaza surrounded by shops and cafés. The sports bar leads directly to the Bank of America Events Arena, which is home to Boise's hockey team. Sports fans should ask for a room overlooking the valley: besides the attractive panorama, you can sometimes hear events taking place in the arena. For a real splurge, consider one of three fully appointed condos on the 14th floor. *245 S. Capitol Blvd., 83702 208/333–8000 208/333–8800 www.westcoasthotels.com/grove 211 rooms, 20 suites, 3 condos 2 restaurants, room service, minibars, indoor pool, gym, piano bar, sports bar, laundry service, concierge, business services, convention center, meeting rooms, no-smoking rooms AE, D, DC, MC, V.*

$–$$ **J. J. Shaw House Bed & Breakfast Inn.** There is no prettier lodging option in Boise's historic North End than this renovated Victorian. Built in 1907, it has rooms overflowing with period antiques. Innkeeper Junia Stephens prides herself on her specialty breakfast: stuffed croissant French toast with huckleberry syrup. Her mother bakes fresh goodies, which magically appear each afternoon on the upstairs buffet. The entire third floor is a single suite, with an elegantly draped king-size bed, skylights, and a shower big enough for two. *1141 W. Franklin St., 83702 208/344–8899 208/344–6677 www.jjshaw.com 4 rooms, 1 suite Breakfast room, Internet; no room TVs, no kids under 10, no smoking AE, DC, MC, V BP.*

$ **Best Western Vista Inn.** Of all the motels clustered between the airport and I–84, this is one of the best. A two-story hallway scattered with tables and chairs runs the length of the building. All rooms open to this pleasant space as well as to the parking lots outside. Milk and cookies are served nightly. *2645 Airport Wy., 83705 208/336–8100 or 800/727–5006 208/342–3060 www.bestwestern.com/vistainn 87 rooms Some refrigerators, cable TV, indoor pool, exercise equipment, spa, video game room, business services, meeting rooms AE, D, DC, MC, V CP.*

★ $ **Idaho Heritage Inn.** Craig and Betti Newburn operate this pretty blue B&B in a former governor's residence about six blocks east of downtown. Each room is different, but all have political themes. The Governor's Suite has a sleigh bed and an enclosed sunporch. Delicately patterned wallpaper and old-style bed frames retain an early 1900s feel. The top-floor room, carved out of the attic, is perfect for those in search of privacy. A full breakfast is included in the rate. *109 W. Idaho St., 83702 208/342–8066 www.idheritageinn.com 6 rooms Dining room AE, D, MC, V BP.*

Camping

Fiesta RV Park. About 2 mi west of Boise, this RV park has good-size campsites, many shaded by old trees. All have paved pads, and most have grass strips separating them from neighbors. The white-tiled bathrooms are very clean. The horseshoe pits and large barbecue pit make this place perfect for family gatherings. *Flush toilets. Full hookups, partial hookups, dump station. Drinking water, guest laundry, showers. Picnic tables. Public telephone. Play area, swimming (pool) 127 full hookups, 18 partial hookups, 6 tent sites 11101 Fairview Ave.,*

83713 ☎ 208/375–8207 Full hookups $28–$32, partial hookups $25, tent sites $23 ▭ DC, MC, V.

Nightlife & the Arts

The city's classic night-on-the-town takes place downtown, where you can stroll from restaurant to coffeehouse to pub to nightclub. All are clustered, more or less, around Capitol and Main. Everyone turns out on weekends, from high school kids cruising the drag in their pickup trucks, to college students dancing frenetically to bands that range from passable to fantastic, to the mellow older crowd listening to acoustic music and munching peanuts.

Nightlife

The **Blues Bouquet** (✉ 1010 W. Main St. ☎ 208/345–6605) is known for its beautiful mahogany bar. There's a small dance floor where you can gyrate to a sampling of national and local blues artists. Although they share an address, **Tom Grainey's** and **J. T. Toad's** (✉ 109 S. 6th St. ☎ 208/345–2505) could hardly be more different. The low ceiling at the cavelike J. T. Toad's seems appropriately grungy for the young crowd. Tom Grainey's is a good place to see local bands. A single cover charge gets you into both venues. If you don't find the music at either place to your taste, both have access to the quieter seating along the sidewalk.

The Arts

In summer, a lovely riverside amphitheater surrounded by a quiet pond and meandering trails hosts nationally acclaimed productions, many of them written by a certain gentleman from Stratford-on-Avon. There's a snack bar, but most people bring a picnic basket and a bottle of wine. You can opt for seats in the bleachers or on the lawn, but the best are at tables where you can turn the experience into dinner theater. For information, contact the **Idaho Shakespeare Festival** (✉ 5657 Warm Springs Ave. ☎ 208/336–9221 🌐 www.idahoshakespeare.org).

Fodor'sChoice ★

The **Morrison Center for the Performing Arts** (✉ 2101 Campus La. ☎ 208/385–1609 🌐 mc.boisestate.edu) has one of the most extensive arts programs in the state. Ballet Idaho, the Boise Opera Company, the Boise Philharmonic, and the Boise Master Chorale all have full seasons, and touring Broadway productions make frequent stops.

Shopping

A rich selection of shops and boutiques lines the downtown streets, especially around the Grove, a plaza with a towering fountain at its center. On hot summer afternoons, children run between the two-story-tall jets of water while their folks window-shop. South of the Grove is the **Eight Street Marketplace** (✉ Capitol Blvd. and Front St.), a brick warehouse converted into stores. North of the Grove, the **Eighth Street Shops** (✉ 8th St. between Grove and Broad Sts.) spice up a restored Victorian-era block with specialty stores and small restaurants. **Capitol Terrace** (✉ Idaho and Main Sts. ☎ 208/384–3901) has a trendy industrial look, with restaurants on the balcony level and shopping on the ground floor.

Boise Factory Outlets (✉ Gowen Rd. off I–84 ☎ 208/331–5000) stretches along the interstate in southeast Boise. High-end stores range from Farber to Eddie Bauer to Coldwater Creek. Inside Boise Towne Square is **Pendleton** (✉ Franklin and Cole Rds. off I–84 ☎ 800/743–9606), the Northwest's best-known maker of high-quality woolens.

SOUTHWESTERN IDAHO

Southwest Idaho is a sagebrush-covered plain broken occasionally by low, infrequently traveled desert mountains. It's split by sometimes startlingly dramatic river gorges and graced with occasional verdant river valleys. Owyhee country, in the extreme southwestern corner of the state, is mostly wilderness. Agriculture is king in this corner of the state. The major attractions of the area are clustered along the Snake River, as are population centers.

Twin Falls

23 *128 mi southeast of Boise via I–84.*

Driving into Twin Falls feels like putting on a comfortable sweater. It's as all-American a city as you'll find anywhere. After a shopping mall was built on the edge of town near the I. B. Perrine Bridge, downtown merchants banded together to take on the competition. The result is a downtown straight out of the 1950s, with neon signs drawing attention to the small shops, bars, and cafés. The only drawback is the town's maddening adherence to the classic Mormon street patterns. For example, there are four streets called 3rd Avenue, one for each point on the compass. The massive Greek Revival **Twin Falls Courthouse** (✉ 425 Shoshone St. N) faces a band shell in the adjoining park, home to summertime concerts.

At the **Herrett Center for Arts & Science,** ancient artifacts from southern Idaho and around the world are on display. But the big draw is the Faulkner Planetarium, with its 50-foot dome and 11,000-watt sound system. Periodically the center hosts "star parties" on the front lawn, at which the center's high-powered telescopes are trained on the night sky. If this gets you interested in astronomy, there are smaller telescopes for sale in the gift shop. *✉ 315 Falls Ave. ☎ 208/733–9554 Ext. 2655 🌐 www.csi.edu/herrett ⏲ Closed Sun. and Mon.*

The town gained its reputation as the site of a pair of waterfalls: Twin Falls and Shoshone Falls. The latter, 1,000 feet wide and 212 feet high, is taller than Niagara Falls by about 50 feet. Milner Dam often reduces the flow over famous Shoshone Falls to little more than a trickle, but during the spring thaw the falls often regain their roaring glory. As you travel south on U.S. 93, just across the Snake River you'll see signs pointing you toward **Centennial Waterfront Park** (✉ Canyon Springs Rd. ☎ 208/733–3974). Because of the sheer canyon walls, the park provides the only river access in the area. You can't see Shoshone Falls from Centennial Waterfront Park, but pontoon boat and canoe trips to the base of the area's most famous falls depart from here.

To see Shoshone Falls from the canyon rim, head for **Shoshone Falls Park** (✉ 3300 East Rd., ☎ 208/736–2265), a scenic overlook 2 mi east of Centennial Waterfront Park. Admission is $3 per vehicle. A little farther east than Shoshone Falls Park, the Idaho Power Company maintains a viewing area at **Twin Falls Park** (✉ 3500 East Rd., ☎ 208/773–3974).

I. B. Perrine Bridge is three attractions in one. On the south side of the bridge, near the visitor center, is the site of daredevil Evel Knievel's 1974 attempt to jump the Snake River canyon on a rocket-powered motorcycle. Second, a paved trail runs from the parking lot along the canyon rim for about 1 mi east and west, providing dramatic peeks into the canyon. Finally, there is no better way to appreciate the 487-foot bridge than to watch humans dive off it. Perrine is the only major bridge in the country from which BASE jumping (skydiving from stationary objects) is legal year-round. In warm weather, the parking lot fills with people in snug, wind-resistant clothing and what look like form-fitting backpacks. ✉ *U.S. 93.*

off the beaten path

SHOSHONE ICE CAVES – Molten basalt flowing across the earth's surface sometimes cools and hardens on the outside while the interior still runs like water, forming long caves called lava tubes. Unlike limestone caves with their entrancing stalactite and stalagmite formations, lava tubes are comparatively featureless, but this one, because it is three football fields long, is lined with ice even in the middle of the summer. It's worth a stop just to cool off. ✉ *Hwy. 93, north of Twin Falls and Shoshone* ☎ *208/886–2058* ⏲ *May–Sept., daily 8–7:15.*

Sports & the Outdoors

ROCK CLIMBING About 77 mi southeast of Twin Falls, the **City of Rocks National Reserve** (✉ Hwy. 27 ☎ 208/824–5519) draws climbers from around the world to its towers of rough granite. The weird formations rise from flat desert floor, creating the equivalent of a huge jungle gym for what in the climbing world are known as "sport climbers," people who rely on the relative safety of ropes affixed to bolts that have been permanently drilled into the rock. Nonclimbers are drawn by the chance to clamber around on the lower rock formations, to camp amidst the oddly jumbled terrain, or to race about on mountain bikes. This place, despite its remoteness, is often packed. The nearest towns are Almo and Oakley.

Where to Stay & Eat

$$–$$$$ ✕ **Rock Creek.** This steak house west of downtown is a throwback to the days when red meat reigned supreme. Today, however, seafood dishes round out the menu. With a dark-red interior lined with chunky booths, this place makes it clear that none of the entrées are going to be too fancy. The bar is known for its wide selection of single-malt whiskeys and vintage ports and for the most comprehensive wine list in town. ✉ *200 Addison Ave. W* ☎ *208/734–4154* ▭ *AE, D, MC, V* ⏲ *No lunch.*

$$–$$$ ✕ **South Pacific Grill.** Seasoned with lemongrass, coconut milk, mango, soy, and sake, the seafood and beef dishes at this popular place taste like the tropics. Jasmine and garlic rice is the perfect accompaniment. The presentations are as creative as the whimsical decor (tropical fishes swimming on the walls, orchids blooming on the tablecloths). Located in tree-lined Main Street's shopping district, the restaurant's limited sidewalk seating is popular with the lunch crowd. ✉ *117 Main Ave. E* ☎ *208/733–5988* ▭ *AE, D, DC, MC, V* ⏲ *Closed Sun. No dinner Mon.*

★ ¢–$ ✕ **Buffalo Café.** Ask anybody in town where to go for breakfast, and you're sure to get the same answer. You might not believe it when you arrive, because the place is squeezed next to a tire store and across from a truck lot surrounded by barbed wire. You shouldn't pass up the Buffalo Chip, a concoction of eggs, fried potatoes, cheese, bacon, peppers, and onion. The brave can ask for a Mexi Chip, made with spicy chorizo sausage. A half order should fill most stomachs. This tiny café (along with its twin in Sun Valley) lets you sit at the counter or one of the tables. If you go on Sunday, expect to wait. ✉ *218 4th Ave. W* ☎ *208/734–0271* ▭ *No credit cards* ⏲ *No dinner.*

$–$$ 🏨 **RedLion Canyon Springs Hotel.** This low-slung building has very well-kept rooms that are larger than those at most nearby motels. Some units have a balcony overlooking the sparkling pool. It's a short drive from

Shoshone Falls. ✉ *1357 Blue Lakes Blvd. N, 83301* ☎ *208/734–5000 or 800/727–5003* 🖷 *208/734–5000* 🌐 *www.redlion.com* *112 rooms* *Restaurant, pool, exercise equipment, sauna, bar, business services, meeting rooms* 💳 *AE, D, DC, MC, V.*

$ **AmeriTel Inn Twin Falls.** This motel has large rooms with dark-wood furnishings and a color scheme that runs toward blues, greens, and mauves. Whirlpool tubs are a treat after a day of exploring the area. A Continental breakfast is served each morning, and freshly baked cookies are a delightful surprise in the afternoon. ✉ *1377 Blue Lakes Blvd. N, 83301* ☎ *208/736–8000 or 800/822–8946* 🖷 *208/734–7777* *118 rooms* *Kitchenettes, indoor pool, gym, hot tubs, lounge, business services, meeting room* 💳 *AE, D, DC, MC, V* 🍽 *CP.*

CAMPING **Anderson Camp.** Just off the interstate but far enough away to be free of highway noise, Anderson Camp has a pair of swimming pools (one with a waterslide), a miniature-golf course, a horseshoe pit, a game room, and a snack bar serving hamburgers and hot dogs cooked to order. When the fruit ripens on nearby trees, you're welcome to pick some. The convenient location means that during the summer months campsites fill quickly. *Flush toilets. Full hookups, dump station. Drinking water, guest laundry, showers. Grills, picnic tables. Public telephone. General store, service station. Play area, swimming (pool)* *61 full hookups, 16 tent sites* ✉ *1188 E. 990 S* ☎ *208/825–9800 or 888/480–9400* *Full hookups $24–$27, tent sites $19* 💳 *AE, DC, MC, V.*

Nat-See-Pah Hot Springs & RV Park. About 16 mi from Twin Falls, this tree-shaded RV park is known for its peace and quiet (unless a big family reunion is taking place). The swimming pool, fed by an underground spring, stays at about 92°F. The water is an odd shade of green because of dissolved minerals. You can rent a bathing suit if you don't want to take the color home as a souvenir. There is also a hot tub, and a snack bar serving candy bars. The place is off South Blue Lakes Boulevard. *Flush toilets. Fire pits and grills at many sites. Picnic tables. Public phone. Swimming (pool).* *24 full hookups, 46 partial hookups, tent area* ✉ *2738 E. 2400 N, 83303* ☎ *208/655–4337* *Full hookups, partial hookups, and tent sites $12* 💳 *No credit cards* ⏲ *May–mid-Sept.*

Nightlife & the Arts

NIGHTLIFE **Dunken's** (✉ 102 Main Ave. ☎ 208/733–8114), an homage to the region's microbreweries, has become a regular stop for downtown workers. There are 21 taps dispensing most of the better Northwestern brews. Regulars come for a beer, some good conversation, and a few games of cribbage, dominoes, or chess. They stay for the delicious sandwiches, especially the New Orleans–style muffaletta (ham, salami, and cheese) served on focaccia bread.

Shopping

Downtown Twin Falls has a variety of small stores. Ducking into the stores along Main Avenue where it intersects with Shoshone Street is much like shopping in small American towns used to be before the coming of malls. You'll find plentiful off-street parking (free and big enough for RVs), shady sidewalks, and small storefronts filled with clothing boutiques, jewelry shops, and the like.

en route

The I. B. Perrine Bridge crosses the Snake River just north of Twin Falls. You may feel a sudden sense of vertigo as you cross the massive canyon, justly known for its dramatic setting. (A similar effect occurs to travelers who cross the Hansen Memorial Bridge, a few miles east of town.) The flat plain to the north simply falls away into the chasm below. About 15,000 years ago, a massive inland sea called Lake

Bonneville (the remnant of which is the Great Salt Lake) crashed through its natural dikes in southeastern Idaho and poured into the Snake River. For about six weeks, a volume of water many times greater than the flow of the Amazon acted like a giant plow as it thundered down the Snake River and carved out the canyon.

Hagerman

24 *34 mi west of Twin Falls via I–84 and Hwy. 46.*

The Hagerman Valley is home to the state's most famous fossil, a complete skeleton of a small horse dating back to the last Ice Age. But that's not why Idahoans come to this 20-mi-long and 4-mi-wide valley dominated by the alternately placid and turbulent Snake River. The valley is a hot spot for hot water, and spring-fed pools are found everywhere.

One of the most beautiful spots is called Thousand Springs, where waterfalls trickle and spurt from high on the canyon walls, plunging into the Snake River below. Before dams and diversions, these displays were vastly more dramatic. Now much of the water that does emerge, clean enough to drink at a steady 58°F, is captured and used in the valley's thriving trout-farming industry. (Some 70% of the nation's commercially grown trout hail from here.) Along the way, look for large round boulders scattered over the landscape. These "melon rocks" were eroded into that shape and dumped here by the Lake Bonneville Flood about 15,000 years ago.

Customers still make deposits and withdrawals at the **Idaho State Bank** (✉ State and Hagerman Sts. ☎ 208/837–6464), an interesting building dating back to 1887. It served as a general store between stints as a bank. The teller area has been restored to a wooden-and-brass showplace, just the way a bank would have looked in the 1880s.

The **Hagerman Fossil Beds National Monument** sprawls across 4,000 acres, most of which is closed to visitors to protect the world's richest deposit of Pliocene-era fossils. About 3½ million years ago, creatures who would disappear in the Ice Age still roamed through this landscape. There are two ways to see these unique fossil beds. One is with a self-guided 10-mi driving tour (pick up a map and other materials at the visitor center or online); the other is along a series of short but occasionally steep hiking trails. The visitor center, on U.S. 30 across from Hagerman High School, houses fossils of the famous Hagerman horse, *Equus simplicidens,* along with some of the 90 other distinct species, from camels to turtles, that have been found here. Seven have been found nowhere else in the world. Guided tours of the fossil beds are available. ✉ *221 N. State St.* ☎ *208/837–4793* 🌐 *www.nps.gov/hafo* *Free* *Visitor center June–Aug., daily 9–5; Sept.–May, Thurs.–Mon. 9–5.*

Perhaps the greatest architect of the 20th century, Frank Lloyd Wright believed that buildings should be in harmony with their surroundings. An excellent example of his philosophy is the state's only **Frank Lloyd Wright House,** built into a hillside overlooking the Snake River and its magnificent canyon. The house, still a private residence, is about 2½ mi west of Hagerman off U.S. 30. At the Snake River Pottery sign, just west of the Malad River Bridge, turn left and drive 1½ mi. To the left you'll spot this stone structure. The house can also be seen from an overlook 1 mi farther uphill on U.S. 30.

Built in 1920, **Banbury Hot Springs** has a spring-fed pool that varies between 88°F and 94°F, depending on the weather. Two springs constantly feed the pool, but only one is hot; on warmer days more cold water is added. Five private soaking tubs are emptied between each use. The facility, popular with families, has a campground with full hookups, a dock and boat ramp, and a picnic area. ✉ *Banbury Rd., 9 mi south of Hagerman off Hwy. 30 and River Rd.* ☎ *208/543–4098* *$7* ⏲ *June–Sept., daily; Apr. and May, weekends.*

The prettiest of all the resorts in the area, **Miracle Hot Springs** also has by far the most pleasant private tubs. There are indoor changing areas that lead to deep little hot tubs open to the sky. The larger tubs are worth the higher price ($4 per hour, versus $2 for a smaller tub). The outdoor swimming and soaking pools are pleasant and clean. The resort borders pretty Salmon Falls Creek and has a campground with a few 16-foot geodesic domes for rent. The warm water allows the owners to keep three 5-foot-long alligators as pets. You can sign up to feed them, but it's strictly BYOM (bring your own meat). ✉ *19073-A Hwy. 30, 9 mi south of Hagerman off Hwy. 30.* ☎ *208/543–6002* 🌐 *www.mhsprings.com* *$6* ⏲ *Closed Sun.*

Where to Stay & Eat

$–$$$ ✕ **Snake River Grill.** You can get a good burger or steak here, but chef Kirt Martin specializes in wild game such as alligator, which he then prepares in classic French style. The ambience is a bit more upscale than at other nearby places, all brass, glass, and polished wood. Breakfast is standard diner fare, with nice touches such as warm syrup. Ask about the fried chicken that's packed up so you can take it on a picnic. ✉ *611 Frogs Landings* ☎ *208/837–6227* ▭ *MC, V* ⏲ *No dinner Mon.*

★ ¢ **Billingsley Creek Lodge & Retreat.** Legend has it that novelist Ernest Hemingway slept and wrote in the cabin named in his honor and that author Vardis Fisher planted the giant Douglas fir out back. Rooms are quaint and old-fashioned, each individually decorated. Both cabins have private hot tubs. Of the pair, Creekside is the most pleasant, near enough to Billingsley Creek that from its screen porch you can hear the water trickle. The grounds are designed to make you wander; lights are strung in the trees, goldfish swim in one of the ponds, and a bridge leads you into an island in Billingley Creek, where benches invite you to linger. ✉ *17940 Hwy. 30, 83332* ☎ *208/837–4822* 🌐 *www.billingsleycreeklodge.com* *4 rooms, 2 suites, 2 cottages* *Some kitchens, hot tub, spa; no room phones, no room TVs* ▭ *MC, V.*

CAMPING **Sligar's Thousand Springs Resort.** Campsites here are on a grassy slope near the Snake River, with some spots for tents right on the water. Across the river, several waterfalls plunge down the basalt cliffs like giant faucets someone left running. Campers can use the indoor spring-fed swimming pool (ranging from 89°F in summer to 95°F in winter) and private hot tubs. There is a boat ramp right at the resort. *Flush toilets. Full hookups. Drinking water, showers, Grills at some sites, picnic tables. Public phone* *15 full hookups, 47 tent sites* ✉ *18734 Hwy. 30* ☎ *208/837–4987* 🌐 *www.1000springs.com* *Full hookups $20, tent sites $13* ▭ *No credit cards* ⏲ *Pool closed Mon.*

en route

From Hagerman, take U.S. 30 east; the road gradually tumbles into the Snake River Canyon until it is nearly level with the river near Thousand Springs. Here you'll see dozens of springs literally pour out of the canyon wall. Geologists think the water comes from mountains to the north and that it may take up to 100 years for it to make the underground journey to the Snake River.

Glenns Ferry

25 *29 mi west of Hagerman via Hwy. 30, I–84.*

Now a bucolic community of 1,300 people (many of them descendants of pioneers), Glenns Ferry sits adjacent to what was once the most dangerous river crossing on the 2,000-mi Oregon Trail. Those who made it this far had to decide whether to risk their possessions, their livestock, and possibly their lives crossing the fast-flowing Snake River, which would significantly shorten their journey, or plod south through the barren, rocky desert that offered little in the way of water or food.

Some 300,000 people are believed to have crossed the river at Glenns Ferry in a 30-year period beginning in the early 1840s. Among the first to try were two missionaries named Marcus Whitman and Henry Spalding, whose wagon was destroyed by the current. They salvaged the pieces, constructed a much smaller cart, and continued on their way.

The town is named for Gus Glenn, who in 1869 began offering pioneers a safer ferry crossing about 2 mi upriver.

Housed in a stone schoolhouse built in 1909, the **Glenns Ferry Historical Museum** has artifacts from the Oregon Trail, as well as ranch and railroad memorabilia. Check out the photographs of the horse teams dragging 1,000-pound sturgeon out of the Snake River. ✉ *200 W. Cleveland St.* ☎ *No phone* ⏲ *June–Sept., Fri. and Sat. noon–5* 🎫 *Donations accepted.*

Listed on the National Register of Historic Places, the town's newly restored **Opera Theater** was built in 1914. When it debuted, famous opera stars would perform while waiting to change trains or while waiting out a blizzard en route from Salt Lake City to Seattle. During the summer, you can attend the mystery dinner theater on Friday and old-time melodramas on Saturday. ✉ *208 E. Idaho Ave.* ☎ *208/366–7408* ⏲ *Memorial Day–Labor Day.*

You can still see wagon ruts from the Oregon Trail at **Three Island Crossing State Park.** About 1 mi southwest of town, the park is a great place for hiking, biking, or camping. The visitor center is filled with life-size dioramas, replicas of old-time wagons, diaries of the pioneers, and displays that tell about the Oregon Trail from the perspectives of the newcomers and those who were already here. To get here, head south on Commercial Street for about ½ mi until you see signs for the park. The entrance is 1 mi down the paved road. ✉ *1083 Three Island Park Dr.* ☎ *208/366–2394* 📠 *208/366–2060* 🌐 *www.idahoparks.org* 🎫 *$3 per vehicle.*

Carmela Vineyards. This family-owned winery overlooks the Snake River near Three Mile Crossing. You can sample a variety of wines when you take a tour, then choose your favorite to enjoy during lunch at the restaurant. There's also a 9-hole golf course and a pro shop. ✉ *795 W. Madison Ave.* ☎ *208/366–2313* 🎫 *Free* ⏲ *June–Aug., 9–9.*

Where to Stay & Eat

$–$$$ ✕ **Carmela Vineyards Restaurant.** A family-style restaurant with an enviable view of the river, this place has fresh seafood such as halibut and sturgeon, as well as hamburgers and other kid-friendly fare. Whatever you order, your server can suggest the perfect accompaniment from the vineyard's own cellars, such as a chardonnay or merlot. ✉ *795 W. Madison Ave.* ☎ *208/366–2313* 💳 *MC, V.*

¢ **Great Basin Bed & Breakfast.** Built in 1917 as a boardinghouse for railroad workers and once the site of a bootleg whiskey operation, this downtown inn now pampers weary travelers with nicely decorated rooms filled with period antiques. Each has a name taken from the town's history books. The Walker Ranch Room, for example, commemorates a nearby stage stop, and the Kitty Wilkins Room is named for a horse trader. The ranch-style breakfasts should leave you feeling satisfied. *319 E. 1st Ave.* *208/366–7406* *4 rooms, 1 with bath* *Breakfast room* *MC, V.*

Mountain Home

26 *29 mi west of Glenns Ferry via I–84.*

Originally known as Rattlesnake Station, this town got its start in 1864 as a stagecoach stop. The route was popular for another 20 years until the Union Pacific Railroad came to town in 1883. The current name is something of a misnomer; the town actually sits on a sagebrush flat, with the nearest mountains about 60 mi away.

Mountain Home is becoming a destination for adventure travelers. Hikers like the challenge of 1,000-foot Teapot Dome. The town also serves as a gateway for white-water rafting excursions on the Owyhee, Jarbidge, and Snake rivers to the south.

About 25 mi south of Mountain Home is **Bruneau Dunes State Park,** where you'll find the largest sand dune in North America. The massive pile of sand towers up to 470 feet. Scientists believe the sediment collected in the basin about 12,000 years ago, during the Lake Bonneville Flood, one of the largest floods in the history of the world. Water slammed against a lava wall on the park's outskirts and swirled around in what is now called Eagle Cove. The huge eddy deposited the sand, which eventually formed the dunes. They remain in place because prevailing winds blow alternately from the southeast and northwest.

Within the park's 2,800 acres, you can pitch a tent (the campground is very shady and, because of this, filled with raucous birds), search out wildflowers (prince's plum, storkbill, and pale evening primrose are found here, among others), or watch for birds (the lakes are stopovers for migrating waterfowl). If you are a photographer, the knife-edged summit ridge makes a wonderful subject, especially in early morning or just before sunset. Some hike to the top of the largest dune with sleds, old snowboards, or skis and catch a fast ride down. *3 mi southeast of Bruneau on Hwy. 51* *208/366–7919* *www.idahoparks.org* *$3 per car.*

Sports & the Outdoors

HIKING Head to Teapot Dome, 7 mi north of Mountain Home, for a good view of the Boise Basin. Travelers heading west along the Oregon Trail often used the dome as a landmark. Well-preserved ruts marking the route of the Oregon Trail are still visible in many places. You can hike up the 1,000-foot dome, but there is no developed trail.

SKIING A family-oriented resort that many people consider an affordable alternative to Sun Valley, **Soldier Mountain Ski Area** is about 70 mi from Mountain Home. The vertical drop at this quiet hill is 1,500 feet from the top elevation of 7,150 feet. You can try downhill skiing, or grab a snowboard and skid down the mountain. You can rent ski packages and arrange for lessons. A snack bar serves fast food. *10 mi north of Fairfield* *208/764–2300 or 208/764–2626* *Mid-Nov.–early Apr.*

WHITE-WATER RAFTING The Owyhee, Bruneau, and Jarbidge rivers start in the mountains of northern Nevada and flow through remote high deserts until they reach the Snake River in southern Idaho. These rivers are navigable for only a few months each spring, roughly from April to June. The Owyhee's five runs vary in difficulty, but all are spectacularly beautiful as they pass by sheer rhyolite walls. The upper and middle sections of the Owyhee, as well as its southern and eastern forks, are some of the most challenging in the area. The 40-mi-long Bruneau squeezes through a narrow basalt-walled canyon that is, at places, 800 feet deep and 1,300 feet wide from rim to rim. It offers generally Class III to Class IV rapids. The 29-mi-long Jarbidge is steep, and the rapids are strewn with boulders. Jarbidge is a Shoshone Indian word for "monster," and the name probably refers to Jarbidge Falls, generally bypassed by river runners even today.

Trips usually last four to five days, but it's possible, especially on the Owyhee, to design a trip lasting two weeks or even longer. Permits are not required to run these rivers privately, but only experienced wilderness white-water rafters should attempt them. Everyone else should consider an outfitter. Jon Barker specializes in running these desert rivers and makes a point of being on each trip his company runs. Contact **Barker River Expeditions** (✉ 2124 Grelle St., Lewiston 83501 ☎ 208/836–5551 🌐 www.barker-river-trips.com).

Where to Eat

✕ **Stoney Desert Inn.** Renowned for its tasty soups and homemade pies, the restaurant has the casual environment and modest prices of a diner. It's open 24 hours a day, so it's the perfect place for a midnight snack. It's a local favorite, so be prepared to wait for a table. ✉ *1500 Sunset Strip* ☎ *208/587–9931* ▭ *AE, DC, MC, V.*

Nampa

27 *63 mi west of Mountain Home via I–84.*

Nampa, along with its sister city of Caldwell, is practically a suburb of booming, bustling Boise. Named after a Shoshone chief whose name meant "Big Foot," Nampa was founded in 1883 as a stop along the Oregon Short Line Railroad. The stately brick depot, built in 1903, is now a museum and one of the town's main attractions. There are more than a dozen other notable buildings dating from the early 1900s. Surrounding Nampa are fields teeming with orchards and fragrant mint, and vineyards that spread across the sloping hillsides. Two-thirds of the state's wineries are in the area as well, including Ste. Chapelle, Hells Canyon, and Koenig near Caldwell, and Sawtooth near Nampa.

Caldwell's claim to fame is agriculture. The completion of the Deer Flat dams and the creation of Lake Lowell in 1908 boosted agricultural development in the area, making Canyon County one of the most productive in the nation. Potato baron J. R. Simplot started dehydrating onions and later potatoes at a Caldwell plant in the 1940s. This was the start of Simplot's food-processing operations, among the biggest in the world today.

Housed in a Victorian-era train depot, the **Canyon County Historical Society Museum** displays artifacts from the Oregon Short Line Railroad and the Union Pacific Railroad. There is also a hodgepodge of blacksmith and farm tools, medical instruments, and other relics from the region's settlement in the late 1800s. ✉ *1200 Front St., Nampa* ☎ *208/467–7611* 🎟 *$2* ⏲ *Tues.–Sat. 1–5.*

Three days a week you can peer into the old **Swiss Village Cheese Factory** as workers in white pants, shirts, and plastic helmets work with long, troughlike vats, each holding 5,000 pounds of cheese curds. (There's a much larger and newer plant nearby that processes up to 3 million pounds per day.) A small museum of cheese making explains the entire process. If all this makes you hungry, there's a small café on the premises, as well as an outlet store where you can buy squeaky cheese curds to take back home. Taste a few types before you decide. ✉ *4912 Franklin, Nampa* ☎ *208/463–6620* 🎫 *Free* ⏲ *Call ahead for appointment.*

Along 81 mi of the Snake River, the 482,640-acre **Snake River Birds of Prey Natural Conservation Area** has become a key stop for those fascinated by North American raptors. Eagles, ospreys, hawks, falcons, and owls nest in the rocks and soar overhead. In all, 15 raptor species make their homes here and 9 others use the area during migrations. To get here from Nampa, take Highway 69 south. Beyond the town of Kuna the road is not paved. ✉ *Rte. 69, south of I–84* ☎ *208/384–3463* 🌐 *www.id.blm.gov/bopnca* 🎫 *Free.*

Idaho's largest wine producer, **Ste. Chapelle Winery & Vineyards** is surrounded by the Winery Hill Vineyard and overlooks the Snake River valley. The winery began on a small scale back in 1976 but now produces 130,000 cases of premium varietals each year. You can take a tour that explains the fermentation, aging, and bottling processes, then step into the tasting room to sample a few of the vintages. In summer, a Sunday afternoon jazz concert series at a small park below the winery is popular with locals. ✉ *19348 Lowell Rd., Caldwell* ☎ *208/459–7222* 📠 *208/459–9738* 🌐 *www.idahowines.com* 🎫 *Free* ⏲ *Mon.–Sat. 10–5, Sun. noon–5.*

The **Warhawk Air Museum** at the municipal airport houses a rare collection of WWII aircraft, but its best attractions are its volunteer guides, nearly all retired pilots. Many of them flew the planes on display and can tell you stories that will make your hair stand on end. ✉ *201 Municipal Dr., Nampa* ☎ *208/455–6446* 🌐 *www.warhawkairmuseum.org* 🎫 *$5* ⏲ *Mon.–Sat. 10–5, Sun. 11–5.*

The natural hot springs along the Snake River first attracted Native American tribes who spent the winters here for about 5,000 years. Homesteaders built a pool in the 1880s, and the springs became a popular stopping point for pioneers on the Oregon Trail. The original resort at **Givens Hot Springs** burned to the ground in 1939 but was rebuilt in 1952. Today the resort is a great place to swim and soak in the 95°F water. The springs are about 17 mi south of Nampa on Highway 45. ✉ *8 mi west of Hwy. 45 on Hwy. 78* ☎ *208/495–2000* 🎫 *$6* ⏲ *Daily noon–10.*

Sports & the Outdoors

The Snake River Birds of Prey Natural Conservation Area attracts raptor lovers from all over the world. **Birds of Prey Expeditions** (☎ 208/327–8903 🌐 www.birdsofpreyexpeditions.com) has guided float tours of the protected area from February to November.

Where to Stay & Eat

$–$$$ ✕ **Copper Canyon.** Linen-draped tables fill the small dining room at this upscale eatery. The menu is American fare with Asian and Mediterranean touches, so the shrimp and scallops, steak and salmon, pastas and salads are all a bit out of the ordinary. Everything from the salad dressing to the whipped cream is made in house by chef Brian Inaba, former executive chef for the Columbia Gorge Hotel. This is a very small place, so reservations should be made far in advance. ✉ *218 12th Ave. S, Nampa* ☎ *208/461–0887* ⚠ *Reservations essential* 💳 *MC, V* ⏲ *Closed Sun. and Mon. No lunch Sat.*

$–$$ ✕ **Tacos Michoacan.** Named for a lush region along Mexico's Pacific coast, this restaurant reflects the owner's heritage. Murals, piñatas, and ornately carved wooden booths and chairs create a festival atmosphere.

FAMOUS POTATOES

THE HUMBLE POTATO was first grown in the north woods of Idaho by a Presbyterian missionary, Henry Harmon Spalding, at a Lapwai mission in the 1830s. The next notable milestone in the potato's history in Idaho was in 1860, when Mormon pioneers from Salt Lake City settled in the southeastern corner of the state near Franklin. The settlers lived in their wagons, built irrigation ditches, and harvested bushels of potatoes and onions the first year. Just 16 years later, farmers from the same area shipped more than 2.5 million pounds of potatoes to mining camps as far away as California. By the early 1870s, botanist Luther Burbank had developed the Burbank tuber, which was then succeeded by the Russet Burbank. Idaho would make the Russet Burbank famous. Thanks to widespread irrigation initiatives in the early 1900s and ongoing research, the Snake River Plain, once an arid, sagebrush-dotted region, began producing enormous harvests of high-quality potatoes.

It was J. R. Simplot who became the true spud king. After reaping a handsome profit on a small hog operation at age 17, he rented 160 acres near Declo and planted potatoes. Simplot used his business savvy to add value to the simple tuber, and became a billionaire as a result. He produced freeze-dried potatoes for the troops in World War II and backed the development of frozen french fries in the 1940s. Today's farmers in southern Idaho raise the nation's largest crop of potatoes, about 30 percent of the total yield in the United States. In addition to starting with good potatoes and abundant water, they can rely on the porous, fertile volcanic soil and arid growing conditions to produce uniform growth with few imperfections.

8

Here you can find traditional dishes that taste the way they would in Mexico, including some, such as *menudo* (beef tripe soup) and *ceviche* (raw fish soaked in lemon or lime juice), that are not often found in this part of the country. The only downside is the location, in a worse-for-the-wear area a few blocks from Caldwell's downtown district. ✉ *3623 Lake Ave., Caldwell* ☎ *208/863–2826* ▭ *No credit cards.*

$ **Best Western Caldwell Inn & Suites.** Convenient to the interstate but in a quieter location than other hotels nearby, this three-story lodging is a good choice. Remember to drop by the pleasant lobby in the afternoon, when freshly made cookies are set out for guests. There's an attractive indoor pool and a small landscaped patio where you can enjoy your complimentary Continental breakfast. ✉ *908 Specht Ave., Caldwell 83605* ☎ *208/454–7225 or 888/454–3522* 🖷 *208/454–3522* 🌐 *www.bestwestern.com* *51 rooms, 18 suites* *Microwaves, refrigerators, indoor pool, hot tubs, exercise equipment, guest laundry facilities, business services, meeting room* ▭ *AE, D, DC, MC, V* 🍽 *CP.*

$ **Shilo Inn Nampa Suites.** The newer of two hotels of the same name, this modern building has suites decorated with contemporary furnishings. Rooms have nice touches such as coffeemakers and wet bars. ✉ *1401 Shilo Dr., Nampa 83687* ☎ *208/465–3250* 🖷 *208/465–5929* 🌐 *www.shiloinns.com* *83 suites* *Restaurant, room service, in-room data ports, some kitchenettes, microwaves, refrigerators, cable TV, indoor pool, exercise equipment, hot tub, sauna, laundry facilities, business services, meeting rooms, airport shuttle, some pets allowed (fee)* ▭ *AE, D, DC, MC, V.*

¢ **Alpine Villa Motel.** This motel offers cottagelike accommodations for budget-minded travelers. It's in downtown Nampa. ✉ *124 3rd St. S, Nampa 83651* ☎ *208/466–7819* *11 rooms* *Cable TV* ▭ *AE, DC, MC, V* 🍽 *CP.*

Weiser

28 *60 mi north of Nampa via I–84 and Hwy. 95.*

The history of Weiser reads like a romance novel. In 1863 William Logan and his sweetheart, Nancy Harris, having passed through the region while traveling the Oregon Trail, eloped and returned to build a primitive home of willows, rocks, and mud. Their home soon became a stop on the trail. A year later, a general store was added, then a gristmill, and by 1870, the little community along the banks of the Weiser River had taken root. Brick homes from the early 1900s and edifices such as the castlelike Knights of Pythias Building are still standing.

If you ask locals about the town, they'll tell you that it bears the name of a Revolutionary War veteran who served as a cook on the Lewis and Clark expedition. Weiser serves as a gateway to the southern end of Hells Canyon on the Snake River, from which rafters launch three- to six-day trips through one of the deepest river gorges in the world. The town also provides access to the massive reservoirs created by Brownlee and Hells Canyon dams, popular with anglers and boaters.

Fodor's Choice ★ Weiser is famous around the region and, among folk musicians, around the nation, for the **National Oldtime Fiddlers' Contest.** Whether or not old-time fiddling appeals to you, something at this weeklong festival almost certainly will. An old-fashioned parade that runs through the center of town is popular with kids. There are cowboy poets showing off their best rhymes in one park, cooks enticing you to try their barbecued ribs in another. There are dances and movies and cow-pie bingo (don't ask) and, of course, fiddlers everywhere. The contest itself takes place at the high school, with competitors broken into categories ranging from kids so small they don't look much bigger than their fiddles to world-renowned performers whose bows move so fast that you worry they'll set their fiddles on fire. Buy tickets for the end of the week, as the caliber of the competitors just gets better and better. All the talent isn't inside the auditorium, however. Surrounding the school are folk and bluegrass players who are less interested in competing than in simply jamming with each other. The contest takes place over the course of the third full week of June. ✉ *309 State St.* ☎ *800/437–1280* 🌐 *www.fiddlecontest.com* 🎫 *$8–$10.*

The sprawling **Hells Canyon National Recreation Area** has plenty of outdoor opportunities. The reserve centers on the Snake River as it roars through one of the few remaining stretches that haven't been dammed or diverted. The river runs north, defining the border between Idaho and Oregon and, farther north, between Idaho and Washington. At Hells Canyon it has carved a dramatic gorge best appreciated from below, although scenic overlooks in the Seven Devils Peaks near the town of Riggins also have breathtaking views. Activities in Hells Canyon include fishing, white-water rafting, strenuous but rewarding hiking and backpacking, and wildlife watching. The reserve is rich in history. Old homesteads can be found on benches above the river, and even where the buildings have long since fallen down, the stone fences that once surrounded them remain. Fruit trees planted by settlers draw bears and other wildlife in summer. Earlier inhabitants, the Nez Perce and their ancestors, have left the shallow, hollowed-out remains of their pit houses. ☎ *208/628–3916* 🌐 *www.fs.fed.us/hellscanyon.*

Sports & the Outdoors

HIKING The 84-mi **Weiser River Trail** runs along the route of a former railway, making it suitable for hiking, biking, horseback riding, and (in the winter) cross-country skiing. The trail surface has been smoothed but has not yet been paved, which preserves the feeling that you're in the wilderness. The route passes through farmland, forests, steep-sided canyons, and wildflower-covered meadows. It also runs through three small towns—Midvale, Cambridge, and Council—before coming to an end near New Meadows. In one 8-mi section south of Tamarack, 16 trestle bridges span the Weiser River. For more information on the Weiser River Trail, contact the **Weiser Chamber of Commerce** (✉ 309 State St., 83672 ☎ 208/414–0452 🌐 www.weiserrivertrail.org).

WHITE-WATER RAFTING Of the state's wilderness white-water runs, the only place where you'll find a dam is on Snake River near where it passes through Hells Canyon. This is both a plus and a minus for those who like running the rapids. On the plus side, when free-flowing rivers are either too high or too low, the levels at the Snake River are often moderate. On the minus side, a visible "bathtub ring" mars the sheer canyon walls, the salmon that once swam up this river in stunning numbers are gone or nearly so, and the sandy beaches have mostly washed away. Wild Sheep and Granite, the river's two biggest rapids, are the highlights of a trip that also contains plenty of placid stretches for wildlife and scenery watching. Private permits to run the Snake River are available through a lottery system run by the Forest Service, but the easiest way to see Hells Canyon is with an outfitter. Based near Weiser, **Hughes River Expeditions** (✉ Hwy. 71 and Hwy. 95 ☎ 208/257–3477 or 800/262–1882 🌐 www.hughesriver.com) is one of the most venerable white-water rafting companies in Idaho. Owner Jerry Hughes runs three- to five-day trips through Hells Canyon.

Where to Stay & Eat

$–$$ ✕ **Judy's Weiser Inn.** Some small-town restaurants try to be everything to everybody, and sometimes they succeed. That's the case at Judy's, which has the obligatory biscuits and gravy for breakfast, roast beef sandwiches for lunch, and sirloin steaks for dinner. But there's also a "heart smart" section on the menu that includes entrées that make good use of egg whites and low-fat cheeses. There are also plenty of options for vegetarians. *✉ 1800 E. 6th St. ☎ 208/414–4962 ▭ MC, V ⊙ Closed Sun.*

$ ✕ **Homestead Café.** Because this is Weiser, an old fiddle and banjo figure prominently in the decor of this restaurant. Down-home meals such as roast beef, fried chicken, and chicken-fried steak make Homestead Café a favorite among the locals, who say they get a lot of bang for their buck. Many turn out for the breakfasts. *✉ 813 State St. ☎ 208/414–3962 ▭ MC, V.*

¢–$ 🏨 **Galloway Inn.** This charming brick abode, a Queen Anne–style house dating back to 1900, has covered porches where you can enjoy the breeze. In the music room hangs a photo of the family who originally lived here, standing on their lawn wearing their Sunday best. The house, seen behind them, was at the time the most expensive private residence in Weiser. Now it's the most expensive, and perhaps the most pleasant, lodging option. Breakfast is plentiful but not pretentious, served buffet style when the inn is full and made to order when it is not. *✉ 1120 E. 2nd St., 83672 ☎ 208/549–1719 ⇨ 5 rooms, 2 with bath ♨ Hot tub; no smoking ▭ MC, V 🍴 BP.*

¢ 🏨 **Indianhead Motel.** On the edge of town, this motel is most pleasant in the summer when the sweet-smelling vines are in bloom. The basic rooms have a cared-for look not typical of lodgings in this price range. A few RV hookups are in back, surrounded by a few picnic areas and horseshoe pits. *✉ 747 Hillcrest Dr., 83672 ☎ 208/549–0331 ⇨ 7 rooms, 1 suite ♨ Horseshoes ▭ MC, V.*

SOUTHERN IDAHO A TO Z

To research prices, get advice from other travelers, and book travel arrangements, visit www.fodors.com.

AIR TRAVEL

CARRIERS Boise, the regional hub, is served by many of the nation's larger airlines, including Delta, Northwest, Southwest, United, and America West. Commuter airlines Horizon Air and Sky West serve the airports in Hailey, Idaho Falls, and Pocatello, whereas Twin Falls is served only by Sky West. Charter flights can be arranged through McCall Aviation or Salmon Air into the many smaller airports and airstrips scattered around Idaho. Many of these airstrips are unpaved and therefore are open only in summer and fall.

Airlines & Contacts **America West** ☎ 800/235–9292 ⊕ www.americawest.com. **Delta** ☎ 800/221–1212 ⊕ www.delta.com. **Horizon Air** ☎ 800/547–9308 ⊕ www.horizonair.com. **McCall Aviation** ☎ 208/634–7137 or 800/992–6559 ⊕ www.mccallaviation.com. **Northwest** ☎ 800/225–2525 ⊕ www.nwa.com. **Salmon Air** ☎ 208/756–6211 or 800/448–3413 ⊕ www.salmonaire.com. **Sky West** ☎ 800/453–9417 ⊕ www.delta.com. **Southwest** ☎ 800/435–9792 ⊕ www.southwest.com. **United** ☎ 800/241–6522 ⊕ www.united.com.

AIRPORTS

Boise Airport, in the southern part of the city, is the main gateway to the region. Commuter flights head to other cities. Friedman Memorial Airport serves Hailey and the surrounding communities. Other popular gateways are Idaho Falls Regional Airport and Pocatello Regional Airport.

Airport Information **Boise Airport** ✉ 3201 Airport Way, Boise ☎ 208/383–3110. **Friedman Memorial Airport** ✉ 1616 Airport Wy., Hailey ☎ 208/788–4956. **Idaho Falls Regional Airport** ✉ 2140 N. Skyline Dr., Idaho Falls ☎ 208/529–1221. **Pocatello Regional Airport** ✉ 1950 Airport Wy., Pocatello ☎ 208/234–6154.

BUS TRAVEL

Greyhound has service to Boise, as well as to Twin Falls and Idaho Falls. Boise-Winnemucca Stages serves the U.S. 95 corridor and has several stops in towns around Boise. Sun Valley Stages runs buses between Twin Falls, Boise, and Sun Valley.

In Boise, ValleyRide runs frequently between major points around the city. An hour-long historical tour on the open-air Boise Tours train helps you get your bearings. Pick up the bus at Julia Davis Park, several blocks south of the capitol.

Ketchum Area Rapid Transit serves downtown Ketchum, and the River Run and Warm Springs ski lifts in Sun Valley. Buses run about every 20 minutes. Getting around Pocatello is no problem with Pocatello Urban Transit.

Bus Information **Boise Tours** ☎ 208/342–4796 ⊕ www.boisetourtrain.com. **Boise-Winnemucca Stages** ☎ 208/336–3300. **Greyhound** ☎ 800/231–2222 ⊕ www.greyhound.com. **Ketchum Area Rapid Transit** ☎ 208/726–7140. **Sun Valley Stages** ☎ 208/821–9064. **Pocatello Urban Transit** ☎ 208/254–2287. **ValleyRide** ☎ 208/336–1010.

CAR RENTAL

Avis, Budget, Dollar, Hertz, and National car rental companies operate out of Boise Airport, Idaho Falls Regional Airport, and Twin Falls Regional Airport. At smaller airports around the region, expect to find Avis, Budget, and Hertz.

At Friedman Memorial Airport, the airport closest to Hailey, make sure to book well ahead of time at the height of the summer or winter season.

Avis ☎ 800/831-2847 🌐 www.avis.com. **Budget** ☎ 800/527-0700 🌐 www.budget.com. **Dollar** ☎ 800/800-4000 🌐 www.dollar.com. **Hertz** ☎ 800/654-3131 🌐 www.hertz.com. **National** ☎ 800/227-7368 🌐 www.nationalcar.com.

CAR TRAVEL

If you plan on seeing southern Idaho, the only way is by car. Interstates and the much more interesting two-lane state and federal highways are uncrowded, with rare exceptions (such as Boise to McCall on Friday evenings, or Idaho Falls to Island Park on the first day of fishing season). Best of all, a car allows you to travel back roads, where you'll find some of Idaho's unique sights. Be sure to keep an eye on your gas gauge; in some parts of the state, the nearest gas station may be a long distance away.

The region's main highway is I–84, which stretches from Boise in the west to Twin Falls in the central part of the state, then continues south into Utah. A more scenic route from Boise to Twin Falls is U.S. 30, which turns off at Bliss and follows the Snake River Canyon. From Boise to Sun Valley, there are several options. In summer, Highway 21 and Highway 75 through Stanley and the Sawtooth National Recreation Area make for a long but beautiful drive. In winter, the road is often closed, so be sure to call ahead about road conditions. The shortest route from Boise is to head east on I–84 to Mountain Home and then take U.S. 20 east to U.S. 75 north. From Twin Falls or points farther east along I–84, take U.S. 93 and U.S. 75 north. For the most part, this road passes through the high desert. If there is snow, it is cleared or melts quickly.

In the east, I–15 runs through Idaho Falls and Pocatello, where it intersects I–86 (the main route west, which eventually becomes I–84). In winter, I–15 can be closed even if there has not been a recent storm, as blowing and drifting snow is a common problem. Call ahead for road conditions.

In winter, travel in southwest Idaho is usually not problematic, whereas travel in central and southeastern Idaho can be unpredictable, with many highways and smaller roads impassable for short periods. Snowstorms in the mountainous areas can make tire chains a good idea, although they are not mandatory. Many of Idaho's unpaved roads are not accessible to low-clearance vehicles, although four-wheel-drive vehicles are usually not necessary. Backcountry roads are usually not plowed in winter, which effectively turns them into snowmobile routes. Major newspapers carry road-condition reports on their weather pages. It's always a good idea to call the state's road report hotline for information about possible closures.

ROAD EMERGENCIES

Anywhere in southern Idaho, you can contact the Idaho State Police if you have troubles on the road. Members can also call AAA.

AAA Emergency Road Service ☎ 800/222-4357. **Idaho State Police** ☎ 800/233-1212.

ROAD CONDITIONS

For up-to-date information on road conditions, construction, and travel-weather advisories, contact the Idaho Transportation Department.

Idaho Transportation Department ☎ 888/432-7623 🌐 www.state.id.us/itd.

RULES OF THE ROAD

In Idaho you may make a right turn on red after stopping, unless there is a sign specifically forbidding it. It is illegal to delay more than three vehicles on winding roads where pull-outs are available.

HOSPITALS

The Wood River Medical Center is in the east end of Sun Valley Village, near the golf course.

Hospitals **Eastern Regional Medical Center** ✉ 3100 Channing Way, Idaho Falls ☎ 208/529-6111. **Magic Valley Regional Medical Center** ✉ 650 Addison Ave. W, Twin Falls ☎ 208/737-2000 or 208/737-2114 TTY. **Pocatello Regional Medical Center** ✉ 777 Hospital Way, Pocatello ☎ 208/234-0777. **St. Alphonsus Regional Medical Center** ✉ 1055 N. Curtis Rd., Boise ☎ 208/378-2121, 208/378-2121 emergency room. **St. Luke's Regional Medical Center** ✉ 190 E. Bannock St., Boise ☎ 208/381-2222, 208/386-2344 emergency room. **Wood River Medical Center** ✉ Sun Valley ☎ 208/622-3333.

Walk-in Medical Care **Boise Family Medicine Center** ✉ 10798 W. Overland, Boise ☎ 208/377-3368. **Family Emergency Centers East** ✉ 250 S. Skyline Dr., Idaho Falls ☎ 208/525-2600. **Family Emergency Center West** ✉ 1995 E. 17th St., Idaho Falls ☎ 208/529-5252. **Physicians Immediate Care Center** ✉ 1246 Yellowstone Ave., Pocatello ☎ 208/237-1122.

LODGING

The *Idaho Official State Travel Guide* contains information about lodging, dining, and activities across the state in a magazine format. Contact the Idaho Travel Council. A helpful Web site maintained by the Idaho Department of Commerce can point you at lodging options as well as events, recreational opportunities, and much more. Reservations can be made through this site as well.

Since the 1920s, the Dude Ranchers' Association has inspected guest ranches in the region and allowed some few to become members. Many fine northern Idaho guest ranches are not members, but every member is, as the association likes to say, "actually a ranch and not just a hotel with horses out back."

Dude Ranchers' Association ☎ 307/587-2339 🌐 www.duderanch.org. **Idaho Department of Commerce** ☎ 208/334-2470 or 800/842-5858 🌐 www.visitidaho.org. **Idaho Travel Council** 📫 Box 83720, Boise 83720 ☎ 800/847-4843.

CAMPING

Campgrounds in Idaho are either public (run largely by the Idaho Department of Parks and Recreation, the U.S. Forest Service, or the Bureau of Land Management), or they are private. One-stop shopping for campgrounds and campground reservations is most easily accomplished, however, by going straight to one of two resources, the Idaho Department of Commerce Web site or ReserveAmerica. Both let you browse among southern Idaho campgrounds and reserve sites at most campgrounds, public or private, that accept reservations.

Idaho Department of Commerce 🌐 www.visitidaho.org. **ReserveAmerica** ☎ 877/444-6777 🌐 www.reserveamerica.com.

MEDIA

NEWSPAPERS & MAGAZINES

The region's biggest daily paper for national and regional news is the *Boise Statesman*. Boise also has an alternative weekly that covers arts and entertainment called the *Boise Weekly*. Eastern Idaho and the Yellowstone region are better covered by the state's second-largest daily, the *Idaho Falls Post Register*. Twin Falls, Pocatello, Nampa, and Mountain Home also have daily papers. Smaller towns usually have weekly publications.

SPORTS & THE OUTDOORS

GUIDED OUTDOOR ACTIVITIES

Guided recreation is big business in Idaho. Members of the Idaho Outfitters & Guides Association are licensed for the activities they offer, whether horseback riding, fishing, mountain biking, or white-water rafting. Individual guides are also required to be licensed. The IOGA,

as it's called, puts out a membership directory categorized by activity and can help you find the right outfitter.
Idaho Outfitters & Guides Association 208/342-1919 or 800/847-4843 www.IOGA.org.

FISHING Learn the state's fishing regulations from the Idaho Department of Fish and Game.
Idaho Department of Fish and Game 208/334-3700 or 800/554-8685 www.state.id.us/fishgame.

TRAIN TRAVEL

Amtrak's *California Zephyr* is the only train that passes near southern Idaho. Its closest stop is Salt Lake City, three hours south of Pocatello.
Train Information **Amtrak** 800/872-7245 www.amtrak.com.

VISITOR INFORMATION

Local Information **Boise Convention & Visitors Bureau** 312 S. 9th St., Suite 100, 83702 208/344-7777 or 800/635-5240 www.boise.org. **Caldwell Chamber of Commerce** 704 Blaine St. 83605 208/459-7493 www.caldwellid.org. **Eastern Idaho Visitor Information Center** 505 Lindsay Blvd., Idaho Falls 83402 208/523-1010 or 800/634-3246 www.yellowstoneteton.org. **McCall Chamber of Commerce** 102 N. 3rd 83638 208/634-7631 www.mccall-idchamber.org. **Greater Pocatello Convention & Visitors Bureau** 343 W. Center 83204 208/233-7333 www.pocatelloidaho.com. **Sun Valley/Ketchum Chamber of Commerce** 4th and Main Sts., Sun Valley 83353 208/726-3423 or 800/634-3347 www.visitsunvalley.com. **Salmon Valley Chamber of Commerce** 315 Hwy. 93 N, 83467 208/756-2100 www.salmonbyway.com. **Stanley-Sawtooth Chamber of Commerce** Hwy. 75, Stanley 83278 208/774-3411 or 800/878-7950 www.stanleycc.org. **Weiser Chamber of Commerce** 309 State St., 83672 208/414-0452.
State Information **Idaho Department of Fish and Game** Box 25, Boise 83707 208/334-3700, 208/334-3417, or 800/554-8685. **Idaho Travel Council** 700 W. State St., Box 83720, Boise 83720-0093 208/334-2470 or 800/635-7820 www.visitid.org.

9

NORTHERN IDAHO

NEZ PERCE COUNTRY, THE PANHANDLE

FODOR'S CHOICE

Hells Canyon, *Lewiston*
Paradise Valley Inn Lodge, *Bonners Ferry*
Route of the Hiawathas, *bike path in Silver Valley*
The Veranda, *restaurant in Kellogg*

HIGHLY RECOMMENDED

RESTAURANTS
Floating Restaurant, *Hope*
Italianna Inn, *Lewiston*
Red Door Restaurant, *Moscow*
Roosters Waterfront Restaurant, *Clarkston*
The 1313 Club Historic Saloon & Grill, *Silver Valley*
Wolf Lodge Inn, *Coeur d'Alene*

HOTELS
Best Western Edgewater Resort, *Sandpoint*
Best Western Salmon Rapids Lodge, *Riggins*
Clark House on Hayden Lake, *Hayden Lake*
Coeur d'Alene Resort, *Coeur d'Alene*
Gregory's McFarland House, *Coeur d'Alene*
Wolf Lodge Inn, *Coeur d'Alene*

SIGHTS
Dworshak National Fish Hatchery, *Orofino*
Heavens Gate Observation Site, *Riggins*
Lake Coeur d'Alene, *Coeur d'Alene*
Sierra Silver Mine, *Silver Valley*
Wolf Education & Research Center, *Winchester Lake State Park*

By Jo Deurbrouck

SOUTHERN IDAHOANS CONSIDER THE SALMON RIVER the unofficial boundary between north and south, since it bisects the state almost perfectly, separates the more highly populated inhabitable areas of the state from the least, and defines the Pacific and Mountain time zones. The Salmon River is also one of the state's great scenic attractions. It is the longest wild river left in the United States, outside of Alaska, and its largest tributary, the Middle Fork, which begins as runoff from the Sawtooths and flows through the Frank Church–River of No Return Wilderness Area, is recognized around the world for one of the wildest, most gorgeous white-water journeys on earth. The river system is a magnet for anglers, too. South of the Salmon, Idaho's terrain is generally arid: mountain shoulders are covered with sage, and all but the lowest peaks are bare and jagged. North of White Bird Summit, Idaho begins to feel more like the Northwest than the Rockies. Mountains are densely forested to their low, rounded summits. The climate is milder, because of moister air and generally lower elevations. Lewiston, the largest city in northern Idaho, is an inland port whose traffic comes from the Columbia River; it's also a portal to Hells Canyon, a natural wonder that forms the border between Oregon and Idaho.

The panhandle of Idaho (and the only area a true North Idahoan is likely to call North) is a logging and mining region that has been "discovered" by refugees from larger cities in California, Washington State, and elsewhere. The resort towns of Coeur d'Alene and Sandpoint are the sort of places that compel vacationers to thumb through real estate brochures.

Exploring Northern Idaho

Peruse a map of northern Idaho and you'll quickly realize that in this state, choosing which road to take is easy. There are usually only one or two ways to get where you're going. Rugged terrain has limited road building statewide, but nowhere is this more obvious than in northern Idaho, where the largest contiguous wilderness in the United States outside Alaska crashes against the rugged Bitterroot Range, which defines the border with Montana. Northern Idaho's highways had to be forced into river-carved routes through the mountains, so it's no surprise that they pass through some breathtaking scenery. In fact, with only a couple of eastward detours—one on the improbably lovely Highway 12, the other on I–90, one of Idaho's two stretches of interstate—driving the length of Highway 95 will give you a fine overview of northern Idaho.

About the Restaurants

Idaho is not an indoor state, and eating out is not a popular pastime for residents. This quickly becomes clear when you start looking for a great restaurant outside the major tourist centers of Coeur d'Alene and, to a lesser extent, Sandpoint. What Idahoans want and every town has is a meat-and-potatoes-type restaurant or diner serving lots of food for little money. Salads tend to rely on iceberg lettuce, and dessert options are often limited to pie and ice cream. As is true across the state, Mexican food is usually a good bet. The typical cantina serves marvelous meals made from recipes that the owner brought from Mexico.

About the Hotels

Northern Idaho is thin on full-service hotels (Lewiston, the area's largest town, has only one). But anything else you might long for can be found here, from cozy bed-and-breakfasts to relaxing ranches to mountainside cabins to kitschy roadside motels. There are also plenty of national chains such as Super 8 and Best Western. In general, expect to enjoy more novel—and expensive—choices in the tourist centers, Coeur d'Alene and Sandpoint, and a range of fairly standard options in the regional economic hubs, Moscow and Lewiston. In smaller towns, expect basic but clean roadside accommodations for drop-dead deals, along with a few surprising and unique woodsy lodges well worth the drive out of town.

WHAT IT COSTS					
	$$$$	$$$	$$	$	¢
RESTAURANTS	over $22	$16–$22	$11–$16	$7–$11	under $7
HOTELS	over $220	$160–$220	$110–$160	$70–$110	under $70

Restaurant prices are for a main course at dinner, excluding sales tax of 5%. Hotel prices are for two people in a standard double room in high season, excluding service charges and 11% tax.

Timing

In summer northern Idaho blooms, and not just with wildflowers. Recreational opportunities abound, especially near key attractions such as Lake Coeur d'Alene and Lake Pend Oreille, the lower Salmon River, and the pretty Silver Valley. Tiny Sandpoint can experience gridlock of near-urban dimensions on a sunny Friday afternoon, and there are weekends in Coeur d'Alene when a motel room cannot be had for love or money. But crowded or not, summer and early fall are definitely the best times to visit this region. Most towns stage their big arts festivals and concert events during this part of the year to catch the crowds. (The exceptions are Moscow and Lewiston, both college towns whose populations swell with students in winter.) But summer is the time to visit because of the mild weather. Winter and spring often bring rain and chill to the valleys and more than enough snow in the mountains to draw skiers and snowmobilers. One concern across the state is that travel often requires navigating mountainous areas and less-traveled roads. In winter, it's worth a call ahead to see if your chosen route is open.

NEZ PERCE COUNTRY

Not exactly north and not exactly south, Nez Perce Country is where you'll find the Salmon, Snake, and Clearwater rivers. Historically, it was home to the Nez Perce people, who befriended Meriwether Lewis and William Clark on their westward journey in 1805. Now it is home to the dying logging and mining industries, slowly being replaced by agriculture and, of course, tourism. Visitors to the area mostly seek natural beauty and outdoor activities, something that the locals know quite well; in tiny Riggins, rafting companies outnumber restaurants at least three to one.

Riggins

➊ *45 mi from McCall via Rte. 55 and U.S. 95 north.*

The Little Salmon River and the Salmon River meet at the bottom of a deep, dramatic gorge, and this is where you'll find the tiny town of Riggins. This wide spot in the road, about 33 mi north of the junction of Route 55 and U.S. 95, is the last stop in the Mountain Time Zone; across the river, it's an hour earlier. Hunters flock here for chukar (a type of partridge) and elk, and anglers get excited about the salmon and steelhead. Adrenaline-crazed rafters come for the Salmon River's rapids—the Riggins stretch is one of only three spots where the famous river's waves can be readily accessed from a road. The river's importance to the local economy is clear from the rafting and fishing companies scattered along both sides of the highway.

Numbers in the text correspond to numbers in the margin and on Northern Idaho map.

If you have 3 days Be warned: Idaho is a big state and most of its top attractions are not enjoyed on the run. This trip, mostly following Highway 95, covers only a small sliver of northern Idaho. On your first day, run the rapids at **Riggins** 1, the white-water capital of the state. Grab a bite to eat in town and then head north on Highway 95 along the Salmon River and up the Whitebird Grade. Spend the night in **Lewiston** 5, perhaps after taking a stroll on paved paths along the Clearwater River. The next morning, drive out of the canyon and onto rolling, grain-covered hills to **Moscow** 9. Stop and wander this college town's pretty downtown streets before heading up to **Coeur d'Alene** 11 via Highway 97, which runs along the east shore of the lake before intersecting with Interstate 90. Be sure to stop along the way to hike the Mineral Ridge Trail. Book a sunset cruise on shimmering Lake Coeur d'Alene. Spend your last day enjoying the lake's broad beaches.

If you have 5 days Two more days takes you a bit farther into the wilderness. Spend an extra day in **Riggins** 1 exploring those dramatic canyons. Drive the slow, steep route up into the Seven Devils Mountains. Soon you'll reach Heavens Gate, an overlook that allows you to peer down into both the Salmon and Snake river valleys and see four states at once. If you can't get enough of the bird's-eye view, wander along the trail on the ridge dividing those two massive rivers. Then head up to **Lewiston** 5, this time more slowly: stop at Spalding, where you'll find the headquarters of the Nez Perce National Historic Park. Here you can learn more about the tribe's history. On Day 3, book a jet-boat trip up the Snake River into Hells Canyon. You'll find yourself deep in the dramatic landscape you peered down into the day before. The last two days you can follow the three-day itinerary through **Moscow** 9 and **Coeur d'Alene** 11.

If you have 7 days In a week you can see much more of northern Idaho. Follow the five-day itinerary above. On Day 6, drive east on I–90 up the **Silver Valley** 12. Stop at the Cataldo Mission in Cataldo and the Staff House Mining & Smelting Museum in Kellogg, but save plenty of time for wandering around the historic town of Wallace. Spend the night in the Silver Valley before retracing your steps on the last day and heading north into **Sandpoint** 13, on the shores of massive, lovely Lake Pend Oreille. Enjoy biking, hiking, and berry picking (in season), but if you haven't wet a line yet in a state that prides itself on its stellar fishing, perhaps your last act in Idaho should be to pull a lake trout out of the clear waters. Consider it your contribution to preserving native fisheries beleaguered by this non-native invader.

Learn about area hiking, history, wildlife, and more at the **Hells Canyon National Recreation Area Visitors Center,** south of Riggins. Travel books, river guides, and maps are available for purchase, as well as free, typed directions to key attractions in the Wallowa-Whitman National Forest and other protected lands. *189 Hwy. 95 208/628–3916 Free Weekdays 8–noon and 1–5.*

★ Riggins sits in a dramatic canyon that hides from view equally dramatic mountains, the Seven Devils. **Heavens Gate Observation Site,** 18 mi from Highway 95 on a steep gravel road, is the easiest place to enjoy them. The observation site sits at 8,429 feet and is accessed by a short trail from the parking area. Other trails continue along the ridge that separates the Salmon River from the Snake River. Check road conditions and your vehicle's capabilities with the ranger station near the turnoff before you start up. ✉ *Forest Rd. 517* ☎ *208/628–3916* 🎫 *Free* 🕒 *Open July–mid-Oct.*

Sports & the Outdoors

FISHING Try for steelheads in October and November and again in March from a comfortable drift boat. Many of the white-water outfitters in Riggins also offer steelhead fishing on the more accessible section of the lower Salmon River. Try **Exodus Wilderness Adventures** (✉ 606 N. Main St., ☎ 208/628–4109 or 800/992–3484 🌐 www.riverescape.com), which offers drift-boat and jet-boat fishing trips. It also has white-water rafting excursions near Riggins on the famous Salmon River, and below it on the less-well-known but perhaps more lovely lower Salmon River.

WHITE-WATER RAFTING Ride the Class III white water on a section of the Salmon River that, for half its length, parallels Highway 95. The more adventurous types can go solo in a "duckie," or inflatable kayak. Guided half-day to two-day trips are available through several companies scattered along Riggins's main drag. **Northwest Voyageurs** (✉ 1 Pollock Rd., Pollock ☎ 208/628–3021 or 800/727–9977 🌐 www.voyageurs.com) focuses on day-long adventures but also runs five-day white-water rafting trips on the Lower Salmon and three- to five-day trips on the section of the Snake River where it runs through Hells Canyon. In fall, the company offers drift-boat steelhead fishing.

Where to Stay & Eat

$ ✕ **Salmon River Inn.** The atmosphere is pure pool hall—dark, cavernous, and, on hot summer days, refreshingly cool. Video games line one wall. The jukebox pours out classic country. Perfectly fine pizza and sandwiches are served on picnic tables in plastic baskets. In cooler month, some old-timers sit on the front porch watching the traffic on Highway 95 (also known in Riggins as Main Street). ✉ *129 S. Main St.* ☎ *208/628–3813* 💳 *AE, MC, V.*

★ $–$$ 🏨 **Best Western Salmon Rapids Lodge.** On the site of the old town lumber mill is a sure sign of things to come for tiny Riggins: a modern hotel with an upscale feel, thanks to a wall of glass in the spacious lobby that faces the confluence of the Salmon and the Little Salmon. The high-ceilinged rooms have pleasant lodge-style furnishings. For a bit extra you can get a room with a tiny private balcony where you can enjoy the view. It's money well spent. ✉ *1010 S. Main St., 83549* ☎ *208/628–27443 or 877/957–2743* 📠 *208/628–3834* 🌐 *www.salmonrapids.com* 🛏 *51 rooms, 4 suites* 👍 *Refrigerators, cable TV, exercise equipment, hot tub, laundry facilities, meeting room, some pets allowed (fee), no-smoking rooms* 💳 *AE, D, DC, MC, V* 🍽 *CP.*

¢ 🏨 **Salmon River Motel.** The rooms are clean and comfortable at this little motel at the south end of town. You can drift off to sleep to the sounds of the river (along with the inescapable traffic on busy Highway 95). The motel's staff is known for being helpful. One of Riggins's four restaurants, This Old House, is next door, serving breakfast, lunch, and dinner. ✉ *1203 S. Hwy. 95, 83549* ☎ *208/628–3231 or 888/628–3025* 🛏 *16 rooms* 👍 *Cable TV, laundry facility, some pets allowed* 💳 *AE, D, DC MC, V.*

Getting Away from It All

Look at a map of northern Idaho and you quickly notice how few paved roads are here. Highway 95 is the major north–south route, bisecting the major east–west route of Interstate 90. Get even a couple of miles from these thoroughfares and you'll leave the summer crowds behind, increasing the odds of seeing a bear or a moose and enjoying the solitude that residents treasure. Fishing is better far from the main roads. So is berry picking. Campgrounds are often half deserted, even in the middle of the high season. Getting off the beaten path is easy. The national forests of the panhandle offer the best opportunities in northern Idaho, with 3,300 mi of trail and 8,500 mi of well-maintained roads. Hikers should carry plenty of food and water (don't drink from streams no matter how clear they appear), protective clothing (the weather can change quickly in the mountains), and a map of the area. It's a good idea to let someone know your route.

White-Water Rafting

Thanks to its rugged terrain, Idaho has more white water than any other state in the country. Some enthusiasts run the waves in hard-shell kayaks, a skill that takes a bit of dedication to master, or in white-water canoes, which is even harder. Luckily, there are also white-water paddle and oar rafts, and inflatable kayaks, jokingly called duckies (as in "rubber duckies"). Passengers in oar rafts need have no experience—just the ability to hang on through the rough patches. Rafts are available for rent in every town where there's a river nearby, but the easiest and safest way for first-timers to get their feet wet is to go with an outfitter. Rafting trips in northern Idaho are mostly one- and two-day affairs. The best are the wild Lochsa, the wide Moyie, and pretty little St. Joe rivers, which are at their best for 6 to 12 weeks in the spring.

CAMPING

Forest Service Campgrounds. The Forest Service maintains nine campgrounds in the Riggins area, most very small with no camping fee. Three—Spring Bar, Van Creek, and Allison Creek—are on the Salmon River. The rest are at higher elevations, which means they open later in the spring and close earlier in fall. One of the most scenic is Seven Devils Campground near Heavens Gate overlook. Spring Bar has a paved boat ramp. *Pit toilets. Drinking water at some campgrounds. Fire pits, picnic tables* ✉ *189 Hwy. 95, 83549* ☎ *208/628–3916* *Free–$10* *No credit cards* *May–Nov.*

Prospectors Gold RV Park. Campsites at this RV park are on a grassy, rosebush-dotted patch of land in a bend of the Salmon River. Except during salmon season, this place tends to be quiet. Facilities are well cared for and pleasant, although the showers are metered. A café serving breakfast, lunch, and dinner is at the top of the hill beside Highway 95. *Flush toilets. Partial hookups, dump station. Drinking water, guest laundry, showers. Fire grates, picnic tables. General store. Swimming (river)* *24 partial hookups, tent area* ✉ *Hwy. 95, at milepost 204, Lucile 83542* ☎ *208/628–3773* *Partial hookups $16–$17, tents $4 per person* *No credit cards.*

Riverside RV. Tucked up against the rollicking Little Salmon River, this small RV park hidden from the highway is popular with anglers during salmon and steelhead runs. All but two sites are adjacent to the river. Some get all-day shade from the mature trees on nearly every site. Cable

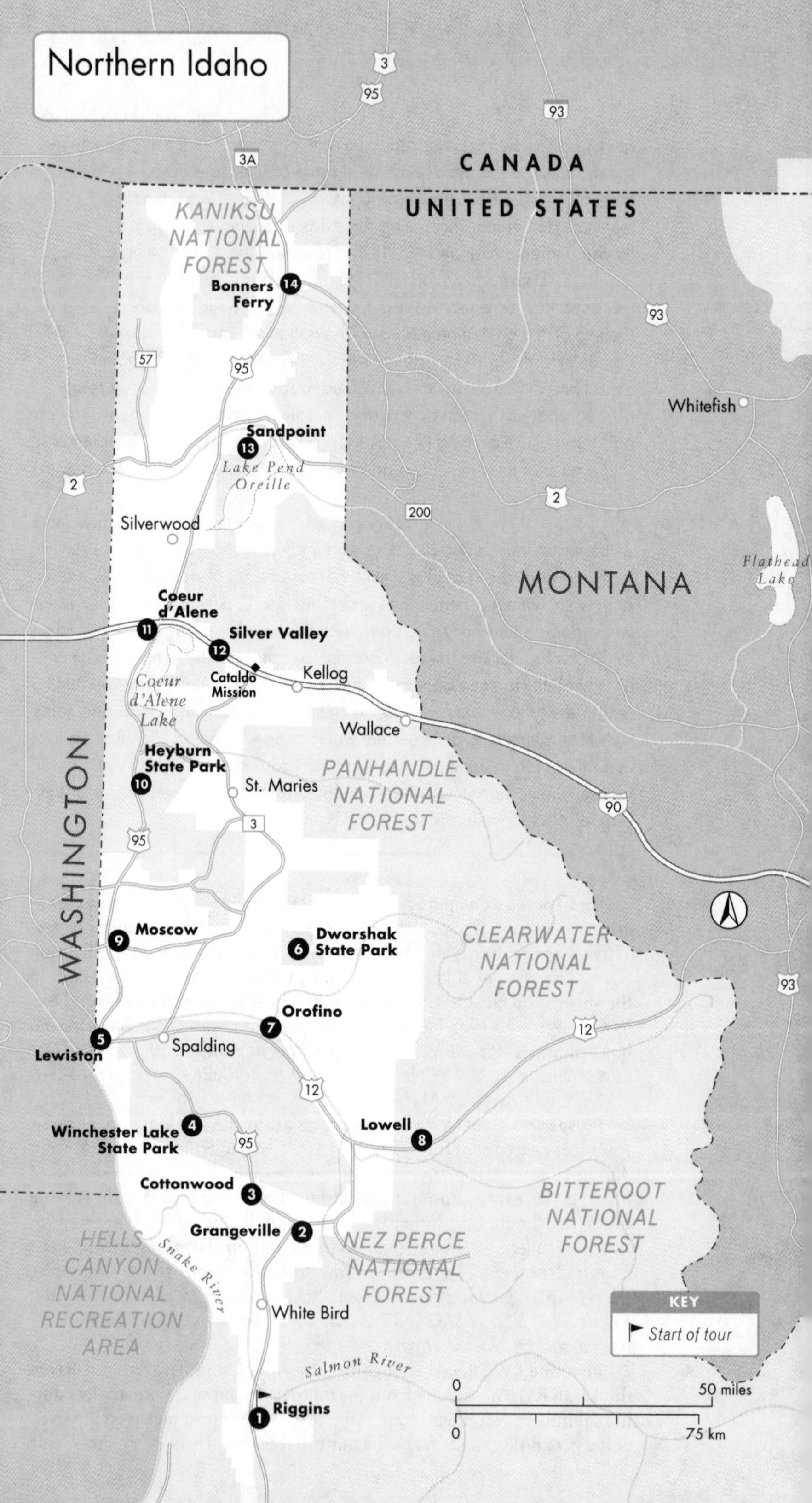

Northern Idaho
CANADA
UNITED STATES
KANIKSU NATIONAL FOREST
Bonners Ferry
Whitefish
Sandpoint
Lake Pend Oreille
Silverwood
MONTANA
Flathead Lake
Coeur d'Alene
Silver Valley
Cataldo Mission
Kellog
Coeur d'Alene Lake
Wallace
Heyburn State Park
St. Maries
PANHANDLE NATIONAL FOREST
WASHINGTON
Moscow
Dworshak State Park
CLEARWATER NATIONAL FOREST
Orofino
Lewiston
Spalding
Winchester Lake State Park
Lowell
Cottonwood
BITTEROOT NATIONAL FOREST
Grangeville
HELLS CANYON NATIONAL RECREATION AREA
Snake River
NEZ PERCE NATIONAL FOREST
White Bird
KEY
Start of tour
Salmon River
Riggins
0
50 miles
0
75 km

TV hookup is available. *Flush toilets. Full hookups, partial hookups. Picnic tables. Public telephone* *17 full hookups* *Hwy. 95, 83549* *208/628–3698* *$15* *No credit cards.*

en route

Immediately outside Riggins, U.S. 95 crosses the Salmon River and begins the 40-mi climb toward **White Bird Summit,** which rises to 4,245 feet above sea level. There were no roads from northern to southern Idaho until 1915, when the White Bird Grade was finished. It climbed nearly 3,000 feet in 14 mi of agonizing hairpins and switchbacks. The new road was finished in 1975. A little more than halfway up the new grade, a small scenic overlook sits above the valley where the Nez Perce War started. In 1877, Chief Joseph and his band of Nez Perce, who had not signed a treaty with the whites (as had other bands), were nevertheless on their way to resettle at the nearby reservation when trouble broke out. About 80 Native Americans decimated a much larger white force without losing a person. The army retreated, but the legendary pursuit of Chief Joseph's band across 1,500 mi of Idaho and Montana began. An interpretive shelter tells the story of the battle. From White Bird Summit, U.S. 95 plunges rapidly into the Camas Prairie and into Grangeville, a farming town. Here, the Nez Perce dug the roots of the camas plant, a dietary staple.

Grangeville

2 *46 mi north of Riggins via Hwy. 95.*

Grangeville was first a supply town to serve the mining districts in the Gospel Mountains and Buffalo Hump. When a Grange Hall was built in 1874, the building was the first in the fledgling town and is thought to have been the first local chapter of the National Grange of the Patrons of Husbandry, a secret fraternal organization for farmers, in the Northwest. The organization helped determine the town's name. In 1902, the town had grown so much that it became the county seat of Idaho County. Today Grangeville is a town of 3,500 and the northern gateway to Hells Canyon and four of the state's five wilderness areas. Fishing and hunting outfitters and river runners use the town as a base camp. The town sits on the edge of the Camas Prairie, a 200,000-acre stretch of rolling foothills bordered by the Clearwater and Snake rivers and at the base of the 6,000- to 7,000-foot Bitterroot Mountains.

At the **Bicentennial Historical Museum** you'll find an extensive collection of Nez Perce items, including a beaded buckskin jacket worn by Eagle Boy, a scout for General Oliver O. Howard during the Nez Perce War of 1877. Several buckskin ceremonial dresses decorated with shells are also on display. One ceremonial costume is made of red Hudson Bay trade cloth and trimmed with ribbons and coins. Other Nez Perce items are corn-husk bags, beaded bags, saddlebags, pipes, moccasins, gloves, dolls, an awl holder, and a pack saddle. *305 N. College* *208/983–2104* *www.grangevilleidaho.com/historical_museum.htm* *Donation suggested* *June–Sept., Wed. and Fri. 1–5.*

You'll need a high-clearance vehicle and most of a day to drive the 53 mi up unpaved **Elk City Wagon Road.** For centuries it was used by Native Americans traveling through the Clearwater Mountains to the Bitterroot Valley and other points to the east. After 1861, thousands of miners used the same route to reach the goldfields of Newsome, Elk City, Buffalo Hump, and Thunder Mountain. So heavy was the traffic that a new road had to be built along the route. The road to Elk City, funded mostly by public subscription, was completed July 15, 1895. To help you follow the road there are "Elk City Wagon Road" posts and 22 interpretive signs, and you can get a tour guide book from Nez Perce National Forest Headquarters in Grangeville or any other ranger district in the forest. In Elk City there is a ranger station where you can get additional information. ✉ *Starts in Harpster, 10 mi east of Grangeville on Rte. 13 and 3 mi north on U.S. 12* ☎ *208/842–2245 or 208/983–1950* 🌐 *www.fs.fed.us/r1/nezperce* ⏲ *Summer and fall, weather permitting.*

Where to Stay & Eat

$–$$$ ✕ **Oscar's Restaurant.** Grab a table near the big picture windows and you can watch locals make their way down Main Street. Oscar's serves the usual burgers, steaks, and seafood. The prime rib dip, thin-sliced prime rib topped with sautéed onions and Swiss cheese and served on a roll, is one of the most popular dishes. ✉ *101 E. Main St.* ☎ *208/983–2106* ▭ *MC, V* ⏲ *No dinner Sun.*

¢ **Downtowner Inn.** Grangeville's only downtown motel is about a block from Main Street. Rooms are quiet, simple, and clean. Flower beds outside the office and along the parking lot create a homey feel. ✉ *113 E. North St., 83530* ☎ *208/983–1110* *17 rooms* *Some microwaves, refrigerators, cable TV* ▭ *AE, DC, MC, V.*

Cottonwood

❸ *17 mi northwest of Grangeville via Hwy. 95.*

A quiet agricultural community of about 1,000 people, Cottonwood sits on the rolling Camas Prairie above the Salmon River. The prairie gets its name from a flowering plant that was ground into a fine flour by the Nez Perce and their ancestors. Most people you encounter here are visiting the Historical Museum at St. Gertrude or passing through on their way to one of the access points to the lower Salmon River.

The **Historical Museum at St. Gertrude** houses an extensive collection of military artifacts, including many from the Nez Perce War of 1877. Look for uniforms from the Spanish-American War and a collection of 19th-century firearms. Gold scales from 1880 and a miner's rocker cradle are among the items in exhibits on mining in the region. Objects from everyday pioneer life include a complete cobbler's bench with sewing machine, shoe lasts, and leather tools; a Hoosier cabinet with old bowls and serving pieces; a kitchen work table from about 1900; handmade tools dating back to 1834; and clocks, dolls, butter churns, and lanterns dating to 1865. ✉ *121 Keuterville Rd.,* ☎ *208/962–7123* 🌐 *www.historicalmuseumstgertrude.com* *$4* ⏲ *May–Sept., Tues.–Sat. 9:30–4:30, Sun. 1:30–4:30; Oct.–Apr., Tues.–Sat. 9:30–4:30.*

Where to Stay & Eat

$–$$ ✕ **Country Haus Restaurant.** Breakfast, lunch, and dinner are all served at this down-home cookery. The menu includes consistently well-prepared dishes such as chicken-fried steak and homemade apple pie. It's all brought to you by friendly servers. Locals like the little extras, such as the baskets of fresh, hot bread and the homemade salsa and chips. ✉ *407 Foster St.* ☎ *208/962–3991* ▭ *MC, V.*

$ **Dog Bark Park.** A three-story-tall beagle nicknamed Sweet Willy Colton just might be your home for the night. He wears a red collar and has 14-foot-long ears made from indoor-outdoor carpet. You can sleep in the dog-shape cabin's main room or climb a ladder into the loft. Owners Dennis Sullivan and Frances Conklin are chain-saw artists whose work keeps getting bigger and bigger. At their adjacent gift shop, much smaller versions of Willy and other critters are for sale. Reserve well ahead. ✉ *Hwy. 95,, at the dog, 83522* ☎ *208/962–3647* *1 room* *Kitchenette, pets allowed; no a/c, no room phone, no room TV, no smoking* 💳 *MC, V* ⏲ *Closed Nov.–Mar.*

Winchester Lake State Park

4 *23 mi north of Cottonwood via U.S. 95.*

The namesake of this state park is a man-made lake that was once a log storage pond for a nearby mill that closed in the 1960s after the area's mature timber was mostly depleted. At the forested base of the Craig Mountains, Winchester Lake State Park happens to have the nicest campgrounds in the area. Turkey, grouse, great blue herons, and several duck species frequent the area, as do beavers, white-tailed deer, muskrats, otters, and painted turtles. The big draw, however, is the fishing. The Idaho Department of Fish and Game stocks the lake with rainbow trout each year. Crappie, largemouth bass, and bluegill are also pulled from these waters. Fishing is most pleasant from canoes or other small craft, but no gas motors are allowed on the lake. Swimming in the lake is not recommended because of potential health hazards associated with its large population of waterfowl. In the winter, cross-country skiing and ice fishing are popular pastimes. The adjacent town of Winchester is where everyone goes for supplies.

When documentary filmmaker Jim Dutcher wanted to film a wolfpack in the 1990s, he collected captive-bred wolves, built a fenced enclosure, and named his wolves the Sawtooth Pack. At project's conclusion the wolves, socialized to humans and therefore unsuitable for release, were ★ brought to the **Wolf Education & Research Center.** Seven of them remain in a 20-acre enclosure. Guided tours take place morning and evening and provide the best chance to see wolves. Self-guided walks to the wolf-viewing platform are allowed during the day. In winter, the center is open by appointment only. ✉ *Off Hwy. 95, near Winchester* ☎ *208/924–6960* 🌐 *www.wolfcenter.org* *$5–$10* ⏲ *June–Aug., daily; May and Sept., weekends.*

Sports & the Outdoors

BOATING Rent canoes and kayaks by the hour, or by the half or full day from **Park Headquarters** (☎ 208/924–7563) on the far side of Lake Winchester.

Camping

Winchester Lake State Park. The park's campground straggles up a hillside, with many spacious sites hidden among the trees. Tent sites are down by the lake and tend to be a bit quieter. The three lattice-and-canvas-walled, Mongolian-style yurts come with outside cooking grills, skylights in the roofs, and bunk beds. They sleep five comfortably. *Flush toilets, pit toilets. Drinking water, showers. Fire grates, picnic tables. Public telephone. Ranger station* *45 partial hookups, 20 tent sites, 3 yurts* ✉ *Forest Rd., 83555* ☎ *208/924–7563* *Partial hookups $16, tent sites $12, yurts $35–$55* 💳 *MC, V.*

Lewiston

5 *32 mi northwest of Winchester Lake State Park via Hwy. 95 and Hwy. 12.*

The hardworking mill town of Lewiston is tucked into the grain-gold hills where the Snake River and Clearwater River meet. Although it was once the capital of the Idaho Territory, Lewiston is now known mostly for the giant paper mill on its eastern edge. Despite its long stretches of waterfront, it has yet to attract much tourism.

Fodor'sChoice ★

Lewiston and Clarkston (its twin city across the border in Washington) are known as the gateways to **Hells Canyon,** a geologic wonder considerably deeper than the Grand Canyon. The hills in the canyon resemble ancient Maya temples as they rise high above the water. Columnar basalt, rock formations that look like giant black pencils, frame the river. In some spots, ancient Native American pictographs can be seen on smooth rock faces. Bald eagles swoop down from cliffs to hunt for fish, and deer graze among the plants on the hillsides.

Miners tried to exploit the area, but they gave up. Today a few hardy sheep and cattle ranchers are all that's left of the pioneers who first settled here. The **Kirkwood Historic Ranch** (☎ 208/628–3916), a dramatic, 5-mi hike up the Snake River from Pittsburg Landing, past mining-camp sites and petroglyphs, or a four-hour jet-boat ride from Lewiston, has been preserved to show how canyon pioneers lived.

off the beaten path

NEZ PERCE NATIONAL HISTORICAL PARK – This is really a series of 24 sites spread across three states, but park headquarters and the site most visited is in Spalding, 11 mi east of Lewiston, where a well-designed visitor center gives a detailed look at the history of the Nez Perce, or Ne-Mee-Poo (The People), as they call themselves. A 30-minute film details the tribe's contacts with Lewis and Clark and their lives today. The museum exhibits artifacts from chiefs Joseph and White Bird, including textiles; pipes; and, poignantly, a ribbon and a coin given to the tribe by Meriwether Lewis as thanks for help. ✉ *Hwy. 95* ☎ *208/843–2261* 💵 *Donation* ⏲ *Memorial Day–Labor Day, daily 8–5:30; Labor Day–Memorial Day, daily 8–4:30.*

Sports & the Outdoors

BOATING Jet-boat tours are the easiest way to see Hells Canyon if you don't have the time or inclination for white-water rafting from Hells Canyon Dam or Pittsburg Landing. **Snake River Adventures** (✉ 227 Snake River Ave. ☎ 208/746–6276 or 800/262–8874 🌐 www.snakeriveradventures.com) runs one-day, 200-mi trips up into Hells Canyon on 42-foot jet boats. The 28-foot jet boat is used for guided fishing or camping trips lasting from one to three days.

FISHING Riding into Hells Canyon on a guided jet-boat fishing trip is one of the truly amazing experiences of an angler's life. Giant sturgeon, often more than 6 feet long, are caught here in the kind of epic battles that make you think you're fighting a small whale. Sturgeon were once anadromous, living part of their lives in the ocean but spawning in fresh water. Dams now prevent the fish from reaching the sea, and the sturgeon's future is in doubt. All sturgeon must be released, but part of the fun is watching this giant, boneless, toothless, and scaleless creature glide majestically out of your grip after an hour of fight. **Hells Canyon Resort** (✉ 35909 Snake River Rd., Asotin, WA ☎ 509/243–4869) offers both fishing trips and upscale lodge-style accommodations near Hells Canyon. The company's 25- and 29-foot-long jet boats chase sturgeon year-round. Although sturgeon fishing is generally better in winter, guides say they can practically guarantee your hooking a fish. The company also specializes in steelhead fishing.

Where to Stay & Eat

$$–$$$ ✕ **Bojack's.** This popular downtown eatery has been pleasing locals with the same menu for 30 years. Get ready for tasty steaks and seafood with a dollop of spaghetti on the side. Both price and quantity are more than fair: doggie bags are frequently required. There's a dark bar upstairs. ✉ *311 Main St., Lewiston* ☎ *208/746–9532* 💳 *AE, MC, V* ⏲ *Closed Sun. No lunch.*

★ $–$$$ ✕ **Roosters Waterfront Restaurant.** Ask locals for the best restaurant in town, and they'll point across the Snake River. Roosters Landing, as most people call it, is in Washington in the town of Clarkston. The restaurant has a massive deck overlooking a marina, and a party feel, thanks to the insistent rock music and the whimsical decor, which includes a plastic marlin. Fish-and-chips, dished out generously enough to feed two, is a popular option, as are other seafood offerings. Pasta dishes and well-aged steaks are also good bets. There is a full bar where bands sometimes play in the evenings. ✉ *1550 Port Dr., Clarkston, WA* ☎ *509/751–0155* ▭ *AE, DC, MC, V.*

$–$$$ ✕ **Tomato Brothers.** Wood-fired pizzas and well-prepared pasta dishes are the specialty at this eatery on the Washington side of the Snake River. Especially creative are the sandwiches, which are equally good served the regular way or "smashed" (grilled between two cast-iron plates). Extra touches include the butcher paper and crayons awaiting your creative attention, and the "honor bottle" of house red, from which you can pour as soon as you reach your table. At the end of the meal, just tell your server how many glasses you drank. ✉ *300 Bridge St., Clarkston, WA* ☎ *509/758–7902* ▭ *AE, D, MC, V.*

★ $–$$$ **Italianna Inn.** The owner may have left Tuscany at 12, but she's re-created a bit of her history right here in Lewiston. From the red tile roof to the white stucco walls, from the grapevines to the rosebushes, her villa would be at home in any Italian town. Anna serves what she calls simple country fare: fritatas made with garden vegetables, fresh breads based on her grandmother's recipes, and Italian sausage. Two generously oversize guest rooms have private entrances. One smaller room is an art-deco dream with crimson and green walls (like Italy's flag) and a black-and-white tile floor. ✉ *2728 11th Ave., 83501* ☎ *208/743–4552* 🌐 *www.italiannainn.com* *4 rooms, 3 with bath* *Pool, meeting rooms; no room phones, no room TVs* ▭ *No credit cards.*

¢ ✕ **Sacajawea Motor Inn.** The basic rooms at this motel are a good bargain. It's near Lewiston's historic downtown. Lots of locals eat at the Helm because they know exactly what to expect: good, reliable food for breakfast, lunch, or dinner. The menu includes steaks, chops, burgers, and a variety of sandwiches. ✉ *1824 Main St., 83501* ☎ *208/746–1393 or 800/333–1393* 🖷 *208/743–3620* *90 rooms* *Restaurant, pool, gym, hot tub, laundry facilities, some pets allowed (fee)* ▭ *AE, D, DC, MC, V.*

$ **Red Lion Hotel.** On a hill overlooking the entrance of town, this hotel is a stone's throw away from many shops and restaurants. The airy atrium is a welcome sight when you return from a fishing or rafting expedition. Meriwether's, the excellent restaurant, serves a Sunday brunch buffet that draws people from miles around. The on-site microbrewery, MJ Barleyhoppers, hosts a comedy night on Wednesday that showcases local talent. ✉ *621 21st St., 83501* ☎ *208/799–1000 or 800/232–6730* 🖷 *208/748–1050* 🌐 *www.redlionlewiston.com* *132 rooms, 51 suites* *2 restaurants, room service, some microwaves, some refrigerators, cable TV, pool, health club, outdoor hot tub, pub, laundry facilities, meeting rooms, some pets allowed, no-smoking rooms* ▭ *AE, DC, MC, V.*

¢ **Inn America.** Don't be put off by the unpromising facade of this roadside motel. It's perched on a hill, so many rooms have views of the Snake River. The accommodations are generously proportioned, particularly the oversize "family rooms." Look for extras such as refrigerators and coffeemakers. The hotel is a snap to get to from Highway 12. ✉ *702 21st St., 83501* ☎ *208/746–4600* 🖷 *208/748–1050* *61 rooms* *Refrigerators, pool, laundry facilities* ▭ *AE, D, DC, MC, V* 🍽 *CP.*

CAMPING **Hellsgate State Park.** On the banks of the placid, dam-slowed Snake River, Hellsgate State Park has a boat ramp that makes it a hit with speedboat fans. It's just as popular with those looking for a full-service campground for a good price. Campsites are on a flat, grassy area. *Flush toilets. Full hookups, dump station. Drinking water, showers. Grills, picnic tables. Play area, swimming (river) 11 full hookups, 54 partial hookups, 28 tent sites 3620 Snake River Ave., 83501 208/799–5015 www.idahoparks.org Full hookups $22, partial hookups $20, tent sites $16 MC, V.*

Shopping

Lewiston is not a tourist town, so its tree-shaded Main Street shopping district is pleasantly devoid of souvenir shops. Most of the interesting shopping and dining opportunities are clustered between 3rd and 9th streets, centering on a brick pedestrian walkway with benches surrounding a fountain. Offstreet parking is available on D Street, which parallels Main Street. Expect the stores a small town needs: a cigar shop, a bookstore, and jewelry shops.

A few blocks from most of the other shops on Main Street, **Meacham Mills** (1305 Main St. 208/798–1682) is worth a walk. It is literally crammed to the ceiling with kitchen gadgets, specialty foods, and more. You can buy adzuki beans, buckwheat honey, and six kinds of lentils, including some that are a vivid crimson. An entire room is filled with scented bath products and candles.

en route

Driving east from Lewiston is one long adventure that doesn't end until you reach the border of Montana. Highway 12 first parallels the Clearwater River up a pretty and increasingly forested canyon, passes through several small logging towns, then turns northeast to follow the wild Lochsa River up to its divide near Lolo Pass. On the far side of the Lochsa River lies the largest wilderness area in the lower 48 states. Spotting elk and deer on this tortuously twisting section of road is common. It's called the **Northwest Passage Scenic Byway** because it parallels the route Lewis and Clark took on their 1805 westward journey.

Dworshak State Park

6 *61 mi northeast of Lewiston via Hwy. 12 and County Rd.*

About 45 minutes from the nearest town, Dworshak State Park is reached via a slow, two-lane road. The final 2 mi are paved but twisting, leading down to the western shore of the reservoir that is the point of this 850-acre park. Campsites, a picnic area, hiking trails, two boat launches, a lodge available for groups, and a fish-cleaning station are the park's primary facilities.

Completed in 1972 and originally known as Bruce's Eddy Dam project, **Dworshak Dam** is the highest straight-axis dam in North America (which means it is unarched, sitting like an improbably tall wall across the canyon). It's also the third-tallest dam in the country, and it holds back a 54-mi-long reservoir. The visitor center is on top of the dam, and exhibits here cover the dam's history, local logging history (some of the last big log drives in the country took place on the now-buried North Fork of the Clearwater), and native wildlife. *3 mi past Orofino Bridge 208/476–1255 Free Daily 10–4.*

A narrow, deep reservoir snaking through what was once the canyon home of the North Fork of the Clearwater, the **Dworshak Reservoir** is heaven if you own a speedboat. Besides state park boat launches, there are also launches at Canyon Creek, Bruce's Eddy, and Dent Acres. The reservoir's great length means it never feels too crowded. Fishing for kokanee and rainbow trout is good year-round. Bass fishing is often good in the spring near the mouths of creeks. Water levels fluctuate by more than 100 feet, although Dworshak Reservoir is usually kept brimming until after the big tourist weekend of July 4. The shoreline is steep and undeveloped, alternating between thick forest and wildflower-filled meadow.

Camping

Freeman Creek Campground. Some sites in this campground are lakeside, affording nice views. Temperate weather warms the reservoir quickly in spring; swimmers start hitting the protected sand beach as early as Memorial Day. One of the park's two boat launch facilities is here. *Flush toilets, pit toilets. Partial hookups, dump station. Drinking water, showers. Fire pits, picnic tables. Swimming (reservoir). 46 partial hookups Freeman Creek Rd., 208/476–5994 www.idahoparks.org Partial hookups $16, tent sites $12 MC, V Apr.–Sept.*

U.S. Army Corps of Engineers Mini-Camps. Not part of the state park but accessible from its boat launches, these tiny sites offer basic facilities and the kind of solitude campgrounds can't usually provide. Seven are accessible by trail, but the rest can be reached only by boat. There's one downside: sites get farther and farther from shore as the reservoir level drops, so although technically they're open year-round, by mid-August most are not conveniently located. *Some pit toilets, some portable toilets. Fire pits, picnic tables 118 sites Dworshak Reservoir 208/476–1261 Free Reservations not accepted.*

Orofino

7 *42 mi east of Lewiston via Hwy. 12.*

Meaning "fine gold" in Spanish, Orofino is a gold-rush town that was established in 1898. Lewis and Clark passed what would later become Orofino when they made their westward trek along the Clearwater River in 1805. The town straddles the river and reaches up a narrow tree-lined valley with an elevation of 1,097 feet, adjacent to the Nez Perce reservation. Orofino's proximity to the North Fork of the Clearwater, a perfect highway for moving great quantities of cut trees out of the rugged country and down to the mills, made lumbering important to the economy. At one time, Clearwater County was home to 20-odd lumber mills. One of the last small mills in the region still operates in Orofino. These days, the town is better known as a gateway to Dworshak Dam and reservoir, Dworshak State Park, and the Nez Perce National Historical Park.

★ The U.S. Fish and Wildlife Service's **Dworshak National Fish Hatchery** is one of the largest anadromous hatcheries in the world, releasing some 6 million fish annually. Self-guided tours give you access to most of the facility. Come during the right time of year (late January through early May for steelhead, mid-August for chinook) and you can visit holding ponds full of fish as big as a toddler, and, with luck, watch broodstock being sorted, their eggs collected for artificial spawning. With advance reservation, guided tours are available. *4147 Ahsahka Rd., Ahsahka 208/476–4591 dworshak.fws.gov Free Daily 7:30–4.*

The **Clearwater Historical Museum** displays artifacts from the Nez Perce, including a dugout canoe and a braided hair rope. Other items date to the Lewis and Clark era and the gold-rush and settlement days. Easy to read and informative explanatory placards are unusually well done for such a small museum. The old house in which the museum resides dates to the 1920s and is interesting in its own right. ✉ *315 College Ave.* ☎ *208/476–5033* 🎫 *Free* ⏲ *Tues.–Sat. 1:30–4:30.*

Sports & the Outdoors

FISHING Fishing is almost a religion around here. If large numbers of salmon and steelhead successfully navigate eight dams between the Pacific and Lewiston, anglers in and around Orofino will have the time of their lives. The steelhead season runs from August to April. When the Idaho Department of Fish and Game approves a salmon season, it typically runs May to July. Both species can grow to more than 20 pounds. Good places to try are the waters below Dworshak Dam and around the hatcheries to which most of the fish are trying to return.

Clearwater Drifters & Guideshop (✉ 14010 Hwy. 12, milepost 40 ☎ 208/476–3531 🌐 www.theguideshop.com) is a well-established local fishing shop and guide service. The company fishes Dworshak Reservoir from jet boats from April to July for kokanee, bass, and rainbow trout. Lunkers are not uncommon. The company's drift boats and jet boats patrol the Clearwater River for salmon. The company's Web site posts an updated fishing report every Wednesday.

SKIING At the small **Bald Mountain Ski Resort** (✉ 42 mi east, 6 mi north of Pierce on Rte. 11 ☎ 208/464–2311 or 208/743–6397), run by the Idaho Parks and Recreation Department, the vertical drop is 975 feet. It's popular with locals, and the only way to get to the top is a T-bar. However, the price is right and the slopes are never crowded. The resort is open from December through mid-March. The lodge has a snack bar and rentals and offers lessons to get beginners started.

Where to Stay & Eat

$–$$$ ✕ **Ponderosa Restaurant & Lounge.** On the edge of town, this is a family establishment by day and a lounge in the evening. Dinners range from sandwiches to seafood to the house favorite, prime rib. There's a separate rooms for non-smokers called the Garden Room. ✉ *220 Michigan Ave.* ☎ *208/476–4818* 💳 *MC, V.*

$–$$ ✕ **Fiesta en Jalisco.** Authentic southern Mexican dishes served in a festive family atmosphere have made this small regional chain a big success. The restaurant gets its name from the part of Mexico's Pacific coast known for its unique cuisine, so expect more than the usual burritos and fajitas. Locals return again and again for entrées such as *carne asada* (marinated grilled beef) at very reasonable prices. ✉ *307 Johnson Ave.* ☎ *208/476–7506* 💳 *AE, DC, MC, V.*

¢ ✕ **Flamingo Café.** The freshest ingredients go into the soups and quiches at this popular eatery. Everything is served with creative flair. Breakfasts are pancake and egg affairs. Lunches are sandwiches, burgers, and salads. While you're waiting, browse for bargains in the attached antiques shop. ✉ *235 Johnson Ave.* ☎ *208/476–0200* 💳 *MC, V* ⏲ *Closed Sun. No dinner.*

¢ ✕🏨 **Konkolville Motel.** When the mill runs cedar, the sweet aroma drifts past this motel owned by an old lumbering family. Rooms are simply furnished but spacious and pin-neat. Don't spoil your appetite, because the motel's grill-it-yourself restaurant is a must for meat lovers. As you tackle your baked potato, the staff drops a seasoned New York strip steak on the grill in the courtyard. You flip it a few times and then chow down. During salmon and steelhead runs, the indoor fish-cleaning room, with stainless-steel counter and sink, gets a workout. ✉ *2000 Konkolville Rd., 83544* ☎ *208/476–5584 or 800/616–1964* 📠 *208/476–3268* 🌐 *konkolvillemotel.com* 🛏 *40 rooms* 👍 *Refrigerators, pool, outdoor hot tub, laundry facilities, some pets allowed (fee), no-smoking rooms* 💳 *AE, DC, MC, V* 🍽 *CP.*

$ **High Country Inn.** The Clearwater River rushes by just below the garden-rimmed patio of this delightful little inn. The place has an open, airy feel. The high-ceilinged great room is filled with mounted elk, deer, and moose. If you like the breakfast whipped up by owner Jo Moore, she'll be happy to cook you a gourmet dinner. Better yet, she offers cooking classes. This is a popular place, so call ahead. *4232 Old Ahsahka Grade, Ahsahka 83520 208/476–7570 www.thehighcountryinn.com 2 rooms Some pets allowed; no room phones, no room TVs, no smoking AE, DC, MC, V BP.*

¢ **Helgeson Place Hotel Suites.** The suites at this low-cost lodging have touches more often found in higher-end accommodations, such as the fluffy terry robes. The two-bedroom suites are perfect for families is search of a little alone time. Located in the heart of downtown, this place is an easy walk from several restaurants. *125 Johnson Ave. 208/476–5729 or 800/404–5729 19 rooms Kitchens, hot tub, exercise equipment, some pets allowed (fee), no-smoking rooms AE, DC, MC, V.*

Lowell

8 *54 mi east of Orofino via Hwy. 12.*

More wilderness outpost than a real town, Lowell has a population of about 30 people. It clings to the edge of the Selway-Bitterroot Wilderness at the confluence of two famous rivers protected under the Wild and Scenic Rivers Act, the Lochsa and the Selway. Residents delight in telling stories about the cougar that trapped a camper in a glass-walled phone booth and the other big cat that trotted into Three Rivers Resort.

Tree-covered canyons lead up to rugged ridges at the **Clearwater National Forest,** which includes 1.8 million acres at elevations ranging from 1,600 feet to nearly 9,000 feet. The climate varies greatly, and much of the area is snowbound from December through May. There are more than 1,700 mi of hiking trails leading past buttes and to waterfalls. Some easily reached trailheads are found in the White Pine Scenic Drive area along U.S. 12, Route 247, and Forest Road 250, next to the North Fork of the Clearwater River. You can see herds of elk as well as moose, mountain goats, white-tailed and mule deer, mountain lions, and black bears. *12730 U.S. 12 208/476–4541 www.fs.fed.us/r1/clearwater Free Daily 24 hrs.*

A quarter of the 9,767 acres that make up the **Selway-Bitterroot Wilderness** are within the Clearwater National Forest. Elevations range from 1,800 feet near the Selway and Lochsa rivers to 8,800-foot mountain peaks along the Bitterroot Divide. Hundreds of miles of trails are maintained through the park. The Selway-Bitterroot Wilderness is reachable via forest roads off U.S. 93. Mechanized vehicles, including bicycles, are not permitted in the park itself or on trails leading into the park.

The **Mallard-Larkins Pioneer Area** is a 33,000-acre region of rugged mountains between the St. Joe and Clearwater rivers. The park lies partly in the St. Joe National Forest and partly in the Clearwater National Forest. There are no roads through the park, but a trail system provides easy access to both halves.

A trio of waterfalls, known collectively as **Elk Creek Falls,** is a popular area for hiking, camping, and picnicking. A ½-mi trail leads to the falls.

The **Lochsa River** (Lochsa means "rough water" in Nez Perce) originates in the Bitterroot Mountains and joins the Selway and Clearwater rivers after 26 mi. It includes 40 Class III to Class IV rapids. U.S. 12 parallels the river for much of its course. The river-running season is short, from mid-May to late June. Most outfitters offer trips lasting from one to three days.

The backcountry **Lochsa Historical Ranger Station** (✉ Hwy. 12, 24 mi north of Lowell ☎ no phone 🎟 Donation suggested ⏲ June–Sept., daily 10–5), built in the early 1920s, was accessible only on foot until 1956, when the Lewis and Clark Highway (now U.S. 12) was constructed. The old station has been restored to show how rangers lived. Retired Forest Service employees greet visitors, answer questions, and guide tours. If you're interested in hiking and other outdoor activities, this is a good place to stop.

The **Lolo Pass Visitor Center** (✉ Hwy. 12, near the Montana state line ☎ no phone ⏲ Daily 9–5), a refurbished log cabin, stands at a rest stop at the Idaho-Montana state line. Exhibits at the center trace Lewis and Clark's journey through Idaho. If you reached this point via Lewiston, you have already traced much of their route.

Sports & the Outdoors

WHITE-WATER RAFTING

The Lochsa River draws thrill seekers from across the region when the rapids are at their peak, usually from mid-May to early July. Few road-accessible rafting runs offer so many big rapids (Class III and IV) in such a short distance. Most outfitters insist that you wear wet suits and helmets and have previous white-water rafting experience. A good choice is **River Odysseys West** (☎ 208/765–0841 🌐 www.rowinc.com). Based in Coeur d'Alene, the company has an office in Lochsa and runs the river nearly every day during the height of the season.

Where to Stay

¢ **Three Rivers Resort.** The Lochsa River rolls by this string of rustic A-frame cabins not far from the Clearwater National Forest. (A little farther downstream it joins the Selway and the Clearwater, hence the name.) You can relax on your wide porch or cook dinner on your own grill. A small grocery, lounge, and a restaurant serving simple American dinners are on the premises. The resort also offers RV and tent camping. The nearest town with full services is Kooskia, 23 mi back down Highway 12. ✉ *Hwy. 12, 83539* ☎ *208/926–4430 or 888/926–4430* 🖷 *208/926–7526* 🌐 *threeriversresort.com* *13 rooms, 17 cabins* *Restaurant, pool, hot tub, 2 outdoor hot tubs, basketball, horseshoes, shuffleboard, lounge; no room phones* 💳 *AE, D, DC, MC, V.*

¢ **Weitas Butte, Austin Ridge, and Castle Butte Lookouts.** Although no longer used for fire detection, this trio of extremely basic lookout stations is available for overnight stays during the summer. They offer dramatic views of the Clearwater National Forest but are not recommended for families with small children. All three are on roads that may not be passable in wet weather. ✉ *12730 U.S. 12* ☎ *208/476–4541* 🌐 *www.fs.fed.us/r1/clearwater* *3 lookout stations* 💳 *AE, D, DC, MC, V.*

CAMPING

Clearwater National Forest Campgrounds. Nearly 20 beautifully maintained campgrounds are all clustered along the Clearwater, Selway, and Lochsa rivers. One of the nicest areas is off Highway 12 at Wilderness Gateway. This also happens to be the only campground in the area with flush toilets. Across the river from the road, Wilderness Gateway is a few minutes' drive from the Lochsa Historical Ranger Station. *Pit toilets. Drinking water at some campgrounds. Fire pits, picnic tables* ✉ *Lowry St., Kooskia 83539* ☎ *208/926–4274* 🎟 *Free–$8* 💳 *No credit cards* ⏲ *June–Aug.*

THE ORIGINAL NORTH IDAHOANS

FOR PERHAPS 10,000 YEARS, *the plains and river canyons of northern Idaho were home to the Nez Perce people and their ancestors. For most of that time, change came slowly: homes that were little more than lean-tos built against overhanging ledges became cylindrical pit houses, hollowed into the ground and roofed over with rushes and perhaps hides.*

The Nez Perce moved with their food sources, visiting the Camas Prairie when the camas lily was ready to harvest and fishing the Clearwater, Salmon, and Snake rivers during salmon and steelhead runs. When the horse arrived in the 1700s, the Nez Perce adopted it, developing the hardy Appaloosa over the course of centuries.

For a people generally slow to change, the Nez Perce adapted quickly to the presence of white people, welcoming adventurers Lewis and Clark into their villages, making sure they were well fed, and providing them with transportation. This won the Nez Perce unusually fair treatment from the normally harsh American government; an 1855 treaty gave them ownership of most of their homeland, a vast area that stretched not only across northern Idaho but into what is now Washington and Oregon.

That changed five years later, when trespassers on the reservation discovered gold. Pressure from would-be miners and homesteaders led to a new treaty, which most of the Nez Perce refused to sign. That was fine with government officials, who ceded about a tenth of the original reservation to one band of Nez Perce (whose leaders did sign). The refusal of most Nez Perce people to move onto the smaller reservation led finally to the military action the bands had so carefully worked to avoid. Less than a century after the first Nez Perce encountered a white man, the bands had been decimated and their lands mostly parceled out to strangers.

To learn about the struggles of the Nez Perce, both past and present, visit the Nez Perce National Historical Park. As was once true of the Nez Perce themselves, the park spreads across northern and central Washington and Idaho, western Montana, and eastern Oregon. There are 38 individual sites along the way.

Moscow

9 *34 mi north of Lewiston via Hwy. 95.*

From Lewiston, U.S. 95 climbs 2,000 feet out of the valley and up into the Palouse, an area of gentle hills with extremely fertile soil that at the height of growing season looks like a sea of green velvet and in fall a sea of gold. About 30 mi later, the road cuts through the middle of Moscow, cradled by the Rocky Mountains to the east and the Palouse Hills to the west. From Moscow Mountain, a few miles northeast of town via Mountain View Road, you get a panoramic view of the entire area.

Moscow is also home to the University of Idaho, which was established in 1889, the year before Idaho became a state. Students often joke that the university was placed in Moscow because there is absolutely nothing to do here except study. It does feature a fine set of late-19th-century buildings, however, and, in February, the Lionel Hampton Jazz Festival, a weeklong musical event.

Moscow's **Appaloosa Museum & Heritage Center** highlights the history of the Appaloosa, a type of horse known for its distinctive markings. Saddles, riding gear, and other artifacts associated with the Appaloosa are on display, including Native American items. The Nez Perce tribes who lived in the area practiced selective horse breeding and produced large herds of high-quality horses, including Appaloosas. ✉ *2720 W. Pullman Rd.* ☎ *208/882–5578* 🌐 *www.appaloosa.com* 🎫 *Free* 🕑 *Tues.–Fri. 10–5, Sat. 10–4.*

Built in 1886 by Idaho's third governor, the **McConnell Mansion** is an eclectic combination of Eastlake, Queen Anne, and Victorian Gothic styles. Period-furnished rooms display artifacts and Victorian-style furniture from the early 1900s to the 1930s. The mansion also houses the Latah County Historical Society, which presents changing exhibits on county history on the second floor. ✉ *110 S. Adams St.* ☎ *208/882–1004* 🌐 *www.moscow.com* 🎫 *$2 suggested donation* 🕑 *Tues.–Sat. 1–4.*

off the beaten path

EMERALD CREEK GARNET AREA – Dig for the state's gemstone, star garnet, on federal government land about 30 mi south and west of St. Maries. The crystals are 12-sided and range from pinhead-size to—very rarely—fist-size. The most prized garnets are those that display, in bright light, four- or six-ray stars that seem to float inside the stone. ✉ *Forest Rd. 447 off Hwy. 3 south of St. Maries* ☎ *208/245–2531* 🎫 *$10* 🕑 *June–Aug., daily 8–5.*

Where to Stay & Eat

★ **$$–$$$** ✕ **Red Door Restaurant.** It calls itself a "slow food restaurant," and everything about this casually elegant restaurant backs up that description. It's easy to linger over meals prepared with such high-quality ingredients, from aged cheeses to the freshest herbs. The mashed potatoes, for example, are made from buttery-tasting Yukon Gold spuds. Polenta makes the hush puppies anything but average. And the lamb is raised in the region, so it's always flavorful. The only problem here is the sometimes irritating noise levels, a result of odd acoustics that makes quiet conversations impossible. ✉ *215 S. Main St.* ☎ *208/882–7830* ▭ *AE, DC, MC, V* 🕑 *Closed Sun. and Mon. No lunch.*

$–$$ ✕ **Basilio's.** In the Moscow Hotel, this restaurant offers updated Italian cuisine in a bright dining room fitted with artwork from ceiling to floor. The menu has a good variety of pastas. For those who like variety, the dinner menu offers unusual duos like lasagna and prime rib. ✉ *313 S. Main St.* ☎ *208/892–3848* ▭ *MC, V.*

¢ ✕ **Moscow Food Co-op.** You can make your stomach happy and keep your heart healthy when you grab a meal at this neighborhood food co-op. On weekends you can also get no-frills breakfasts of huevos rancheros or breakfast burritos. The menu changes daily, but there are always plenty of soups and salads to choose from. One option is usually vegan. Several small tables are scrunched into a corner near the front door, but a more pleasant option is to wander back toward Main Street and relax on one of the benches in Friendship Square. ✉ *221 E. 3rd St.* ☎ *208/882–8537* ▭ *MC, V.*

$ 🏨 **Best Western University Inn.** Near the western gate of the University of Idaho, this lodging is the nicest in town. Rooms are decorated with light-wood furniture and floral print fabrics. ✉ *1516 Pullman Rd.* ☎ *208/882–0550* 📠 *208/883–3056* *173 rooms* *2 restaurants, room service, some refrigerators, cable TV, indoor pool, wading pool, hot tub,* *sauna, bar, laundry service, business services, airport shuttle, some pets allowed (fee)* ▭ *AE, D, DC, MC, V.*

¢ ▣ **Mark IV Motor Inn.** It's been around for years, but spacious rooms and traditional furnishings make this downtown hotel a pleasant place to stay. It's near the university. ✉ *414 N. Main St.* ☎ *208/882–7557* 🖷 *208/883–0684* *86 rooms* *Restaurant, room service, cable TV, indoor pool, hot tub, bar, business services, airport shuttle, pets allowed (fee)* ▭ *AE, D, DC, MC, V.*

Nightlife & the Arts

THE ARTS The **University of Idaho Lionel Hampton Jazz Festival** (☎ 208/885–6765), a weeklong event held annually in February, is known for the appearances by more than 50 of the world's great jazz artists.

Shopping

Moscow's main shopping district, along Main Street between 1st and 6th, is pedestrian-friendly by careful design (for instance, free parking lots are away from the crowded streets). Specialty stores include a shop selling tie-dye clothing and another selling guitars. Cafés, bakeries, and restaurants are scattered throughout the area.

Shop for gems and minerals, both in their natural forms and fashioned into rings or pendants, at **Gem State Crystals** (✉ 404 S. Main St. ☎ 208/883–0939). The shop lapidaries are happy to do custom work.

An old-fashioned independent bookstore proud of its focus on local and regional authors, **Bookpeople of Moscow** (✉ 521 S. Main St. ☎ 208/882–7957) is a browser's paradise.

en route

Leaving Moscow and its rolling hills, first on Highway 95 north and then on Idaho Highway 6 and 3 toward the intersection with I–90, the **White Pine Scenic Byway** rises quickly into pine forests, crosses the pretty St. Joe River, passes through the little logging town of St. Maries, and wanders past marshlands and lakes in the lower Coeur d'Alene River basin before reaching Cataldo in the Silver Valley, home to the oldest standing building in Idaho.

THE PANHANDLE

For North Idahoans, the panhandle *is* Idaho. Anyplace south of Coeur d'Alene is of little concern to a true North Idahoan. The panhandle differs from the rest of the state in terms of climate (milder and rainier because of the influence of coastal weather patterns) and in its terrain (rugged but not nearly as high). Historically the region relied on logging and mining, but those industries have been superceded, to a degree greater than that of any other region of the state, by tourism. The big draws are two massive bodies of water, Lake Pend Oreille and Lake Coeur d'Alene, both with resort communities booming on their forested shores. North of Sandpoint you notice there aren't nearly as many tourists. Bonners Ferry, near the Canadian border, is one of the last towns in northern Idaho that don't make their living as as vacation destinations. There the temperate climate has led to the creation of a thriving agricultural community.

Heyburn State Park

⑩ *53 mi south of Coeur d'Alene via Hwy. 95 and Idaho Hwy. 5.*

Created from the Coeur d'Alene Indian Reservation in 1908, Heyburn State Park is the oldest protected area in the Pacific Northwest. It's also one of the more popular state parks in Idaho. Spanning 5,505 acres near Chatcolet Lake (which was once a separate lake but, because of a dam on the Spokane River, is now the southern tip of Lake Coeur d'Alene), it's a great spot for birders. Herons and ospreys are especially common. Each fall a festival highlights the wild rice harvest. The Hawleys Landing Amphitheater presents lectures, slide shows, and other programs on summer weekends. There are six hiking trails at the west end of the lake totaling more than 20 mi, most of them passing through stands of 400-year-old ponderosa pines. The historic Mullan Trail starts at the Chatcolet Campground. There are boat ramps at Rocky Point, Benewah, and the Chat. ⊠ *Rte. 5, 7 mi west of Hwy. 95* ☎ *208/686–1308* 🌐 *www.idahoparks.org* 🎫 *$3 per car* ⏲ *Daily.*

An 87-passenger cruise boat called ***The Idaho*** (⊠ Chat Marina ☎ 208/686–1308) chugs up the St. Joe and around Lake Coeur d'Alene. It operates from May to October.

Sports & the Outdoors

BOATING You can rent rowboats, kayaks, canoes, and paddleboats from out of the **Rocky Point Marina** (☎ 208/686–0157).

Camping

There's no doubt about it: the best camping deals in the Coeur d'Alene area are in Heyburn State Park. Of the three campgrounds, only Hawleys Landing takes reservations. It is also the busiest and most developed of the three. Chatcolet, a tent-only campground, tends to be quieter than the other two. Hawleys Landing and Benewah are both within a mile of a boat ramp, but the Benewah ramp is marshy and inconvenient when water levels drop in Lake Coeur d'Alene.

⛺ **Benewah.** This campground has many of the amenities Hawleys Landing has, but it doesn't fill up quite as fast, partly because it is smaller and less conveniently located (it's 8 mi from the park headquarters). *Flush toilets. Full hookups, partial hookups. Drinking water, showers. Grills, picnic tables* *6 full hookups, 8 partial hookups, 24 tent sites* ⊠ *409 Benewah Lake Rd.* ☎ *208/686–1308* 🎫 *Full hookups $18, partial hookups $16, tent sites $12* *Reservations not accepted* 💳 *MC, V* ⏲ *June–Oct.*
⛺ **Chatcolet.** If your idea of camping is setting up your tent, then this is the place for you. Located above the Chat Marina, it has some lovely views of the lake. Even when the other campgrounds are full, there are almost always campsites available here. *Flush toilets. Drinking water. Grills, picnic tables* *40 tent sites* ⊠ *52 Chatcolet Upper Rd.* ☎ *208/686–1308* 🎫 *Tent sites $12* *Reservations not accepted* 💳 *MC, V* ⏲ *June–Oct.*
⛺ **Hawleys Landing.** This campground has the most amenities, and therefore it is the first to fill up. There is an amphitheater where rangers give lectures about the local flora and fauna on summer weekends. Hawleys Landing is less than a mile from Rocky Point, the best boat ramp facility in the park. It's also near a beach popular with swimmers. *Flush toilets. Full hookups, partial hookups, dump station. Drinking water, showers. Grills, picnic tables* *7 full hookups, 35 partial hookups, 10 tent sites* ⊠ *55 Chatcolet Rd.* ☎ *208/686–1308* 🎫 *Full hookups $18, partial hookups $16, tent sites $12* 💳 *MC, V* ⏲ *June–Oct.*

Coeur d'Alene

⓫ *86 mi north of Moscow via Hwy. 95.*

Sitting on the shores of lovely Lake Coeur d'Alene, this resort town is surrounded by evergreen-covered hills. Originally a French fur trading post (the French provided the name, which means "heart of the awl," or, less literally, "sharp-hearted" and referred to the savvy trading practices of the locals), Coeur d'Alene later became an army outpost called Fort Sherman, then a logging and lumbering town. Many of the turn-of-the-last-century mansions built by the timber barons still stand in and around the old downtown, particularly on tree-shaded Foster Avenue.

The town has long drawn those who love the water. A century ago, paddle wheelers steamed to and from Coeur d'Alene full of sightseers. In the 1920s, the first pair of water skis was fashioned and demonstrated here by a man named John Finney. More and more tourists are discovering Coeur d'Alene, but so far the town has managed to hang on to a pleasant, laid-back atmosphere, especially along Sherman Avenue, the old main drag, and along the waterfront. Although primarily known as a summer destination, Coeur d'Alene has boosted tourism during the winter months by promoting Silver Mountain, a ski area about 50 mi to the east. Its greatest claim to fame is that the terrain forced the construction of the world's longest gondola.

★ Massive **Lake Coeur d'Alene** is the one attraction that no visitor could possibly miss. The lake is more than 25 mi long and has 135 mi of heavily forested shoreline. Its remarkably clear waters average 120 feet in depth. Fed by the pretty St. Joe and Coeur d'Alene rivers, the lake drains into the Spokane River. It is home to the largest population of osprey in the West, which can be seen plummeting lakeward for fish or flying home clutching their catch like bombs beneath a fighter plane.

See the lake at your own pace from Highway 97, known in these parts as the Lake Coeur d'Alene Scenic Byway. It runs up much of the eastern shore. Stop along the way at Mineral Ridge Trail to take in some breathtaking views. Start your drive at I–90 a few miles east of Coeur d'Alene, or from Idaho Highway 3 north of St. Maries.

Lake Coeur d'Alene Cruises sets off on 90-minute trips around the lake, six-hour excursions up the St. Joe River, and sunset cruises. The boats have climate-controlled cabins as well as plenty of deck space for enjoying the weather. Trips begin and end at Independence Point. ✉ *Independence Point* ☎ *208/765–4000 or 800/365–8338 Ext. 7123* 🎟 *$16–$33* ⏲ *May–Oct.*

A broad curve of sand and protected water backed by a shady park, **City Beach** is popular for sunning, swimming, and picnicking. City Beach is part of a ribbon of shoreline that begins near the Spokane River and continues all the way to Tubbs Hill. Beyond that are quieter beaches visited mostly by locals. ✉ *Spokane River–Tubbs Hill* 🎟 *Free* ⏲ *Daily sunrise–sunset.*

In between all the water sports on Coeur d'Alene, make sure to visit **Tubbs Hill.** Here you'll find a 2-mi trail that loops around a 120-acre hill. Small wooden signs describe the types of flora found in the area as well as the remnants of historical buildings. The trails begin at the southern end of 3rd Street. ✉ *221 S. 5th St.* ☎ *208/769–2250* 🎟 *Free* ⏲ *Daily sunrise–sunset.*

off the beaten path

COEUR D'ALENE CASINO – About 30 minutes south of Lake Coeur d'Alene on the Coeur d'Alene Reservation is an ever-expanding resort. The casino has more than 1,400 slot machines, some in designated no-smoking rooms. There's an arena for professional boxing and big-name concerts with stars such as Willie Nelson and Wayne Newton. ✉ *Hwy. 95, Worley* ☎ *800/523–2464* 🌐 *www.cdacasino.com* 🎟 *Free* ⏲ *Daily 24 hrs.*

Silverwood Theme Park, 14 mi north of Coeur d'Alene, is the biggest amusement park in the Northwest. It features a reconstructed turn-of-the-20th-century mining town where you can ride on a narrow-gauge steam train or go for a spin in a vintage biplane. Don't miss the old-fashioned barnstorming show. The eight-story-tall wooden roller coaster dubbed "Tremors" will make you shake, rattle, and roll. New in 2003 was Boulder Beach Water Park, whose prime attraction is an oversize wave pool. *26225 N. U.S. 95, Athol 208/683–3400 www.silverwood4fun.com/ $22, plus $4 for parking Memorial Day–Labor Day, daily; hrs vary.*

Sports & the Outdoors

CYCLING The most popular cycling route is the **Centennial Trail,** a paved path running from east of Coeur d'Alene 7 mi along the shore of the lake and continuing 16 mi to the Washington border. If you have the energy, you can bike all the way to Spokane. The best place to rent bikes is at the activities desk of the **Coeur d'Alene Resort** (2nd and Front Sts., 83814 208/765–4000 208/667–2707 www.cdaresort.com)

GOLF **Avondale-on-Hayden Golf Club** (10745 Avondale Loop, Hayden Lake 208/772–5963) offers 18 challenging holes on beautifully manicured grounds running between Hayden Lake and Avondale Lake. The clubhouse has an excellent restaurant and a pro shop. The 18-hole course at the **Coeur d'Alene Resort** (900 Floating Green Dr. 208/765–4000) is without a doubt the area's more popular destination for golfers. It also has what may be the only floating green in the nation, out in Lake Coeur d'Alene and equipped with adjustable anchors so its position can be varied to alter the difficulty. The affordably priced **Highlands Golf Course** (701 N. Inverness Dr., Post Falls 208/773–3673) is an 18-hole course characterized by narrow, tree-lined fairways and plenty of water hazards, traps, and ravines, some of which are invisible from the tees.

Where to Stay & Eat

★ $$–$$$$ **Wolf Lodge Inn.** Spokane residents drive 50 mi to eat here, because the price is right and the steaks are large and cooked to perfection. Side dishes such as piping-hot popovers and slow-cooked baked beans are equally as popular. Locals say all of this practically guarantees you'll walk out with a doggie bag. *11741 E. Frontage Rd. 208/664–6665 AE, DC, MC, V No lunch. Closed Mon. Oct.–Apr.*

$$–$$$ **Cedars Floating Restaurant.** Yes, this restaurant is actually *on* Lake Coeur d'Alene, drawing diners from miles away for its wonderful views. If you're a little peckish when you're motoring around the lake, simply pull your boat up to the full-service dock. A supper-club atmosphere takes hold on the deck most evenings. Beer-marinated charbroiled steak is a specialty. The selection of wines from Washington State can't be beat. *U.S. 95, ¼ mi south of I–90 208/664–2922 AE, DC, MC, V No lunch Sept.–May.*

$$–$$$ **Stone Grill at Jimmy D's.** This comfortable spot across from the lake is a favorite with locals, especially hoteliers who have the food delivered to their own establishments. Brick walls hung with art, candlelighted tables, and a small bar create a bistrolike atmosphere. The menu is uncomplicated but well executed. The steaks, chicken, and fish dishes are always wonderful. The seasonal weekend brunch is a winner. There is also a good selection of wines, perhaps because the former owner runs the wine shop across the street. *320 Sherman Ave. 208/664–9774 AE, D, DC, MC, V.*

¢–$ **Coeur d'Alene Brewing Company.** The best seller among the 11 or so beers brewed on the premises is the Huckleberry Ale, which smells strongly of berries but carries only a hint of their flavor. The best reason to come here is the creative menu of sandwiches, soups, and pasta dishes. Many of the recipes include beer, such as the chipotle meat loaf, which is served with mushrooms sautéed in Pullman Porter. The pub is a lively place, with a wood-and-brass U-shape bar that seems to attract a youngish crowd. ✉ *204 N. 2nd St.* ☎ *208/664–2739* ▭ *AE, D, MC, V.*

¢ ✕ **Hudson's Hamburgers.** When they say hamburgers, they mean it. Aside from ham and cheese or egg sandwiches, that's all she wrote. But these sizzling slabs of chopped steak are more than enough for their devoted fans. The place has been in business since 1907, and even rivals have been forced to admit that the burgers are the best in town. Sit at the counter and get a load of how burgers used to be made. ✉ *207 Sherman Ave.* ☎ *208/664–5444* ▭ *No credit cards* ⏲ *Closed Sun. No dinner.*

★ $$–$$$$ ✕ **Coeur d'Alene Resort.** There's hardly any reason to leave this resort, because the lobby is full of cafés, shops, and sunny nooks where you can sit and watch the people pass. The older rooms are smaller and have very basic amenities, whereas the newer ones in the tower are spacious and beautifully decorated. Many have fireplaces and balconies with terrific views of Lake Coeur d'Alene. Atop the hotel, wide windows create an open, airy setting for the Northwest-inspired menu at Beverly's ($$–$$$). Don't miss the grilled salmon drizzled with huckleberry salsa. Tableside preparations are elaborate and entertaining. ✉ *115 S. 2nd St., 83814* ☎ *208/765–4000 or 800/688–5253* 🖷 *208/667–2707* 🌐 *www.cdaresort.com* *336 rooms* *4 restaurants, 18-hole golf course, indoor pool, health club, sauna, spa, beach, bowling, 3 bars, lobby lounge, recreation room, shops, children's programs (ages 4–14), travel services* ▭ *AE, D, DC, MC, V.*

★ $$–$$$ **Clark House on Hayden Lake.** Half hidden in the trees near Hayden Lake is the historic Clark Mansion, which was the most expensive private home in Idaho when it was completed in 1910. The colonial-style home was scheduled to be burned down as practice for local firefighters when it was rescued by the current owners. The expansive walled garden, well-appointed rooms, and hardwood floors in public areas add to the feeling of luxury. The hotel's wedding-cake appearance apparently inspires many couples; it's a popular place for taking vows. A formal, four-course breakfast (included in the rate) and dinner (reservations essential) are served. ✉ *E. 4550 S. Hayden Lake Rd., Hayden Lake 83835* ☎ *208/772–3470 or 800/765–4593* 🖷 *208/772–6899* 🌐 *www.clarkhouse.com* *10 rooms* *Dining room* ▭ *AE, D, DC, MC, V* *BP.*

★ $$–$$$ **Gregory's McFarland House.** This country inn dates from the early 1900s, and the grace with which it's run also recalls a bygone era. Afternoon tea and leisurely breakfasts are served in the glassed-in conservatory, furnished with nothing but wicker. Lacy curtains cover the windows and tables in the small formal dining room. Fir beams are an elegant, rich shade of brown. Each guest room is uniquely furnished with an English country house feel. Book far ahead. ✉ *601 Foster Ave., 83814* ☎ *208/667–1232* *5 rooms* *No room phones, no room TVs, no kids under 14, no smoking* ▭ *DC, MC, V* *BP.*

$$–$$$ **Wolf Lodge Creek Bed & Breakfast.** Although it's practically in the woods, this secluded little inn is far from rustic. The two-story cathedral ceiling, soaring windows, and wide expanses of hardwood floors give it an open, airy feel. Rooms have gas fireplaces to keep out the chill. From the long, inviting front porch you can hear nothing but whispering aspens. The buffet-style breakfast, with a selection of homemade breads and muffins, is heavenly. The inn is about 15 mi from Coeur d'Alene. ✉ *715 N. Wolf Lodge Creek Rd., 83814* ☎ *208/667–5902 or 800/919–9653* 🖷 *208/667–1153* 🌐 *www.wolflodge.com* *5 rooms* *Hot tub; no TV in some rooms, no smoking* *BP* ▭ *AE, D, DC, MC, V.*

$–$$ **Best Western Coeur d'Alene Inn.** Just off the interstate, this hotel is a sister property to the lakeside Coeur d'Alene Resort, which means you can stay at this budget lodging and still get preferred start times at the Coeur d'Alene Resort Golf Course. You also have access to resort facilities such as the spa and private beach. The glass-walled pool area with roll-back roof is a great place for kids. ✉ *414 Appleway, 83814* ☎ *208/765–3200 or 800/251–7829* 🖷 *208/664–1962* 🌐 *www.cdainn.com-rkeyser@cdainn.com* 🛏 *121 rooms, 2 suites* 👍 *Restaurant, in-room data ports, in-room safes, some microwaves, refrigerators, room TVs with movies, indoor-outdoor pool, exercise equipment, hot tub, lounge, laundry service, meeting rooms, no-smoking rooms* 💳 *AE, D, DC, MC, V.*

$ **Flamingo Motel.** One of the least-pricey options for staying within walking distance of the shops and restaurants on Sherman Avenue is the Flamingo Motel. The shocking-pink doors do little to hide its previous life as a roadside dive. It's a dive no longer, though. Rooms are immaculately clean and have updated baths. Each has been uniquely decorated with humor and panache. ✉ *718 Sherman, 83814* ☎ *208/664–2159 or 800/955–2159* 🛏 *11 rooms, 2 suites* 👍 *Some kitchens, refrigerators, cable TV; no smoking* 💳 *AE, D, DC, MC, V.*

CAMPING **Blackwell Island RV Park.** This busy new RV park lies on a former marsh on the grassy banks of the Spokane River. The facilities are pleasant, although the lack of trees may bother some people. The location, only a few minutes from town and a short stroll from Cedars Floating Restaurant, is ideal for those who plan to spend part of their time in town. A boat launch is available. 👍 *Flush toilets, full hookups, dump station. Drinking water, guest laundry, showers. Picnic tables. Public telephone. Swimming (river)* 🛏 *122 full hookups* ✉ *800 S. Marina Dr., 83814* ☎ *208/665–1300 or 888/571–2900* 🖷 *208/667–5853* 🎫 *$28–$38* 💳 *MC, V* 🕒 *Apr.–Nov.*

Coeur d'Alene Ranger District Campgrounds. The district maintains eight campgrounds, including Bell Bay Campground in Lake Coeur d'Alene. Mokins Bay Campground is closer to Hayden Lake. 👍 *Pit toilets. Drinking water at some campgrounds. Fire grates, picnic tables* ✉ *2502 E. Sherman Ave., 83814* ☎ *208/769–3000* 🎫 *$8–$12 for first vehicle of your party* 💳 *No credit cards* 🕒 *May–Sept.*

Squaw Bay Resort. About 10 minutes by boat from downtown Coeur d'Alene, Squaw Bay has lakeside campsites, some with full hookups. Cabins are also available, most with kitchens. Boat moorage, boat rentals, and a gas dock make this place practical for those into water sports. The sandy swimming area has two waterslides. 👍 *Flush toilets. Full hookups, partial hookups, showers. Fire pits, food service, picnic tables. General store. Swimming (lake)* 🛏 *11 full hookups, 24 partial hookups, 12 tent sites* ✉ *Hwy. 97 near Beauty Bay, Harrison 83833* ☎ *208/664–6782* 🌐 *www.squawbayresort.com* 🎫 *Full hookups $28, partial hookups $22–$26, tent sites $18–$24* 💳 *AE, DC, MC, V* 🕒 *May–Sept.*

Nightlife & the Arts

NIGHTLIFE Loud rock music reaches out into the street from the get-down-and-party capital of Coeur d'Alene, the **Iron Horse Bar & Grill** (✉ 413 Sherman Ave. ☎ 208/667–7314). In warmer weather, patrons sit outside at tables on the sidewalk. Even locals who don't care for the smoky bar come to hear the occasional big-name bands.

Shopping

The **Plaza Shops at the Coeur d'Alene** (✉ 210 Sherman Ave., at 2nd St. ☎ 208/664–1111) contains 22 small shops, several selling merchandise with a Northwestern emphasis. There are clothiers, including United Colors of Benetton and Worn Out West, which specializes in shirts bearing wildlife designs; an espresso shop; and a bistro-style restaurant called Tito Macaroni's.

Journeys American Indian Arts (✉ 117 S. 4th St. ☎ 208/664–5227) carries beads and other jewelry supplies, as well as a wealth of Native American drums, moccasins, baskets, and books. **Northwest Artists** (✉ 217 Sherman Ave. ☎ 208/667–1464) is a cooperative that carries work by regional artists and artisans. One of the creators is nearly always behind the counter. The **Original Penny Candy Store** (✉ 325 Sherman Ave. ☎ 208/667–0992) resembles a turn-of-the-last-century dry-goods store. You'll be tempted with exotic candies from around the world, from sour-apple balls to strawberry bonbons. **Wilson's Variety** (✉ 401 Sherman Ave. ☎ 208/664–8346) carries a wide selection of books about Idaho, including guides on geology and history, as well as topographical maps.

en route

Driving east out of Coeur d'Alene on I–90, make sure to watch over your shoulder for lovely views of Lake Coeur d'Alene. The highway then shoots straight east up the Silver Valley, which becomes prettier as it gets narrower.

Silver Valley

12 *24 mi east of Coeur d'Alene via I–90.*

This was a rootin', tootin' mining community not so very long ago: Silver Valley's last bordello didn't close down until 1989. Today, the tiny town of Wallace, listed in its entirety with the National Register of Historic Places, is almost unbearably cute. Window shopping was never more fun than here on a sunny summer afternoon. Kellogg is several times larger than Wallace and still bears a touch of gritty reality, although as the base for Silver Mountain, an up-and-coming ski resort, it's growing a healthy tourist trade of its own. The two major mines still active in the valley are the Galena and the Lucky Friday. Silver is the predominant ore, but gold, lead, zinc, and copper have also been extracted from time to time.

Influenced by trappers and visited by missionaries, a group of people from Coeur d'Alene took up Roman Catholicism. In 1850, together with Father Anthony Ravalli, they began construction of **Cataldo Mission,** now the oldest building in Idaho and one of the region's most interesting historical sites. The mission church is massive, considering that it was built almost totally by hand with an ax and a few other hand tools. Behind the altar you can see the mud-and-stick construction used on the walls. The giant beams overhead were dragged from the forest, and rock for the foundation was quarried from a hill ½ mi away. The adjacent mission house, home to generations of priests, is furnished the way it would have been at the turn of the last century. The Cataldo Mission is accessible to travelers with mobility impairments. ✉ *Old Mission State Park, Exit 39, I–90, Cataldo* ☎ *208/682–3814* 🎫 *$2 per vehicle* ⏲ *Memorial Day–Labor Day, daily 8–6; Labor Day–Memorial Day, daily 9–5.*

Retrace a colorful era in the mining region by visiting the historic towns of Murray, Pritchard, and Enaville in the **Kellogg Mining District.** Some still thrive, whereas others are deserted shells of decaying wood. Maps and other information are available at the Kellogg Chamber of Commerce. ✉ *10 Station Ave.* ☎ *208/784–0821* 🌐 *www.nidlink.com/~kellogg* 🎫 *Free* ⏲ *Daily dawn–dusk.*

Exhibits at the **Staff House Mining & Smelting Museum** trace the history of the Bunker Hill Mining & Smelting Company, one of the oldest and largest mining companies in the Coeur d'Alene district. On display in the historic home are a scale model of the Bunker Hill mine, mineral and metallurgical exhibits, and mining and smelting equipment. ✉ *820*

McKinley Ave., Kellogg ☎ 208/786–4141 🌐 www.kellogg-id.org 🎫 $3 ⏲ Late May–Sept., daily 10–5.

Visible from I–90, the **Sunshine Mine Disaster Memorial** honors the 91 miners who died in the 1972 Sunshine Mine Fire, the worst mining disaster in recent history. Set against the cliff, north of Big Creek Canyon, the memorial is a 12-foot-tall sculpture of a miner with his drill raised. It is surrounded by plaques listing the names of those who perished. A nearby local landmark is a building constructed in the shape of a miner's hat that was once a tavern and now houses a real-estate office. ✉ *I–90 Exit 54 ☎ 208/784–0821 🌐 www.nidlink.com/~kellogg 🎫 Free ⏲ Daily dawn–dusk.*

The historic mining town of **Wallace,** 37 mi east of Coeur d'Alene off I–90, is one of the few towns to be included in its entirety on the National Register of Historic Places. It was first settled in the 1880s gold rush, and today much of the town center and many of the private homes look (at least from the outside) exactly as they did at the turn of the last century.

In a historic building that once housed Rice's Bakery, the **Wallace District Mining Museum** has been educating people about life in the mines since 1956. The museum includes exhibits on the history of mining methods dating back to the 1880s. Miners would have been in the dark if it weren't for lighting devices ranging from old-fashioned stearic candles and oil lamps to today's rechargeable electric lamps mounted right on their hard hats. In addition, the museum has the only complete steam-driven diamond drill known to have been preserved. The video *North Idaho's Silver Legacy* relates the 150-year history of the region. ✉ *509 Bank St., Wallace ☎ 208/556–1592 🎫 $2.*

★ Put on your yellow hard hat and tour the **Sierra Silver Mine,** which was such a poor producer of lead and silver that it was more useful as a classroom for local kids than as a working mine. Guides are current or former miners with firsthand stories about working underground. Much of the equipment, although outdated, is still running and is put to good use during the course of the tour. Transportation to and from the mine is via open-air trolley, so you also get a brief narrated tour of Wallace. ✉ *405 5th St., Wallace ☎ 208/752–5151 🎫 $9 ⏲ May–Sept.*

The history of railroading in the Coeur d'Alene mining district is the subject of the **Northern Pacific Depot Railroad Museum.** On display is a rare 13-foot glass map of the Northern Pacific Railroad route. ✉ *219 6th St., Wallace ☎ 208/752–0111 🎫 $2 ⏲ Apr.–mid-Oct.*

Wallace's **Oasis Bordello Museum** depicts the glory days of the Oasis Rooms, one of the town's most infamous brothels. These "dens of iniquity" operated until 1973, when a newspaper article charged a politician with going easy on them in exchange for a $25,000 campaign contribution. The brothels soon closed for good. At halftime during a University of Idaho football game, students unfurled a 40-foot-long banner inscribed GIVE WALLACE BACK ITS HOUSES. Today, proprietor Michelle Mayfield will take you on a tasteful tour of the establishment, and her anecdotes range from poignant to hilarious. In addition to a peek at the second-floor brothel, the tour includes a look at an old wine press in the basement and stroll through the Bi-Metallic Building, which began as a hotel and saloon in 1895. The building is one of the few structures to have survived the 1910 fire that ravaged the town. Of particular interest are its mosaic floor tiles imported from China. ✉ *605 Cedar St. ☎ 208/753–0801 🌐 www.silver-country.com 🎫 Donation suggested ⏲ May–Oct., daily.*

Sports & the Outdoors

BICYCLING
Fodor's Choice ★
The **Route of the Hiawathas** bike path makes use of old railroad track bed, which gives it an almost unnoticeable slope that is nearly as easy to ride up as down. It is generously wide and fully paved. The Route of the Hiawathas is 15 mi long and runs through nine tunnels and across seven trestle bridges. The **Trail of the Coeur d'Alenes** starts in Mullan near the Montana border and finishes 72 mi later in the Washington town of Plummer.

Your best choice if you want to travel the Trail of the Coeur d'Alenes is **Excelsior Cycle** (✉ 21 Railroad Ave., Kellogg ☎ 208/786–3751). Located mere yards from the trail, it has everything you need to make the journey memorable. **Lookout Pass Ski & Recreation Area** (✉ I–90, Exit 0, at Lookout Pass ☎ 208/744–1301 Ext. 11), at the top of the Route of the Hiawathas, rents front-suspension mountain bikes that can take a lot of punishment. A shuttle bus makes pickups at the end of the trail every 90 minutes during the day from June through September.

SKIING
The ski resort of **Silver Mountain** was difficult to reach until someone hit on the bright idea of installing the world's longest single-stage gondola. Near Kellogg, Silver Mountain offers lessons for people of every skill level, from beginners to experts. Locals think the advanced terrain at nearby Schweitzer is better, but Silver Mountain offers some excellent powder skiing and some steep runs. More than 50 trails cover a vertical drop of 2,200 feet and are reached by a quad, two triple chairs, two double chairs, and a surface lift in addition to the gondola. In January and February there's night skiing until 9 on Friday and Saturday. ✉ *610 Bunker Ave., Kellogg 83837* ☎ *208/783–1111* ⏲ *Mid-Nov.–Apr., Wed.–Sun. 8–4.*

Lookout Pass Ski & Recreation Area, Idaho's second-oldest ski area, opened in 1938 and remains popular for families. The area includes 150 skiable acres with 14 runs and a vertical drop of 850 feet. The double chairlift carries you to an elevation of 5,650 feet, and from there you can ski to St. Regis Basin. Also available are guided snowmobile trips into Montana. The annual snowfall is 389 inches, and there are 50 new acres of expert terrain for snowboarders. Rental packages are available at the ski lodge. ✉ *12 mi east of Wallace on I–90, in Idaho Panhandle National Forest* ☎ *208/744–1392* 📠 *208/744–1227* 🌐 *www.skilookout.com* ⏲ *Mid-Nov.–mid-Apr.*

Where to Stay & Eat

$$–$$$
Fodor's Choice ★
✕ **The Veranda.** Owned (and decorated) by the proprietor of the nearby Mansion on the Hill Bed & Breakfast, this restaurant couldn't be more charming. The intimate upstairs dining room resembles a sidewalk café (thanks largely to the sky-and-clouds mural on the ceiling). Two elegant private dining rooms are available by reservation. The only fine dining restaurant in Kellogg, The Veranda serves an eclectic mix of meat, fish, and pasta dishes. ✉ *2 E. Portland Ave., Kellogg* ☎ *208/783–2625* 💳 *AE, MC, V* ⏲ *Closed Sun. and Mon. No dinner Tues., no lunch Sat.*

$–$$ ✕ **Albi's Steak House.** Housed in a historic building in the historic center of Wallace, this restaurant has an old-fashioned air. Sizzling steaks and other meat dishes are the order of the day. (Locals are particularly partial to the prime rib.) Freshly caught fish and heaping platters of pastas round out the menu. ✉ *220 6th St., Wallace* ☎ *208/753–3071* 💳 *AE, D, MC, V.*

$–$$ ✕ **Edelweiss.** You get great views of the valley if you ask to be seated by the window at this casual eatery. The menu is strong on fresh seafood as well as steaks. Smoking is permitted. ✉ *210 McKinley Ave., Kellogg* ☎ *208/783–0114* 💳 *No credit cards.*

$–$$ **Enaville Resort.** Known also as the Snakepit, Josie's, and what the proprietors characterized as a slew of "unprintable names," this is definitely not a resort. The weathered old wood-frame house at a fork of the Coeur d'Alene River has served as a bar, a hotel, and a house of ill repute since it was built sometime in the 1880s. An Old West flavor dominates the interior, with hunting trophies hanging above the rock fireplace and comfy twig and log furniture scattered about. The restaurant serves plates heaped high with buffalo burgers, barbecued ribs, and succulent steaks. Friday nights there's a seafood buffet. ✉ *Coeur d'Alene River Rd. 1½ mi from I–90 Exit 43* ☎ *208/682–3453* ▭ *AE, D, MC, V.*

★ ¢ **The 1313 Club Historic Saloon & Grill.** Order burgers, hot and cold sandwiches, and to-die-for beer-battered fries at this local hangout. Enjoy them under the watchful eyes of the bison, moose, beaver, boar, and bear heads hanging on the walls. The odd name reflects the fact that the original bar area, back in the late 1800s, was 13 feet wide by 13 feet long. The owners, transplants from Seattle, couldn't be friendlier. ✉ *608 Bank St., Wallace* ☎ *208/752–9391* ▭ *No credit cards* ⊗ *Closed Sun.*

$ **Jameson Inn.** A ghost reportedly haunts a third-floor room at the 1889 Jameson Building, which now houses a saloon and restaurant on the first floor and cozy accommodations above. Legend has it that she's still waiting for her lover to return after striking it rich at nearby Burke Canyon. The decor here is reminiscent of a saloon—not surprising, as that was the building's first function. The rooms are small but have been carefully furnished with choice antiques. A complimentary Continental breakfast is served in your rooms or the parlor. The Jameson Restaurant ($–$$) serves classic American cuisine. ✉ *304 6th St., Wallace 83873* ☎ *208/556–6000* 🖷 *208/753–0981* *6 rooms, 1 with bath* *Restaurant, meeting rooms* ▭ *MC, V* *CP.*

★ $$ **Mansion on the Hill Bed & Breakfast.** Owner Dana Musick has the deft hand of a decorator and a love for country French ambience. Her full-time gardener performs similar magic on the acre of immaculate grounds surrounding this historic home. Inside the house are two guest rooms, each with tiny private veranda. Across a paved patio lies a cottage with vaulted ceiling and private hot tub. Also on the premises is a family suite with two bedrooms and a full kitchen. You won't believe your luck—there's a day spa just steps from your room. Book far ahead. ✉ *105 S. Division St., Kellogg 83837* ☎ *208/786–4455* 🖷 *208/786–0157* ⊕ *www.mansionbnb.com* *4 rooms* *Refrigerators, hair salon, spa; no room phones, no room TVs, no smoking.* ▭ *AE, DC, MC, V.*

$ **Best Western–Wallace Inn.** The newest hotel in town, this pumpkin-colored building is near all the attractions downtown. The rooms and suites are all spacious, and some have lovely views. The glass-walled pool area is particularly pleasant. ✉ *100 Front St., Wallace 83873* ☎ *208/752–1252 or 800/643–2386* ⊕ *www.bestwestern.com* 🖷 *208/753–0981* *59 rooms, 4 suites* *Restaurant, room service, minibars, refrigerators, cable TV, indoor pool, gym, hot tub, business services* ▭ *AE, D, DC, MC, V.*

$ **Silverhorn Motor Lodge.** This half-timber hotel has shutters and window boxes that call to mind a Bavarian inn. And it's less than ½ mi from the Silver Mountain gondola, so it's a good choice for skiers. The hot tub is reportedly the biggest in Kellogg. Native American crafts are available at the gift shop. ✉ *699 W. Cameron Ave., Kellogg 83837* ☎ *208/783–1151 or 800/437–6437* 🖷 *208/784–5081* ⊕ *www.silverhornmotorlodge.com* *40 rooms* *Restaurant, room service, cable TV, hot tub, shop, laundry facilities, business services, some pets allowed* ▭ *AE, D, DC, MC, V.*

¢ **Stardust.** This budget-friendly lodging in the center of Wallace is immediately identifiable by its corner turret. Rooms are well maintained and squeaky clean. ✉ *410 Pine St., Wallace 83873* ☎ *208/752–1213*

☎ 208/753–0981 ⇆ *42 rooms* ♨ *Cable TV, some pets allowed; no a/c in some rooms* ▭ *AE, D, DC, MC, V.*

CAMPING ⛺ **Coeur d'Alene River Ranger District Campgrounds.** The Forest Service maintains four campgrounds in the area, all with potable water. Kit Price Campground is the largest of them, with 52 campsites and direct access to the Coeur d'Alene River. Big Hank Campground is also near the river. ♨ *Some pit toilets. Drinking water. Grills, picnic tables* ✉ *Exit 60 off I–90, Silverton 83876* ☎ *208/752–1221* ▭ *$10 for first vehicle in your party* ▭ *No credit cards* ⊙ *Closed Sept.–mid-May.*

⛺ **Down by the Depot RV Park.** There's nothing fancy about this mid-size RV park, but the bathrooms are immaculate and a two-minute walk brings you to downtown Wallace and its historic buildings. Nine Mile Creek runs along one side of the property. The trees along a narrow valley create some late-afternoon shade. Hook into cable TV for $2 per day. ♨ *Flush toilets. Guest laundry, showers. Public telephone* ⇆ *44 full hookups* ✉ *108 Nine Mile Rd., Wallace 83837* ☎ *208/753–7121* ▭ *$22* ▭ *No credit cards.*

⛺ **Kellogg/Silver Valley KOA Kampground.** Between the hot tub, the outdoor pool, and the playground, this RV park has more amenities than any other campground in Silver Valley. Cable television hookups are free, and Internet access is available. Reservations are strongly suggested for the cabins and the cottage, which has a fully furnished kitchen with its own private hot tub. ♨ *Flush toilets. Dump station. Guest laundry, showers. Public telephone. General store. Play area, swimming (pool)* ⇆ *27 full hookups, 8 partial hookups, 16 tent sites; 6 cabins, 1 cottage* ✉ *801 N. Division, Pinehurst 83850* ☎ *208/682–3612 or 800/562–0799* ⊕ *kelloggsilvervalleykoa.com* ▭ *Partial hookups $30, full hookups $32, tent sites $22* ▭ *AE, DC, MC, V* ⊙ *Closed mid-Dec.–Apr.*

Shopping

Locally mined silver fashioned into a wide range of jewelry is available at **Silver Capital Arts** (✉ 524 Bank St., Wallace ☎ 208/556–7081). There's also an interesting selection of regional arts and crafts, as well as a collection of Idaho minerals.

Shop for Idaho star garnets and other precious gems at **Idaho Silver** (✉ 606 Bank St., Wallace ☎ 208/556–1171). The staff can point you to jewelry and other items made from locally mined silver.

Sandpoint

⓭ *40 mi north of Coeur d'Alene via U.S. 95.*

Sandpoint sits on the shore of Lake Pend Oreille, the second-deepest body of water in the United States. Nestled between the lake and the Selkirk and Cabinet mountain ranges, Sandpoint has been a railroad depot and a timber town but relies increasingly on tourism. The town is tiny—five blocks of shops and restaurants form the historic district—and the brick and stone buildings are little changed since the early 1900s. Increasingly hectic Highway 95 runs through the center of town, but a bypass is planned that will reroute all the traffic. Locals say the town is 20 years behind Coeur d'Alene, and they mean it as a compliment. Like Coeur d'Alene, this is a summer destination with fine beaches, extensive woodlands, and breathtaking mountains. However, the local ski hill is transforming itself into a first-class resort area. Sandpoint, it has been said, is what places such as Vail, Colorado, and Jackson, Wyoming, were like just before they boomed.

Lake Pend Oreille, Idaho's largest lake, measures 65 mi long and 15 mi wide. Formed when an ice dam broke 25,000 years ago, it sinks to an astonishing depth of 1,200 feet. Maybe that's why this intensely blue body of water is a fisherman's paradise. More than a dozen species of game fish inhabit its waters, including kokanee, largemouth bass, and bluegill. Mackinaw (also called lake trout) the length of your forearm are regularly caught here. The name Pend Oreille (pronounced pond-or-*ray*) comes from the term used by early French trappers to describe the pendants the local Native Americans wore in their earlobes.

One great way to see the lake is on afternoon or evening cruises with **Lake Pend Oreille Cruises.** In spring and fall when the pretty *Shawnodese* is not making scheduled trips, cruises can still be arranged on other vessels. Wildlife-watching cruises on which you can spot nesting eagles are periodically available. ✉ *106 Bridge St.* ☎ *208/255–5253* 🌐 *www.lakependoreillecruises.com* 🎟 *$14–$29* ⏲ *Mid-June–early Sept.*

Relaxing **City Beach,** little more than a block from downtown, has several hundred feet of sand, protected swimming areas, and sweeping views of the Cabinet Mountains to the east. The large and bustling park surrounding the beach has volleyball, basketball, tennis, and other diversions. ✉ *End of Bridge St.* ☎ *208/263–2161* 🌐 *www.sandpoint.com* 🎟 *Free* ⏲ *Memorial Day–Labor Day, daily dawn–dusk.*

The smooth curves of the polished concrete bar are fun and the eclectic selection of housewares makes for good browsing, but the best reason to visit the **Pend d'Oreille Winery** is to taste lovely wines. Founded in 1995, it began racking up awards in 1997 and hasn't stopped. The grapes are sometimes grown in Idaho, more often in Washington's Columbia basin. ✉ *220 Cedar St.* ☎ *208/265–8545* 🌐 *www.powine.com.*

off the beaten path

PRIEST LAKE – North of the diminutive Priest River are two lakes as pretty as Pend Oreille, but much less frequently visited. Lower Priest Lake connects by an easily canoeable outlet to Upper Priest Lake, where backcountry camping, hiking, and fishing are the prime activities. Snowmobiling and cross-country skiing are popular here in winter, when it is possible to snowmobile more quickly to Schweitzer than to take your car across the icy roads. Lodging options include five Forest Service campgrounds. ✉ *Hwy. 57* ☎ *208/443–2512.*

Sports & the Outdoors

BOATING You can rent watercraft of all sorts, including Jet Skis, ski boats (with skis or wakeboards), canoes, and kayaks, from **All Season Recreational Rentals** (✉ 106 Bridge St. ☎ 208/255–2431 or 888/246–6181). The company is conveniently located at the Lakeside Inn's dock, a few minutes' walk from town. The company will deliver to most area lakes at no extra charge.

FISHING Sandpoint's main attraction is Lake Pend Oreille, and almost all the region's summer activities take place on or near the water. Kayaking is becoming increasingly popular, but powerboating of all flavors is the perennial favorite. Fishing is often very good, and because rangers are trying to save native kokanee runs from the voracious non-native lake trout, you're encouraged to keep every lake trout you can catch. Area food banks will take what you can't eat.

GOLF About 8 mi east of Sandpoint, **Hidden Lakes Golf Resort** (✉ 151 Clubhouse Way, off Hwy. 200 ☎ 208/263–1642 or 888/806–6673) has a well-regarded course with a river and other water hazards on 16 of the 18 holes. One hazard not mentioned in the brochure is the grazing moose. Upscale amenities include the traveling beverage carts that cruise the course and the courtesy phone on the 9 tee from which you can call in lunch orders. The resort also has a massive, lovely log clubhouse that houses a fine restaurant and a fully equipped pro shop.

SKIING For many years, only people in Spokane and Sandpoint knew about **Schweitzer,** but it's becoming a top Western ski destination. Open-bowl and glade skiing are available for intermediate and advanced skiers, and beginners can choose from half a dozen tree-lined runs. There is a vertical drop of 2,400 feet. One six-person chair and one quad high-speed chair and four double chairs bring you up to 61 runs. Night skiing takes place throughout Christmas week and on Friday and Saturday between January and March. The resort maintains nearly 30 km of Nordic trails and a terrain park that features a 250-foot-long half pipe. It also offers a full-service ski school. ✉ *10,000 Schweitzer Mountain Rd., 11 mi northwest of Sandpoint off U.S. 95, Sandpoint 83864* ☎ *208/263–9555 or 800/831–8810* ⏲ *Late Nov.–early Apr., daily 9–4.*

Where to Stay & Eat

$$–$$$$ ✕ **Swan's Landing.** Waterfront dining on the wisteria-draped patio is the draw at this romantic retreat on the Pend Oreille River. Inside, a fireplace gives the dining room a lodgelike atmosphere. Known for its contemporary Northwest cuisine, the restaurant serves creative dishes such as roast rack of lamb pressed in rosemary and garlic pepper accompanied by roasted mashed potatoes. Whatever you order, your server can suggest the right wine from the well-stocked cellar. Sunday brunch is a local tradition. ✉ *Hwy. 95 and Lakeshore Dr.* ☎ *208/265–2000* 💳 *AE, D, MC, V.*

★ **$$–$$$** ✕ **Floating Restaurant.** Sunset is a magical time here: the docks on which the restaurant sits have quieted down, letting you enjoy the brilliant colors that streak across the sky. It's the perfect accompaniment to the restaurant's well-prepared entrées, ranging from steak to salmon. In nice weather nearly everyone sits outside on floating platforms that bob subtly beneath the umbrella-shaded tables. For a bit more stability, dine indoors. Sunday brunch is popular. Moorage is available if you decide to arrive by boat. ✉ *Hwy. 200 E, Hope* ☎ *208/264–5311* 💳 *AE, DC, MC, V* ⏲ *Closed Nov.–mid-May and weekdays Oct. and Apr.*

$–$$$ ✕ **Ivano's.** Some of the Northwest's most highly regarded northern Italian cuisine is served here beneath the cathedral ceiling that graces the main dining room. Try creative dishes such as the ravioli *della casa* (with a butter and sage sauce) or the tortellini *al campo* (with spinach, porcini mushrooms, and onions in a cream sauce). You can enjoy a memorable meal indoors by candlelight or outside on the brick-lined terrace. ✉ *124 S. 2nd Ave.* ☎ *208/263–0211* 💳 *AE, D, DC, MC, V* ⏲ *No lunch.*

$–$$ ✕ **Hydra.** Stained glass, polished wood, and lots of greenery decorate this intimate little restaurant. The prime rib and steak are the main draws, but there are also excellent seafood dishes such as mesquite-seared shrimp and sautéed scallops. Sunday brunch is popular, as is the lunch buffet Tuesday through Friday. ✉ *115 E. Lake St.* ☎ *208/263–7123* 💳 *AE, D, MC, V.*

$$$$ 🏨 **BC&M Houseboat Vacations.** Half lodging and half recreation, a houseboat buys you from three days to a week of water, water, everywhere. These houseboats range from the 44-foot *Pike Minnow,* which sleeps 8, to the 55-foot *Dream Catcher,* which sleeps up to 16. They come with amenities such as hot tubs, full kitchens, and televisions. Shoulder season rates are significantly more affordable. The houseboats are docked at Hope Marine Services in Hope. ✉ *1245 Hwy. 200, Hope 83836* ☎ *208/666–0915* 🌐 *www.sandpoint.com* *3 houseboats* *Kitchens, hot tubs* 💳 *MC, V* ⏲ *Closed Oct.–May.*

$$–$$$$ 🏨 **Inn at Sand Creek.** Placid Sand Creek flows past the rear of this historic old building, which was built as a bank in 1906. Each one-bedroom suite is gracefully appointed with a gas fireplace, four-poster bed, and an armoire filled with terry robes. The fridges come stocked with juices and locally baked pastries. The only downside to this tiny hotel is that there is no on-site management. Downstairs is The Sand Creek Grill, an elegant lunch and dinner spot with indoor and outdoor seating and occasional live music. ✉ *105 S. 1st Ave., 83864* ☎ *208/255–2821* 🌐 *www.innatsandcreek.com* *3 suites* *Some kitchens, refrigerators* 💳 *AE, MC, V.*

$$–$$$$ **Selkirk Lodge at Schweitzer Mountain.** Ski right up to your door in this ski-in/ski-out lodge at the base of Schweitzer Mountain. The sharply peaked roof gives the hotel the feel of an alpine country inn. Many rooms have a view of the lake or the slopes. The on-site coffeehouse is a pleasant place for people-watching both summer and winter, with oversize windows facing toward the valley floor far below. ✉ *10000 Schweitzer Mountain Rd., 11 mi northwest off U.S. 95, 83864* ☎ *208/265–0257 or 800/831–8810* 📠 *208/265–0257* 🌐 *www.schweitzer.com* *82 rooms, 2 suites* *Two restaurants, microwaves, refrigerators, cable TV with movies, pool, gym, hot tub* 💳 *AE, D, MC, V.*

★ $–$$$ **Best Western Edgewater Resort.** This rambling old hotel within sight of the nearby beaches and volleyball courts also enjoys easy access to downtown shops and restaurants. Every room has views of the lake. You can drive to the ski slopes in half an hour. The outdoor dining area makes the restaurant especially popular. ✉ *56 Bridge St., 83864* ☎ *208/263–3194 or 800/635–2534* 📠 *208/263–3194* 🌐 *www.bestwestern.com* *55 rooms* *Restaurant, room service, in-room data ports, cable TV, pool, exercise equipment, hot tub, sauna, beach, business services* 💳 *AE, D, DC, MC, V.*

$$ **La Quinta Inn & Suites.** Rooms at this chain hotel are tastefully decorated, with thoughtful touches such as refrigerators and microwaves. One two-room suite with a whirlpool tub and a wet bar feels downright decadent. A full breakfast buffet, including delicious Belgian waffles, comes with the room rate. The restaurant and lounge are as popular with locals as they are with guests. ✉ *415 Cedar St., 83864* ☎ *208/263–9581* 📠 *208/263–3395* 🌐 *www.laquinta.com* *60 rooms, 10 suites* *Restaurant, microwaves, refrigerators, pool, gym, hot tub, lounge, meeting room* 💳 *AE, D, MC, V* 🍽 *BP.*

$ **Western Pleasure Guest Ranch.** A trio of secluded cabins and a sprawling A-frame lodge building are set among towering pines on a 960-acre ranch. Rooms in the lodge are comfortably furnished and have private baths. Cabins have wide front porches and are heated with wood. In summer the main activity is horseback riding; in winter you'll enjoy cross-country skiing, snowshoeing, or sledding. ✉ *1413 Upper Gold Creek Rd., 83864* ☎ *208/263–9066* 📠 *208/265–0138* 🌐 *www.westernpleasureranch.com* *6 rooms, 3 cabins* *Dining room, kitchens, hot tub, horseback riding, cross-country skiing, recreation room* 💳 *MC, V.*

¢–$ **Lakeside Inn.** Beside Sand Creek and only a block from Lake Pend Oreille, this motel couldn't have a better location. It's also an easy walk from downtown. The exterior is a bit weathered, but the rooms are well maintained. Some have tiny private balconies literally steps from the creek. The motel's dock is home to the popular Lake Pend Oreille Cruises, which offers public cruises and private charters. ✉ *106 Bridge St., 83864* ☎ *208/263–3717 or 800/543–8126* 📠 *208/265–4781* *56 rooms, 4 suites* *Some kitchenettes, cable TV, hot tub, sauna, laundry facilities, airport shuttle, some pets allowed (fee)* 💳 *AE, D, DC, MC, V.*

CAMPING **Sandpoint Ranger District Campgrounds.** The Forest Service maintains four campgrounds in the area, three on Lake Pend Oreille. Whiskey Rock Bay Campground and Green Bay Campground are both small and feel miles away from the crowds. Sam Owen Campground is the largest, with 80 sites, flush toilets, and a dump station. *Some flush toilets, pit toilets. Some dump stations. Drinking water at some campgrounds. Fire pits, picnic tables* ✉ *1500 Hwy. 2, Suite 110, 83864* ☎ *208/263–5111* *Free–$13* *May–Sept.*

Nightlife

A couple hundred beer taps hang from the ceiling at **Eichardt's** (✉ 212 Cedar St. ☎ 208/263–4005). Behind the long bar, a dozen more are ready to pour, from American micros to that old standby, Guinness. Locals and tourists alike come for burgers with toasted buns, garlic and herb fries, and other high-end pub grub. Four nights a week, the bar hosts live music. Monday is open mike night. Wednesdays expect mellow acoustic guitar, and on weekends the volume goes up as bands playing blues, funk, and rock crowd the tiny stage.

Shopping

Sandpoint is home to more than its share of artisans. Weekdays you can peer from the second-floor gallery into the workshop at **Misty Mountain** (✉ 502 Cedar St. ☎ 208/265–1553), which makes and sells log furniture. The shop carries the work of 65 regional craftspeople, many of them woodworkers from the area. From china-thin wooden bowls to massive peeled-log bedsteads, **Northwest Handmade Furniture** (✉ 308 N. 1st Ave. ☎ 877/880–1962) carries the work of more than 90 regional woodworkers. The gallery is near Coldwater Creek on the most pleasant street for window shopping in Sandpoint.

Cabin Fever (✉ 113 Cedar St. ☎ 208/263–7179 ✉ 309 1st St. ☎ 208/263–7178) has one of the best assortments of home-decor items, garden adornments, and curios for cabins in northern Idaho. The 1st Street store sells casual, Northwestern-style clothing. The original retail outlet for the mail-order **Coldwater Creek** (✉ 1st and Cedar Sts. ☎ 208/263–2265) took over the Cedar Street Bridge Public Market, which now comprises six stores and restaurants in a split-level arcade of native tamarack and fir timbers spanning a creek. Merchandise includes wildlife-inspired jewelry, posters, and books; bird feeders; and other nature-oriented gifts.

The next time you need a custom-made yurt, try **Little Bear Trading Company** (✉ 324 1st St. ☎ 208/263–1116). The shop owner, Bear (yes, just Bear), makes these Mongolian-style tents for clients around the country. The small store also carries Native American crafts, beads, and feathers, as well as materials from Africa and Central and South America.

Bonners Ferry

⓮ *33 mi north of Sandpoint via Hwy. 95.*

An 1863 gold rush gave rise to the town of Bonners Ferry, a small community on the banks of the Kootenai River. The town, roughly 35 mi from the Canada and 20 mi from Montana, is a convenient stopover for those heading for either border. The town is named after Edwin L. Bonner, who began ferrying people across the river in 1864. Long before that, the area was inhabited by the lower band of the Kootenai (pronounced *koot*-n-nee) people. In 1855, the Kootenai were not represented at the Hellsgate Treaty and were left without tribal lands of their own. They declared war on the United States in 1974. As a result they were ceded a tiny forested hill of some 18 acres in the middle of flat, agricultural Kootenai Valley. The tribe also runs the Kootenai Casino in Bonners Ferry, which echoes with the sound of several hundred slot machines.

Another group that has had an effect on the local landscape is the Mennonites, a religious group that values modesty both in possessions and ambitions. Locals say part of the reason Bonners Ferry has not boomed with large-scale tourism is the stabilizing influence of the Mennonites. Another reason is that the area's pretty mountains aren't as breathtaking as the jagged peaks of Glacier National Park to the east.

Learn about the national forests in Idaho's panhandle at the **Bonners Ferry Ranger Station.** The area, home to Selkirk Mountain and Purcell Mountain, contains more than 350 mi of trails and five campgrounds. It is sprinkled with pretty lakes, some easily reachable and others accessible only to hikers and horseback riders. Popular activities are berry picking, fishing (especially on the Moyie River), and wildlife watching. ✉ *Hwy. 95* ☎ *208/267–5561* 🌐 *www.fs.fed.us/outernet/ipnf* 🎫 *Free* 🕙 *Weekdays.*

Less than 20 mi from the Canadian border, the 3,000-acre **Kootenai National Wildlife Refuge** includes ponds, grasslands, and a timbered region to the west. One popular destination is lovely Myrtle Falls. Wetland birds found here include many species of ducks—mallards, the main nesting species, and wigeon and pintails, which are migratory. Canada geese typically number more than 2,500 in the fall. In spring you can spot migrating tundra swans. Both white-tailed and mule deer and coyotes are common; rarely seen are black bears, elk, and moose. Grizzlies live in the area but seldom come so close to the valley floor. ✉ *Riverside Rd., 5 mi west of Bonners Ferry* ☎ *208/267–3888* 📠 *208/267–5570* 🌐 *www.fws.gov* 🎫 *Free* 🕙 *Daily dawn–dusk.*

off the beaten path

COPPER FALLS SELF-GUIDED NATURE TRAIL – Copper Falls, an 80-foot-high waterfall, is a 10-minute stroll up a gradually rising, well-maintained trail past feathery cedars and imposing larch. Pick up a brochure at the ranger station in Bonners Ferry or at the trailhead and watch for the marked stopping points. The trail loops to the bottom of the falls and back to the road in less than a mile. The hike begins after a 45-minute drive up the Kootenai Valley. ✉ *Forest Rd. 2517 off Hwy. 95* ☎ *208/267–5561* 🎫 *Free* 🕙 *Daily when road is passable.*

Sports & the Outdoors

RAFTING Relaxing summer floats on the Kootenai and Moyie rivers are made easy by **Twin Rivers Canyon Resort** (✉ County Rd. 70, 2 mi south of Hwy. 2 ☎ 208/267–5932). The company will rent you the raft and shuttle you to and from the river. Some trips begin at the resort and end downstream at Bonners Ferry, whereas others start higher on the Kootenai and end right back where you started. Exciting white-water action awaits on the wide Moyie River and on the smaller St. Joe River. **River Odysseys West** (☎ 208/765–0841 🌐 www.rowinc.com) runs well-organized, daylong guided paddle raft trips as long as the water lasts, which is usually about six weeks in late spring.

Where to Stay & Eat

$$–$$$$ ✕ **The Den.** Bonners Ferry's best dining option is this cathedral-ceilinged dining room with fresh flowers on each of the glass-top tables. The menu is surf and turf. Fresh sourdough bread and French onion soup keep you satisfied while you wait for your meal. Regional beers and wines are available at the bar. Since the restaurant is open only on weekends, tables generally fill quickly. ✉ *S. Hwy. 95* ☎ *208/267–7268* ⚠ *Reservations essential* 💳 *AE, D, MC* 🕙 *Closed Sun.–Wed. No lunch.*

$–$$ ✕ **Feist Creek Falls Resort.** In a secluded setting along the Moyie River not far from Feist Creek Falls, this place is known for lip-smacking steaks and barbecue ribs. There are also plenty of seafood dishes. A meal here is a great reward after a hike to Copper Falls. ✉ *Rte. 34 and Meadow Creek Rd., 45 mi north on U.S. 95 to Good Grief, then 3 mi south on Rte. 34* ☎ *208/267–8649* ▭ *AE, MC, V.*

$–$$ ✕ **The Panhandle.** This homey diner, with big picture windows looking onto historic downtown Bonners Ferry, serves stick-to-your-ribs food at modest prices. ✉ *7168 Main St.* ☎ *208/267–2623* ▭ *D, MC, V.*

$–$$$ Fodor's Choice ★ **Paradise Valley Inn Lodge.** A luxurious lodge set on 64 wooded acres, this secluded retreat is only 10 minutes from Bonners Ferry. The generously sized guest rooms have the same stunning valley views as the cathedral-ceilinged great room and the deck. Understated contemporary furnishings complement the art on the walls, most by Idaho artists. Also available are the cozy mountain cabin, tucked out of sight on a finger of ridge, and the smaller garden cabin, set amid the flowers. A full breakfast is included. ✉ *300 Eagle Way, 10 mi south of Bonners Ferry off U.S. 95, 83805* ☎ *208/267–4180 or 888/447–4180* 🖷 *208/267–3673* 🌐 *www.paradisevalleyinn.com* *5 rooms, 2 cabins* *Some room phones, some in-room VCRs, hot tub, laundry facilities; no smoking* ▭ *AE, MC, V.*

$ **Best Western Kootenai River Inn.** All the rooms at this low-slung lodging have views of the broad, placid Kootenai River and easy access to cafés and shops in the tiny downtown historic district. All have balconies that overlook the water or the well-groomed grounds. The on-site casino is often crowded with busloads of would-be winners. ✉ *7169 Plaza St., 83805* ☎ *208/267–8511* 🖷 *208/267–3744* *69 rooms* 🌐 *www.bestwestern.com* *Restaurant, room service, cable TV, indoor pool, exercise equipment, hot tub, bar* ▭ *AE, D, DC, MC, V.*

¢ **Bonners Ferry Log Inn.** Lush greenery surrounds this modern motel with the comfortable feel of a log cabin. Tree-shaded rooms are arranged along a long, covered boardwalk with plenty of outdoor seating. You'd hardly know you're a stone's throw from busy Highway 95. The gift shop carries interesting crafts and souvenirs. ✉ *Hwy. 95 W, 2 ½ mi north of Bonners Ferry, 83805* ☎ *208/267–3986* 🌐 *www.bonnersferryloginn.com* *27 rooms* *Hot tub* ▭ *AE, DC, MC, V.*

CAMPING **Bonners Ferry Ranger District Campgrounds.** The Forest Service maintains five campgrounds in the area, including two that are free. Meadow Lake Campground is near the Moyie River. Robinson Lake Campground is on Robinson Lake and has a boat ramp. The smallest of the campgrounds, Brush Lake, has only four sites and no drinking water. *Pit toilets. Drinking water at most campgrounds. Fire pits, picnic tables* ✉ *Hwy. 95 south of Bonners Ferry, 83805* ☎ *208/267–5561* *Free–$8* ▭ *No credit cards* *May–Sept.*

Löwenshaw Vineyards Retreat & RV Park. On a tree-covered hillside near a lily-pad-bedecked private lake, this quiet RV park is about 8 mi south of Bonners Ferry. *Flush toilets. Dump station. Drinking water, guest laundry, showers. Picnic tables. Swimming (lake)* *20 full hookups, 22 partial hookups, 10 tent sites* ✉ *Hwy. 95, Naples 83847* ☎ *208/267–2029* *Full hookups $26, partial hookups $22.70, tent sites $15* ▭ *No credit cards* *May–Oct.*

Twin Rivers Canyon Resort. Hidden on a broad bench at the bottom of the canyon formed by the Kootenai and Moyie rivers, this may be Idaho's prettiest RV retreat. Mature cedars and Douglas fir provide good shade. Willows and other shrubbery make many of the oversize sites feel secluded. Kids love the miniature golf course and shaded playground. There's a primitive boat launch and a diving platform in the pond, and enough open ground that even when the park is full (which is often, despite the fact that it's several miles off the highway) the atmosphere is peaceful. *Flush toilets. Full hookups, dump station. Drinking water,* *guest laundry, showers. Grills, picnic tables. Public telephone. General store. Play area, swimming (pond)* 26 *full hookups, 22 partial hookups, 16 tent sites* ✉ *County Rd. 70, Moyie Springs 83845* ☎ *208/267–5932 or 888/258–5952* 🌐 *twinriversresort.com* *Full hookups $24.50, partial hookups $22.50, tent sites $16* ▭ *MC, V* ⏲ *Apr.–Oct.*

Shopping

An independent bookstore that specializes in a startling range of new and used books, **Bonners Books** (✉ 7195 Main St. ☎ 208/267–2622) is a bibliophile's heaven. The 18,000-odd titles are shelved by subject, and mixed among the new ones are great deals on hard-to-find titles. The wood floors creak as you wander among the stacks. Owner John O'-Connor is here most days, quiet but helpful if you ask. He has run the place since 1986.

NORTHERN IDAHO A TO Z

AIR TRAVEL

Most major airlines serve Spokane International Airport, across the border in Spokane, Washington. Horizon Air, the largest regional carrier, serves Moscow and Lewiston. Salmon Air flies between all major Idaho airports as well as smaller town and backcountry airstrips. Many of these airstrips are unpaved and therefore are open only in summer and fall. Charter flights can be arranged through Salmon Air or McCall Aviation.

Airlines & Contacts **Horizon Air** ☎ 800/547–9308 🌐 www.horizonair.com. **McCall Aviation** ☎ 208/634–7137 or 800/992–6559 🌐 www.mccallaviation.com. **Salmon Air** ☎ 208/756–6211 or 800/448–3413 🌐 www.salmonair.com.

AIRPORTS

If you're flying to northern Idaho, you might actually end up in Washington. Spokane International Airport, a gateway to the panhandle, is only 40 minutes by car from Coeur d'Alene. Also across the border is tiny Moscow-Pullman Regional Airport, about 4 mi west of Moscow.

Lewiston-Nez Perce County Regional Airport is the biggest facility in northern Idaho and receives direct flights via Horizon from Boise, Seattle, and Portland.

Airport Information **Lewiston-Nez Perce County Regional Airport** ✉ 406 Burrell Ave., Lewiston ☎ 208/746–7962 🌐 www.lcairport.com. **Moscow-Pullman Regional Airport** ✉ 3200 Airport Complex North, Pullman, WA ☎ 509/338–3223 🌐 www.ci.pullman.wa.us. **Spokane International Airport** ✉ 9000 W. Airport Dr., Spokane, WA ☎ 509/455–6455 🌐 spokaneairport.net.

BUS TRAVEL

Northwestern Trailways runs between Boise and Spokane, stopping in Lewiston, Moscow, and other small towns along the way. The route does not pass through Coeur d'Alene. Greyhound runs buses to Coeur d'Alene from Spokane. The bus does not serve Sandpoint or Bonners Ferry.

Greyhound ☎ 800/231–2222 🌐 www.greyhound.com. **Northwestern Trailways** ☎ 800/366–3830 🌐 www.northwesterntrailways.com.

CAR RENTAL

All of the major rental car companies operate out of Spokane International Airport, the major gateway to northern Idaho. Two of them, Hertz and Budget, also operate out of Lewiston-Nez Perce County Regional Airport and Moscow-Pullman Regional Airport.

Avis ☎ 800/831–2847 🌐 www.avis.com. **Budget** ☎ 800/527–0700 🌐 www.budget.com. **Dollar** ☎ 800/800–4000 🌐 www.dollar.com. **Hertz** ☎ 800/654–3131 🌐 www.

hertz.com. **National** ☎ 800/227-7368 🌐 www.nationalcar.com. **Thrifty** ☎ 800/367-2277 🌐 www.thrifty.com.

CAR TRAVEL

The best way to see northern Idaho is by car—this is the West, after all, and interesting sights are spread out. Remember that Westerners often have an expanded view of distance. So when an Idahoan says "right around the corner," translate that as less than an hour's drive. Interstates and the much more interesting two-lane state and U.S. highways are never crowded (with the exception of Highway 95 on a summer afternoon). Best of all, a car allows you to travel back roads, where some of Idaho's unique sights await. Be sure to keep an eye on your gas gauge; the next gas station may be no closer than "right around the corner."

As a rule of thumb, the region's network of major roads is open year-round. Winter driving conditions can be rough, especially on the passes, and fall and spring bring fog, but conditions seldom make the roads unpassable. Winter snowstorms in mountainous areas can make tire chains advisable, but nowhere in northern Idaho are they mandatory. Major newspapers carry road-condition reports on their weather pages. Many of Idaho's back roads and forest roads are accessible by two-wheel-drive vehicles in summer driving conditions. Most shut down for the winter. On all roads, keep an eye peeled for wildlife—the most significant driving hazard.

Any time you leave the major roads, 95, I–90 and 12, or the major byways such as Idaho 6 and 3, carry a working jack and spare tire, as well as motor oil and engine coolant. And be prepared to stay a while with extra clothing, good walking shoes, food, and water. If you have engine trouble or get stuck trying to turn around on a one-lane dirt road, the 21st century's best car repair tool, your cell phone, may let you down as well.

ROAD EMERGENCIES Anywhere in northern Idaho, you can contact the Idaho State Police if you have troubles on the road. Members can also call AAA.

AAA Emergency Road Service ☎ 800/222-4357. **Idaho State Police** ☎ 208/799-5144.

ROAD CONDITIONS For up-to-date information on road conditions, construction, and travel-weather advisories, contact the Idaho Transportation Department.

Idaho Transportation Department ☎ 888/432-7623 🌐 www.state.id.us/itd.

RULES OF THE ROAD In Idaho you may make a right turn on red after stopping, unless there is a sign specifically forbidding it. It is illegal to delay more than three vehicles on winding roads where pull-outs are available.

HOSPITALS

Bonner General Hospital (✉ 3rd and Fir, Sandpoint ☎ 208/263–1441 or 208/265–4733 emergency). **Kootenai Medical Center** (✉ 2003 Lincoln Way, Coeur d'Alene ☎ 208/667–6441). **St. Joseph Hospital** (✉ 5th Ave. and 6th St., Lewiston ☎ 208/743–2511).

Ambulance or Police **Emergencies** ☎ 911.

Walk-in Medical Care **Express Care at Valley Medical Center** ✉ 2315 8th St., Lewiston ☎ 208/746-1383. **North Idaho Immediate Care** ✉ 1701 Lincoln Way, Coeur d'Alene ☎ 208/667-9110.

LODGING

The *Idaho Official State Travel Guide* contains information about lodging, dining, and activities across the state in a magazine format. Contact the Idaho Travel Council. A helpful Web site maintained by the Idaho Department of Commerce can point you to lodging options as well as events, recreational opportunities, and much more. Reservations can be made through this site as well.

Since the 1920s, the Dude Ranchers' Association has inspected guest ranches in the region and allowed some few to become members. Many fine northern Idaho guest ranches are not members, but every member is, as the association likes to say, "actually a ranch and not just a hotel with horses out back."

Dude Ranchers' Association 307/587-2339 www.duderanch.org. **Idaho Department of Commerce** 208/334-2470 or 800/842-5858 www.visitidaho.org. **Idaho Travel Council** Box 83720, Boise 83720 800/847-4843.

CAMPING Campgrounds in Idaho are either public (run largely by the Idaho Department of Parks and Recreation, the U.S. Forest Service, or the Bureau of Land Management), or they are private. One-stop shopping for campgrounds and campground reservations is most easily accomplished, however, by going straight to one of two resources, the Idaho Department of Commerce Web site or ReserveAmerica. Both let you browse among northern Idaho campgrounds and reserve sites at most campgrounds, public or private, that accept reservations.

Idaho Department of Commerce www.visitidaho.org. **ReserveAmerica** 877/444-6777 www.reserveamerica.com.

MEDIA

NEWSPAPERS & MAGAZINES The region's big daily newspaper for national and regional news is the *Spokane Spokesman-Review.* The *Coeur d'Alene Press, Moscow-Pullman Daily News,* and the *Lewiston Morning Tribune* all put out daily newspapers with a tighter focus on their towns in particular and northern Idaho in general. Smaller towns usually have weekly newspapers that focus on local issues and events.

SPORTS & THE OUTDOORS

FISHING Learn the state's fishing regulations from the Idaho Department of Fish and Game.

Idaho Department of Fish and Game 208/334-3700 or 800/554-8685 www.state.id.us/fishgame.

GUIDED OUTDOOR ACTIVITIES Guided recreation is big business in Idaho. Members of the Idaho Outfitters & Guides Association are licensed for the activities they offer, whether horseback riding, fishing, mountain biking, or white-water rafting. Individual guides are also required to be licensed. The IOGA, as it's called, puts out a membership directory categorized by activity and can help you find the right outfitter.

Idaho Outfitters & Guides Association 208/342-1919 or 800/847-4843 www.IOGA.org.

TRAIN TRAVEL

Amtrak's fabled *Empire Builder* makes a highly scenic run paralleling much of the route first traveled by Lewis and Clark. Starting in Chicago, it stops in Sandpoint on its way to Spokane and various other destinations. In summer, a national park ranger hops on at Montana's Glacier National Park to act as your guide through the area.

Train Information **Amtrak** 800/872-7245 www.amtrak.com. **Sandpoint Station** 409 Railroad Ave., Sandpoint 800/872-7245.

VISITOR INFORMATION

Coeur d'Alene Area Chamber of Commerce 1121 N. 3rd, 83816 208/664-3194 or 877/782-9232 www.coeurdalene.org. **Lewiston Chamber of Commerce** 111 Main St., 83501 208/743-3531 lewistonchamber.org. **Moscow Chamber of Commerce** 411 S. Main, 83843 208/882-1800 www.moscowchamber.com. **Greater Sandpoint Chamber of Commerce** 900 N. 5th Ave., 83864 208/263-0887 www.sandpointchamber.com.

UNDERSTANDING MONTANA, WYOMING & IDAHO

BOOKS & MOVIES

Books

A good place to begin your background reading about the Montana, Wyoming, and Idaho region is with America's quintessential explorers, Meriwether Lewis and William Clark. From 1804 to 1806, at the behest of President Thomas Jefferson and Congress, the pair traveled with their team of soldiers, surveyors, and interpreters over then-uncharted territory in 11 present-day western states—including Montana and Idaho. Among the many excellent accounts of Lewis and Clark's journey, *Undaunted Courage: Meriwether Lewis, Thomas Jefferson, and the Opening of the American West,* by acclaimed historian Stephen Ambrose, is arguably the finest.

If you like going directly to the source, try *The Journals of Lewis and Clark,* a compilation of the notes the explorers kept during their travels. While it's not a work of fine literature, it's fascinating as an unmediated record of the expedition as it unfolded. Bernard DeVoto, who edited *The Journals of Lewis and Clark,* also wrote *Across the Wide Missouri,* a look at fur trappers and their role in the expansion of the American West, for which he won a Pulitzer Prize in 1948.

Classic fiction from the region includes the work of another Pulitzer prize-winning author, A. B. Guthrie Jr., whose historical novel *The Big Sky* is a saga of frontier Montana. *The Virginian,* by Owen Wister, is a time-tested masterpiece of the Western genre. For more contemporary fiction, check out the story collections *Rock Springs,* by Richard Ford, and *Half in Love,* by Maile Meloy, and anything by Montana's writer-in-residence, Ivan Doig.

Each state swears by its own must-read standard history. Montana's is the 1991 *Montana: A History of Two Centuries,* by Michael Malone, Richard Roeder, and William Lang. T .A. Larson, possibly the single greatest authority on Wyoming's past, has written and edited not one but three authoritative histories about the state: *Wyoming: A Guide to its History, Highways, and People,* first distributed by the Works Progress Administration in 1941, is now considered a classic, while *The History of Wyoming* and its condensed version, *Wyoming: A Bicentennial History,* are Larson's two other monumental works. For a solid primer on Idaho, pick up the two-volume *History of Idaho* by Leonard J. Arrington.

You get history laced with personal experience in Jonathan Raban's *Bad Land,* a rumination on the stark beauty of the Montana plains and the broken dreams of homesteaders who tried to make a living off the land in the early 20th century. *Great Plains* by Ian Frazier is a more picaresque exploration of some of the same territory, with historical asides about Native Americans, early settlers, and whatever else captures Frazier's imagination.

Perhaps the most famous chronicler of the region is Norman Maclean. His autobiographical novella, *A River Runs Through It,* has taken on near religious significance for lovers of fly-fishing, while his nonfiction *Young Men & Fire* is the definitive story of the smoke jumpers of the U.S. Forest Service.

If a picture is worth a thousand words, then a must-see is Donna Lucey's *Photographing Montana 1894–1928, The Life and Work of Evelyn Cameron,* a collection of more than 150 black-and-white photographs that capture frontier life at the turn of the 20th century. Susan Anderson and Zbigniew Bzdak's *Living in Wyoming* offers beautiful glimpses into the modern-day lives of Wyoming's people. *Idaho Unbound: a Scrapbook & Guide*—"part guidebook, part reminiscence, part black-and-white photo album"—is a unique compilation by Clay Morgan and Steve Mitchell.

Movies

Before there was digital movie editing—making it possible to insert a rugged mountain peak into a movie scene with the click of a mouse button—there were the Rockies. With their jagged peaks looming over open plains, they've been the backdrop for many a motion picture. And with such terrain, it's only natural that the list of movies filmed in Montana, Idaho, and especially Wyoming (the "Cowboy State") contains a fair share of Westerns, dating as far back as Cecil B. DeMille's *The Plainsman* (1937), which the writer Graham Greene heralded as "perhaps the finest western in the history of the film."

In another classic, *Little Big Man* (1970), starring Dustin Hoffman, Faye Dunaway, and Chief Dan George (who was nominated for an Oscar), was shot in Montana; it's generally hailed as having altered the way Hollywood portrays Native Americans. The prolific Clint Eastwood, an actor whose very name is synonymous with the West, shot a number of his movies in Wyoming (*Thunderbolt and Lightfoot,* 1974; *Any Which Way You Can,* 1980) and Idaho (*Bronco Billy,* 1980; *Pale Rider,* 1985).

Sweeping landscapes aren't the only things that have drawn filmmakers to the region. After a brutal, fatal 1998 hate crime against 21-year-old Matthew Shepherd, a gay student in Laramie, Wyoming, HBO's *The Laramie Project* (2002) examined the emotional wounds and bitter recovery of a town cast into the national spotlight. For something lighter, rent *Sun Valley Serenade* (1941), a musical comedy set at the Idaho ski resort, with a legendary cast that includes ice-skating queen Sonja Henie, Milton Berle, John Payne, Glenn Miller, and Dorothy Dandridge. More recent star-studded action includes the noirish *Red Rock West* (1992), with Nicolas Cage and Dennis Hopper, and *The River Wild* (1994), a rafting thriller with Meryl Streep and Kevin Bacon; both were filmed in Montana.

Portions of Montana, Wyoming, and Idaho have made cameos in the unlikeliest of movies, from 1987's Chicago mob flick *The Untouchables* (the Hardy Creek Bridge in Montana is where Ness intercepts the shipment of Canadian whiskey) to *Star Trek: The Motion Picture* in 1979 (parts of the Planet Vulcan sequence were filmed in Wyoming). Sun Valley, Idaho, put the "country" in *Town & Country* (2001), and the Newton family took their vacation, St. Bernards in tow, to Glacier National Park in the innocuous family comedy *Beethoven's 2nd* (1993).

Devils Tower National Monument is the landmark of choice for visitors from outer space in Steven Spielberg's sci-fi classic *Close Encounters of the Third Kind* (1977), and if you visit there it's easy to understand why. When Robert Redford shot two of his later movies—*A River Runs Through It* (1992, based on the Norman Maclean novella) and *The Horse Whisperer* (1998)—in the region, he chose to showcase more subtle, but equally compelling qualities: a quiet river, an open plain, and the healing power of nature.

CHRONOLOGY

Montana

30,000–10,000 BC Asiatic peoples enter North America via the land bridge formed across the Bering Strait. Some venture into present-day Montana to hunt and scavenge.

5000–4000 BC Migrant foragers from the desert southwest inhabit the state's western valleys.

3000–2000 BC The "late hunters," the last wave of prehistoric visitors, enter Montana from the south and west.

AD 1500 The Flathead arrive in western Montana.

1620 Plains tribes begin arriving in Montana.

1803 United States purchases Louisiana Territory from France, including that part of Montana east of the Rocky Mountains, for 3¢ an acre.

1805–06 Explorers Meriwether Lewis and William Clark travel through Montana on their transcontinental expedition. Their journals confirm the presence of beaver, otter, and other fur-bearing animals.

1807 American fur trade begins with Manuel Lisa's construction of the Missouri Fur Company's trading post at the confluence of the Bighorn and Yellowstone rivers.

1828 Fort Union Trading Post is established at the mouth of the Yellowstone River by John Jacob Astor's American Fur Co.

1859 The first steamboat from St. Louis arrives in Fort Benton, the farthest-inland port in the world.

1862 Montana's first major gold strike occurs near the present-day town of Dillon. John Bozeman founds the Bozeman Trail, which will be abandoned in 1868 after frequent Sioux attacks. Congress passes the Homestead Act, opening thousands of acres to pioneer settlers.

1863 Gold is discovered near Virginia City and Nevada City, attracting thousands of prospectors seeking the new El Dorado.

1864 Montana Territory is created on May 26, with its capital at Bannack. John Bozeman leads first wagon train over Bozeman Trail.

1875 Helena becomes Montana's third territorial capital (following Bannack and Virginia City, sites of major gold strikes).

1876 Lt. Col. George Armstrong Custer and his 7th Cavalry fall victim to Sioux and Cheyenne warriors at the Battle of the Little Bighorn.

1877 The Nez Perce, led by Chief Joseph, surrender to the U.S. Army near present-day Chinook after leading troops on a six-month, 1,170-mi trek that included nearly a dozen battles.

1880 Hide hunters shoot buffalo to near extinction.

1882 A thick vein of copper is discovered beneath the played-out gold-mining camp of Butte, the richest cache of copper ore in the world.

1888 Sweetgrass Hills Treaty establishes boundaries for Fort Peck, Fort Belknap, and Blackfeet reservations.

1889 Montana is admitted to the Union on November 8 as the 41st state.

1894 Helena is voted Montana's capital in a run-off against Anaconda following a $3 million campaign financed by rival copper barons.

1910 Glacier National Park is established by act of Congress.

1916 Construction begins on Glacier National Park's Going-to-the-Sun Road. The engineering marvel takes 16 years to complete. Rocky Boy's Indian reservation is established near Havre.

1934 Construction begins on Fort Peck Dam, one of the world's largest earth-filled dams. At its peak in 1936, the project employs 11,000 workers. Its price tag: $156 million.

1951 Geologists discover Williston Basin—a massive oil field beneath eastern Montana, western North Dakota, and southern Saskatchewan.

1959 An evening earthquake registering 7.1 on the Richter scale topples half a mountain into the Madison River canyon, dams the river, creates Quake Lake, and buries 28 campers in an unmarked grave.

1970 Newsman Chet Huntley and Chrysler Corp. announce plans for the massive Big Sky resort complex north of Yellowstone National Park.

1977 Oil giant Atlantic Richfield Co. (ARCO) buys Anaconda Co.

1980 ARCO closes Anaconda copper smelter and Great Falls refinery, putting more than 1,000 employees out of work.

1983 After more than a century of mining operations and $4 billion in mineral production, ARCO closes all its Butte mines.

1995 Wolves are reintroduced to Yellowstone National Park. Montana becomes the only state without a specified daytime speed limit.

1996 Theodore Kaczynski, suspected "Unabomber" serial bomber, is arrested at his remote Lincoln-area cabin. After an 81-day standoff near Jordan, a group of "Freemen" surrender to the FBI.

1999 After the State Supreme Court declares Montana's lack of a speed limit unconstitutional, the state re-establishes speed limits.

Wyoming

8,300 BC Prehistoric people live in the Bighorn Basin.

AD 1500 Modern Indian tribes first establish homes and territories.

1743 The Verendrye brothers are the first white men to visit Wyoming when they reach the Bighorn Mountains on an exploratory trip.

1803 The United States concludes the Louisiana Purchase, which includes what will eventually be Wyoming.

1807–08 John Colter, a member of Lewis and Clark's Corps of Discovery, explores Wyoming, becoming the first non-native to lay eyes on the geyser basins of the Yellowstone National Park ecosystem.

1811 Wilson Price Hunt's Astorians head east from Fort Astoria, crossing through Wyoming on a route that later becomes the Oregon Trail.

1825 The first trappers' rendezvous is held on Black Fork of the Green River.

1834 The first permanent non-native settlement develops at Fort William near the confluence of the Laramie and North Platte rivers; it is eventually renamed Fort Laramie.

1843 Migration begins over the Oregon Trail.

1847 Brigham Young forges the Mormon Trail.

1849 Gold seekers head to California over the California Trail.

1860–61 The Pony Express delivers the mail by horseback courier.

1861 The Creighton Telegraph begins operation in October, bringing to an end the need for the Pony Express.

1865 Trail travel shifts south from the Oregon-Mormon-California corridor to the Overland Trail in southern Wyoming.

1868 Wyoming Territory is established on July 25.

1869 On Dec. 10 Wyoming grants women the right to vote, hold office, and serve on juries.

1872 Congress designates Yellowstone the first national park.

1874 An army expedition led by Lt. Col. George Armstrong Custer finds gold in the Black Hills, leading to a rush to the region with a primary route from Cheyenne to Deadwood, South Dakota.

1870 Cowboys begin trailing cattle to the northern ranges over the Texas, Goodnight-Loving, and other trails, bringing them into and through Wyoming. Some herds are kept in the state, beginning an industry that remains strong more than a century later.

1880 Wealthy cattlemen form the Cactus Club in Cheyenne. It later becomes the Cheyenne Club and is a base where anti-rustling activities are planned.

1886–87 A severe winter kills thousands of head of cattle. It becomes known as "The Great Die-Up."

1890 Wyoming becomes a state on July 10.

1892 A cattlemen's army invades Johnson County, killing two men before the army itself is surrounded and must be "rescued" by the U.S. Army. Although charges are filed, the case never goes to trial. The incident becomes known as the Johnson County Invasion or Johnson County War.

1903 Shoshone National Forest, the nation's first, is created in northwestern Wyoming.

1906 Devils Tower becomes the first national monument.

1913 The Lincoln Highway—the first transcontinental road in the nation—opens across southern Wyoming; it is later replaced by Interstate 80.

1922 Scandal erupts in the oil fields when the Teapot Dome federal naval reserve is leased without competitive bids. The Colorado River Compact determines ownership of water in the Colorado River drainage by six states: Wyoming, Colorado, Utah, Nevada, Arizona, and California.

1929 Congress establishes Grand Teton National Park; it is expanded in 1950 to its present size.

1936 The cowboy silhouette first appears on Wyoming license plates.

1942 Federal officials develop Heart Mountain Relocation Center between Powell and Cody, an internment camp for people of Japanese ancestry used throughout World War II.

1982 The world's largest wind turbine goes into operation near Medicine Bow.

1998 A new wind-energy project is developed east of Elk Mountain; it provides power throughout the Pacific Northwest.

Idaho

Pre-history From 13,000 BC, evidence suggests that Native American cultures inhabit Idaho, as shown in rock shelters, petroglyphs, and stone tools.

1805 Meriwether Lewis and William Clark enter the area of present-day Idaho at Lemhi Pass, cross into north Idaho over the Lolo Trail, then meet with Nez Perce at Weippe Prairie.

1806 Lewis and Clark spend more than six weeks with the Nez Perce in the Kamiah area before returning eastward across the Lolo Trail. Canadian David Thompson establishes a fur-trading post near Bonners Ferry. Missouri Fur Company establishes Fort Henry near St. Anthony, the first American trading post.

1810–11 The Pacific Fur Company expedition explores the Snake River valley en route to the Columbia River and discovers the Boise Valley.

1818 Trappers explore southern Idaho on a Snake River expedition, and a treaty of joint occupancy between Great Britain and the United States maintains that the Oregon region, including Idaho, is open to settlement by citizens of both nations.

1820 A treaty between Spain and the United States establishes the southern boundary of Idaho at the 42nd Parallel.

1824 Alexander Ross and Jedediah Smith lead expeditions throughout the Salmon River region; Russia cedes the Northwest Territory to the United States.

1832 Captain B.L.E. Bonneville leads covered wagons across the Rockies.

1834–42 Fort Hall becomes a hub for trails and roads to the western United States. Several Jesuit missions are established in northern Idaho.

1843 The Oregon Trail is established, entering the state to the east near Montpelier, passing by Fort Hall, and continuing westward along the Snake River before crossing into Oregon.

1848 The Oregon Territory, which includes Idaho, is established.

1849 More than 20,000 gold-rush immigrants pass through southeastern Idaho on the California Trail.

1852 French Canadians discover gold on the Pend Oreille River.

1857–59 Oregon becomes a state, leaving all of Idaho in the Washington Territory. Gold is discovered on Orofino Creek and Lewiston becomes a mining supply town.

1863–65 The Idaho Territory is organized, with Lewiston as its capital. The town of Boise is laid out and replaces Lewiston as the capital. Idaho's population climbs to 17,804.

1877–78 Indian War with battles at White Bird.

1880–84 Idaho's population almost doubles in 10 years to 32,619. Lead and silver lodes are discovered in the Wood River valley. The Northern Pacific railroad is completed across the northern part of the Territory and the Oregon Short Line is completed through the southern region. The Coeur d'Alene rush creates boomtowns in the Silver Valley.

1887 A bill to annex north Idaho to Washington Territory passes Congress but is not signed by President Cleveland and therefore does not become law.

1890 Idaho reaches a population of 88,548 and becomes the 43rd state.

1893 The Panic of '93 causes lead and silver prices to collapse and Coeur d'Alene's mines shut down.

1900 Idaho's population reaches 161,772.

1903–06 The Carey Act supports irrigation projects around Twin Falls. The largest sawmill in the nation opens at Potlatch.

1910 Idaho's population reaches 325,594. Fires consume almost 20% of northern Idaho's forests and destroy many communities.

1915 Arrowrock Dam, the tallest in the world, is completed on the Boise River. Irrigation contributes to the development of three important crops—potatoes, peas, and sugar beets.

1920 The northern and southern portions of the state are connected for the first time by an improved roadway, Whitebird Hill grade. The state capitol is completed.

1924 Craters of the Moon National Monument is established.

1925 The Union Pacific Railroad begins service to Boise.

1930s Idaho's population reaches 445,032. Gold- and silver-mining industries redevelop; Idaho becomes the top U.S. producer of silver.

1936 The Union Pacific establishes Sun Valley, the nation's first destination ski resort, near the mining town of Ketchum. Former governor William Borah becomes the state's first presidential candidate.

1939–45 During World War II Idaho becomes a relocation center for 10,000 Japanese nationals and Japanese-Americans from Washington and Oregon. The state is also the site of 18 German and Italian prisoner-of-war camps.

1970s Governor Cecil Andrus spearheads the passage of legislation emphasizing the conservation of natural resources, rivers, and streams. Many parts of Idaho are designated national forests or wilderness areas, including the Hells Canyon National Recreation Area, the River of No Return, and Sawtooth National Wilderness Areas.

1980s The mining industry continues a steady decline that started in the mid-1960s. Tourism becomes increasingly important in the state, helping to offset the decline in mining and timber revenues.

1981 One of Idaho's largest employers, Bunker Hill Mine and Smelter, near Kellogg, shuts down, leaving 2,000 workers unemployed.

1990s Idaho ranks 42nd in the United States with a population of a little over 1 million. It is the sixth most sparsely populated state. Food processing is the state's chief industry, followed by the manufacture of industrial machinery, lumber and wood production, and the manufacture of electronic equipment.

1992 Randy Weaver, a white separatist living in the northern Panhandle region, draws national attention during an 11-day siege and shoot-out with federal officials. During the siege, several people are killed, including a federal officer. Weaver and Kevin Harris are tried and acquitted, and the Weaver family wins a multimillion-dollar lawsuit against the federal government for using lethal force during the siege.

INDEX

R

S

T

U